The United States
AIR
NATIONAL
GUARD

The United States
AIR
NATIONAL
GUARD

René J. Francillon

WORLD
AIR POWER
JOURNAL

Aerospace Publishing London
Airtime Publishing USA

Published by
Aerospace Publishing Ltd
179 Dalling Road
London W6 0ES
England

Published under licence in USA
and Canada by
Airtime Publishing Inc.
10 Bay Street,
Westport, CT 06880
USA

Distributed in the UK,
Commonwealth and Europe by
Airlife Publishing Ltd
101 Longden Road
Shrewsbury SY3 9EB
England
Telephone: 0743 235651
Fax: 0743 232944

Distributed to retail bookstores in
the USA and Canada by
Airtime Publishing Inc.
10 Bay Street,
Westport, CT 06880
USA
Telephone: (203) 226-3580
Fax: (203) 221-0779

US and Canadian readers wishing
to order by mail, please contact
Airtime Publishing Inc. at (203)
226-3580. The publishers also
welcome inquiries from model and
hobby stores.

Aerospace **ISBN: 1 874023 27 1**
Airtime **ISBN: 1-880588-03-X**

Publisher: Stan Morse
Editor: David Donald
Production Editor:
  Karen Leverington
Design: Barry Savage
Artist: Chris Davey
Typesetting: SX Composing Ltd
Origination and printing by
  Imago Publishing Ltd
Printed in Singapore

Portions of the text have
previously appeared in *The Air
Guard* by René J. Francillon,
published by Aerofax Inc.

The publishers gratefully
acknowledge the assistance
given by the units of the Air
National Guard and aviation
corporations, who have
generously helped with this
publication.

World Air Power Journal is
published quarterly and
provides an in-depth analysis
of contemporary military
aircraft and their worldwide
operators. Superbly produced
and filled with extensive color
photography, World Air Power
Journal is available by
subscription from:

UK, Europe and
Commonwealth:
Aerospace Publishing Ltd
179 Dalling Road
London W6 0ES
England

USA and Canada:
Airtime Publishing Inc.
Subscription Dept
10 Bay Street
Westport, CT 06880
USA

CONTENTS

The Air National Guard of the Several States

Mission Aircraft of the Air National Guard   **178**

Tables

Index   **222**

Preface and Acknowledgements

Compiling a history spanning eight decades and covering the more than 100 Air National Guard flying units which have served and, in most cases, continue to serve in each of the 50 states, the Commonwealth of Puerto Rico and the District of Columbia, would have been an impossible task without the cooperation of these same units, the National Guard Bureau, the Office of National Guard History, the National Guard Association of the United States and fellow historians.

Shortly after immigrating to the United States in 1961, I came into contact with Air Guardsmen and soon was awed by their remarkable *esprit de corps*, intense pride, quiet professionalism and deep love for our nation. In the last 12 years I have, with the support of the National Guard Bureau, visited ANG units and flown with them whenever I could, and my admiration for ANG men and women has deepened. These visits have been the source of some of the richest and most heart-warming moment in my life and I am deeply indebted to my ANG hosts, from Florida to Alaska, and from Hawaii to the Atlantic Coast, for their warm hospitality and support. I am proud and humbled that many of my hosts from yesteryear are now my friends.

In addition to being able to count on the assistance of virtually every ANG unit, state headquarters and other official organizations to gather historical data, I have been most fortunate in receiving invaluable assistance from leading experts in this field. In particular, I want to single out Marty Isham, whose knowledge of active and ANG air defense units is unrivalled; Bill Larkins, the doyen of American aviation historians; and Dave Menard, whose knowledge of the history of active and reserve USAF components is encyclopedic. I am also most grateful for the considerable help and encouragement provided by Major General Wayne C. Gatlin, MN ANG (Ret.), and Major General H. Robert Hall, CA ANG (Ret.).

Even though help was available from so many people, there remain a number of events for which accurate dates could not be determined. Furthermore, some readers will question dates appearing in this book. This is particularly the case for dates of conversion, as the conversion process to modern aircraft is a lengthy one, especially when it entails a change in mission. In this book, dates of conversion are either those of official completion of the conversion process (i.e. 30 June 1990 in the case of the F-4C to F-15A conversion for the 123rd FIS) or that of official redesignation (i.e. 1 July 1986 for the redesignation from 183rd TAS/172nd TAG to 183rd MAS/172nd MAG, Mississippi ANG, which converted from Lockheed C-130Hs to Lockheed C-141Bs).

While 'pretty pictures' of aircraft currently in service are easily obtainable from various official and private sources or can be specially taken to illustrate a book or article, color photos of older aircraft are not easily available as the years have not been kind to official collections. There again, I was most fortunate in being able to rely on the unselfish assistance of many friends who dug into their archives to locate color slides and color prints of A-26s, F-47s, F-51s, F-80s, F-84s and other aircraft long retired from ANG service. At the risk of being presumptuous, I dare say that many readers will join me in thanking these genuine historians, unlike those who horde their photos and never share them with the public, and to realize that keeping one's slides for private showing is a strange way to contribute to aviation history.

The publisher and I made every attempt to credit photos accurately to the original photographers and to identify those who made them available for use in illustrating this book. We especially want to thank the following photographers for their contributions: Charles Arrington, Brian Baker, William Balough, Jim Benson, Jean-Pierre Bézard, Gordon Blake, Peter Bowers, Tom Brewer, Donald Brown, Bob Burgess, Jack Callaway, Robert Casari, Gary Chambers, Roger Cook, Bill Curry, John Dean, Dave Donald, N. Donald, Robert Dorr, Jim Dunn, Walter Fleming, John Funk, Wayne Gatlin, Jerry Geer, Jim Goodall, Charles Graham, Norris Graser, Robert Greby, Michael Grove, Robert Hall, Tom Hildreth, Robert Hopkins, Marty Isham, Clay Jansson, Randy Jolly, Tom Kaminski, John Karpiej, Robert Kling, William Larkins, Geoffrey LeBaron, William Lightfoot, Don Logan, David Lucabaugh, Frank MacSorley, Peter Mancus, Patrick Martin, David McLaren, David Menard, John Michaels, Larry Milberry, Paul Minert, Rick Morgan, Douglas Olson, Pat Paulsen, William Peake, Geoff Pearce, Dennis Peltier, Robert Pfannenschmidt, Carl Porter, Jim Retter, Charles Robbins, Brian Rogers, Harrison Rued, Vikki Schandle, John Sheets, Warren Ship, Douglas Sloviak, Daniel Soulaine, Don Sperring, Jim Sullivan, David Swearingen, Norm Taylor, Scott Van Aken, Wally Van Winkle, Rick Wargo and Gordon Williams. *Primus inter pares*, my sincerest thanks go to my long-time friend Pete Lewis; his unselfishness and modesty are inspirations.

With help from these friends and from ANG units, every effort has been made to have text and illustrations reflect the organization of the Air National Guard as of the end of Fiscal Year 1992. However, as so many changes have taken place in recent months and continue to take place daily, some could not be recorded prior to going to press. We apologize for these few omissions.

On a more personal basis, I thank my wife, Carol McKenzie, for her patience in enduring my 'Guard monologues' and for substituting for me in Duluth; my son, Edric Francillon, for encouraging me to keep working on this book when I needed prodding; and my nephew, Chris Jacquet, for carting my bags on so many Guard ramps and for sharing my passion for aviation.

René J. Francillon
Vallejo, California
October 1992

Foreword

This is only one of very many books about aviation that René Francillon has written. It is his most important to the citizen soldiers of the Air National Guard. It is our history – the story of the success of the militia concept in air power.

René and I met in 1982, when I was asked to carry him on a C-130 mission to Korea from the California Air Guard Base at NAS Moffett. A civilian passenger on a military mission, in the painfully noisy C-130, is usually to be avoided. René was, however, an asset to the mission. His warmth, his cooperation, and especially his knowledge of things that fly all added greatly to the enjoyment of the mission.

René is well known as an aviation historian and astute photographer of aircraft. He has flown in almost all of the aircraft presently in the Air Guard inventory. But he is also an excellent writer – remarkable since English is a second language for this European-born and -educated American. He does his research carefully, verifying those things he writes as facts.

He has been impressed, as many are, to learn of the extensive missions the Air Guard has for the 50 states, the District of Columbia, Guam, Puerto Rico and the Virgin Islands. In each, the governor can call up the Guard for emergencies. In California, for example, the Air Guard did life-saving airlift in the floods of 1986; flew relief missions after the 1989 earthquake; and every summer fights wildfires.

Additionally, the Air Guard can be seen at parades, dedications, and civic ceremonies.

The Air Guard – about 120,000 men and women – is best known for its role as a component of the Total Force, supporting the active-duty USAF. For example, in Just Cause, Panama, the ANG flew airlift and A-7 close air support missions.

And the real worth of the Air Guard was shown brightly in Desert Shield/Desert Storm. From the beginning, its tankers refueled fighters, its C-130, C-141 and C-5 airlifters were transporting people and material, its LOROP-equipped RF-4s looked deep behind the Iraqi border, and its support people were placed where needed – throughout the nation, Europe and the Persian Gulf. After fighting broke out, ANG F-16s struck targets in Iraq and occupied Kuwait, and its RF-4s brought back BDA intelligence.

The Air National Guard is, of course, entirely volunteers – and no military draft drives them to volunteer, as in the 1960s and 1970s. These men and women of the Air Guard, as we so proudly proclaim, are Americans at their best.

H. Robert Hall
Major General, CA ANG (Retired)
Commander, California Air National Guard, 1987-1991

A Uniquely American Concept

Main picture: Carrying on traditions inherited from the Minutemen who helped the Thirteen Colonies to gain their independence, Air Guardsmen from New York's 138th TFS proved the validity of the Total Force concept by flying combat missions from Day One of Operation Desert Storm.

The National Guard concept – placing military forces under the control of local governments instead of the central government – is a uniquely American phenomenon. True, provincial regiments were a traditional feature in Europe, but their control was quickly wrested from local lords as central governments fought to establish their control. Their manning by young men from limited geographical areas fell into disfavor during World War I when nearly the entire young male population of some of these areas was wiped out. Today, none of the world's other federative states, such as Brazil, Germany, Mexico, the former Soviet Union and Switzerland, has the equivalent of the National Guard, and all their front-line military forces are directly under the control of their federal governments.

The world's fifth-largest air force

At the end of Fiscal Year 1992 (30 September 1992), when the effects of the world's political realignment and the Iraqi invasion of Kuwait were beginning to impact on its organization, the Air National Guard possessed 1,500 combat and transport aircraft and had a total strength of 118,923 officers and enlisted personnel. It thus was the world's fifth-largest air force, surpassed only by the the the air forces of the Commonwealth of Independent States, the active-duty components of the USAF, the United States Navy and Marine Corps, and China's Air Force of the People's Liberation Army.

The Air National Guard is composed of 1,378 flying and non-flying units in all 50 states, the District of Columbia, and Puerto Rico, as well as non-flying units in Guam and the Virgin Islands, having status as both federal and state military forces. In non-mobilized status these units are commanded by the governors of the 50 states, the Commonwealth of Puerto Rico, the Territories of Guam and the Virgin Islands, and the Commanding General of the District of Columbia. Each governor is represented in the state or territory chain of command by the adjutant general. Upon being called to federal active service by the

Right: The forebears of the men and women of the Army National Guard and Air National Guard first went into battle for America at Concord Bridge on 19 April 1775, when they 'fired the shot heard 'round the world' at Lord Percy's redcoats.

President, Congress or both, ANG units have, like all other units of the United States Armed Forces, the President of the United States as their commander-in-chief.

Under the Total Force Policy which was implemented at the beginning of the 1970s, the Air National Guard is a combat-ready force that is immediately available for mobilization to support active Air Force requirements. In addition to the mobilization-ready forces, it supports USAF worldwide missions in a non-mobilization status (e.g. in 1992 the entire air defense of the United

Right: The first muster of militiamen of the Massachusetts Bay Colony at Salem, MA, in 1637.

States was provided by ANG squadrons flying F-15As and F-16A ADFs under state control).

While its federal role has been steadily strengthened, the Air National Guard of each state, and those of the Commonwealth of Puerto Rico, the Territories of Guam and the Virgin Islands, and the District of Columbia remain constitutionally a state- (commonwealth, territory or federal district) administered military force. Their state (commonwealth, territory or federal district) mission is to provide units organized, equipped and trained to function

effectively (**1**) in the protection of life (such as by flying search-and-rescue missions) and property (such as by providing specially-fitted C-130s to fight forest fires), and (**2**) the preservation of peace, order and public safety (for example, by airlifting riot-control units) under competent orders of federal or state authorities.

Even though this book deals only with the ANG flying units, it is appropriate to note that these units (100 squadrons, and the 24 wings and 68 groups to which they are attached) are only a small portion of the 1,378 units con-

Inset, above: Officers of the 111th Observation Squadron, Texas National Guard, in front of one of the unit's Douglas O-2Hs. Jodphurs and riding boots were standard for Air Corps officers.

Above: Powered by a Pratt & Whitney R-1535-7, the Douglas O-46A entered service with the Guard in 1936. Maintenance personnel from the 118th Observation Squadron, Connecticut National Guard, work on a spotless engine in the maintenance hangar at Brainart Field, Hartford.

Top right: A Douglas BT-1 of the 109th Observation Squadron, Minnesota National Guard, undergoing an engine change at Holman Field in St Paul. The engine is a World War I-vintage 435-hp Liberty V-1650-1.

Above right: Inspection time for pilots and observers of the 104th Observation Squadron and their Douglas O-38Es. The flying unit of the Maryland National Guard had received federal recognition on 20 June 1921.

stituting the total strength of the Air National Guard. Non-flying ANG units – including notably aeromedical evacuation flights and squadrons, clinics and hospitals, consolidated aircraft maintenance squadrons, aerial port flights and squadrons, communications/electronics units, civil engineering units (Red Horse and Prime Beef), weather units, state headquarters, etc. – perform a vital support role without which the flying units could not fulfill their missions and 'fly and fight'.

The unique dual status of the Air National Guard, and of its counterpart the Army National Guard, is rooted in the concept of the privilege and responsibility of able-bodied citizens of the United States to be ready at all times to bear arms, under federal control, for the common defense, and to augment civil authorities, under state control, during disasters and disturbances that exceed the capabilities of civilian agencies.

Forebears of the National Guard

To place the development of aviation in the National Guard in proper historical perspective, it is appropriate to summarize its history and traditions.

One hundred and forty years before the United States of America declared its independence, home defense units ('train bands') in several Massachusetts Bay Colony settlements were incorporated into the Colony's first formally-structured military force, the Old North Regiment or Middlesex County Militia Regiment. (Thus, the 182nd Infantry Regiment of the Massachusetts National Guard can today proudly trace its ancestry to 1636.) In the years that followed, more units were formed in the colonies and, as part of the Colonial Organized Militia, fought alongside the King's Regulars in King William's War (1689-97), Queen Anne's War (1701-13), King George's War (1744-48) and the French and Indian War (1745-63).

The next significant event in the history of the Organized Militia – the true forebear of the modern National Guard – took place in 1775, when the Second Continental Congress formally organized the militias raised by the several colonies into the overall defense force of the country. On 19 April 1775, 130 'minute men' of the Lexington Company of the Massachusetts Volunteer Militia under the command of Captain John Parker 'fired the shot heard 'round the world' when they stood their ground against Lord Percy's redcoats during the fight at Concord Bridge. The forebears of today's Guardsmen had begun a long tradition of service to their nation.

The formation of volunteers, recruited and officered by the 13 states to form individual State Lines,[1] quickly became the nucleus of the Continental Line under the command of General George Washington. Coming from the militia himself, the nation's father had become a full colonel in command of the 1st Regiment of the Organized Militia, Colony of Virginia, after unsuccessfully seeking a Crown's commission in the King's Regulars. Eventually, some 165,000 of the 396,000 troops raised during the Revolutionary War for General Washington came from the State Lines. Personnel recruitment for these units was through volunteering and was expedited by bounties and pressures of state laws for compulsory military service. In

addition, the 13 states organized Home Guard units, which provided locally-limited support for the troops of the Continental Line; these units, however, cannot be considered as being forebears of today's Guardsmen as their duty had a much narrower scope.

After the United States had won its independence, the Continental Line was disbanded because it was argued that no regular army would be needed, and the troops returned to their home states. It was not until the first session of the First Congress in 1789 that the need for the establishment of troops in the service of the United States was recognized. Three years later the provision for and recognition of the militia, which was included in the second amendment of the Bill of Rights,[2] was further clarified in the Federal Militia Act of 8 May 1792.

According to this Act, the federal government was to organize and arm 'a well regulated Militia', and the states were to provide officers and control. No action was taken, however, and for several years troops were separately formed and trained by each state entirely under state control. Further developments took place in 1795, when Congress gave the President authority to call out the Militia in cases of invasion and other emergencies, and in 1808, when legislation provided $200,000 in federal aid to be paid annually to the states to support forces remaining under their control.

In 1798 President John Adams was authorized to call up 50,000 officers and militiamen for planned offensive operations against the French in Louisiana and Florida. This war, however, ended after only a few naval engagements and the troops were demobilized. During the following century, militia troops were called four times to serve their nation during major incidents. In the war of 1812-15 against Great Britain, troops from the Organized Militia on extended active duty accounted for almost half of the total force available at the time of peak strength and, during the Battle of New Orleans (the final US victory in

---

[1] The term 'Line' came into being during the American Revolution to differentiate the militia units raised by a state for federal duty from those retained under state control (Home Guard) for local defense. The Continental Line was the federal army and was composed of the Line of each of the 13 states and of regulars.

[2] Amendment 2: "A well regulated Militia, being necessary to the security of a free state, the right of the people to keep and bear arms, shall not be infringed."

OH ANG

January 1815), more than 60 per cent of General Andrew Jackson's troops belonged to the Tennessee and Kentucky Regiments and to the Louisiana Artillerymen and Infantrymen.

The next federal call that went to all states – more limited calls having been made during the intervening period to provide troops in Indian wars – was caused by the war with Mexico, April 1846-March 1848. Initially, General Zachary Taylor's regular troops were supplemented by citizen-soldiers of the Republic of Texas and by other Militia units from neighboring states. Later, during the same war, President James Polk was authorized to call up to 50,000 volunteers for 12 months or for the duration. Eventually, just over 80 per cent of the American troops operating against Mexico served with the Volunteer Regiments and the smaller units from 24 states.

By far the largest call made on the Organized Militia during the 19th century was brought about by the Civil War, as the armies of the United States of America and the Confederate States of America both relied mainly on militia troops. In the union, 90 per cent of the aggregate equivalent of 2,080 regiments serving during the war volunteered into the Organized Militia of the individual states and were inducted into federal service. The Organized Militia (National Guard)[3] of the State of New York alone provided, as befitted the most populous state in the Union, the equivalent of 294 regiments, 25 companies and 35 batteries, whereas the regular army fielded only the equivalent of 135 regiments, 22 companies and 11 batteries. With the Confederacy, the role of the militiamen was even more significant as only 11 of the grand aggregate of 764 regiments taking part in 'The War Between the States' carried Confederate States Army designations; the Organized Militia of the Commonwealth of Virginia led the pack with 90 regiments, 21 battalions and 53 batteries. The price paid, however, was horrendous, as battle deaths, for

regular and Militia units, reached an estimated total of 140,414 Union officers and men and 74,524 Confederate personnel; more than twice as many troops on both sides had been wounded.

After Appomattox, the troops of the late Confederate States of America were disarmed and disbanded, while within eight months 80 per cent of the 1,000,000 officers and men serving in the Union Army at the end of the Civil War were mustered out. During the next 25 years the Organized Militia played only a small role in the development of the nation and the regulars carried the brunt of the responsibility of military actions against Indians. While the population of the United States grew by leaps and bounds, personnel strength of the Organized Militia increased slowly from the post-Civil War nadir until 1893 when the aggregate strength of the Organized Militia (National Guard) of all the states and territories reached 112,507 officers and men (of which 22 per cent served in

Above: Parachute training from a Consolidated PT-1 of the 112th Observation Squadron, Ohio National Guard. In 1927, the table of organization of flying units of the National Guard was revised to include five of these trainers and three observation aircraft.

Left: A bulky camera is installed in the rear cockpit of a Douglas O-2H of the 112th Observation Squadron, Ohio National Guard. Based at the Hopkins Airport in Cleveland, the aviation unit of the 37th Division was federally recognized on 20 June 1927.

units organized in the 11 states which had formed the Confederacy).

The slow increase in strength was due mainly to the lack of military threats – with only the citizen-soldiers in western states and territories being called upon occasionally to fight Indians until federal troops arrived – and to the unpopularity of the need for the Organized Militia to maintain order in their own states during periods of labor unrest (as was notably the case during the Great Railroad Strike of 1877). Furthermore, almost 70 years after Congress had authorized annual appropriations of $200,000 in federal aid to the Organized Militia, funds available for this purpose had increased only to $400,000, while the national population had increased eightfold.

Nevertheless, the National Guard was called into active duty one further time in the 19th century. On 15 February 1898 the battleship *Maine* exploded and sank in Havana Harbor and the long tension between Spain and the United States quickly reached war fever, with Congress declaring war on 24 April. The previous day, President William McKinley addressed a Call to the States for 125,000 men from their National Guard units. Eventually, the National Guard contributed almost 173,000 officers and men who fought in Cuba, Puerto Rico and the Philippines, and served in the United States until the late summer of 1899. During the Spanish-American War the regular army had been reinforced not only by National Guard units but also by US volunteer regiments directly recruited by the federal government and manned to a large extent by ex-militiamen.

The Dick Act, foundation of today's National Guard

Following the end of the war, serious attempts were made to downgrade the roles of the National Guard to those of a mere training school and recruiting preserve for the United States Volunteer Army. This nearly occurred, even though supporters of the National Guard pointed out that the regular army had never won a major war without the active assistance of the Organized Militia/National Guard. Fortunately for the future of the Guard, these attempts failed, and the Dick Act of 21 January 1903 set the foundations on which today's National Guard and Air National Guard are based.

This act provided, for the first time, a clearly defined federal legal differentiation between the organized strength of the National Guard and the unorganized, military-obligated manpower within statutory ages. Moreover, it provided the National Guard with both state and federal support and stipulated that within five years after the signing of the law

> " . . . the organization, armament, and discipline of the Organized Militia – shall be the same as that which is now, or may thereafter be prescribed, for the regular and volunteer armies of the United States."

The states were assigned the responsibility of furnishing personnel and armory facilities. The federal government became responsible for issuing arms and equipment to the Guard without charge and for providing instructors and inspection teams detailed from the regular army. Furthermore, federal appropriations were to be used for military stores, professional publications, pay and subsistence during joint maneuvers with the regular army and attendance at Fort Leavenworth and the Army War College, and for ammunition for target practice during summer encampments at regular army posts.

From then on, the National Guard developed into an effective military force with well-organized and adequately trained units. Their supervision within the Office of the Secretary of War was first entrusted to the Division of Militia Affairs, which was established on 12 February 1908. General Order No. 24, dated 6 July 1916,

pursuant to the National Defense Act of 3 June 1916, reorganized the Division into the Militia Bureau. In 1933 the name was changed to National Guard Bureau. As detailed in subsequent chapters, the Division/Bureau oversaw the organization and development of aviation units in the National Guard and, today, the director of the Air National Guard reports to the chief, National Guard Bureau (NGB). The last-mentioned office is a Joint Bureau of the Departments of the Army and the Air Force, and channels the communications between the states and these departments. Its chief, a lieutenant general, is appointed by the President, with the advice and consent of the Senate, from a list of National Guard officers recommended by the respective governors.

[3] The title 'National Guard' was coined by the Marquis de La Fayette, the founder of France's Garde Nationale, during his 1824 visit to the New York Organized Militia. During the Civil War this term was adopted by a change in the statute of the State of New York and, for example, the 10th New York Volunteer Infantry became known as the 'National Guard Zouaves'. By 1896 most states had adopted this title and finally, in 1933, it received full sanction when the War Department reorganized the Militia Bureau into the still-in-existence National Guard Bureau.

The title 'Air National Guard' came into being after the National Security Act of 1947, which created the United States Air Force as a service equal to the Army and the Navy, was passed by Congress and signed by President Harry Truman on 26 July 1947. At that time, the fighter and bomber squadrons of the National Guard became part of the Air National Guard of their states, and their gaining federal service was the USAF. Therefore, throughout the remainder of this book, the titles 'National Guard' and 'Air National Guard' are used in their proper historical context (i.e. National Guard prior to 18 September 1947, the official date of organization of the United States Air Force, and Air National Guard thereafter).

Maj Gen H. Robert Hall

René J. Francillon

C. Graham, courtesy of David W. Menard

Above left: During the Cold War years, the Air National Guard provided a steadily-increasing share of the air defense units. Bearing the griffin markings of the 194th FIS, California ANG, this F-86L was photographed over Great Salt Lake, Utah.

Above: Among the many benefits which Americans derive from their Air National Guard is added protection against forest fires. This C-130B of the 187th TAS, Wyoming ANG, is seen dropping a load of water during a fire-fighting training exercise in California on 17 June 1987.

Below: A pair of F-16A ADFs of the 194th Fighter Interceptor Squadron, 144th Fighter Interceptor Wing, California ANG, is silhouetted against the sunset during a training sortie off the Big Sur Coast on 25 April 1990. The Air National Guard now mans all interceptor units in the United States.

René J. Francillon

The Guard's
Early Days

CHAPTER 2

USAF coutesy of Robert Casari

Main picture: Purchased by the Aero Club of America and donated to the New Mexico National Guard, the prototype of the Curtiss Twin-JN was shipped to Columbus, New Mexico, in June 1916 to take part in the Mexican Punitive Expedition.

Inset, above: The Curtiss Twin-JN prototype, seen here being reassembled by New Mexico Guardsmen, crashed before making a concrete contribution to the Mexican Punitive Expedition.

The New York National Guard, which organized an 'Aeronautic Corps' on 30 April 1908 and its Aviation Detachment, 1st Battalion, Signal Corps, on 1 November 1915 but did not get federal recognition for either unit, and the Minnesota National Guard, which obtained federal recognition for its 109th Squadron on 17 January 1921, are generally recognized as the two organizations with the most genuine claims to having the first aviation units in the National Guard.

Other states, however, can soundly claim 'firsts' in this field: Rhode Island, which had the first two 'flyers' to serve their nation (James Allen and William H. Helme, who brought their balloons with them when joining the Army of the Potomac at the beginning of the Civil War); Michigan, which in 1911 was the first to pay expenses incurred by one of its officers (Captain George MacKay) to obtain a Fédération Aéronautique Internationale civilian pilot licence; Ohio, which had one of its officers (Lieutenant Colonel Charles B. Winder) obtain the first Reserve Military Aviator rating in 1912; and Maryland, which in 1923 became the first to have a National Guard unit (the 104th Squadron) equipped with its own aircraft.

Arkansas, New Jersey, Tennessee and Washington can proudly point out that theirs were the first observation squadrons to be called to active duty before America was drawn into World War II (the 154th, 119th, 105th and 116th going on active duty on 16 September 1940). Finally, Colorado and Missouri were first in the post-World War II era to obtain federal recognition for fighter and bombardment

units (the 120th Fighter Squadron on 30 June 1946 and the 180th Bombardment Squadron on 22 August 1946, respectively).

The first attempts at creating aviation units in the National Guard and the post-World War I organization of federally recognized squadrons, the true forebears of today's Air National Guard units, are detailed later.

The Militia shows the way

When they joined the First Regiment, Rhode Island Militia, James Allen and Dr William H. Helme took along with them the two balloons in which, as private citizens, they had made several ascents. Convinced that balloons would be ideal machines to observe the disposition of enemy forces, the two Rhode Island militiamen diligently sought to place their balloons at the disposal of Union forces assembled under the command of General Irvin McDowell at the onset of the Civil War. Finally succeeding, Allen and Helme attempted their first military ascent in Washington, DC, on 9 June 1861. While their effort failed when the balloon could not be inflated properly, this attempt – and an equally unsuccessful one on 14 July 1861 when both balloons were set to observe Confederate forces before the Battle of Bull Run (the first major engagement of the Civil War) – marked the start of military aviation in the United States. Accordingly, Guardsmen can proudly claim that two of their forebears showed the way to the regulars.

Balloons were used a few times in Virginia during the

National Air & Space Museum

Board of Ordnance and Fortification. Thus, it was only in February 1908 that they were rewarded by the placing of an order for the first US military aircraft. Delivered to Fort Myer, Virginia, on 20 August 1908, this aircraft was first demonstrated in flight by Orville Wright two weeks later. In the afternoon of 17 September, the airplane crashed, injuring Orville Wright and killing his passenger, Lieutenant Thomas E. Selfridge.[4] In spite of this first military air casualty, the Wright Flyer was rebuilt and on 2 August 1909 was officially accepted, giving the United States the world's first military airplane.

New York's Aeronautic Corps

Guardsmen had already begun evincing much interest in aviation, as on 30 April 1908, 17 officers and men[5] of the 1st Company, Signal Corps, New York National Guard, had been placed under the command of Major Oscar Erlandsen to form an 'Aeronautic Corps'. Twice during the first month of existence of the Aeronautic Corps its personnel received instruction by means of then modern training techniques: First Lieutenants Frank Lahm and Thomas E. Selfridge, the first officers selected to learn to fly the yet-to-be-delivered Wright airplane, and Leo A. Stevens, a civilian who had a balloon factory in New York, used a film of a Farman airplane, and lantern slides, to illustrate their training lectures. During the next three years pro-

Above: Attempts at forming flying units in the Naval Militia were short-lived. This Curtiss F flying-boat belonged to the Aviation Detachment, First Battalion, New York Naval Militia, at Bay Shore, Long Island, in 1916.

Below: Lieutenant Colonel Charles B. Winder, Ohio National Guard, became on 22 May 1912 the first Guard officer to obtain a Reserve Military Aviator rating. Standing to his left are Lieutenants Hazelhurst and Milling, and Captain Beck, of the Signal Corps, US Army; Mr Walsh, their civilian instructor, is at the controls.

Civil War, notably by Union forces during the battle of Fair Oaks on 31 May and 1 June 1862, the crossing of the Rappahannock River in December 1862, and at the battle of Chancellorsville in April-May 1863, but US military interest in this new instrument of war remained almost nonexistent for 25 years. However, after investing $50,000 in 1898 to help Professor Samuel P. Langley finance the development of a man-carrying airplane, the Army again lost interest as Langley's attempt to fly his 'Aerodrome' proved unsuccessful.

Thirteen months after making the world's first powered, sustained and controlled flight at Kitty Hawk, North Carolina, on 17 December 1903, the Wright brothers in turn sought to interest the US Army in their airplane. Their efforts, however, were frustrated by the lack of understanding of the military potential of heavier-than-air machines displayed by members of the Army

USAF

[4] The airfield, which was activated in July 1917 at the storage depot in Mount Clemens, Michigan, was named Selfridge Field in memory of the first Army officer to be killed in an air crash. In July 1971, Selfridge AFB was transferred to the Michigan Air National Guard and was redesignated Selfridge ANGB. It currently houses the 127th TFW and 191st FIG, MI ANG, as well as units from the AFRES, USAF, USCG, USMCR and USNR.

[5] First Lieutenant Hallahan; Sergeants Bacon, Huelser, Thomas and Tack; Corporals La Roche, Everett, Stewart and Mohr; Privates First Class Coffin and Crassi; and Privates Brokaw, Carolin, Doty, Overton, Veeder and Wilcox.

The Guard's Early Days

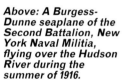

Above: A Burgess-Dunne seaplane of the Second Battalion, New York Naval Militia, flying over the Hudson River during the summer of 1916.

Right: Private Beckwith Havens, an exhibiton pilot working for the Curtiss Aeroplane Company, joined the Aeronautics Corps, 1st Company, Signal Corps, New York National Guard, in 1911. He used his own airplane to familiarize fellow Guardsmen with the potential of flying machines.

gress was slow, as the National Guard lacked funds to finance a venture which most people considered ludicrous. The New York Guardsmen did learn to assemble and handle a 35,000-cubic foot balloon under the guidance of Leo Stevens; however, the first balloon ascent by one of their members, if indeed one was made officially, has remained unrecorded. Most of the Guardsmen's duty time was spent receiving standard Signal Corps training in signaling, firearms practice, equitation and field services.

Following the acceptance of the Wright Flyer by the regulars, Guard interest in aeronautics increased markedly, but the subsequent events have since become confused due to ill-recorded claims and counterclaims by Guard units of the various states. Most claims regarding the formation of aeronautic units remain largely unsubstantiated as often they only reflected the dream of early civilian flyers to place their aeronautical experience at the disposal of the Guard and their country. However, in most instances these aspirations were not carried forth.

Pioneering attempts

Perusal of contemporary documents has brought to light several significant attempts which went beyond mere idle talk and grandstanding. The most significant ones are summarized in chronological order.

By General Order No. 19, dated 12 August 1909, the commanding general of the Missouri National Guard directed that a 15-man aero detachment be organized under the command of Lieutenant Chester E. Burg in Company A, Signal Corps, based in St Louis. It is of interest that all men of this aero detachment were coincidentally members of the St Louis Aero Club, which had been organized by Major Albert Bond Lambert (a Guard officer after whom Lambert Field is named) to train balloon pilots for the 1907 international balloon races held in St Louis. No further developments in the use of balloons or airplanes were reported by the Missouri National Guard until 1923 when, as noted later on, the 110th Observation Squadron was organized under the command of William Robertson.

Secretary of War Jacob Dickinson and President William Taft asked Congress in 1910 for a $500,000 appropriation (later scaled down to $250,000) to procure aeronautical equipment and instruction for the Army and the National Guard. In support of this request for appropriation, General James Allen, Chief of the Army's Signal Corps, clarified the plans of the War Department for the development of aeronautical activities, first in the Regular Army and then, eventually, in the National Guard. In particular, he stated:

"We can do nothing further in the matter until we are provided with means for buying more aeronautical devices, such as aeroplanes, dirigible balloons and other flying equipment, each of which, it is believed, has a special fitness in war . . . When the work is sufficiently developed for the Signal Corps in the Regular Army and accepted as part of the military equipment of the army, there is no doubt that similar work will be taken up amongst the Signal Corps companies of the National Guard, the same as with other signal corps work. These machines will be furnished to the National Guard as other war material . . . It is to be hoped that an appropriation will be made this year to enable this work to be carried on. The Militia Bureau has never had a definite appropriation for aero work, and the Signal Corps can do nothing further until Congress appropriates."

Unfortunately, appropriations actually approved by Congress in this and subsequent years were insufficient to enable the Signal Corps to equip the National Guard with airplanes.

Undaunted, in August 1910, Guardsmen of the Aeronautic Corps, 1st Company, Signal Corps, New York National Guard, came through with $500 to pay for shipping to Army maneuvers at Pine Camp, New York, the copy of an early Farman airplane built by one of their original members, Private Phillip W. Wilcox. This airplane could not be flown during the maneuvers, however, and subsequently crashed at Garden City, New York. Wilcox survived the crash, to become a major in the Army Air Service. Two years later the New York National Guard had a Curtiss airplane flying during joint Army-Guard maneuvers in Connecticut.

On the West Coast, the first aeronautic unit was formed on 12 March 1912 in the 7th Company, Coast Artillery Corps, California National Guard. Among its first mem-

National Air and Space Museum

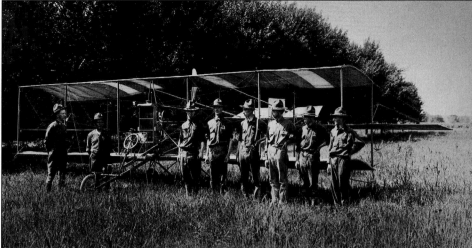

National Guard Association

bers the unit counted a private by the name of Eugene B. Ely. Ely, the famous earlybird who, on 14 November 1910, had made the first airplane take-off from the deck of a warship (the USS *Birmingham*) and who, on 18 January 1911, had made the first deck landing aboard the USS *Pennsylvania*, contributed not only his experience but also personal funds to enable the California Guard to obtain some aviation experience. Commissioned on 27 June 1911 as a second lieutenant in the California National Guard, Ely was not on Guard duty when he was killed in a crash at Macon, Georgia, a few weeks later. Following his death, the California Guardsmen continued toying with airplanes, notably by experimenting in association with the Southern California Aeronautical Society, with early wireless equipment. However, little state support was available and these experiments with aviation ended soon thereafter. Likewise, an Aeronautical Section in the California Naval Militia, which had been mustered on 11 December 1915, disappeared within 17 months when the Naval Militia was inducted into federal service.

In July 1911, John B. Moisant, the founder of an early flying school and of the Moisant International Aviators group, offered to train free of charge any National Guardsmen chosen by the Governor of the State of Michigan. Captain George W. MacKay of Company A, Signal Corps, Michigan National Guard, was chosen by Governor Osborn, and his expenses while attending Moisant's aviation school at Garden City, Long Island, were paid by the Guard's Signal Corps. Thus, Captain MacKay became the first Guard officer to earn a Fédération Aéronautique Internationale civilian pilot's license while in service with the Guard.

During the same year, Beckwith Havens, an exhibition pilot working for the Curtiss Airplane Company, joined the Aeronautic Corps, 1st Company, Signal Corps, New York National Guard. Even though he only held the rank of private, Havens brought with him his aircraft and thus further familiarized fellow New York Guardsmen with the potential of flying machines.

Reserve Military Aviators

Whereas Captain MacKay of the Michigan National Guard had learned to fly in a civilian school and had obtained an FAI license, Lieutenant Colonel Charles B. Winder of the Ohio National Guard became the first Guard officer to obtain a Reserve Military Aviator (RMA) rating. The events leading to Lieutenant Colonel Winder's rating began when the War Department detailed Lieutenant Benjamin D. Foulois, the nation's third military aviator and future Chief of the Air Corps, to visit the National Guard headquarters of the various states and institute a comprehensive system of aeronautic instruction for the Guard. During these visits Lieutenant Foulois informed the Guardsmen that, to qualify as military pilots, officers would have to (**1**) reach an altitude of at least 2,500 ft (760 m), make a cross-country flight of at least 10 miles (16 km) and return, at a minimum height of 1,000 ft (305 m); (**2**) fly for at least five minutes in 15-mph (24-

km/h) wind; (**3**) carry a passenger to at least 500 ft (150 m) altitude; (**4**) fly a 20-mile (32-km) reconnaissance mission at an average altitude of 1,500 ft (460 m); and (**5**) land within 150 ft (45 m) of a designated point after gliding from an altitude of at least 500 ft (150 m). Availing itself of the flight training offer made by the War Department, the Ohio National Guard instructed Lieutenant Colonel Winder, on 6 March 1912, to attend the Aviation School at Augusta, Georgia. The school was moved to College Park, Maryland, the following month and there Lieutenant Colonel Winder soloed on 20 May and qualified for his RMA rating two days later.

When, in August of that year, the 1st Company, Signal Corps, New York National Guard, joined other Guard and Army units for training maneuvers along the Housatonic River, Private Havens took along his Curtiss Model E. Most Guard officers did not know what to do with the strange flying contraption and Private Havens was sent to join the regulars. Whereas Havens' lack of military training made his observation work worthless, the arrival of his aircraft increased by 50 per cent the equipment of the flying unit! After these maneuvers, the 1st Company received from a Mrs Russell Sage a donation of $5,000, with which it acquired the first aircraft to belong to the National Guard, and $650 to cover the expense of its operation.

The year 1912 also saw attempts at forming aviation units in at least two other states, Colorado and Pennsylvania. In the former state, Private First Class James E. Helpling joined the Guard after being discharged from the Army Signal Corps in which he had qualified as an expert aviator. Two Curtiss graduates also joined the Guard as instructors, but lack of funds prevented that state from implementing its projected aviation activities. In the Pennsylvania National Guard, the members of Company A, Third Regiment, were bitten by the aviation bug when they were joined by Lieutenant Hammis, the inventor of an airship, and Private Hungerliter, a then well-known aviator. However, there too, monetary restrictions soon cured the disease.

Better luck attended efforts during 1913 by officers and men of the Nebraska National Guard to assemble a biplane, which appears to have been a Curtiss Model D. This aircraft was flown at Fremont and may have been taken along during the annual encampment; however, there was as yet no official recognition of an aviation branch by the State of Nebraska.

Even though the European fighting powers had committed their fledgling aviation units immediately after the outbreak of World War I in August 1914 (the first aerial victory was claimed on 5 October 1914 by France's Aviation Militaire), military aviation continued to be neglected in the United States. Here and there efforts were being made to achieve some results, and forward-thinking Guardsmen

Above: Personnel of the Aviation Corps, Nebraska National Guard, in front of the Curtiss Model D of Captain Ralph E. McMillen in the summer of 1915. The two officers on the left appear to be Captains Schaffer and McMillen.

Above left: The LWF Model V of the Michigan National Guard was flown both with a land undercarriage and with twin pontoons before being extensively damaged at Camp Ferris, Grayling, during a storm on 18 August 1916.

Above: Following the lead of two Rhode Island militiamen, James Allen and Dr William H. Helme, who twice attempted to fly their balloon before the first Battle of Bull Run, Union forces made limited use of balloons during the Civil War.

Above right: In 1912, the War Department authorized aviation training for Guard officers. Trained in Augusta, GA, and College Park, MD, Lieutenant Colonel Charles B. Winder of the Ohio National Guard obtained the first Reserve Military Aviator rating in May 1912.

played a major part in this venture. In Nebraska, Captain Castle W. Schaffer was appointed chief of aviation in the Guard and was joined by Ralph E. McMillen, a qualified pilot and aircraft owner. Under the leadership of these two officers, Nebraska officially organized, on 15 July 1915, an Aviation Corps, and during the following month Captain McMillen flew the Curtiss Model D he owned during the encampment of the 4th and 5th Infantry Regiments, Nebraska National Guard.

During the following 12 months, the Nebraskans continued their aviation endeavors and Second Lieutenant Edgar W. Bagnell learned to fly. Both Bagnell and McMillen were sent to the Curtiss Atlantic Coast Aeronautical Station, Newport News, Virginia. There, both officers apparently obtained their FAI licenses but, on 2 September 1916, Captain McMillen was killed while flying a display at St Francis, Kansas. In spite of the loss of his mentor, Second Lieutenant Bagnell carried on and, after the United States declared war on Germany in April 1917, he joined the Third Aero Squadron, Air Service, at San Antonio, Texas.

By the fall of 1915, the development of aviation in the National Guard took a leap forward as the Aero Club of America, worried by the slow development of military aviation in the United States, endeavored to encourage fund-raising for aircraft to be used by the National Guard and Naval Militia of the states. Specifically, the Aero Club set up a National Aeroplane Fund and pledged to contribute an amount equivalent to 10 per cent, but not to exceed $10,000 per state, of all donations which would be collected by the states. This pledge was backed by the offer of Mr Emerson McMillin, a prominent New York banker, who offered $100 for every $900 raised, up to a maximum of $500,000.

New Yorkers take the lead

During the encampment of the New York National Guard in the fall of 1915, Captain Raynal C. Bolling – who less than three years later died in France while trying to avoid capture during a ground reconnaissance mission, and after whom Bolling AFB, DC, is named – rented an airplane and learned to fly. Upon returning to New York, Bolling and James E. Miller, with the support of General John F. O'Ryan, began recruiting personnel to organize an aviation unit for which two Gallaudet tractor airplanes – one with a 100-hp and one with a 50-hp Gnome engine – were rented and for which flying instructions were provided by Filip A. Bjorklund and, later, Overton M. Bounds, A. B. Thaw and H. W. Blakely. The success of this venture led the State of New York to organize the first genuine aviation unit in the National Guard on 1 November 1915: the Aviation Detachment, 1st Battalion, Signal Corps, under the command of Captain Bolling.

Spurred by the availability of money through the National Aeroplane Fund, the joint decision of the Division of Militia Affairs, the aviation section of the Signal Corps and the Department of the Navy to provide, upon state request, flight training for militiamen, numerous aviation developments took place during 1916 in the National Guard and the Naval Militia.[6] In the latter organization, aviation units were formed in at least five states. In California, an Aeronautical Section was

mustered on 11 December 1915, but it disappeared within 17 months when the Naval Militia was inducted into federal service. The Massachusetts Naval Militia acquired two airplanes, one of which was a Burgess Model U, which it used during a two-week encampment on Mystery Island in September 1916. In Rhode Island, the Naval Militia obtained a total of $25,000, including a $7,500 gift from Miss Lyra Brown Nickerson through the National Aeroplane Fund, with which a Sturtevant seaplane was acquired in 1916 and personnel trained. Meanwhile, the First and Second Battalions, New York Naval Militia, respectively acquired a Curtiss F flying-boat and two Burgess-Dunne seaplanes and operated respectively from Bay Shore, Long Island, and Rhinebeck on the Hudson River under the command of Ensign Vincent Astor and Lieutenant Harris. To assist these units of the Naval Militia, as well as the one planned for Connecticut, the Navy trained a number of pilots and maintenance personnel at Pensacola, Florida. However, none of these units survived after being inducted into federal service during World War I.

Within a year of its organization, the National Aeroplane Fund had collected $171,031.17 and more than 85 per cent of the money had been distributed. The timing of these disbursements was most favorable, as a troublesome situation along the Mexican border had deteriorated while the nation was slowly moving towards a state of belligerence with the Central Powers in Europe. Besides partially financing the previously mentioned purchase of aircraft for the New York and Rhode Island Naval Militia, as well as that of an LWF Model V donated in 1916 to the Michigan National Guard, the National Aeroplane Fund provided a substantial portion of pilot training cost for National Guard officers. Thus, by the end of 1916 at least 20 Guardsmen had earned RMA ratings, among them Captain H. Fleet[7], Washington.

Even though the above contributions were significant, it was the New York National Guard which became the

---

[6] The first Naval Militia units, four companies forming the Naval Battalion of the Volunteer Militia, had been organized in Massachusetts on 28 March 1890 and 23 other states had followed suit prior to World War I. However, the planned naval counterpart of the National Guard did not find as much favor and, even though some states still have the necessary statutes, it has now virtually disappeared.

[7] This National Guard officer, who obtained his RMA in April 1917, became Officer-in-Charge of the Aerial Mail Service in May 1918 and organized the Consolidated Aircraft Corporation – the principal forebear company of today's General Dynamics – in May 1923.

Left: *The balloon* Intrepid *being inflated by union troops during the Battle of Fair Oaks, six miles east of Richmond, Virginia, on 31 May–1 June 1862.*

largest recipient of the National Aeroplane Fund when it received $21,535.74 during 1916. With this money, the 1st Aero Company, as the original New York unit had been redesignated, was able to replace in early 1916 the two unsatisfactory Gallaudet machines it rented with five new airplanes: a Curtiss JN-4 with a 90-hp OX-2 engine, an LWF with a 140-hp Sturtevant, a Sloane-Day with a 125-hp Hall-Scott, a Sturtevant with a 140-hp Sturtevant engine and a Thomas T2 with a 90-hp OX-2. Within a few months the LWF and Sturtevant aircraft were taken out of the inventory but, soon after, a second Curtiss JN-4 was added. In addition to providing the means with which to expand the activities of its 1st Aero Company, the financial assistance received from the National Aeroplane Fund enabled the New York National Guard to organize the 2nd Aero Company in Buffalo. This new unit was mustered on 30 June 1916 under the command of Captain John Sutterfield.

Mexican Punitive Expedition

While these activities were taking place, the United States had been forced in March 1916 to launch the Mexican Punitive Expedition to avenge Pancho Villa's raid on Columbus, New Mexico. To support this expedition and beef up the regular troops of General Pershing, President Woodrow Wilson mobilized a major portion of the National Guard under a call issued on 18 June 1916. Eventually, some 100,000 Guardsmen served for six months on the Mexican border and some of the fledgling aviation elements of the Guard got their first taste of federal duty. Even though it remained at Mineola, New York, for additional training, the 1st Aero Company of the New York National Guard was the most noteworthy of these elements.

Called to active duty on 13 July 1916, the 1st Aero Company had four officers on flying status. None of its 27 additional members who had been recommended for such status qualified for their RMA rating while on 16-week active duty. During this period, the 1st Aero Company was placed under the command of Captain Joseph E. Carberry, and was enlarged by the addition of a dozen Guard officers from other states, six regular officers, and a 25-man Army detachment, to bring its total complement to about 130 officers and enlisted personnel. Flight training at Mineola (by that time identified as a Signal Corps Aviation Station) was stepped up and the 1st Aero Company remained in federal service until 2 November 1916 and continued as a New York Guard unit until 23 May 1917 when, in turn, it was disbanded. Although it served on active duty, the 1st Aero Company never received federal recognition. (The first aviation unit in the Guard to reach this milestone was the 109th Observation Squadron, Minnesota National Guard, which was organized after World War I, as detailed later on.)

As its contribution to the Mexican Punitive Expedition,

the Signal Corps of the US Army had initially been able to send only its 1st Aero Squadron, which was commanded by Captain Benjamin Foulois and equipped with eight Curtiss JN-3s. Within five weeks of its arrival in New Mexico, this first regular aviation unit was reduced to 25 per cent strength and the sorry condition of military aviation in the United States became the subject of much criticism. Leading the fight for a quantitative and qualitative increase in American military aviation was Alan R. Hawley, the President of the Aero Club of America, who actively campaigned for a congressional appropriation of $2,000,000 and the training of 2,000 military aviators. To bring attention to its president's proposal, the Aero Club contributed $7,500 towards the $10,000 purchase price of the prototype Curtiss Twin-JN and donated it to the New Mexico National Guard. Shipped from Washington, DC, at the end of May 1916, the Twin-JN was reassembled in New Mexico but it apparently crashed on a flight from Hachita to Columbus prior to making a concrete contribution to the war's effort.

Of equally minor material importance was the use of a Goodyear Kite Balloon from the Ohio National Guard, which was sent to Texas in the winter of 1916-17. In addition, the Michigan National Guard was scheduled to contribute its LWF Model V, but this aircraft was damaged in a hurricane at Camp Ferris, Grayling, Michigan, on 18 August 1916. Likewise, attempts by the Nebraska National Guard to contribute its aviation unit under Lieutenant Bagnell for service in Mexico were never sanctioned.

Towards the end of Fiscal Year 1916,[8] the National Defense Act was passed by Congress on 3 June, and among its many features was an affirmation of the role and importance of the National Guard. The Guard became fully a part of the organized peacetime military establishment of the United States and the organization of its units was made to conform to that of regular Army units. Early in the following fiscal year, Congress approved a recommendation from the Militia Bureau and appropriated $76,000 to purchase and maintain material and equipment necessary for the proper instruction in military aviation of such officers and enlisted men of the National Guard as authorized by the War Department to attend the United States Signal Corps Aviation School. Thus, during FY17, 18 Guardsmen received training in Signal Corps schools in San Diego, CA, Mineola, NY, and Memphis, TN. At long last it appeared that aviation was about to become a recognized activity in the National Guard.

---

[8] Up to 1975, the Fiscal Years as used by the US government extended from 1 July through 30 June. Thus, Fiscal Year 1916 ran from 1 July 1915 until 30 June 1916. The system was changed in 1976 and, beginning with FY77, Fiscal Years have started on 1 October of the preceding calendar year (e.g. FY90 covered the 12 months from 1 October 1989 through 30 September 1990).

The Guard's Early Days

Right: On 18/19 November 1916, less than three weeks after the 1st Aero Company, New York National Guard, had been returned to state control after the first federal activation of a National Guard aviation unit, 10 of its Curtiss JN-4s were flown from Mineola to Princeton and back.

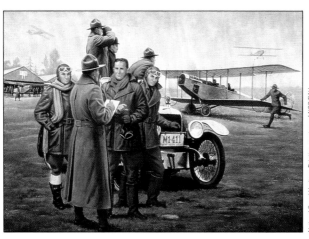

Above right: First Lieutenant Reed M. Chambers, a former Tennessee Guardsman serving in France with the 94th Aero Squadron, AEF, shot down two Fokker D VIIs on 2 November 1918 to raise his score to five enemy aircraft destroyed, thus becoming the first Guardsman to reach ace status.

At that time, however, availability of aircraft and provision for flight training were not the pacing elements in the development of National Guard aviation. In this respect, reports by Captain R. C. Bolling, the commanding officer of New York's 1st Aero Company, and First Lieutenant J. E. Carberry,[9] the regular Signal Corps officer assigned to supervise this unit and its CO during the unit's period of active duty, made interesting reading in the report of the Chief of the Militia Bureau submitted at the end of Fiscal Year 1916. In particular, Captain Bolling noted:

"There is no difficulty in obtaining any desired number of men of education, character and intelligence to take up military aviation. Men qualified by character, intelligence and education to become officers and not merely aviators can be readily obtained. If men of this sort are desired, there is no need to take men of a different sort.

"It is extremely difficult – and, in my opinion, will not generally prove possible – to obtain the right sort of mechanics as enlisted men in National Guard aviation units.

"The expert mechanical work required in an aviation unit is very great in amount and most exacting in character. The utmost skill and care are required at all times and in every detail. This work must be done by mechanics regularly and constantly employed on the aeroplanes and motors. Mechanics who report at the aviation field only once or twice a week for a few hours according to the established rule of the National Guard duty cannot keep the aeroplanes in condition to be used, nor can such mechanics themselves be trained successfully. Furthermore, except in war times, men do not enlist in the National Guard merely to work nights and Saturday afternoons and Sundays at their regular trade. For these reasons and from our experience I am convinced that it will always be necessary to employ an adequate force of expert professional mechanics to maintain and repair the aeroplanes of any National Guard organization. *(Time proved Captain Bolling to have been right. Today, ANG aircraft are maintained by full-time ANG Technicians.)*

"It is very doubtful whether men will join National Guard aviation units unless they can be reasonably sure that sooner or later they will be given a chance to fly."

Center, top: The Curtiss Oriole which was rented by the State of Minnesota for the flight to Washington, DC, in September/ October 1920 by Captain Ray Miller, Lieutenant Colonel William Harris, and Brigadier General Walter Rhinow.

Likewise, Lieutenant Carberry reported:

"The First Aero Company was mustered into federal service 13 July 1916; it has been in active training since November 1915, a period of nine months; it possesses four aeroplanes of a military type; it has had the service of highly paid aviation instructors and mechanics; the consistent devotion of its members has been wholly admirable, but as an aero company, in the military sense, it is non-existent. The intention at the time of its creation was the training of a corps of officer aviators. In that it has succeeded, but it lacks, and under present condition will continue to lack, the

Center, bottom: Curtiss JN-6H of the 116th Observation Squadron, Washington National Guard, getting some extra horse power after making a forced landing on a farm.

[9] Shortly after taking command of the activated 1st Aero Company, Joseph Carberry was promoted to Captain (the rank used earlier in this narrative).

trained personnel that makes an aero company not only efficient, but even possible. No one will more candidly admit the truth of this statement than its own commanding officer.

" . . . Is it to be expected that other states will have greater success? Quite the reverse, considering the field of selection that is here open. *(Prior to World War I, Long Island, New York, was known in the United States as 'The cradle of aviation'. Later on, of course, the US aviation industry shifted westward.)* It is not too much to predict that if in each state an aviation unit, or group of units, is raised, that the training of these units will be inadequate, except at a prohibitive cost, ununiform, due to the impossibility of federal supervision *(In that respect, Lieutenant Carberry was less prophetic as today ANG units are effectively supervised by their gaining commands.)*, so far as preparation for war is concerned."

The United States enters World War I

The opinions expressed by these two respected officers weighed heavily in the decision made by the War Department that National Guard units called to active duty when America entered the World War in April 1917 would not include aviation elements. Thus, all Guard aviation units ceased to exist at that time and their personnel tendered their services as individuals. The survivors, however, along with many of the young men who served with the American Expeditionary Force in 1917-1918, were to become the founders of the observation squadrons formed in the National Guard beginning in January 1921.

When on 6 April 1917 the United States declared war on the Central Powers (Germany, Austria-Hungary, Bulgaria and Turkey), its military aviation was in a sorry state. The Aviation Section of the Signal Corps consisted of 35 pilots, 1,987 men and 55 aircraft suitable only for training, while New York's 1st Aero Company, the only aviation unit then in Guard service, was about to be disbanded. Fortunately, three and one-half months later Congress approved a first massive air appropriation of $640,000,000. Moreover, the Allies were ready and willing to assist the United States by providing training and a large quantity of aircraft (by war's end France had supplied 4,500 aircraft to the American Expeditionary Force, Great Britain had delivered 258 and Italy had contributed 19 trainers). Concurrently, a massive industrial effort was mounted at home and its chief results were the license-built de Havilland D.H.4 bombers (entering combat operation with the 135th Corps Observation Squadron on 2 August 1918; 1,213 American-built D.H.4s eventually reached the Western Front), the Curtiss JN (Jenny) series of trainers, and the excellent 8- and 12-cylinder Liberty engines.

On the war front, active participation by US aviation units began on 18 February 1918 when the 103rd Aero Squadron, the famous American volunteer unit previously known as the 'Escadrille Lafayette' or SPA 124, began

Above: The Douglas O-2H was the first aircraft to prove effective in National Guard service. This aircraft of the 111th Observation Squadron, Texas National Guard, was photogaphed at Ellington Field, Houston, on 3 June 1928.

Left: The first aircraft to be issued to National Guard aviation units were Curtiss Jennies of various models. These two are JN-4Ds built by the St Louis Aircraft Company.

operations under the tactical control of France's Aviation Militaire. The first original US combat unit, the 94th Pursuit Squadron, made its first flight across the lines one month later, while the 1st Corps Observation Squadron and the 96th Aero Squadron respectively became, on 11 April and 12 June 1918, the first American observation and bombardment squadrons to be operational in France. Combat experience soon mounted as additional American units joined the fray, and by war's end the Air Service, AEF, claimed a total of 781 enemy aircraft and 73 balloons for the loss in combat of 237 officers and men. By that time, the Army Air Service had a total of 195,024 personnel, of whom 20,568 were officers, and operated 8,403 aircraft, of which 3,538 were with the AEF. Indeed, American air power had grown spectacularly in the space of only 19 months.

Following the signing of the Armistice on 11 November 1918, a swift military demobilization took place with the Army Air Service being slated to be reduced to 24,000 officers and men. By 1920, this figure was further reduced to some 10,000 personnel, or only a mere five per cent of the peak wartime strength. This drastic reduction, however, released large numbers not only of pilots and observers but also of mechanics and other skilled specialists and created a talent pool from which the National Guard was soon able to draw, thus overcoming the manning problem noted in 1916 by Captain Bolling and First Lieutenant Carberry.

Air Service units for the Guard

Even though the post-World War I period was not a good one in which to organize new military units (since the American people were satiated with military matters much as they were to become in the post-Vietnam War era), the Militia Bureau was keen to exploit the pool of talents made available by the demobilization. Accordingly, on 14 February 1919, just three months after the end of the war, it sent back to the director of Military Aeronautics its Circular No. 9 of 1916 requesting information and suggestions to update that circular as regards the formation and operation of aero units in the National Guard. The matter was discussed by the director of Military Aeronautics, the chief of the Air Service and their staffs until 9 February 1920, when they communicated the results of this review to the Militia Bureau. In paragraph two of this communication, the director of Military Aeronautics stated:

"National Guard divisions should be organized the same as is contemplated for the divisions of the regular army and authority is hereby granted for including in each National Guard Division one aero unit consisting of the following: one observation squadron, one balloon company, one photo section and one branch G-2 (military intelligence). Each aero squadron, balloon company, photo section and branch G-2 will be organized as are similar units in the regular army."

On the strength of this communication, the Militia Bureau issued on 1 June 1920 its Circular No. 1, covering the organization of aero units in the National Guard. At that time, anticipating the formation of these units, the Air Service reserved the numbers 101 through 199 for the National Guard flying squadrons. The Air Service further decided to limit the role of National Guard squadrons to observation and planned initially to equip these units with Curtiss JN-4s and JN-6s, both of which it had in large numbers. Furthermore, the Air Service undertook to assign to each Guard squadron one of its regular officers to act as inspector for the squadron and to assure that each unit would reach the appropriate level of training.

First federally-recognized squadron

As the Militia Bureau's Circular No. 1 was issued during the last month of FY20, no squadron could be formed in the National Guard during that year. However, several states soon expressed interest and the honor of gaining the first federally-recognized squadron went to Minnesota. Soon after Governor Burnquist had passed a copy of Circular No. 1 to Brigadier General W. F. Rhinow, the Adjutant General, a first meeting was held in St Paul to chart the

Above: The 116th Observation Squadron, 41st Division, Washington National Guard, was initially equipped with JN-4Ds and was federally recognized at Felts Field, Spokane, on 6 August 1924.

Above: Differing from the O-2H mainly in having the Liberty engine replaced by a 600-hp Curtiss Conqueror, the Douglas O-25 was a relatively rare aircraft in National Guard service. Belonging to Tennessee's 105th Observation Squadron, this O-25 was photographed during gunnery practice at Valparaiso, Florida, on 19 August 1936.

Top right: Powered by a 90-hp OX-5 engine, this JN-4H of the 101st Observation Squadron, Massachusetts National Guard, is typical of the Curtiss Jennies which equipped 16 National Guard squadrons between July 1921 and September 1927.

Above right: Curtiss JNSs of the 110th Observation Squadron, Missouri National Guard. The letters FAI on the white rudder stripe indicate that the aircraft have been rebuilt by the Fairfield Air Intermediate Depot in Ohio.

organization of an observation squadron in the 34th Division, Minnesota National Guard. Attending this meeting were Lieutenant Colonel William Garis, the state's Assistant Adjutant General; T. Glen Harrison, a local newspaper reporter; and Lieutenant Ray S. Miller, a recently discharged Air Service pilot who was chief pilot for the Curtiss Northwest Airplane Company. In July 1920, Miller became a captain and was designated the commanding officer of the yet-to-be-born squadron, while Harrison was commissioned a first lieutenant and appointed squadron adjutant. With the full support from Governor Burnquist and Brigadier General Rhinow, plans were drawn for a flight to Washington, DC, to consult with the chief of the Militia Bureau and the chief of the Air Service. By Special Order No. 161 issued on 24 September 1920 by the Adjutant General, Captain Miller, Lieutenant Colonel Garis and Brigadier General Rhinow were instructed to proceed from St Paul to Washington. For this purpose the state of Minnesota rented an Oriole[10] from the Curtiss Northwest Airplane Company. With Captain Miller as pilot, the three officers departed on 26 September and completed their 1,600-mile (2560-km) flight on 2 October after stopping in LaCrosse and Madison, WI, Chicago, IL, Van Wirt and Cleveland, OH, and Amsterdam, Albany, Poughkeepsie and Garden City, NY. In Washington, the Minnesotans held a series of fruitful meetings with Major General Jessie Carter, chief of the Militia Bureau, Major General Mason Patrick, chief of the Air Service, and Brigadier General Billy Mitchell, assistant chief of the Air Service, resulting in the official organization of the 109th Squadron.

Proceeding with the same vigor with which it sought approval of its efforts, the state of Minnesota had fully organized the 109th Squadron by 10 January 1921, under the command of Ray Miller, who had by then been promoted to Major. With a personnel strength of 21 officers and 90 men, the 109th was extended federal recognition on 17 January 1921, thus becoming the first National Guard aviation unit to achieve this distinction. The 109th Squadron, however, had not yet satisfied the federal requirement for "reasonably permanent hangars, preferably of steel, and provided with concrete floors, electric lights, heating and water systems" to care for aircraft assigned to the National Guard but remaining federal government property. Accordingly, the unit did not receive its nine Curtiss JN-6Hs until February 1922, 13 months after having been federally recognized, when it moved into permanent facilities at Speedway Field (now the site of the Minneapolis-St Paul International Airport).

Twice during 1921, in spite of its lack of flying equipment, the 109th Squadron was called to active duty by the state of Minnesota: the first time, within days from having obtained federal recognition, it was asked to mount an aerial search for the Cook County commissioner, who had disappeared during a boat trip on Lake Superior; and the second time, in the fall of 1921, it flew forest fire patrols over northern Minnesota. In both cases, the unit had to rent a Curtiss Oriole to discharge its duty.

Following in the footsteps of Minnesota, Maryland organized its Guard squadron beginning in November 1920 when Adjutant General Milton Reckord met in Baltimore with members of the American Flying Club, among whom were several World War I veteran pilots including Major George Jones, Captains Paul Burwell, John Hambleton and William Tipton, and First Lieutenants Harold Hinds and Charles Masson. By April 1921, these men were authorized to proceed with the recruitment of members sufficient to form an observation squadron in the 29th Division, Maryland NG. Designated the 104th Squadron, the new unit was extended federal recognition on 29 June. Like the 109th Squadron, the 104th was not issued its own aircraft until suitable facilities were built at Logan Field, but its personnel were able to obtain some experience by borrowing Curtiss JN-4s from a regular unit stationed at Bolling Field, DC.

Jennies for the Guard

Between July and October 1921, the 104th Squadron received 13 Curtiss JN-4Ds, thus becoming the first National Guard unit to be equipped with airplanes supplied by the Air Service. In July of the following year, the 104th gained further renown by becoming the first flying unit to attend a summer encampment (at Langley Field, VA).

In order to assemble the necessary personnel for an observation squadron in the Indiana National Guard, another war-trained pilot, Major Wilbur Fagley, organized a headquarters battery in the 81st Field Artillery and flew to Washington to drum up support. Succeeding in his attempt, Major Fagley became the first commanding officer of the 137th Squadron. This unit received federal recognition on 1 August 1921 as a Corps Aviation unit attached to the Indiana NG. Its first facility, including two steel hangars, was located on a field outside Kokomo and it is there that the 137th received its Curtiss JN-4Ds shortly before the end of FY22. Less than six weeks later, the squadron took its aircraft to Wright Field, OH, for its first encampment.

The history of the 102nd Squadron, which was activated in the 27th Division, New York NG, on 17 November 1921, is an interesting one, as the unit received its Jennies some months before receiving federal recognition on 4

---

[10] The Curtiss Oriole was a three-seat (with passengers seated side-by-side and the pilot seat in a separate cockpit slightly aft) light commercial and sports biplane powered by either a 90-hp Curtiss OX-5 or 160-hp Curtiss C-6 (the more powerful engine powering the aircraft rented by the Minnesotans).

ron's inspector/instructor. Thus, by 30 June 1922, 53 Jennies had been issued to six Guard squadrons, while Massachusetts' 101st Squadron, the only unit without aircraft, had to await completion of its facilities at Logan Field to receive its aircraft during the summer of 1922. The wisdom of the federal insistence on proper hangar facilities being provided to house government-furnished equipment was soon vindicated as a unit lost three of its aircraft to freeze damage when, following suspension of operations due to cold weather, they were left in unheated Bessoneau canvas-covered hangars.

Fiscal Year 1923 saw a series of changes in unit designation as on 3 January the 137th Squadron was transferred from Corps Aviation to the 38th Division, Indiana NG, and was redesignated the 113th Squadron. This change of designation, however, was short-lived as 20 days later the full designations of the 101st, 102nd, 104th, 109th, 113th, 135th and 136th became 'Observation Squadron' instead of 'Squadron' or 'Squadron (Observation)'. Next, on 1 May 1923, the 135th Observation Squadron, upon being transferred to the 39th Division, Alabama NG, became the 114th Observation Squadron.

During the last week of FY23, three additional units were activated: the 110th Observation Squadron, 35th Division, Missouri NG, on 23 June; the 120th Observation Squadron, 45th Division, Colorado NG, on 27 June; and the 111th Observation Squadron, 36th Division, Texas NG, on 29 June. Commanded by Major William Robertson and based at the Anglum Airport, near Bridgeton, the 110th initially had to rely for flight training on a surplus Jenny purchased by its officers, but in 1924 it received the first of its federally-supplied JN-4Ds. The Colorado Guardsmen were not quite as fortunate. They did not receive their Curtiss JNSs until May 1924, when their facil-

November 1922. Led by Major Kenneth Littauer, a much-decorated Air Service veteran, the unit was initially composed of 19 wartime pilots, while its enlisted personnel were primarily obtained by transferring personnel from an infantry unit. Operations were initially split between Hempstead, where enlisted personnel were trained, New York City, where officers studied aerial observation, and Mitchel Field, where flight training was conducted. However, in 1922 all operations were concentrated at Miller Field on Staten Island and it is there that the 102nd was federally recognized at the end of the first year in the service of the New York NG.

Federally recognized on 18 November 1921 as the Air Service, 26th Division, Massachusetts NG, the 101st Squadron came into being as the result of the combined efforts of Major Leonard Drennan (a regular Army officer serving in the Boston area) and of members of the Archie Club (an organization of wartime flyers residing in New England). Initially commanded by Major James Knowle, a World War I ace, the 101st held its first summer encampment in 1922 at Mitchel Field, NY, with borrowed aircraft, as its own flying equipment was not delivered until after appropriate facilities were built at Jeffries Point on the site now occupied by Boston's Logan IAP.

For more than one year a group of Tennessee Guardsmen drilled without pay and strained to meet all requirements to obtain federal recognition for an observation squadron. Since a prerequisite was access to a landing field with suitable facilities, the group used a $10,000 donation by H. O. Blackwood to acquire a 100-acre (40.5-hectare) cornfield adjoining the Hermitage estate of President Andrew Jackson and to arrange the transfer of an old wartime hangar from Memphis Park Field to the newly named Blackwood Field outside Nashville. Federal recognition was finally obtained on 4 December 1921 and shortly thereafter the 136th Squadron, Corps Aviation, Tennessee NG, received 10 Curtiss JN-6Hs.

Another Corps Aviation Unit, the 135th Squadron, was activated in the Alabama NG under the command of a wartime ace, Major James Meissner. Based at Robert's Field outside Birmingham, the unit, initially equipped with seven Curtiss JN-4Ds, took its aircraft to Maxwell Field, Montgomery, for its first encampment during the summer of 1922.

In practice, aircraft complements still varied from squadron to squadron; however, during FY22 the Militia Bureau and the Air Service agreed to standardize on a complement of nine Jennies (JN-4D, JN-6H or JNS) per squadron with an additional aircraft, usually an American-built D.H.4, for the Air Service officer assigned as the squad-

Left: In the early years, Air Service instructors assigned to National Guard squadrons were usually issued a US-built de Havilland DH-4s. This DH-4M belonged to the Air Service officer supervising the 109th Observation Squadron, Minnesota National Guard.

Left: Colorado Guardsmen of the 120th Observation Squadron being inspected at Lowry Field, Denver, on 1 June 1925. Because of the high altitude of this field, the 120th was forced to fly its underpowered Jennies from Pueblo during the hot summer months.

Below: Three JN-6Hs of the 105th Observation Squadron, and the DH-4B of the Air Service advisor assigned to this Tennessee National Guard unit, at Blackwood Field in Nashville shortly before the unit phased out the last Guard Jennies in September 1927.

Left: The Douglas O-2C had been selected in 1926 to become the standard National Guard observation aircraft but, as its handling characteristics were found unsatisfactory, it was rapidly supplanted by the O-2H with staggered wings.

Left: Roaring twenties: Amateur jazz players of the 107th Observation Squadron, Michigan National Guard, are seen in front of a Consolidated PT-1 at Rouge Park Airport on the west side of Detroit.

Above: Competing for Air Service/Air Corps orders against Douglas biplanes, Curtiss observation biplanes did not fare as well. With the Guard, the Curtiss aircraft were the exception rather than the rule. This O-11 served relatively briefly with Maryland's 104th Observation Squadron.

Top right: The O-17, such as this aircraft from the 104th Observation Squadron, Maryland National Guard, was a derivative of the PT-1 trainer with provision for light armament and 180-hp Wright E replaced by a 220-hp Wright R-790-1 radial.

Above right: In Guard service, the O-38 seldom carried its armament. This aircraft from Minnesota's 109th Observation Squadron is an exception as evidenced by the weapon racks below the lower wings, the gunsight ahead of the front cockpit, and the flexible gun in the rear cockpit.

ities were completed at Lowry Field, outside Denver; however, because on hot summer days Jennies performed poorly at Denver's elevation, the 120th Observation Squadron was forced to split into two flights, with Flight B being assigned to Pueblo. In the Texas NG, the 111th Observation Squadron, led by Major Bernard Law, began drilling in downtown Houston until receiving its first JN-4Ds in September 1923, at which time the unit transferred the center of its activities to Ellington Field.

In spite of difficulties stemming from the lack of service-type flying equipment (an insufficient number of Jennies being available to provide the nine authorized aircraft per squadron), the lack of suitable replacements for the flying personnel leaving the Guard, and the lack of sufficient funds to cover the cost of maintenance and supply, the Militia Bureau and the states were able during FY24 to increase personnel assigned to National Guard air units by over 54 per cent and to form three new squadrons.

In the small and not-heavily-populated New England states, the Guard's 43rd Division was made up of officers and men from Connecticut, Rhode Island and Vermont. As only one squadron was to be assigned to this division, it was initially planned to locate the flying unit in Rhode Island as neither Connecticut nor Vermont had suitable airfields. The decision was fought by Connecticut, the wealthiest and most populated of the three states, and the opening of Brainart Field, Hartford, in October 1922, enabled Governor Trumbull to secure the 118th Observation for the 'Constitution State'. The 118th received federal recognition on 1 November 1923 and, after receiving its first Jennies seven months later, began flight operations at Brainart Field during the summer of 1924.

In California, the forebear of today's 115th Airlift Squadron, 146th Airlift Wing, was activated on 16 June 1924 under the command of Corliss Moseley, who held concurrently the positions of inspector/instructor (as a lieutenant in the Air Service Reserve) and of Commanding Officer (as a major in the California National Guard). Designated the 115th Observation Squadron and based at Clover Field, Santa Monica, until it moved to Griffith Park Airfield in January 1925, the unit counted among its first members Captain Paul Baer who, on 11 March 1918, as a lieutenant in the 103rd Aero Squadron, had become the first pilot in American uniform to destroy an enemy aircraft. Upon moving to Griffith Park in Los Angeles, the 115th received its first aircraft: a D.H.4 for use by Major Moseley, two Dayton-Wright TW-3 trainers and six Jennies.

Finally, as FY24 was drawing to a close, the 103rd Observation Squadron was activated in Philadelphia on 27 June as part of the 28th Infantry (Keystone) Division of the Commonwealth of Pennsylvania's National Guard.

FY24 had also seen two flying units being renumbered when transferred. The 136th Observation Squadron, Tennessee NG, was renumbered the 105th Observation Squadron upon passing from Corps Aviation to the 30th Division on 16 January 1924. The 114th Observation Squadron (ex-135th Squadron and ex-135th Observation Squadron), Alabama NG, was renumbered, once again, as the 106th Observation Squadron when it was transferred from the 39th to the 31st Division.

In the spring of 1924, when the 41st Division, Washington National Guard, was authorized to organize an observation squadron, the state's Adjutant General offered to the cities of Seattle, Spokane and Tacoma the opportunity to become the base of the new unit. Spokane was the first to raise the necessary $10,000 for the erection of hangars and, based at that city's Felts Field, the 116th Observation Squadron became on 6 August 1924 the only Guard squadron to be federally recognized during FY25.

New aircraft for the Guard

Besides being marked by the activation of two more squadrons – the 154th Observation Squadron on 24 October 1925 at Little Rock as a Corps Aviation unit in the Arkansas NG, followed on 7 May 1926 by the 107th Observation Squadron at East Jefferson, Detroit, in the 32nd Division, Michigan NG – FY26 saw the initiation of the first major change in equipment for the air units of the National Guard. So far these units had received as 'free issue' Curtiss Jennies (of which there were 112 in service in mid-1926; Guard units then also had seven Dayton-Wright TW-3s and were to get 11 more of these trainers), for which the Air Service was reimbursed by the Militia Bureau the sum of $2,000 per aircraft to meet the cost of reconditioning the equipment. However, by 1926 the stock of Jennies with which to offset attrition and equip new units was practically exhausted.

Consequently, a special board, consisting of three National Guard officers and three regular Army officers, was convened by the War Department at the request of the chief of the Militia Bureau to study the replacement question and the general problem of the supply of National Guard observation squadrons. After protracted discussions, the Board recommended that each National Guard squadron be equipped with three Air Service observation aircraft and five advanced trainers, or special National Guard airplanes. This recommendation was endorsed by the chief of the Militia Bureau who transferred available funds to the Air Service for the purchase of 14 Douglas O-2C observation biplanes (serials NG26-001 through

Gordon S. Williams

Above: The only O-38D (33-001) built was acquired by the Militia Bureau as a command aircraft.

IL ANG

Left: Douglas BT-1 of the 108th Observation Squadron, Illinois National Guard, with blind flying hood over the rear cockpit. When America was forced into World War II, National Guardsmen were among the best-qualified instrument flying pilots available to the Army Air Forces.

NG26-014) to be issued to the older squadrons. In order to complete the re-equipment program during FY28, additional funds were scheduled to be made available in the FY27 and FY28 budgets.

The Air Corps Act of 1926, which became law on 2 July 1926, changed the name of the Air Service to Army Air Corps, but left unaltered its status as a combatant arm of the Army as well as its obligations to assist and support air units of the National Guard and to supply training and cadres for these units. Furthermore, when ordered into federal service, the air units of the National Guard now were to be incorporated into the Army Air Corps.

Fiscal Year 1927 also saw one additional unit, the 112th Observation Squadron, 37th Division, Ohio NG, acti-

vated on 20 June 1927, bringing the total number of National Guard air units to 17 squadrons manned by 330 officers and 1,636 enlisted men. During the year, as they had done in the past, these squadrons took part in a number of emergency and relief operations (e.g. mail service operated by the 105th Observation Squadron, Tennessee NG, when communications were cut off by flooding of the Cumberland River; aerial delivery of mail and medication by the 120th Observation Squadron, Colorado NG, following unusually heavy snow storms; and flood relief work performed in the Mississippi Valley by the 154th Observation Squadron, Arkansas NG).

Fourteen of the 17 squadrons were recipients of a Douglas O-2C at some point during FY27, when delivery

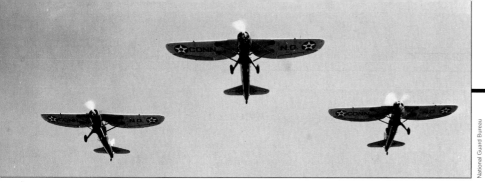

Above: Three Douglas O-46As of the 118th Observation Squadron, Connecticut National Guard, flying near their home base, Brainart Field in Hartford, on 30 June 1937. Entering service in 1936, these Douglas parasol monoplanes were the first 'state-of-the-art' aircraft assigned to the Guard.

Right: The stiletto and ace of spades emblem seen here on the fuselage of a Douglas O-38B of the 116th Observation Squadron at Spokane's Felts Field is now carried by KC-135Es of the 116th Air Refueling Squadron, Washington ANG, at Fairchild AFB.

Right: North American O-47Bs of the 105th Observation Squadron, Tennessee National Guard. The O-47, the first National Guard monoplane with retractable undercarriage, entered service in September 1940.

Right: Forebears of the AT-6s and Harvards of World War II fame, North American BC-1A trainers were first ordered for the National Guard during FY39. This BC-1A wears the gull emblem and O1NG designator of Massachusetts' 101st Observation Squadron.

was made of aircraft ordered during the previous year. However, the O-2C proved not entirely satisfactory and plans to order 27 additional aircraft of this type were shelved in favor of an order for 35 Curtiss O-11s (serials NG27-001 to NG27-035; two subsequent orders added 32 aircraft, NG27-098 to NG27-107 and NG28-196 to NG28-217). In addition, 46 Consolidated PT-1 trainers, out of 70 aircraft of this type (serials 27-108 to 27-177) ordered by the Air Corps, were paid with funds made available out of the Militia Bureau's budget and were intended to complement the three observation aircraft (O-2Cs or O-11s) of each Guard squadron with five trainers. Thus, although 104 Jennies were still on strength at the end of FY27, the phase-out of these antiquated Curtiss biplanes, which had been the mainstay of National Guard air units since the inception of the program, was planned to be completed by 1 September 1927.

The equipment modernization program initiated during FY26 was completed during FY28 when all Curtiss Jenny trainers were phased out and the Guard squadrons received their complement of three observation aircraft and five Consolidated PT-1s or O-17s (the latter combined a modified PT-1 airframe with 225-hp Wright R-790-1 radial and had provision for a 0.30-in gun on a Scarff ring; they were given serials 28-260 to 28-365, 28-396, 28-397 and 30-89). However, while satisfactory as a Jenny replacement, the Consolidated PT-1 was not ideally suited as it was a primary trainer with relatively limited performance.

The first day of FY28 had also seen the activation of the 18th National Guard air unit, the 108th Observation Squadron, 33rd Division, Illinois NG. Manpower now exceeded 2,000 officers and enlisted men for the first time since the first air unit of the National Guard had received federal recognition on 17 January 1921.

Fiscal Year 1929 was a year of consolidation rather than a year of growth, and saw the table of equipment for each of the National Guard observation squadrons changed to include four observation aircraft and four training aircraft. To cope with this change additional Douglas O-2Cs were transferred from the Air Corps inventory, while the first of 10 improved Douglas O-2Hs (serials 28-349 to 28-358) ordered by the Militia Bureau during FY28 were delivered. Additional orders for 40 O-2Hs (serials 29-342 to 29-351 and 29-375 to 29-404) and 20 O-2Ks (serials 29-413 to 29-432) were placed in 1929.

On 30 January 1930, the last of the 19 squadrons initially allotted to the National Guard – the 119th Observation Squadron, 44th Division, New Jersey NG – was activated. From that time until 27 September 1939, when the first of 10 additional Guard squadrons authorized by Congress as part of the Air Corps expansion program was activated, manpower available to National Guard air units fluctuated between 2,250 and 2,400 officers and enlisted men.

Fiscal Year 1930 was marked by an upgrading of equipment to improve the overall effectiveness of the National

Guard units. Orders were placed for one Douglas O-38A (serial 30-407) for use by the Militia Bureau and 12 O-38s (serials 30-408 to 30-419) for assignment to squadrons. Powered by Pratt & Whitney R-1690 Hornet radials, these aircraft, being much improved versions of the long series of Douglas observation biplanes, were destined to be the standard mount of Guard observation squadrons during much of the 1930s. Other improvements included the substitution of Browning machine guns for the obsolete Lewis gun previously used on a flexible mount, the supply of photo-cameras and camera guns, and the replacement of older SCR 109-A radios with more reliable SCR 136 sets.

In spite of this re-equipping, the effectiveness of the Guard flying units was much diminished as insufficient funds during the lean Depression years prevented expansion and proper maintenance of existing facilities. So serious was the situation that several states had to be warned by the Militia Bureau that federal recognition of their National Guard air unit might have to be withdrawn if they continued failing to provide proper facilities.

Thirty-three O-38s (serials 31-349 to 31-379, 31-406 and 31-407) were ordered during FY31 to supplement the 12 aircraft from the previous year's contract. More significantly, as satisfactory progress was made towards providing adequate facilities for 12 of the 19 squadrons, nine of them each received five O-38s while, beginning in September 1931, three others received O-38Bs which had been ordered by the Army Air Corps. Meanwhile, the seven remaining squadrons retained older Liberty-powered Douglas O-2Hs as their observation aircraft.

During FY32 a change in the number of observation aircraft allocated to each squadron, from four to six, necessitated the placing of an order for 39 O-38Bs (serials 32-102 to 32-116 and 32-325 to 32-342). Thus, at the end of FY32, 13 squadrons were primarily equipped with Douglas O-38s and O-38Bs, while six were still flying O-2Hs. Moreover, all National Guard squadrons continued to use either Consolidated O-17s or Douglas BT-1s (redesignated O-2Ks) as trainers.

The composition of National Guard squadrons was again changed during FY33 as the World War I-vintage Liberty engines were beginning to show their age and as no suitable replacements for the Liberty-powered O-2Hs and BT-1s were immediately available. Likewise, the Consolidated O-17s had proved poor substitutes for the more powerful observation aircraft. It was thus urgently necessary to replace BT-1s, O-2Hs and O-17s with addi-

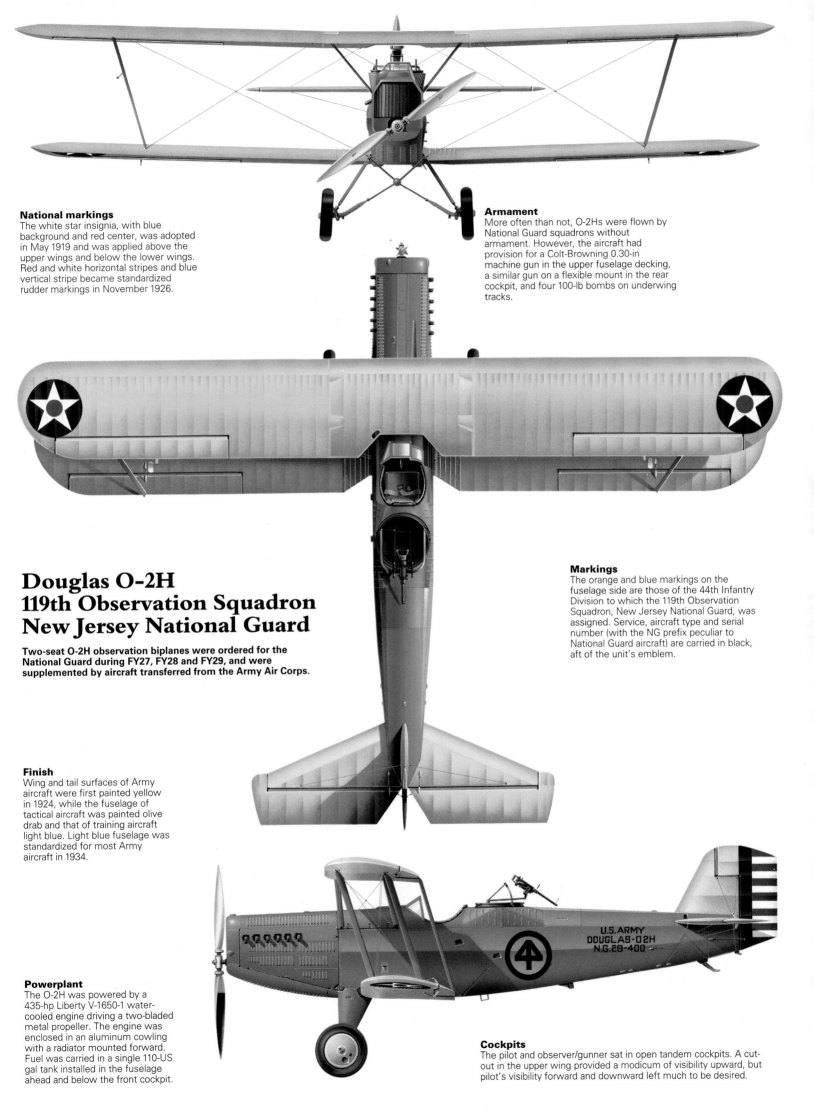

National markings
The white star insignia, with blue background and red center, was adopted in May 1919 and was applied above the upper wings and below the lower wings. Red and white horizontal stripes and blue vertical stripe became standardized rudder markings in November 1926.

Armament
More often than not, O-2Hs were flown by National Guard squadrons without armament. However, the aircraft had provision for a Colt-Browning 0.30-in machine gun in the upper fuselage decking, a similar gun on a flexible mount in the rear cockpit, and four 100-lb bombs on underwing tracks.

Douglas O-2H
119th Observation Squadron
New Jersey National Guard

Two-seat O-2H observation biplanes were ordered for the National Guard during FY27, FY28 and FY29, and were supplemented by aircraft transferred from the Army Air Corps.

Markings
The orange and blue markings on the fuselage side are those of the 44th Infantry Division to which the 119th Observation Squadron, New Jersey National Guard, was assigned. Service, aircraft type and serial number (with the NG prefix peculiar to National Guard aircraft) are carried in black, aft of the unit's emblem.

Finish
Wing and tail surfaces of Army aircraft were first painted yellow in 1924, while the fuselage of tactical aircraft was painted olive drab and that of training aircraft light blue. Light blue fuselage was standardized for most Army aircraft in 1934.

Powerplant
The O-2H was powered by a 435-hp Liberty V-1650-1 water-cooled engine driving a two-bladed metal propeller. The engine was enclosed in an aluminum cowling with a radiator mounted forward. Fuel was carried in a single 110-US gal tank installed in the fuselage ahead and below the front cockpit.

Cockpits
The pilot and observer/gunner sat in open tandem cockpits. A cut-out in the upper wing provided a modicum of visibility upward, but pilot's visibility forward and downward left much to be desired.

This Douglas O-46A of the 104th Observation Squadron, Maryland National Guard, bears the fuselage emblem of the 29th Division.

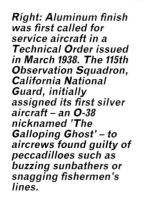

Right: Aluminum finish was first called for service aircraft in a Technical Order issued in March 1938. The 115th Observation Squadron, California National Guard, initially assigned its first silver aircraft – an O-38 nicknamed 'The Galloping Ghost' – to aircrews found guilty of peccadilloes such as buzzing sunbathers or snagging fishermen's lines.

tional observation aircraft to bring normal squadron allocation to eight aircraft of a single type.

To implement this plan, the National Guard Bureau (as the Militia Bureau had been renamed in 1933) ordered an O-38D (serial 33-001) for its own use, and 15 O-38Es (serials 33-002 to 33-016) and eight O-38Fs (serials 33-322 to 33-329) for use by the squadrons. In spite of receiving these aircraft and of ordering, early during the year, an additional batch of 22 O-38Es (serials 34-001 to 34-022), the National Guard ended FY34 by being 40 per cent short of its authorized strength of 153 aircraft (eight aircraft per squadron plus one for the NGB). However, as the Douglas O-38 series was rapidly approaching obsolescence, the National Guard Bureau elected to await the availability of aircraft of monoplane design rather than ordering additional biplanes.

On 5 December 1933, an amusing facet of the National Guard observation squadrons' story – if not of their history – came to an end as Congress ratified the Twenty-First Amendment, which repealed the Eighteenth Amendment prohibiting the manufacture, sale and transportation of intoxicating liquors. Prior to that time, an attractive, if highly unofficial, 'fringe benefit' from flying with the Guard had provided opportunities to 'tank up' during occasional 'goodwill' flights into Canada and Mexico. Whether or not the loss of this 'incentive' was real is most debatable; nonetheless, this anecdote became in some minds part of the undeserved flying-club image given to the contemporary activities of the Guard.

Monoplanes for the Guard

To bring the observation squadrons of the National Guard to statutory strength, the Army Air Corps transferred to the Guard a number of O-38Bs it had ordered during FY31 as well as BT-2 trainers (unarmed and lower-powered derivatives of the O-38 series). Furthermore, the Army Air Corps scheduled for delivery to the National Guard 46 of the 71 Douglas O-46A observation parasol

monoplanes (serials 35-161 to 35-231) it had on order. With the influx of most of these aircraft, the flying Guardsmen were able, at last, to step up their activities and during FY35 they exceeded for the first time the minimum of 40,000 flight hours per year which had been set as a goal for the 19 National Guard squadrons.

Scheduled to commence in January 1936, the delivery of the 46 O-46As ordered by the Army Air Corps did not materialize during FY36; nevertheless, an additional 19 aircraft of this type (serials 36-128 to 36-144, 36-147 and 36-148) were ordered for the Guard. Still depending on the reliable O-38 series, the observation squadrons of the National Guard continued to increase their level of activities and recorded a total of 45,852 flight hours during FY36.

It was during the early part of that year that the War Department elected to identify closely the National Guard squadrons with their Air Service forebears with which they shared the same unit number. Thus, for example, by a letter dated 16 October 1936, the War Department reconstituted the Air Service's 112th Aero Squadron and consolidated it with the 112th Observation Squadron, Ohio NG. In a like manner, other Guard squadrons were consolidated to perpetuate the history and traditions of their Air Service forebears.

With the delivery of the last O-46A taking place on 3 April 1937 and the transfer of O-38s from newly re-equipped units to other observation squadrons, the Guard was able to increase the statutory strength of each squadron to nine aircraft. FY37 also saw the placing of an order for 45 North American O-47As (serials 37-324 to 37-368), the first type of aircraft with a retractable undercarriage to be acquired by the National Guard.

A new increase in total allotment from 171 to 195 aircraft was authorized during FY38 to provide training or similar-type aircraft for use by regular Army Air Corps officers giving instrument flying instructions and flight checks to Guardsmen. Moreover, to continue the modernization of the flying equipment of its squadrons, the National Guard Bureau placed an order for 48 additional O-47As (serials 38-271 to 38-318). Furthermore, the NGB took delivery on 8 July 1937 of the Guard's first multi-engined aircraft: the Y1C-37 (a military staff transport version of the Lockheed 10-A twin-engined airliner).

Pre-mobilization build-up

The rapidly deteriorating international situation prompted President F. D. Roosevelt to propose an ambitious Army Air Corps expansion program to more than triple the inventory from 1,775 to 5,500 aircraft. Under this program, which was approved by Congress on 3 April

Below: A North American O-47A of the 115th Observation Squadron, California National Guard, flying past 14,495-ft Mount Whitney, the highest point in the lower 48.

Right: The number 4 and the designator 1260 identify this O-47A as the fourth aircraft of the 126th Observation Squadron, Wisconsin National Guard. Revised designators were adopted for all units of the Army Air Corps, including National Guard squadrons, in mid-1940.

1939, not only were the personnel strength and aircraft allocation of the 19 existing squadrons of the National Guard to be increased, but the organization of 10 new observation squadrons was authorized as well.

To implement the intent of this program, plans were made to increase the strength of each observation squadron to a total of 14 aircraft including 10 observation aircraft, three short-range observation aircraft and one combat trainer. Consequently, orders for 50 O-47Bs (serials 39-089 to 39-138) and 19 North American BC-1A trainers (serials 39-798 to 39-816) were placed in FY39, while the ordering of short-range observation aircraft was postponed to the next year.

The first two of the 10 additional squadrons[11] authorized as part of the expansion program were activated during FY40: the 153rd Observation Squadron, Mississippi NG, on 27 September 1939, and the 152nd Observation Squadron, Rhode Island NG, on 13 October 1939. Following the formation of these two squadrons and the increase in strength of previously formed units, total manpower available to air units of the National Guard exceeded for the first time 2,500 officers and enlisted men. Nevertheless, efficient growth was deterred by a major shortage of field servicing trucks.

Record orders totaling 187 aircraft were placed by the National Guard Bureau during FY40 and included 19 Curtiss O-52s (part of a contract for 203 aircraft of this type, serials 40-2688 through 40-2890, issued by the War Department), 10 North American BC-1As (serials 40-707 to 40-716), and 18 Stinson O-49s (part of a contract for 100 of these short-range observation aircraft – later redesignated L-1s – serials 40-192 through 40-291).

As FY41 started, Belgium, Denmark, France, Luxembourg, the Netherlands and Norway had already fallen to Nazi invasions and the British sky was about to become the arena for one of the epic battles in aviation history. The United States, fortunately, was still spared the new war's miseries and thus was able to develop its armed forces. In so doing, the nation drew upon land and air units of the National Guard which, for the most part, had reached a high standard of training. In particular, some of its aircrews had seven to eight years of military flying experience and were better trained than regular Army Air Corps/Army Air Forces[12] personnel.

To better utilize the Guardsmen's flight experience, it was proposed to train as pursuit pilots three of the most proficient officers from each National Guard squadron and to use these pilots as cadres for new Guard fighter squad-rons which were to provide local air defense. However, while on the one hand not enough fighter aircraft were yet available to implement this plan, on the other hand the Army Air Corps/Forces had an urgent need for experienced flight crews. Consequently, the idea of training Guardsmen as fighter pilots was not carried forth and instead some of these pilots volunteered for transfer to the Army Air Forces to serve as cadres for new units being organized in that service.

In spite of this drain of experienced aircrews and the late deliveries of aircraft ordered during FY40 – none of the O-52s and only a few O-49s were received by the National Guard prior to 30 June 1941 due to changes in priority for airplane manufacture and delivery – seven new units were activated as follows: 121st Observation Squadron, District of Columbia NG, on 10 April 1941; 122nd Observation Squadron, Louisiana NG, on 2 March 1941; 123rd Observation Squadron, Oregon NG, on 18 April 1941; 124th Observation Squadron, Iowa NG, on 25 February 1941; 125th Observation Squadron, Oklahoma NG, on 10 February 1941; 126th Observation Squadron, Wisconsin NG, on 12 November 1940; and 128th Observation Squadron, Georgia NG, on 1 May 1941.

Nevertheless, pursuant to President Roosevelt's call to active duty on 27 August 1940, the National Guard Bureau lost control of 21 of its observation squadrons during FY41 as, beginning on 16 September with the 105th, 116th, 119th and 154th Observation Squadrons, these units were ordered into federal active duty. Thus, on 30 June 1941, only seven squadrons – the 121st, 122nd, 123rd, 124th, 125th, 128th and 153rd – were still under state control.

Less than two months later, on 4 August, the last authorized Guard flying unit, the 127th Observation Squadron, was activated in Kansas. However, this unit was almost immediately called to active duty, as were the seven squadrons which had still been under state control at the end of FY41. Thus, at the time of the Japanese attacks in the Pacific and Southeast Asia, all 29 National Guard observation squadrons and the more than 3,500 officers and enlisted men manning them were on federal active duty.

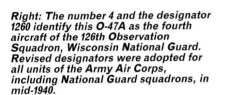

Top: A Stinson O-49 of the 107th Observation Squadron at Beaumont, Texas, on 14 August 1941. This Michigan National Guard unit had been placed on active duty on 15 October 1940. The circle on the fuselage is the marking used to identify aircraft of the 'White Force' during the Louisiana Maneuvers.

Above left: Curtiss O-52s were ordered during FY40 and were delivered to National Guard squadrons on active duty in 1941. The Owl proved unsatisfactory and was not taken into combat.

[11] By that time Guard squadrons were no longer assigned to specific divisions as the Air Corps was evolving into a more independent branch not restricted to providing support to ground troops.

[12] On 20 June 1941, Army Regulation 95-5 created the Army Air Forces with the Air Corps and the Air Force Combat Command as its principal components.

The Call to Duty

Above: Once the United States found itself drawn into the fight, the first combat task assigned to most of the 29 National Guard squadrons which had been placed on active duty beginning in the summer of 1940 was anti-submarine patrol along the coast of the United States. This O-47 from an unidentified ex-National Guard squadron bears stars without red center as specified by the Combined Chiefs of Staff on 12 May 1942.

Above right: ASW patrols were flown by Guardsmen on active duty not only along the East Coast and over the Gulf of Mexico to counter the threat of German submarines, but also along the Pacific Coast to counter Japanese submarines. This pair of O-47As is from the 115th Observation Squadron.

To prevent the US Navy from interfering with their operations in Southeast Asia, the Philippines, and the southwest and central Pacific, the Japanese struck against American forces on Oahu in the early morning hours of Sunday, 7 December 1941. A few hours later, US installations in the Philippines, Guam and Wake also came under attack. With these acts of unprovoked aggression, the United States of America was drawn into World War II and the next day war on Japan was declared. Four days later Congress declared war on Germany and Italy.

Although the attack on Pearl Harbor came as a surprise, America's involvement in World War II had been expected since September 1939, when Germany invaded Poland on 1 September and France and Great Britain declared war on Germany on 3 September in compliance with their alliance with Poland. Notwithstanding a strong isolationist movement in the United States, President Franklin D. Roosevelt had almost immediately initiated preparation for war and, two months after the fall of France, had moved to in-

duct all federally-recognized elements of the National Guard into active military service. By executive order issued on 27 August 1940, the 21 federally-recognized Guard squadrons began their preparations for federal service while the organization of eight additional squadrons was accelerated.

On active duty but still at peace

On 16 September 1940, in answer to the Presidential call to active duty, the 105th Observation Squadron from Tennessee, the 116th from Washington, the 119th from New Jersey and the 154th from Arkansas became the first National Guard flying units to come under federal control. As shown in Table 3, they were followed by eight additional squadrons before the end of 1940, by nine squadrons during the first six months of 1941, and finally by the eight remaining squadrons. The last of these units to be activated was the 153rd Observation Squadron, Mississippi NG, which was federalized on 15 October 1941.

Initially it had been planned that these squadrons would be on active duty for one year during which, retaining their personnel and identity, they would undergo intensive training in preparation for any national emergency that might arise; however, the pressing need for cadres to help organize and train regular AAF units soon resulted in the transfer of some key personnel. Furthermore, as the impending war created an equally urgent need for maintaining an efficient airline industry capable of supplementing the then-limited capability of the newly formed Air

USAF

USAF

USAF

Corps Ferrying Command, airline pilots serving in Guard squadrons were released to resume their critical civilian occupation. In spite of these personnel drains, the 29 Guard squadrons on active duty were able to increase their combat capabilities. More often than not they were relocated, immediately upon being activated, to bases with only minimal facilities and were thus forced to operate under conditions resembling those they would find once assigned to combat zones.

Primary activities during this period consisted of aerial observation, anti-tank reconnaissance, liaison, navigation and gunnery sorties in support of ground forces. In addition, several of these squadrons deployed for brief periods to take part in major maneuvers in the southeast United States.

ASW patrol and Combat Team X

The National Guard squadrons were placed on full alert immediately after the news of the attack on Pearl Harbor had been received. However, as their observations and liaison aircraft were definitely obsolete for use in combat zones (see Table 4) and, more particularly, as enemy submarines operating off US shores presented a greater immediate threat, most of these squadrons were retained for use on anti-submarine patrols. To fulfill their new mission, they were quickly redeployed from the 18 states where they had been based on 7 December 1941 to 14 states and Panama. Thus, by mid-January 1942, 17 of the 29 mobilized squadrons were flying ASW patrols along the

eastern seaboard, three were doing so over the Gulf of Mexico, five squadrons patrolled the Pacific Coast, three were training with ground forces in the central United States and one had been transferred to the Canal Zone.

When the former Guard squadrons (upon being called to active duty they had become units of the United States Army Air Corps/Air Forces) began flying antisubmarine patrols they were still equipped, for the most part, with their prewar aircraft as well as with new light observation aircraft. With the obsolete Douglas O-38 biplanes now on their way out, the main observation types were Douglas O-46s, North American O-47A/Bs and Curtiss O-52s; in addition, Stinson O-49s, Taylorcraft O-57s, Aeronca O-58A/Bs and Piper O-59s (which respectively became L-1s, L-2s, L-3s and L-4s in 1942) were operated by these squadrons in the battlefield reconnaissance/liaison role while North American BC-1As were used for advanced and instrument training. Among this motley collection of obsolete and obsolescent aircraft, only the O-47A/Bs could then be regarded as semi-modern combat aircraft, as they possessed fully enclosed cockpit and retractable undercarriage, were capable of a top speed of 221 mph (356 km/h),[13] and could carry two 325-lb (147-kg) depth charges.

O-47s, in addition to serving if not glamorously at least reliably with squadrons searching for enemy submarines along the American shores, were selected to equip, as part

---

[13] To provide some points of comparison, one should remember that contemporary enemy fighters were 50 to 90 per cent faster than the O-47, with the German FW 190A-3 reaching 418 mph (673 km/h), the Italian M.C. 202 Folgore 370 mph (595 km/h), and the Japanese A6M2 'Zero' 332 mph (534 km/h). The most common US fighter then in squadron service, the Curtiss P-40E, had a top speed of 362 mph (582 km/h).

of Combat Team X, a unit specially formed with 10 aircraft and crews from as many ex-National Guard squadrons. Bound for Singapore, where they were scheduled to fly coastal patrols, the crews were shipped out of San Francisco on 12 January 1942 aboard the *President Coolidge*, while their aircraft left the next day on board the SS *Mariposa*. While at sea, the situation in Malaya deteriorated rapidly (eventually Commonwealth forces which had been pushed back to Singapore were forced to surrender to the Japanese on 15 February 1942) and both vessels were diverted to Australia. There Combat Team X reassembled its aircraft and used them briefly for antisubmarine duties. However, the crews were soon transferred to other USAAF units in the area and, like their sister ships in the United States, the antipodean O-47s were not called to perform more bellicose activities.

During the first six months of 1942, more modern equipment began to trickle down to the ex-Guard squadrons. However, as AAF combat and operational losses could be made up only barely by new aircraft deliveries, priority had to be given to units facing the Japanese onslaught in the Pacific and to those being prepared for deployment to England. Nonetheless, a small number of fighters (such as Bell P-39s, Curtiss P-40s and Republic P-43s), attack aircraft (Douglas A-20s and A-24s), and twin-engined bombers (Douglas B-18s and Lockheed B-34s) were added to the inventory of these squadrons, enabling their crews to familiarize themselves with aircraft of performance similar to those they would soon be called to operate in combat. At the same time, the drain of experienced personnel continued, with some officers and men being transferred to other AAF units. (All in all, and counting personnel retained in their original units, the Guard contributed 468 pilots to the USAAF.)

The menace of submarines peaked in February 1942 when, in addition to having to deal with Kriegsmarine U-boat operations in the Gulf of Mexico, the Caribbean and the eastern seaboard, the United States had to contend with the threat of Japanese submarine operations off the West Coast.[14] The danger gradually receded as better defensive methods prompted U-boats to operate further out in the Atlantic and as the US Navy victory during the Battle of Midway in early June 1942 forced the Imperial Japanese Navy to focus its operations in the Solomons. Thus, the ex-Guard squadrons were progressively able to concentrate their efforts in support of training ground troops and, in the case of several squadrons, in preparation for their deployments overseas.

Right: Fighter aircraft began to be assigned to the former National Guard squadrons in early 1942. This Curtiss P-40F of the 120th Observation Squadron was photographed at Biggs Field, Fort Bliss, Texas, on 12 October 1942.

Below: During the summer of 1942, Douglas A-20Bs were issued to the three mobilized Guard squadrons earmarked for operations in North Africa.

First overseas deployments

The first squadrons to be alerted for assignment to overseas theatres of operations were the 107th, 109th and 153rd which, as part of the 67th Observation Group, were to move to England, and the 111th, 122nd and 154th which, forming the 68th Observation Group, were to take part in Operation Torch, the Allied invasion of French North Africa. Leaving their aircraft in the United States, the pilots and ground personnel of the 67th OG were shipped across the Atlantic in August-September 1942. Setting up station at Membury, Wiltshire, on 7 September, the 107th,

[14] On 23 February 1942, the Japanese submarine I-17 shelled the California coast north of Santa Barbara. Although damage to piers and oil wells was only slight, this event caused much concern at the time.

USAF

109th and 153rd became the first ex-Guard squadrons to take up duty in a theater of operations. However, as related later, they remained without combat aircraft for an extended period and, thus, were preceded in combat by the three squadrons of the 68th Observation Group.

Equipped in the United States with combat-worthy Douglas A-20Bs, the squadrons of the 68th OG were earmarked for operations in North Africa. Beginning in late September 1942, their flight crews ferried the A-20Bs across the South Atlantic while their ground crews and equipment were shipped via the North Atlantic and the United Kingdom. The first duty station was Fedala, French Morocco, where the 122nd arrived on 9 November and St Leu, Algeria, where the 111th and 154th arrived the following day. Shortly after the group began operations, its squadrons were detached for separate duty to carry out diverse activities over a wide area. In the process, these squadrons soon flew a mix of aircraft including A-20s, P-38s, P-39s, P-40s and P-43s, as most of their A-20Bs were needed to make up combat attritions in the 47th Bombardment Group.

Transferred from Algeria to French Morocco, the 111th Observation Squadron flew anti-submarine and convoy escort patrols, as well as patrols along the border with Spanish Morocco, until March 1943 when it was taken out of operations. Redesignated as the 111th Reconnaissance Squadron (Fighter) on 31 May 1943, the unit was retrained with Allison-powered North American Mustangs (P-51s, P-51As and A-36As). Ready to return to combat in time for the Allied invasion of Sicily, the 111th went back to operations at Bou Ficha, Tunisia, on 7 July 1943, distinguishing itself while performing in the tactical reconnaissance role. Following advancing troops, the unit operated from Sicily beginning on 14 July 1943, from bases on the Italian mainland starting on 16 September 1943, from Corsica in July and August 1944 and, finally, commencing in mid-August 1944, from bases in southern and eastern France. During its two years as a combat unit in the MTO and ETO, the 111th Tactical Reconnaissance Squadron (a designation which was adopted on 13 November 1943) flew an assortment of P-51/F-6 Mustangs, with Merlin-powered versions replacing Allison-powered models in 1944. One of its pilots, Lieutenant V. S. Rader, became an ace during the last month of the war in Europe and was credited with the destruction of 6½ enemy aircraft.

Also initially flying antisubmarine and convoy patrols from French Morocco, the 122nd Observation Squadron was transferred on 22 March 1943 to Berrechid, French Morocco, to become part of the newly formed 12th Training Command. Equipped with a mix of fighter aircraft, the unit trained Allied crews arriving in North Africa in the radio and tactical procedures peculiar to that theater. While performing this necessary but lackluster duty, the squadron had most of its personnel transferred out, as experienced pilots and ground personnel were needed by combat units. Finally, on 8 November 1943, the last 16 officers and men, as well as the files of the 122nd, were taken over by a new unit, the 885th Bombardment Squadron (Heavy). With its Boeing B-17s later supplemented by

Consolidated B-24s, the 885th BS flew special Carpetbagger missions from Algerian and Italian bases. These activities, which included transporting agents and supplies to partisans in occupied Europe and dropping leaflets, were carried out with distinction between October 1943 and VE Day.

After flying antisubmarine patrols from Algerian and Moroccan bases for three weeks in December 1942-January 1943, the 154th Observation Squadron (the third squadron initially assigned to the 68th Observation Group) soon relinquished its A-20Bs. Re-equipped with P-38s, P-39s and P-51s, and serving as a tactical reconnaissance unit during the Algeria-Tunisia campaign, it became in April 1943 the first USAAF unit to take the Allison-powered Mustang into combat. During this period its personnel also modified P-38s into photographic reconnaissance aircraft by installing cameras in the aircraft's nose, as was later done at depots in the United States to produce the F-4 and F-5 variants of the Lockheed Lightning. On 11 May 1943, while based in Tunisia, the squadron was taken out of operations to be reorganized. Equipped with Lockheed P-38G/Js and F-4s and redesignated the 154th Weather Reconnaissance Squadron, it was assigned to the Fifteenth Air Force and, from February 1944 until the end of the war, it operated from Bari, Italy, in support of the heavy bombers. In so doing, its pilots not only flew ahead of the bombers to provide weather data but, often, they remained with the bombers to give a steady flow of information and to report on target damage.

In the Mediterranean theater of operations these three units were later joined by three other ex-Guard squadrons. Activated on 1 May 1941, the 128th Observation Squadron, Georgia NG, was still in its home state when the war started. While flying the usual anti-submarine patrols during the first months of the war, this unit was redesignated the 21st Antisubmarine Squadron. On 28 September 1943, after 29 months on active duty in the southeast United States, the unit was reorganized at Ephrata AAB, WA, as a B-17 unit and became the 840th Bombardment Squadron (Heavy). As part of the 483rd BG, Fifteenth Air Force, it began combat operations from Sterparone, Italy, on 12 April 1944 with an attack against an aircraft component factory at Fischamend Markt in Austria. After VE Day, the 840th transported redeployed personnel between Italy and French Morocco; it was finally inactivated at Pisa, Italy, on 25 September 1945.

Inactivated on 18 October 1942, after having flown the usual early wartime antisubmarine patrols, the unit from the District of Columbi NG received a new lease of life

Below left: Allison-powered North American F-6A of B Flight, 111th Tactical Reconnaissance Squadron, 68th Observation Group, during operations in Italy. Looking decidedly war-weary, 'The Snoopers' has a rather impressive mission tally painted on its engine cowling.

Below: Supermarine Spitfire Mk VB, 107th Tactical Reconnaissance Squadron, at Membury, England. The 107th originated in the Michigan National Guard as a prewar observation squadron, was called to active duty on 15 October 1940, and served in the ETO between September 1942 and July 1945.

National Guard Heritage Painting courtesy of NGB/PAH

*Above: After exchanging its **Spitfires** for North American **F-6As**, the 107th TRS distinguished itself by photographing most of the Normandy coast before D-day.*

some six months later when it was organized anew as the 121st Liaison Squadron. After training in the United States the unit was sent to Algeria, where it remained for three months during the spring of 1944. Finally, having moved to Italy in July 1944, the 121st Liaison Squadron went operational in September of that year. Equipped with Piper L-4s and Stinson L-5s, it flew in support of US ground troops fighting in France and northern Italy until the German surrender. Another unit tracing its lineage to a prewar Guard unit, Rhode Island's 152nd Observation Squadron, had an even shorter combat history. Redesignated the 37th Photographic Reconnaissance Squadron on 29 March 1944 while still stateside, this unit arrived in Italy eight months later and was operational with Lockheed F-5s between February and March 1945 only.

ETO operations

As previously mentioned, the three squadrons forming the 67th Observation Group had become, in September 1942, the first ex-Guard units to arrive, though without aircraft, in the European theater of operations. With the assignment of a few Stinson L-5s, flying activity was resumed at a slow pace. The availability of additional aircraft, including Piper L-4s and de Havilland Tiger Moth trainers, Douglas Bostons (the export version of the A-20 which was then in RAF service), and Supermarine Spitfire MkVB fighters, enabled the units' personnel to continue training and to furnish support activities such as target towing and liaison flights. In addition, some air-defense sorties were flown with Spitfires while individual Boston crews began operating with RAF squadrons.

On 31 May 1943, the 107th and 109th were redesignated Reconnaissance Squadrons (Fighter) while responsibility for the liaison activities was given to the group's third squadron, which became the 153rd Liaison Squadron. This change, however, was not accompanied by an increase in activity as long as the 67th Reconnaissance Group (changed from Observation Group in May 1943) remained assigned to the Eighth Air Force. In preparation for the Allied invasion of Europe, the 67th was redesignated a Tactical Reconnaissance Group and, effective 13 November 1943, it was transferred to the Ninth Air Force. At that time the 107th and 109th moved to Middle Wallop, Hampshire, and received their first North American F-6As (a camera-equipped version of the Allison-powered Mustang) while the 153rd Liaison Squadron relocated to Keevil, Wiltshire, and was wholly equipped with Stinson L-5s.

Combat operations began on 20 December 1943, when the 107th Tactical Reconnaissance Squadron flew its first two sorties over France. During the following months this unit, joined by the 12th TRS of the 67th TRG,[15] photographed 'Noball' sites (V1 launching pads) in the Pas de Calais area. Beginning on 23 February 1944, the squadrons of the 67th TRG were assigned responsibility for photographing, from an altitude of 3,000 to 6,000 ft (915 to 1830 m), a 160-mile (260-km) strip of French coastline and two 120-mile (195-km) inshore strips, covering all possible invasion areas. In the process the 67th TRG flew 83 missions (67 of which were credited to the 107th TRS) without losing an aircraft and brought back 9,500 photographs which were put to good use in planning and carrying out Allied landings in Normandy.

Launched during the night of 5-6 June 1944, Operation Overlord took the Nazis by surprise and, despite fairly heavy losses in some areas, solidly established Allied beachheads in France. Following the advancing troops for which they were providing tactical reconnaissance, the 107th and 109th TRSs moved to the continent, with the 107th operating from Landing Strip A-4 at Deux Jumeaux for seven days beginning on 28 June, and then moving to A-9 at Le Molay to join the 109th TRS. Subsequently, these two squadrons, by then flying Merlin-powered F-6C/Ds, moved from base to base in northern France, Belgium (from which they operated with conspicuous success during the fierce Battle of the Bulge), and Ger-

---

[15] During 1944-45 the 67th TRG comprised the two ex-Guard squadrons (Michigan's 107th and Minnesota's 109th) and of regular USAAF squadrons – the 12th TRS, until June 1944, and the 30th and 33rd TRSs, from June 1944. The previously assigned 153rd Liaison Squadron was directly attached to the Ninth Air Force in March 1944 and went on to serve with the IX and XII Tactical Air Commands in support of the Twelfth Army Group and the Seventh Army operating in France, Belgium and Germany during the last year of the war.

Following General MacArthur's return to the Philippines, the 110th TRS took up station at Dulag, Leyte, from where it was operating when 11 of its P-40Ns wiped out a small convoy on 24 November, killing 1,500 Japanese troops. It repeated this success on 26 December when 20 of its pilots warded off a Japanese naval force threatening the American beachhead on Mindoro. Soon thereafter, it received North American F-6Ds and F-6Ks and with these aircraft it moved to Lingayen, Luzon, in January 1945. Shortly before the Japanese surrender the 110th TRS moved to Ie Shima, its last wartime station.

Redesignated from the 106th Observation Squadron to the 106th Reconnaissance Squadron (Bombardment) on 2 April 1943, the former Alabama NG unit was then stationed at Camp Campbell, KY, where it began training on North American B-25s. First alerted for deployment overseas in August 1943, the squadron eventually joined the Thirteenth Air Force on Guadalcanal in mid-November 1943. Assigned to that Air Force's 42nd BG and based on Sterling Island, the 106th flew its first combat sorties on 30 January 1944. Retaining its B-25s until the end of the war, but redesignated the 106th Bombardment Squadron (Medium), the unit successively operated from New Guinea (Hollandia and Sansapor), Morotai and Palawan.

Starting on 28 March 1944, when the 118th TRS began flying defensive patrols in India in the rear of the combat zone, five ex-Guard squadrons were operational against the Japanese in the China-Burma-India theater of operations. By far the most active was the 118th Tactical Reconnaissance Squadron, which was transferred in June 1944 from the Tenth Air Force in India to the Fourteenth Air Force in China. Within the Fourteenth, the squadron was first attached to the 23rd Fighter Group, the heir of the famous Flying Tigers, with which it flew its first ground-support sorties from Kewilin on 18 June 1944 to help blunt a Japanese offensive. Operating successively from Liuchow, Suichwan and Laohwangping, the 118th TRS saw its status within the 23rd FG changed in January 1945 when it became a full component of that prestigious group.

In 14 months of heavy operations, during most of which it was equipped with North American F-6Cs after having entered operations with Curtiss P-40Ns, the squadron earned an impressive combat record. At least five of its pilots became aces: Lieutenant Colonel E. O. McComas

Above left: Called to active duty on 23 December 1940, Missouri's 110th Observation Squadron had been redesignated 110th TRS before it flew P-40Ns in support of General MacArthur's return to the Philippines in October 1944.

Above: With the 110th TRS, P-40Ns gave place to North American F-6Ks during the last year of the war. These Mustangs were photographed on Ie Shima on 12 August 1945. Three days before VJ Day, protecting the cockpit from the tropical sun had become more important than hiding the aircraft in protective revetments. The imperial sun was about to set but that provided by Mother Nature was still a force to be reckoned with.

many, to end the war at Eschwege in the ruins of the Third Reich.

Later arrivals in the ETO included the 112th (ex-Ohio NG) and 125th (ex-Oklahoma NG) Liaison Squadrons, which, having arrived in England in June 1944 and moved to the continent two months later, flew courier and liaison sorties for American troops operating in northern Europe. In addition, two Photographic Reconnaissance Squadrons serving in this theater were the scions of Observation Squadrons: the 101st of Massachusetts, which became the 39th PRS on 29 March 1944, and the 126th of Wisconsin, which was redesignated the 34th PRS on 11 August 1943. The latter unit arrived in England in March 1944 and began operations from Chalgrove, Oxfordshire, on the 19th of the following month. Assigned to the 10th Photographic Group, Ninth Air Force, and equipped primarily with Lockheed F-4s and F-5s (with some North American F-10s[16] and Douglas A-20s being added later), the 34th PRS operated from French bases from August 1944 until VE Day. The combat career of the 39th PRS spanned only two months as, after arriving in France on 24 January 1945, it did not become operational until 16 March; war's end saw it based at Wiesbaden, Germany.

The war against Japan

In the Southwest Pacific, after the previously related aborted debut of Combat Team X, only two ex-Guard squadrons took part in the war against the Japanese. The 110th Reconnaissance Squadron (Fighter), equipped with Bell P-39Qs when it arrived in Brisbane, Australia, on 5 December 1943, moved almost immediately to New Guinea. While stationed at Port Moresby, the 110th detached flights to Gusap to commence combat operations on 21 January 1944 as part of the 71st Group, Fifth Air Force. Moving along the north coast of New Guinea, the 110th TRS (designation adopted on 10 May 1944) was re-equipped with Curtiss P-40Ns in the late summer of 1944.

---

[16] The F-10 was a photographic reconnaissance version of the B-25 twin-engined bomber.

Right: Former Guard units which remained in the United States flew a motley collection of aircraft on sundry duties. This Douglas A-24 was with the 102nd Observation Squadron at Camp Robinson, Arkansas, in 1942.

Below: Not all former Guard units got to fly fighters or bombers in combat, but all performed superbly. Heir of California's 115th Observation Squadron, the 1115th Liaison Squadron was flying Stinson L-1 As and float-equipped L-1Fs from Myongon, Burma, in November 1944.

(17 air victories); Captain M. M. Lubner and Brigadier General C. D. Vincent (six victories each); and Captains L. F. Jones and O. S. Watts (five victories each).

During September 1944 the former Pennsylvania (103rd Observation Squadron) and Oregon (123rd Observation Squadron) Guard units became operational in the CBI theater as Photographic Reconnaissance Squadrons equipped with Lockheed F-5s. The first of these units, which had become the 40th PRS on 21 October 1943, arrived at Guskhara, India, in July 1944, flew its first combat sortie on 6 September 1944, and remained a component of the India-based 8th Photographic Group, Tenth Air Force, until the end of the war. The 35th PRS (designation given on 11 August 1943) had arrived at Guskhara one

month before the 40th PRS but, before entering combat in September 1944, was transferred to China for service with the Fourteenth Air Force. Two weeks before VJ Day, while stationed at Laohwangping, the 35th PRS was again assigned to the Tenth Air Force.

In the CBI theater of operations, two Liaison Squadrons, the 115th (ex-California NG) and 127th (ex-Kansas NG) flew observation, light transport and medical evacuation sorties for ground forces in the battle areas. Equipped with Stinson L-1s and L-5s, and with some Piper L-4s, the 115th arrived in India during November 1944. Entering combat operations on 3 December 1944, the 115th was successively based at forward fields in India, Burma and China. The 127th began its combat career at Cox's Bazaar within five weeks of its arrival in India on 16 December 1944. However, on 19 May 1945, the unit was withdrawn from the front to be shipped to Okinawa, where it arrived one month after the end of the war.

Service in the ZI and Canal Zone

To round up the history of the Guard's contribution to the American wartime effort, mention must be made of the seven squadrons which were retained in the Zone of the Interior and of the squadron which served in the Canal Zone. After serving for periods of up to 43 months in a variety of duties, these squadrons were inactivated prior to the end of the war. The first to go was the 105th Recon-

naissance Squadron (Bombardment) which was phased out on 15 August 1943; it was followed on 30 November 1943 by the 113th, 116th and 120th Tactical Reconnaissance Squadrons; on 15 April 1944 by the 102nd TRS; and finally on 1 May 1944 by the 124th TRS and the 489th and 490th Fighter Squadrons (previously designated the 104th and 119th Observation Squadron respectively).

After engaging in maneuvers and joint exercises in Illinois, Tennessee, Arkansas and Louisiana during most of 1941, the 108th Observation Squadron was back at its home base in Chicago when, shortly after the Japanese attack against Pearl Harbor, it was ordered to Panama. Ground personnel and supplies left Chicago on 28 December 1941 and, on 9 January 1942, were loaded in New Orleans aboard the SS *Algonquin* for the four-day voyage to Panama. The O-47A/Bs and O-49s were ferried by their crews from Chicago to the Canal Zone with stops in Nashville, TN; Texarkana, TX; Mobile, AL; Houston and Brownsville, TX; Tampico and Vera Cruz, Mexico; Guatemala City, Guatemala; and Managua, Nicaragua. When on 14 January 1942 the 108th Observation Squadron, now part of the 72nd Observation Group, Caribbean Air Force (redesignated Sixth Air Force in February 1942), took up its new assignment, it became the first ex-Guard flying unit to be stationed outside the 48 contiguous states. Successively based at Rio Hato and Howard Field, the unit flew a motley collection of aircraft (A-18s, B-18s, L-4s, O-47s, O-49s, P-36s and P-39s) in defense of the Canal Zone until its inactivation on 1 November 1943.

After VJ Day, 18 of the 20 ex-Guard squadrons were rapidly inactivated between 25 September 1945, when the 840th Bombardment Squadron (ex-128th Observation Squadron, Georgia NG) was released, and Christmas Day 1945, when the 115th Liaison Squadron was phased out. The 110th Tactical Reconnaissance Squadron soldiered on into 1946, being finally released on 20 February, while the heir of the 101st Observation Squadron, Massachusetts NG, remained on active duty until 29 July 1946 (and, by then designated 39th TRS, got to fly some of the first Lockheed P-80A jet fighters from March Field, CA).

When the inactivation process was finally completed, all 29 units were again assigned their old squadron numbers and were allotted back to their original states. Together with 55 ex-AAF regular squadrons, which had also been inactivated after the war, they were reorganized to constitute the air component of the expanded postwar National Guard.

Below: Whether former Guardsmen or young draftees, maintenance personnel adapted remarkably well to the harsh conditions prevailing in the CBI. These 'wrench-benders' work on a Stinson L-1A of the 115th Liaison Squadron at Myitkyina, Burma, in late 1944.

Postwar Development

Above: After the end of World War II, old units were returned to state control and new Guard units were organized. All proudly proclaimed their home state and, for several years, played down their USAAF/USAF affiliation. Flying over the San Francisco Bay on a typically fog-shrouded day, this F-51D-30-NA belongs to the 194th Fighter Squadron (SE).

Just as had been the case after World War I had ended, the United States quickly demobilized most of its forces following VJ Day. Thus, between September and December 1945, the Army Air Forces shrank from 2,253,000 personnel to fewer than 889,000, while the number of aircraft on strength went from 63,745 on 10 August 1945 to 34,195 on 30 June 1946. Rapid demobilization and its attendant losses of skilled personnel weakened the AAF.

Fortunately, as became obvious less than five years after World War II had ended when the US was drawn into another war, handsome pay-offs were seen from the work initiated in July 1943 by a Special Planning Division set up to coordinate detailed War Department planning for demobilization and the postwar Army, its air units, and ground and air reserve components. Already at that time, however, problems surfaced as service rivalries and the desire of some senior officers within the air staff to rely solely on active-duty forces, rather than to supplement regular units with Reserves or National Guard air strength, threatened the future of aviation in the National Guard. Effective lobbying by the National Guard Association of the United States (NGAUS), the Adjutant Generals' Association and the National Guard Bureau in the War Department's Special Staff, however, insured the future of the Guard and its air components.

The original plan for the organization of postwar National Guard air units was prepared by the Army Air Forces and presented to the air staff on 9 October 1945. Less than seven weeks later, on 26 November, a revised plan was approved by the Commanding General, Army Air Forces, and forwarded to the Chief of Staff, United States Army, with recommendations that it be approved for initial implementation and further planning. However, pending decisions as to the organization, strength and composition of the postwar Regular Army, no action was taken to implement this plan. Finally, on 30 January 1946, the Army Chief of Staff directed that National Guard air units be activated and, 10 days later, the plan was announced to the several states. Unit allotments, revised on the basis of comments from the several states, were announced on 24 May 1946 and the organization of the National Guard air units proceeded without further delay.

While these planning activities were taking place, the dual (federal and state) mission of the National Guard was defined as follows in the Report of the Chief of the National Guard Bureau, Fiscal Year 1946:

operations, including the offensive, either in the United States or overseas.

2. Mission of the National Guard of the several states: To provide sufficient organizations in each state so trained and equipped as to enable them to function efficiently at existing strength in the protection of life and property and the preservation of peace, order and public safety, under competent orders of the state authorities."

Its mission having been confirmed and the basis of its organization having been agreed to, the National Guard proceeded with personnel recruitment and the planning required to obtain federal recognition.

According to the modified organization plan, a total of 541 units of the air arm of the National Guard was allotted to the states. Most were support units, such as weather detachments, anti-aircraft batteries, bands, aircraft warning control organizations, etc, while the combat elements were to be organized into 12 wings.[17] As programmed, these 12 wings were to be assigned under the overall umbrella of the Air Defense Command, to the First, Second, Fourth, Tenth, Eleventh and Fourteenth Air Forces (as shown in Table 5). These wings were to be divided into 20 fighter groups (with a total of 62 squadrons), two light bombardment groups (four squadrons), and five composite groups (with 12 fighter squadrons and six bombardment squadrons).

Each fighter squadron was scheduled to be equipped with 25 mission aircraft (North American P-51D Mustangs for units in the midwest and the west, and Republic P-47D or P-47N Thunderbolts for units in the east and the south), four target-towing aircraft (modified Douglas A-26 Invader light bombers), two instrument trainers (North American AT-6 Texans), two liaison air-

Above: Before the 1947 National Security Act and the resulting organization of the United States Air Force as a separate branch, Guard aircraft were identified by the letters NG for National Guard. After September 1947, NG rapidly gave place to the now-familiar ANG. This P-47N-5-RE is an aircraft of the 142nd Fighter Squadron (SE), Delaware National Guard.

Left: The 194th Fighter Squadron (SE) received federal recognition as a unit of the California Air National Guard on 2 March 1949. One of its North American T-6Ds is seen wearing NG markings in October 1949, more than two years after 'NG' was supposed to have been replaced by 'ANG'.

"1. Mission of the National Guard of the United States: To provide a reserve component of the Army and Army Air Forces of the United States, capable of expansion to immediate war strength, able to furnish land and air units fit for service anywhere in the world, trained and equipped to: a. defend critical areas of the United States against land, seaborne or airborne invasion; b. assist in covering the mobilization and concentration of the remainder of the reserve forces; and c. participate, by unit, in all types of

[17] Readers who are used to today's wings, which are made up of two to four flying squadrons, are reminded that during World War II, and immediately after the war, wings were larger units comprised of two or more groups. Groups, in turn, were made up of two or more squadrons. Hence, early National Guard groups were equivalent to today's wings in terms of flying squadrons. Unlike today's wings, however, the wartime and postwar groups did not include support and administrative units.

Right: Republic P-47D and P-47N Thunderbolts (F-47Ds and F-47Ns after 11 June 1948) equipped no fewer than 28 NG/ANG squadrons between 1946 and 1954. Tennessee's 105th Fighter Squadron (SE) received federal recognition on 3 February 1947 and converted from F-47Ds to F-51Ds in April 1951.

Right: Along with Mustang and Thunderbolt fighters, Douglas A-26 (B-26 after 11 June 1948) Invader light bombers were the mission aircraft initially assigned to Guard units after World War II. This pair of B-26Cs of the 122nd Bombardment Squadron (Light) was photographed over the Louisiana coast on 25 September 1948.

Far right: Jet fighters made their appearance in Guard service in 1948 when specially-ordered Lockheed F-80Cs were delivered to five ANG squadrons, including Maine's 132nd Fighter Squadron (Jet).

craft (Stinson L-5 Sentinels), and one Douglas C-47 Skytrain transport (or, in a few instances, two transport aircraft; a few units had Curtiss C-46 Commandos instead of Skytrains). The 10 light bombardment squadrons were each to receive 20 Douglas A-26B and A-26C Invaders, two AT-6s and/or two Beech AT-11 Kansans, two L-5s and one C-47 or C-46.

The first ANG flying units

The military authorities in the 48 states, the District of Columbia and the territories of Hawaii and Puerto Rico immediately began recruiting personnel and organizing the ground and air units which they had been allotted. Working at a frantic pace, the State of Colorado succeeded in manning and organizing the 120th Fighter Squadron (Single Engined) prior to the end of Fiscal Year 1946 and, on 30 June 1946, this squadron became the first Guard unit, ground or air, to be extended federal recognition after World War II.

The organization of new air units did not proceed as rapidly as scheduled during FY47, as the result of the transfer of $53 million from the National Guard appropriation to the Regular Army (having reduced earlier the military budget, Congress then had to allow the War Department to divert funds from the Guard to the active-duty components) and the difficulty for some states to obtain the needed airfield facilities (notwithstanding that the War Assets Administration sold most wartime air bases to local authorities for a nominal amount and that the federal government undertook to pay 75 per cent of the oper-

ational expenses of airfields used by the Guard). Nonetheless, during the year no fewer than 56 squadrons were organized in 42 states, the District of Columbia and the Territory of Hawaii (see Table 6). Thirty of these squadrons were initially equipped with P-51Ds (as had been Colorado's 120th Fighter Squadron), 18 received P-47Ds or Ns, and eight were light bomber squadrons with A-26Bs or Cs.

By the end of FY47, a total of 1,965 fighters, light bombers and support aircraft had been delivered to equip the 57 federally-recognized squadrons and headquarters units. To bring all units to their full allotment and to provide 10 per cent reserve aircraft, an additional 359 aircraft were required and were expected to be delivered by August 1947. Unfortunately, delays were encountered and by the summer of 1948, when the number of federally-recognized squadrons had grown to 73, the Guard only had 76.6 per cent of its authorized aircraft.

Passed by Congress and signed into law by President Harry S. Truman on 26 July 1947, the National Security Act (Public Law 253) created the United States Air Force. Coming into its own on 18 September 1947, the USAF became through its Air Defense Command the gaining service for the fighter and bomber squadrons of the Guard which, together with their supporting units, now officially formed the Air National Guard.[18]

During the course of FY48, 16 additional squadrons – nine with Mustangs, five with Thunderbolts and two with Invaders – were extended federal recognition. These additional units were located in 11 states and Puerto Rico and brought the Air National Guard to a total strength of 73 mission squadrons and 320 support units, or 76.5 per cent of the units which had been allotted to and accepted by the several states after World War II.

The Guard's first jets

Fiscal Year 1948 also saw the ANG make its belated entry into the jet age.[19] The first of 107 Lockheed P-80C Shooting Stars, which were ordered in FY47 and FY48 specifically for the Guard and received serial numbers prefixed with the letters NG,[20] were delivered to five ANG squadrons – the 132nd at Bangor, Maine; the 158th at Savannah, Georgia; the 159th at Jacksonville, Florida; the 173rd at Lincoln, Nebraska; and the 196th at San Bernardino, California. The latter unit was the first to convert and, effective 16 June 1948, it was redesignated 196th Fighter Squadron (Jet). Three of the other squadrons, the 132nd, 158th and 173rd, completed their conversions in August while the 159th did so in January 1949.

Above: In addition to being used as mission aircraft by 14 ANG bombardment squadrons, including California's 115th Bombardment Squadron (Light) to which 41-39324 belonged when photographed at Oakland in 1949, Douglas Invaders were used by Guard fighter squadrons as target-towing aircraft.

Left: New Mexico's 188th Fighter Squadron (SE) was extended federal recognition on 7 July 1947. It flew Mustangs until August 1953 when it converted to F-80s.

Above left: Hawaii's 199th Fighter Squadron (SE) was the last US unit to fly Thunderbolts. It converted from Republic F-47Ns to North American F-86Es in February 1954.

The third significant change to take place during that period was a change in reporting procedure. With the establishment of the Continental Air Command on 1 December 1948 as a major command with jurisdiction over Air Defense Command, Tactical Air Command, the Air National Guard and the Air Force Reserve, CONAC replaced ADC as the Air Force's command responsible for the organization, training and maintenance of the Air Guard.

The last of the 84 flying squadrons allotted to the Air National Guard in the original postwar program were federally recognized during FY49 and included four units with Mustangs, five with Thunderbolts and two with Invaders. The planned jet conversion of a number of squadrons could not be accomplished during the year as scheduled due to the need to modify the Republic F-84Bs and F-84Cs being transferred from USAF inventory. Thus, on 30 June 1949, the Air National Guard was organized into 12 wings, 27 groups and 84 squadrons with the following types of mission aircraft: Shooting Stars (five squadrons); Mustangs (41 squadrons); Thunderbolts (26 squadrons); and Invaders (12 squadrons). Including support and training aircraft, these units had 104 jets and 2,159 piston-powered aircraft, representing 82 per cent of the ANG authorization.

Few notable events marked FY49 for the Guard save for the fact that the 171st Fighter Squadron (SE) of the Michigan ANG made the first postwar mass formation flight of an entire Guard squadron when, in the last five days of

[18] Since their organization in 1946, aviation units had been properly designated National Guard Air Units. Unofficially, however, the name Air National Guard was already used frequently prior to the signing of the 1947 National Security Act.

With the separation of the National Guard into the Army National Guard (ARNG) and the Air National Guard (ANG) came the need to organize aviation units within the ARNG. Initially, the ARNG aviation units were equipped mostly with single-engined observation and liaison aircraft, the principal types being the Aeronca L-16, the North American (Ryan) L-17, the Piper L-4 and the Stinson L-5. The history of ARNG aviation units is not part of the history of the Air National Guard but it should be indicated that ARNG aviation has grown in importance over the years. In 1990, the ARNG operated over 2,700 helicopters (AH-1s, AH-64s, CH-46s, CH-47s, OH-6s, OH-58s and UH-1s) and fixed-wing aircraft (C-7s, C-12s, U-8s and U-21s) and had its own training facilities, the Eastern Army National Guard Aviation Training Site (EAATS) in Pennsylvania and the Western Army National Guard Aviation Training Site (WAATS) in Arizona.

[19] By way of comparison, the first operational sorties with jet fighters were made in April 1944 by the Erprobungskommando 262 of the Luftwaffe (then based at Lechfeld and equipped with the revolutionary Messerschmitt Me 262A-1a); three months later, No. 616 Squadron of the Royal Air Force flew Gloster Meteor I twinjet fighters against V1 flying bombs. Although Bell P-59s and Lockheed P-80s were delivered to operational units of the Army Air Forces prior to the end of World War II, neither type was used in combat (two YP-80As had been dispatched to Italy and two to the UK as part of Project Extraversion but were too late to fly combat sorties). With the USN, VF-17A became the first squadron to complete its carrier qualifications, doing so in May 1948 with McDonnell FH-1s aboard the USS *Saipan* (CVL-48).

[20] F-80Cs ordered for the Guard were included in USAF contract W33- 038 – AC- 16132 and were given serials NG47-551/NG47-600 (50 F-80C-5-LOs), and NG47-601/NG47-604, NG47-1380/NG47-1411 and NG48-376/NG48-396 (57 F-80C-1-LOs).

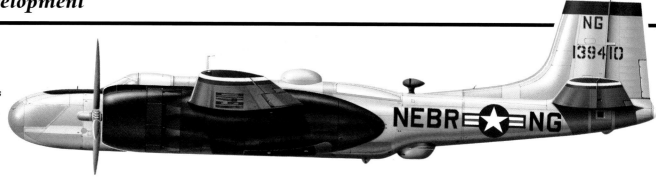

Right: Representative of the Invaders used in the target-towing role by the Guard's fighter squadrons, 41-39410 was built as an A-26B-30-DL but had lost its bomber nose and weapons before being assigned to Nebraska's 173rd Fighter Squadron.

Above: Republic Thunderjets first went into Guard service in early 1950. Delaware's 142nd Fighter Squadron (Jet) flew F-84Cs between February 1950 and September 1951.

Above right: In an age when humor was more easily accepted by senior staff officers, Guard units often opted for catching names. Thus, the Florida ANG, to which belonged this F-80C photographed on 26 March 1950 at Las Vegas AFB (now Nellis AFB), became known as the FANG. Other examples were Georgia's GANG, Hawaii's HANG, Pennsylvania's PANG, and Puerto Rico's PRANG.

December 1948, its Mustangs covered a distance of some 4,500 miles (7200 km). During the following month, the Air National Guard contributed approximately 400 aircraft to participate in the inauguration ceremonies for President Truman on 20 January 1949.

Typical of the 84 squadrons then serving the ANG was the 199th Fighter Squadron (SE), Territory of Hawaii, which on 4 November 1946 had become the 25th squadron to be extended federal recognition. This unit had received its first support aircraft, A-26C 44-35433, on 19 March 1947 and its first mission aircraft, P-47N 44-88529, on 9 July 1947 while it was based at Bellows Field. By 28 October 1947, the 199th had moved to Hickam AFB where better facilities were available. It was there that the squadron undertook, during FY49 (its second year of flying operations), to become a combat-ready unit. To do so, flying activities were stepped up with 'dawn patrols' being flown between 0550 and 0715 hours – giving pilots time to get to their civilian jobs for a normal work schedule – and 'twilight patrols' being scheduled after normal business hours. More flying hours were accumulated during the squadron's summer encampment held between 14 and 28 June 1949 at Hickam AFB.

During the year, the 199th received an unexpected boost in equipment when the 81st Fighter Group, USAF, was inactivated at Wheeler AFB. The TH ANG was given responsibility for reclaiming the unit's F-47s (the Air Force had changed the type letter 'P' for pursuit to 'F' for fighter effective 11 June 1948) for transfer to ANG squadrons on the mainland. The best airframes and engines were retained by the 199th after 'acquiring' the number plates of those in its inventory, and the squadron's stock level was increased from a normal 45-day supply to a whopping two-year supply.

During February 1949, in addition to its normal training activities, the squadron used its two Curtiss C-46F transports to fly 76 airlift missions (carrying in the process 1,452 passengers and 180,758 lb of freight) to provide relief to flash flood victims at the Waimea River on the island of

Kauai. By the end of FY49, the 199th and its support units had a strength of 352 personnel – 100 per cent of authorized airmen but 13 short of authorized officers. Its aircraft inventory included 27 F-47Ns, four TB-26Cs, five T-6Ds and two C-46Fs. During FY49 it had flown 4,462 hours and had suffered five aircraft accidents resulting in the loss of one F-47N and damage to four other fighters; fortunately, no personnel loss resulted from these accidents.

On the eve of the Korean War

Prior to being handed over to the Guard, Republic F-84B and F-84C Thunderjets had to be put through an $8-million modification and modernization program to strengthen their wings, adapt their engines to the use of a new type of jet fuel and incorporate some 100 other structural and engineering modifications. Their entry into ANG service was further complicated by the insufficient number of specialized ground equipment items such as auxiliary starting units, jacks, stands and sling assemblies. Nonetheless, beginning in early 1950, Thunderjets began equipping 10 fighter squadrons (jet) – the 101st (MA), 107th (MI), 116th (WA), 121st (DC), 127th (KS), 138th (NY), 142nd (DE), 166th (OH), 171st (MI) and 174th (IA). In addition, the Wisconsin ANG's 126th Fighter Squadron converted during the year from F-51Ds to F-80As to bring the Guard's complement of fighter squadrons (jet) to a total of 16 units. Fifty-six other fighter squadrons continued to fly piston-powered aircraft while the 12 bombardment squadrons retained their Invaders.

In its fourth year following post-World War II organization, the Air National Guard faced a number of problems. Personnel strength, notably, was below authorization with 40,995 officers and men carried on the rolls versus a planned strength of 49,500 personnel – a more than 17 per cent shortfall. More significant was the fact that the ANG only had some 3,000 pilots assigned to tactical units, a 25 per cent shortfall, and was faced with an annual attrition rate of 18 per cent as increased responsibility in their civilian careers and to their families made it increasingly difficult for some aircrews to keep their Guard commitment. To provide the required replacement pilots, the ANG was authorized to train younger officers already serving in non-flying capacity, to appoint qualified airmen as aviation cadets, and to commission 200 second lieutenants annually and send them to Air Force flying schools for training. Pilots already assigned to tactical units were authorized 110 flying hours per year while ANG pilots fly-

With triple fuselage bands on its aft fuselage, this F-51D-25-NA is identified as the aircraft assigned to the squadron commander of the 192nd Fighter Squadron (SE), Nevada ANG.

The District of Columbia's 121st Fighter Squadron converted from Republic F-47Ds to F-84Cs in December 1949 and from Thunderjets to Lockheed F-94Bs in July 1951.

ing support missions were limited to 80 hours annually. Nearly one-fourth of these flying hours were normally accumulated during two-week summer encampments when each fighter squadron and its 30 pilots typically consumed 62,534 US gal (236712 liters) of aviation gasoline, and expended 18,889 rounds of 0.50-caliber ammunition, 85 bombs and 195 rockets. More flying hours, both during encampments and the remainder of the year, had been planned when the FY50 budget for the Guard was prepared; however, budgetary limitations imposed on 10 October 1949 resulted in a drastic curtailment.

In spite of staffing, equipment and budgetary constraints, the Air National Guard had reached a fairly satisfactory training status when, just before the end of FY50, the United States found itself drawn into another war following the North Korean invasion of South Korea on 25 June 1950. Five days later, before the new mobilization brought Guardsmen back into federal active duty, the ANG possessed 373 jet fighters, 1,489 piston-powered fighters, 317 twin-engined light bombers, 306 trainers and 170 transport aircraft.

Above: Shortly after receiving federal recognition on 4 April 1957, New Hampshire's 133rd Fighter Squadron was equipped with Republic F-47Ds. It converted to North American Mustangs in November 1952 (with these F-51H-NAs seen here at Grenier Field in July 1953).

USAF

National Guard Heritage Painting courtesy of NGB/PAH

FL ANG

Above: F-84Es at Taegu (K-2), Korea. The first four aircraft bear on their vertical surfaces the diagonal stripe of the 136th Fighter-Bomber Wing and the insignia of Texas' 111th FBS. Those in the background are from the 49th FBW.

Right: During the Korean War, the all-ANG 136th Fighter-Bomber Wing, which included Texas' 111th FBS and 182nd FBS and Arkansas' 154th FBS, flew combat operations with F-84Es between June 1951 and July 1952. The squadrons were then returned to state control but many ANG pilots and ground personnel elected to remain in Korea.

Above right: After being called to active duty, Florida's 159th Fighter-Bomber Squadron converted from F-80Cs to F-84Es before being sent to Korea.

The Korean War

When the war broke out in Korea, the Air National Guard had just undertaken a major organizational change to bring its units into conformity with the new combat wing organization of the regular Air Force. To do so necessitated the reorganization of 111 units, the activation of 150 new units and the inactivation of 207 old-type units. The previously existing 12 wings were to be replaced by 27 self-contained combat wings with a like number of fighter and bomber, maintenance and supply, air base and medical groups. Twenty-two of the new combat wings were organized during the first quarter of FY51 but, because of the partial mobilization of ANG units which was ordered in October 1950, the five remaining combat wings were to be organized only after their return from federal active duty.

During the summer of 1950, five squadrons converted to jet aircraft with the 107th Bombardment Squadron (Light) of the MI ANG becoming the 107th Fighter Squadron (Jet) upon exchanging its Invaders for Thunderjets, while the 125th (OK), 128th (GA), 181st (TX) and 197th (AZ) Fighter Squadrons converted from piston-engined fighters to Thunderjets. Conversely, Nebraska's 173rd Fighter Squadron lost its F-80Cs shortly before being activated and converted back to F-51Ds.

The Air National Guard was not activated at the onset of the Korean War, but some of its personnel volunteered on an individual basis for active service while 145 of its 764 F-51Ds were taken over by the USAF. Shipped from Alameda, California, to the Far East Air Force, these F-51Ds were rushed to Korea as they were the only fighter aircraft capable of operating from unimproved Korean airfields. They were replaced in ANG service during FY51 by F-51Ds and F-51Hs taken out of storage and overhauled.

Beginning on 10 October 1950, when 15 squadrons were inducted into federal active service, a total of 67 ANG squadrons was called for 21 months of active duty (see Table 7). Fifty-one of the activated units served in the continental United States while three went to Korea, three to Japan (from where they flew combat sorties over Korea), six to continental Europe and four to the United Kingdom. Following the initial 15 squadrons, 18 squadrons were activated on 1 February 1951, 15 squadrons on 1 March and 19 squadrons on 1 April. These last units were released from active duty on 30 December 1952, more than six months before the war ended, but individual Guardsmen remained voluntarily on active duty until after hostilities ended. The 17 ANG squadrons remaining under state control retained their obsolete piston-engined aircraft and lost a substantial number of their pilots and technicians who volunteered for active duty.

Upon being called to active duty, the 111th Fighter Squadron, TX ANG (normally stationed at Ellington Field, Houston), the 154th Fighter Squadron, AR ANG (at Adams Field, Little Rock) and the 182nd Fighter Squadron, TX ANG (at Brooks AFB, San Antonio) were organized into the all-ANG 136th Fighter-Bomber Group which was assigned to Tactical Air Command and initially headquartered at Hensley Field, Dallas. Two weeks later, the 136th Group moved to Langley AFB, VA, where it began its conversion from F-51D Mustangs to F-84E Thunderjets in preparation for its deployment overseas. Rumors[21] circulated that the 136th would be assigned to Europe[21] but, finally, on 1 May 1951 its personnel were

---

[21] The most prevailing rumor, according to which the unit was to deploy to Cannes, was typical of rumors circulating among the uninformed in all the world's armies. To be stationed on the French Riviera would indeed have been lovely. Unfortunately for all concerned, the rumor mongers had not taken the trouble to confirm a most essential fact: the availability of airfield facilities suitable for jet operations. In 1951, Cannes-Mandelieu was most certainly not ready for jet fighter operations.

Mason collection, courtesy of David W. Menard

Left: The 116th Fighter-Bomber Wing, which was made up of ANG squadrons from California, Florida and Georgia, was selected to conduct combat air refueling tests as part of Operation High Tide. Its F-84Es were specially fitted with refueling probes on the inside of the tip tanks.

alerted for shipment to the Far East to take over the Thunderjets of the veteran 27th Fighter Escort Wing which was rotated back to the States.

The first combat mission by pilots of the 136th was flown eight weeks later from Itazuke AB, Japan, when on 26 June four flights of the 182nd Fighter-Bomber Squadron joined two flights manned by pilots of the 27th Wing on a strike against the airfield at Yongyu. In the process, the Guardsmen tangled for the first time with MiG-15s, and Captain Underwood and Lieutenant Oligher shared credit for the destruction of an enemy jet fighter. Four days later, the 136th Fighter-Bomber Wing was officially declared operational and for the next three months it remained based at Itazuke AB. Finally, in October 1951, it moved to K-2 airfield at Taegu where a 9,000-ft (2745-m) asphalt and PSP runway had been built to accommodate the pavement-hungry Thunderjets.

Now closer to the battlefront, the ANG unit intensified its operations (B-29 escort and ground-attack sorties). Among its increasing losses was that of its CO, Colonel Albert C. Prendergast, who was shot down on 5 November 1951 while leading the wing. Another loss was narrowly avoided in a spectacular mid-air rescue which occurred after Captain J. Paladino lost consciousness due to a malfunction of his oxygen system. Two pilots of the 154th Fighter-Bomber Squadron – Captain J. Miller and Lieutenant W. MacArthur – reacted swiftly. While Captain Miller placed his left wing beneath the right wing of Paladino's aircraft, MacArthur positioned his aircraft in a similar fashion beneath the other wing of Paladino's Thunderjet. Thus preventing the disabled pilot's aircraft from spinning or diving, they proceeded to descend in tight formation until reaching a lower altitude, where Paladino regained consciousness in time to regain control of his aircraft and land back safely at Taegu. While not all missions were that eventful, the 136th completed its 5,000th combat sortie on 31 October 1951 and its 10,000th sortie less than

Mason collection, courtesy of David W. Menard

three months later. Finally, after being singled out as the outstanding fighter-bomber unit in Korea, the 136th completed its 21 months on active duty on 9 July 1952.

In the Far East the 136th had been joined by another all-ANG unit, the 116th Fighter-Bomber Wing, composed of the 158th (GA), the 159th (FL) and the 196th (CA) Fighter-Bomber Squadrons. Shortly after being activated on 10 October 1950, these three squadrons had taken their Shooting Stars to George AFB, CA, where they converted to F-84Es in preparation for their planned assignment to NATO in Europe. However, the urgent need for more aircraft and pilots to fight the war in Korea resulted in the transfer of the 116th to Misawa AB, Japan, where it arrived

Above: Bomb-laden F-84Es of the 159th Fighter-Bomber Squadron are lined up on the apron at Misawa AB, Japan, before an air-refueled combat mission.

Postwar Development

Above: Mounted on the inside of the tip tanks of F-84Es, the refueling probe was well located for the pilot to keep it in sight during air refueling. However, the probe was too far outboard for easy line-up with the basket.

in late July 1951. Four months later the squadrons of the 116th began rotating one at a time to K-2 to relieve, on a temporary basis, squadrons of the battle-weary 49th and 136th Fighter-Bomber Wings. In addition, another squadron of the 116th was rotated to Chitose AB to provide air defense for northern Japan.

As no other airfield with a runway long enough for Thunderjets carrying bombs or full external tanks was available in Korea, and as F-84s had insufficient loiter time over the front when operating from Japanese bases, the 116th was selected in February 1952 as the first unit to experiment under combat conditions with inflight refueling.

Also eventually moving overseas was a third all-ANG wing equipped with Thunderjets, the 123rd Fighter-Bomber Wing. With its three squadrons, Kentucky's 165th, North Carolina's 156th and West Virginia's 167th, then flying Mustangs and Thunderbolts, the 123rd was ordered to active duty at the Standiford Municipal Airport, Louisville, KY, on 10 October 1950. Assigned to Tactical Air Command, the 123rd moved to Godman AFB, KY, some 10 days later for intensive training and jet conversion. Transferred to USAFE in late 1951, the 123rd set up station at RAF Manston, Kent, England, where on 10 December they took over the F-84Es previously used by two TDY SAC units, the 31st and 12th Fighter-Escort Wings. Seven months later the 123rd and its three squadrons were returned to state control. Its aircraft and most of its personnel, however, were retained in the UK for use by the specially established 406th FBW, USAFE.

The three squadrons of the 123rd Fighter-Bomber Wing and their F-84Es had been preceded in England by the 116th Fighter Interceptor Squadron. This unit, while serving in the Washington ANG, had begun its conversion to Thunderjets in April 1950 and was fully jet qualified when, on 1 February 1951, it was ordered to active duty. Soon thereafter, the 116th became the first mobilized Guard unit to be equipped with North American F-86As, then the world's most advanced fighter aircraft. Accelerated training soon bore fruit and the 116th FIS was declared ready to

bolster NATO's defense. Flying its Sabres across the North Atlantic, with several refueling stops along the way, the squadron arrived at RAF Shepherds Grove, Suffolk, England, in late August 1951. Fourteen months later, having completed their tour of active duty, the Guardsmen of the 116th were returned to the States while their F-86As were absorbed into the USAFE inventory.

On the European continent, NATO's strength was increased during the Korean War period by six Guard squadrons. First to arrive were the Douglas Invaders of the 126th Bombardment Wing (Light) and its 108th (IL), 168th (IL) and 180th (MO) Squadrons. Activated on 1 April 1951, the personnel of these three squadrons underwent stepped-up training first at their home base and then, from July, at Langley AFB, VA. On 30 October 1951, the first echelon of B-26 bombers left Langley AFB and, stopping in Boston, Labrador, Greenland, Iceland, Scotland and England, proceeded to its assigned station at Bordeaux-Mérignac, France. There the 126th BW became the first US tactical air unit stationed in France since the end of World War II. The unit remained at Mérignac AB until May 1952 and then transferred to Laon AB in northern France to complete its tour of active duty by 31 December 1952.

Even though the 157th Fighter Squadron (SC ANG) and 160th Fighter Squadron (AL ANG) had been among the first 15 ANG units to be activated on 10 October 1950, they very nearly did not get an assignment overseas. Together with the 112th Fighter Squadron (OH ANG) they had been assigned a tactical reconnaissance role shortly after being activated and were grouped into the 117th Tactical Reconnaissance Wing at Lawson AFB, GA. Trained initially on RF-51Ds, the 157th and 160th Tactical Reconnaissance Squadrons converted to RF-80As while the 112th received RB-26Cs. Delays then prevented the wing from being deployed overseas until its personnel had less than 12 months to serve prior to the end of their 21-month call-up when, according to Air Force regulations, they could no longer be sent overseas. However, by signing Indefinite Career Reserve Statements, many of the officers were

Opposite page, top left: Operation High Tide. A Republic F-84E of the 159th F-BS is refueled by a Boeing KB-29M of the 91st Air Refueling Squadron.

Mason collection, courtesy of David W. Menard

USAF

The first North American F-86As to be based in Europe were those of the 116th Fighter Interceptor Squadron, the flying unit of the Washington ANG which had been placed on active duty on 1 February 1951. The Sabres reached RAF Sheperds Grove, Suffolk, on 27 August 1951 after the Guardsmen had converted from F-84Bs.

William J. Balogh Sr courtesy of David W. Menard

Left: A Douglas B-26C-35-DT of the 126th Bombardment Wing on 27 May 1950. Illinois' 108th and 168th Bombardment Squadrons (Light) and Missouri's 180th BS were called to active duty on 1 April 1951 and the wing was assigned to USAFE in November 1951.

Left: Republic F-84Gs of the 127th Fighter-Bomber Squadron at Alexandria AFB, Louisiana, in the spring of 1952 during the Korean War activation of this Kansas ANG squadron.

Courtesy of David W. Menard

Below: While on active duty during the Korean War, Mississippi's 153rd FBS continued to fly Republic F-47Ns in the United States. After its return to state control, the 153rd was reorganized as a tactical reconnaissance unit and converted to North American RF-51Ds.

again qualified to go overseas and, finally, in January 1952 the 157th and 160th TRSs left for Europe. As their intended facilities at Toul-Rosières AB, France, were not yet ready, both squadrons first went to Fürstenfeldbrück AB in Germany. The 160th TRS later transferred to Neubiberg AB, Germany, and finally to Toul-Rosières. The officers who signed Indefinite Career Reserve Statements were retained on active duty until May 1953, while most other personnel were released as scheduled on 9 July 1952.

Shortly after their activation on 10 October 1950, the Thunderjet-equipped 125th (OK ANG), 127th (KS ANG) and 128th (GA ANG) Fighter-Bomber Squadrons forming the 137th Fighter-Bomber Wing moved as a unit to Alexandria AFB, LA. After delays were incurred, some personnel signed Indefinite Career Reserve Statements and were supplemented by regular Air Force personnel to man the 127th FBS. Equipped with Thunderjets of the latest model, the F-84G fitted with inflight-refueling equipment and capable of delivering tactical nuclear weapons, this squadron was deployed to Chaumont AB, France, on 13

R. Uppstrom courtesy of David W. Menard

Postwar Development

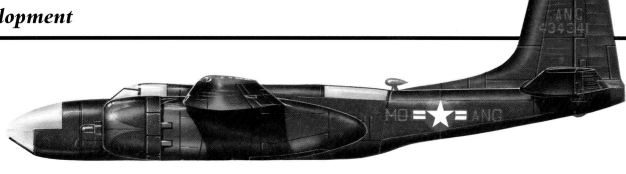

After serving 21 months on active duty during the Korean War activation, the two bombardment squadrons of the Missouri ANG were returned to state control and flew B-26Cs during the mid-1950s.

Above: Having flown Boeing RB-29As during its Korean War activation, Pennsylvania's 103rd was reorganized as a fighter-bomber squadron in January 1953 and flew F-51Ds for approximately 21 months. This F-51D-25-NA was photographed at the Philadelphia Airport in March 1953.

Above right: During the Korean War, the 127th Pilot Training Wing trained Thunderjet pilots at Luke AFB, AZ. Its squadrons were ANG units on active duty, Arizona's 197th and Michigan's 107th and 171st. This F-84E was photographed at Luke AFB on 19 March 1951 after the wing had converted from earlier Thunderjet models.

May 1952 as part of the reorganized 137th Fighter-Bomber Wing. The other Guardsmen remained at Alexandria AFB until demobilized on 9 July 1952. The 125th, 127th and 128th FBSs were returned to state control and the 137th FBW and its three squadrons of F-84Gs were absorbed into USAFE on 10 July to become the 48th Fighter-Bomber Wing.

While the Guard units deployed to Korea and Europe during the Korean War retained their unit number, they lost their Guard identity as most became manned by a mix of ANG and USAF personnel when their own crews volunteered for service with regular USAF units serving in Korea and elsewhere. The same situation prevailed to an even larger extent with mobilized ANG units which remained stateside and in the 17 ANG flying squadrons which were kept under state control.

Upon activation of their units, large numbers of aircrews and maintenance personnel from the activated ANG squadrons which did not deploy overseas were transferred to regular Air Force units for service in Korea, Europe and elsewhere. Partially manned by replacement personnel, these ANG squadrons were retained within their newly-formed wings as follows:

101st Fighter Interceptor Wing: This wing was activated on 1 February 1951 and comprised the 132nd FIS (flying Mustangs from Bangor, ME), the 133rd FIS (with F-47Ds at Grenier Field, NH), the 134th FIS (with F-51D/Hs at Burlington, VT) and the 136th FIS (F-47Ds at Niagara Falls, NY).

106th Bombardment Wing: Activated on 1 March 1951 as the 106th Bombardment Group (Light), this unit was transferred to SAC two months later to fly Boeing B-29As from March AFB, CA, as the 106th Bombardment Wing (Medium). In addition to its two original NY ANG squadrons, the 102nd and 114th, the wing also included the 135th BS, a newly organized squadron manned mostly by Guardsmen from various states.

108th Fighter-Bomber Wing: With three squadrons of Thunderbolts (the 141st, NJ; 149th, VA; and 153rd, MS), the 108th FBW served on active duty from 1 March

1951 until 30 November 1952. First assigned to SAC, it took up station at Turner AFB, GA, on 14 March 1951, and, upon being transferred to TAC in December of the same year, it was relocated to Godman AFB, KY.

111th Bombardment Wing (Light): The wing, which was equipped with Invaders and made up of two Pennsylvania squadrons, the 103rd and 117th Bombardment Squadrons, and of Louisiana's 122nd BS, received its call to active duty on 1 April 1951. However, the 117th and 122nd Bombardment Squadrons were soon transferred out to provide B-26 crew training at Langley AFB, VA, until returned to state control at the end of 1952. Upon being separated from the other Guard squadrons, the 103rd Squadron was joined by two new ANG-manned squadrons, the 129th and 130th, to form at Fairchild AFB, WA, the 111th Strategic Reconnaissance Wing (Medium) equipped with Boeing RB-29As.

113th Fighter Interceptor Wing: Prior to being activated on 1 February 1951, two of the squadrons of the 113th FIW, Delaware's 142nd and the District of Columbia's 121st, had converted from Thunderbolts to Thunderjets but its third squadron, Pennsylvania's 148th, was still flying Mustangs. However, as neither their F-84s nor their F-51s were satisfactory for the air-defense mission, the three squadrons were promptly converted to more suitable aircraft. The first two received Lockheed F-94Bs at the New Castle County Airport in Delaware to protect the mid-Atlantic states. The 148th FIS moved from its home base, which was unsuitable for jet operations, to Dover AFB, Delaware, where it successively flew F-86A day fighters and F-94B all-weather interceptors.

118th Tactical Reconnaissance Wing: Redesignated from 118th Composite Group to 118th TRG (later TRW) in February 1951, this unit was equipped with RF-51Ds upon being activated on 1 April 1951. Transferred to Shaw AFB, SC, its three squadrons (the 106th, AL; 155th, TN; and 185th, OK) were converted to RF-80As in January 1952. All three squadrons lost their jets upon being returned to state control at the end of 1952.

122nd Fighter Interceptor Wing: For the duration of their period of active duty (1 February 1951 to 31 October 1952) Indiana's 113th and 163rd Fighter Interceptor Squadrons and Ohio's 166th FIS were assigned to the 122nd FIW. The Indiana squadrons kept flying Mustangs (F-51Ds and Hs) and were initially based at Baer Field, Fort Wayne, IN. The 113th later had a detachment at Sioux City, IA, prior to moving on 24 May 1951 to Scott AFB, IL. The Ohio unit operated F-84Cs from two stations in its home state, Lockbourne AFB and the Youngstown MAP.

William T. Larkins

D. L. Brown courtesy of David W. Menard

Far left: Early during the Korean War, the Air National Guard transferred 145 of its 764 F-51Ds to the Air Force for shipment to Korea. Several of the stateside ANG units then supplemented their remaining F-51Ds with F-51Hs.

Left: Replacing its F-51Ds with F-51Hs in May 1950, Ohio's 162nd FIS was not called to active duty and remained at the Cox-Dayton Municipal Airport.

F. Crain Collection courtesy of David W. Menard

Above: While on active duty at its home base, Oregon's 123rd FIS became in the spring of 1952 one of the first units to be equipped with the F-86F version of the Sabre.

127th Pilot Training Wing: Providing type conversion and operational training to USAF Thunderjet pilots, the 127th Pilot Training Group (later Wing) operated F-84Bs, Cs and Es from Luke AFB, AZ. On 21-month active duty from 1 February 1951, this wing comprised one squadron from the Arizona ANG (the 197th) and two from the Michigan ANG (the 107th and 171st).

128th Fighter Interceptor Wing: Assisting regular USAF squadrons in providing air defense for the midwestern states from 1 February 1951 until 31 October 1952, three squadrons of the 128th FIW each flew different types of aircraft. Michigan's 172nd FIS, which was based at Selfridge AFB, MI, continued to fly F-51Ds. Based at Truax Field in their home state, Wisconsin's 126th and 176th Fighter Interceptor Squadrons respectively converted from F-80As to F-86As and from F-51Ds to F-89Bs.

131st Fighter-Bomber Wing: Strengthening SAC upon being called to active duty on 1 March 1951, the 131st FBG (later FBW) was transferred to TAC in November of that year. Equipped with F-51Ds and based at Bergstrom AFB, TX, for SAC duty, and at George AFB, CA, for TAC duty, it was made up of Illinois' 170th FBS, Missouri's 110th FBS and Nevada's 192nd FBS.

132nd Fighter-Bomber Wing: This wing was called up on 1 April 1951 for service with SAC at Dow AFB, DE,

and was transferred to Alexandria AFB, LA, in November 1951 for service with TAC. Initially its 174th FBS (IA ANG) was equipped with Thunderjets but it was quickly converted back to F-51Ds, with which the other two squadrons (Iowa's 124th and Nebraska's 173rd) were already equipped.

133rd Fighter Interceptor Wing: As was typical with other FIWs on active duty, the 133rd had its three squadrons (Minnesota's 109th and 179th and South Dakota's 175th) assigned to different bases – respectively, Holman Field and Wold-Chamberlain Field in Minnesota, the Duluth Municipal Airport in the same state, and Ellsworth AFB in South Dakota. All three squadrons flew F-51Ds while on active duty between 1 March 1951 and 30 November 1952.

140th Fighter-Bomber Wing: The wing was on active duty from 1 April 1951 until 31 December 1952 and served with TAC at Clovis AFB, New Mexico. Its three squadrons were the 120th from Colorado, the 187th from Wyoming and the 191st from Utah.

146th Fighter-Bomber Wing: On active duty from 1 April 1951 until the end of 1952, the wing's three Mustang squadrons (Idaho's 190th, Montana's 186th and North Dakota's 178th) served at Moody AFB, GA, while under SAC and at George AFB, CA, under TAC.

Above left: Republic F-84D Thunderjets equipped Georgia's 128th FIS between the winter of 1952 and the summer of 1955, and that state's 158th FIS between July 1953 and March 1957.

North American F-51H-10-NA 131st Fighter Interceptor Squadron Massachusetts ANG

Built during the last few months of World War II, most P-51Hs were placed in storage after flying only a few hours. Less sturdy than the more numerous F-51Ds, F-51Hs were taken out of storage and issued to Air National Guard units during the Korean War years.

Unit
A healthy rivalry has long existed between the two Massachusetts ANG units. During the 1950s, the 101st FIS was based in Boston, a city which has a large Irish-descent population, whereas the 131st FIS was organized in the southwestern part of the state where Polish descent prevails. Not surprisingly, the 101st became known as the 'Irish Guard' and adopted green for its aircraft markings, while the 131st became the 'Polish Guard' with red markings.

Powerplant
The F-51H was powered by Packard-built Rolls-Royce Merlin V-1650-9 12-cylinder liquid-cooled engine. Driving a four-bladed Aeroproducts propeller, the engine was rated at 1,380 hp on take-off but, according to the Tech Order, maximum power was boosted to 2,220 hp at 10,000 ft under War Emergency Rating.

Handling
Pilots generally found the H to be even more delightful to fly than the D. However, they did not fully trust the H's lighter structure and felt that the latter Mustangs lacked the sturdiness and dependability of the Ds.

Lightweight Mustang
The H version of the legendary Mustang was developed from the principal production version, the D, as a lighter, faster and longer-ranged aircraft. Externally, the H differed from the D in having a longer fuselage, taller fin and rudder, smaller canopy, and straight wing leading edges.

Markings
Spinner bands, fintip, wingtips and squadron commander stripes are in the traditional 'Polish Guard' red of the 131st Squadron.

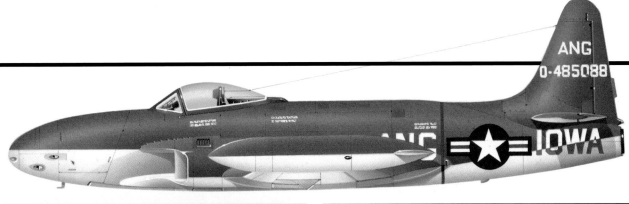

Left: When used to tow targets during all-ANG gunnery meets at Gowen Field in Idaho, Mustangs, Shooting Stars, Thunderjets and Sabres were usually given extensive coats of red or yellow as displayed by this F-80C-11-LO, 124th FIS.

In addition to the above-mentioned 42 squadrons serving as part of stateside-based wings and to the previously mentioned squadrons (112th, 125th and 128th) which did not deploy overseas as part of their wing, six squadrons were placed on active duty as individual units but remained CONUS-based . They were the 105th, TN; 115th, CA; 118th, CT; 123rd, OR (during spring 1952, the 123rd became one of the first squadrons equipped with F-86Fs; however, the Sabres were once again replaced by F-51Ds when the squadron was returned to state control in December 1952); 188th, NM; and 195th, CA. Their equipment and duty stations are listed in Table 7.

Finally, the 17 squadrons not activated during the Korean War included 10 squadrons flying Mustangs (101st, MA; 138th and 139th, NY; 146th and 147th, PA; 162nd and 164th, OH; 169th, IL; 181st, TX; and 194th, CA), four which converted from Thunderbolts to Mustangs (104th, MD; 119th, NJ; 131st, MA; and 137th, NY), and three which retained their obsolete Thunderbolts (152nd, RI; 198th, PR; and 199th, HI). All remained at their home bases.

Two of the squadrons which remained under state control took part in an experiment which had a long-lasting impact on the Air National Guard. In a memorandum to the Commander of the Continental Air Command on 20 May 1952, CONAC's Deputy for Air National Guard Matters had recommended at the suggestion of the National Guard Bureau that a small number of Guard pilots at strategic locations be placed on short tours of active duty to augment ADC's runway alert program. At first opposed by some senior Air Force officers, this plan was implemented on an experimental basis before the end of the Korean War, ADC being critically short of aircraft and crews as the result of the war. Starting on 1 March 1953, the 138th FIS at Syracuse, NY, and the 194th FBS at Hayward, CA, each started maintaining two F-51Ds and five pilots on alert status from one hour before sunrise until one hour after sunset, seven days a week. The experiment, which ended on 30 June 1953, was considered a success and continuous participation of the Guard in the runway alert program was implemented in 1954, as detailed in the next chapter.

Altogether, 45,594 Guardsmen – nearly 80 per cent of the total strength of the Air National Guard – had entered federal service during the Korean War. The mobilization, however, had revealed a number of deficiencies. Some were inherent to the way Guard units had been organized and equipped while others resulted from haphazard mobilization of reserve forces by the Department of Defense, from the use of trained Guardsmen who volunteered for active duty before the call-up of their units as 'fillers' for regular Air Force units, and from the transfer of aircraft from Guard squadrons to regular units (notably F-51Ds which were rushed to Korea and F-80Cs which were used as attrition replacements). The most critical problems stemming from the way ANG units were manned, trained and equipped at the onset of the war included understaffing (in the late 1940s, budget restrictions had limited actual manning to approximately 80 per cent of full authorization), insufficient training (especially as regards flying operations at squadron or wing strength), and obsolete aircraft (F-51s and F-47s were certainly past their prime and would have been no match for Soviet aircraft had all-out war broken out in Europe as was feared at the time). Consequently, Air Guard units required from three to six months of intensive post-mobilization reorganization, re-equipment and retraining before they could be declared combat ready.

Notwithstanding these initial problems, Guardsmen could be justly proud of their deeds when fighting in Korea ended with the signing on 27 July 1953 of the Panmunjon armistice. Considering that at the start of the Korean War the USAF had only 48 combat wings, the influx of 22 mobilized ANG wings had indeed contributed greatly – directly through deployment overseas or indirectly by providing pilots and trained maintenance personnel to bring regular units to full combat status or freeing regular units for such deployments – to the nation's ability to oppose the Communist aggression in Korea and to deter further Soviet moves on the European continent. The price paid by the Air National Guard was, however, high, both in terms of personnel loss and in terms of the initial lack of organization and equipment (in particular, the Air Force retained the jet fighters which had equipped some of the mobilized units) which followed the return of ANG units to state control.

Above: Returned to state control on 1 December 1952, Delaware's 142nd FIS lost the F-94Bs it had flown while on active duty and was reorganized as the 142nd Fighter-Bomber Squadron with late model Mustangs, including this F-51H-5-NA.

Above left: The F-51D-25-NT of the squadron commander, 190th Fighter Interceptor Squadron, Idaho ANG. Based at Gowen Field in Boise, the 124th FIS converted from F-51Ds to F-86As in November 1953.

Cold War & Vietnam

Above: Back from a gunnery training flight, a North American F-86H-5-NH of the 138th TFS, NY ANG, poses for the photographer. The 'Boys from Syracuse' flew F-86Hs between the summer of 1958 and the fall of 1970.

By 30 June 1953, less than four weeks before the signing of an armistice in Panmunjon, all Guard flying units had been back under state control for at least six months. The demobilized ANG squadrons, however, once again faced severe problems. Many of their experienced air and ground crews were still serving with the USAF after signing Indefinite Career Reserve Statements, while many old timers were rapidly approaching retirement age or, at least, were to be reassigned to non-flying positions. Equipment, particularly aircraft, was in short supply, as all ANG jet aircraft had been turned over to the USAF. The F-47s had reached the end of their useful lives and the F-51s were fast approaching the same point. Furthermore, in anticipation of their re-equipment with jets, many units needed either to improve their facilities and lengthen/strengthen the runways from which they operated, or, when the former was not feasible, to relocate in order not to lose the opportunity of converting to jets.

On the other hand, as the end of the war in Korea approached, the prospects for the Air National Guard markedly improved as both experienced crews and modern aircraft were anticipated to become available in quantities sufficient not only to bring up existing units to strength, but also to enable the formation of new ones.

On 1 July 1953, the first day of FY54, two new units, both still without aircraft – the 144th Fighter-Bomber Squadron, Territory of Alaska ANG, and the 183rd Tactical Reconnaissance Squadron, Mississippi ANG – were extended federal recognition and joined the 84 pre-Korean War squadrons. Sixty-five of these flying units were equipped with F-51Ds or Hs and were designated either fighter-bomber or fighter interceptor squadrons, two fighter units still flew Thunderbolts (the 198th in Puerto Rico and the 199th in Hawaii), six bombardment squadrons had Invaders, four TRSs operated RF-51Ds and two further tactical reconnaissance squadrons had been assigned RB-26Cs. In addition, five squadrons had already begun their jet conversion with the 117th in Pennsylvania, the 124th in Iowa, the 164th in Ohio and the 185th in Oklahoma slated to receive Shooting Stars (for the most part early F-80As and F-80Bs respectively brought up to F-80C-11 and F-80C-12 standards), while New York's 137th FIS acquired Lockheed F-94A/B all-weather interceptors. Admittedly, however, as of 1 July 1953, the Air National Guard had received only six jet aircraft.

The lack of jet aircraft was known to be temporary as aircraft released by the USAF were being overhauled and modernized prior to being delivered to ANG squadrons. Thus, operational plans and budget estimates for FY54 included conversion of all fighter squadrons. However, mainly due to the lack of facilities suitable for jet operations, the allocation of jets to the ANG failed to materialize as programmed. By 30 June 1954, the 674 jet aircraft on hand (of which approximately 150 were T-33A trainers and the remainder mission aircraft including RF-80A and F-80C Shooting Stars, F-84D and E Thunderjets, F-86A Sabres, and F-94A and B Starfires) enabled the ANG to convert, or initiate the conversion of, only 53 of its 79

J. E. Michaels courtesy of David W. Menard

Maj Gen Wayne C. Gatlin

AR ANG

Top: *Lockheed F-80Cs soldiered on with the ANG until 1958, Oklahoma's 185th becoming one of the last Shooting Star units when in May 1958 it exchanged its F-80Cs for F-86Ls and became a fighter interceptor squadron.*

Above: *Minnesota's 179th FIS flew 'Deuces' for less than five years, but during that period won the F-102 Category and came second overall during the 1970 William Tell meet at Tyndall AFB.*

Left: *Lockheed RF-80As entered ANG service in 1954 and equipped five squadrons, including Arkansas' 184th TRS, to which belonged 44-85019.*

fighter and tactical reconnaissance squadrons. The Sabre, the most modern of these types, had emerged from the Korean War as the world's outstanding fighter aircraft and was assigned in the fall of 1953 to the 186th FIS, MT ANG, and to the 190th FIS, ID ANG. Previously, F-86s had been flown by other ANG squadrons while they were on active duty.

Jet conversion and base construction

In support of this sweeping conversion endeavor, the National Guard Bureau undertook during FY54 the largest construction program in its history. Contracts were awarded at 34 ANG bases where construction was performed on property owned by, or under lease to, the United States government. In addition, construction of facilities and runway extensions at airfields not previously used by the Air National Guard was initiated. In spite of the magnitude of this effort, however, it became evident that several units would not be able to obtain the facilities necessary for jet operations and would have to be either relocated or assigned new missions not requiring the use of jet aircraft.

FY54 also saw the 144th FBS at Elmendorf AFB, Territory of Alaska, and the 183rd TRS at Hawkins Field, Jackson, Mississippi, (both of which had been federally recognized on 1 July 1953) receive their mission aircraft, F-80Cs

Warren Ship, courtesy of Cloud 9 Photography

Right: With the Guard, the superlative day fighter versions of the North American F-86 Sabre had a relatively short career, the first being taken on in November 1953 and the last being phased out seven years later. One of the 31 ANG squadrons equipped with day Sabres was Utah's 191st FIS, which flew F-86As between July 1955 and August 1958.

Right: Built by Canadair, this F-86E-6-CAN of the 107th Fighter Interceptor Squadron, MI ANG, is the wing commander's aircraft as shown by fuselage stripes in the colors of the three squadrons.

and RB-26Cs respectively. Another new unit, the 184th TRS, became the 87th flying squadron in the Air National Guard when it was federally recognized at Fort Smith, Arkansas, on 15 October 1953.

Following the success which attended the experimental assignment of pilots and aircraft of the 138th FIS and 194th FBS to the runway alert program, plans were made to expand the role of the Air National Guard in the defense of North America. This expanded responsibility led to switching primary mobilization assignments for all Guard fighter squadrons from Tactical Air Command to Air Defense Command and to expediting conversion of seven squadrons from obsolete, piston-powered, single-seat day fighters to all-weather, two-seat, jet-powered Lockheed F-94As and Bs. More importantly, the alert program was made a permanent ANG assignment.

The Air Defense Augmentation Program was implemented on 15 August 1954, when eight squadrons began maintaining two aircraft on five-minute readiness alert during daylight hours, and was expanded on 1 October, when nine additional squadrons went on alert. As members of the air-defense teams, pilots and radar operators were to be ready at all times to become immediately airborne and challenge unidentified aircraft. The overall value of this plan, which was implemented at the height of the Cold War period when the Soviet Union was known to possess hydrogen bombs and long-range jet bombers,[22] was two-fold: (**1**) it augmented ADC with additional combat-ready personnel and aircraft; and (**2**) it provided valuable tactical training for a maximum number of air and ground personnel, thus increasing the overall readiness capability of the Air National Guard.

The facilities construction program, initiated in FY54 and expanded during FY55, started to bear fruit rapidly, and enabled the Guard to convert 12 more fighter squadrons to jets during FY55. Deliveries of more modern aircraft were also accelerated and included two new types: the Republic F-84F Thunderstreak, first assigned to the 146th F-BS, PA ANG, in October 1954, and the Northrop F-89B and C Scorpion, first assigned to the 126th and 176th FISs, WI ANG, in October 1954. Nevertheless, the ANG

inventory at the end of FY55 remained short, with only 60 per cent of the authorized fighter and jet reconnaissance aircraft, and 90 per cent of the night photo-reconnaissance and light bomber aircraft being available. Total number of aircraft on hand reached 2,060 by 30 June 1955 and included 1,063 jet fighters (F-80, F-84, F-86, F-89 and F-94), 38 RF-80A jet reconnaissance aircraft, 179 T-33A jet trainers, 288 F-51 fighters, and 105 B/RB-26 twin-piston engined light bomber and reconnaissance aircraft, 175 T-6 piston-powered trainers, 146 twin-engined transports (C-45, C-46 and C-47) and 68 aircraft of various types.

At the end of FY55, these aircraft were assigned to 27 combat wings and various support units. Distribution among the combat wings was as follows: of the 73 squadrons composing the six fighter interceptor wings and 17 fighter-bomber wings, eight flew F-51s, 18 flew F-80s, six flew F-84s, seven flew F-84Fs, 18 had F-86s, four had F-89s and 12 had F-94s; the six squadrons composing the two bombardment wings flew B-26s; and two RB-26 squadrons and four RF-80 squadrons formed the two tactical reconnaissance wings.

New missions, new units and new bases

To replace fighter aircraft in units based at airfields which were not adaptable to jet operations and for which relocation proved ill-advised, and to organize new units at sites left vacant by the relocation of squadrons re-equipping elsewhere with jets, the Air National Guard was authorized during FY55 to form four air resupply groups, each with one squadron to be equipped with a mix of piston-engined Grumman SA-16 amphibians and

---

[22] The Soviets exploded their first thermonuclear device on 12 August 1953 and the twinjet Tupolev Tu-16 'Badger' entered Aviatsiya Dal'nevo Deistviya service in late 1954. The fear of a Soviet nuclear attack on the United States became so great that ADC was glad not only to have its regular fighter force, which was completely equipped with all-weather jet interceptors beginning in February 1955, augmented by alert detachments of the Air National Guard, but also accepted help from the US Navy. On 1 December 1955, the Navy began placing fighters on alert at San Diego, California.

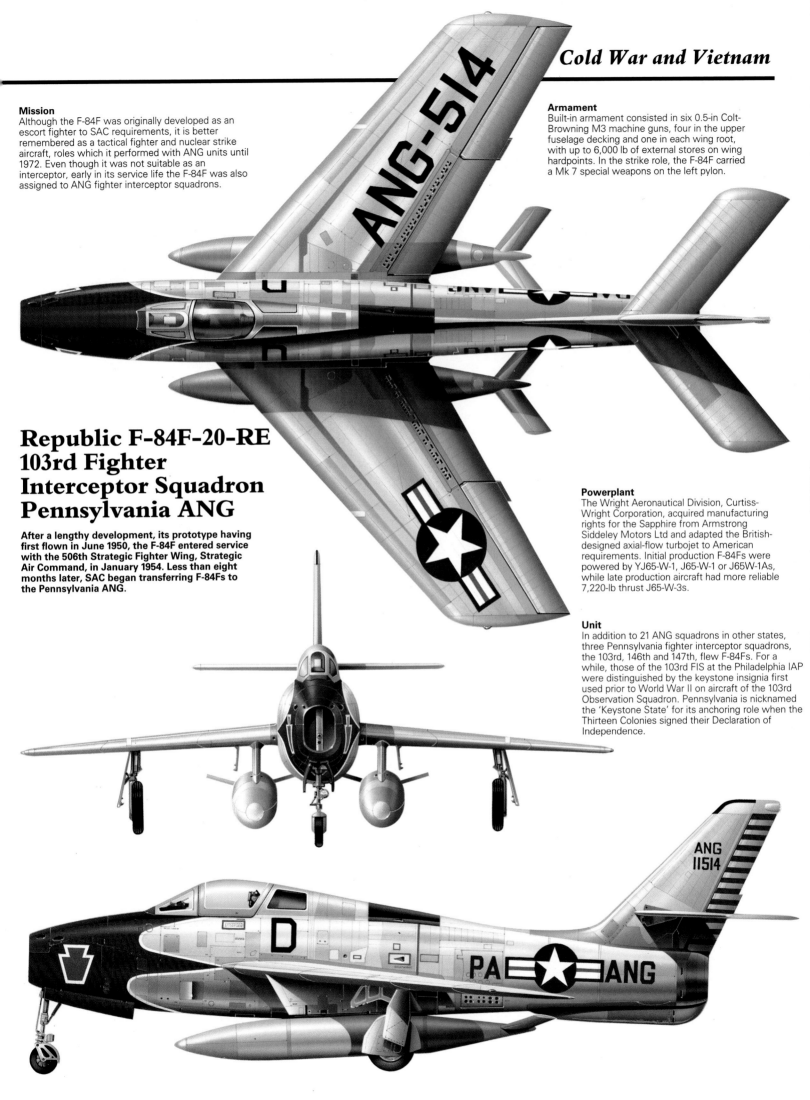

Mission
Although the F-84F was originally developed as an escort fighter to SAC requirements, it is better remembered as a tactical fighter and nuclear strike aircraft, roles which it performed with ANG units until 1972. Even though it was not suitable as an interceptor, early in its service life the F-84F was also assigned to ANG fighter interceptor squadrons.

Armament
Built-in armament consisted in six 0.5-in Colt-Browning M3 machine guns, four in the upper fuselage decking and one in each wing root, with up to 6,000 lb of external stores on wing hardpoints. In the strike role, the F-84F carried a Mk 7 special weapons on the left pylon.

Republic F-84F-20-RE 103rd Fighter Interceptor Squadron Pennsylvania ANG

After a lengthy development, its prototype having first flown in June 1950, the F-84F entered service with the 506th Strategic Fighter Wing, Strategic Air Command, in January 1954. Less than eight months later, SAC began transferring F-84Fs to the Pennsylvania ANG.

Powerplant
The Wright Aeronautical Division, Curtiss-Wright Corporation, acquired manufacturing rights for the Sapphire from Armstrong Siddeley Motors Ltd and adapted the British-designed axial-flow turbojet to American requirements. Initial production F-84Fs were powered by YJ65-W-1, J65-W-1 or J65W-1As, while late production aircraft had more reliable 7,220-lb thrust J65-W-3s.

Unit
In addition to 21 ANG squadrons in other states, three Pennsylvania fighter interceptor squadrons, the 103rd, 146th and 147th, flew F-84Fs. For a while, those of the 103rd FIS at the Philadelphia IAP were distinguished by the keystone insignia first used prior to World War II on aircraft of the 103rd Observation Squadron. Pennsylvania is nicknamed the 'Keystone State' for its anchoring role when the Thirteen Colonies signed their Declaration of Independence.

Maj Gen Wayne C. Gatlin

Courtesy of David W. Menard

P. Paulsen courtesy of David W. Menard

Top: A Lockheed F-94B-5-LO of the 179th FIS, MN ANG. The three flights of the 179th FIS painted the rudder in their respective colors of blue, red and yellow.

Above: Assigned target-towing duty during the ANG Gunnery Meet held in October 1954 at Gowen Field, ID, this F-84D-5-RE of the 118th Fighter-Bomber Squadron has received high-visibility markings.

Top right: When ANG fighter interceptor squadrons first converted to all-weather fighters, they were assigned radar trainers. Fitted with a Hughes E-1 fire-control system, this North American TB-25K was used in the mid-1950s by Oregon's 123rd FIS to train backseaters for its Lockheed F-94Bs.

Curtiss C-46 transports. The first two C-46s were delivered to the 129th Air Resupply Squadron, which was federally recognized on 3 April 1955 and which replaced the 194th Fighter Interceptor Squadron, CA ANG, at the Hayward Municipal Airport. The 194th FIS was then relocated to Fresno where jet operations presented no problems.

During Fiscal Year 1956, the availability of additional F-89 and F-94 two-seat interceptors, and the scheduled delivery of single-seat F-86D all-weather interceptors, enabled the Air National Guard to convert eight of its fighter interceptor (day fighter) wings to air defense (all weather) wings. In addition, one of the eight fighter squadrons still flying the decidedly antiquated F-51D was converted to jet fighter aircraft. Further modernization, however, was impeded by the impracticality of providing suitable facilities for jet operations at a number of bases. Thus, for example, the state of Rhode Island could not improve the facilities for its 152nd FIS and was forced to inactivate it[23] on 19 November 1955. On the same date, the RI ANG received federal recognition for a replacement unit, the 143rd Air Resupply Squadron, which took over the personnel and installation of the inactivated fighter squadron and was equipped with Curtiss C-46 twin-engined transports and Grumman SA-16 twin-engined amphibians. A similar fate befell the 148th Fighter-Bomber Squadron, PA ANG, which was replaced at Spaatz Field, Reading, by the C-46-equipped 140th Aeromedical Transport Squadron.

Four other states were more fortunate, as each gained a flying unit when transport-equipped squadrons were organized to take over facilities vacated by fighter squadrons being transferred to new locations within their state. Thus, in Maryland, the 135th Air Resupply Squadron moved into the facilities vacated by the 104th FIS when fighter operations were transferred from Harbor Field, Baltimore, to that city's Friendship Airport. In New Jersey, the 119th FIS moved to McGuire AFB and was replaced at the Newark Airport by the 150th Air Transport Squadron (Medium). In Ohio, the 145th Air Transport Squadron (Light) received federal recognition at the Akron-Canton Airport after the 112th FIS was forced to move to Toledo in order to convert to jets. Finally, the 130th Air Resupply Squadron was organized at the Kanawha Airport in Charleston when the 167th FIS moved to Martinsburg.

Thus, at the end of FY56, the Air National Guard had 23 all-weather fighter squadrons, 50 day fighter squadrons, six bombardment squadrons, eight tactical reconnaissance squadrons, three aeromedical transport squadrons and four air resupply/air transport squadrons. To equip these 84 flying squadrons and their support units, the Guard had a total of 2,138 aircraft, of which more than two-thirds were jet powered.

Fiscal Year 1956 was also marked by the inception of organizational changes which shaped up the squadron/group/wing relationship still prevailing today. In 1946, when National Guard Air Units were organized after World War II, squadrons were assigned to groups in batches of two to four. In turn, two or more groups were assigned to regional wings (see Table 5). The intent of this organization, which cut across state boundaries, was to provide the framework for group-sized units along the then-current USAF practice. In theory, the groups were to provide the administrative and support structure required for the activation of individual squadrons. Shortly before the Korean War, however, the USAF had dropped its previous squadron/group/wing hierarchy to adopt the wing/base concept. Thus, all of the support units which achieved self-contained status were added to the old groups, which then became wings (i.e. after being so reorganized, the 4th Fighter Interceptor Group had become the 4th Fighter Interceptor Wing on 20 January 1950).

To match changes in the active force, the ANG was reorganized so that, at each base, administrative and support units were to be added to each flying squadron to achieve self-supporting group status. The parent organizations,

[23] The 152nd FIS was then transferred on a WOPE (without personnel or equipment) basis to the Arizona ANG. Equipped with F-84Fs and based in Tucson, the 152nd Tactical Fighter Squadron was extended federal recognition on 18 May 1956.

Left: Northrop F-89Bs of the 190th Fighter Interceptor Squadron wore some of the most attractive markings applied to Scorpions. The Idaho unit was equipped with F-89Bs between July 1956 and April 1959.

Left: A 'Class B' Douglas B-26C-30-DT still wearing the markings of the 108th Bombardment Squadron (Light) in January 1956. Three years earlier, this Illinois ANG unit had become a fighter-bomber squadron when it converted from Invaders to F-51Ds.

incorporating one flying squadron and its supporting units, were to be designated groups, while the multi-squadron organizations (ex-groups) were to be redesignated wings.[24]

The long-delayed phase-out of the piston-powered North American F-51D was finally accomplished during the third quarter of FY57[25] when the 167th FIS, WV ANG, handed its last two Mustangs to the Air Force Museum and to Post 20, American Legion, in Charleston. As previously indicated, seven ANG squadrons were still flying Mustangs at the end of FY56 as the lack of suitable facilities had delayed their conversion. The problem was finally solved as follows:

109th FIS, MN ANG: Pending completion of adequate facilities, the unit was re-equipped with piston-engined North American T-28A basic trainers. Its first jets were F-94As and Bs which had previously belonged to the other flying squadron in Minnesota, the 179th FIS, and which were used between June and December 1957 prior to the squadron receiving its F-89Hs.

112th FIS, OH ANG: In order to convert to jets, this squadron was forced to move from the Akron-Canton Airport (where, as mentioned earlier, it was replaced by the 145th ATS) to the Toledo Municipal Airport. Prior to moving to its new base and re-equipping with F-84Fs, it flew T-28As.

148th FBS, PA ANG: Plans were made to reactivate this unit and to move it to York, where it could have operated jets; the unit, however, was not reactivated.

165th FIS, KY ANG: After the runway at Standiford Field, Louisville, was extended, the 165th converted to F-86As during the fall of 1956.

167th FIS, WV ANG: Moving from Charleston to Martinsburg, the 167th flew T-28As until its new facilities were ready for operations with F-86Hs.

169th FBS, IL ANG: Based at Peoria, this squadron flew T-28As until it converted to F-84Fs in April 1958.

182nd FBS, TX ANG: In August 1956, the 182nd F-BS moved from Brook AFB to Kelly AFB, where it converted to F-80Cs and was redesignated 182nd FIS.

Other significant changes during the year included the transfer of the 117th FIS from the PA ANG to the KS ANG – in which it was extended federal recognition on 23 February 1957 – and the conversion of two tactical bomb wings (the 106th and 131st) to fighter interceptor wings. FY57 was also noteworthy in that aircraft straight from the

Above: Unable to convert to jets due to the lack of a suitable facility, the 152nd FIS was inactivated in Rhode Island on 19 November 1955. Its place on the ANG roster of 'Little Rhody' was taken by the 143rd Air Resupply Squadron, which was initially equipped with Curtiss C-46Ds.

production line – Republic RF-84Fs – were phased into the Air National Guard inventory (with the 160th TRS in Alabama) for the first time since the Korean mobilization, and in that the F-86D made its debut in the ANG (with the 159th FIS in Florida).

The ANG goes supersonic

Truly a banner year, FY58 saw the introduction into the ANG inventory of two significant new types: the Northrop F-89H and the North American F-100A. The H version of the Scorpion, the first ANG aircraft to be armed with guided missiles, was first used by the 109th FIS, MN ANG, in December 1957, and the Super Sabre, the first supersonic fighter in the Guard, was received by the 188th FIS, NM ANG, in April 1958. During the year the Douglas B-26 bomber, the last piston-powered combat

[24] This organizational structure has been retained since that time; the only change being made in the mid-1970s when, for cost-saving purposes, groups co-located with wings were inactivated. At each base where groups were disbanded, the local flying squadron and its supporting units were then placed directly under the control of the parent wing.

[25] As this was happening, the Soviet Air Force – the main potential adversary of the ANG – was phasing in supersonic MiG-19s with more than twice the top speed of the Mustang (902 vs 437 mph). It was fortunate that the Cold War did not then warm up significantly!

Cold War and Vietnam

Courtesy of Cloud 9 Photography

Top: Conspicuously marked F-86Es equipped the 144th FIS in Anchorage before Alaska became the 49th state. Statehood deprived the 144th of its fighters and the squadron has operated transport aircraft ever since.

Above: The 159th FIS, FL ANG, converted from F-80Cs to F-86Ds in August 1956. The Sabre Dogs were exchanged for F-86Ls in June 1959, but the days of subsonic interceptors were numbered and F-102As replaced F-86Ls in July 1960.

Top right: Huge tip tanks dominated the silhouette of late model F-89s. 54-0383 is a Northrop F-89H-5-NO of the 103rd FIS, PA ANG.

aircraft in the ANG inventory, was also phased out as a mission aircraft[26] when the 114th (NY) and 168th (IL) Tactical Bombardment Squadrons were inactivated.[27] On 9 September 1957, the ANG began full-time operations of its own jet instrument school. Run by the 111th FIS, TX ANG, at Ellington AFB and equipped with Lockheed T-33As, this school provided the instrument phase of advanced pilot training and thus relieved ANG squadrons throughout the country of the necessity of conducting such training at home stations.

During FY58, the Air Defense Augmentation Program was expanded as two of the 20 participating squadrons increased their alert coverage from 14 to 24 hours a day. However, at the end of that year, two squadrons were temporarily withdrawn from the program. In a related development, 11 Fighter Interceptor Squadrons (Special Delivery) were assigned in June 1958 a new combat-type training mission to become proficient in the LABS (Low Altitude Bombing System) bombing technique required to deliver tactical nuclear weapons.[28]

By 30 June 1958, all of the Air National Guard's 84 combat squadrons were equipped with jet aircraft. Forty-three squadrons possessed F-86D/Ls, F-89C/D/Hs, F-94B/Cs and F-100A/Fs to perform fighter interceptor (all-weather) missions;[29] 26 squadrons were equipped with F-80Cs, F-84Es, F-84Fs and F-86A/E/Hs to perform tactical (day)

missions; and 15 squadrons had RB-57A/Bs and RF-84Fs to provide tactical reconnaissance. In addition, nine support squadrons were equipped with SA-16s, C-119s and C-47s for aeromedical, air resupply and transport missions.

No significant new types of aircraft were taken on strength by the ANG during FY59 but, as the result of aircraft availability following the deactivation of 10 Tactical Air Command wings, several obsolete models of combat aircraft (F-80Cs, F-84Es, F-86As and Es, F-89Cs and F-94Bs) and the last of the T-28As were phased out. At the end of the year, the ANG had 2,421 aircraft in its inventory which were distributed in 43 all-weather interceptor squadrons (29 with F-86D/Ls, 11 with F-89D/Hs, one with F-94Cs and two with F-100As), 25 tactical fighter squadrons (12 with F-84Fs, 12 with F-86Hs and one with F-100As), 14 tactical reconnaissance squadrons (10 with RF-84Fs and four with RB-57A/Bs), and 10 tactical support squadrons (four with SA-16As, five with C-119Js and one with C-47As).

Renamed the Air National Guard Air Defense Alert Program, the ADC mobilization assignment was expanded to include 22 ANG squadrons. Of this number, seven squadrons provided alert coverage on a 24-hour schedule with the remaining 15 units on a 14-hour daylight commitment. In a related event, the team representing Florida's 159th FIS at the 1958 William Tell air-to-air meet achieved a perfect score and won in the F-86D/L category.

---

[26] In a support role, the Invader soldiered on for 14 more years until aircraft 44-34160, a VB-26B assigned to the National Guard Bureau, was finally retired.

[27] The numerical designations of these two units were eventually restored to Guard squadrons. Equipped with McDonnell F-4Cs and based at Kingsley Field, Klamath Falls, the 114th Tactical Fighter Training Squadron received federal recognition in the Oregon ANG on 1 February 1984. Based at Eielson AFB and equipped with Boeing KC-135Es, the 168th Air Refueling Squadron, AK ANG, was federally recognized on 1 October 1986.

[28] Equipped with F-84Fs, these squadrons were the 110th (MO), 113th (IN), 119th (NJ), 128th (GA), 141st (NJ), 149th (VA), 162nd (OH), 163rd (IN), 166th (OH), 169th (IL) and 170th (IL). Their pilots trained to deliver tactical nuclear weapons and their munition personnel trained to store, handle and arm nuclear weapons. However, no such weapons were stored at ANG bases.

[29] Included among these units was the latest addition to the ANG roster, the 151st FIS, TN ANG, which was federally recognized on 15 December 1957 and was initially equipped with F-86Ds.

Left: With Missouri ANG markings replaced by standard USAF markings, this F-84F-30-RE is seen departing St Louis on its way to France in October 1961 after the 110th TFS had been called to active duty as the result of the Berlin Crisis.

Courtesy of Maj David P. Swearingen

Above: Showing off in front of Idaho Guardsmen, the pilot of this Martin RB-57B of Nevada's 192nd TRS has quickly tucked up the gear and stays low over runway 10 Left as he departs Gowen Field.

Above left: Lockheed F-104As entered Guard service in 1960 and equipped Arizona's 197th FIS, South Carolina's 157th FIS, and Tennessee's 151st FIS. All three were deployed to Europe during the Berlin Crisis activation and lost their Starfighters when they were returned to state control on 15 August 1962.

Gaining command concept, Mach 2 fighters, and four-engined transports

During the fall of 1959, after the Eisenhower administration and Congress had agreed to make drastic reductions in the military budget, plans were prepared for the closure of several bases and the inactivation of active Air Force units. To offset these reductions in defense capability, the Department of the Air Force sought to increase its dependency on the Guard and the Reserve. A specially organized Reserve Forces Review Group recommended that ANG units be placed directly under the control of the major air commands which would gain these units upon mobilization instead of continuing to be administered by CONAC. This so-called gaining command concept was adopted in July 1960 when the Guard's fighter interceptor units became ADC-gained, its tactical fighter and reconnaissance squadrons TAC-gained and its transport and aeromedical evacuation squadrons MATS-gained.

Four new aircraft types and two new models offering substantially increased capability were introduced during the year. The new types included the Convair F-102A, a supersonic all-weather interceptor, which first went to the 182nd FIS, TX ANG, in July 1960; the Lockheed F-104A, the first ANG aircraft capable of Mach 2+ performance, which was first assigned to the 157th FIS, SC ANG, in February 1960; the Boeing C-97A, the first four-engined transport to be used by the Guard, which reached the 133rd Air Transport Squadron, NH ANG, in September 1960 and also replaced fighters in the 115th and 195th (CA), 109th (MN), 139th (NY) and 125th (OK) squadrons; and the Fairchild C-123J, a twin-engined transport with auxiliary turbojets on its wingtips, which equipped the 144th ATS, AK ANG, beginning in December 1960. The improved models were the F-89J, a version of the Northrop Scorpion capable of carrying nuclear-tipped missiles, and the F-100C, the first tactical fighter version of the North American Super Sabre. Mission aircraft phased out during the year were the Douglas C-47A[30] and the Lockheed F-94C.

During FY61 the scope of activities for ANG squadrons was once again expanded. Prior to World War II, all Guard flying units had been observation squadrons and in the initial postwar period they had served either as fighter or bombardment squadrons. The 1950s had seen the introduction of two new missions (tactical reconnaissance and transport), the deletion of the bombardment mission and the division of the fighter mission into interception and fighter-bomber/tactical specializations. During FY61 this broadening of the ANG's activities was accelerated, with 14 squadrons changing missions. Thus, on 30 June 1961, the ANG was composed of 32 fighter interceptor squadrons, 22 tactical fighter squadrons, 12 tactical reconnaissance squadrons, 11 air transport squadrons (heavy), 10 aeromedical transport squadrons, four troop carrier squadrons (formerly air resupply squadrons) and one air transport squadron (medium) based in all 50 states, the District of Columbia, and Puerto Rico.

An innovative change in annual training was adopted by some units in 1962 when they went under the 'Texas Plan' year-round training program. Rather than having entire units go on 'summer camps' as in the past, the Texas Plan allowed individual Guardsmen to schedule their annual training any time during the year. For flying organizations with a continuing mission – such as the fighter interceptor and transport units – and revolving around a cadre of full-time air technician employees, the Texas Plan offered more flexibility in meeting mission requirements while at the same time it gave some choice to individuals in performing their annual training requirement at a more convenient time. However, before this plan could be adopted by more ANG units, Guardsmen were called to active duty for the third time.

[30] The AK ANG's 144th Air Transport Squadron was the only Guard unit to use C-47s as mission aircraft and became the sole operator of C-123Js, as this type was particularly well suited to Alaskan operations.

Courtesy of Cloud 9 Photography

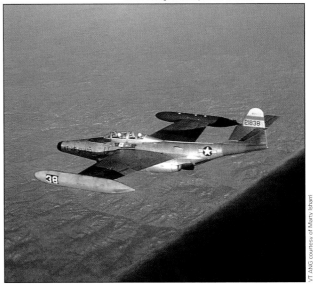

William J. Balogh Sr courtesy of David W. Menard

*Inset, above: South Carolina's 157th FIS took its F-104As to Moron AB, Spain, during the Berlin Crisis. While on active duty, the 'SC AIR GUARD' title adorning 56-0687 and other Starfighters was replaced by standard **USAF** markings.*

Main picture, above: In addition to standard RF-84Fs, the tactical reconnaissance squadrons of the Michigan Air National Guard operated a few RF-84Ks, including this RF-84K-17-RE photographed in June 1960.

Right: Vermont's 134th FIS converted from F-94Bs to F-89Ds in April 1958. It traded its Northrop Scorpions for Convair Delta Daggers during the summer of 1965.

The Berlin Crisis mobilization

During the summer of 1961, the threat of a separate peace treaty being signed by the Soviet Union and the German Democratic Republic, and the anticipated unilateral termination of Western access rights to Berlin, forced President John F. Kennedy to announce an American military build-up and to consider mobilization of selected ANG units. Preparation for the mobilization of ANG flying squadrons was still underway when, on 13 August 1961, the Soviets and East Germans began erecting the infamous Berlin Wall. The American response was prompt and included the mobilization, effective 1 October 1961, of 28 Guard squadrons: 18 tactical fighter squadrons – three equipped with F-100Cs, three with F-86Hs and 12 with F-84Fs; four tactical reconnaissance squadrons with RF-84Fs; and six air transport squadrons with C-97As (see Table 9). One month later, three fighter interceptor squadrons flying F-104As were also activated. To man the units on active duty, 2,760 officers and 18,392 NCOs and airmen, representing 29.8 per cent of the total ANG strength, were mobilized.

The Guard's reaction was swift and effective. Before the end of October, eight of the recalled squadrons with 216 F-84Fs, RF-84Fs, F-86Hs and T-33As assembled at Loring AFB, Maine, and McGuire AFB, New Jersey, for deployment to Europe under Operation Stair Step and assignment to the 17th Air Force, USAFE. With little experience in overwater flying, the pilots of these units crossed the Atlantic without an accident or the loss of a single aircraft. Beginning on 30 October, the three F-86H squadrons (the 101st TFS and 131st TFS from the MA ANG and the 138th TFS from the NY ANG) flew from Loring AFB to Phalsbourg AB, France, via Newfoundland, Greenland, Iceland and Scotland. Two days later, the five squadrons flying F-84Fs and RF-84Fs left McGuire AFB for French bases which they reached via Newfoundland, the Azores and Spain. The 163rd TFS (IN ANG) went to Chambley AB, the 141st TFS (NJ ANG) to Chaumont AB, the 106th TRS (AL ANG) to Dreux AB, the 166th TFS (OH ANG) to Etain AB, and the 110th TFS (MO ANG) to Toul-Rosières AB.

In Europe, the Stair Step tactical squadrons were joined by three interceptor squadrons but, as their range was insufficient for the Atlantic crossing, the F-104As of these FISs were ferried in C-124 Globemasters of the Military Air Transport Service during Operation Brass Ring. On the continent, Starfighters of the 151st (TN ANG) and 197th (AZ ANG) Fighter Interceptor Squadrons went on alert at Ramstein AB, Germany, while those of the 157th FIS (SC ANG) did so at Moron AB, Spain.

The other activated Tactical Fighter Squadrons (120th, CO; 121st, DC; 169th and 170th, IL; 113th, IN; 119th, NJ; 136th, NY; 112th, 162nd and 164th, OH; and 149th, VA) and Tactical Reconnaissance Squadrons (106th, AL; 184th, AR; and 153rd, MS) remained in the United States and, with the exception of the 119th TFS which moved within New Jersey from its base at McGuire AFB to the Atlantic City NAFEC, operated from their home bases. Likewise, the six Air Transport Squadrons (115th and 195th, CA; 109th, MN; 133rd, NH; 139th, NY; and 125th, OK) stayed

Left: 'Defenders of paradise' would have been a fitting nickname for the 199th Fighter Interceptor Squadron. As the sole unit responsible for the defense of Hawaii, the 199th flew F-102As between January 1961 and October 1976.

Above: Black aircraft, black mission. The 129th Air Resupply Squadron, CA ANG, was trained to 'infil/ exfil' special operations teams. Other air resupply squadrons which were given that mission were Maryland's 135th, Rhode Island's 143rd, and West Virginia's 130th.

based at their home stations but, utilizing the long-range capability of their Boeing Stratofreighters, they augmented MATS airlift by flying worldwide missions.

Although eight ANG squadrons were operating in Europe five weeks after being called to active duty, the Berlin mobilization once again brought to light quite a few problems. Some critics afterwards went so far as to claim that the mobilized squadrons had been of limited value. This was a gross and unfair exaggeration.

Nevertheless, there was no denying the need for boosting the preparedness of the Guard if its flying squadrons were indeed to make a significant contribution to the national defense by being combat-ready as soon as mobilized. Manning, training and equipment problems needing attention were for the most part out of the control of the National Guard Bureau and individual units. They had been caused by budget reductions which in the early 1960s forced the Department of Defense to limit squadrons to 83 per cent of their authorized strength, enough for peacetime training but not enough to turn these squadrons into effective combat units. Moreover, nearly one out of every eight mobilized Guardsmen had requested, and obtained, release from active duty due to exceptional family or professional hardship. Finally, the DoD had neither devoted sufficient planning effort nor provided adequate funding to stockpile spare parts, fuel and ammunition, and to prepare overseas bases for utilization by units transferred from CONUS. Consequently, mobilized Guardsmen lost much time in foraging for supplies and in making their bases operational and livable.

Tankers for the Guard

Ten of the 61 squadrons remaining under state control underwent aircraft conversions and/or mission changes during FY62. Most significant among these changes were those affecting the 108th FIS (IL), 126th FIS (WI) and 145th ATS (OH) which, respectively, converted from F-86Ls, F-89Js and MC-119Js to Boeing KC-97F tankers, became TAC-gained and were redesignated air refueling squadrons in July and August 1961. In the process, they pioneered in the Guard the air refueling mission. FY62 also

saw the arrival in the ANG inventory of the first two Lockheed C-121C four-engined transports, the commencement of crew training on the Super Constellation and the assignment of one C-121C each to the 156th (NC) and 183rd (MS) Aeromedical Transport Squadrons, which were scheduled to complete their conversion from MC-119Js early in the following year.

Of special interest was another development which affected the 185th ATS as this OK ANG unit had its Stratofreighter transports supplemented by a single C-97E specially fitted as an airborne command post. Coded 'Talking Bird,' this aircraft saw much use during this and subsequent years.

In the second half of August 1962, the 31 units which had been mobilized during the Berlin Crisis were returned to state control. However, as the USAF needed their aircraft to help equip five new active wings, six F-84F squadrons and the three F-104A units were divested of their aircraft. Upon returning to their home bases, the six tactical fighter squadrons which had left their Thunderstreaks with USAFE were converted to F-100Cs (two squadrons), to F-86Hs (two squadrons) and to RF-84Fs. Although these latter were reconnaissance aircraft, the two units involved – Indiana's 113th and 163rd TFSs – retained their tactical fighter mission. Two of the FISs, the 151st and 157th, converted to F-102As, while the third ex-Starfighter unit received Boeing C-97Gs and was redesignated the 197th Air Transport Squadron. Other aircraft conversions taking place during FY63 involved six aeromedical transport squadrons which exchanged their C-119Js for C-97Gs (two units) or C-121Cs (four units).

The demobilized squadrons had barely settled back into normal operations when, on 22 October 1962, President Kennedy informed the nation of a new Communist challenge: the installation of Soviet offensive missiles in Cuba. Although they were not called to active duty during the Cuban contingency, 14 ANG fighter units were placed in an accelerated training status and prepared for possible 'no notice' deployment. At the same time, ANG heavy transport units augmented MATS worldwide airlift capability. In addition, 26 ANG bases became hosts for SAC B-47E

New Jersey's 150th Aeromedical Transport Squadron converted from Fairchild MC-119Js to Lockheed C-121Cs in October 1962. Thrice redesignated, the squadron traded its Super Connies for de Havilland Caribous during the spring of 1973. It was designated 150th MAS when 54-0153 was photographed at McClellan AFB, CA, on 28 October 1967.

Peter B. Lewis

USAF

USAF

Above: Beginning in August 1965, ANG volunteers began flying aeromedical evacuation and cargo supply operations within the United States and abroad, thus freeing USAF assets for operations in Southeast Asia. This C-121G of Pennsylvania's 140th ATS was flown to Torrejon AB, Spain, in 1965 during one of these support missions.

Above right: Washington's 116th FIS received its first 'Deuce' on 30 June 1965 and disposed of its last on 1 December 1969. This TF-102A was photographed at Geiger Field in Spokane, where the 116th was based between August 1949 and July 1976.

units and ADC F-101B, F-102A and F-106A units which were dispersed during the Cuban contingency.

A new degree of preparedness was reached by the Air National Guard during FY64 when tactical squadrons, as the result of deficiencies brought to light during the Berlin call-up, were provided with fly-away kits and full clothing bags to enable them to be more mobile and capable of being deployed to Europe in nine hours non-stop. To demonstrate the effectiveness of this new program,[31] the Alabama ANG flew 12 RF-84Fs 3,500 miles non-stop to Alaska in August 1963 (Operation Minutemen Alpha) while the DC and MO ANG sent 18 F-100Cs on a non-stop flight to Puerto Rico (Operation Canecutter). In both instances ANG tankers refueled the tactical aircraft.

New aircraft types being readied for service with the ANG included Republic F-105Bs, which were delivered to the 141st TFS, NJ ANG, and jet-augmented KC-97Ls which were pioneered by the 108th AREFS of the Illinois ANG. Other aircraft conversions undertaken during the year were less drastic and resulted in an ANG roster on 30 June 1964 comprised of 26 air transport squadrons, 24 fighter interceptor squadrons, 23 tactical fighter squadrons, 11 tactical reconnaissance squadrons, four air refueling squadrons and four air commando squadrons (previously designated air resupply or troop carrier squadrons). These 92 squadrons, together with headquarters units, operated a total of 1,810 aircraft.

During Fiscal Year 1965 the make-up of the ANG was again revised as one squadron, the 181st, TX ANG, switched from fighter interception to the air-refueling role, and one Tactical Fighter Squadron, the 173rd, NE ANG, became a tactical reconnaissance squadron. Two other FISs exchanged F-86Ls for more capable F-102A Delta Daggers, while three TFSs converted from F-86Hs to F-84Fs and one traded F-86Hs for F-100Cs.

A convincing demonstration of the Guard's readiness was given during Operation Ready Go which saw units from 23 states and the District of Columbia deploy fighters and reconnaissance aircraft to Europe. With the help of three mid-air refuelings from ANG KC-97s, the fighters and reconnaissance aircraft flew 4,600 miles non-stop in nine hours and 20 minutes. Forty-five minutes after landing in Europe, the tactical aircraft were fully armed, refueled, crewed with fresh pilots and ready for combat. Furthermore, the usefulness of the Guard was also proven during the US intervention in the Dominican Republic in

[31] This programme came about when DoD began implementing Air Force Regulation 45-60 which, published in February 1963, called for the Air Reserve Forces (i.e. the Air Force Reserve and the Air National Guard) to provide operationally ready units immediately available to augment the active duty Air Force rather than requiring extensive post-mobilization preparation as had been the case in the past.

Peter B. Lewis

USAF

Jim Retter courtesy of Jim Dunn

May 1965 when ANG transports supplemented MATS airlift, and the Oklahoma ANG deployed its C-97E 'Talking Bird' communications command post to Ramey AFB, Puerto Rico.

The 12-year-old ANG Air Defense Alert Program continued to provide a much needed boost in ADC capability and, during FY65, involved 22 fighter interceptor squadrons providing alert coverage on a 24-hour schedule with two or three aircraft on five- or 15-minute alert. Two of these units, the 198th FIS, PR ANG, and the 199th FIS, HI ANG, provided sole air defense coverage of their islands.

With the USAF increasingly committed in Southeast Asia (the first combat sorties in South Vietnam had been flown by Farm Gate crews in December 1961; the first jet strikes in Laos were flown in June 1964; Flaming Dart strikes against targets in North Vietnam were undertaken in February 1965; and Rolling Thunder operations were initiated the following month) and active-duty units experiencing a serious shortage of aircrews, the ANG stepped in to fill vital gaps in the nation's defense establishment:

1) TAC-gained fighter squadrons took over training responsibilities from the USAF in air-ground support exercises for regular Army units.

2) MATS-gained (which became MAC-gained when on 1 January 1966 the Military Air Transport Service was reorganized and renamed Military Airlift Command) transport squadrons expanded the pace of their global commitments, including cargo flights to the war zone in Southeast Asia, and provided a CONUS-based aeromedical evacuation system with regularly scheduled routes.

3) Nine tactical fighter squadrons and four tactical reconnaissance squadrons, all TAC-gained, became fully-manned, equipped and geared for instant mobilization. Known as the Beef Broth (later Combat Beef) force, these units soon were operationally ready and prepared, if need be, for rapid deployment overseas.

4) Short-term exercises saw several ANG units deployed from CONUS to Europe, Panama and Alaska.

5) ANG pilots volunteered for short tours of duty overseas to replace active-duty pilots transferred to units in Southeast Asia, and served with F-102 squadrons in Alaska, Germany, the Netherlands, and the far East.

As the training pace was increased, the Air National Guard became a more mature force and no squadrons underwent a mission change during FY66. However, four of its 22 FISs converted from F-89Js to F-102As and three of its 12 TRSs substituted McDonnell Voodoos for their Martin RB-57s. These Voodoos, the first assigned to the ANG, were unique in that they were F-101A and C tactical fighters phased out by the 81st TFW, USAFE, and modified as unarmed reconnaissance aircraft by Lockheed Aircraft Service for assignment to the 154th (AR), 165th (KY) and 192nd (NV) Tactical Reconnaissance Squadrons.

Top left: The Air National Guard added air refueling to its scope of missions during FY62. This KC-97L belonged to the 197th AREFS, an AZ ANG unit which flew C-97 transports for 10 years before converting to jet-augmented tankers in August 1972.

Top right: Drag chute deployed, a F-100C of the ANG-manned 355th TFS, 37th TFW, lands at Phu Cat AB after flying an air support sortie over South Vietnam.

Above: Seldom photographed in the air, the RF-101H was a reconnaissance version of the McDonnell Voodoo obtained by replacing the gun nose of the F-101C with a camera pack. These RF-101Hs of the 192nd TRS were seen over Utah in January 1968.

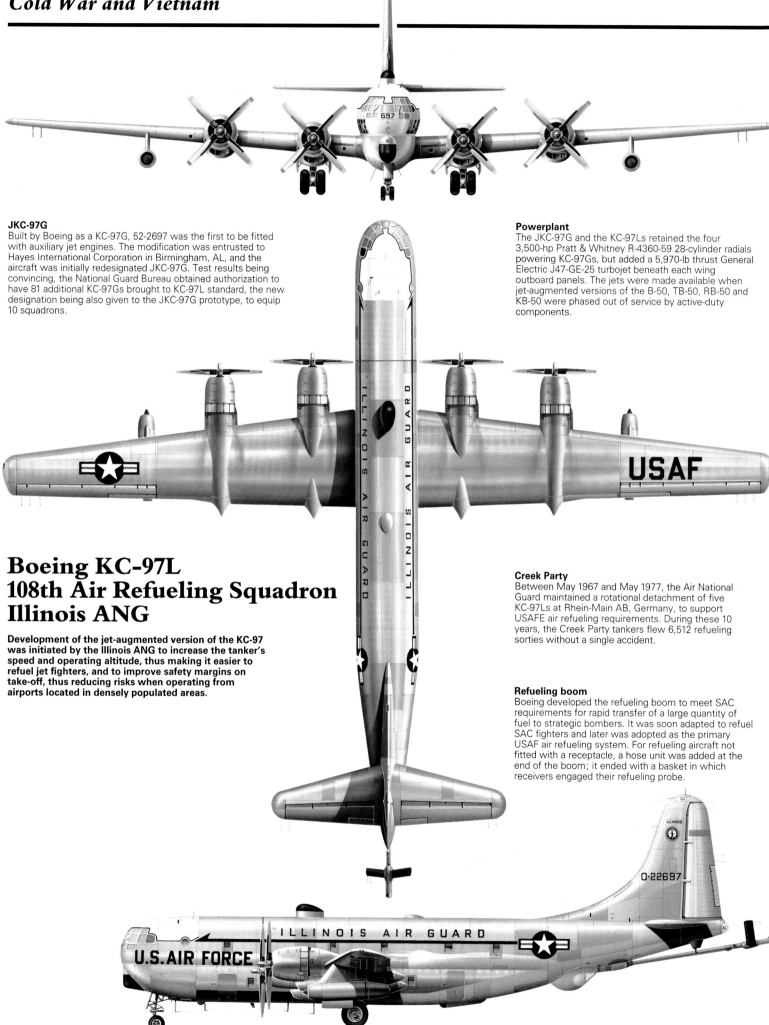

JKC-97G
Built by Boeing as a KC-97G, 52-2697 was the first to be fitted with auxiliary jet engines. The modification was entrusted to Hayes International Corporation in Birmingham, AL, and the aircraft was initially redesignated JKC-97G. Test results being convincing, the National Guard Bureau obtained authorization to have 81 additional KC-97Gs brought to KC-97L standard, the new designation being also given to the JKC-97G prototype, to equip 10 squadrons.

Powerplant
The JKC-97G and the KC-97Ls retained the four 3,500-hp Pratt & Whitney R-4360-59 28-cylinder radials powering KC-97Gs, but added a 5,970-lb thrust General Electric J47-GE-25 turbojet beneath each wing outboard panels. The jets were made available when jet-augmented versions of the B-50, TB-50, RB-50 and KB-50 were phased out of service by active-duty components.

Boeing KC-97L
108th Air Refueling Squadron
Illinois ANG

Development of the jet-augmented version of the KC-97 was initiated by the Illinois ANG to increase the tanker's speed and operating altitude, thus making it easier to refuel jet fighters, and to improve safety margins on take-off, thus reducing risks when operating from airports located in densely populated areas.

Creek Party
Between May 1967 and May 1977, the Air National Guard maintained a rotational detachment of five KC-97Ls at Rhein-Main AB, Germany, to support USAFE air refueling requirements. During these 10 years, the Creek Party tankers flew 6,512 refueling sorties without a single accident.

Refueling boom
Boeing developed the refueling boom to meet SAC requirements for rapid transfer of a large quantity of fuel to strategic bombers. It was soon adapted to refuel SAC fighters and later was adopted as the primary USAF air refueling system. For refueling aircraft not fitted with a receptacle, a hose unit was added at the end of the boom; it ended with a basket in which receivers engaged their refueling probe.

The 144th Tactical Airlift Squadron, AK ANG, was the only Guard squadron to fly jet-augmented, ski-equipped Fairchild C-123Js. It did so for 16 years beginning in June 1960.

A Boeing C-97G of the 185th Military Airlift Squadron at the Will Rogers Field, Oklahoma City MAP, on 5 July 1968. In addition to its C-97 transports, Oklahoma's 185th also operated the sole C-97E 'Talking Bird' airborne communications and command post.

During FY67, the ANG logged a total of 540,060 flying hours to establish a Guard record which has yet to be broken. This achievement was the direct result of the intensified training of Beef Broth units, of the all-out participation of ANG transport units in support of Southeast Asia airlift requirements and of intensified aeromedical evacuation missions over a network at home and abroad (Labrador, Newfoundland, Bermuda, Puerto Rico, the Canal Zone and Cuba).

Again no units changed mission and the ANG roster of flying units remained at a total of 92 squadrons (26 ATSs, 23 TFSs, 22 FISs, 12 TRSs, five AREFSs and four ACSs). The only new type in the inventory was the Douglas C-124C, which became available with the entry into MAC service of the Lockheed C-141A, and replaced C-121s in the 156th (NC) and 183rd (MS) ATSs and C-97s in the 128th ATS (GA). Three Fighter Interceptor Squadrons – the 178th in North Dakota, the 179th in Minnesota and the 186th in Montana – converted from Northrop F-89Js to Convair F-102As.

A significant development took place on 1 May 1967 when the 136th Air Refueling Wing inaugurated a new mission for the ANG. Named Creek Party, this operation involved support of an overseas command – USAFE – on a regular basis and provided for five KC-97Ls to be based at Rhein-Main AB, Germany, on a rotational basis. These aircraft provided refueling training and emergency capability to USAFE tactical aircraft.

The *Pueblo* Crisis mobilization

Already heavily committed to the Southeast Asia War (on 31 December 1967, US Armed Forces in Vietnam totalled 487,300 men, to which were added 47,000 men in Thailand and 25,000 men serving offshore on USN ships), the United States found itself facing a new challenge when, on 24 January 1968, the North Koreans seized the USS *Pueblo* (AGER-3). Reacting swiftly, President Lyndon B. Johnson issued the next day a Presidential Executive Order

mobilizing eight tactical fighter squadrons and three tactical reconnaissance squadrons, with necessary support elements. Thirty-six hours later, 1,076 officers (including 447 pilots) and 8,102 airmen were on federal active duty. A second Presidential Executive Order, issued on 11 April 1968, added two tactical fighter squadrons, one aeromedical airlift squadron and 1,333 Air Guardsmen to the units and personnel on federal active duty as of 13 May. Thus, at the end of FY68, the Air National Guard only retained 78 flying squadrons under state control (see Tables 8 and 10).

Four of the Tactical Fighter Squadrons on active duty used 11 or 12 air-to-air refuelings to fly their F-100Cs to South Vietnam. First to reach the war zone was the 120th TFS, CO ANG, which joined the 35th TFW at Phan Rang AB and entered combat on 5 May 1968. It was followed by the 174th TFS, IA ANG, with the 37th TFW at Phu Cat AB, and by the 136th TFS, NY ANG, and 188th TFS, NM ANG, with the 31st TFW at Tuy Hoa AB. In addition, volunteer personnel from the 119th (NJ) and 121st (DC) – whose units formed an F-100 training unit at Myrtle AFB, SC, during the *Pueblo* Crisis Mobilization – provided 85 per cent of the manning for the 355th TFS, 37th TFW, at Phu Cat AB. The two remaining F-100C squadrons on active duty – the 127th TFS, KS ANG, and the 166th TFS, OH ANG – deployed to Kunsan AB, Korea, in the latter part of June 1968.

During FY68 the other six mobilized units remained in the United States. The three squadrons (154th, AR; 165th, KY; and 192nd, NV) of the 123rd TRW were relocated to Richards-Gebaur AFB, MO, for intensive training prior to overseas deployment. The 104th TFS (MD ANG) and 138th TFS (NY ANG) moved to Cannon AFB, NM, where their F-86Hs were flown in support of the Air Force training program for forward air controllers and liaison officers. Finally, Pennsylvania's 147th Aeromedical Airlift Squadron operated out of its home station, the Greater Pittsburgh Airport.

Right: Nicknamed 'Old Shaky', the Douglas Globemaster proved reliable and equipped 10 ANG squadrons. The last C-124Cs were phased out by the 158th Military Airlift Squadron, GA ANG, in September 1974.

Right: When in 1969 forward air control was added to the repertory of the Air National Guard, Cessna O-2s were not immediately available. Accordingly, Pennsylvania's 103rd TASS, in the markings of which 58-2174 is shown, New York's 137th and Illinois' 169th were temporarily equipped with a mix of Cessna U-3As and U-3Bs.

Opposite page, top: The Lockheed EC-121S was unique to the 193rd Tactical Electronic Warfare Squadron, PA ANG. Four of the unit's C-121Cs were modified by Lockheed as airborne radio/television stations for use in Coronet Solo psychological warfare operations. Operation Commando Buzz saw two of these aircraft operating from Korat RTAFB, Thailand, between July and December 1970.

The C-124 conversion program continued at an accelerated pace with six units switching from C-97s to Globemasters. Two military airlift squadrons of the Pennsylvania ANG retained their Lockheed C-121s but were assigned new missions. The 147th MAS in Pittsburgh became an aeromedical airlift squadron, while the 140th MAS at the Olmsted State Airport in Harrisburg was inactivated and replaced by the 193rd Tactical Electronic Warfare Squadron. Manned by the personnel of the former 140th MAS, the 193rd TEWS soon operated Super Constellations modified to the EC-121S configuration. Meanwhile, in Puerto Rico, the 198th TFS converted from F-86Hs to F-104Cs and Ds.

Excluding the aircraft assigned to its mobilized units, the ANG ended FY68 with a force of 1,220 aircraft including 414 interceptors (40 F-89Js and 374 F-/TF-102As), 319 tactical fighters (250 F-84Fs, 22 F-100C/Fs, 19 F-104C/Ds and 28 F-105Bs), 166 reconnaissance aircraft (136 RF-84Fs and 30 RB-57A/C/Es), 55 KC-97L tankers, 200 four-engined transports (102 C-97s, 26 C-121s and 72 C-124s), and 66 sundry tactical aircraft (18 HU-16Bs, 24 U-10Ds, 16 C-119Cs and 8 EC/C-121s).

At the start of FY69, six mobilized units were in Asia and eight remained in the United States. However, soon thereafter the 154th TRS deployed to Itazuke AB, Japan, on 24 July 1968. It was rotated back to CONUS on 18 November 1968, and its place at Itazuke was taken on that date by the 192nd TRS. In turn, on 3 February 1969, this NV ANG squadron was replaced in Japan by the 165th TRS. The KY ANG unit returned to Richards-Gebaur AFB[32] on 24 April 1969 to end the rotation of squadrons of the 123rd Tactical Reconnaissance Wing.

Beginning on 12 December 1968 with the 147th Aeromedical Airlift Squadron, the mobilized units were progressively returned to state control. The last three units (the 121st, 166th and 174th TFSs) ended their period of federal active service on 18 June 1969. Once again, the Guardsmen's service to the nation had been truly outstanding; however, due to the antiwar feelings dampening the country's morale, their deeds were too often not fully appreciated. During their 11-month combat tour in Vietnam, the five Guard-manned F-100 squadrons lost 10 aircraft to enemy gunfire, one to an unknown cause, one due to an engine failure, and two in a probable mid-air collision. Four of their pilots were killed and two were missing.

Notwithstanding that the Army National Guard and Air National Guard units called to active duty and sent to Vietnam served with distinction, the Guard came in for some bitter and undeserved criticism due to the Johnson administration's reliance on draftees to fight the war and its reluctance to call up Reservists and Guardsmen (only 22,745 Guardsmen were called to active duty during the Southeast Asia War as opposed to the call-up of 183,600 Guardsmen during the Korean War and 65,438 Guardsmen during the Berlin Crisis). There is no denying that during the Southeast Asia War a fair number of draft-age males joined the Guard to avoid being drafted and sent to Vietnam. However, the very large majority of Guardsmen were ready to serve their country and expected the President to call them to active duty.

On 30 June 1969, following the return of all mobilized units, the assignment of a new mission (tactical air support with Illinois' 169th TFS, New York's 137th MAS and Pennsylvania's 103rd MAS re-equipping with Cessna U-3As and becoming the 169th, 137th and 103rd TASSs[33]), changes in mission and aircraft affecting five squadrons, and aircraft conversions for two squadrons, the Air National Guard was composed of 27 fighter interceptor squadrons (all now equipped with F/TF-102As), 22 Tactical Fighter Squadrons, 12 tactical reconnaissance squadrons, 21 military airlift squadrons and aeromedical airlift squadrons, six air refueling squadrons, four special operations squadrons, three tactical air support squadrons, one tactical airlift squadron and one tactical electronic warfare squadron.

---

[32] While based at Richards-Gebaur AFB, Missouri, the Guard's reconnaissance squadrons made deployments to Elmendorf AFB, Alaska, in support of the Alaskan Air Command, and to Howard AFB, Panama, in support of the Southern Command.

[33] These three squadrons became in May 1969 the first ANG unit to be assigned the tactical air support (forward air control) mission.

PA ANG

North American F-100C-25-NA 120th Tactical Fighter Squadron 35th Tactical Fighter Wing

Called to active duty on 26 January 1968 as a result of the *Pueblo* Crisis, the 120th TFS, CO ANG, was sent to Vietnam to join the 35th TFW, on active-duty USAF unit based at Phan Rang AB. The Coloradans flew the first of 5,905 combat sorties on 8 May 1968.

Markings
When deploying to Vietnam, the Coloradans of the 120th TFS proudly continued to display on the nose gear door of their F-100Cs the mountain lion head insignia of their squadron. The 'VS' tailcode was applied in country.

'Huns' for the Guard
Twenty-six ANG squadrons flew Super Sabres, with F-100As being first assigned to the 188th FIS NM ANG, in April 1958. Ten years later, four ANG squadrons which had been called to active duty took their F-100Cs to Vietnam for in-country combat operations. F-100Ds and F-100Fs soldiered on with the Guard until November 1970 when Indiana's 113th TFS sent its last Huns to MASDC.

ANG F-100C Losses in South Vietnam

Date	Serial	Squadron	Cause	Pilot's Fate
14 Jul 68	54-2004	174th TFS	AAA	KIA
25 Jul 68	54-1912	136th TFS	Gunfire	KIA
2 Aug 68	54-1775	136th TFS	Gunfire	Recovered
8 Aug 68	53-1713	136th TFS	Eng. failure	Recovered
27 Sep 68	53-1765	174th TFS	Gunfire	Recovered
18 Dec 68	54-1931	136th TFS	Gunfire	Recovered

Date	Serial	Squadron	Cause	Pilot's Fate
29 Dec 68	54-1973	120th TFS	Gunfire	Recovered
4 Jan 69	54-2051	188th TFS	Midair collision?	MIA
4 Jan 69	54-2030	188th TFS	Midair collision?	MIA
31 Jan 69	54-2041	188th TFS	Gunfire	Recovered
14 Mar 69	53-1740	174th TFS	Gunfire	Recovered
27 Mar 69	54-1897	120th TFS	Unknown	KIA
4 May 69	53-1741	188th TFS	Gunfire	KIA

Total Force
Component

Above: The 128th TFS, 116th TFW, converted from F-100Ds to F-105Gs during the summer of 1979. The Georgia ANG unit kept its 'Wild Weasels' for just over three years before converting to F-4Ds. 62-4438 was photographed taking off from Dobbins AFB on 20 October 1982, just as the 128th TFS was transitioning to Phantoms.

Opposite page, bottom: Flying off the coast of central California on 23 February 1985, three F-4Ds of the 194th FIS formate with one of the unit's T-33As. Just received from an active-duty unit, 66-0279 has not yet been repainted in the air defense gray scheme and has not yet received its California fin band.

CHAPTER 6

During the 1960s the effectiveness of the Air National Guard as a first-line combat reserve force had improved steadily, with units activated in 1961 for the Berlin Crisis being operational much faster than units activated in 1950 during the Korean War, and those activated in 1968 during the *Pueblo* Crisis, particularly the tactical fighter squadrons sent to Vietnam, doing even better.

Nevertheless, at the beginning of the 1970s the ANG remained a mere adjunct to the Air Force and its units were often equipped with aircraft long withdrawn from active units. For example, at the beginning of 1970, subsonic North American F-86Hs still equipped three Guard squadrons, whereas this type had been withdrawn from TAC service in 1958. Likewise, at the beginning of 1970, subsonic Republic F-84Fs and RF-84Fs, which had been withdrawn from TAC service in 1965 and 1958, respectively, continued to equip 10 TFSs and seven TRSs of the Air National Guard. Fortunately, the obsolescence of the ANG inventory was soon remedied as the result of recommendations made by the RAND Corporation and a change in US defense policy planned and implemented by the Nixon administration.

Requested in 1966 by the Air Force Chief of Staff, General John P. McConnell, and completed in July 1967, the Air Reserve Forces Study prepared by the RAND Corporation – a non-profit research organization head-quartered in Santa Monica, California – pointed out that the ANG then possessed one-fourth of the tactical fighters available to the Air Force and that ANG units were passing operational readiness inspections just as effectively as active-duty units. The study also stressed that the availability of well-trained ANG units was a particularly cost effective means to maintain forces in a period of reduced budgets. As it turned out, the RAND study provided a partial basis for the reorganization of US military forces undertaken by a new Republican administration.

During the 1968 presidential campaign, the Republican candidate, Richard M. Nixon, had pledged to bring American ground troops home from Vietnam, to seek an honorable peace in Southeast Asia and to reduce drastically the military budget. The first of these pledges resulted in the implementation of the Vietnamization Program, the second in the eventual signing of the Paris Agreement and the third in the promulgation in 1970 by Secretary of Defense Melvin R. Laird of the Total Force Policy.

Implementing the Total Force Policy

In accordance with the Total Force Policy, and as later provided in detail in Air Force Regulation 45-1 – Purpose, Policy and Responsibility for Air Reserve Force – the role of the Air National Guard as a combat-ready force was expanded, its equipment modernized and its authorized strength kept at a level such that its units were at all times

Peter B. Lewis

Carl E. Porter

Peter B. Lewis

Above: Landing at McClellan AFB, CA, on 14 July 1972, a Douglas C-124C from Oklahoma's 125th MAS flies over a TF-101B and an RF-101B from the 192nd TRS, NV ANG.

Left: Photographed at the Van Nuys Airport in April 1971, this C-130A of the 'Hollywood Guard' (California's 146th TAW) was transferred to South Vietnam during Operation Enhance Plus.

immediately available for mobilization to support active Air Force requirements.

The big gainers of the initial implementation of this policy were the TAC-gained units, which during FY70 increased in number and received more modern equipment. Additions to this segment of the Air National Guard came through the conversion of four FISs to the tactical fighter role, the switch of two squadrons from the transport to the air tanker role, and of one squadron from military airlift to tactical airlift. New aircraft types entering service with TAC-gained squadrons were the Lockheed C-130A (with California's 115th TAS), the Cessna A-37B (with Maryland's 104th TFS) and the Cessna O-2A (with the 103rd TASS, PA ANG; the 137th TASS, NY ANG; and the 169th TASS, IL ANG).

Now numbering only 18 squadrons, the ADC-gained units gained in capability as three of them (Maine's 132nd, North Dakota's 178th and Washington's 116th) converted from the F-102A to the more potent F-101B. In addition, some of the remaining F-102A squadrons re-equipped with upgraded models of the Delta Dagger which had been fitted with infra-red detecting equipment and other improved systems. Several of these aircraft were ferried by ANG crews from Europe to CONUS and others were shipped from Southeast Asia to Hawaii when F-102As became surplus to USAFE and PACAF requirements. Furthermore, the 111th FIS, TX ANG, assumed the added

René J. Francillon

Both types of Convair's delta-wing interceptors – the F-102A and the F-106A, shown here in the markings of Florida's 159th FIS and Montana's 186th FIS – saw much service with the ANG.

Above: The 170th TFS, IL ANG, became in January 1972 the first ANG fighter unit to receive Phantoms. With their fin cap and band on the nosewheel door painted in the color of their respective flights, these three F-4Cs were photographed at Capital Airport in Springfield during the summer of 1979.

Above right: Redesignated 127th TFTS on 25 March 1971, the Kansas ANG unit provided crew training for F-105 pilots. In addition to its Thunderchiefs, the 127th TFTS was assigned T-39Bs fitted with the NASARR/ Doppler radar and navigation system of the F-105D.

responsibility of training new pilots in the aerospace defense role, thus becoming the first Guard squadron to function as a replacement training unit (RTU).

Meanwhile, MAC-gained squadrons continued to fly in support of the Southeast Asia War and to operate aeromedical evacuation flights within CONUS. However, their combined capacity had been reduced by approximately 20 per cent from the peak reached in 1968-69 due to the transfer of several units to TAC roles (air refueling, air support and tactical airlift).

Just as was the case with MAC-gained squadrons supporting the war efforts, Pennsylvania's TAC-gained 193rd Tactical Electronic Warfare Squadron did not have to be inducted into federal active service to make a significant contribution to the war's effort, as its personnel volunteered for Operation Commando Buzz. On 26 July 1970 a 75-man detachment, two Lockheed EC-121S Coronet Solo electronic warfare aircraft and two support C-121Cs departed Pennsylvania for Korat RTAFB. For the next five months, the EC-121Ss provided radio relay for Phnom Penh broadcasts, and their crews and maintenance personnel served in Thailand on 30- to 60-day tours of duty with replacement personnel being flown to and from CONUS in the unit's C-121Cs. Commando Buzz, for which 252 officers and airmen had volunteered, ended on 24 December 1970.

Phantoms and Delta Darts for the Guard

In its 50th anniversary year[34] the Air Guard achieved a new peak in strength as its aircraft inventory, which had reached a post-World War II low of 1,659 aircraft at the end of FY63,[35] climbed back to 1,938 on 30 June 1971. In the process an unprecedented number of units – 34 squadrons or almost 37 per cent of the ANG's roster – underwent aircraft conversion and/or change in mission and gaining command. Two units of the Alabama ANG, the 106th and 160th Tactical Reconnaissance Squadrons, became the first Guard units to fly Phantom IIs when they converted from

RF-84Fs to RF-4Cs during the first half of 1971. Furthermore, as additional A-37s, C-130s, F-100s, F-101s, F-105s,[36] O-2s and RF-101s replaced older aircraft, the ANG boosted markedly its effectiveness as an adjunct to the USAF.[37]

In spite of the drain imposed by the Southeast Asia War on its parent service, the USAF, the Air National Guard was able during FY72 to pursue aggressively its modernization program and to retire its subsonic and decidedly obsolete Republic F-84Fs and RF-84Fs. New aircraft types added to the ANG inventory included the Convair F-106A, first assigned to Montana's 186th FIS, and the McDonnell F-4C, which first replaced the F-84F in the 170th TFS, IL ANG. Four more tactical airlift squadrons, including the 183rd TAS, MS ANG, which received the longer-ranged C-130E version instead of C-130A or B as previously assigned to other ANG units, converted to Lockheed Hercules. Also notable was the conversion of the 117th TRS, KS ANG, which became a bombardment tactical squadron after converting from RB-57A/Bs to

---

[34] As described in Chapter 2, the 109th Squadron, Minnesota National Guard, had become on 17 January 1921 the first flying squadron in the Guard to be extended federal recognition.

[35] A lower aircraft inventory in FY62 and FY68 reflected the fact that several ANG squadrons and their aircraft were then on federal active duty.

[36] On 25 March 1971, after converting from F-100Cs to F-105Ds, the 127th TFS/184th TFG, KS ANG, became the Guard's F-105 RTU and was redesignated 127th TFTS/184th TFTG.

[37] This increase in operational capability is perhaps best illustrated by the fact that in the 1970 William Tell Meet at Tyndall AFB, Florida, ANG crews captured first place in the F-101 (178th FIS, ND ANG) and F-102 (179th FIS, MN ANG) categories, posted the highest score among all nine teams in the weapons loading event, and one of the ANG crews won top individual scoring honors. Four years later, ANG units won first place in all three categories (F-101 – Maine's 132nd FIS; F-102 – Idaho's 190th FIS; and F-106 – Montana's 186th FIS) and at the 1980 William Tell meet California's 144th FIW became the first overall meet winner.

Left: A Sikorsky CH-3E of the 129th AR&RS at the Hayward Air Terminal on 14 October 1977.

Below: Project Pacer Angler was initiated during FY75 and saw KC-135As assigned for the first time to Guard units. The first squadron to convert to jet tankers was the 145th AREFS, OH ANG.

Left: During the spring of 1972, the Massachusetts squadron based at Otis AFB converted from Super Sabres to Delta Darts and was redesignated from 101st TFS to 101st FIS. While flying F-106As, the 101st took part regularly in William Tell competitions. 57-2503 was photographed at Tyndall AFB, FL, during the 1978 meet.

Some of the many missions given to the Guard are illustrated, from top to bottom, far left, by a C-119G-84-KM of California's 129th SOS (with the radio call of a T-33A, 53-6074, instead of the correct 53-8074), a B-57G of Kansas' 117th TBS, and an F-101C-40-MC of Kentucky's 165th TRS (soon to be brought to the RF-101H configuration by Lockheed Aircraft Service).

the B-57G night-interdiction version of the twin-jet Martin aircraft. Also significant was the fact that during FY72 women were first authorized to enlist in the Air National Guard.

Main gainer during FY73 was the ADC-gained component, which was increased by three squadrons following the mission change undertaken by Michigan's 171st TRS, New Jersey's 119th TFS and New York's 102nd AREFS (the 119th FIS and the 171st FIS received F-106A/Bs, whereas the 102nd FIS got F/TF-102As).

Finally, with the winding down of the Southeast Asia War, in support of which its MAC-gained units had flown a substantial number of missions without ever being mobilized, the Air National Guard lost much of its airlift capability. During FY73, three of its military airlift squadrons were reorganized into air refueling squadrons and converted to KC-97Ls, two MASs switched to the tactical fighter role and re-equipped with F-100Ds, and New Jersey's 150th Aeromedical Airlift Squadron exchanged its C-121Cs for de Havilland C-7As to become a tactical airlift squadron. In addition, during the fall of 1972, several ANG tactical airlift squadrons were stripped of many of their C-130A/Bs, which were delivered to the Air Force of the Republic of Vietnam (VNAF) as part of Operation Enhance Plus prior to the signing of the Paris Agreement on 27 January 1973.

The first oil crisis

As the first full year following United States disengagement from the war in Southeast Asia, FY74 saw reductions in the active forces being announced. Full implementation of the Total Force concept placed increased reliance on reserve forces – notably the Air and Army National Guard – which received further support to meet the nation's defense needs in spite of cuts in active forces. At the same time, fuel shortages brought about by the Arab embargo on oil shipments to the United States following American military assistance to Israel during the

October 1973 Yom Kippur War resulted in curtailments in ANG operations (for example, a total of 432,206 flying hours had been programmed for the year but actual flight hours were limited to 405,428, for a variance of 6.2 per cent).

The reduced level of activities was also evidenced by the fact that only six units underwent aircraft conversions during FY74. Two of these conversions were minor, as they involved only exchange of early aircraft models for later models of the same type (C-130A to C-130B for California's 115th TAS and F-100C to F-100D for Iowa's 174th TFS), but two others resulted in the introduction in ANG service of a new type as New Mexico's 188th and Colorado's 120th traded their F-100D/Fs for LTV A-7Ds. The remaining conversions involved not only a change in aircraft (to Martin EB-57B/Es) but also a change in mission, as the 117th Bombardment Tactical Squadron, KS ANG, and the 134th Fighter Interceptor Squadron, VT ANG, became defense systems evaluation squadrons. In their new role, the crews of these two squadrons were ADC-gained and provided electronic countermeasure training to Army and Air Defense forces of the United States and Canada.

Budgetary limitations, resulting in part from fuel price increases, led to the streamlining of the Air National

Total Force Component

During the 1970s, the McDonnell Voodoo and the Convair Delta Dart respectively equipped seven and six ANG squadrons. The F-101B is shown in the markings of Minnesota's 179th FIS and the F-106A in those of Florida's 159th FIS.

Above: Gear and flaps down, this F-101B-100-MC is on final approach to Duluth International Airport. The Minnesotans of the 179th FIS flew 'One-Oh-Wonders' for nearly five years beginning in April 1971.

Above right: Refueling is a home state affair for this KC-135A of the 108th AREFS and these F-4Cs of the 170th TFS.

Guard organization to avoid unnecessary duplications. In the process, the ANG began to inactivate groups at bases where wings were also located. Thus, flying squadrons located at the same base as their wing headquarters were made to report directly to the wing, while the other flying squadrons in the wing continued to receive support (maintenance, administration, etc) through groups.

The 19 groups inactivated during FY75 included nine tactical fighter groups (108th, NJ; 113th, DC; 116th, GA; 121st, OH; 122nd, IN; 127th, MI; 131st, MO; 132nd, IA; and 140th, CO), five tactical airlift groups (118th, TN; 133rd, MN; 137th, OK; and 146th and 195th, CA), three air refueling groups (126th, IL; 136th, TX; and 171st, PA), and two tactical reconnaissance groups (117th, AL; and 123rd, KY). In the case of the 195th TAG, the inactivation involved not only the group but also its flying squadron, the 195th TAS, as its C-130Bs and personnel were absorbed into the 115th TAS/146th TAW, with which it had shared facilities at the Van Nuys Airport.

Another significant change which occurred as a result of organizational changes within the Air Force[38] was the transfer from TAC-gained to MAC-gained status of the Air National Guard's tactical airlift fleet equipped with C-7s, C-123s and C-130s.

Aircraft conversions taking place during FY75 affected 12 squadrons. Half of these conversions did not result in mission changes and involved the following units: two interceptor squadrons – California's 194th and Florida's 159th, which traded F-102As for F-106As; three airlift squadrons – Georgia's 158th, Oklahoma's 185th and Tennessee's 155th, which exchanged C-124s for Hercules; and Ohio's 166th TFS which received A-7Ds to replace its F-100Ds. Two squadrons (the 146th, PA ANG, and 157th,

SC ANG) switched from an air-defense role to a tactical fighter role upon converting from F-102As to A-7Ds, while two other FISs (California's 196th and Wisconsin's 176th) underwent a more drastic change and became tactical air support squadrons upon exchanging their F-102A jet fighters for piston-powered O-2A light aircraft.

Life-saving mission for the Guard

The other FY75 conversions and mission changes affected the 102nd FIS of the NY ANG and the 129th SOS of the CA ANG, which respectively exchanged 18 F-102As and eight C-119Ls for a mix of four HC-130H/Ps and six Sikorsky CH/HH-3Es. These two conversions, which resulted in the two units being redesignated aerospace rescue and recovery squadrons, marked 'firsts' for the Air National Guard in terms of both the rescue mission and the assignment of rotary-wing aircraft.

The nation's bicentennial year was another banner year for the Air National Guard. Four F-100 TFWs (10 squadrons) and the 117th TRW deployed to Europe for two weeks of theater indoctrination and training as part of ongoing Reforger (Return of Forces to Germany) exercises. Seven squadrons (three with F-100Ds, three with A-7Ds and the 193rd TEWS) participated in multi-threat simulated combat training at Nellis AFB, Nevada, during the first Red Flag exercises.[39] In addition, the ADC-gained fighter interceptor squadrons and defense systems evaluation squadrons continued their active participation in the peacetime NORAD alert program and the KC-97L-equipped Air Refueling Squadrons completed their ninth successful year providing refueling support for fighter/reconnaissance forces in Europe (Operation Creek Party).

---

[38] The consolidation of Tactical Air Command airlift resources with those of the Military Airlift Command had been ordered on 1 December 1974.

[39] Since then, ANG squadrons have participated in almost all Red Flag exercises.

Pacer Angler: ANG units join SAC

Project Pacer Angler, which had begun in the third quarter of FY75 with the installation of Aerospace Ground Equipment at the initial conversion site – the OH ANG base at the Akron-Canton Municipal Airport – and the receipt on 18 April 1975 by the 145th AREFS/160th AREFG of its first Boeing KC-135A, moved into full-swing during the bicentennial year and involved the conversion of ANG refueling squadrons to jet tankers. During this conversion, one of these units, Ohio's 145th AREFS, merely replaced its KC-97Ls with the new aircraft, while the other four squadrons also underwent a mission change: from tactical airlift for New Hampshire's 133rd; from tactical reconnaissance for Arkansas' 154th; and from fighter interception for Maine's 132nd and Washington's 116th. In addition to its mission change, the latter, together with its parent 141st AREFW, moved from Geiger Field to Fairchild AFB. With the start of the conversion to jet tankers, all ANG air refueling units, whether they were equipped with KC-135As or with KC-97Ls, switched from TAC- to SAC-gained status to preclude dual command management of tanker forces.

During FY76 two groups, Maine's 101st FIG and Washington's 141st FIG, were inactivated, as their flying squadrons, the 132nd and 116th, began reporting directly to the 101st AREFW (ex-101st FIW) and the 141st AREFW (ex-141st FIW) upon converting from F-101Bs to KC-135As. During the Transitional Quarter[40] it was the turn of the 102nd FIG (MA ANG) and 144th FIG (CA ANG) to be inactivated.

Beside these conversions to KC-135As, the Air National Guard undertook during FY76 and the Transitional Quarter the conversion of 12 other squadrons, with six of these also switching missions as detailed below:

State	Squadron	Mission Aircraft From	To
AK ANG	144th TAS	C-123J	C-130E
AZ ANG	152nd TFTS[41]	F-100D	F-100D & A-7D
HI ANG	199th FIS to 199th TFS	F-102A	F-4C
ID ANG	190th FIS to 190th TRS	F-102A	RF-4C
KY ANG	165th TRS	RF-101C	C-130B
MN ANG	179th FIS to 179th TRS	F-101B	RF-4C
NV ANG	192nd TRS	RF-101B	RF-4C
NY ANG	139th TAS[42]	C-130A	C-130D
OH ANG	164th TFS to 164th TAS	F-100D	C-130B
PR ANG	198th TFS	F-104C	A-7D
RI ANG	143rd SOS to 143rd TAS	C-119C	C130A
WV ANG	130th SOS to 130th TAW	C-119C	C-130A

At the end of the Transitional Quarter (30 September 1976), the Air National Guard was composed of 24 wings (four AREFWs, three FIWs, two TASWs, four TAWs, nine TFWs and two TRWs) with 69 groups (none of which was on bases where wings existed as the duplication of wings and groups had been eliminated in July 1976 with the inactivation of California's 144th FIG at Fresno ANGB and Massachusetts' 102nd FIG at Otis AFB) and 91 squadrons.

---

[40] During 1976 the United States government went from a 1 July-30 June fiscal year to a fiscal year starting on 1 October of the preceding year and ending on 30 September of the corresponding calendar year. Therefore, to make up the difference between FY76, which ended on 30 June 1976, and FY77, which began on 1 October 1976, a Transitional Quarter (TQ – from 1 July 1976 to 30 September 1976) was added at the end of FY76.

[41] Having functioned as an F-100 Combat Crew Training School since January 1970, the 152nd TFTS assumed responsibility for A-7D conversion transition training in July 1976 when it began a two-stage conversion in preparation for the phasing out of the F-100 from the Guard's inventory.

[42] After completing its conversion to ski-equipped C-130Ds, the 139th TAS assumed responsibility for Volant DEW, the Arctic DEW Line Support mission.

Above: Beginning during FY74, Kansas' 117th DSES and Vermont's 134th DSES took on the defense systems evaluation mission with Martin EB-57s. In that role, Guardsmen provided specialized support during major exercises such as Brave Shield XV in October 1976, when 52-1499 was photographed.

Above left: Several versions of the Martin twinjets, née English Electric, were modified for use in the defense systems evaluation role. This EB-57C of the 134th DSES, VT ANG, was built as a B-57C transition trainer.

Middle left: A Boeing T-43A of Det 1, HQ District of Columbia ANG, taxis in front of the control tower at McClellan AFB, CA, on 13 February 1982.

Bottom left: The 'Flying Yankees' of the 118th TFS, CT ANG, flew F-100Ds and Fs between the spring of 1971 and the summer of 1979. Earlier, while designated 118th FIS, the squadron had flown F-100As before converting to F-102As.

Creek Party ends – Volant Oak starts

Phase-out of the KC-97L tankers, scheduled to be completed during FY78, resulted in the conversion of three squadrons to KC-135As[43] and of one squadron to C-130A during FY77, and in the termination in May 1977 of Operation Creek Party, the air-refueling support by ANG tankers to Air Force tactical aircraft in Europe. During 10 years of accident-free operations, the Creek Party tankers had flown 6,512 sorties, completed 47,207 hook-ups, and off-loaded 137,398,620 lb of jet fuel.

Aircraft conversions and mission changes taking place during FY77 were the following:

State	Squadron	Mission Aircraft From	To
IA ANG	124th TFS	F-100D	A-7D
IA ANG	174th TFS	F-100D	A-7D
IL ANG	108th AREFS	KC-97L	KC-135A
MD ANG	135th TASS to 135th TAS	O-2A	C-7A/B
MO ANG	180th AREFS to 180th TAS	KC-97L	C-130A
ND ANG	178th FIS	F-101B	F-4D
NJ ANG	150th TAS to 150th AREFS	C-7A/B	KC-135A
PA ANG	147th AREFS	KC-97L	KC-135A
PA ANG	193rd TEWS	C/EC-121	EC-130E
SD ANG	175th TFS	F-100D	A-7D
TN ANG	151st AREFS	KC-97L	KC-135A

Volant Oak, the Joint Chiefs of Staff-directed rotation of Guard and Reserve C-130s to Howard AFB in support of USSOUTHCOM (the US Southern Command) in Panama, was initiated on 1 October 1977. Since then, C-130 squadrons from the AFRES and the ANG have rotated six aircraft, seven crews and support personnel on one-month deployments, with six successive Guard detachments operating from Panama for half of each year and six AFRES detachments operating from Panama during the other six months.[44]

During FY78 four more air refueling squadrons underwent Pacer Angler conversion to KC-135As to complete the ANG planned force of 13 jet tanker squadrons. As shown in the following tabular listing, three of these units had previously flown KC-97Ls while the fourth, Kansas' 117th, had been a defense systems evaluation squadron equipped with Martin EB-57s. This loss of one of the two DSESs was partially offset by increasing the UE strength of the 134th DSES, VT ANG, from nine to 15 EB-57B/C/Es.

Snowbird and Coronet Cove – Places in the sun for the Guard

FY78 also saw the beginning of Operation Snowbird, an NGB-funded program which since then has seen northern-based tactical fighter and tactical air support squadrons rotate to Davis-Monthan AFB for two-week deployments and training in the more clement Arizona winter weather.

Aircraft conversions and mission changes taking place during FY78 were the following:

State	Squadron	Mission Aircraft From	To
AZ ANG	197th AREFS	KC-97L	KC-135A
KS ANG	117th DSES to 117th AREFS	EB-57	KC-135A
MI ANG	171st FIS	F-106A	F-4C
OH ANG	162nd TFS	F-100D	A-7D
OK ANG	125th TFS	F-100D	A-7D
TX ANG	181st AREFS to 181st TAS	KC-97L	C-130B
UT ANG	191st AREFS	KC-97L	KC-135A
WI ANG	126th AREFS	KC-97L	KC-135A

The Air National Guard attained its highest combat-ready status to date (97 per cent) during FY78 as its units continued participating in the enhanced Operational Readiness Inspection (ORI) program.[45] Evaluated under the same criteria as applied to active Air Force units, all ANG units undergoing ORI during the year passed with satisfactory ratings.

Coronet Cove, a year-round commitment through which the Guard's A-7 squadrons were to support the US Southern Command in Panama, was initiated in December 1978. Thereafter, squadrons took turns sending a five- or six-aircraft detachment to Howard AFB for a month, with the pilots and support personnel being rotated at the two-week mid-point.

---

[43] One of these squadrons, the 197th AREFS, AZ ANG, became the first Guard unit to be assigned a female pilot, First Lieutenant Marilyn Koon.
During FY77, Airman Linda Jean Hall of the 193rd TEWS became the Guard's first female airborne radio operator.

[44] Since inception of this mission, the six Volant Oak aircraft have typically flown an average of 52 missions per month, for a monthly total of 144 sorties and 382 flying hours, while providing intra-theater movement of USSOUTHCOM personnel and material throughout Central and South America. Each month they have transported an average of 208 tons of cargo and 842 passengers, and airdropped 224 troops and 1,650 lb of equipment and supplies.

[45] During ORIs, units are expected to generate sorties at wartime rates and must operate under realistic combat scenarios. Inspections test coordination between the command and control, intelligence, operations, security and maintenance functions in response to a simulated threat.

During the last year of the 1970s two states exchanged tactical air support headquarter units as New York's 105th TASW was replaced at the Westchester County AP by the 105th TASG, while Wisconsin's 128th TASG at Truax Field became the 128th TASW. The 105th TASG became the direct parent unit for the 137th TASS, while the 128th TASW became that of the 176th TASS. No squadrons changed missions during the year but 13 aircraft conversions took place. Two long-serving types, the F-100 and RF-101, were phased out; jet-powered OA-37Bs began replacing piston-powered O-2As; F-105Gs and the 'Wild Weasel' defense-suppression mission went to Georgia's 128th TFS; and the number of ANG squadrons flying F-4s trebled. More importantly, FY79 witnessed the delivery of brand new Fairchild Republic A-10As to the three squadrons of the 174th Tactical Fighter Wing and the replacement of war-weary C-130As in Oklahoma's 185th TAS with factory-fresh C-130Hs.

VIP transport and support for the Air Force Academy

Jet transports and navigation trainers were first operated by the Guard late in 1978 when six Boeing T-43As were assigned. Before going to Det 1, DC ANG, at Andrews

AFB, to fly administrative airlift missions through MAC scheduling, four of these aircraft were converted back to the transport configuration (the T-43A being a military version of the 737-200 jetliner) and were fitted with only 64 seats so that they would have non-stop transcontinental capability. The other two went to Det 1, CO ANG, at Buckley ANGB, to provide support for the United States Air Force Academy at Colorado Springs.

No fewer than 13 aircraft conversions took place during FY79 as the last F-100s and RF-101s were phased out and older C-130As replaced by new C-130Hs:

State	Squadron	Mission Aircraft From	To
AR ANG	184th TFS	F-100D	F-4C
CT ANG	118th TFS	F-100D	A-10A
GA ANG	128th TFS	F-100D	F-105G
IN ANG	113th TFS	F-100D	F-4C[46]
IN ANG	163rd TFS	F-100D	F-4C[46]
LA ANG	122nd TFS	F-100D	F-4C
MA ANG	131st TFS	F-100D	A-10A
MI ANG	107th TRS	F-100D	A-7D
MO ANG	110th TFS	F-100D	F-4C
MS ANG	153rd TRS	RF-101C	RF-4C
OH ANG	112th TFS	F-100D	A-7D
OK ANG	185th TAS	C-130A	C-130H
TX ANG	182nd TFS	F-100D	F-4C

Into the 1980s

The new decade began with the relocation of two units – California's 129th AR&RS/129th AR&RG moving from the Hayward Air Terminal to NAS Moffett Field, and Rhode Island's 143rd TAS/143rd TAG from the T. F. Green Airport to the Quonset State Airport – and saw a

[46] The aircraft assigned to the two IN ANG units had in fact been modified earlier to the EF-4C 'Wild Weasel' configuration. However, in service with the IN ANG these aircraft were operated in the normal tactical fighter role rather than in the 'Wild Weasel' defense-suppression role and were once again designated F-4Cs.

Above: McDonnell Douglas F-15As entered ANG service during the summer of 1985 when they were first delivered to the 122nd TFS, LA ANG, at NAS New Orleans

Above left: Much regretted in these days of dull gray tactical schemes, markings applied on the tail of Delta Darts of the 194th FIS were inspired by the 'California Republic' flag of the 'Golden State'. They were proudly worn in October 1980 when the Californians became the first overall winners at William Tell.

Top: An F-4D of the 179th FIS, MN ANG, at Ramstein AB, Germany, in June 1986 during Creek Klaxon.

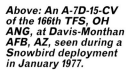

Above: An A-7D-15-CV of the 166th TFS, OH ANG, at Davis-Monthan AFB, AZ, seen during a Snowbird deployment in January 1977.

Right: Returning from the Nellis range, an A-10A of the 118th TFS, CT ANG, lands at Nellis AFB, NV during Gunsmoke '87.

Top right: Based at the Fort Smith MAP, Arkansas' 184th TFS completed its conversion from F-4Cs to F-16As on 1 April 1989.

Above right: Unless fitted with their clip-on antenna arrays, EC-130E 'Comfy Levi' EW aircraft modified under the Senior Scout program are hard to distinguish from standard C-130Es. The Pennsylvania unit to which they have been assigned since 1980 was redesignated from 193rd TEWS to 193rd ECS in March 1983, and to 193rd SOS in November 1983.

Task Force (PTTF) at Andersen AFB, Guam, aircraft conversions picked up gain.[50] Those undertaken during FY81 affected nine squadrons as follows:

State	Squadron	Mission Aircraft From	To
CA ANG	115th TAS	C-130B/E	C-130E
DC ANG	121st TFS	F-105D	F-4D
IL ANG	170th TFS	F-4C	F-4D
MD ANG	135th TAS	C-7A/B	C-130B
MI ANG	172nd TASS	O-2A	OA-37B
MS ANG	183rd TAS	C-130E	C-130H
NJ ANG	141st TFS	F-105B	F-4D
OR ANG	123rd FIS	F-101B	F-4C
PA ANG	103rd TASS	O-2A	OA-37B

Towards the end of FY81, the Air Force held its first air-to-ground weapons meet in 19 years with four ANG units competing against AAC, AFRES, PACAF, USAFE and TAC teams. The overall winner of the first Gunsmoke meet was the A-7D team from Colorado's 140th TFW, and the 'Top Gun' was a pilot from the same unit.

It should be noted that the success of the ANG interceptor units at William Tell meets and of its tactical fighter units at Gunsmoke was matched all along by good performance at tactical reconnaissance competitions (i.e. Idaho's 124th TRG winning Photo Derby '80, Photo Derby '84 and Photo Finish '85, Nevada's 152nd TRG winning at Reconnaissance Air Meet '86 and RAM '90, and Nebraska's 155th TRG winning the 'top day' award at RAM '88) and airlift meets (i.e. North Carolina's 145th TAG gaining top honors at Volant Rodeo '86).

marked slowdown in conversions, with those completed during FY80 involving only five units:

State	Squadron	Mission Aircraft From	To
IL ANG	169th TASS	O-2A	OA-37B
KS ANG	127th TFTS to 127th TFS	F-105D/F	F-4D[47]
MD ANG	104th TFS	A-37B	A-10A
NY ANG	138th TFS	A-37B	A-10A
WI ANG	176th TASS	O-2A	OA-37B

During FY80 the primary mission of the 13 AREFSs continued to be to provide strategic refueling in support of SAC's Single Integrated Operational Plan (SIOP), and to that end they continued to keep KC-135As and crew on alert, an assignment first given to Guard tankers in FY76. The 13 AREFSs also continued to provide two aircraft and crews to the European Tanker Task Force (a duty which they had first assumed during FY77) and the Alaska Tanker Task Force (participation in which had begun during FY79) and supported numerous deployments and exercises in the United States and abroad. Other developments in the Guard tanker force were its participation for the first time in Red Flag exercises and the winning by New Hampshire's 157th AREFG of the Tanker Navigation Trophy during the 1980 SAC Bomb/Nav Competition.

Other notable events during the first year of the 1980s were: (**1**) the switch of fighter interceptor units from ADCOM-gained to TAC-gained status;[48] (**2**) the winning of the William Tell air-to-air weapons meet by California's 144th FIW;[49] and (**3**) the initial participation of Guard units in a Maple Flag exercise at CFB Cold Lake, the first participants being Oklahoma's 125th TFS and South Dakota's 175th TFS, which took their A-7Ds to Canada in April-May 1980.

During the following Fiscal Year, which saw the first 11 A-7K two-seaters delivered to the RTU in Arizona and KC-135 units starting to participate in the Pacific Tanker

[47] When it converted from 18 F-105D/Fs to 30 F-4Ds, the KS ANG unit received a dual role as an operational fighter squadron and as the Guard's F-4D RTU. Accordingly, it dropped the training designation from its title and was redesignated 127th Tactical Fighter Squadron/184th Tactical Fighter Group on 8 October 1979.

[48] The Air Defence Command (ADC), the gaining command for the Guard's FISs, had been redesignated Aerospace Defense Command (ADCOM) on 15 January 1968, and ADCOM had been designated a specified command on 1 July 1975. The Air Force announced on 19 March 1979 its decision to transfer all aerospace defense resources from ADCOM to other major commands. Active-duty fighter interceptor squadrons and the responsibility for FISs to be gained from the ANG in the event of mobilization were transferred to Air Defense, Tactical Air Command (ADTAC). ADCOM was inactivated on 31 March 1980.

[49] The Guard's domination of William Tell '80 was further evidenced by the Texas ANG's win in the F-101 category, the winning of the 'Top Gun' award in the F-101 and F-106 categories by Guardsmen from Texas and Massachusetts, the winning by the Californians of the 'Top Maintenance' trophy in the F-106 category and the winning of the 'Top Weapons Load' award by a Michigan ANG crew.

Above: Republic F-105D Thunderchiefs were assigned to the 149th TFS, VA ANG, for 11 years beginning in February 1971.

Above: McDonnell F-4C of the 137th FIS, NY ANG.

In 1982 the capability of the Guard's tanker force began to be significantly upgraded as the first nine re-engined KC-135Es were distributed among three air refueling squadrons – Arizona's 197th, Tennessee's 151st and Utah's 191st – with plans calling for the re-engining of all KC-135As to be completed during FY85.[51]

Aircraft conversions and mission changes taking place during FY82 were the following:

		Mission Aircraft	
State	Squadron	From	To
AK ANG	144th TAS	C-123J	C-130E
NY ANG	107th FIS	F-101B	F-4C
PA ANG	103rd TASS	O-2A	OA-37B
TX ANG	111th FIS	F-101B	F-4C
VA ANG	149th TFS	F-105D	A-7D
VT ANG	134th DSES to 134th TFS	EB-57	F-4D
WI ANG	176th TASS to 176th TAS	OA-37B	A-10A

In October 1983, as the United States prepared to intervene in Grenada, an EC-130E from Pennsylvania's 193rd SOS[52] and 17 volunteers were sent to NAS Roosevelt Roads, Puerto Rico, to be in position to begin psychological warfare operations at the onset of Operation Urgent Fury on 25 October. Later operating from Barbados, the detachment of the 193rd SOS remained in the area until the end of October, as its ability to broadcast news to the Grenadan population proved invaluable to offset propaganda by sympathizers of the socialist New Jewel Movement.

Aircraft conversions – which included initial assignment of F-16s to the Guard – and mission changes taking place during FY83 were the following:

		Mission Aircraft	
State	Squadron	From	To
AL ANG	160th TRS to 160th TFS	RF-4C	F-4D
CA ANG	196th TASS to 196th TFS	O-2A	F-4C
GA ANG	128th TFS	F-105G	F-4D
GA ANG	158th TAS	C-130E	C-130H
SC ANG	157th TFS	A-7D	F-16A

Organization of new CCTU and RTUs

New A-7D/K and F-4D replacement training units, Arizona's 195th TFTS and Kansas' 177th TFTS, were integrated with the co-located 162nd TFG at the Tucson IAP and the 184th TFG at McConnell AFB to eliminate the expense of organizing and staffing new groups.[53] Both were

[50] Unfortunately, gains resulting from these conversions were partially offset by the loss of eight A-7Ds (72-0189, 72-0219, 72-0221, 72-0222, 73-0994, 73-1005, 74-1748 and 74-1755) which were destroyed on the ramp of the 198th TFS, Puerto Rico ANG, during a terrorist attack at Muniz ANGB on 12 January 1981.

[51] The re-engining program was completed on schedule with Maine's 132nd AREFS becoming the last squadron to exchange its KC-135A for KC-135Es in FY85. The re-engining of KC-135As with Pratt & Whitney TF33-P-102 turbofans (second-hand JT3D turbofans which had become surplus to airline requirements with the phase-out of 707s) resulted in a 14 per cent increase in fuel efficiency, a 90 per cent reduction in air pollution and a 25 per cent increase in take-off thrust.

[52] The designation of this squadron and parent group had been changed on 1 October 1983 from Electronic Combat to Special Operations.

[53] Likewise, when on 15 October 1985 the 148th TFTS was organized in Tucson as an F-16A/B RTU it became part of the existing 162nd TFG. The 161st TFTS, another F-16A/B RTU at McConnell AFB, was similarly added to the 184th TFG when it received federal recognition on 1 July 1987.

Above: Photographed in January 1989 at the Suffolk County Airport, this HC-130H then belonged to the 102nd AR&RS, 106th AR&RG, NY ANG. On 15 March 1992, the designators for the squadron and group were changed to RQS and RQG.

Top left: Guard units from most states make frequent use of the Air National Guard Permanent Training Site, Volk Field, WI. This KC-135E of the 108th AREFS, IL ANG, was taking part in Sentry Independence when photographed at Volk Field on 14 June 1990.

Above left: 'Comfy Levi' and 'Rivet Rider' 'Herks' of Pennsylvania's 193rd SOS confusingly bear the same EC-130E designation. No prize is given for identifying the latter.

Top: A C-130B of the 187th TAS, WY ANG, making a water drop in the morning of 17 June 1987 during a MAFFS fire-fighting training exercise in the Rouse Ridge area of the San Bernardino National Forest.

Above: Taking off from Volk Field, WI, on 14 June 1990, this KC-135E of the 126th AREFS, WI ANG, is on its way to refuel thirsty Sentry Independence participants.

Top right: Maryland's 104th TFS converted from OA-37Bs to A-10As in the fall of 1979. Still flying 'Warthogs', the Marylanders took first place during Gunsmoke '91 by scoring higher than Gulf War veterans.

Above right: The 138th TFS, NY ANG, is the only Guard unit cleared to carry a GPU-5/A 30-mm gun pod beneath its F-16As. Limited use of that pod was made during Desert Storm when the squadron operated from Al Kharj in Saudi Arabia.

extended federal recognition on 1 February 1984. On the same date, a new Oregon ANG unit, the 114th TFTS at Kingsley Field in Klamath Falls, received federal recognition as an air-defense combat crew training school responsible for providing advanced flying training for ANG pilots and WSOs assigned to ADTAC-gained squadrons.

Next, on 1 September 1984, the Guard organized an RF-4C combat crew training unit (CCTU) in Idaho. Based at Gowen Field in Boise and attached to the 124th TRG, this 189th Tactical Reconnaissance Training Flight did not receive its own aircraft but began sharing aircraft with the 190th TRS. Subsequently, the number of RF-4Cs assigned to the 124th TRG was increased twice to enable the 190th TRS to keep its operational commitment while the 189th TRTF provided training for increasing numbers of reconnaissance crews.

During 1984 significant progress was also made in upgrading the capability of ANG flying squadrons as (**1**) threat simulators were installed at the Volk Field Training Site in Wisconsin as part of the 'Sentry Dawg' program to provide Guard aircrews with regular opportunity to train against aircraft equipped with ECM pods; (**2**) the aircraft of several squadrons were equipped with 'Have Quick' jam-resistant UHF radios; and (**3**) MAC gave priority to ANG squadrons for equipping their aircraft with 'Have Quick' radios, ALE-40 countermeasures dispensing sets and radar-warning receivers.

Fiscal Year 1984 also saw New York's 105th TASS reorganized as the 105th MAS, as it underwent conversion from the smallest and lightest aircraft in the ANG inventory, the Cessna O-2A, to its largest and heaviest, the Lockheed C-5A Galaxy. Two other squadrons underwent aircraft conversions to complete the following changes:

State	Squadron	Mission Aircraft	
		From	To
MN ANG	109th TAS	C-130A	C-130E
MN ANG	179th TRS to 179th FIS	RF-4C	F-4D
NY ANG	105th TASS to 105th MAS	O-2A	C-5A

Fiscal Year 1985 was essentially a year of consolidation during which only two squadrons underwent aircraft conversions, merely involving trading older aircraft for newer versions of the same types:

State	Squadron	Mission Aircraft	
		From	To
AK ANG	144th TAS	C-130E	C-130H
MO ANG	110th TFS	F-4C	F-4E

Whereas 1985 had been a year of relative calm as regards the organization and operations of the Air National Guard, Fiscal Year 1986 was a year rich in events. Mississippi's 183rd TAS was redesignated the 183rd MAS, after completing its conversion from C-130Hs to C-141Bs on 1 July 1986. Work continued to convert Arkansas' 154th AREFS into the 154th Tactical Airlift Training Squadron[54] and to replace its KC-135Es with C-130Es (officially, however, the conversion process was completed only on the first day of the following fiscal year, 1 October 1986), and to organize a new tanker unit in Alaska, the 168th AREFS, which received federal recognition at Eielson AFB on 1 October 1986.

In a significant move reflecting the Air Force's confidence in the readiness of the ANG interceptor force, 22 ANG F-4 units were given a one-year defense-alert commitment at Ramstein AB, Germany, to enable the 86th TFW, USAFE, to stand down from alert duty while converting from F-4Es to F-16Cs. Initiated in April 1986, Operation Creek Klaxon saw the Guard provide eight Phantoms and 96 'Zulu Warriors', with pilots and WSOs being rotated every three months and support personnel remaining in Germany for 90 to 139 days.

Continued modernization saw McDonnell Douglas

---

[54] The selection of this squadron to become the Combat Crew Training Unit for the Guard's C-130 units was logical, as Little Rock AFB already was the site of the active-duty C-130 training unit (the 34th TATG) and thus housed the required complement of simulators.

McDonnell F-4C-16-MC
171st Fighter Interceptor Squadron
191st Fighter Interceptor Group
Michigan ANG

With the Guard, F-4Cs were assigned both to fighter interceptor squadrons and to tactical fighter squadrons. The first were delivered to the 170th TFS, IL ANG, in January 1972 and the last were phased out by the 123rd FIS, OR ANG, in October 1989.

Peter B. Lewis

F-4C interceptors
Four fighter interceptor squadrons flew F-4Cs: Michigan's 171st, New York's 136th, Oregon's 123rd and Texas' 111th. In addition, although they were respectively designated tactical fighter squadron and tactical fighter training squadron, Hawaii's 199th and Oregon's 114th flew their F-4Cs primarily in the air defense and air defense training role.

Nose art
While equipped with F-4Cs the 171st FIS, MI ANG, gained much attention as their aircraft were adorned with nose arts at a time when the practice was shunned by the Air Force. A close-up of 'Shadow Demon', the nose art carried by 63-7442, is illustrated (left).

F-15As assigned to Louisiana's 122nd TFS, a first in the Guard. Other squadrons underwent aircraft conversions, with the following changes taking place during FY86:

		Mission Aircraft	
State	Squadron	From	To
AR ANG	154th AREFS to 154th TATS	KC-135E	C-130E
AZ ANG	152nd TFS	A-7D/K	F-16A/B
LA ANG	122nd TFS	F-4C	F-15A
MI ANG	171st FIS	F-4C	F-4D
MS ANG	183rd TAS to 183rd MAS	C-130H	C-141B
NJ ANG	141st TFS	F-4D	F-4E
TX ANG	182nd TFS	F-4C	F-16A

New support aircraft and accelerated modernization of mission aircraft inventory

The ANG Operational Support Turboprop Aircraft (ANGOSTA) program was begun in 1987 to replace piston-powered Convair C-131s with smaller Beech C-12J and Fairchild C-26A twin-turboprop aircraft. Deliveries of C-12Js began in the last quarter of 1987 and those of C-26As in the spring of 1989.

Modernization of two long-serving aircraft types saw Alabama's 106th TRS become the first RF-4C unit in the

Harrison W. Rued

Above: Beech twins were among the first type of transport assigned as support aircraft to state headquarters. This C-45H of the California ANG was photographed in January 1959.

Above right: For many years, 'Gooney Birds' were the most common state support aircraft. Illinois' C-47A was caught in good light at Battle Creek on 17 July 1968.

Guard to have aircraft fitted with the KS-127A Long-Range Oblique Photography (LOROP) system, and New Mexico's 188th TFS initiate qualification, operational testing and evaluation (QOT&E) for A-7Ds fitted with the Low-Altitude Night Attack (LANA) system. The successful completion of this test program led to the modification of 75 A-7Ds and eight A-7Ks to the LANA configuration[55] and the assignment of modified aircraft to the 124th (IA ANG), 125th (OK ANG) and 188th (NM ANG) Tactical Fighter Squadrons.

A new F-16A RTU, the 161st TFTS, received federal recognition in the Kansas ANG on 1 July 1987, and 11 aircraft conversions and one aircraft conversion/mission change occurred during FY87, as follows:

State	Squadron	Mission Aircraft	
		From	To
CA ANG	196th TFS	F-4C	F-4E
DE ANG	142nd TAS	C-130A	C-130H
GA ANG	128th TFS	F-4D	F-15A
HI ANG	199th TFS	F-4C	F-15A
MO ANG	180th TAS	C-130A	C-130H
MT ANG	186th FIS	F-106A	F-16A
NY ANG	107th FIS	F-4C	F-4D
NY ANG	139th TAS	C-130D	C/LC-130H
TX ANG	111th FIS	F-4C	F-4D
TX ANG	181st TAS	C-130B	C-130H
VT ANG	134th TFS to 134th FIS	F-4D	F-16A
WV ANG	130th TAS	C-130E	C-130H

Creek Corsair, a new rotational deployment of Air Guard A-7Ds to Germany, began in July 1988. Three units each contributed two aircraft and support equipment for the full six-week duration of the deployment to Spangdahlem AB, each unit providing 72 officers and enlisted personnel for two-week periods. Iowa's 185th TFG led off the first two-week rotation and ferried the aircraft to Germany with support from ANG KC-135Es. Aircrews and support personnel from Ohio's 121st TFW were in Germany for the middle two-week period. Finally, New Mexico's 150th TFG provided personnel for the last period and ferried the aircraft back to CONUS.

The following aircraft conversions, which notably saw the Convair F-106A being phased-out by New Jersey's 119th FIS, took place during FY88:

State	Squadron	Mission Aircraft	
		From	To
AL ANG	160th TFS	F-4D	F-16A
FL ANG	159th FIS	F-106A	F-16A
IL ANG	170th TFS	F-4D	F-16A
IN ANG	113th TFS	F-4C	F-4E
IN ANG	163rd TFS	F-4C	F-4E
KS ANG	127th TFS	F-4D	F-16A
MA ANG	101st FIS	F-106A	F-15A
NJ ANG	119th FIS	F-106A	F-16A

Rumors as to the impending phase-out of the RF-4C from Guard service and the ensuing reorganization of tactical reconnaissance squadrons into airlift units appeared to be confirmed when, in early 1989, Kentucky's 165th TRS became the 165th TAS upon reluctantly exchanging its RF-4Cs for C-130Bs. This conversion, however, was an isolated situation, and by mid-1990 no other RF-4C squadron was expected to suffer this fate. Pennsylvania's 103rd TASS was more fortunate, as its conversion entailed trading OA-37Bs for OA-10As. More significant than either of these conversions was that undergone by Oregon's 114th TFTS which, after initiating its conversion to the Fighting Falcon with unmodified F-16A/Bs, received its first F-16 ADF[56] in April 1989.

Including the above-mentioned conversions and mission changes, those taking place during FY89 were the following:

State	Squadron	Mission Aircraft	
		From	To
AR ANG	184th TFS	F-4C	F-16A
KY ANG	165th TRS to 165th TAS	RF-4C	C-130B
OR ANG	114th TFTS	F-4C	F-16 DF
PA ANG	103rd TASS	OA-37B	OA-10A
RI ANG	143rd TAS	C-130A	C-130E

---

[55] The LANA modification resulted in the addition of a pod-mounted AN/AAR-49 FLIR, and endowed the aircraft with automatic terrain-following (ATF) capability.

[56] The Air Defense Fighter version of the Fighting Falcon had been selected in October 1986 as the new interceptor for the Air National Guard. Orders were placed for conversion kits to be fitted at the Ogden Air Logistics Center to 270 F-16As and F-16Bs. The modified aircraft were to be assigned exclusively to the Guard to replace the F-4Ds and unmodified F-16As equipping its 11 operational fighter interceptor squadrons and its air defense RTU (the 114th TFTS).

Although the F-16 ADFs are not new-build aircraft, they have substantially upgraded capability and are effective interceptors. Principal avionics upgrades incorporated in the ADF version include (**1**) the modification of the AN/APG-66 radar to provide continuous wave illumination and thus enable the aircraft to be armed with medium-range radar missiles (one AIM-7 Sparrow or AIM-120 AMRAAM beneath each wing); (**2**) the incorporation of radar software modifications to improve small target detection; (**3**) the addition of a radar HUD display visual identification mode; (**4**) the installation of night identification spotlight; (**5**) the addition of an HF radio; and (**6**) the installation of the latest IFF interrogator.

Operation Just Cause

Late in FY89 and early in FY90, when the Air Force's intent to phase out its trisonic Lockheed SR-71As ran into Congressional opposition, serious consideration was given to transferring the last operational 'Blackbirds' and the strategic reconnaissance mission to the California ANG. This exciting proposal, however, was not implemented, as maintaining and flying a squadron of SR-71As would have taken a disproportionate portion of the Guard's budget.

In December 1989, on the eve of Operation Just Cause (the US intervention to protect the lives of American citizens in Panama and restore its democratic government) the Air National Guard had nine aircraft at Howard AFB on regularly scheduled Coronet Cove and Volant Oak deployments. During Just Cause the Guard also used the assets of three of its other flying units for specific support operations and alerted four of its tactical airlift units, but the additional C-130s were not needed.

In place with five A-7Ds and 56 people when fighting broke out in the early hours of 20 December 1989 was Ohio's 180th TFG, which flew 22 close air support sorties before its scheduled replacement on 23 December by the 114th TFG from Sioux Falls. The South Dakotans then flew 54 sorties before fighting subsided at the end of the month.

Some 120 Volant Oak personnel from seven units (California's 146th TAW, Delaware's 166th TAG, Missouri's 139th TAG, Oklahoma's 137th TAW, Tennessee's 118th TAW, Texas' 136th TAW and Wyoming's 153rd TAG) and four aircraft (a C-130E from the 146th TAW and one C-130H from each of the 136th TAW, the 139th and 166th TAGs) were at Howard AFB on 20 December. During Just Cause the crews of these four Hercules flew 97 sorties, including aeromedical evacuation flights to CONUS, and airlifted 416.4 tons of cargo and 2,395 people.

Units not scheduled to be in Panama, but which provided essential support, were Mississippi's 172nd MAG, New York's 105th MAG and Pennsylvania's 193rd SOG. The MS ANG unit flew 87 C-141B sorties from its home station in Jackson and transported 931 people and 319.7 tons of cargo to Panama. The NY ANG group flew 49 C-5A sorties from Stewart ANGB to airlift 637 people and over 1,000 tons of cargo both within CONUS and to Panama. The 193rd SOG, which had been alerted and had deployed two of its EC-130Es to Panama immediately prior to the start of Operation Just Cause, flew 137 hours in 19 missions before the end of that operation. Several of these missions required air refueling, as the aircraft were needed on station nearly continuously during the first three days to broadcast news and jam stations controlled by General Manuel Noriega's Panama Defense Forces.

Notwithstanding the splendid performance of the two A-7D detachments during Just Cause – weapons delivery was accurate, all scheduled sorties were flown, all taskings were met and all take-offs were on time – the 11-year Coronet Cove commitment[57] was terminated on 1 February 1990 due to budgetary cuts and the diplomatic need to reduce the size of US forces in Panama.

---

[57] Between December 1978 and January 1990, the Guard's A-7Ds had logged 16,959 flight hours in the course of some 13,000 Coronet Cove sorties. Soon thereafter, a new rotational deployment of ANG units was instituted, rather discreetly, as F-16 ADF units began sending Sentry Nighthawk detachments to Howard AFB as part of the Guard's role in the anti-drug war.

Top: In 1968, the mission aircraft of the 120th FIG were F-102As. The unit also maintained Montana's VC-54G state support aircraft.

Above: Vietnam War-era camouflage hid the fact that this VT-29A, photographed at Tucson IAP on 13 May 1973, was the state support aircraft for Arizona and that its accommodation was not all that spartan.

Total Force Component

René J. Francillon

General Dynamics

Above: Based at Andrews AFB, MD, as there are no suitable fields within the District of Columbia, the 121st TFS converted to F-16As in 1989. This bomb-laden Fighting Falcon was one of the six F-16As of the DC ANG taking part in a Red Flag exercise in June 1991.

Top right: Tennessee's 151st AREFS and South Carolina's 157th TFS were both called to active duty in December 1990 and took part in Desert Storm.

Above right: 'Rivet Rider' EC-130Es of the 193rd SOS, PA ANG, took part in Operations Just Cause, Desert Shield and Desert Storm.

PA ANG

Budget cuts, however, did not yet impact on the modernization of ANG units. Two versions of the Phantom, the F-4C and the F-4D, were phased out during FY90. Cuts also did not preclude the activation of a new flying unit, the 210th Air Rescue Squadron which received federal recognition in Alaska, nor did they interfere significantly with the previously funded move of California's 146th TAW from old facilities at the Van Nuys Airport to brand new installations at Channel Islands ANGS on the edge of NAS Point Mugu.

The mission change of California's 196th TFS, which had been initially scheduled to re-equip with OA-10As and to be once again designated 196th TASS, was changed before the delivery of the unwanted OA-10As. Instead, the unit traded its F-4Es for RF-4Cs and became the 196th TRS on 1 July 1990. Fourteen other aircraft conversions – including those of five fighter interceptor squadrons which received F-16As but were to have their aircraft upgraded to the F-16 ADF configuration within the next two years – were completed, or at least initiated, during FY90:

State	Squadron	Mission Aircraft From	To
CA ANG	194th FIS	F-4D	F-16 ADF
CA ANG	196th TFS to 196th TRS	F-4E	RF-4C
DC ANG	121st TFS	F-4D	F-16A
KS ANG	177th TFTS	F-4D	F-16C
MD ANG	135th TAS	C-130B	C-130E
MI ANG	107th TFS	A-7D	F-16A
MI ANG	171st FIS	F-4D	F-16A
MN ANG	179th FIS	F-4D	F-16 ADF
ND ANG	178th FIS	F-4D	F-16 ADF
NY ANG	137th FIS	F-4C	F-16 ADF
NY ANG	138th TFS	A-10A	F-16A
OR ANG	123rd FIS	F-4C	F-15A
TN ANG	105th TAS	C-130A	C-130H
TX ANG	111th FIS	F-4D	F-16A
WV ANG	167th TAS	C-130B	C-130E

Desert Shield/Desert Storm – The Gulf War

Two hundred and fifteen years after their forebears had fired that famous shot, Guardsmen were once again asked to stand in defense of freedom. In doing so, they convincingly demonstrated that the nation's reliance on the Total Force concept was well founded.

In answer to Iraq's invasion of Kuwait on 2 August 1990, President George Bush committed American forces first to help defend Saudi Arabia in the event of further Iraqi aggression and then to free Kuwait in compliance with United Nations resolutions. As both the short- and long-term goals of the coalition required an unprecedented build-up of forces, the most urgent need to supplement active-duty USAF components was for airlifters and tankers rather than for combat aircraft. Accordingly, a call for volunteers was issued before the end of the first week of August. The response by Guardsmen and Reservists was overwhelming, far exceeding the initial requirements of military planners. Noteworthy was the response of KC-135E and C-130 units, as the number of volunteers was such that there was no need to call up tanker and tactical airlift until three weeks before the United Nations deadline for Iraq to withdraw from Kuwait. Hence, the only ANG flying units called to active duty at the onset of Desert Shield were the much-needed C-141 and C-5 squadrons.

Mississippi's 183rd MAS and New York's 137th MAS were activated on 24 August 1990 and remained nominally based at their home stations, but crews and support personnel were constantly shuttling between CONUS and the Persian Gulf. The immensity of their task is indicated by the fact that they flew 13,752 hours before 17 January 1991, and carried 19,480 people and 55,000 tons of cargo. After fighting began, they flew an additional 7,708 hours, and carried 7,022 passengers and 20,726 tons of cargo prior to 13 February. Their activities continued at this hectic

Powerplant
The F-15A is powered by a pair of Pratt & Whitney F100-P-100 turbofans, each rated at 14,670 lb thrust dry and 23,830 lb thrust with afterburning.

Armament
The standard armament consists of an internal M61A1 20-mm cannon with 940 rounds, four AIM-9M Sidewinders and four AIM-7M Sparrows. AIM-120 AMRAAM is being issued to active-duty Eagle units, and will eventually be supplied to ANG squadrons.

McDonnell Douglas
F-15A-12-MC Eagle
128th Tactical Fighter Squadron
116th Tactical Fighter Wing
Georgia Air National Guard

Radar
Guard F-15As retain the original APG-63 radar. No plans exist yet to put the aircraft through MSIP, which upgrades the radar to APG-70.

Six ANG squadrons are equipped with the Eagle, one on each coast dedicated to the air defense role (Massachusetts and Oregon). Of the remainder, three (Georgia, Louisiana and Missouri) are assigned a battlefield air defense role, while Hawaii's 199th Fighter Squadron defends the island group and is gained by PACAF.

Markings
This aircraft carries the standard Eagle two-tone gray camouflage, with full-color markings for the commander of the 116th TFW. Normal squadron aircraft wear similar markings but in shades of gray. The unit has dropped the 'Tactical' from its designation, in line with recent Guard policy.

pace not only during the last two weeks of Desert Storm but also afterwards, as they helped to redeploy troops, equipment and supplies to Germany and the United States. Finally, the 137th and 183rd Military Airlift Squadrons were released from active duty on 15 May 1991.

C-130s manned by volunteers from virtually every ANG squadron supplemented active-duty tactical airlifters from the early phases of Desert Shield. Some flew within CONUS, others went to Germany and the United Kingdom (between August 1990 and April 1991, volunteers from the 133rd TAW, MN ANG; 146th TAW, CA ANG; 135th TAG, MD ANG; 143rd TAG, RI ANG; and 167th TAG, WV ANG shared 30-day rotational deployments, with four Hercules and 90 to 100 people, to Rhein-Main AB and RAF Mildenhall), and others went to the

Persian Gulf (a provisional tactical airlift squadron composed of 16 C-130Hs crewed by volunteers from Delaware, Missouri, Tennessee, Texas and West Virginia, deployed to the Gulf on 4 September 1990).

As time went by and the build-up of forces in the Gulf continued, the need for intra-theater airlift increased significantly and led to the activation of Texas' 181st TAS and West Virginia's 130th TAS on 5 October 1990, of Missouri's 180th TAS on 27 December 1990, of Delaware's 142nd TAS on 22 January 1991, and of Rhode Island's 143rd TAS on 23 February 1991. In theater, tactical airlifters, primarily from the activated squadrons but also including volunteers from other units, were assigned mostly to the 1630th Tactical Airlift Wing (Provisional). Known unofficially as the 'First DAWG' (First Desert Airlift Wing),

Jim Dunn

Above: Having won Gunsmoke '89, when this photograph was taken as a 'Swamp Fox' F-16 was departing for the Nellis range, South Carolina's 157th TFS was ready when it was called to fight during Desert Storm.

Right: ANG C-130s assigned to the 1630th Tactical Airlift Wing (Provisional) carried nearly one-third of the intra-theater cargo during Desert Shield and Desert Storm, thus playing a vital part in ensuring the success of General Schwarzkopf's Hail Mary tactic. This C-130H was photographed over a US Army installation in the desert.

this ANG-manned temporary unit was originally based in the United Arab Emirates but later moved to near Riyadh, Saudi Arabia, and went on to perform more than a third of all intra-theater airlifts. Altogether, in support of Desert Shield, ANG C-130s flew 10,275 hours in the course of 2,018 support and tactical airlift sorties, during which they carried 13,521 military and civilian passengers and more than 86,000 tons of cargo. During the first four weeks of Desert Storm they flew 11,511 hours, performed 2,406 support and tactical airlift sorties, and carried 13,858 passengers and 4,646 tons of cargo. The end of the fighting, however, did not terminate the need for ANG support, as C-130s were still urgently needed to help reposition troops, equipment and supplies. The last squadron to be released from active duty was Rhode Island's 143rd TAS.

Although C-130 units had been quick to volunteer, some of the first ANG Hercules in Saudi Arabia were the EC-130Es of Pennsylvania's 193rd SOS. Crewed, maintained and supported throughout Desert Shield/Desert Storm by volunteers, 'Rivet Rider' and 'Comfy Levi' EC-130Es played a significant, but discreet, role.

From the very onset of Desert Shield, all ANG tanker squadrons provided KC-135Es, crews and support personnel, with some squadrons being left virtually without aircraft at their home bases. Later, as it became increasingly evident that Iraq would not willingly withdraw from Kuwait, 12 of the 13 ANG tanker squadrons were activated on 20 December 1990 (the exception being Alaska's 168th

AREFS, as its KC-135Ds would have encountered interoperability problems; however, volunteers from the Alaska Guard did fly the squadron's KC-135Es in support of Desert Storm and during the postwar redeployment phase).

In most instances, and whether crewed and supported by volunteers or federalized personnel, the Guard KC-135Es were dispersed as the squadrons were splintered. Consequently, crews and aircraft from most squadrons were sent to different locations to support air operations not only in the Gulf and vicinity but also from bases in CONUS and Europe. The primary units to which they were assigned in or near the Gulf were the 1701st Air Refueling Wing (Provisional) and later the 1709th AREFW(P) at the King Abdul Aziz IAP in Jeddah, Saudi Arabia, the 1706th AREFW(P) at Cairo West AB in Egypt, the 1712th AREFW(P) at the Abu Dhabi IAP in the United Arab Emirates, and the 1713th AREFW(P) at Dubai IAP, also in the UAE. Other forward-deployed Guard tankers operated from Diego Garcia AB in the Indian Ocean, Masirah AP in Oman, and Incirlik AB in Turkey.

The one tanker squadron that was not splintered during Desert Shield/Desert Storm was Kansas' 117th AREFS. Following Kansas Governor Mike Hayden's approval of the participation of some 500 members of the 190th AREFG to support activities for the movement of US troops to the Persian Gulf, the first group of volunteers from that unit deployed to Saudi Arabia on 10 August

Above: The fight is on and the Guard belongs: a KC-135E of the 108th AREFS, IL ANG, refuels a pair of F-14As from VF-84 over the northern Arabian Gulf on 30 January 1991.

Far left and left: Nose art and mission markings are revealed on a pair of KC-135Es of the 1709th AREFW(P) at King Abdul Aziz IAP in Jeddah, Saudi Arabia. 56-3641 is an aircraft of the 117th AREFS, KS ANG, while 57-1455 belongs to the 151st AREFS, TN ANG.

1990. Their commander, Colonel Charles 'Mick' Baier, was then selected to command the 1701st AREFW(P) being organized at the Prince Abdullah AB on the edge of the King Abdul Aziz IAP in Jeddah to support SAC, AFRES and ANG tankers on TDY to Saudi Arabia. In being so chosen, Colonel Baier became the first Reserve officer on a voluntary TDY assignment to take command of a line combat unit. Subsequently, with the addition of SAC B-52s, KC-10s and KC-135A/Qs, the 1701st AREFW(P) was redesignated the 1701st Strategic Wing to assume responsibility for base operations and support, while the bombers were formed into the 1708th BMW(P) and the tankers into the 1709th AREFW(P). During Desert Storm the 1708th and 1709th had up to 115 aircraft under their control. The tankers of the 1709th (including all 10 KC-135Es of the 117th AREFS) averaged 75 refueling sorties a day, most of them along the Iraq-Saudi border, with periodic missions into Iraq. In addition, other 190th AREFG personnel supported the war effort from their home base and other locations. The Kansas Guardsmen returned to Forbes ANGB on 14 March 1991 and were released from FAD on 15 April 1991.

During the five months prior to the start of hostilities, ANG tankers flew 7,661 hours in the course of 1,989 sorties, refueled 5,553 receivers, and offloaded 90.4 million lb of fuel in support of Operation Desert Shield. Between 17 January and 12 February 1991, they worked at an even sprightlier pace as they flew 8,935 hours in 1,865

sorties, refueled 7,512 receivers, and transferred 95.7 million lb of fuel. That frantic pace[58] continued until the last day of the war, and then gave place to less hectic activities as KC-135Es provided refueling support for tactical units being brought back to their home bases and to strategic airlifters bringing back troops and supplies. ANG air refueling squadrons were released from active duty beginning on 15 April and ending on 31 May 1991.

The first tactical ANG flying unit to deploy to Southwest Asia was the 117th TRW, Alabama ANG, which was alerted on 15 August, as its LOROP-equipped RF-4Cs were assets vitally needed to conduct surveillance of Iraqi forces in occupied Kuwait and along the Saudi Arabia-Iraq border. Within nine days 156 volunteers were ready to depart Birmingham for the Persian Gulf. With support and maintenance personnel, spare parts and supplies carried aboard two KC-10As, six RF-4Cs of the 106th TRS departed on 24 August bound for the United Arab

---

[58] Typical of this effort was that of the 1713th Air Refueling Wing (Provisional). This almost all-ANG wing (non-ANG support personnel accounted for 15 per cent of the wing's manning) had 12 crews from the 147th AREFS, PA ANG, and six crews from each of Ohio's 145th AREFS and Tennessee's 151st AREFS. Between 13 January and 28 February 1991, the 1713th AREFW(P) flew 556 sorties and transferred 30.2 million lb of fuel to 2,921 receivers while operating from the Dubai IAP. No sorties were canceled for maintenance or operational reasons.

David Donald

Above: The RF-4C arrived in the Gulf in August 1990, flown by Alabama volunteers. Until the end of the conflict, the photo-Phantom was used to gather intelligence on enemy defenses.

Below: Photographed in Reno on 11 April 1991, a couple of days after a triumphant return to Nevada, this RF-4C shows that the Nevadans quickly claimed possession of their borrowed aircraft.

Emirates. Later attached to the 35th Tactical Fighter Wing (Provisional) at the Sheikh Isa AB in Bahrain, the Alabamans first flew in-theater familiarization sorties and, tragically, lost one of their crews – Major Barry K. Henderson, pilot, and Lieutenant Colonel Stephen G. Schramm, WSO – in an RF-4C operational accident on 8 October. A replacement aircraft and crew were later flown from Alabama. The volunteers from the 117th TRW went on to perform flawlessly in support of the USCENTAF requirement for long-range photography. In the process, the Alabama volunteers flew within 12 nm of enemy territory to complete 87 Eager Light sorties, during which they provided what Lieutenant General Charles A. Horner, USCENTAF Commander, later described as "a unique capability that was a critical part of our collection effort against Iraq and was an extremely important part of our overall intelligence effort."

To relieve the Alabama volunteers, the Nevada ANG was notified at the end of October 1990 that volunteers from its 152nd TRG would deploy in December to the Persian Gulf and that six pilots and six WSOs from the 192nd TRS would be called to FAD to fly the RF-4Cs brought to Bahrain by the Alabama ANG. Going on active duty on 3 December, the 'High Rollers' relieved the "bamers' on 18 December and were fully familiar with local operating conditions when the war started on 16 January 1991. During the following six weeks, crews from the 192nd TRS flew combat sorties without experiencing either a single cancellation due to mechanical problems or a single combat loss, in spite of intense Iraqi AAA and SAM activity. However, following the end of hostilities, one of the Alabama's RF-4Cs crashed in the Persian Gulf; fortunately, both NV ANG crew members ejected and were safely recovered. After having flown 412 Desert Shield/ Desert Storm sorties, the 192nd TRS crews flew the Alabama RF-4Cs and two of their own aircraft back to May ANGB in Reno where, along with support personnel, they arrived on 9 April 1991. All were demobilized on 20 April 1991.

Shortly after being alerted in November 1990, New York's 174th TFW and South Carolina's 169th TFG began sending food service, billeting and laundry service personnel to Al Kharj AB, a 'bare base' southeast of Riyadh, to help prepare facilities for the 4th Tactical Fighter Wing (Provisional). This wing was formed to group at that base with two TAC F-15E squadrons (the 335th and 336th TFSs), a USAFE F-15C squadron (the 53rd TFS), and two ANG F-16A squadrons (the 138th and 157th TFSs), plus supporting AFRES and ANG C-130s. So primitive were the conditions at Al Kharj that the base became known as

René J. Francillon

Above: Flying from Al Kharj, Saudi Arabia, the 'Boys from Syracuse' flew 1,050 combat sorties during Desert Storm without losing an aircraft to the enemy.

Right: Such was the need for tankers that 12 of the 13 air refueling squadrons of the Air National Guard were called to active duty, along with those of the Air Force Reserve.

the 'Camel Lot', but that rather uncomplimentary nickname soon was changed to the more acceptable 'Camelot' spelling.

Called to active duty at the end of December 1990, the two Guard units were ready for immediate deployments and their F-16As departed from McEntire ANGB on 29 December 1990 and from Hancock Field on 2 January 1991. Flying directly to Saudi Arabia with KC-10A support, the Guardsmen immediately prepared for combat operations (in the process, an aircraft from the 138th TFS was lost on 13 January but its pilot was safely recovered) and were flying over Iraq and occupied Kuwait on the first day of Desert Storm. Operating against a variety of ground targets, the two units primarily dropped Mk 82 and Mk 84 bombs, cluster-bomb units (CBU-58s, CBU-87s and Mk 20 Rockeyes), and AGM-65 Maverick missiles. The 138th TFS also made extremely limited use of its GPU-5/A 30-mm gun pod. By the time a ceasefire was declared, the 138th TFS had flown 1,050 combat sorties, while the 157th TFS had flown 1,729 sorties (including sorties flown between the ceasefire and 8 May 1991, when its last aircraft were readied to be flown back to South Carolina). Neither suffered combat losses (one of the aircraft from the 138th TFS, however, did suffer much damage when hit by a surface-to-air missile, but was skillfully brought back to base) and the New York and South Carolina Guardsmen earned much praise from senior Air Force officers. Most remained in Saudi Arabia for several months after the end of hostilities, and the 138th TFS and 157th TFS were not released from active duty until 30 June and 22 July 1991, respectively.

While this brief overview of ANG operations during Desert Shield/Desert Storm has, as the remainder of the book, dealt primarily with flying squadrons operations, it is important to note that the vast majority of the more than 10,500 Air Guardsmen who volunteered or served on active duty were non-aircrews. They included personnel from aeromedical evacuation flights, civil engineering squadrons, combat communications squadrons, joint chiefs of staff squadrons, medical squadrons, mobile aerial port flights, public affairs detachments, security police

flights, services flights, and tactical clinics and hospitals. Going mostly unheralded, their work did much to prove once again that citizen soldiers can be relied upon to protect the nation's interests in war as well as in peace. In the words of Air Force Chief of Staff General Merrill A. McPeak:

> "They *(The Guardsmen and Reservists)* were ready when called on, they were moved immediately, and they were employed the minute combat began . . . The Total Force policy works for the Air Force, and we're proud of their performance."

Clearly, 'The Guard belongs' is more than just a snappy motto!

Below: For the Air National Guard, the role played by its men and women in helping the coalition free Kuwait marked the end of yet another day in its long tradition in support of freedom.

The Changing World

CHAPTER 7

Far right: A sure sign that the world is changing: a Minnesota ANG F-16A ADF flies in close formation with a visiting MiG-29UB. For 36 of the 44 years since the 179th Fighter Squadron received federal recognition, the Duluth unit had one clearly defined mission: intercept and shoot down any Soviet aircraft entering US airspace . . .

Below: After 16 years as a reconnaissance unit, Idaho's 190th FS returned to the fighter business when, during the summer of 1991, it became the only Guard squadron to fly F-4Gs in the defense suppression role.

Below right: The 183rd MAS was called to active duty on 24 August 1990, barely three weeks after Iraq invaded Kuwait. The Mississippians and their C-141Bs played a vital role during the build-up, combat and redeployment phases of the Gulf War.

During FY92, lessons from the Gulf War, the breakup of the Warsaw Pact, the fall from power of the Soviet Communist Party and fast-breaking changes in the Commonwealth of Independent States led to considerable pressure to reduce the budget of the Defense Department and to drastically reassess the structure and management of the Air Force. Together with previously approved aircraft conversions and mission changes, these developments have brought about a significant reorganization in the Air National Guard.

In keeping with changes implemented in the active force, the designations of ANG flying units (or the abbreviations of these designations) were changed on 15 March 1992 as follows:

From	To
Air Refueling Heavy (AREFG/AREFS/AREFW)	Air Refueling (ARG/ARS/ARW)
Air Rescue (ARG/ARS)	Rescue (RQG/RQS)
Military Airlift (MAG/MAS/MAW)	Airlift (AG/AS/AW)
Tactical Airlift (TAG/TAS/TAW)	Airlift (AG/AS/AW)
Tactical Airlift Training Squadron (TATS)	Training Squadron (TS)
Tactical Air Support (TASG/TASS/TASW)	Fighter (FG/FS/FW)
Tactical Fighter (TFG/TFS/TFW)	Fighter (FG/FS/FW)
Fighter Interceptor (FIG/FIS/FIW)	Fighter (FG/FS/FW)
Tactical Fighter Training (TFTG/TFTS)	Fighter (FG/FS)
Tactical Reconnaissance (TRG/TRS/TRW)	Reconnaissance (RG/RS/RW)
Tactical Reconnaissance Training Flight (TRTF)	Training Flight (TF)
Composite Group (COMPG)	Composite Group (CG)
Special Operations (SOG/SOS)	No change

As announced in the White Paper *Air Force Restructure* published in September 1991, Military Airlift Command (MAC), Strategic Air Command (SAC) and Tactical Air Command (TAC) were to be inactivated and replaced on 1 June 1992 by two new commands – Air Combat Command (ACC) and Air Mobility Command (AMC). Moreover, overseas commanders of Pacific Air Forces (PACAF) and US Air Forces in Europe (USAFE) were to command not only their traditional combat assets but also the tanker, theater airlift and reconnaissance assets stationed in their theaters (assets which previously remained resources of MAC, SAC and TAC).

Headquartered at Langley AFB, Virginia, ACC became on 1 June 1992 the gaining command for ANG flying units which had been previously TAC-gained. Headquartered at Scott AFB, Illinois, AMC became the new gaining command for most ANG airlift and transport units which had been previously gained by MAC and SAC. Headquartered at Hickam AFB, Hawaii, PACAF remained the gaining command for units of the Hawaii ANG but also gained the airlift, rescue and tanker units of the Alaska ANG which had been previously gained by MAC and SAC. Headquartered at Hurlburt Field, Florida, the Air Force Special Operations Command (AFSOC) – the USAF component of the United States Special Operations Command (USSOCOM) – remained the gaining command for the 193rd Special Operations Group, Pennsylvania ANG.

In addition to these changes resulting from the restructuring of the United States Air Force, changes occurring in the ANG during FY92 were the results of the following previously-approved aircraft conversions (including the phase-out of the last F-4Es and the phase-in of KC-135Rs) and mission changes.

Geoff LeBaron

René J. Francillon

Maj. Gen. Wayne C. Gatlin/MN ANG

State	Squadron	Mission Aircraft	
		From	To
CO ANG	120th FS	A-7D/K	F-16C/D
IA ANG	174th FS	A-7D/K	F-16C/D
ID ANG	190th TRS to 190th FS	RF-4C	F-4G
IL ANG	169th TASS TO 169th FS	OA-37B	F-16A/B ADF
IN ANG	113th FS	F-4E	F-16C/D
IN ANG	163rd FS	F-4E	F-16C/D
KY ANG	165th AS	C-130B	C-130H
MI ANG	107th FS	A-7D/K	F-16A/B
MI ANG	172nd TASS to 172nd FS	OA-37B	A-10A/OA-10A
MO ANG	110th FS	F-4E	F-15A/B
MS ANG	153rd TRS to 153rd ARS	RF-4C	KC-135R
NJ ANG	141st TFS to 141st ARS	F-4E	KC-135E
OH ANG	112th FS	A-7D/K	F-16C/D
OH ANG	145th ARS	KC-135E	KC-135R
PA ANG	146th TFS to 146th ARS	A-7D/K	KC-135E
SD ANG	175th FS	A-7D/K	F-16C/D
TN ANG	155th TAS to 155th AS	C-130A	C-141B
VA ANG	149th FS	A-7D/K	F-16C/D
WI ANG	126th ARS	KC-135E	KC-135R

OH ANG

Deliveries of KC-135Rs have continued the upgrading of the Guard tanker fleet. Ohio's 145th ARS (illustrated) and Wisconsin's 126th ARS were the first ANG recipients of the F108-powered Stratotanker. During the last decade of the 20th century, the number of ANG air refueling squadrons is expected to increase significantly as the Air Force reorganizes to meet the defense requirements of a changing world.

Particularly noteworthy was the accelerated phase-out of the A-7D as the reduction in force affecting active-duty components made late-model F-16C/Ds available to the Guard and rendered unnecessary plans to upgrade Corsair IIs to the A-7F configuration. Also of note was the assignment of additional tankers to the Guard as, much to the dismay of such long-time fighter squadrons as New Jersey's 141st, Ohio's 166th and Pennsylvania's 146th, the USAF sought to retain combat aircraft preferentially for its active-duty units and to transfer more tankers and transports to its reserve components.

Less significant changes occurring during FY92 included further modernization of the operational support fleet with the addition of C-26Bs and the reorganization of the airlift support detachments of the Colorado ANG and

District of Columbia ANG into the 200th Airlift Squadron (with four T-43As) and the 201st Airlift Squadron (with four C-21As and four C-22Bs). In addition, the C-26A assigned to the Texas ANG was fitted with a Westinghouse AN/APG-66 radar to evaluate its usefulness in the drug interdiction role; redesignated UC-26C, it was assigned on 15 June 1992 to OL-DI (Operating Location-Drug Interdiction) at Ellington Field.

Participation in the nation's drug interdiction campaign was not limited to the evaluation of the C-26C, as a discrete program saw F-16 ADF detachments operating regularly from Howard AFB, Panama. Little was said officially about this Sentry Nighthawk program but the Guard acknowledged the fact that in 1992 it provided all 216 interceptors assigned to the air defense of the United

States[59]. Obviously, with the importance of these interceptors bearing little resemblance to that of their Cold War forebears, the use of a few aircraft to keep track of unauthorized air traffic from the Guajira Peninsula in Colombia and other points in Latin America made much sense.

In addition to contributing 100 per cent of the interceptors assigned to the air defense of the United States, the Air National Guard provided during FY92 the following share of the Total Force:

Tactical reconnaissance	100.0%
Tactical airlift[60]	38.6%
Rescue[61]	32.4%
Tactical fighters	31.1%
Tactical air support	30.8%
KC-135 tankers	27.9%
Support aircraft[62]	26.5%
Strategic airlift	6.7%

Above: In recent years nose art has returned to the strategic fleet, a practice accelerated by the Gulf War. Many Guard tankers sport World War II-style artwork, this example being Utah ANG KC-135E 59-1489.

Below right: While the mission aircraft inventory has undergone a major re-equipment, so the support fleet has also been rejuvenated, principally with the ANG version of the Fairchild Swearingen Metro. This is a C-26B, serving with the New Mexico Guard.

Below: Flying along the Point Reyes National Seashore, north of San Francisco, an HH-60G of California's 129th Rescue Squadron takes on fuel from one of the unit's HC-130Ps during a May 1991 training sortie.

[59] Recent and announced changes in CONUS alert locations are the move of Det 1, 158th FIG, VT ANG, from Bangor IAP to Langley AFB on 1 October 1991; that of Det 1, 144th FW, CA ANG, from George AFB to March AFB on 15 June 1992; and that of Det 1, 102nd FW, MA ANG, from Loring AFB to Bangor IAP on 1 July 1993.

[60] In addition to routine airlift operations and regularly-scheduled operations from Panama during Volant Oak deployments, three squadrons (California's 115th, North Carolina's 156th, and Wyoming's 187th) have a secondary mission during the summer months when crews are kept available to operate two Hercules fitted with MAFFS (Modular Airborne Fire Fighting System) for fighting forest fires. Developed by FMC Corporation, MAFFS can be installed in a C-130 in less than two hours and enables Hercules to drop 3,000 US gal (11,355 liters) of fire retardant in six to eight seconds over an area 150 ft (45 m) wide and 2,000 ft (610 m) long. The fire retardant is discharged through two nozzles protruding from the C-130's open aft ramp. Typically, the fire retardant is dropped using push-over maneuvers initiated 150 to 200 ft (45 to 60 m) above a ridge at a speed of 110 to 140 kt (125 to 160 mph; 205 to 260 km/h).

[61] As of September 1992, the last day of FY92, the 102nd ARS/106th ARG and the 129th ARS/129th ARG had been credited respectively with having saved 254 and 214 lives since they were organized in 1975.

[62] AFSOC-gained, Pennsylvania's 193rd Special Operations Squadron at the Harrisburg IAP, is unique in being equipped with eight EC-130Es of two different models, neither of which is operated by other USAF units. The four 'Rivet Rider' aircraft have been permanently fitted with distinctive antennas and are used as radio and television airborne transmitters for psychological warfare operations, whereas the four 'Comfy Levi' aircraft have been modified to carry specially configured mission packages with tailored antennas and have 'back-end' crews provided by the Electronic Security Command as required for intelligence gathering and electronic countermeasures missions.

The Air National Guard at the end of FY92

At the end of FY92, flying components of the Air National Guard included 55 ACC-gained squadrons (51 with fighters and four with RF-4Cs), 38 AMC-gained squadrons (21 with airlifters, 15 with tankers and two with rescue aircraft), four PACAF-gained squadrons (one with C-130s, one with KC-135s, one with F-15s and one with HC-130s and HH-60s), and one AFSOC-gained squadron. (At the time of writing, the wing/group/squadron alignment resulting from recent conversions, changes of mission and assignment to new gaining commands was not expected to be finalized for several months. Hence, the last officially approved wing/group/squadron alignment, that prevailing on 30 September 1991, is shown on Table 11, whereas Table 16 lists flying units by gaining command and state as of 30 September 1992.)

In addition to mission aircraft equipping its 98

[63] Prior to receipt of the current types, the principal types of support aircraft assigned to state headquarters for transport and liaison duties had been successively the Beech C-45, the Douglas C-47 and C-54, and the Convair T-29 and C-131. Today, most states have a Beech C-12, Fairchild C-26 or Lockheed C-130 support aircraft, the exceptions being states in which tactical aircraft squadrons are based close to the state capital. States typically assign their dedicated support aircraft to the flying squadron closest to the state capital (e.g. the C-26A and C-26B of the California ANG are assigned to the 144th FIW in Fresno; in addition to flying the usual variety of state support missions, these aircraft are also used to ferry personnel between Fresno and March AFB where the 144th FIW has its Det 1 on alert).

[64] Late in 1978 Det 1, HQ CO ANG, received two T-43As to provide instruction and training on the principles of celestial, inertial, radar and radio navigation to cadets at the United States Air Force Academy in Colorado Springs. When not providing cadet training, the CO ANG's T-43As were to provide limited airlift support. In the mid-1980s, following the replacement of the T-43As with C-22Bs at Andrews AFB, Colorado's Det 1 doubled its T-43A inventory. On 15 March 1992, the 200th Airlift Squadron was activated at Buckley ANGB to take over personnel, aircraft, equipment and mission of Colorado's Det 1.

[65] Detachment 1 of the DC ANG was organized in February 1951 as Air Base Flight H and was initially attached to the Air Section of the District of Columbia National Guard. Based at Andrews AFB, Maryland, this flight was equipped at first with Douglas VB-26s, C-47s, and C-53s for transport/liaison duties and to enable Guard pilots assigned to the Pentagon and other administrative locations to maintain their flight qualifications; for the latter role, the flight also had North American F-51s on strength. Reassigned to the Headquarters of the District of Columbia ANG in November 1951 and given its Det 1 designation in June 1954, this unit has since flown a broad variety of aircraft – including Beech C-45s, L-23s, and U-8s; Boeing T-43s, Cessna LC-126s and U-3s; Convair C-131s and T-29s; de Havilland L-20s; Douglas C-54s; Hiller H-23s; Lockheed C-121s and T-33s; and North American T-39s and F-86s (the latter were the last fighters assigned to Det 1 and were phased out in 1958) – prior to receiving in the mid-1980s four Boeing C-22Bs and four Gates Learjet C-21As. The four C-22Bs, which are ex-National Airlines/Pan American 727-100 jetliners, were procured as replacement for transport-configured T-43As to carry inspection and training teams, as well as senior officers and distinguished visitors. Prior to being assigned to Det 1, DC ANG, these four aircraft were fitted with additional fuel tanks and a strengthened undercarriage. The C-21As, which are similar to Learjet Model 35A business jets, were purchased new in 1986. The detachment was elevated to squadron status with the activation of the 201st Airlift Squadron on 15 March 1992.

Bernard Thouanel

AFSOC-, ACC- or AMC-gained flying squadrons, the ANG has transport aircraft assigned in a support capacity to 39 of the 50 states, the Commonwealth of Puerto Rico[63], and two specialized squadrons, the 200th Airlift Squadron of the Colorado ANG[64], which primarily provides support for the Air Force Academy, and the 201st Airlift Squadron of the District of Columbia ANG[65], which mainly provides logistic support for the National Guard Bureau. (Assignments of support aircraft as of 30 September 1992 are shown on Table 13.)

Geoffrey Pearce/Aviagraphics

Above: The 199th Fighter Squadron, Hawaii ANG is a PACAF-gained unit, with a principal commitment to defend the island group. The unit converted from F-4Cs to F-15A/Bs in 1987.

Left: The tiger marking on the tail of this KC-135E of New Jersey's 141st ARS is a carryover from the days when the unit flew F-4Es with a similar marking on the nose. This unit was the first of several to make the transition from tactical missions to a tanker tasking in the 1990s. It has already attended its first NATO 'Tiger Meet' with the Stratotanker.

Left: During the third quarter of FY93 the sun will finally set on the RF-4Cs of the Idaho ANG, as its 189th Training Flight will dispose of its last recce Phantoms to concentrate on 'Wild Weasel' training.

ID ANG

Above: Photographed over the Winslow air refueling track in northern Arizona in May 1992, 70-1034, 75-0386 and 72-0225 were among the last flyable A-7Ds of the 188th Fighter Squadron. The New Mexico unit was about to convert to F-16C/Ds.

René J. Francillon

Aircrew training

Guard's aircrews flying missions and support aircraft are either former Air Force, Marine or Navy pilots, navigators, flight engineers, boom operators and loadmasters, or are trained for the Air National Guard by the Air Training Command with pilots going through the usual T-41/T-37/T-38 curriculum and navigators/WSOs receiving their training from the 323rd Flying Training Wing at Mather AFB, California[66]. As tabulated below, training on mission aircraft is provided either by replacement training units and combat training units operated by the Air National Guard or by active Air Force units, depending on the type of aircraft.

From Aircraft types	To Training unit
A-10/OA-10	ACC: 355th Wing, Davis-Monthan AFB, AZ
C-5	AMC: 443rd Airlift Wing, Altus AFB, OK
C-130	AR ANG: 154th Training Squadron, Little Rock AFB, AR
(Also trains USAF, AFRES, USCG, USMC, USN, and allied aircrews)	
HC-130	AMC: 542nd Crew Training Wing, Kirtland AFB, NM
KC-135	ACC: 93rd ARS, 93rd Wing, Castle AFB, CA
C-141	AMC: 443rd Airlift Wing, Altus AFB, OK
RF-4C/F-4G	ID ANG: 189th Training Flight, Gowen Field, Boise, ID
(Also trains USAF crews)	
F-15	ACC: 325th Fighter Wing, Tyndall AFB, FL
F-16A/B	AZ ANG: 148th Fighter Squadron, Tucson IAP, AZ
(Also trains USAF, AFRES, and KLu pilots)	
F-16C/D	KS ANG: 161st and 177th Fighter Squadrons, McConnell AFB, KS
(Also trains USAF and AFRES pilots)	
F-16 ADF	OR ANG: 114th Fighter Squadron, Kingsley Field, Klamath Falls, OR
HH-60	AMC: 542nd Crew Training Wing, Kirtland AFB, NM

Advanced combat training is provided for ANG, AFRES, USMC and NATO tactical airlift and special operations aircrews at the Advanced Airlift Tactics Training Center (AATTC) operated by the 139th Airlift Group, Missouri ANG, at the Rosecrans Memorial Airport in St Joseph.

ANG personnel

The majority of Air Guardsmen are traditional Guardsmen who, after receiving initial active-duty training/initial entry training (IADT/IET lasting a minimum of 72 days), fill 'drill positions' and are obligated to enlist for six years (if they have no prior military service), attend one unit training assembly (UTA or drill week-end) each month, and take part in 15 days of annual training (AT). The Air National Guard, however, would not function

Below: Another example of ANG tanker nose art, this time a KC-135D of the 168th ARS, Alaska ANG at Eielson AFB. The decorations of this unit naturally tend toward the unique wildlife and climate of the Last Frontier state.

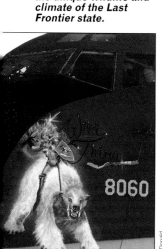

David Donald

[66] Every year during the late 1980s an average of 140 Guard pilots and 55 Guard navigators have earned their wings.

[67] Typically, full-time personnel account for about 20 to 25 percent of the total staffing. For example, at the end of FY89, the New York Air National Guard had 1,714 full-time staff and 6,567 drill positions.

without a large cadre of full-time personnel[67] falling into one of the following categories:

ANG Technicians (Air Techs) are full-time career Federal Civil Service employees of the Guard who provide day-to-day continuity and support (administration, maintenance, logistic, etc.) for their unit. Administrative control and supervision for ANG technicians is retained at the state level with the Adjutant General acting as the sole employing agent. Most ANG technicians are also regular members of their unit (as many as 95 per cent are military technicians) and as such have the same UTA and AT obligations as Guardsmen whose primary employment is outside the Guard (e.g. the majority of ANG aircrews work for airlines).

Active (duty) Guard/Reserve Personnel (AGRs) are Guardsmen on active duty who provide full-time support (administration, recruitment, training, active-duty missions including air defense and air refueling alert missions, etc.) for their unit or for various ANG organizations (such as the National Guard Bureau, State Headquarters, the ANG Support Center at Andrews AFB, the ANG Fighter Weapons Office in Tucson, replacement training units, the full-time recruiter force, and permanent field training sites and gunnery ranges, etc.).

Active Duty Component Personnel are Air Force officers and enlisted personnel assigned to Guard units as Air Force advisors.

ADT (Active Duty for Training) personnel are traditional Guardsmen who are temporarily placed on active duty for specific training purposes. This is notably the case of personnel receiving initial training (BMT – basic military training, or UPT – undergraduate pilot training) and of aircrews and maintenance personnel attending

**Above: The primary
mission of the 138th
Fighter Squadron is
close air support.
Having converted from
slow A-10As to swift
F-16As in 1989, the 'Boys
from Syracuse' now
proudly identify their
mission as 'Fastass
CAS'. The F-16s carry
conventional ordnance
underwing, and the
bulky 30-mm GPU-5/A
gun pod on the
centerline.**

**Left: A Galaxy for
Manhattan: a C-5A from
the 137th AS, 105th AG,
flies over New York
City on a crisp, clear
day. The New York
Guard heavylifters saw
much use during Desert
Shield/Storm.**

General Dynamics

schools when their unit converts to a new aircraft and/or a new mission.

Air Guardsmen can be mobilized by their state governors for short periods of state active duty (SAD), such as following natural disasters or during periods of unrest[68], and for usually longer periods of federal active duty (FAD) by the President or Congress. The President can either **(1)** call up to 200,000 members of the Selected Reserve (Reserve plus Guard) for up to 180 days without declaring a national emergency or **(2)** order up to one million Reservists and Guardsmen for up to 24 months after declaring a national emergency. Congress, after declaring war or a national emergency, can order all or portions of the Reserve forces for the duration of the war or emergency and for six months thereafter.

When units of the Air National Guard are called to active duty by the President, Guardsmen retain their ANG identity and their state continues to appoint the officers. Conversely, when units are ordered to active duty by the Presi-

René J. Francillon

dent or the Congress, Guardsmen lose their ANG identity and become members of the United States Air Force until released from federal active duty.

National Guard Bureau

The National Guard Bureau (NGB), which is located in the Pentagon, formulates and administers programs to ensure the continued development and maintenance of ARNG and ANG units. It is directed by the Chief and Vice Chief, National Guard Bureau, and the Director and Deputy Director of the Army National Guard and Air National Guard. These positions are filled by National Guard general officers serving on statutory tours. The Air Guard Directorate administers the personnel budget, facilities, training and equipment.

ANG funding

To support its many activities the Air National Guard, in addition to receiving substantial contributions from each of the 50 states, the District of Columbia, the Commonwealth of Puerto Rico, and the Territories of Guam and the Virgin Islands, relied during FY92 on four major federal sources as appropriated by the United States Congress. The largest of these, the Operation and Maintenance appropriation, us used to finance the recurring operation and maintenance of ANG organizations and facilities. The Military Personnel appropriation covers training, pay and allowances, while the Military Construction appropriation pays for major construction and facilities upgrading projects. Finally, Other Procurement funds are used for miscellaneous items of equipment. Total federal appropriations in FY92 amounted to over $3.7 billion, as follows:

Operation & Maintenance	$2,346,400,000
Military Personnel	1,148,500,000
Military Construction	217,260,000
Total	$3,712,160,000

Inflation and the expanding role assigned to the ANG have resulted over the past 10 years in a 68 per cent increase in total appropriations, and increases of 41, 140 and 260 per cent, respectively, in O&M, Personnel and Construction.

---

[68] During calendar year 1990, 23,795 ANG and ARNG personnel spent 210,786 mandays on SAD. They were involved in 313 support missions during which they provided assistance to authorities responding to several civil disturbances, 82 natural disasters, and 244 other situations.

B. Colin

Far left: Two hundred and seventy Block 15 ADFs have been reworked to ADF standard to equip the ANG's air defense units (apart from two equipped with F-15s). The squadrons are strategically positioned to encircle the nation, one link in the defensive chain being provided by the 136th FS at Niagara Falls, NY.

René J. Francillon

82-0926
Built as a F-16A-15K-CF, this Fighting Falcon was delivered to the 388th TFW at Hill AFB, Utah, on 28 July 1983. When the 388th TFW converted to F-16Cs, 82-0296 was earmarked to be upgraded to the ADF configuration by the OALC (Ogden Air Logistics Center at Hill AFB). After being modified, it went to the 178th FIS on 29 March 1990.

ADF recognition features
Three features are unique to the single-seat ADF version of the Fighting Falcon: the 150,000-candlepower night identification spotlight on the port side of the nose, the MK XII IFF antennas forward of the windshield and below the air intake, and the fairings over the relocated rudder servo actuators.

General Dynamics F-16A ADF
178th Fighter Squadron
119th Fighter Group
North Dakota ANG

The ADF (Air Defense Fighter) version of the Fighting Falcon was specially developed to provide the Air National Guard with replacements for the F-4Ds and F-106As equipping most of its fighter interceptor squadrons.

The 'Happy Hooligans'
The North Dakota Guardsmen have proudly carried this nickname ever since it was bestowed on them after a particularly boisterous annual training encampment. When TAC mandated that colorful markings be removed from tactical aircraft, North Dakota's State legislature came to the rescue and passed a resolution to enable the Fargo unit to retain its distinctive tail band.

Sparrow and AMRAAM
A key requirement for the ADF was the addition of medium-range missiles. To that end, the AN/APG-66 radar was modified to provide continuous wave illumination and an AIM-7F/M missile was to be carried on stations 3 and 7. Later, AIM-120A AMRAAMs are to be carried on stations 1, 2, 3, 7, 8, and 9 in lieu of the current mix of AIM-7/AIM-9s.

'Rough Riders'
During the Spanish-American War of 1898, then Lieutenant Colonel Theodore Roosevelt – soon to be the 26th President of the United States – led the 'Rough Riders' of the 1st Volunteer Cavalry Regiment in a gallant charge up San Juan Hill. Many of the 'Rough Riders' were Dakotans and Teddy Roosevelt had spent several years in western Dakota, hence his 'Rough Rider' portrait on the tail of 82-0926.

James Benson

Above: In ANG service, KC-135Es re-engined with airline-surplus JT3Ds have proved highly satisfactory, as their turbofans significantly improve safety, reduce pollution and increase the amount of fuel available for offloading. E models will remain with the Guard well into the next millenium.

Freedom has its price but, for the US taxpayer, the Air National Guard is, without a doubt, one of the most cost-effective insurance policies to preserve the freedom made possible back on 19 April 1775 when the 'minute men' of the Lexington Company, Massachusetts Volunteer Militia, 'fired the shot heard 'round the world'.

Forthcoming changes

Announced aircraft conversions, which will see the last A-7D/Ks being phased out and night-capable F-16C/Ds phased in, and mission changes which have been programmed for FY93 and FY94 are as follows:

State	Squadron	Mission Aircraft From	To
CT ANG	118th FS	A-10A	F-16C/D
HI ANG	New unit	none	KC-135R
IA ANG	124th FS	A-7D/K	F-16C/D
MA ANG	131st FS	A-10A	F-16C/D
MD ANG	104th FS	A-10A	A-10A/0A-10A
NM ANG	188th FS	A-7D/K	F-16C/D
OH ANG	162nd FS	A-7D/K	F-16C/D
OH ANG	166th FS to 166th ARS	A-7D/K	KC-135R
OK ANG	125th FS	A-7D/K	F-16C/D
PR ANG	198th FS	A-7D/K	F-16A/B ADF
WI ANG	176th FS	A-10A	F-16C/D

Other announced changes include the award in September 1992 of a contract for 20 C-130Hs with which to replace the C-130Bs equipping North Carolina's 156th AS and Wyoming's 187th AS, the closure of Rickenbacker ANGB during FY94, and the resulting relocation of Ohio's two KC-135R units to Wright-Patterson AFB.

It is quite likely that in coming years deeper cuts will be made in the military budget and the force structure. Fortunately, for the time being, the Air National Guard has not been requested to inactivate flying units. Quite to the contrary, the ANG is proceeding with the planned activation during the second quarter of FY93 of a KC-135R tanker unit in Hawaii.

Regardless of changes which might be implemented in the future, it is certain that the United States will continue to rely for much of its defense on citizen soldiers of the Army National Guard and their flying brethren of the Air National Guard.

Above: Support of Arctic installations is entrusted to the 139th Airlift Squadron, New York ANG, for which it operates ski-equipped LC-130Hs.

Right: Aircraft 91-1231, the 2,000th Hercules built by Lockheed, was delivered to the 165th AS, Kentucky ANG, at Standiford Field on 16 May 1992. In common with Air Mobility Command practice, the 'Herks' are receiving an all-over gray scheme.

Charles W. Arrington

As active-duty F-16 units convert to night attack Block 40/50 aircraft, so the Block 30 F-16C/Ds are cascaded to Guard units, joining existing F-16A/B users. As far as tactical assets are concerned, the ANG is moving towards a single-type force, F-16A Air Defense Fighters complementing the battlefield ground attack machines. This cavorting pair is from Ohio's 112th FS 'Stingers', one of a crop of units to convert in 1992.

General Dynamics

The Air National Guard of the Several States

Brief historical synopses covering each of the flying squadrons which are serving, or have served, in the Air National Guard are arranged by states and complement the first part of this book which relates the history of the ANG from the national point of view.

For ease of reference, Table 17 cross-indexes squadron numbers with the corresponding wings, groups and states. Table 18 lists current groups and wings in numerical sequence and gives the corresponding squadrons and states.

Alabama Air National Guard

Alabama became the seventh state to have a federally-recognized Guard aviation unit when the 135th Squadron was activated in Birmingham in January 1922. Successively redesignated 114th and 106th Observation Squadron, that unit went on FAD in November 1940 and, as the 100th Bombardment Squadron (Medium), flew B-25s in combat in the Pacific from January 1944 until the end of World War II. Postwar, the unit was reorganized in the Alabama NG as the 106th Bombardment Squadron (Light) and the 160th FS was federally recognized in October 1947.

At the end of FY92, 3,169 officers and enlisted personnel manned 32 AL ANG units, including the 106th RS flying RF-4Cs from the Birmingham IAP and the 160th FS flying F-16A/Bs from Dannelly Field in Montgomery.

106th Reconnaissance Squadron
117th Reconnaissance Wing

Lineage: *Organized at Kelly Field, TX, as the 106th Aero Squadron on 27 August 1917, this Air Service unit moved to France in January 1918, was redesignated 800th Aero Squadron on 1 February 1918, served as an Artillery Aerial Observation School with the AEF in France, and was demobilized between May and July 1919. In 1936, its lineage and honors were consolidated with those of the Alabama NG unit which had been activated in January 1922 as the 135th Squadron.*
21 Jan 1922: 135th Squadron extended federal recognition at Roberts Field, Birmingham, as a Corps Aviation unit in the Alabama NG.
25 Jan 1923: Redesignated 135th

Observation Squadron.
1 May 1923: Redesignated 114th OS as aviation unit in the 39th Division.
16 Jan 1924: Redesignated 106th OS as aviation unit in the 31st Division.
1922-1940: Initially equipped with **Curtiss Jennies**, the Alabama NG squadron was equipped over the years with the mix of aircraft typical of prewar Guard units, including **Consolidated PT-1s** and **O-17s; Curtiss O-11s; Dayton-Wright TW-3s; Douglas BT-1s, O-2s** and **O-38s;** and **North American O-47s** and **BC-1s.**
25 Nov 1940: Called to active duty and placed under the command of the Fourth Corps Area. Initially remaining at Fort Sumpter Smith in Birmingham, the 106th OS had one **BC-1A**, one **O-38B** and nine **O-47A/Bs** on 31 December 1940.
World War II: Moving to Miami, FL, in December 1941, the unit remained in the United States until October 1943 but changed stations eight times, was

redesignated on four occasions, flew ASW patrols over the Caribbean and trained in preparation for overseas deployment. As the 100th BS (Medium) it was assigned to the 42nd BG, Thirteenth Air Force, with which it flew combat operations with **North American B-25s** in the South and Southwest Pacific between January 1944 and VJ Day. Inactivated at Camp Stoneman, CA, on 11 December 1945, it was redesignated 106th BS (Light) and allotted back to the Alabama NG on 24 May 1946.
25 Nov 1946: 106th BS (Light) extended federal recognition at the Birmingham MAP (Sumpter Smith Field) and equipped with **Douglas A-26B/Cs** (plus support aircraft).
1 Feb 1951: Redesignated 106th TRS (Night-Photo) and equipped with **Douglas RB-26Cs.**
1 Apr 1951: Called to active duty as part of the Korean War call-up.

5 Jan 1952: Transferred to Shaw AFB, SC, and assigned to CONAC.
9 Jan 1952: Redesignated 106th TRS and assigned to the 118th TRG (TAC).
1 Jan 1953: Returned to state control at the Birmingham MAP as part of the 117th TRG.
1 May 1957: Redesignated 106th TRS (Photo Jet) and converted from RB-26Cs to **Republic RF-84Fs.**
1 Jul 1960: Became TAC-gained upon implementation of gaining command concept.
1 Oct 1961: Called to active duty as part of the Berlin Crisis call-up.
Nov 1961: Transferred to Dreux AB, France, and assigned to the 7117th TRW, USAFE.
20 Aug 1962: Relieved of active duty.

A Republic RF-84F-10-RE (51-1882) of the 106th Tactical Reconnaissance Squadron, 117th Tactical Reconnaissance Group.

and returned to state control at the Birmingham MAP (Sumpter Smith ANGB).

15 Oct 1962: Reached group status with federal recognition of the 117th TRG.

1963-1964: Exercise Poncho: Using air refueling, 10 RF-84Fs deployed non-stop to Puerto Rico. Exercise Minutemen Alpha: Using air refueling, 12 RF-84Fs deployed non-stop to Alaska. Exercise Ready-Go: Using air refueling, 12 RF-84Fs deployed non-stop to Europe.

Feb 1971: Converted from RF-84Fs to McDonnell RF-4Cs.

9 Dec 1974: 117th TRG inactivated and 106th TRS placed directly under the control of the 117th TRW.

1987: Became the first ANG unit equipped with the KS-127 Long-Range Oblique Photography (LOROP) system.

24 Aug 1990: Volunteers deployed to Bahrain's Sheikh Isa AB with six LOROP-equipped RF-4Cs and attached to the 35th TFW (Provisional) as part of Operation Desert Shield.

18 Dec 1990: Volunteers relieved by activated personnel from the Nevada ANG. RF-4Cs left in Bahrain to be flown by crews from the 192nd TRS.

15 Mar 1992: Unit designation changed to 106th Reconnaissance Squadron, 117th Reconnaissance Wing.

1 Jun 1992: As part of the Air Force restructuring program, gaining command changed to ACC.

64-1044 of the 106th TRS at NAS Fallon, NV, during Photo Derby '84. Major Barry K. Henderson and Lieutenant Colonel Stephen G. Schramm were killed when this RF-4C-22-MC crashed in Saudi Arabia on 8 October 1990.

160th Fighter Squadron
187th Fighter Group

1 Oct 1947: 160th FS (SE) extended federal recognition at the Birmingham MAP (Sumpter Smith Field) and equipped with **North American P-51Ds** (plus support aircraft).

10 Oct 1950: Called to active duty as part of the Korean War call-up.

Nov 1950: Redesignated 160th TRS, transferred to Lawson AFB, GA, and equipped with RF-51Ds.

Jul 1951: Redesignated 160th TRS (Photo Jet) and converted from RF-51Ds to Lockheed RF-80As.

Jan 1952: Deployed to Europe and temporarily stationed at Fürstenfeldbrück AB and Neubiberg AB, Germany, pending completion of facilities at Toul-Rosières AB, France.

1 Jan 1953: 160th TRS returned to state control to be reorganized at Dannelly Field, Montgomery, and again equipped with RF-51Ds.

Jun 1955: Converted from RF-51Ds to RF-80As.

May 1956: Converted from RF-80As to Republic RF-84Fs.

1 Jul 1960: Became TAC-gained upon implementation of gaining command concept.

1 Oct 1961: Called to active duty as part of the Berlin Crisis call-up but

In March 1990, 18 months after completing its conversion to F-16As, the 160th Tactical Fighter Squadron was back at Nellis AFB, NV, to take part in Red Flag 90-3. Alabama's 160th FS will fly F16s for the rest of the decade.

remained based at Dannelly Field.

20 Aug 1962: Released from active duty.

15 Oct 1962: Reached group status with federal recognition of 187th TRG.

Jun 1971: Converted from RF-84Fs to McDonnell RF-4Cs.

1 Jul 1983: Redesignated 160th TFS, 187th TFG, and converted from RF-4Cs to F-4Ds.

1 Oct 1988: Completed conversion from F-4Ds to **General Dynamics F-16A/Bs**.

15 Mar 1992: Unit designation changed to 160th Fighter Squadron, 187th Fighter Group (160th FS, 187th FG).

1 Jun 1992: As part of the Air Force restructuring program, gaining command changed to ACC.

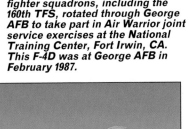

Below: During the 1980s ANG fighter squadrons, including the 160th TFS, rotated through George AFB to take part in Air Warrior joint service exercises at the National Training Center, Fort Irwin, CA. This F-4D was at George AFB in February 1987.

Alaska Air National Guard

For a few months in 1990, the organizational structure of the Alaska ANG was without equivalent in the Air National Guard. A single group, the 176th Composite Group at Kulis ANGS, supported three flying squadrons having different missions (air refueling, air rescue and tactical airlift), based at two different locations (Kulis ANGS in Anchorage and Eielson AFB southeast of Fairbanks), and gained by two major Commands (MAC and SAC). That situation changed with the activation on 1 July 1990 of the 168th AREFG, and the transfer of the 168th AREFS from the 176th COMPG to the new group.

The first Alaskan unit, the 8144th Air Base Squadron, was allotted in February 1952 and was organized in September 1952, more than six years before Alaska became the 49th state in the union. Its first

aircraft were North American T-6Gs, but these trainers were supplemented by Lockheed F-80Cs soon after the 144th Fighter-Bomber Squadron received federal recognition on 1 July 1959 as the first operational unit in the Territory of Alaska ANG. By the time Alaska achieved statehood on 3 January 1959, the squadron had been reorganized as a transport unit and was flying Douglas C-47As. The 144th has remained a transport unit ever since, but was joined as a flying component of the 176th Composite Group by the 168th Air Refueling Squadron, in October 1986, and by the 210th Air Rescue Squadron, in April 1990.

At the end of FY92, 1,720 officers and enlisted personnel manned 24 AK ANG units, including the 144th AS and 210th RQS at the Anchorage IAP and the 168th ARS at Eielson AFB.

Alaska ANG

144th Airlift Squadron
176th Composite Group

15 Sep 1952: 8144th Air Base Squadron constituted at Elmendorf AFB as first unit of the Territory of Alaska ANG. Shortly afterward, the 8144th ABS received a **North American T-6G**, the first aircraft assigned to the Alaska Guard.
1 Jul 1953: 144th FBS extended federal recognition at Elmendorf AFB and equipped with **Lockheed F-80Cs.**
1 Jul 1955: Redesignated 144th FIS upon converting to **North American F-86Es** and being transferred to Kulis ANGS at the Anchorage IAP.
1 Jul 1957: Redesignated 144th ATS (Light) upon converting to **Douglas C-47As.**
1 Jul 1960: Became AAC-gained upon

implementation of gaining command.
1 Dec 1960: Redesignated 144th ATS (Medium) upon converting to ski-equipped **Fairchild C-123Js.**
1 Apr 1969: Reached group status with federal recognition of the 176th TAG, squadron redesignated 144th TAS.
1 Dec 1974: Became MAC-gained upon transfer of tactical airlift resources from other commands to MAC.

Below: Kulis ANGS, home of the 144th Airlift Squadron, 176th Composite Group, and its C-130Hs, is located on the edge of the Anchorage International Airport.

FY76: Converted from C-123Js to Lockheed C-130Es.
FY85: Converted from C-130Es to C-130Hs.
1 Oct 1986: Group redesignated 176th COMPG upon activation of the 168th AREFS.
Aug 1990: Volunteers began flying missions in support of Operation Desert Shield.
15 Mar 1992: Unit designation changed to 144th Airlift Squadron, 176th Composite Group (144th AS, 176th CG).
1 Jun 192: As part of the Air Force restructuring program, gaining command changed to PACAF.

Above: A ski-equipped Fairchild C-123J of the 144th TAS at the Anchorage IAP. This Alaska squadron was the only ANG unit to be equipped with Providers and flew this piston-cum-turbojet aircraft for almost 16 years.

Below: When it converted from C-130Es to C-130Hs during FY85, the 144th TAS was issued eight consecutively numbered aircraft, 82-0054 through 82-0061. Flying the State of Alaska flag, 82-0057 was photographed at the Reno-Stead Airport.

168th Air Refueling Squadron
168th Air Refueling Group

Lineage: *When in 1986 the Alaska ANG was authorized to organize an air refueling squadron, that unit was given the numerical designation of the 168th Fighter Interceptor Squadron, which had*

been inactivated as an Illinois ANG unit on 31 May 1958.
1 Oct 1986: 168th AREFS extended federal recognition at Eielson AFB as an SAC-gained unit and, initially equipped with four **Boeing KC-135Es**, was assigned to the 176th COMPG based at Kulis ANGS.
1 Jul 1990: 168th AREFG activated at

Eielson AFB as new parent organization for the 168th AREFS. The number of assigned tankers has been doubled and now includes four KC-135Es and four KC-135Ds which have been re-engined with TF33-P-102 turbofans.
Aug 1990: Volunteers began flying missions in support of Operation Desert Shield.

15 Mar 1992: Unit abbreviation changed to 168th ARS, 168th ARG.
1 Jun 1992: As part of the Air Force restructuring program, gaining command changed to PACAF.

Only four air-refuelable KC-135D tankers were built. 63-8060 'Wild Thing' serves with the 168th ARS.

210th Rescue Squadron
176th Composite Group

D. Donald

Lineage: *Nicknamed 'The second 10th', the 210th ARS has been bestowed the lineage and honors history of the 10th ARS, an active-duty squadron organized at Elmendorf Field in 1946 and mostly manned by Alaskans. Expanded into the 10th Air Rescue Group on 4 November 1952, this Alaskan Air Command unit pioneered Arctic search and rescue techniques prior to its deactivation on 8 January 1958.*

Upon being activated as the 10th Rescue Squadron, the 10th had itself inherited the tradition of the 924th Quartermaster Company, Boat (Aviation), a rescue unit which had been constituted in Alaska on 14 June 1942, saw action during the Aleutian Island Campaign, was redesignated the 10th Emergency Rescue Boat Squadron on 3 July 1944, and was deactivated on 8 March 1946.

Above: Extended federal recognition on 4 April 1990, the 210th Air Rescue Squadron was the lucky recipient of brand new tankers and helicopters, including four HH-60Gs (88-26105/88-26107 and 88-26109). For operations in Alaska, the HH-60Gs are fitted with skis.

Right: The first of two HC-130H(N)s, 88-2101 and 88-2102, for the 210th Air Rescue Squadron was handed over at the Lockheed plant in Marietta, Georgia, on 15 October 1990.

4 Apr 1990: 210th ARS extended federal recognition at the Anchorage IAP, as an MAC-gained unit, but not yet equipped with helicopters and tankers.
6 Jul 1990: First of four Sikorsky MH-60Gs accepted at Kulis ANGB.
15 Oct 1990: First of three Lockheed HC-130H(N)s delivered to Kulis ANGB.
Fall 1991: MH-60G designation

D. Donald

changed to HH-60G.
15 Mar 1992: Unit designation changed to 210th Rescue Squadron, 176th Composite Group (210th RQS,

176th CG).
1 Jun 1992: As part of the Air Force restructuring program, gaining command changed to PACAF.

Arizona Air National Guard

Starting with a single unit, the 197th FS which was federally recognized in December 1946, the Arizona ANG has grown into a four-squadron force. The second of these squadrons, the 152nd FIS, was activated in May 1956 and served between September 1969 and July 1979 as a replacement training unit. Two specialized RTUs were organized in February 1984 (195th TFTS) and October 1985 (148th TFTS).

At the end of FY92, 3,032 officers and enlisted personnel manned 28 AZ ANG units, including the 197th ARS flying KC-135Es from the Sky Harbor IAP in Phoenix and the 148th, 152nd and 195th FSs flying F-16A/Bs from Tucson. Since January 1990, the 148th TFTS has been training F-16 pilots not only for other ANG squadrons but also for the Royal Netherlands Air Force.

148th Fighter Squadron
162nd Fighter Group

Lineage: *When in 1985 the Arizona ANG was authorized to organize a replacement training unit to train F-16 pilots for the Guard, the new squadron was given the numerical designation of the 148th F-BS, which had been*

inactivated as a Pennsylvania ANG unit on 31 October 1957.
15 Oct 1985: 148th TFTS extended federal recognition at the Tucson IAP as a TAC-gained unit and equipped with F-16A/Bs.
Jan 1990: Added 14 F-16A/Bs (four from US inventory and 10 from the Netherlands) and five Dutch instructors, as activities were expanded to include training of F-16 pilots for the Royal Netherlands Air Force (Koninklijke Luchtmacht or KLu).
15 Mar 1992: Unit designation changed to 148th Fighter Squadron, 162nd Fighter Group (148th FS, 162nd FG).
1 Jun 1992: As part of the Air Force restructuring program, gaining command changed to ACC.

Tucson International Airport, 6 May 1989: An F-16B of Arizona's 148th TFTS shares the Guard ramp with A-7s of the 162nd TFG. The 148th FS now also trains Dutch F-16 pilots.

Chris Jacquet

101

Arizona ANG

Fighting Falcons entered service with the Arizona ANG at the end of 1985 when F-16As and F-16Bs were delivered to the 148th Tactical Fighter Training Squadron which had been activated on 15 October 1985 to function as a F-16 replacement training unit for the Guard. Arizona's good flying weather, uncongested airspace, and proximity to the 2.7-million acre Barry M. Goldwater Bombing and Gunnery Range are valuable assets for the tactical training unit.

152nd Fighter Squadron 162nd Fighter Group

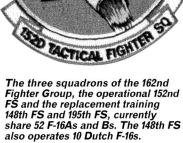

Lineage: *When in 1956 the Arizona ANG was authorized to organize a new FIS, this unit was given the numerical designation of the 152nd FIS, which had been inactivated as a Rhode Island ANG unit on 19 November 1955.*

18 May 1956: 152nd FIS extended federal recognition at the Tucson IAP and equipped with North American F-86As.

Jun 1957: Converted from F-86As to Republic F-84Fs.

25 May 1958: Reached group status with federal recognition of 162nd FIG.

May 1958: Converted from F-84Fs to North American F-100As.

1 Jul 1960: Became ADC-gained upon implementation of gaining command concept.

Early 1966: Converted from F-100As to Convair F/TF-102As (first received in Feb 1966).

Summer 1969: Converted from F/TF-102As (last left on 16 September 1969) to North American F-100C/Fs.

16 Sep 1969: Redesignated 152nd TFTS, 162nd TFTG, assigned responsibility for training F-100 pilots for the ANG and added F-100F two-seat trainers, and became TAC-gained.

Jun 1972: Converted from F-100Cs to F-100Ds, but retained F-100Fs.

Jul 1975: Unit notified that it would

The three squadrons of the 162nd Fighter Group, the operational 152nd FS and the replacement training 148th FS and 195th FS, currently share 52 F-16As and Bs. The 148th FS also operates 10 Dutch F-16s.

also train A-7D pilots for the ANG.
FY76: A-7Ds added to F-100D/Fs.
Jan 1977: First A-7D classes began.
Mar 1978: Last F-100D/Fs phased out.
24 Jul 1979: Redesignated 152nd TFS, 162nd TFG, but continued functioning as the A-7 RTU.
FY81: A-7Ks added to A-7D.
FY84: Function as A-7 RTU transferred to the co-located 195th TFTS, which received federal recognition on 1 Feb

Chris Jacquet

1984.
Mar 1986: Began conversion from A-7D/Ks to General Dynamics F-16A/Bs.
15 Mar 1992: Unit designation changed to 152nd Fighter Squadron, 162nd Fighter Group (152nd FS, 162nd FG).
1 Jun 1992: As part of the Air Force restructuring program, gaining command changed to ACC.

Below: 56-0981, a Convair F-102A-55-CO of the Tucson IAP-based 152nd FIS, photographed at nearby Davis-Monthan AFB on 16 March 1969. The 152nd Fighter Interceptor Squadron converted from F-100As during FY66 and received its first Delta Dagger in February 1966. It disposed of its last 'Deuce' in September 1969.

195th Fighter Squadron
162nd Fighter Group

Lineage: *When in 1984 the Arizona ANG was authorized to organize a replacement training unit to train A-7D pilots for the Guard, the new squadron was given the numerical designation of the 195th TAS, which had been inactivated as a California ANG unit on 30 September 1974.*

1 Feb 1984: 195th TFTS extended federal recognition at the Tucson IAP as a TAC-gained unit and equipped with A-7D/Ks.

1990-1991: Inventory of A-7D/Ks reduced progressively as requirement for training A-7 pilots diminished. Conversion to F-16A/Bs was completed during FY91 and A-7D/K operations ended on 26 July 1991.

15 Mar 1992: Unit designation changed to 195th Fighter Squadron,

162nd Fighter Group (195th FS, 162nd FG).

1 Jun 1992: As part of the Air Force restructuring program, gaining command changed to ACC.

The 195th TFTS was federally recognized in February 1984 as an A-7 Replacement Training Unit. A-7 operations ended in July 1991 and the 195th FS now trains F-16 pilots.

197th Air Refueling Squadron
161st Air Refueling Group

Lineage: *Constituted in May 1943 and activated at Westover Field, MA, on 15 August 1943, the 412th FS was assigned to the 373rd FG, Ninth Air Force. Successively based in England, Belgium, Holland and Germany, it flew Republic P-47Ds in combat between May 1944 and May 1945. Inactivated at Mitchel Field, NY, on 7 November 1945, the unit was reconstituted as the 197th FS and was allotted to the Arizona NG on 24 May 1946.*

12 Dec 1946: 197th FS (SE) extended federal recognition at Luke Field and, beginning during the summer of 1947, equipped with North American F-51Ds (plus support aircraft).

Winter 1950: Converted from F-51Ds to Republic F-84Bs.

1 Feb 1951: Called to active duty as part of the Korean War call-up but remained at Luke AFB to serve as a component of the 127th Pilot Training Wing (with F-84E/Gs later supplementing and finally supplanting the initially assigned F-84B/Cs).

1 Nov 1952: Returned to state control to be reorganized at the Sky Harbor Airport in Phoenix as the 197th FBS and equipped with F-51D/Hs.

1 Mar 1954: Redesignated 197th FIS.

Mar 1954: Converted from F-51D/Hs to

The 'Copperheads' of the 197th Fighter-Bomber Squadron flew F-51Hs (including 44-64455) and F-51Ds after being returned to state control in November 1952.

North American F-86As.

2 Oct 1957: Reached group status with federal recognition of the 161st FIG.

Jun 1958: Converted from F-86As to F-86Ls.

Jul 1960: Converted from F-86Ls to Lockheed F-104A/Bs.

1 Jul 1960: Became ADC-gained upon implementation of gaining command concept.

1 Nov 1961: Called to active duty as part of the Berlin Crisis call-up.

Nov 1961: F-104A/Bs, pilots, and maintenance and support personnel airlifted to Ramstein AB, Germany, for assignment to USAFE.

15 Aug 1962: Returned to state control but F-104A/Bs retained by Air Force.

Sep 1962: First Boeing C-97Gs arrived

to commence conversion process.

1 Oct 1962: Redesignated 197th ATS and became MATS-gained.

1 Jan 1966: Redesignated 197th MAS and became MAC-gained following MATS redesignation.

16 Aug 1968: Redesignated 197th Aeromedical Evacuation Squadron.

1 Dec 1969: Redesignated 197th MAS.

1 Aug 1972: Redesignated 197th AREFS, became TAC-gained, and equipped with KC-97Ls.

1 Jul 1976: Gaining command changed from TAC to SAC.

Oct 1977: Converted from KC-97Ls to Boeing KC-135As.

26 Jul 1982: Received first ANG KC-135E and converted from KC-135As to KC-135Es.

Aug 1990: Volunteers began flying missions in support of Operation Desert Shield.

20 Dec 1990: Called to active duty as part of Operation Desert Shield call-up.

15 May 1991: Released from active duty after taking part in Desert Shield/Desert Storm.

15 Mar 1992: Unit abbreviation changed to 197th ARS, 161st ARG.

1 Jun 1992: As part of the Air Force restructuring program, gaining command changed to AMC.

The Phoenix-based 197th became an air refueling squadron in August 1972. Since then, it has successively flown KC-97Ls, KC-135As and KC-135Es.

Arkansas Air National Guard

Organized in October 1925 and placed on FAD in September 1940, the 154th Observation Squadron served with distinction in North Africa and Italy from November 1942 until the end of World War II. Reconstituted in August 1946 as the 154th FS and based at Little Rock AFB since October 1962, the 154th TS currently serves as the C-130 RTU for the Air National Guard.

The second flying unit in the Arkansas ANG was organized after the Korean War as the 184th TRS and became a tactical fighter squadron in June 1972. The 184th FS currently flies F-16A/Bs from Fort Smith MAP.

At the end of FY92, 2,237 officers and enlisted personnel manned 31 AR ANG units, including the above-mentioned two flying squadrons.

154th Training Squadron
189th Airlift Group

Lineage: *Organized at Kelly Field, TX, on 8 December 1917 as the 154th Aero Squadron, Air Service, this repair and maintenance unit moved to England in March 1918 and to France in September 1918. It was demobilized at Garden City, NY, on 1 February 1919. In 1936, its lineage and honors were consolidated with those of the Arkansas NG unit which had been activated in October 1925.*

24 Oct 1925: 154th OS extended federal recognition at the Little Rock Airport as a Corps Aviation unit and initially equipped with **Curtiss JN-4** and JN-6 trainers.

1925-1940: Remaining based in Little Rock, the 154th OS was equipped over the years with the mix of aircraft typical of prewar Guard units, including **Consolidated PT-1s; Douglas BT-1s, O-2s and O-38s; and North American BC-1s and O-47s.**

16 Sep 1940: Called to active duty and placed under command of Eighth Corps Area.

World War II: Moved to Post Field, OK, in September 1940, the 154th OS had one BC-1A, two O-38Es and 10 O-47A/Bs on 31 December 1940. Thereafter, the unit moved four times within CONUS and flew ASW patrols over the Gulf of Mexico before deploying to North Africa, via the UK, in November 1942. Equipped with **Douglas A-20s,** the 154th OS briefly flew ASW patrols along the Moroccan coast. It then flew **Bell P-39s and North American P-51s** on tactical reconnaissance missions in Algeria and Tunisia until May 1943, served as a fighter training unit in Algeria between June 1943 and January 1944, and was redesignated 154th Weather Reconnaissance Squadron (Medium).

AR ANG

Equipped with **Lockheed P-38Js** and assigned to the Fifteenth Air Force, the 154th WRS flew weather reconnaissance sorties from Bari, Italy, until VE Day. Inactivated at Drew Field, FL, on 12 December 1945, the squadron was designated 154th FS and allotted back to the Arkansas NG on 24 May 1946.

23 Aug 1946: 154th FS (SE) extended federal recognition at Adams Field, Little Rock, and equipped with **North American P-51Ds** (plus support aircraft).

10 Oct 1950: Called to active duty,

Based at Little Rock AFB, Arkansas' 154th TATS became the Guard's C-130 replacement training unit in October 1986. This is a C-130E photographed at Reno.

redesignated 154th F-BS, and moved to Langley AFB, VA, within two weeks.

Mar 1951: Converted from F-51Ds to Republic F-84Es.

Jul 1951: Moved to Itazuke AB, Japan.

Aug 1951-Jul 1952: Combat operations with F-84Es from Itazuke AB and Taegu AB (K-2), Korea.

10 Jul 1952: Returned to state control to be reorganized as 154th TRS and equipped with **RF-51Ds** at Adams Field.

Dec 1954: Converted from RF-51Ds to Lockheed RF-80As.

1 Jan 1955: Redesignated 154th TRS (Photo Jet).

May 1957: Converted from RF-80As to Republic RF-84Fs.

Feb 1958: Converted from RF-84Fs to Martin RB-57A/B/Es.

1 Jul 1960: Became TAC-gained upon

The sheer beauty of smoothly cowled Rolls-Royce Merlin engines: North American P-51D Mustangs of the 154th Fighter Squadron (SE) at Little Rock, Arkansas, in 1947.

implementation of gaining command concept.

15 Oct 1962: Reached group status with federal recognition of 189th TRG. Permanent change of station from Adams Field to Little Rock AFB.

Jul 1965: Converted from RB-57s to McDonnell RF-101G/Hs.

26 Jan 1968: Called to active duty and soon moved to Richards-Gebaur AFB, MO. TDY deployments to Howard AFB, Panama, and deployment to Itazuke AB, Japan (24 Jul – 18 Nov 1968).

20 Dec 1968: Returned to state control at Little Rock AFB.

FY72: Converted from RF-101G/Hs to RF-101Cs.

1 Jan 1976: Redesignated 154th AREFS as a SAC-gained unit and converted from RF-101Cs to **Boeing KC-135As.**

FY84: Converted from KC-135As to KC-135Es.

1 Oct 1986: Redesignated 154th TATS/189th TAG, became MAC-gained, and was equipped with **Lockheed C-130Es** to serve as the ANG C-130 RTU.

15 Mar 1992: Unit designation changed to 154th Training Squadron, 189th Airlift Group (154th TS, 189th AG).

1 Jun 1992: As part of the Air Force restructuring program, gaining command changed to AMC.

Peter B. Lewis

184th Fighter Squadron
188th Fighter Group

Peter B. Lewis

15 Oct 1953: 184th TRS (Night Photo) extended federal recognition at the Ft Smith Municipal Airport and soon equipped with **Douglas RB-26Cs** (plus support aircraft).
Jun 1956: Converted from RB-26Cs to Lockheed RF-80As.
1 Jan 1957: Redesignated 184th TRS (Photo Jet), with the 'Photo Jet' soon being dropped from the designation.
Jan 1957: Converted from RF-80As to Republic RF-84Fs.
1 Jul 1960: Became TAC-gained upon implementation of gaining command concept.
1 Oct 1961: Called to active duty but remained in Ft Smith.
20 Aug 1962: Returned to state control.
15 Oct 1962: Reached group status with federal recognition of the 188th TRG.
Dec 1970: Converted from RF-84Fs to McDonnell RF-101Cs.
Spring/Summer 1972: Converted from RF-101Cs to North American F-100D/Fs.
15 Jun 1972: Redesignated 184th TFS/188th TFG.

Above: Republic RF-84F-40-RE Thunderflash (53-7605) of the 184th Tactical Reconnaissance Squadron at McClellan AFB, California, on 3 March 1969.

Right: The flagship of the 188th Tactical Fighter Group, complete with the unit's 'Flying Razorbacks' nickname and razorback insignia incorporated in a shooting star on the fin. The nickname comes from the pride Arkansans take in their skill at hunting sharp-ridged wild hogs in the Ozarks.

Summer 1979: Converted from F-100D/Fs to McDonnell F-4Cs.
1 Apr 1989: Completed conversion from F-4Cs to General Dynamics F-16A/Bs.
15 Mar 1992: Unit designation

changed to 184th Fighter Squadron, 188th Fighter Group (184th FS, 188th FG).

1 Jun 1992: As part of the Air Force restructuring program, gaining command changed to ACC.

California Air National Guard

After two inconclusive attempts at organizing aviation units in its National Guard (in 1911) and Naval Militia (in 1915), California gained its first Guard squadron in June 1924 when the 115th Observation Squadron was activated in Santa Monica. That squadron was placed on FAD in March 1941 and, as the 115th Liaison Squadron, flew combat operations in India during the last year of World War II.

In the immediate postwar period, California was allotted four squadrons, the reconstituted 115th and the 194th, 195th and 196th: the last-mentioned unit becoming in January 1948 the first ANG squadron to be equipped with jet fighters). A fifth squadron, the 129th Air Resupply Squadron, was federally recognized in April 1955 to take the place of the 194th FIS in the San Francisco Bay area when the fighter squadron was transferred to Fresno to operate jets in a less noise-sensitive area. (The newly constituted 129th Air Resupply

Squadron was the first ANG unit to be assigned transport aircraft; in May 1975 it became the first Guard unit to be given the search and rescue mission and to fly helicopters.)

Although the 195th TAS was inactivated in September 1974 to eliminate some duplication of personnel with the collocated 115th TAS, the California ANG retained most of its capability as the 115th TAS was reorganized as an augmented squadron and was assigned twice the normal number of C-130s.

At the end of FY92, 5,588 officers and enlisted personnel manned 64 CA ANG units, including four flying squadrons: the 115th AS flying C-130Es from the Channel Islands ANGS, the 129th RQS flying HC-130H/Ps and HH-60Gs from NAS Moffett Field, the 194th FS flying F-16A/B ADFs from the Fresno Air Terminal MAP, and the 196th RS flying RF-4Cs from March AFB.

115th Airlift Squadron
146th Airlift Wing

Lineage: *Organized at Kelly Field, TX, on 29 August 1917 as the 116th Aero Squadron, this Air Service unit moved to France in December 1917. It was redesignated 636th Aero Squadron on 1 February 1918, constructed facilities and engaged in supply and related base-support activities for the AEF, and was demobilized at Garden City, NY, on 8 April 1919. In 1936, its lineage and honors were consolidated with those of the California NG unit which had been activated in June 1924.*
16 Jun 1924: 115th OS extended federal recognition at Clover Field, Santa Monica, as the aviation unit of the 40th Division, California NG, and initially equipped with **Curtiss JN-4H** trainers.
Jan 1925: 115th OS relocated to Griffith Field, Los Angeles.

The California grizzly bear had been part of the 115th Squadron's insignia since 1924, and is seen here on a B-26C in August 1950.

William T. Larkins

California ANG

1925-1940: Remaining based at Griffith Field, the 115th OS was equipped over the years with the mix of aircraft typical of prewar Guard units, including **Consolidated PT-1s** and **O-17s; Dayton-Wright TW-3s; Douglas BT-1s, O-2s** and **O-38s;** and **North American BC-1s** and **O-47s.** On 31 December 1940, it had one BC-1A, three O-38B/Es and six O-47A/Bs.

3 Mar 1941: Called to active duty and assigned to III Army Corps; 10 days later moved to Paso Robles, CA.

World War II: Between March 1941 and September 1944, the unit remained in the United States, changed station seven times, was redesignated on three occasions, flew ASW along the California coast (and flew covert sorties along the coast of Baja California after it had been alleged that Japan had built submarine pens in Mexico), and trained in preparation for overseas deployment. As the 115th Liaison Squadron, the unit moved to India in the fall of 1944 and flew **Stinson L-1s** and **L-5s** (and finally **Piper L-4s**) in support of the Tenth and Fourteenth Air Forces until VJ Day. It was inactivated at Ft Lewis, WA, on 23 December 1945, and was allotted to the California NG on 24 May 1946 after being redesignated the 115th BS.

8 Oct 1946: 115th BS (Light) extended federal recognition at the Van Nuys Airport and equipped with **Douglas A-26B/Cs** (plus support aircraft).

1 Apr 1948: Relocated to the Lockheed Air Terminal in Burbank.

1 Apr 1951: Called to active duty as part of the Korean War call-up and soon after transferred to Langley AFB, VA, where it became part of the 47th BG.

Sep 1951: Converted from B-26B/Cs to **North American B-45As.**

Feb 1952: Redesignated 4430th CCTS and, still based at Langley AFB, re-equipped with B-26B/Cs.

1 Jan 1953: Returned to state control to be organized at the Van Nuys Airport as the 115th FBS with North American F-51D/Hs.

Feb 1955: Converted from F-51D/Hs to North American F-86As.

1 Jul 1955: Redesignated 115th FIS.

10 Dec 1958: Redesignated 115th TFS.

15 Jan 1960: Redesignated 115th ATS and converted from F-86As to **Boeing C-97A/Gs.**

1 Jul 1960: Became MATS-gained upon implementation of gaining command concept.

1 Oct 1961: Called to active duty as part of the Berlin Crisis call-up to conduct worldwide airlift missions from its base in Van Nuys.

1 Sep 1963: Returned to state control.

1 Jan 1966: Redesignated 115th MAS and became MAC-gained following MATS redesignation.

11 Apr 1970: Redesignated 115th TAS and became TAC-gained.

Apr 1970: Converted from C-97A/Gs to Lockheed C-130As.

Jul 1971: Conducted operational testing of the Modular Airborne Fire-Fighting System (MAFFS) at Edwards AFB. Initially the nozzles through which the fire retardant mixture was dispensed protruded through the parachute doors on both sides of the aft fuselage. Later, they protruded from the partially open aft cargo ramp.

Spring 1974: C-130As supplemented by C-130Bs.

1 Dec 1974: Became MAC-gained upon transfer of tactical airlift resources from TAC to MAC.

9 Feb 1975: 146th TAG inactivated and 115th TAS placed directly under the control of the 146th TAW.

FY75: Mix of C-130A/Bs replaced by C-130B/Es.

FY81: C-130Bs phased out.

Dec 1988: Began operations from new

René J. Francillon

Flying over farmland near Oxnard, 62-1181 approaches runway 21 at NAS Point Mugu at mid-day on 31 August 1989. The 115th TAS completed its move to brand new facilities at Channel Islands ANGS, on the edge of NAS Point Mugu, in September 1990.

facilities at Channel Island ANGS.

Dec 1989: Participated in Operation Just Cause in Panama.

Aug 1990: Volunteers began flying missions in support of Operation Desert Shield.

Sep 1990: Move from Van Nuys to Channel Island ANGS completed.

15 Mar 1992: Unit designation changed to 115th Airlift Squadron, 146th Airlift Group (115th AS, 146th AG).

1 Jun 1992: As part of the Air Force restructuring program, gaining command changed to AMC.

129th Rescue Squadron
129th Rescue Group

Lineage: *When in 1955 the California ANG was authorized to organize a new squadron to replace its 194th FIS at the Hayward Municipal Airport, the new unit was given the numerical designation of the 129th SRS (Medium), an ANG-manned unit which had been activated during the Korean War in August 1951 and had been assigned to the 111th SRW to serve alongside a Pennsylvania ANG squadron, the 103rd. The 129th SRS was inactivated on 1 January 1953 after the PA ANG unit was returned to state control.*

3 Apr 1955: 129th Air Resupply Squadron extended federal recognition at the Hayward MAP and equipped with Curtiss C-46Ds.

Summer 1956: C-46Ds supplemented by Grumman SA-16As.

FY58: C-46Ds phased out.

1 Nov 1958: Redesignated 129th Troop Carrier Squadron (Medium).

1 Jul 1960: Became TAC-gained upon implementation of gaining command concept.

20 Jan 1962: Reached group status with federal recognition of the 129th Troop Carrier Group.

Early 1963: HU-16As supplemented with Helio U-10As.

Jul 1963: Converted from HU-16As to Fairchild C-119Cs but U-10As retained.

1 Jul 1963: Redesignated 129th ACS.

1966-1967: U-10As temporarily replaced with de Havilland Canada U-6As.

1 Aug 1968: Redesignated 129th SOS.

FY68: Converted from C-119Cs to C-119Gs.

FY73: Converted from C-119Gs to C-119Ls.

Feb 1974: Plans to deactivate the 129th SOS in mid-1975 were announced but were later countermanded.

3 May 1975: Redesignated 129th AR&RS, converted from C-119Ls and U-10As to Lockheed HC-130H/Ps and Sikorsky HH/CH-3Es, and became MAC-gained.

1 May 1980: Permanent change of station from the Hayward Air Terminal to NAS Moffett Field.

1 Oct 1989: Redesignated 129th ARS.

Fall 1990: Converted from HH-3Es to Sikorsky MH-60Gs but HC-130H/Ps retained.

Fall 1991: MH-60G designation changed to HH-60G.

15 Mar 1992: Unit designation changed to 129th Rescue Squadron, 129th Rescue Group (129th RQS, 129th RQG).

1 Jun 1992: As part of the Air Force restructuring program, gaining command changed to AMC.

1 Jan 1993: Unit scheduled to become ACC-gained.

Peter B. Lewis

Above: While flying C-119s, the 129th was successively a troop carrier unit, an air commando unit and a special operations unit. This is a C-119G of the 129th SOS.

Below: To commence training on Pave Hawks prior to receipt of its own HH-60Gs, the 129th Air Rescue Squadron borrowed 88-26107 from Alaska's 210th ARS.

René J. Francillon

A pair of HH-60Gs from the 129th Air Rescue Squadron prepares to refuel from one of the squadron's HC-130Ps during a training sortie over fog-shrouded San Francisco Bay on 29 May 1991. As this book was going to press, it was announced that the unit would switch from AMC-gained to ACC-gained status on 1 January 1993.

René J. Francillon

194th Fighter Squadron
144th Fighter Wing

Lineage: *Constituted in October 1943 and activated at Hamilton Field, CA, on 15 October 1943, the 409th FS, 372nd FG, Fourth Air Force, served in the ZI as a Bell P-39, Curtiss P-40 and North American P-51 replacement training unit until its inactivation at Alexandria AAFld, LA, on 7 November 1945. Reconstituted and redesignated 194th FS, the unit was allotted to the California NG on 24 May 1946.*

2 Jun 1948: Utility Flight, 194th FS (SE) extended federal recognition at the Oakland Airport and equipped with support aircraft (North American T-6s and Douglas B-26s).
2 Mar 1949: 194th FS (SE) extended federal recognition at the Hayward Airport and equipped with North American F-51Ds.
Summer 1952: F-51Ds supplemented with F-51Hs.
1 Oct 1952: Redesignated 194th FIS.
15 Dec 1952: Redesignated 194th FBS.
1 Mar 1953-30 Jun 1953: Maintained two F-51Ds on alert from sunrise to

The 144th FIW (144th FW since 15 March 1992) has traditionally been tasked with maintaining and flying California's support aircraft. These have included this VC-131D photographed on 25 Oct 1984.

sunset as part of an experimental program to determine feasibility of augmenting active ADC units with ANG squadrons.
Jun 1953: 194th FBS pilots flew North American F-86As during USAF Worldwide Gunnery Meet at Nellis AFB, NV.
Sep 1954: Received first Lockheed T-33A jet trainers.
1 Nov 1954: 194th FBS moved to the Fresno Air Terminal and converted from F-51D/Hs to North American F-86As.
1 Jul 1955: Redesignated 194th FIS.
7 Apr 1956: 194th FIG extended federal recognition.
Apr 1958: Converted from F-86As to F-86Ls.

1 Jul 1960: Became ADC-gained upon implementation of gaining command concept.
Jul 1964: Converted from F-86Ls to Convair F/TF-102As.
Jan 1970: Ferried 20 F/TF-102As from Hahn AB, Germany, to Fresno as part of Coronet East.
Summer 1974: Converted from F/TF-102As (last left in Jul 1974) to Convair F-106A/Bs.
9 Jul 1976: 194th FIG inactivated and 194th FIS placed directly under the control of the 144th FIW.
1 Apr 1980: Became TAC-gained following ADC inactivation.
Sep 1980: Won William Tell '80 competition.

When aviation units were again organized in the National Guard following the end of World War II, all received North American AT-6s (redesignated T-6s in June 1948) along with their mission aircraft. This T-6G of the 194th FS was photographed in July 1951.

Winter 1984: Converted from F-106A/Bs (last F-106A flown out on 18

The 194th Fighter Interceptor Squadron flew F-86Ls between April 1958 and July 1964. 53-0947 was photographed at the Military Aircraft Storage & Disposition Center in May 1965.

William T. Larkins

Peter B. Lewis

Peter B. Lewis

Above: Bearing the griffin markings of the 194th FIS on its fin, this two-seat 'Deuce' was photographed in May 1966.

René J. Francillon

Right: Flying training intercept sorties against an ECM-configured Learjet of Flight International is a pair of F-16A ADFs of the 194th FS.

Jan 1984) to McDonnell F-4Ds.
Apr 1986-Apr 1987: Provided aircraft and personnel to Operation Creek Klaxon, the ANG's assumption of air defense commitment at Ramstein AB, Germany, while the 86th TFW, USAFE, was converting to F-16C/Ds.
Oct 1989: Completed conversion from F-4Ds to General Dynamics F-16A/B ADFs.

15 Mar 1992: Unit designation changed to 194th Fighter Squadron, 144th Fighter Wing (194th FS, 144th FW).
1 Jun 1992: As part of the Air Force restructuring program, gaining command changed to ACC.
15 Jun 1992: Det 1 alert relocated from George AFB, CA, to March AFB, CA.

195th Tactical Airlift Squadron
195th Tactical Airlift Group

Lineage: *Constituted in May 1943 and activated at Westover Field, MA, on 15 August 1943, the 410th FS was assigned to the 373rd FG, Ninth Air Force. Successively based in England, Belgium, Holland and Germany, it flew Republic P-47Ds in combat between May 1944 and May 1945. Inactivated at Mitchel Field, NY, on 7 November 1945, the unit was reconstituted as the 195th FS and was allotted to the California NG on 24 May 1946.*

29 Sep 1946: 195th FS (SE) extended federal recognition at the Van Nuys Airport, and equipped with North American P-51Ds (plus support aircraft).
1 Mar 1951: Called to active duty as part of the Korean War call-up but remained based in Van Nuys.
Oct 1952: F-51Ds supplemented by F-51Hs.
1 Dec 1952: 195th FBS returned to state control.
Mar 1954: Redesignated 195th FIS and converted from F-51D/Hs to North American F-86As.

15 Jan 1960: Redesignated 195th ATS and converted from F-86As to Boeing C-97A/Gs.
1 Jul 1960: Became MATS-gained upon implementation of gaining command concept.
1 Oct 1961: Called to active duty as part of the Berlin Crisis call-up to conduct worldwide airlift missions from its base in Van Nuys.
1 Sep 1963: Returned to state control.
1 Jan 1966: Redesignated 195th MAS and became MAC-gained following MATS redesignation.

11 Apr 1970: Redesignated 195th TAS and became TAC-gained.
Apr 1970: Converted from C-97A/Gs to Lockheed C-130As.
Spring 1974: C-130As supplemented with C-130Bs.
30 Sep 1974: 195th TAS inactivated at the Van Nuys Airport.

The 195th Air Transport Squadron came into being in January 1960 when the Van Nuys-based 195th FIS traded its F-86As and took on the transport mission.

USAF

196th Reconnaissance Squadron
163rd Reconnaissance Group

Lineage: *Constituted in May 1943 and activated at Westover Field, MA, on 15 August 1943, the 411th FS was assigned to the 373rd FG, Ninth Air Force. Successively based in England, Belgium, Holland and Germany, it flew Republic P-47Ds in combat between May 1944 and May 1945. Inactivated at Mitchel Field, NY, on 7 November 1945, the unit was reconstituted as the 196th FS and was allotted to the California NG on 24 May 1946.*
9 Nov 1946: 196th FS (SE) extended federal recognition at the San Bernardino

Concern over noise pollution plus anti-military feelings forced the 196th FIS to trade its 'Deuce' for FAC-configured O-2As in 1975.

CA ANG

Air Materiel Area (SBAMA) and initially equipped with two **North American T-6s** and two **Stinson L-5s**.
Feb 1947: Equipped with **North American P-51Ds** and support aircraft.
Jun 1948: Converted from F-51Ds to Lockheed F-80Cs.
16 Jun 1948: Redesignated 196th FS (Jet) as the ANG's first jet fighter unit.
Mar 1950: San Bernardino Air Materiel Area renamed Norton AFB.
10 Oct 1950: Called to active duty as part of the Korean War call-up.
1 Nov 1950: Redesignated 196th FBS and moved to George AFB, CA.
Jan-Jun 1951: Several F-80Cs, their pilots and support personnel sent TDY to Eniwetok to provide air defense during Operation Greenhouse nuclear tests.
Apr 1951: Converted from F-80Cs to Republic F-84Es.
Jul 1951: 196th FBS and other squadrons from the 116th FBW moved to Japan.
25 Jul 1951: 196th FBS arrived at Misawa AB, Japan.
Aug 1951-Jul 1952: While at Misawa AB, the 116th FBW rotated one of its squadrons to Chitose AB, to provide air defense for northern Japan (beginning on 1 Sep 1951 with the 196th FBS), and to Taegu AB (K-2) to combat operations in Korea (beginning on 30 Nov 1951 with the 159th FBS). Beginning in Feb 1952, the three squadrons of the 116th FBW also trained in the new air-refueling technique and flew four High Tide combat missions with F-84Es fitted with tip-tank-mounted refueling probe.
10 Jul 1952: Returned to state control at the Ontario International Airport but not immediately activated.
Oct 1952: 196th FIS re-equipped with North American F-51Hs.
1 Jan 1953: Redesignated 196th FBS.
Mar 1954: Redesignated 196th FIS and

Convair F-102A-75-CO (56-1391) of the 196th Fighter Interceptor Squadron. The Ontario-based unit flew 'Deuces' between May 1965, when it converted from F-86Ls, and March 1975, when it was re-equipped.

began conversion from F-51Hs to North American F-86As.
12 May 1958: Reached group status with federal recognition of 163rd FIG.
1 Jul 1960: Became ADC-gained upon implementation of gaining command concept.
Feb 1961: Converted from F-86As to F-86Ls.
May 1965: Converted from F-86Ls to Convair F/TF-102As.

8 Mar 1975: Redesignated 196th TASS, converted from F/TF-102As to Cessna O-2As, and became TAC-gained.
Summer 1982: Permanent change of station from the Ontario International Airport to March AFB.
1 Oct 1982: Redesignated 196th TFS and converted from O-2As to McDonnell F-4Cs.
Spring 1987: Converted from F-4Cs to F-4Es.

Spring 1990: Converted from F-4Es to RF-4Cs.
1 Jul 1990: Redesignated 196th TRS.
15 Mar 1992: Unit designation changed to 196th Reconnaissance Squadron, 163rd Reconnaissance Group (196th RS, 163rd RG).
1 Jun 1992: As part of the Air Force restructuring program, gaining command changed to ACC.
FY94: Scheduled to convert from RF-4Cs to Boeing KC-135Es and to become an AMC-gained air refueling unit.

Equipped with F-4Es, the 196th TFS was to have converted to OA-10As in 1990 but instead received RF-4Cs, including 66-0444 photographed at Hill AFB, Utah, in April 1991, and was redesignated the 196th TRS.

Colorado Air National Guard

The sole flying unit in the Colorado Guard was activated in June 1923 and has remained based in the Denver area except during four periods of federal active duty. During World War II, the Colorado unit remained stateside. Allotted once again to Colorado, the 120th FS on 30 June 1946 became the first Guard flying unit to receive federal recognition after World War II.

Once again activated during the Korean War and the Berlin Crisis, the unit served in CONUS (when a substantial number of its pilots were transferred to active units for service overseas), whereas its activation as the result of the *Pueblo* Crisis saw it flying combat operations in Vietnam.

At the end of FY92, 1,601 officers and enlisted personnel manned 20 CO ANG units, including the 120th FS and the 200th AS which respectively fly F-16C/Ds and T-43As from the Buckley ANGB in Aurora.

120th Fighter Squadron
140th Fighter Wing

Lineage: *Organized at Kelly Field, TX, on 28 August 1917 as the 120th Aero Squadron, this Air Service unit moved to England in March 1918 and to France in September 1918 to undertake aircraft maintenance for the AEF. It was demobilized at Mitchel Field, NY, on 17 May 1919. In 1936, its lineage and honors were consolidated with those of the Colorado NG unit which had been activated in June 1923.*
27 Jun 1923: 120th OS extended federal recognition at Lowry Field, Denver, as the aviation unit of the 45th Division, Colorado NG, and equipped with **Curtiss JNS-E** trainers beginning in

May 1924.
1924-1940: Remaining based in the Denver area (initially with a flight operating from Pueblo where the lower elevation was more suitable for aircraft

operations) but moving from Lowry Field to the Denver Municipal Airport in 1938, the 120th OS was equipped over the years with the mix of aircraft typical of prewar Guard units, including

The F-80Cs of the 'Minute Men', the ANG official precision flying team, were flown by Coloradans of the 120th FIS between 1953 and 1958.

Colorado ANG

Consolidated PT-1s and O-17s; Douglas BT-1s and O-38s; North American O-47s and BC-1s; and Thomas-Morse O-19s. In February 1939 the 120th OS was transferred from the 45th Infantry Division to the 24th Cavalry Division. On 31 December 1940, it had one BC-1A and eight O-47A/Bs.
6 Jan 1941: Called to active duty and placed under the command of the Third Army, the 120th OS was moved to Biggs Field, TX, during the following month to fly patrols along the Mexican border.
World War II: Remaining based in the United States and providing close air support for training ground troops, the unit changed stations five times and was redesignated on four occasions before being disbanded at the Birmingham AAFld, AL, on 30 November 1943. Redesignated 120th FS, it was allotted back to the Colorado NG on 24 May 1946, and less than six weeks later became the first Guard squadron to receive federal recognition after World War II.
30 Jun 1946: 120th FS (SE) extended federal recognition at Buckley Field, Aurora, and equipped with North American P-51Ds (plus support aircraft).
1 Oct 1946: 140th FG extended federal recognition.
1 Nov 1950: 140th FW extended federal recognition.
1 Apr 1951: Called to active duty as

part of the Korean War call-up.
12 Apr 1951: Redesignated 120th FBS and moved to Clovis AFB, NM.
1 Jan 1953: Returned to state control at Buckley Field.
Jul 1953: Converted from F-51Ds to Lockheed F-80Cs.
1 Jul 1955: Redesignated 120th FIS.
Fall 1956: 'Minute Men' precision aerial flying team designated by NGB as the official ANG team.
Early 1958: Converted from F-80Cs to North American F-86Es.
1960: Converted from F-86Es to F-86Ls.
1 Jul 1960: Became ADC-gained upon implementation of gaining command concept.
1 Jan 1961: Redesignated 120th TFS,

began conversion from F-86Ls to North American F-100C/Fs, and became TAC-gained.
1 Oct 1961: Called to active duty as part of Berlin Crisis call-up but remained based at Buckley ANGB.
24 Aug 1962: Returned to state control.
26 Jan 1968: Called to active duty as part of the *Pueblo* Crisis call-up.
3 May 1968: Arrived at Phan Rang AB, Vietnam, with F-100Cs.
8 May 1968: First sorties flown over South Vietnam (Colorado Guardsmen went on to fly 5,905 combat sorties in 11 months).
30 Apr 1969: Returned to state control at Buckley ANGB.
Oct 1971: Converted from F-100C/Fs to F-100D/Fs.
Apr 1974: Converted from F-100D/Fs to LTV A-7Ds.
9 Dec 1974: 140th TFG inactivated and 120th TFS placed directly under the control of the 140th TFW.
Oct 1981: Won Gunsmoke '81 competition.
FY92: Converted from A-7D/Ks to General Dynamics Block 30 F-16C/Ds (first F-16C received on 28 Aug 1991 and last A-7D left on 5 Feb 1992).
15 Mar 1992: Unit designation changed to 120th Fighter Squadron,

Left: 86-0339, a three-year-old F-16C-30E-CF, was among the first Fighting Falcons delivered to the 120th Fighter Squadron when it converted from A-7Ds to F-16Cs.

Back from flying combat operations from Phan Rang AB in Vietnam, F-100C-15-NA (54-1836) was photographed at Buckley ANGB in July 1971. While on federal active duty, the Coloradans flew 5,905 combat sorties in Southeast Asia, losing four F-100Cs. Two pilots were reported MIA and one was killed in action.

140th Fighter Wing (120th FS, 140th FW).
1 Jun 1992: As part of the Air Force restructuring program, gaining command changed to ACC.
11 Sep 1992: Completed conversion to F-16C/Ds.

Below: Flying Corsair IIs between April 1974 and the summer of 1991, Colorado's 120th TFS gained notoriety in October 1981 when it won the first Gunsmoke competition at Nellis AFB and one of its pilot, Lieutenant Colonel Wayne Schultz, took the 'Top Gun' trophy.

200th Airlift Squadron
140th Fighter Wing

Lineage: *Detachment 1, HQ Colorado CO ANG, was organized at the end of 1978 and was initially assigned two T-43As to provide instruction and training on the principles of celestial, inertial, radar and radio navigation to cadets at the United States Air Force Academy in Colorado Springs. When not used for cadet training, the T-43As provided limited airlift support. In the mid-1980s, Det 1 doubled its T-43A inventory.*
15 Mar 1992: Det 1, HQ Colorado ANG redesignated 200th Airlift Squadron without change of station, equipment, or mission.

Boeing T-43As were first delivered to the Headquarters, 140th Tactical Fighter Wing, at the end of 1978 to enable the Colorado ANG to provide celestial, inertial, radar and radio navigation instruction to cadets at the Air Force Academy in Colorado Springs. This detachment was elevated to squadron status with the activation on 15 March 1992 of the 200th Airlift Squadron. The 200th AS is currently assigned four T-43As and has recently adopted an all-white scheme with thin cheat-line and 'United States of America' titles.

Connecticut Air National Guard

The 'Flying Yankees' were organized in Connecticut in November 1923 after the state of Rhode Island, to which the 118th Squadron had been allotted, was unable to provide facilities for the flying unit of the 43rd Division. During World War II, the 118th TRS flew fighter and recce combat missions in the CBI theater of operations from

February 1944 until the Japanese surrender.

Reorganized as the 118th FS after the war, the Connecticut flying unit has flown fighter aircraft ever since, and provided air defense for the New York/New England area during its Korean War activation. In early 1991 the 118th TFS continued to fly A-10As with which it has been equipped since 1979.

At the end of FY92, 1,275 officers and enlisted personnel manned 13 CT ANG units, including the 118th TFS which was converting to F-16C/Ds at Bradley ANGS in Windsor Locks.

118th Fighter Squadron
103rd Fighter Group

Peter B. Lewis

Lineage: *Organized at Kelly Field, TX, on 31 August 1917 as the 118th Aero Squadron, this Air Service unit moved to France in January 1918. It was redesignated 639th Aero Squadron on 1 February 1918, constructed facilities and engaged in supply and related base-support activities for the AEF, and was demobilized at Mitchel Field, NY, on 6 June 1919. In 1936, its lineage and honors were consolidated with those of the 118th OS, which had been allotted to the Rhode Island NG but was activated as a Connecticut NG unit in November 1923.*

1 Nov 1923: 118th OS extended federal recognition at Brainart Field, Hartford, as the aviation unit of the 43rd Division, Connecticut NG, and initially equipped with **Curtiss Jennies.**
1923-1940: Remaining based in Hartford, the 118th OS was equipped over the years with the mix of aircraft typical of prewar Guard units, including **Consolidated PT-1s** and **O-17s; Curtiss XO-12s; Dayton-Wright TW-3s; Douglas BT-1s, O-2s, O-38s** and **O-46s;** and **North American O-47s** and **BC-1s.** On 31 December 1940, it had one BC-1A, seven O-46As and three O-47As.
24 Feb 1941: Called to active duty and placed under command of IV Army Corps. Moved to Jacksonville, FL, three

Above: Convair F-102A-70-COs, formerly operated by the 118th FIS, at MASDC, Davis-Monthan AFB in May 1974.

weeks later.
World War II: Remaining based in CONUS until December 1943, the squadron moved seven times, was redesignated on four occasions, flew ASW patrols over the Caribbean and trained as a reconnaissance unit prior to deployment overseas. As the 118th TRS, it arrived in February 1944 in India, where it flew North American P-51s on air-defense patrols for four months. Attached to the 23rd FG, Fourteenth Air Force, the 118th TRS flew North American P-51s and F-6s in combat from June 1944 until VJ Day. Inactivated at Camp Kilner, NJ, on 7 November 1945, the unit was redesignated 118th FS and was allotted back to the Connecticut NG on 24 May 1946.
7 Aug 1946: 118th FS (SE) extended federal recognition at Bradley Field, Windsor Locks, and equipped with **Republic P-47Ns** (plus support aircraft).
28 Sep 1950: Redesignated 118th FIS.
1 Feb 1951: Called to active duty as part of the Korean War call-up and transferred to Suffolk County AFB, NY, to provide air defense for the New York/ New England area.
1 Dec 1952: Returned to state control to be reorganized as the 118th FBS with **North American F-51Hs.**

Jan 1953: Converted from F-51Hs to Republic F-84Ds.
Spring 1956: Converted from F-84Ds to Lockheed F-94Bs.
1 May 1956: Redesignated 118th FIS.
Fall 1957: Converted from F-94Bs to North American F-86Hs.
30 Nov 1957: Redesignated 118th TFS.
1 Jul 1960: Became TAC-gained upon implementation of gaining command concept.
Summer 1960: Converted from F-86Hs to North American F-100As.
1 Sep 1960: Redesignated 118th FIS and became ADC-gained.
Jan 1966: Converted from F-100As to Convair F/TF-102As.
Spring/Summer 1971: Converted from F/TF-102As (last left on 11 June 1971) to North American F-100D/Fs.

Over the past 10 years, the 118th TFS has been a regular participant in Gunsmoke competitions. 78-0615 was photographed on the approach to Nellis AFB returning from a Gunsmoke '87 sortie.

12 Jun 1971: Redesignated 118th TFS and became TAC-gained.
Summer 1979: Converted from F-100D/Fs to **Fairchild Republic A-10As.**
15 Mar 1992: Unit designation changed to 118th Fighter Squadron, 103rd Fighter Group (118th FS, 103rd FG).
1 Jun 1992: As part of the Air Force restructuring program, gaining command changed to ACC.
FY93: Scheduled to convert from A-10As **to General Dynamics Block 25 F-16C/Ds.**

Delaware Air National Guard

Extended federal recognition in September 1946, the sole Delaware flying unit flew fighter aircraft until 1961 and provided air defense for the mid-Atlantic area during its Korean War activation. Equipped with C-97 transports, the 142nd Tactical Airlift Squadron was on federal active duty during the Berlin Crisis. It converted to C-130As

in 1971 and to its current C-130Hs in 1985.

At the end of FY92, 969 officers and enlisted personnel manned 15 DE ANG units, including the 142nd AS at the New Castle County Airport in Wilmington.

Peter B. Lewis

142nd Airlift Squadron
166th Airlift Group

Lineage: *Constituted and activated at Mitchel Field, New York, in September 1942, the 342nd FS was assigned to the 348th FG, Fifth Air Force, with which it flew combat operations with Republic P-47Ds in the Southwest Pacific theater beginning in July 1943. Re-equipped with North American P-51Ds in January 1945, it was inactivated in Japan in May 1946. Reconstituted and redesignated the 142nd FS, the unit was allotted to the Delaware NG on 24 May 1946.*
6 Sep 1946: 142nd FS (SE) extended federal recognition at the New Castle County Airport and, beginning in Feb

Upon converting from F-86Hs to C-97s, the Delaware ANG's squadron was redesignated the 142nd Air Transport Squadron (Heavy) in April 1962. This Delaware C-97G was photographed at MASDC in May 1971.

1947, equipped with **Republic P-47Ns** (plus support aircraft).
Feb 1950: Converted from F-47Ns to Republic F-84Cs.
1 Feb 1951: Called to active duty as part of the Korean War call-up but retained at its home base to provide air defense for the mid-Atlantic states.
17 May 1951: Redesignated 142nd FIS.
Sep 1951: Converted from F-84Cs to Lockheed F-94Bs.

Above: P-47N-25-RE of the 142nd FS (SE). As the P-47N only entered service toward the end of World War II, the postwar Guard became the primary operator.

Below: C-130Hs of the 142nd TAS at the New Castle County Airport in Wilmington on 27 June 1990. Two months later, volunteers began flying in support of Desert Shield.

1 Dec 1952: Returned to state control to be reorganized as the 142nd FBS and equipped with **North American F-51Hs**.
Mar 1954: Converted from F-51Hs to North American **F-86As**.
Winter 1955: Converted from F-86As to **F-86Es**.
Summer 1956: Converted from F-86Es to **F-86Hs**.
10 Nov 1958: Redesignated 142nd TFS.
1 Jul 1960: Became TAC-gained upon implementation of gaining command concept.
Jun 1961: New Castle County Airport renamed Greater Wilmington Airport.
Spring 1962: Converted from F-86Hs to **Boeing C-97F/Gs**.
7 Apr 1962: Reached group status with federal recognition of 166th ATG, squadron redesignated 142nd ATS (Heavy), and became MATS-gained.
1 Jan 1966: Redesignated 142nd MAS and became MAC-gained following

MATS redesignation.
Spring 1971: Converted from C-97F/Gs to **Lockheed C-130As**.
12 May 1971: Redesignated 142nd TAS and became TAC-gained.
1 Dec 1974: Became MAC-gained upon transfer of tactical airlift resources from TAC to MAC.
Oct 1985: First C-130H received.
28 Feb 1987: Completed conversion from C-130As to C-130Hs.
Dec 1989: Participated in Operation Just Cause in Panama.
Aug 1990: Volunteers began flying missions in support of Operation Desert Shield.
22 Jan 1991: Called to active duty as part of Operation Desert Storm call-up.
30 Jun 1991: Released from active duty after taking part in Desert Storm.
15 Mar 1992: Unit designation changed to 142nd Airlift Squadron, 166th Airlift Group (142nd AS, 166th AG).
1 Jun 1992: As part of the Air Force restructuring program, gaining command changed to AMC.

District of Columbia Air National Guard

Unlike the several states, the District of Columbia does not have a governor. Hence, its ARNG and ANG units come directly under the Commanding General of the District of Columbia.

In September 1941, less than five months after being federally recognized, the 121st Observation Squadron, was placed on FAD. Redesignated 121st Liaison Squadron it flew combat operations in the MTO during the last eight months of World War II. Postwar, the

DC unit was reorganized as the 121st FS and since then it has flown nine types of fighter aircraft from Andrews AFB. Since the end of 1989, the 121st TFS has been equipped with F-16A/Bs.

At the end of FY92, 1,485 officers and enlisted personnel manned 15 DC ANG units, the 121st FS and 201st AS at Andrews AFB, with the latter providing support for the National Guard Bureau with C-21As and C-22Bs.

121st Fighter Squadron 113th Fighter Wing

Lineage: *Designated 121st Observation Squadron and allotted to the District of Columbia NG on 30 July 1940.*
10 Apr 1941: 121st OS extended federal recognition at Bolling Field, Washington, and equipped with a mix of aircraft (which by 30 Nov 1941 included one O-38B, one O-38E, one O-46A, one O-47B, four O-58s and one AT-6A).
1 Sep 1941: Called to active duty and assigned to 65th OG at Owens Field, SC.

World War II: Between September 1941 and October 1942, the unit remained in CONUS, moved on three occasions, was redesignated twice, and flew ASW patrols along the mid-Atlantic coast. It was inactivated in October 1942 but was reconstituted as the 121st Liaison Squadron in April 1943. Shipped to the MTO in February 1944, it flew **Piper L-4s** and **Stinson L-5s** in support of ground forces in Italy and France between September 1944 and VE Day. Inactivated at Muskogee AAFld, OK, on 17 November 1945, the unit was redesignated 121st FS and allotted back to the DC NG on 24 May 1946.
20 Oct 1946: 121st FS (SE) extended federal recognition at Andrews AAFld and initially equipped with support aircraft.
Feb 1947: First **Republic P-47Ds** delivered.
Dec 1949: Converted from F-47Ds to **Republic F-84Cs** and redesignated 121st FS (Jet).
1 Feb 1951: Called to active duty as part of the Korean War call-up, redesignated 121st FIS, and transferred to New Castle County AFB, DE.
Jul 1951: Converted from F-84Cs to **Lockheed F-94Bs**.
1 Nov 1952: Returned to state control to be re-equipped with **North American F-51Hs**.

Mar 1954: Converted from F-51Hs to **North American F-86As**.
Late 1955: Converted from F-86As to F-86Es.
Late 1957: Converted from F-86Es to F-86Hs.
1 Nov 1958: Redesignated 121st TFS.
Mid-1960: Converted from F-86Hs to **North American F-100C/Fs**.
1 Jul 1960: Became TAC-gained upon implementation of gaining command concept.
1 Oct 1961: Called to active duty as part of the Berlin Crisis call-up but

remained based at Andrews AFB.
24 Aug 1962: Returned to state control.
Nov 1963: Deployed non-stop to Puerto Rico with the use of air refueling.
Aug 1964: Deployed non-stop to

Among the many aircraft types assigned over the years to the logistic support element of the District of Columbia ANG was this turboprop-powered VC-131H.

Below: Republic F-105F-1-RE (62-4433) of the 121st Tactical Fighter Squadron, District of Columbia ANG. 'Thuds' entered ANG service in April 1964 when New Jersey's 141st TFS converted from F-86Hs to F-105Bs and were phased out during the summer of 1983. F-105s with the 121st TFS replaced F-100Cs and Fs in July 1971 and were kept until the winter of 1981-82.

Above: After being alloted back to the District of Columbia, the 121st FS (SE) was initially equipped with brand new Republic P-47D-30-RA Thunderbolts.

René J. Francillon

Tom Kaminski

Europe with the use of air refueling.

26 Jan 1968: Called to active duty as part of the *Pueblo* Crisis call-up and moved to Myrtle Beach AFB, SC, to operate as an F-100 CCTS.
18 Jun 1969: Returned to state control at Andrews AFB.
Jul 1971: Converted from F-100C/Fs to Republic F-105D/Fs.
9 Dec 1974: 113th TFG inactivated and 121st TFS placed directly under the control of the 113th TFW.
Jul 1981: First F-4D sorties.
Mar 1982: Completed conversion from F-105D/Fs to McDonnell F-4Ds.
Sep 1989: First F-16A received.
Fall 1990: Completed conversion from F-4Ds to General Dynamics F-16A/Bs.

Above right: Conversion time: flagship F-16A and flagship F-4D on the ramp of the 121st TFS at Andrews AFB during the summer of 1990.

Right: Boeing T-43A of Det 1, HQ District of Columbia ANG, on the transient ramp at McClellan AFB, California, on 9 July 1980.

15 Mar 1992: Unit designation changed to 121st Fighter Squadron, 113th Fighter Wing (121st FS, 113th FW).
1 Jun 1992: As part of the Air Force restructuring program, gaining command changed to ACC.

Peter B. Lewis

201st Airlift Squadron
113th Fighter Wing

Lineage: *During Fiscal Year 1951, the District of Columbia ANG was authorized to form a separate unit at Andrews AFB to provide logistic support for the National Guard Bureau and to maintain tactical aircraft for the use of officers*

assigned to the NGB but needing to retain their flying skills. Activated as Air Base Flight H on 1 February 1951, this unit was initially equipped with Douglas B-26Bs, C-47s, and C-53s and with North

One of the recipients of the 80 Learjets acquired by the USAF was Det 1, HQ DC ANG, which obtained four C-21As (including 86-0377).

American F-51s. The unit was redesignated Det 1, HQ DC ANG, on 14 June 1954. At the beginning of the 1990s, Det 1's fleet consisted of four Boeing C-22Bs and four Learjet C-21As.

Activated at Andrews AFB on 15 March 1992 when Det 1, HQ DC ANG was redesignated the 201st Airlift Squadron, the support unit of the DC ANG currently operates four C-21As and four C-22Bs, including this aircraft landing at Pope AFB, North Carolina, during Airlift Rodeo '90.

15 Mar 1992: Det 1, HQ District of Columbia ANG redesignated 201st Airlift Squadron without change of station, equipment or mission.

Bill Curry

Jim Dunn

Florida Air National Guard

Based at the Jacksonville IAP and currently equipped with F-16A/B ADFs, the 159th FS traces its origin to February 1947 when the 159th FS received federal recognition. In its 44-year existence, the sole flying squadron of the Florida ANG has exclusively had fighters as mission aircraft and was called to active duty only once (during the Korean War, when it flew combat operations and some of the first air-refueling sorties).

At the end of FY92, 1,617 officers and enlisted personnel manned 17 FL ANG units, including the 159th FS flying F-16A/B ADFs from the Jacksonville International Airport.

159th Fighter Squadron
125th Fighter Group

Lineage: *Constituted in May 1943 and activated at Mitchel Field, NY, on 1 October 1942, the 352nd FS was assigned to the 353rd FG, Eighth Air Force, with which it flew combat operations with Republic P-47Ds and North American P-51Ds in the ETO between August 1943 and VE Day. Inactivated at Camp Kilner, NJ, in*

October 1945. Reconstituted and redesignated 159th FS, the unit was allotted to the Florida NG on 24 May 1946.

9 Feb 1947: 159th FS (SE) extended federal recognition at the Thomas Cole Imeson Airport, Jacksonville, and equipped with **North American P-51Ds** (plus support aircraft).

Summer 1948: Converted from F-51Ds to **Lockheed F-80Cs**.

1 Aug 1948: Redesignated 159th FS (Jet).

10 Oct 1950: Called to active duty as part of the Korean War call-up.

1 Nov 1950: Redesignated 159th FBS moved to George AFB, CA.

Apr 1951: Converted from F-80Cs to Republic F-84Es.

Jul 1951: 159th FBS and other

F-106As of Florida's 159th Figther Interceptor Squadron fly over the Fort Jefferson National Monument on Garden Key in the Dry Tortugas.

squadrons from the 116th FBW moved to Japan.

25 Jul 1951: 159th FBS arrived at Misawa AB, Japan.

Aug 1951-Jul 1952: While at Misawa AB, the 116th FBW rotated one of its squadrons to Chitose AB, to provide air defense for northern Japan (beginning on 1 Sep 1951 with the 196th FBS), and to Taegu AB (K-2), for combat operations in Korea (beginning on 30 Nov 1951 with the 159th FBS). Beginning in Feb 1952, the three squadrons of the 116th FBW also trained in the new air-refueling technique and flew four High Tide combat missions with F-84Es fitted with tip-tank-mounted refueling probe.

10 Jul 1952: Returned to state control at the Thomas Cole Imeson Airport and reorganized as the 159th FIS but left

The support aircraft assigned in the early 1990s to the Florida ANG is a C-130H, 79-0475 being seen here at the Jacksonville IAP in 1990.

without mission aircraft for two months.

Sep 1952: Re-equipped with **North** American F-51D/Hs.

Summer 1954: Planned conversion to **North American F-86As** cancelled after four Sabres had been delivered to the 159th FIS.

Dec 1954: Converted from F-51D/Hs to **Lockheed F-80Cs** (for a short period of time, the FL ANG had simultaneously four models of mission aircraft – F-51Ds, F-51Hs, F-80Cs and F-86As – and four types of support aircraft – C-45Gs, C-47As, T-6Gs and T-33As).

1 Jul 1956: Reached group status with federal recognition of 125th FIG.

Aug 1956: Converted from F-80Cs to **North American F-86Ds**.

Jun 1959: Converted from F-86Ds to F-86Ls.

1 Jul 1960: Became ADC-gained upon implementation of gaining command concept.

Jul 1960: Converted from F-86Ls to **Convair F/TF-102As**.

24 Oct 1968: Relocated to the Jacksonville IAP.

Jan 1968: Initial batch of F/TF-102As replaced with Configuration 8 updated F/TF-102As.

Summer/Fall 1974: Converted from F/TF-102As (last left in Jul 1974) to **Convair F-106A/Bs**.

1 Apr 1980: Became TAC-gained following ADC inactivation.

Jan 1987: Began conversion from F-106A/Bs to **General Dynamics F-16A/Bs**.

1 Apr 1988: Completed conversion to F-16A/Bs.

FY90: F-16A/Bs upgraded to the ADF configuration.

15 Mar 1992: Unit designation changed to 159th Fighter Squadron, 125th Fighter Group (159th FS, 125th FG).

1 Jun 1992: As part of the Air Force restructuring program, gaining command changed to ACC.

A pair of F-106A ADFs of the 159th FIS in trail behind a KC-135R of the 42nd ARS, 42nd BMW, in May 1989. The 159th FIS began its conversion from F-106A/Bs to F-16A/Bs in early 1987.

Georgia Air National Guard

Organized in May 1941, the 128th Observation Squadron was placed on active duty 15 weeks later, and during the last year of World War II served as a bomber unit in the MTO.

Postwar, it served as a fighter unit between 1946 and 1961 and then as a transport squadron for 12 years. Back in the fighter business in 1973, the 128th TFS successively flew F-100D/Fs, F-105G/Fs and F-4Ds, before completing its conversion to F-15A/Bs at Dobbins AFB in 1987.

The other GA ANG flying unit was organized as the 158th FS in the fall of 1946, served on FAD in Japan and Korea in 1951-52, and became a transport unit in 1962. Since then, the 158th has flown C-97s, C-124s and C-130s (with its current C-130Hs having been operated from Savannah IAP since 1981).

At the end of FY92, 3,494 officers and enlisted personnel manned 36 GA ANG units, including the 128th FS at Dobbins AFB and the 158th AS at Savannah International Airport.

128th Fighter Squadron
116th Fighter Wing

Lineage: *Designated the 128th Observation Squadron and allotted to the Georgia NG on 30 July 1940. In 1944, the history and lineage of the 840th Aero Squadron, Air Service, were consolidated with those of the 128th OS. Organized at Waco, TX, on 1 Feb 1918, the 840th Aero Squadron had moved to England in May 1918 and to France in August 1918, where it served as a repair and maintenance unit. It had been demobilized at Langley, VA, in March 1919.*

1 May 1941: 128th OS extended federal recognition at Candler Field, Atlanta, and initially equipped with two Douglas O-38Es, one Douglas O-46A and one North American BC-1A.

15 Sep 1941: Called to active duty, placed under command of II Air Support Command, and transferred eight days later to Lawson Field, Ft Benning, GA.

World War II: Remaining in CONUS until March 1944, the unit moved five times, was redesignated on six occasions, flew ASW patrols over the Gulf of Mexico, and was trained as a heavy bomber unit. As the 840th BS, it was assigned to the 483rd BG, Fifteenth Air Force, and flew Boeing B-17Gs in combat in the MTO and ETO between April 1944 and VE Day. Inactivated at Pisa, Italy, on 25 September 1945, the squadron was redesignated 128th FS

and allotted back to the Georgia NG on 24 May 1946.

20 Aug 1946: 128th FS (SE) extended federal recognition at Marietta AB and soon after equipped with Republic P-47Ns (plus support aircraft).

6 Feb 1950: Marietta AB redesignated Dobbins AFB.

10 Oct 1950: Called to active duty as part of the Korean War call-up and began conversion from F-47Ns to Republic F-84Ds.

Nov 1950: Transferred to Alexandria AFB, LA, to join other squadrons of the 137th FBW.

10 Jul 1952: Returned to state control at Dobbins AFB to be reorganized as 128th FIS and equipped with North American F-51Hs.

1 Dec 1952: Redesignated 128th FBS.

Winter 1952: Converted from F-51Hs

Afterburner aglow, an F-105G of the 128th TFS lifts off at Dobbins AFB on 20 October 1982. During that month, the Georgia ANG unit received its first F-4D to commence its conversion to Phantom IIs.

to Republic F-84Ds.

1 Jul 1955: Redesignated 128th FIS.

Summer 1955: Converted from F-84Ds to F-84Fs.

Spring 1960: Converted from F-84Fs to North American F-86Ls.

1 Jul 1960: Became ADC-gained upon implementation of gaining command concept.

1 Apr 1961: Redesignated 128th ATS (Heavy) and became MATS-gained.

Spring 1961: Converted from F-86Ls to Boeing C-97Fs.

Winter 1965: Converted from C-97Fs to Douglas C-124Cs.

1 Jan 1966: Redesignated 128th MAS and became MAC-gained following MATS redesignation.

Spring 1973: Converted from C-124Cs to North American F-100D/Fs.

4 Apr 1973: Redesignated 128th TFS and became TAC-gained.

10 Dec 1974: 116th TFG inactivated and 128th TFS placed directly under the control of the 116th TFW.

Summer 1979: Converted from F-100D/Fs to Republic F-105G/Fs.

Oct 1982: Received first F-4Ds.

15 Aug 1983: Completed conversion from F-105G/Fs to McDonnell F-4Ds.

31 Mar 1987: Completed conversion from F-4Ds to McDonnell Douglas F-15A/Bs (first F-15A received in Jun 1986).

15 Mar 1992: Unit designation changed to 128th Fighter Squadron, 116th Fighter Wing (128th FS, 116th FW).

1 Jun 1992: As part of the Air Force restructuring program, gaining command changed to ACC.

Georgia's 128th TFS became the second of five squadrons to be equipped with F-15A/Bs when it converted from F-4Ds in 1986-87. Until such time as active duty squadrons receive F-22s, it is unlikely that additional ANG squadrons will fly Eagles.

158th Airlift Squadron
165th Airlift Group

Lineage: *Constituted in May 1943 and activated at Mitchel Field, NY, on 1 October 1942, the 351st FS was assigned to the 353rd FG, Eighth Air Force, with which it flew combat operations with Republic P-47Ds and North American P-51Ds in the ETO between August 1943 and VE Day. Inactivated at Camp Kilner, NJ, in October 1945. Reconstituted and redesignated 158th FS, the unit was allotted to the Georgia NG on 24 May 1946.*

13 Oct 1946: 158th FS (SE) extended federal recognition at Chatham Field, Savannah, and soon after equipped with

In September 1974, the 158th MAS was the last USAF unit to fly the 'Old Shaky'. Ten years later, this superbly restored C-124C was flown to Travis AFB for display at that California base's museum.

Upon disposing of its Douglas C-124C Globemaster IIs, Georgia's 158th MAS was re-equipped with C-130Es and was redesignated the 158th TAS on 10 December 1974. Aircraft 63-7856 was photographed at its home base, Dobbins AFB, in January 1979.

Republic P-47Ns (plus support aircraft).
Summer 1948: Converted from F-47Ns to **Lockheed F-80Cs.**
1 Aug 1948: Redesignated 158th FS (Jet).
31 Mar 1949: Relocated to Hunter Field, Savannah.
10 Oct 1950: Called to active duty as part of the Korean War call-up.
1 Nov 1950: Redesignated 158th FBS and moved to George AFB, CA.
Apr 1951: Converted from F-80Cs to Republic F-84Es.
Jul 1951: 158th FBS and other squadrons from the 116th FBW moved to Japan.
25 Jul 1951: 158th FBS arrived at

Misawa AB, Japan.
Aug 1951-Jul 1952: While at Misawa AB, the 116th FBW rotated one of its squadrons to Chitose AB, to provide air defense for northern Japan (beginning on 1 Sep 1951 with the 196th FBS), and to Taegu AB (K-2), for combat operations in Korea (beginning on 30 Nov 1951 with the 159th FBS). Beginning in Feb 1952, the three squadrons of the 116th FBW also trained in the new air-refueling technique and flew four High Tide combat missions with F-84Es fitted with tip-tank-mounted refueling probe.
10 Jul 1952: Returned to state control at the Savannah MAP to be reorganized as the 158th FIS and equipped with North American F-51Hs.
1 Dec 1952: Redesignated 128th FBS.

Jul 1953: Converted from F-51Hs to Republic F-84Ds.
1 Jul 1955: Redesignated 158th FIS.
Mar 1957: Converted from F-84Ds to F-84Fs.
10 Jul 1958: Reached group status with federal recognition of the 165th FIG.
1 Jan 1960: Completed conversion from F-84Fs to North American F-86Ls.
1 Jul 1960: Became ADC-gained upon implementation of gaining command concept.
Mar 1962: Initiated conversion from F-86Ls to Boeing C-97Fs.
1 Apr 1962: Redesignated 158th ATS (Heavy) and became MATS-gained.
1 Jan 1966: Redesignated 158th MAS and became MAC-gained following MATS redesignation.

Jul 1967: Converted from C-97Fs to Douglas C-124Cs.
Aug 1974: Initiated conversion from C-124Cs to Lockheed C-130Es.
19 Sep 1974: Last two C-124Cs in Air Force inventory flown to MASDC.
10 Dec 1974: Redesignated 158th TAS.
FY81: Converted from C-130Es to C-130Hs.
Aug 1990: Volunteers began flying missions in support of Operation Desert Shield.
15 Mar 1992: Unit designation changed to 158th Airlift Squadron, 165th Airlift Group (158th AS, 165th AG).
1 Jun 1992: As part of the Air Force restructuring program, gaining command changed to AMC.

Guam Air National Guard

Unlike the other Mariana Islands, which between 1947 and 1986 were administered by the United States under a UN Trusteeship and which in November 1986 became part of the United States as the Commonwealth of the Northern Mariana Islands, Guam is a self-governed US possession administered under the general supervision of the Secretary of the Interior. Guamanians were granted citizenship in August 1950, but have no vote in US presidential elections.

The Headquarters, Guam ANG, was activated at Agana on 21 July 1981, and, at the end of FY92, the GU ANG had 170 officers and enlisted personnel to man five non-flying units.

Hawaii Air National Guard

Organized in November 1946 as the 199th FS, the flying unit of the Hawaii Guard has provided the entire air defense for the Hawaiian Islands since 1969. For that role it has been equipped with F-15A/Bs since the end of 1987.

Its parent unit, the 154th Composite Group, is unique, as it controls not only the 199th FS and the usual support units but also, since November 1978, all other Hawaii ANG assets – including the 154th Tactical Control Squadron and the 150th and 169th Aircraft Control & Warning Squadrons. The diversity of the 154th CG will increase further in early 1993 when a new squadron, initially to be equipped with four KC-135Rs, will be organized at Hickam AFB.

At the end of FY92, 2,159 officers and enlisted personnel manned the 199th FS and 25 other HI ANG units.

199th Fighter Squadron
154th Composite Group

Lineage: *Constituted and activated at Peterson Field, CO, in October 1944, the 464th FS was assigned to the 507th FG, Twentieth Air Force, with which it flew combat operations with Republic P-47Ns in the western Pacific during the last two months of World War II. Inactivated at Yontan, Okinawa, in May 1946, the squadron was redesignated 199th FS and was allotted to the Hawaii NG on 24 May 1946.*
4 Nov 1946: 199th FS (SE) extended federal recognition at Bellows Field, Oahu, Hawaii, and initially equipped with support aircraft only.
Jul 1947: 199th FS (SE) received its Republic F-47Ns.
28 Oct 1947: Permanent change of station from Bellows Field to Hickam AFB.

Conversion from day fighter Sabres to all-weather F-86Ls began for Hawaii's 199th FIS with the arrival at Hickam AFB of Detachment F-86-6 in November 1987. The first batch of cocooned F-86Ls was delivered as deck cargo aboard the USS Windham Bay (CVU-92) on 5 February 1958, and the last F-86Es were phased out on 30 May 1958.

15 Jul 1952: Redesignated 199th FBS.
19 Nov 1952: Redesignated 199th FIS.
Feb 1954: Converted from F-47Ns to North American F-86Es.
Feb 1958: Converted from F-86Es to F-86Ls.
1 Jul 1960: Became PACAF-gained upon implementation of gaining command concept.
1 Dec 1960: Reached group status with federal recognition of 154th FIG.
Winter 1960/Spring 1961: Converted from F-86Ls to Convair F/TF-102As (received in Dec 1960 and first flown on 21 Jan 1961); back on alert status with F-102As beginning in May 1961.
Mar 1965: Initial batch of F/TF-102As replaced with Configuration 8 updated F/TF-102As.
31 Mar 1969: Following the inactivation of the Nike-Hercules SAM batteries of the 298th Artillery Group (Nike), Hawaii ARNG, the 199th FIS became solely responsible for the air

defense of Hawaii.
FY76: Converted from F/TF-102As (last left in Oct 1976) to **F-4Cs** (first received on 31 Oct 1975).
10 Jun 1976: Redesignated 199th TFS, 154th TFG.
22 Oct 1976: Back on alert status after completing conversion to F-4Cs.
3 Nov 1978: 154th TFG redesignated 154th COMPG.
Mar 1987: Initiated conversion from F-4Cs to **McDonnell Douglas F-15A/Bs** (first F-15A received in Jun 1987).
Jan 1988: Completed conversion from F-4Cs to F-15A/Bs.
15 Mar 1992: Unit redesignated 199th Fighter Squadron, 154th Composite Group (199th FS, 154th CG).

The 199th Tactical Fighter Squadron received its first F-15A in June 1987 and completed its conversion from F-4Cs in January 1988. Eagles are likely to equip Hawaii's fighter squadron until at least the end of the 1990s.

Wally van Winkle

Idaho Air National Guard

For the first 29 years after the 190th FS received federal recognition in October 1946, the original flying unit in the Idaho Guard was equipped with fighter-bombers and interceptors. In October 1975, the Idaho ANG switched to tactical reconnaissance and for the next 16 years the 190th TRS was equipped with RF-4Cs. A new change took place in 1991 when in June the 190th received its first F-4G to begin its conversion to the 'Wild Weasel' defense suppression mission.

Beginning in 1983, the Idaho ANG was given the responsibility for training ANG RF-4C replacement crews and to teach advanced tactics to USAF and ANG RF-4C crews. Accordingly, the 189th TRTF and the Reconnaissance Weapons School (RWS) were organized in March of that year.

At the end of FY92, 1,370 officers and enlisted personnel manned 14 ID ANG units, including the 189th TF, with RF-4Cs and F-4Gs, and the 190th FS, with F-4Gs, at the Boise Air Terminal (Gowen Field).

189th Training Flight
124th Fighter Group

1 Sep 1984: Activated at Gowen Field, Boise, as RF-4C replacement training unit. The 189th TRTF shared **RF-4Cs** with the RWS and the 190th TRS.
Mar 1991: Gained responsibility for

training active-duty RF-4C aircrews.
Dec 1991: After absorbing the RWS instructors and receiving six RF-4Cs, the 189th trained RF-4C and F-4G crews.
15 Mar 1992: Redesignated 189th Training Flight, 124th Fighter Group.
FY93: RF-4Cs scheduled to be withdrawn during the third quarter.

Reconnaissance Weapons School
124th Reconnaissance Group

Mar 1983: Activated at Gowen Field, Boise, as the reconnaissance counterpart of the USAF Fighter Weapons School to teach reconnaissance aircrews of the USAF and ANG flying tactics designed to increase their survivability rate.
31 Dec 1991: Inactivated and instructors transferred to the 189th TRTF to begin training F-4G aircrews.

Above: A Convair F-102A-35-CO of the 190th FIS in front of the control tower at Malmstrom AFB, Montana, in September 1968. 'Deuces' equipped this Idaho squadron for 11 years beginning in November 1964.

Chris Jacquet

Peter B. Lewis

190th Fighter Squadron
124th Fighter Group

Lineage: *Constituted in May 1943 and activated at the Richmond AAB, VA, in July 1943, the 405th FS flew Republic P-47Ds in the ETO as part of the 371st FG, Ninth Air Force. Inactivated in November 1945. Reconstituted and redesignated the 190th FS, the unit was allotted to the Idaho NG on 24 May 1946.*
13 Oct 1946: 190th FS (SE) extended federal recognition at Gowen Field,

Back on the ramp at Gowen Field, 65-0904, a RF-4C-28-MC of the 190th TRS, is about to release its drag chute after completing a training sortie over NAS Fallon's tactical range on 16 July 1988.

René J. Francillon

René J. Francillon

Left: Vietnam-era camouflage blended nicely when RF-4Cs of Idaho's 190th TRS flew over farmland near Boise, but was more conspicuous over nearby desert.

Above: The only Guard squadron currently assigned the 'Wild Weasel' defense suppression mission, the 190th FS is one of the last two USAF squadrons to fly F-4Gs.

Boise, and soon equipped with North American P-51Ds (plus support aircraft).
1 Apr 1951: Called to active duty as part of the Korean War call-up. Soon after moved to Moody AFB, GA, and assigned as 190th FBS to the 146th F-BW.
Sep 1951: Moved to George AFB, CA, and assigned to the Ninth Air Force, TAC, as 190th FBS.
1 Jan 1953: Returned to state control to be reorganized as the 190th FIS and equipped with F-51Ds.
Oct 1953: First two Lockheed T-33A trainers received to initiate jet conversion.
Nov 1953: Converted from F-51Ds to North American F-86As.
Dec 1954: Converted from F-86As to Lockheed F-94Bs.
14 Apr 1956: Reached group status with federal recognition of 124th FIG.
Jul 1956: Converted from F-94Bs to Northrop F-89Bs.
Apr 1959: Converted from F-89Bs to North American F-86Ls.
1 Jul 1960: Became ADC-gained upon implementation of gaining command concept.
Apr 1964: Converted from F-86Ls to Convair F/TF-102As.
Fall 1975: Converted from F/TF-102As (last left in Nov 1975) to McDonnell RF-4Cs.
18 Oct 1975: Redesignated 190th TRS/124th TRG and became TAC-gained.
Oct 1980: Won Photo Derby '80 competition.
FY83: 124th TRG given added responsibility as RF-4C RTU.
1 Sep 1984: RTU responsibility transferred to the 189th TRTF upon activation of this co-located unit. The 189th TRTF and 190th TRS share RF-4Cs assigned to the 124th TRG.
Oct 1984: Won Photo Derby '84 competition.
Oct 1985: Won Photo Finish '85 competition.
Summer 1991: Commenced conversion from RF-4Cs to F-4Gs (first F-4G delivered on 21 Jun 1991).
16 Oct 1991: Redesignated 190th TFS/124th TFG.
15 Mar 1992: Unit designation changed to 190th Fighter Squadron, 124th Fighter Group (190th FS, 124th FG).
1 Jun 1992: As part of the Air Force restructuring program, gaining command changed to ACC.

Illinois Air National Guard

The first aviation unit in the Illinois Guard received federal recognition in July 1927 and was placed on active duty in February 1941. Early in the following year, the 108th Observation Squadron became the first Guard unit to be deployed outside the continental United States. The 108th went on to serve in the Panama Canal Zone until disbanded in November 1943. Reconstituted as the 108th BS after World War II, this unit became a fighter squadron in January 1953 upon its return from France at the end of its Korean War activation and, more significantly, became the first ANG air-refueling squadron in July 1961.

In addition to the 108th BS, the Illinois National Guard was allotted three squadrons in the post-World War II era. One of these squadrons, the 168th FIS, was inactivated in May 1958, leaving the Illinois ANG with three flying units.

At the end of FY92, 3,803 officers and enlisted personnel manned 41 IL ANG units, including three flying squadrons (the 108th ARS flying KC-135Es from the O'Hare ARFF in Chicago, the 169th FS at Peoria with F-16A/B ADFs, and the 170th FS at the Capital Airport in Springfield with F-16A/Bs).

108th Air Refueling Squadron 126th Air Refueling Wing

Lineage: *Organized at Kelly Field, TX, on 27 August 1917 as the 108th Aero Squadron, this Air Service unit moved to France in January 1918. It was redesignated 802nd Aero Squadron on 1 February 1918, served as an aircraft maintenance unit in the AEF, and was demobilized at Mitchel Field, NY, on 11 June 1919. In 1936, its lineage and honors were consolidated with those of the 108th OS, which had been activated as an Illinois NG unit in July 1927.*
1 Jul 1927: 108th OS extended federal recognition at the Chicago Municipal Airport as the aviation unit of the 33rd Division, Illinois NG, and initially equipped with Consolidated PT-1s.
1927-1940: Remaining based in Chicago, the 108th OS was equipped over the years with the mix of aircraft typical of prewar Guard units, including Consolidated PT-1s and O-17s; Douglas BT-1s, O-2s, O-31s and O-38s; and North American O-47s and BC-1s. On 31 Dec 1940, it had one BC-1A, one O-31, three O-38Es and 10 O-47A/Bs.
3 Feb 1941: Called to active duty and placed under command of Second Army. Remaining based nominally in Chicago until Dec 1941, the 108th OS deployed to Fort Sheridan, IL, Murfreesboro, TN, and Tallulah, LA, for training and exercises.
World War II: Shipped to Panama in Jan 1942, the squadron was successively based at Rio Hato and Howard Field from which it flew a motley collection of aircraft (A-18s, B-18s, L-4s, O-47s, O-49s, P-36s and P-39s) in defense of the Canal Zone. It

Peter B. Lewis

With smoke billowing from its R-4360-59 radial engines, a KC-97L of the 108th Air Refueling Squadron, Illinois ANG, taxis back to the Guard ramp at the Chicago O'Hare International Airport on 9 May 1967.

Above: The jet-augmented KC-97L was developed as the result of a suggestion made in early 1963 by an officer of the Illinois ANG, Lieutenant Phillip A. Meyer.

Below: 57-1480, a Boeing KC-135E of the 108th AREFS, takes part in an exercise at the Air National Guard Permanent Training Site, Volk Field, Wisconsin, on 14 June 1990.

was redesignated 108th Reconnaissance Squadron in June 1943 but was inactivated at Howard Field, CZ, on 1 Nov 1943. Redesignated 108th BS, the unit was allotted back to the Illinois NG on 24 May 1946.

19 Jan 1947: 108th BS (Light) extended federal recognition at the Chicago Midway Airport and soon equipped with **Douglas A-26B/Cs** (plus support aircraft).

1 Apr 1951: Called to active duty as part of the Korean War call-up, the 108th BS remained in Chicago for three months and then moved to Langley AFB, VA, for additional training.

Oct-Nov 1951: B-26B/Cs ferried across the North Atlantic to Bordeaux-Mérignac, France.

May 1952: Transferred to Laon AB, France.

1 Jan 1953: Returned to state control at the Chicago Midway Airport to be reorganized as the 108th FBS and equipped with **North American F-51Ds** (from mid-May 1953).

Apr 1954: Completed move to O'Hare Field, Chicago.

Summer 1955: Converted from F-51Ds to **Republic F-84Fs**.

1 Jul 1955: Redesignated 108th FIS.

Oct 1957: Converted from F-84Fs to **North American F-86Ls**.

Dec 1958: O'Hare Field renamed Chicago O'Hare IAP.

1 Jul 1960: Became ADC-gained upon implementation of gaining command concept.

Spring 1961: Crew training on Boeing **KC-97** tanker initiated.

1 Jul 1961: Redesignated 108th AREFS and became TAC-gained.

8 Aug 1961: First ANG KC-97F delivered to the 108th AREFS.

6 Sep 1961: First all-ANG air-refueling sortie (the receiver was a Republic F-84F from the 169th TFS, IL ANG).

Early 1963: Addition of pod-mounted J47 turbojets suggested by Lieutenant Phillip A. Meyer to boost performance of KC-97F/Gs.

May 1964: Initial trials of jet-augmented JKC-97G (52-2697).

8-22 Aug 1964: Operation Ready Go: The 108th AREFS and the two other squadrons of the 126th AREFW (Ohio's

145th and Wisconsin's 126th) provided tankers to deploy 31 ANG fighters and reconnaissance aircraft from CONUS to Germany.

Dec 1965: Completed conversion from KC-97F/Gs to jet-augmented **KC-97Ls**.

Jun 1967: 108th AREFS began providing tankers and crews on TDY basis to Rhein-Main AB, Germany, as part of Operation Creek Party.

9 Dec 1974: 126th AREFG inactivated and 108th AREFS placed directly under the control of the 126th AREFW.

1 Jul 1976: Gaining command changed from TAC to SAC.

Dec 1976: Conversion from KC-97Ls to

Boeing **KC-135As** initiated.

FY83: Converted from KC-135As to KC-135Es.

Aug 1990: Volunteers began flying missions in support of Operation Desert Shield.

20 Dec 1990: Called to active duty as part of Operation Desert Shield call-up.

31 May 1991: Released from active duty after taking part in Desert Shield/Desert Storm.

15 Mar 1992: Unit abbreviation changed to 108th ARS, 126th ARW.

1 Jun 1992: As part of the Air Force restructuring program, gaining command changed to AMC.

168th Fighter Interceptor Squadron

Lineage: *Constituted and activated at Barksdale Field, LA, in June 1942, the 437th BS (Medium) was assigned to the 319th BG, Twelfth Air Force, with which it flew combat operations with Martin B-26s and North American B-25s in the MTO between November 1942 and December 1944. Returned to CONUS and re-equipped with Douglas A-26B/Cs, the 437th BS and other squadrons of the 319th BG were reassigned to the Seventh Air Force in April 1945, and flew combat operations from Okinawa during the last month of World War II. Inactivated at Ft Lawton, WA, in January 1946, the squadron was redesignated 168th BS and was allotted to the Illinois NG on 24 May 1946.*

19 Oct 1947: 168th BS (Light) extended federal recognition at the Orchard Place Airport, Park Ridge, and soon equipped with **Douglas A-26B/Cs** (plus support aircraft).

Sep 1949: Orchard Place Airport renamed O'Hare Field.

1 Apr 1951: Called to active duty as part of the Korean War call-up, the 168th BS remained in Chicago for three months and then moved to Langley AFB,

VA, for additional training.

Oct-Nov 1951: B-26B/Cs ferried across the North Atlantic to Bordeaux-Mérignac, France.

May 1952: Transferred to Laon AB, France.

1 Jan 1953: Returned to state control at O'Hare Field, Chicago, to be reorganized as the 168th FBS and equipped with **North American F-51Ds** (from mid-May 1954).

Jul 1955: Converted from F-51Ds to

Republic F-84Fs.

1 Jul 1955: Redesignated 168th FIS.

Oct 1957: Converted from F-84Fs to North American F-86Ls.

31 May 1958: Inactivated due to funding restrictions. The 168th Squadron

Shortly after receiving federal recognition on 19 October 1947, the 168th Bombardment Squadron (Light) was equipped with Douglas Invaders.

designation was retained by the Illinois ANG until 1986, when it was transferred to the Alaska ANG.

169th Fighter Squadron
182nd Fighter Group

Lineage: *Constituted and activated at Morris Field, NC, in July 1942, the 304th FS was assigned to the 337th FG, Third Air Force, and served as a CONUS-based operational training unit. Successively equipped with Bell P-39s, Republic P-43s and Curtiss P-40s, it was disbanded at the Pinellas County Airport, FL, on 1 May 1944. Reconstituted and redesignated the 169th FS, the unit was allotted to the Illinois NG on 24 May 1946.*

*Framed against the main hangar 69-0428 is one of the unit's **OA-37Bs**.*

These F-84F-25-REs were caught at Peoria, Illinois, on 13 May 1967.

21 Jun 1947: 169th FS (SE) extended federal recognition at the Peoria Airport and soon equipped with North American P-51Ds (plus support aircraft).
Aug 1951: Converted from F-51Ds to F-51Hs.
1 Jul 1952: Redesignated 169th FIS.
1 Dec 1952: Redesignated 169th FBS.
Nov 1954: Converted from F-51Hs to F-51Ds.
1 Jul 1955: Redesignated 169th FIS.
Oct 1956: Converted from F-51Ds to North American T-28As. These propeller-driven trainers were assigned as interim equipment pending completion of the runway extension at the Peoria Airport and re-equipment with jets.

Aug 1958: Converted from T-28As to Republic F-84Fs.
10 Nov 1958: Redesignated 169th TFS.
1 Jul 1960: Became TAC-gained upon implementation of gaining command concept.
6 Sep 1961: First all-ANG air-refueling sortie (the tanker was a Boeing KC-97F from the 108th AREFS, IL ANG).
1 Oct 1961: Called to active duty as part of the Berlin Crisis call-up but remained based at Peoria.
16 Aug 1962: Returned to state control.
15 Oct 1962: Reached group status with federal recognition of 182nd TFG.
Spring 1969: Converted from F-84Fs to Cessna U-3A/Bs.
16 May 1969: Redesignated 169th TASS, 182nd TASG.

Jan 1970: Converted from U-3A/Bs to Cessna O-2As.
Winter 1979: Converted from O-2As to Cessna OA-37Bs.
FY92: Converting from from OA-37Bs to General Dynamics Block 15 F-16A/B ADFs (first ADF received on 14 Mar 1992 and last OA-37B flown out on 3 Jun 1992).
15 Mar 1992: Unit designation changed to 169th Fighter Squadron, 182nd Fighter Group (169th FS, 182nd FG).
1 Jun 1992: As part of the Air Force restructuring program, gaining command changed to ACC.
1 Apr 1993: Scheduled to complete conversion to F-16A/B ADFs.

The 169th retired the OA-37 in favour of the F-16ADF, becoming an interceptor unit in the process.

170th Fighter Squadron
183rd Fighter Group

Lineage: *Constituted and activated at Dale Mabry Field, FL, in July 1942, the 305th FS was assigned to the 338th FG, Third Air Force, and served as a CONUS-based replacement training unit. Successively equipped with Bell P-39s, Republic P-47s and Curtiss P-40s, it was*

disbanded at Dale Mabry Field, FL, on 1 May 1944. Reconstituted and redesignated the 170th FS, the unit was allotted to the Illinois NG on 24 May 1946.
30 Sep 1948: 170th FS (SE) extended federal recognition at the Capital Airport in Springfield and, beginning in Dec 1948, equipped with North American F-51Ds (plus support aircraft).
1 Mar 1951: Called to active duty as part of the Korean War call-up and moved two weeks later to Bergstrom AFB, TX.
9 Apr 1951: Redesignated 170th FBS.
20 Jul 1951: Transferred to George AFB, CA.
1 Dec 1952: Returned to state control at the Capital Airport.
Fall 1953: Converted from F-51Ds to North American F-86Es.
Feb 1955: Converted from F-86Es to Republic F-84Fs.
1 Jul 1955: Redesignated 170th FIS.
10 Nov 1958: Redesignated 170th TFS.
1 Jul 1960: Became TAC-gained upon implementation of gaining command concept.
1 Oct 1961: Called to active duty as

part of the Berlin Crisis call-up but remained based at Capital Airport.
24 Aug 1962: Returned to state control.
15 Oct 1962: Reached group status with federal recognition of 183rd TFG.
Nov 1971: Last F-84Fs in ANG service grounded due to structural corrosion.
31 Jan 1972: First McDonnell F-4C assigned to start conversion from F-84Fs to F-4Cs.
Oct 1973-Jul 1975: Two RF-4Cs assigned in addition to F-4Cs.

Bearing more colorful 'FLY'N ILLINI' markings than other aircraft in the squadron, the flagship of the 170th TFS was photographed on its home ramp at the Capital Airport in Springfield, Illinois.

1 Jan 1981: Completed conversion from F-4Cs to F-4Ds.
1 Oct 1989: Completed conversion from F-4Ds to General Dynamics F-16A/Bs.
15 Mar 1992: Unit designation changed to 170th Fighter Squadron, 183rd Fighter Group (170th FS, 183rd FG).
1 Jun 1992: As part of the Air Force restructuring program, gaining command changed to ACC.

The 170th Tactical Fighter Squadron was the first ANG squadron to fly F-4 fighters. It flew F-4Cs between January 1972 and December 1980 and F-4Ds until the spring of 1989. 66-7593 was shot on 15 January 1987.

Indiana Air National Guard

Organized in August 1921 as the 137th Squadron and adopting the 113th Observation Squadron designation in January 1923, the first aviation unit in the Indiana Guard went on FAD in January 1941 and served in CONUS until the end of World War II. After the war, it was reorganized as the 113th FS and was joined by the 163rd FS in October 1947. Both were on active duty in their home state during the Korean War and were again activated during the Berlin Crisis, the 113th TFS remaining at Hulman Field and the 163rd moving to

France. Since their return to state control in August 1962, these two units have undergone almost simultaneous conversions to similar mission aircraft.

At the end of FY92, 2,484 officers and enlisted personnel manned 30 IN ANG units, including two F-16C/D squadrons, the 113th FS at the Hulman Regional Airport in Terre Haute and the 163rd FS at the Ft Wayne Municipal Airport.

113th Fighter Squadron
181st Fighter Group

Peter B. Lewis

Lineage: *Organized at Kelly Field, TX, on 26 August 1917 as the 113th Aero Squadron, Air Service, this supply unit was redesignated 634th Aero Squadron on 1 February 1918 and remained in the United States until demobilized at Middletown, PA, on 31 March 1919. In 1936, its lineage and honors were consolidated with those of the Indiana NG unit which had been activated in August 1921 as the 137th Squadron.*
1 Aug 1921: 137th Squadron extended federal recognition at Fagley Field, Kokomo, as a Corps Aviation unit in the Indiana NG.
3 Jan 1923: Redesignated 113th Squadron as aviation unit in the 38th Division.
25 Jan 1923: Redesignated 113th OS.
Jun 1926: Temporarily relocated to Schoen Field, Ft Benjamin Harrison, in Indianapolis.
Oct 1926: Permanently relocated to Mars Hill Airport (soon renamed Stout Field) in Indianapolis.
1922-1940: Initially equipped with Curtiss Jennies, the Indiana NG squadron was equipped over the years with the mix of aircraft typical of prewar Guard units, including Consolidated PT-1s and O-17s; Curtiss O-11s; Douglas BT-1s, O-2s and O-38s; and North American O-47s and BC-1s. On 31 December 1940, it had two O-38Bs and nine O-47A/Bs.
17 Jan 1941: Called to active duty and placed under command of V Army Corps.
World War II: Between 27 January 1941, when the 113th OS moved to Meridian, MS, and 30 November 1943, when the 113th TRS was disbanded at Birmingham, AL, the mobilized Indiana unit moved 10 times within CONUS, was redesignated on five occasions, flew ASW patrols over the Gulf of Mexico, and provided aerial support for training ground forces. Redesignated 113th FS, the unit was allotted back to the Indiana NG on 24 May 1946.

14 Apr 1947: 113th FS (SE) extended federal recognition at Stout Field, Indianapolis, and soon equipped with North American P-51Ds (plus support aircraft).
1 Feb 1951: Called to active duty as part of the Korean War call-up and operations split between Baer Field in Ft Wayne, IN, and Sioux City, IA.
11 Feb 1951: Redesignated 113th FIS.
24 May 1951: Still on active duty, but by then equipped with F-51Hs, the unit moved to Scott AFB, IL.
1 Nov 1952: Returned to state control at Stout Field to be reorganized as the 113th FBS.
1 Sep 1954: Permanent change of station to Hulman Field, Terre Haute.
1 Jul 1955: Redesignated 113th FIS.
Summer 1955: Converted from F-51Hs to Lockheed F-80Cs.
Mar 1956: Converted from F-80Cs to North American F-86As.
Apr 1958: Converted from F-86As to Republic F-84Fs.
1959: Redesignated 113th TFS.
1 Jul 1960: Became TAC-gained upon implementation of gaining command concept.
1 Oct 1961: Called to active duty as part of the Berlin Crisis call-up but remained at Hulman Field.
20 Aug 1962: Returned to state control but its F-84Fs were transferred to the Air Force.
Oct 1962: Converted from F-84Fs to RF-84Fs. Even though it was equipped with reconnaissance aircraft, the

Lined up with runway 21R at Nellis AFB, Nevada, 68-0412 returns from a sortie during the Gunsmoke competition in October 1989. F-4Es had replaced F-4Cs in the spring of 1988 and equipped the 113th TFS until 1991 when the Terre Haute unit became one of the last four ANG squadrons to fly F-4Es.

Above: Cartridge start for an F-100D-70-NA of the 113th Tactical Fighter Squadron operating from the Tucson IAP, Arizona, during a Snowbird deployment in March 1977. The Terre Haute unit converted to F-4Cs two years later.

Below: Shortly after converting from North American F-86As to Republic F-84Fs, the 113th FIS was redesignated a tactical fighter squadron. This view shows an F-84F-35-RE of the 113th TFS as it appeared on 21 May 1960.

Larry Milberry courtesy of David W. Menard

Jim Dunn

squadron retained its TFS designation and went on training as a fighter unit.
15 Oct 1962: Reached group status with federal recognition of 182nd TFG.
May 1964: Converted from RF-84Fs to F-84Fs.
Sep 1971: Converted from F-84Fs to North American F-100D/Fs.
Summer 1979: Converted from F-100D/Fs to McDonnell F-4Cs (the aircraft actually were 'Wild Weasel' EF-4Cs but were partially demodified and were operated as F-4Cs).
Nov 1979: Last Air Force F-100Ds flown out to MASDC.
1 Apr 1988: Completed conversion from F-4Cs to F-4Es.
FY91/FY92: Converted from F-4Es to General Dynamics Block 25 F-16C/Ds (first Fighting Falcons delivered in Apr

1991 and last Phantom left in Oct 1991).
15 Mar 1992: Unit designation changed to 113th Fighter Squadron, 182nd Fighter Group (113th FS, 182nd FG).
1 Jun 1992: As part of the Air Force restructuring program, gaining command changed to ACC.
1 Jul 1992: Completed conversion to F-16C/Ds.

The 113th FS being based at Terre Haute, not all that far from Indianapolis where the famous '500' car race is held every year during Memorial Day Weekend, 'Racers' is the logical nickname to be applied at the base of the fin of the squadron's F-16Cs and F-16Ds.

163rd Fighter Squadron
122nd Fighter Wing

Lineage: *Constituted in December 1942 and activated at Richmond AAB, VA, in January 1943, the 365th FS was assigned to the 358th FG, Ninth Air Force, with which it flew combat operations with Republic P-47Ds in the ETO between December 1943 and VE Day. Inactivated at La Junta, Colorado, on 7 November 1945, the squadron was redesignated 163rd FS and was allotted to the Indiana NG on 24 May 1946.*
11 Oct 1947: 163rd FS (SE) extended federal recognition at Baer Field, Ft Wayne, and equipped with North American F-51Ds (plus support aircraft).
1 Feb 1951: Called to active duty as part of the Korean War call-up, the unit was soon redesignated 163rd FBS but remained based at Baer Field.
1 Nov 1952: Returned to state control.
Sep 1954: Converted from F-51Ds to Lockheed F-80Cs.
1955: Redesignated 163rd FIS.
Oct 1957: Converted from F-80Cs to F-86As.
Jan 1958: Converted from F-86As to Republic F-84Fs.
Jul 1959: Redesignated 163rd TFS.
1 Jul 1960: Became TAC-gained upon implementation of gaining command concept.
1 Oct 1961: Called to active duty as

part of the Berlin Crisis call-up.
Nov 1951: Transferred to Chambley AB, France, and assigned to the 7122nd TFW, USAFE.
20 Aug 1962: Returned to state control at Baer Field but its F-84Fs were transferred to USAFE.
Oct 1962: Converted from F-84Fs to RF-84Fs. Even though it was equipped with reconnaissance aircraft, the squadron retained its TFS designation and went on training as a fighter unit.
May 1964: Converted from RF-84Fs to F-84Fs.
Jun 1971: Converted from F-84Fs to North American F-100D/Fs.
9 Dec 1974: 122nd TFG inactivated and 163rd TFS placed directly under the control of the 122nd TFW.
Spring 1979: Converted from F-100D/Fs to McDonnell F-4Cs (the aircraft actually were 'Wild Weasel' EF-4Cs but were partially demodified and were operated as F-4Cs).
1 Apr 1988: Completed conversion from F-4Cs to F-4Es.
FY91/FY92: Converted from F-4Es to General Dynamics Block 25 F-16C/Ds (first F-16Cs received in Oct 1991 and last F-4E flown out on 21 Jan 1992).
15 Mar 1992: Unit designation changed to 163rd Fighter Squadron, 122nd Fighter Wing (163rd FS, 122nd FW).
1 Jun 1992: As part of the Air Force restructuring program, gaining command

Above: Prior to serving with the 163rd TFS, 63-7565 had been modified to EF-4C 'Wild Weasel' IV standard.

Below: 68-0411, one of the first F-4Es to receive the 'FW' tailcode of the Fort Wayne unit. The last F-4Es left the 163rd TFS on 21 January 1992.

changed to ACC.
1 Oct 1992: Completed conversion to F-16C/Ds.

Above: Taxiing below the control tower at Luke AFB, Arizona, during a February 1982 deployment, 63-7564 is an F-4E-19-MC which served with the 163rd TFS alongside ex-EF-4Cs.

Right: Now known as the 'Marksmen', the Fort Wayne squadron has been equipped with Block 25 F-16Cs and F-16Ds since the summer of 1991.

Iowa Air National Guard

Extended federal recognition in February 1941 and placed on active duty seven months later, the 124th Observation Squadron served stateside until its inactivation in May 1944. Allotted back to the Iowa Guard in 1946, the 124th FS was supplemented by the 174th FS at the end of that year. Both units served in CONUS while on FAD during the Korean War, and the 174th deployed to Vietnam following its *Pueblo* Crisis activation.

At the end of FY92, 2,161 officers and enlisted personnel manned 24 IA ANG units, including the 124th FS which was converting to F-16C/Ds at the Des Moines International Airport and the 174th FS flying F-16C/Ds from the Sioux City Municipal Airport.

124th Fighter Squadron
132nd Fighter Wing

Lineage: *Designated the 124th Observation Squadron and allotted to the Iowa NG on 30 July 1940.*
25 Feb 1941: 124th OS extended federal recognition at the Des Moines Municipal Airport, Iowa.
15 Sep 1941: Called to active duty, assigned to II Air Support Command, and transferred 11 days later to Sherman Field, Ft Leavenworth, Kansas. On 30 November 1941, it had one Douglas O-38D, one Douglas O-38E, one North American BC-1A and one O-47A.
World War II: Remaining in CONUS, the unit moved five times, was redesignated on three occasions, flew ASW patrols over the Gulf of Mexico, and served as a fighter and reconnaissance replacement training unit before being disbanded at Key Field, MS, on 1 May 1944. The squadron was redesignated 124th FS and was allotted back to the Iowa NG on 24 May 1946.
23 Aug 1946: 124th FS (SE) extended federal recognition at the Des Moines MAP and soon equipped with North American P-51Ds (plus support aircraft).
1 Apr 1951: Called to active duty as part of the Korean War call-up and moved to Dow AFB, ME, for assignment to SAC.
Jun 1952: Redesignated 124th FBS and transferred to Alexandria AFB, LA, for service with TAC.
31 Dec 1952: Returned to state control.
Summer 1953: Converted from F-51Ds to Lockheed F-80Cs.
1 Jul 1955: Redesignated from 124th

Peter B. Lewis

Based at the Des Moines International Airport, the 124th TFS has flown A-7Ds since 1977.

FBS to 124th FIS.
Sep 1956: Converted from F-80Cs to Republic F-84Es.
Apr 1958: Converted from F-84Es to North American F-86Ls.
1 Jul 1960: Became ADC-gained upon implementation of gaining command concept.
Apr 1962: Converted from F-86Ls to Northrop F-89Js.
Summer 1969: Converted from F-89Js to Republic F-84Fs.
2 Aug 1969: Redesignated 124th TFS and became TAC-gained.
Apr 1971: Converted from F-84Fs to

The squadron designation was changed when the 124th converted from F-89Js to F-84Fs.

North American F-100C/Fs.
FY75: Converted from F-100Cs to F-100Ds (but retained F-100Fs) and phased out last ANG F-100Cs.
Jan 1977: Converted from F-100D/Fs to LTV A-7Ds.
FY87: A-7Ds upgraded to LANA configuration.
15 Mar 1992: Unit designation changed to 124th Fighter Squadron, 132nd Fighter Wing (124th FS, 132nd FW).
1 Jun 1992: As part of the Air Force restructuring program, gaining command changed to ACC.
FY93: Converting from A-7D/Ks to General Dynamics Block 52 F-16C/Ds.

Continuing the rapid retirement of the A-7 from ANG service, Iowa's 124th FS joined the state's other squadron as an F-16C/D operator. This is the wing commander's aircraft with full-color markings.

Peter B. Lewis

John A. Sheets

174th Fighter Squadron
185th Fighter Group

Lineage: *Constituted and activated at Richmond, VA, in April-May 1943, the 386th FS was assigned to the 365th FG, Ninth Air Force, with which it flew combat operations with Republic P-47Ds* in the ETO beginning in February 1944. It was inactivated at Camp Myles Standish, MA, in September 1945 and, reconstituted and redesignated the 174th FS, the unit was allotted to the

Before implementation of the Total Force concept, Guard units proudly painted the name of their home state on their aircraft. Iowa's 174th was a TRS between 1958 and 1961.

Jim Sullivan courtesy of Cloud 9 Photography

Jim Dunn

Gary Chambers

Out with state names and in with tactical paint schemes. Fortunately, all signs of unit pride are not gone as Sioux City still appears in script letters on the fin of this A-7D taking off from Nellis.

Iowa NG on 24 May 1946.
2 Dec 1946: 174th FS (SE) extended federal recognition at Sioux City MAP and soon equipped with North American P-51Ds (plus support aircraft).
1 May 1950: Redesignated 124th FS (Jet).
May 1950: Converted from F-51Ds to Republic F-84Bs.
1 Apr 1951: Called to active duty as part of the Korean War call-up and moved to Dow AFB, ME, for assignment to SAC. Most jet pilots transferred to

USAF units in Europe and the Far East and squadron re-equipped with F-51Ds.
Jun 1952: Redesignated 174th FBS and transferred to Alexandria AFB, LA, for service with TAC.
31 Dec 1952: Returned to state control.
Jul 1953: Converted from F-51Ds to Lockheed F-80Cs.
1 Jul 1955: Redesignated from 174th FBS to 174th FIS.
Aug 1956: Converted from F-80Cs to Republic F-84Es.
Spring 1958: Converted from F-84Es to RF-84Fs.
10 Apr 1958: Redesignated from 174th FIS to 174th TRS.
1 Jul 1960: Became TAC-gained upon implementation of gaining command concept.

1 May 1961: Redesignated from 174th TRS to 174th TFS.
Summer 1961: Converted from RF-84Fs to North American F-100C/Fs.
1 Oct 1962: Reached group status with federal recognition of 185th TFG.
26 Jan 1968: Called to active duty as part of the *Pueblo* Crisis call-up and began preparing overseas deployment.
May 1968: Deployed to Phu Cat AB, South Vietnam, and flew combat sorties from June 1968 until April 1969.
28 May 1969: Returned to state control.
Jun 1974: Completed conversion from F-100Cs to F-100Ds but retained F-100Fs.
Dec 1976: Converted from F-100D/Fs to LTV A-7Ds.
FY92/FY93: Converting from A-7D/Ks

Many hope that regulations concerning unit markings will soon be relaxed. This newly-assigned F-16C of the 174th FS already carries distinctive tail markings and state and city names. Add a bit of color and Kodak's profit will be up.

to General Dynamics Block 30 F-16C/Ds (first F-16C arrived on 19 Dec 1991 and last A-7D left on 20 Feb 1992).
15 Mar 1992: Unit designation changed to 174th Fighter Squadron, 185th Fighter Group (174th FS, 185th FG).
1 Jun 1992: As part of the Air Force restructuring program, gaining command changed to ACC.
1 Jan 1993: Scheduled to complete conversion to F-16C/Ds.

Kansas Air National Guard

On 4 August 1941, the 127th Observation Squadron became the 29th and last Guard squadron to receive federal recognition before America's entry into World War II. Placed on FAD two months later, the Kansans ended the war as the 127th Liaison Squadron (Commando) on Okinawa. Reorganized as a fighter squadron in September 1946, the 127th remained the sole flying unit in the Kansas ANG until February 1957 when the 117th was organized. During the

Korean War, the 127th served on active duty in CONUS and during its *Pueblo* Crisis activation it flew F-100C/Fs from Kunsan AB in Korea. For eight years during the 1970s it served as an F-105 RTU. Two specialized training units were organized in the Kansas ANG during the late 1980s.

At the end of FY92, 2,539 officers and enlisted personnel manned 27 KS ANG units, including four flying squadrons: the 117th ARS equipped with KC-135Es at Forbes Field in Topeka and the 127th TFS, 161st and 177th Fighter Squadrons sharing F-16C/Ds at McConnell AFB.

117th Air Refueling Squadron
190th Air Refueling Group

Lineage: *When in 1957 the Kansas ANG was authorized to organize a new FIS, this unit was given the numerical designation of the 117th FIS which had been inactivated as a Pennsylvania ANG unit in January 1957.*
23 Feb 1957: 117th FIS activated at NAS Hutchinson, KS, and equipped with Lockheed F-80Cs.
Spring 1958: Converted from F-80Cs to Martin RB-57A/Bs.
10 Apr 1958: Redesignated from 117th FIS to 117th TRS.
1 Jul 1960: Became TAC-gained upon implementation of gaining command concept.
15 Oct 1962: Reached group status with federal recognition of 190th TRG.
11 Aug 1967: Completed move from NAS Hutchinson to Forbes AFB.
Spring 1972: Converted from

RB-57A/Bs to B-57Gs.
12 Jun 1972: Redesignated from 117th TRS/190th TRG to 117th Bombardment Tactical Squadron/190th Bombardment Tactical Group.

Bil Curry

Oct 1973: Forbes AFB transferred to the Kansas ANG as Forbes ANGB.
Winter 1973: Converted from B-57Gs to EB-57B/Es.
6 Apr 1974: Redesignated from 117th BTS/190th BTG to 117th DSES/190th DSEG, and became ADC-gained.
Summer 1978: Converted from EB-57s to Boeing KC-135As.
8 Jul 1978: Redesignated from 117th DSES/190th DSEG to 117th AREFS/190th AREFG and became SAC-gained.
FY84: Converted from KC-135As to KC-135Es.

Kansas' 117th Squadron had the distinction of flying Martin-built Canberras in the reconnaissance, tactical bombing and defense systems evaluation roles. 52-1521, an EB-57B of the 117th DSES, is seen landing at Shaw AFB, NC, on 27 December 1974.

Aug 1990: Volunteers began flying missions in support of Operation Desert Shield.
20 Dec 1990: Called to active duty as part of Operation Desert Shield call-up.
15 Apr 1991: Released from active duty after taking part in Desert Shield/Desert Storm.
15 Mar 1992: Unit abbreviation changed to 117th ARS, 190th ARG.
1 Jun 1992: As part of the Air Force restructuring program, gaining command changed to AMC.

Back from the Gulf War: a KC-135E of the 190th AREFG sits on the ramp at Forbes Field in March 1991. During the Gulf War, the Commander of the 190th became the Commander of the 1701st AREFW(P) at the King Adbul Aziz IAP in Saudi Arabia.

Jerry Geer

127th Fighter Squadron
184th Fighter Group

Lineage: *Designated the 127th Observation Squadron and allotted to the Kansas NG on 30 July 1940.*
4 Aug 1941: 127th OS extended federal recognition at the Wichita Municipal Airport, Kansas.
6 Oct 1941: Called to active duty, assigned to 68th Observation Squadron, and transferred seven days later to Sherman Field, Ft Leavenworth, KS. On 30 November 1941, it had one **Douglas O-38E**, one **Douglas O-46A** and one **North American BC-1A.**
World War II: Remaining in CONUS until October 1944, the squadron moved eight times, was redesignated on four occasions, flew a variety of observation and liaison aircraft, as well as a few **Douglas A-20s** and **Curtiss P-40s**, before being trained as a liaison unit for overseas deployment. Assigned to the 2nd Air Commando Group, the 127th Liaison Squadron (Commando) flew **Piper L-4s, Stinson L-5s** and **Noorduyn UC-64s** in the CBI theater between January and May 1945. Inactivated on Okinawa in November 1945, the squadron was redesignated 127th FS and was allotted back to the Kansas NG on 24 May 1946.
7 Sep 1946: 127th FS (SE) extended federal recognition at the Wichita MAP and soon equipped with **North American P-51Ds** (plus support aircraft).
Feb 1950: Converted from F-51Ds to **Republic F-84Cs.**
21 Feb 1950: Redesignated 127th FS (Jet).
10 Oct 1950: Called to active duty as part of the Korean War call-up.
1 Nov 1950: Redesignated 127th FBS.
26 Nov 1950: Moved to Alexandria AFB, LA, to join other squadrons of the 137th FBW.

Photographed at McClellan AFB, California, in July 1975, this F-105F was one of the Thunderchiefs then equipping the 127th TFTS, the F-105 replacement training unit at McConnell AFB.

Spring 1952: Converted from F-84Cs to F-84Gs.
May 1952: Moved to Chaumont AB, France.
10 Jul 1952: Returned to state control at Wichita AFB, KS, once again to be equipped with F-51Ds.
Apr 1954: Wichita AFB renamed McConnell AFB.
Jun 1954: Converted from F-51Ds to Lockheed F-80Cs.
1 Jul 1955: Redesignated 127th FIS.
Jan 1958: Converted from F-80Cs to North American F-86Ls.
1 Jul 1960: Became ADC-gained upon

The first Fighting Falcons to equip the 127th TFS were F-16As (including 80-0493 photographed at McConnell AFB in September 1989) and F-16Bs. They replaced F-4Ds during the second half of 1987.

implementation of gaining command concept.
Spring 1961: Converted from F-86Ls to North American F-100C/Fs.
1 Apr 1961: Redesignated 127th TFS and became TAC-gained.
1 Oct 1962: Reached group status with federal recognition of 184th TFG.
26 Jan 1968: Called to active duty as part of the *Pueblo* Crisis call-up.
Jul 1968: Moved to Kunsan AB, Korea, and assigned to the 354th TFW.
18 Jun 1969: Returned to state control at McConnell AFB.
25 Mar 1971: Redesignated 127th TFTS, 184th TFTG.
Spring 1971: Converted from F-100C/Fs to Republic F-105D/Fs.
8 Oct 1979: Redesignated 127th TFS, 184th TFG, but retained training duty as F-4D RTU.
Winter 1979: Converted from

Beginning in the winter of 1990, the three squadrons of the 184th TFG switched from F-16A/Bs to F-16C/Ds. This C model was photographed at McConnell AFB in October 1991.

F-105D/Fs to McDonnell F-4Ds.
Summer/Winter 1987: Converted from F-4Ds to General Dynamics F-16A/Bs.
Winter 1990: Converted from F-16A/Bs to F-16C/Ds.
15 Mar 1992: Unit designation changed to 127th Fighter Squadron, 184th Fighter Group (127th FS, 184th FG).
1 Jun 1992: As part of the Air Force restructuring program, gaining command changed to ACC.

161st Fighter Squadron
184th Fighter Group

1 Jul 1987: Activated at McConnell AFB as a TAC-gained F-16 replacement training unit.
Spring 1991: F-16A/Bs, shared with the two other squadrons of the 184th TFG, replaced with F-16C/Ds.
15 Mar 1992: Unit designation changed to 161st Fighter Squadron, 184th Fighter Group (161st FS, 184th FG).
1 Jun 1992: As part of the Air Force restructuring program, gaining command changed to ACC.

As its 161st and 177th FS function as replacement training units, the 184th FG is a large operator of two-seaters. Before receiving F-16Ds, the 184th operated Bs, including this F-16-B-05-CF.

177th Fighter Squadron
184th Fighter Group

1 Feb 1984: Activated at McConnell AFB as a TAC-gained **F-4D** replacement training unit.
Mar 1990: Last F-4Ds phased out and 177th TFTS began sharing **F-16A/Bs** with the two other squadrons of the 184th TFG.
Spring 1991: Pooled F-16A/Bs replaced by **F-16C/Ds**.
15 Mar 1992: Unit designation changed to 177th Fighter Squadron, 184th Fighter Group (177th FS, 184th FG).
1 Jun 1992: As part of the Air Force restructuring program, gaining command changed to ACC.

*Since the 177th **TFTS** completed its conversion from **F-4Ds**, the F-16s of the three flying squadrons of the 184th **TFG** are pooled.*

Kentucky Air National Guard

Organized as the 165th FS in February 1947, the sole flying unit of the Kentucky ANG served twice on active duty (in England during the Korean War and in Alaska, Panama and Korea during the *Pueblo* Crisis). After flying fighters and tactical reconnaissance aircraft for 42 years, the 165th became the Guard's newest transport squadron in 1989 when it converted from RF-4Cs to C-130Bs.

At the end of FY92, 1,215 officers and enlisted personnel manned 16 KY ANG units, including the 165th AS which was flying C-130Hs from Standiford Field in Louisville.

165th Airlift Squadron
123rd Airlift Wing

Lineage: *Constituted and activated at Westover Field, MA, in January 1943, the 368th FS flew combat operations in the ETO with Republic P-47Ds (from December 1943) and North American P-51Ds (from November 1944 until VE Day) as part of the England-based 359th FG, Eighth Air Force. It was inactivated in November 1945. Reconstituted and redesignated the 165th FS, the unit was allotted to the Kentucky NG on 24 May 1946.*
16 Feb 1947: 165th FS (SE) extended federal recognition at Standiford Field, Louisville, and soon equipped with **North American P-51Ds** (plus support aircraft).
10 Oct 1950: Called to active duty as part of the Korean War call-up and moved 10 days later to Godman Field, KY, for assignment to TAC, redesignation to 165th FBS and subsequent conversion to **Republic F-84Ds** and then to **F-84Es**.
Nov 1951: Moved to RAF Manston, England.
10 Jul 1952: Returned to state control to be reorganized as the 165th FBS and equipped with **North American F-51Hs**.
Nov 1952: Converted from F-51Hs to F-51Ds.

The operational support aircraft currently assigned to Kentucky's 123rd Airlift Wing is this Beech C-12F seen here at Standiford Field, Louisville, in September 1988.

Redesignated the 165th TRS on 15 January 1958 after converting from F-86As, Kentucky's flying squadron operated Martin RB-57Bs until the summer of 1965, when it received Voodoos.

1 Jul 1955: Redesignated 165th FIS.
May 1956: Partial conversion from F-51Ds to **North American T-28As** pending completion of facilities suitable for jet operations.
Sep 1956: First North American F-86As received.
Dec 1956: Converted from F-51Ds/T-28As to F-86As.
15 Jan 1958: Redesignated 165th TRS and re-equipped with **Martin RB-57Bs**.

1 Jul 1960: Became TAC-gained upon implementation of gaining command concept.
15 Oct 1962: Reached group status with federal recognition of the 123rd TRG.
Jul 1965: Received first Voodoos and began conversion from RB-57Bs to **McDonnell RF-101G/Hs**.
26 Jan 1968: Called to active duty as a result of the *Pueblo* Crisis but initially

Wearing the new gray scheme adopted by the Air Mobility Command, the 2000th Hercules, a C-130H, was delivered to the 165th AS on May 1992.

remained at its home station.
18 Jul 1968: Moved to Richards-Gebaur AFB, MO, while on active duty. TDY deployments to Elmendorf AFB, AK, from 16 Aug until 26 Sep 1968, and to Howard AFB, Panama, from 16 Oct 1968 until 16 Jan 1969.
25 Jan 1969: Moved to Itazuke AB, Japan, while on active duty.

9 Jun 1969: Returned to state control.
1972/1973: Converted from RF-101G/Hs to RF-101Cs.
9 Dec 1974: 123rd TRG inactivated and 165th TRS began reporting directly to the 123rd TRW.
Early 1976: converted from RF-101Cs to McDonnell RF-4Cs (first received in Feb 1976).

8 Jan 1989: Redesignated 165th TAS/123rd TAW, re-equipped with Lockheed C-130Bs, and became MAC-gained.
Aug 1990: Volunteers began flying missions in support of Operation Desert Shield.
Early 1992: Commenced conversion from C-130Bs to C-130Hs.

16 May 1992: Received its first C-130H, the 2,000th Hercules built by Lockheed.
15 Mar 1992: Unit designation changed to 165th Airlift Squadron, 123rd Airlift Wing (165th AS, 123rd AW).
1 Jun 1992: As part of the Air Force restructuring program, gaining command changed to AMC.

Louisiana Air National Guard

The 122nd Observation Squadron was organized in New Orleans in March 1941 and was federalized seven months later. Redesignated several times during World War II, the unit served in the MTO from November 1942 until October 1945. At the end of 1946, the squadron was reorganized as the 122nd BS and went on to fly A-26s for 10 years (including 21 months on active duty in the United States during the Korean War). Since the spring of 1957, the 122nd has flown jet interceptors and tactical fighters.

At the end of FY92, 1,656 officers and enlisted personnel manned 16 LA ANG units, including the 122nd FS which was flying F-15A/Bs from NAS New Orleans.

122nd Fighter Squadron
159th Fighter Group

Lineage: *Designated the 122nd Observation Squadron and allotted to the Louisiana NG on 30 July 1940.*
2 Mar 1941: 122nd OS extended federal recognition at New Orleans Airport.
1 Oct 1941: Called to active duty, assigned to 68th Observation Squadron, and transferred five days later to Esler Field, LA. On 30 November 1941, it had three **Douglas O-38B/Es**, one **Douglas O-46A**, one **North American O-47A** and one **BC-1A**.

The 122nd TFS initially operated early production Eagles, including this F-15A-12-MC seen landing at NAS New Orleans.

World War II: The squadron moved eight times, was redesignated on three occasions, and flew ASW patrols over the Gulf of Mexico and along the Atlantic seaboard before being transferred to French Morocco (via England) in the fall of 1942. In North Africa it flew ASW patrols with **Douglas A-20s** until reorganized as a fighter RTU in March 1943. Redesignated 885th BS (Heavy) in May 1944, the unit flew **Boeing B-17s** and **Consolidated B-24s** to transport supplies to partisans and drop leaflets in the MTO. Inactivated in Italy on 4 October 1945, the squadron was redesignated 122nd BS and was allotted back to the Louisiana NG on 24 May 1946.
5 Dec 1946: 122nd BS (Light) extended federal recognition at New Orleans Airport and soon equipped with **Douglas A-26B/Cs** (plus support aircraft).
1 Apr 1951: Called to active duty as part of the Korean War call-up.
13 Apr 1951: Moved to Langley AFB, VA, to become part of the 4400th CCTG.
1 Jan 1953: Returned to state control at New Orleans Airport.
Spring 1957: Converted from B-26B/Cs to **Lockheed F-80Cs.**
1 Jun 1957: Redesignated 122nd FIS and reached group status with federal recognition of 159th FIG.
Fall 1957: Converted from F-80Cs to North American F-86Ds.
Dec 1957: Transferred from New Orleans Airport to NAS New Orleans.
?: Converted from F-86Ds to F-86Ls.
1 Jul 1960: Became ADC-gained upon implementation of gaining command concept.
Jul 1960: Converted from F-86Ls to

Convair F/TF-102As.
Fall/Winter 1970: Converted from F/TF-102As (last left on 4 Dec 1970) to North American F-100D/Fs.
5 Dec 1970: Redesignated from 122nd FIS to 122nd TFS/159th TFG and became TAC-gained.
Apr 1979: Converted from F-100D/Fs to McDonnell F-4Cs.
Summer 1985: Began converting from F-4Cs to McDonnell Douglas F-15A/Bs (first F-15A received in Jun 1985).
FY92: Exchanged early production F-15A/Bs for late model F-15A/Bs

McDonnell F-4Cs of the 122nd TFS seen over NAS New Orleans in November 1984. Seven months later Louisiana's flying squadron received its first McDonnell Douglas F-15A Eagle.

15 Mar 1992: Unit designation changed to 122nd Fighter Squadron, 159th Fighter Group (122nd FS, 159th FG).
1 Jun 1992: As part of the Air Force restructuring program, gaining command changed to ACC.

Maine Air National Guard

At the end of FY92, 1,393 officers and enlisted personnel manned 15 ME ANG units, including the 132nd ARS equipped with KC-135Es and based at Bangor IAP. This squadron, which had first been organized as the 132nd FS in February 1947, was placed on active duty during the Korean War and flew fighters for 29 years. During the spring of 1976, the Guardsmen of Bangor, Maine, converted from supersonic F-101Bs (with which they were known as the 'Maine Bangers') to KC-135A tankers (with which they became the 'Maineacs').

132nd Air Refueling Squadron
101st Air Refueling Wing

Lineage: *Constituted at Will Rogers Field, OK, in January 1942, and activated in March 1942, the 528th Bombardment Squadron (Dive) was redesignated 528th FBS in September 1943, shortly after arriving in India, and 528th FS in May 1944. It flew North American A-36s and P-51s in the CBI theater until VJ Day and was inactivated at Ft Lawton, WA, in January 1946. Reconstituted and redesignated the 132nd FS, the unit was allotted to the Maine NG on 24 May 1946.*

5 Feb 1947: 132nd FS (SE) extended federal recognition at Dow Field, Bangor, ME, and soon equipped with Republic P-47Ds (plus support aircraft).
Summer 1948: Converted from F-47Ds to Lockheed F-80Cs.
1 Aug 1948: Redesignated 132nd FS (Jet).
1 Feb 1951: Called to active duty as part of the Korean War call-up.
25 Feb 1951: Redesignated 132nd FIS and re-equipped with North American F-51Ds to provide air defense for the Northeast US from Dow AFB.
1 Nov 1951: Returned to state control but remained at Dow AFB with F-51Hs.
Jun 1954: Converted from F-51Hs to Lockheed F-94As.
Sep 1957: Converted from F-94As to Northrop F-89Ds.
Dec 1959: Converted from F-89Ds to F-89Js.
1 Jul 1960: Became ADC-gained upon implementation of gaining command.
1 Dec 1960: Reached group status with federal recognition of 101st FIG.
Jun 1968: Dow AFB inactivated and airfield became Bangor IAP.
Jul 1969: Converted from F-89Js to Convair F/TF-102As.
Nov 1969: Converted from F/TF-102As to McDonnell F-101B/Fs.
Spring 1976: Converted from

After the 'Maine Bangers' converted from Voodoos to Stratotankers, their nickname was changed to 'Maineacs'.

René J. Francillon

The 132nd FIS flew F-101B/Fs for just under six years, then sent some Voodoos to museums.

Seen at Edwards AFB, this C-54M was used as a support aircraft by the Maine ANG.

F-101B/Fs to Boeing KC-135As.
1 Apr 1976: Redesignated 132nd AREFS and began reporting directly to the 101st AREFW as a SAC-gained unit.

FY85: Converted from KC-135As to KC-135Es.
Aug 1990: Volunteers began flying missions in support of Operation Desert Shield.
20 Dec 1990: Called to active duty as part of Operation Desert Shield call-up.
30 May 1991: Released from active

duty after taking part in Desert Shield/Desert Storm.
15 Mar 1992: Unit abbreviation changed to 132nd ARS, 101st ARW.
1 Jun 1992: As part of the Air Force restructuring program, gaining command changed to AMC.

Brian C. Rogers

Maryland Air National Guard

Organized in Baltimore, the 104th Squadron was the first National Guard unit to be equipped with its own aircraft (13 Curtiss JN-4D-2s being received between July and October 1921) and the first to attend summer encampment (in July 1922 at Langley Field, VA). Having served on active duty in CONUS between February 1941 and May 1944, the 104th was reconstituted in the Maryland Guard in August 1946 and since then has served as a fighter unit (including seven months on active duty during the *Pueblo* Crisis when it operated as a combat crew training unit). The Maryland ANG added a transport unit, the 135th Air Resupply Group, in September 1955.

At the end of FY92, 1,998 officers and enlisted personnel manned 27 MD ANG units, including the 104th FS and 135th AS both based at the Glenn L. Martin State Airport (Warfield ANGB) and respectively flying A-10As and C-130Es.

104th Fighter Squadron
175th Fighter Group

Lineage: *Organized in June 1921 in the Maryland National Guard as the 104th Squadron.*

29 Jun 1921: 104th Squadron extended federal recognition at Logan Field, Baltimore, as the aviation unit in the 29th Division, Maryland NG, and initially equipped with Curtiss JN-4Ds.
25 Jan 1923: Redesignated 104th OS.

1923-1940: Remaining based in Baltimore, the 104th OS was equipped over the years with the mix of aircraft typical of prewar Guard units, including Consolidated PT-1s and O-17s; Curtiss O-11s; Douglas BT-1s, O-2s, O-38s and

O-46s; and North American O-47s and BC-1s. On 31 December 1940, it had one BC-1As, seven O-46As and five O-47A/Bs.
3 Feb 1941: Called to active duty and placed under command of II Army

As Harbor Field was not suitable for jet operations, the 104th FIS was forced to temporarily split its operations between its home base and Baltimore's Friendship Airport, where this F-86E-10-NA was photographed in June 1957.

David W. Lucabaugh courtesy of David W. Menard

Corps, but remained at Logan Field until September 1941.

World War II: Remaining in CONUS, the unit moved six times, was redesignated on four occasions, flew ASW patrols along the mid-Atlantic coast, and served as a fighter replacement unit until disbanded on 1 May 1944. The squadron was redesignated 104th FS and was allotted to the Maryland NG on 24 May 1946.

17 Aug 1946: 104th FS (SE) extended federal recognition at Harbor Field, Baltimore, and soon equipped with Republic P-47Ds (plus support aircraft).

Aug 1951: Redesignated 104th FIS and converted from F-47Ds to North American F-51Hs.

1 Dec 1952: Redesignated 104th F-BS.

8 Jul 1954: First jet, a Lockheed T-33A, delivered but had to be kept first at Andrews AFB and then at Baltimore's Friendship Airport as Harbor Field was not suitable for jet operations.

Fall 1954: Converted from F-51Hs to F-51Ds for continued operations from Harbor Field.

Sep 1955: Last F-51Ds phased out and 104th left only with T-33A trainers.

Jun 1956: Redesignated 104th FIS and re-equipped with North American F-86Es. Jets were operated from Friendship Airport while the unit remained officially based at Harbor Field.

Jul 1957: Unit moved to the Glenn L. Martin State Airport, on eastern outskirts of Baltimore, and split operations ended with transfer of jets from Friendship Airport.

Flying 'Warthogs' upgraded with LASTE (Low Altitude Safety and Targeting Enhancement), the Marylanders of the 104th TFS stunned the F-16 community by beating Gulf War veterans and taking first place at Gunsmoke '91.

Dec 1957: Converted from F-86Es to F-86Hs.

10 Nov 1958: Redesignated 104th TFS.

1 Jul 1960: Became TAC-gained upon implementation of gaining command.

1 Oct 1962: Reached group status with federal recognition of 175th TFG.

13 May 1968: Called to active duty as part of the *Pueblo* Crisis call-up.

Jun 1968: Moved to Cannon AFB, NM, to operate as a combat crew

A-37Bs were delivered to the 104th TFS directly from the Cessna plant in Wichita. The first of these aircraft arrived at the Glenn L. Martin State Airport, home of the 104th since July 1957, on 25 April 1970 and the last was flown on 8 May 1980.

training unit.

20 Dec 1968: Returned to state control at Martin State Airport.

25 Apr 1970: Received first Cessna A-37B to commence conversion from F-86Hs (last F-86H left on 4 Aug 1970).

28 Sep 1979: Received first Fairchild-Republic A-10A to commence conversion from A-37Bs (last A-37B departed on 8 May 1980).

Oct 1991: Won Gunsmoke '91 competition.

15 Mar 1992: Unit designation changed to 104th Fighter Squadron, 175th Fighter Group (104th FS, 175th FG).

1 Jun 1992: As part of the Air Force restructuring program, gaining command changed to ACC.

Late 1992: Scheduled to add six OA-10As to its 18 A-10As.

René J. Francillon

MD ANG

135th Airlift Squadron
135th Airlift Group

Lineage: *When in 1955 the Maryland ANG was authorized to organize a new squadron to replace its 104th FIS at Harbor Field, the new unit was given the numerical designation of the 135th BS (Medium), an ANG-manned unit which had been activated during the Korean War in May 1951 and was assigned to the 106th BW to serve alongside two New York ANG squadrons, the 102nd and 114th BSs. The 135th BS was inactivated on 1 December 1952.*

MD ANG

10 Sep 1955: 135th Air Resupply Squadron and 135th Air Resupply Group extended federal recognition at Harbor Field, Baltimore, and squadron equipped with Curtiss C-46Ds.

Jan 1956: C-46Ds supplemented by Grumman SA-16As.

10 Oct 1958: Units redesignated 135th TCS (Medium) and 135th TCG; C-46Ds phased out.

1 Apr 1960: 135th TCS and 135th TCG

De Havilland Canada C-7As and C-7Bs equipped the 135th Tactical Airlift Squadron for four years beginning in late 1976. These Caribous had seen prior ANG service with New Jersey's 150th.

64-0520 lifts off at the Glenn L. Martin State Airport on 28 June 1990, shortly after the 135th TAS had exchanged its old C-130Bs for only slightly younger C-130Es.

relocated to Martin AP, Baltimore. At about the same time the SA-16As were supplemented by SA-16Bs.
1 Jul 1960: Became TAC-gained upon implementation of gaining command concept.
1 Jul 1963: Designations changed to

135th ACS and 135th ACG.
Aug 1963: Grumman HU-16A/Bs supplemented by Helio U-10Bs.
Sep 1965: U-10Bs replaced by de Havilland Canada U-6As and HU-16As phased out.
Jul 1967: U-6As replaced by U-10Ds.
8 Aug 1968: Designations changed to 135th SOS and 135th SOG.
Apr 1967: U-10Ds replaced by Cessna O-2As.
14 Jun 1971: Redesignated 135th TASS and 135th TASG as TAC-gained units; HU-16Bs phased out.
Late 1976: Began conversion to de

Havilland Canada C-7A/Bs.
1 Apr 1977: Redesignated 135th TAS and 135th TAG as MAC-gained units.
Fall 1980: Converted from C-7A/Bs to Lockheed C-130Bs.
Spring 1990: Converted from C-130Bs to C-130Es.
Aug 1990: Volunteers began flying missions in support of Desert Shield.
15 Mar 1992: Unit designation changed to 135th Airlift Squadron, 135th Airlift Group (135th AS, 135th AG).
1 Jun 1992: As part of the Air Force restructuring program, gaining command changed to AMC.

Massachusetts Air National Guard

Organized in Boston in November 1921, the 101st Observation Squadron was first called to FAD 19 years later, flew combat operations in Europe for two months just before World War II ended, and was allotted back to the Massachusetts Guard in 1946. Neither the 104th FS nor the 131st FS, which had been organized in eastern Massachusetts in 1947, was called to active duty during the Korean War,

but both served in France during the Berlin Crisis.
At the end of FY92, 2,889 officers and enlisted personnel manned 33 MA ANG units, including the 101st FS flying F-15A/Bs from Otis ANGB and the 131st FS flying A-10As from the Barnes Municipal Airport and preparing to convert to F-16C/Ds.

101st Fighter Squadron
102nd Fighter Wing

The current mission aircraft of the 101st Fighter Squadron are 16 F-15As and two F-15Bs, including 76-0128. The squadron completed its conversion from Delta Darts to Eagles on 1 April 1988.

Lineage: *Organized at Kelly Field, TX, on 22 August 1917 as the 101st Aero Squadron, this Air Service unit moved to France in January 1918. It was redesignated 639th Aero Squadron on 1*

Below and below right: *In August 1968, the 102nd TFG moved to Otis AFB on beautiful Cape Cod. The 'Irish Guard' has since made frequent use of that name. 'Cape Cod' is painted atop the fuselage. On the currently-assigned C-12J, 'Cape Cod' is painted on the engine nacelle.*

February 1918, served an an aircraft maintenance unit with the AEF, and was demobilized at Mitchel Field, NY, on 14 April 1919. In 1936, its lineage and honors were consolidated with those of the 101st Squadron which had been activated as a Massachusetts NG unit in November 1921.
18 Nov 1921: 101st Squadron extended federal recognition at Boston Airport as the aviation unit in the 26th Division, Massachusetts NG, and initially equipped with Curtiss Jennies.
25 Jan 1923: Redesignated 101st OS.
1923-1940: Remaining based in Boston, the 101st OS was equipped over

the years with the mix of aircraft typical of prewar Guard units, including Consolidated PT-1s and O-17s; Curtiss O-11s and XO-12; Douglas BT-1s, O-2s, O-38s and O-46s; and North American O-47s and BC-1s.
25 Nov 1940: Called to active duty and assigned to the First Corps Area. On 31 December 1940, it had one BC-1A, six O-46As and four O-47A/Bs.
World War II: Between 31 July 1941, when the 101st OS moved to Otis Field, Camp Edwards, MA, and December 1944, when the 39th PRS was shipped to France, the mobilized Massachusetts unit moved five times within CONUS,

was redesignated on six occasions, flew ASW patrols along the New England coast and was trained as a photographic reconnaissance unit. Equipped with Lockheed F-5s and assigned to the Ninth Air Force, the 39th PRS flew combat sorties from March to May 1945. Returned to the United States after VE

130

Day and redesignated 39th TRS, the unit flew **North American P-51Ds** and **Lockheed P-80As** until inactivated at March Field, CA, on 29 July 1946. Redesignated 101st FS, the unit was allotted back to the Massachusetts NG on 29 July 1946.

15 Oct 1946: 101st FS (SE) extended federal recognition at Logan Airport, Boston, and soon equipped with Republic P-47Ns (plus support aircraft).

Spring 1950: Converted from F-47Ns to **Republic F-84Bs** and redesignated 101st FIS.

Nov 1951: Converted from F-84Bs to **North American F-51Hs.**

Jul 1954: Converted from F-51Hs to **Lockheed F-94A/Bs.**

Early 1956: Converted from F-94A/Bs to **F-94Cs.**

Fall 1958: Converted from F-94Cs to **North American F-86Hs** and redesignated from 101st FIS to 101st TFS.

1 Jul 1960: Became TAC-gained upon implementation of gaining command concept.

1 Oct 1961: Called to active duty as part of the Berlin Crisis call-up.

Nov 1961: Moved to Phalsbourg AB, France.

21 Aug 1962: Returned to state control at Logan Airport.

Mar 1964: Converted from F-86Hs to **Republic F-84Fs.**

Aug 1968: Moved to Otis AFB, MA.

May 1971: Converted from F-84Fs to **North American F-100D/Fs.**

Spring 1972: Converted from F-100D/Fs to **Convair F-106A/Bs.**

10 Jun 1972: Redesignated from 101st FIS and became ADC-gained.

31 Dec 1973: Otis AFB inactivated and transferred to the MA ANG as Otis ANGB.

9 Jul 1976: 102nd FIG inactivated and 101st FIS directly assigned to 102nd FIW.

1 Apr 1980: Became TAC-gained following ADC inactivation.

1 Apr 1988: Completed conversion from F-106A/Bs to **McDonnell Douglas F-15A/Bs.**

15 Mar 1992: Unit designation changed to 101st Fighter Squadron,

102nd Fighter Wing (101st FS, 102nd FW).

1 Jun 1992: As part of the Air Force restructuring program, gaining command changed to ACC.

A brace of F-106As of the 101st FIS awaits clearance to take off for a competition sortie during William Tell '78 at Tyndall AFB, Florida, in October 1978. The 101st FIS flew Delta Darts for 16 years beginning in the spring of 1972.

Peter B. Lewis

131st Fighter Squadron
104th Fighter Group

Lineage: *Constituted and activated at Bellows Field, HI, in August 1942, the 333rd FS was assigned to the 18th FG and, from January 1943, to the 318th FG, Seventh Air Force. Initially flying patrols in Hawaii, the squadron served as a replacement training unit from July 1943 to June 1944 and, equipped with Republic P-47D/Ns, flew combat sorties in the Western Pacific from July 1944 until VJ Day. Inactivated at Ft Lewis, WA, in January 1946, the unit was reconstituted and redesignated the 131st FS, and was allotted to the Massachusetts NG on 24 May 1946.*

24 Feb 1947: 131st FS (SE) extended federal recognition at Barnes Field, Westfield, MA, and soon equipped with Republic P-47Ds (plus support aircraft).

Nov 1951: Converted from F-47Ds to **North American F-51Hs** and redesignated 131st FIS.

Spring 1954: Converted from F-51Hs

P-47D-30-RE of the 131st Fighter Squadron (SE), Massachusetts' 'Polish Guard'!

to **Lockheed F-94A/Bs.**

Spring 1957: Converted from F-94A/Bs to **F-94Cs.**

Spring 1958: Converted from F-94Cs to **North American F-86Hs.**

10 Nov 1958: Redesignated 131st TFS.

1 Jul 1960: Became TAC-gained upon implementation of gaining command concept.

1 Oct 1961: Called to active duty as part of the Berlin Crisis call-up.

Nov 1961: Moved to Phalsbourg AB, France.

21 Aug 1962: Returned to state control at Barnes Field.

15 Oct 1962: Reached group status with federal recognition of 104th TFG.

Mar 1964: Converted from F-86Hs to **Republic F-84Fs.**

Fairchild-Republic A-10As have equipped the 131st TFS at the Barnes Municipal Airport in Westfield since the summer of 1979. Current plans call for the 131st Fighter Squadron to fly its last 'Warthog' sorties in October 1993 and to complete its conversion to Block 25 F-16C/Ds a year later.

An F-86H-1-NH of the 'Polish Guard', the 131st TFS, photographed at Norton AFB, California, in May 1964. A few years later the same machine (below) was residing in MASDC at Davis-Monthan AFB.

Clay L. Jansson courtesy of Cloud 9 Photography

Jun 1971: Converted from F-84Fs to North American F-100D/Fs.

Jul 1979: Converted from F-100D/Fs to Fairchild-Republic A-10As.

15 Mar 1992: Unit designation changed to 131st Fighter Squadron, 104th Fighter Group (131st FS, 104th FG).

1 Jun 1992: As part of the Air Force

restructuring program, gaining command changed to ACC.

FY93/FY94: Will convert from A-10As to General Dynamics Block 25 F-16C/Ds, with last A-10As to be disposed of by Oct 1993 and conversion to F-16C/Ds to be completed by Oct 1994.

Peter B. Lewis

Daniel Soulaine

Michigan Air National Guard

At the end of FY92, 2,654 officers and enlisted personnel manned 37 MI ANG units, including three flying squadrons (two at Selfridge ANGB, the 107th FS with F-16A/Bs and the 171st FS with F-16A/B ADFs, and the 172nd FS at Battle Creek ANGB with A-10As and OA-10As).

Organized in 1926, the 107th Observation Squadron was activated

in October 1940, served in the ETO from August 1942 until after VE Day, and was allotted back to the Michigan Guard in 1946 to be re-organized as the 107th Bombardment Squadron. Postwar, it was joined by the 171st and 172nd Fighter Squadrons. All three squadrons served on active duty in CONUS during the Korean War.

107th Fighter Squadron
127th Fighter Wing

Lineage: *Organized at Kelly Field, TX, on 27 August 1917, as the 107th Aero Squadron, this Air Service unit moved to France in January 1918. It was redesignated 801st Aero Squadron on 1 February 1918, assembled, serviced and repaired aircraft for the AEF, and was demobilized at Garden City, NY, on 18 March 1919. In 1936, its lineage and honors were consolidated with those of the 107th OS which had been activated as a Michigan NG unit in May 1926.*

7 May 1926: 107th OS extended federal recognition at Wayne County Airport, Romulus, as the aviation unit in the 32nd Division, Michigan NG, and initially equipped with Consolidated PT-1s.

1926-1940: Remaining based in Romulus, the 107th OS was equipped over the years with the mix of aircraft typical of prewar Guard units, including Consolidated PT-1s; Douglas BT-1s, O-2s and O-38s; and North American O-47s and BC-1s.

15 Oct 1940: Called to active duty, assigned to the Fourth Corps Area, and moved 13 days later to Camp Beauregard, LA. On 31 December 1940, it had one BC-1A, two O-38Es and nine O-47A/Bs.

World War II: Before being shipped to England in August 1942, the federalized Michigan unit moved twice, was redesignated on two occasions, and briefly flew ASW patrols along the Carolinas and Georgia coasts. Trained on Supermarine Spitfire Vs but re-equipped with North American P-51/F-6s before being redesignated 107th

TRS, the squadron was assigned to the 67th TRG, Ninth Air Force, and flew tactical reconnaissance missions in the ETO between December 1943 and VE Day. Inactivated at Drew Field, FL, in November 1945, the squadron was redesignated 107th BS before being allotted back to the Michigan NG on 24 May 1946.

29 Sep 1946: 107th BS (Light) extended federal recognition at Wayne City Airport, Detroit, and soon equipped with Douglas A-26B/Cs (plus support aircraft).

Spring 1950: Converted from B-26B/Cs to Republic F-84Bs.

1 Jul 1950: Redesignated 107th FS (Jet).

1 Feb 1951: Called to active duty as part of the Korean War call-up and transferred to Luke AFB to serve as a component of the 127th Pilot Training Wing (with F-84E/Gs later supplementing and finally supplanting

the initially assigned F-84B/Cs).

1 Nov 1952: Returned to state control at the Detroit-Wayne Metro Airport to be reorganized as the 107th FBS and equipped with North American F-51Hs.

Nov 1953: Converted from F-51Hs to North American F-86Es.

Jun 1955: Converted from F-86Es to Northrop F-89Cs.

1 Jul 1955: Redesignated 107th FIS.

Spring 1958: Converted from F-89Cs to Republic RF-84Fs.

12 Apr 1958: Redesignated 107th TRS.

1 Jul 1960: Became TAC-gained upon implementation of gaining command concept.

1 Oct 1962: Reached group status with federal recognition of 127th TRG.

Jan 1971: Moved to Selfridge AFB and converted from RF-84Fs to McDonnell RF-101A/Cs.

Jul 1971: Selfridge AFB inactivated and transferred to Michigan ANG as Selfridge ANGB.

Summer 1972: Converted from RF-101A/Cs to North American F-100D/Fs.

1 Jul 1972: Redesignated 107th TFS.

9 Dec 1974: 127th TFG inactivated and 107th TFS placed directly under 127th TFW.

78-0079, the oldest F-16B serving with an operational unit, photographed at Hill AFB in October 1992, wears the latest markings approved for the 107th FS, 127th FW, Michigan ANG.

'Huns' equipped the 107th TFS between the summer of 1972, when F-100D/Fs replaced reconnaissance Voodoos, and the summer of 1978, when it converted to 'SLUFS'.

Summer 1978: Converted from F-100D/Fs to LTV A-7Ds.

1 Apr 1990: Completed conversion from A-7D/Ks to General Dynamics F-16A/Bs.

15 Mar 1992: Unit designation changed to 107th Fighter Squadron, 127th Fighter Wing (107th FS, 127th FW).

1 Jun 1992: As part of the Air Force restructuring program, gaining command changed to ACC.

171st Fighter Squadron
191st Fighter Group

Lineage: *Constituted at Richmond AAB, VA, in January 1943 and activated during the following month, the 374th FS was assigned to the 361st FG, Eighth Air Force. Equipped with Republic P-47Ds and North American P-51Ds (from May 1944), it flew combat operations in the ETO from January 1944 until VE Day. Inactivated at Camp Kilmer, NJ, in October 1945, the unit was reconstituted and redesignated 171st FS prior to being allotted to the Michigan NG on 24 May 1946.*

25 Apr 1948: 171st FS (SE) extended federal recognition at Wayne City Airport, Detroit, and soon equipped with North American P-51Ds (plus support aircraft).

Spring 1950: Converted from F-51Ds to Republic F-84Bs.

Between 1956 and 1972, 13 ANG squadrons were equipped with RF-84Fs, including two TFSs which flew them in lieu of fighters. The 171st was redesignated a tactical reconnaissance squadron in the spring of 1958, when it converted from F-89Cs.

Right: *Trading reconnaissance Voodoos for Delta Darts, the Michigan unit was redesignated the 171st FIS on 22 July 1972. 56-0463 lands at McClellan AFB, California, on 3 October 1976.*

1 Jul 1950: Redesignated 107th FS (Jet).
1 Feb 1951: Called to active duty as part of the Korean War call-up and transferred to Luke AFB to serve as a component of the 127th Pilot Training Wing (with F-84E/Gs later supplementing and finally supplanting the initially assigned F-84B/Cs).
1 Nov 1952: Returned to state control at the Detroit-Wayne Metro Airport to be reorganized as the 171st FBS and equipped with North American F-51Hs.
Nov 1953: Converted from F-51Hs to North American F-86Es and redesignated 171st FIS.
Jun 1955: Converted from F-86Es to Northrop F-89Cs.
Feb 1958: Converted from F-89Cs to Republic RF-84Fs.
Spring 1958: Redesignated 171st TRS.
1 Jul 1960: Became TAC-gained upon implementation of gaining command concept.
1 Oct 1962: Reached group status with federal recognition of 191st TRG.
Jan 1971: Moved to Selfridge AFB.
Feb 1971: Converted from RF-84Fs to McDonnell RF-101A/Cs.
Jul 1971: Selfridge AFB inactivated and transferred to Michigan ANG as Selfridge ANGB.
Summer 1972: Converted from RF-101A/Cs to Convair F-106A/Bs.
22 Jul 1972: Redesignated 171st FIS

Below: *As did California's 194th FIS, the 171st FIS was forced to trade beloved 'Sixes' for Phantoms. The Michigan unit flew F-4Cs from the spring of 1978.*

and became ADC-gained.
Spring 1978: Converted from F-106A/Bs to McDonnell F-4Cs.
1 Apr 1980: Became TAC-gained upon ADC inactivation.
Jul 1986: Converted from F-4Cs to F-4Ds.
1 Jul 1990: Completed conversion from F-4Ds to General Dynamics F-16A/Bs.
15 Mar 1992: Unit designation changed to 171st Fighter Squadron, 191st Fighter Group (171st FS, 191st FG).

The F-16B flagship of the 191st FIG shares the ramp with one of its more subdued F-16A ADF stablemates during a visit to the Ogden Air Logistics Center at Hill AFB, Utah.

1 Jun 1992: As part of the Air Force restructuring program, gaining command changed to ACC.

172nd Fighter Squadron
110th Fighter Group

Lineage: *Constituted at Richmond AAB, VA, in January 1943 and activated during the following month, the 375th FS was assigned to the 361st FG, Eighth Air Force. Equipped with Republic P-47Ds and North American P-51Ds (from May 1944), it flew combat operations in the ETO from January 1944 until VE Day. Inactivated at Camp Kilmer, NJ, in November 1945, the unit was reconstituted and redesignated 172nd FS prior to being allotted to the Michigan NG on 24 May 1946.*
16 Sep 1947: 172nd FS (SE) extended federal recognition at Kellogg Field, Battle Creek, MI, and soon equipped with North American P-51Ds (plus support aircraft).
1 Feb 1951: Called to active duty as part of the Korean War call-up and soon after moved to Selfridge AFB, MI, for assignment to the 56th FW.
May 1951: Redesignated 172nd FIS.

Nov 1952: Redesignated 172nd FBS and re-equipped with F-51Hs.
1 Dec 1952: Returned to state control at Kellogg Field.
Mar 1954: Converted from F-51Hs to North American F-86Es.
Apr 1955: Converted from F-86Es to Northrop F-89Cs.
18 Aug 1955: Redesignated 172nd FIS.
Spring 1958: Converted from F-89Cs

Martin RB-57As, with the original cockpit configuration inherited from its British forebear, equipped four ANG squadrons from 1958. Shining like a jewel, 52-1485 was photographed 10 years later on the ramp at the W. K. Kellogg Field.

to Martin RB-57As.
12 Apr 1958: Redesignated 172nd TRS.

Internal fuel tank capacity of the OA-37B, including fuel in tip tanks, was only 507 US gal (1920 liters). Hence, cross-country flights required the carriage of several external tanks as shown by 69-6369 at NAS New Orleans in June 1984.

1 Jul 1960: Became TAC-gained upon implementation of gaining command concept.
15 Oct 1962: Reached group status with federal recognition of 110th TRG.
1968-1969: RB-57As supplemented by RB-57B/Es.
Spring 1971: Converted from RB-57A/B/Es to Cessna O-2As.
11 Jun 1971: Redesignated 172nd

Previously flown by the 343rd TFW in Alaska, 80-0266 was one of the first A-10As to be assigned to the 172nd TASS in 1991. The tactical air support squadron and group designations were changed for fighter designations in March 1992.

TASS.
Fall 1980: Converted from O-2As to Cessna OA-37Bs.
FY91/FY92: Converted from OA-37Bs to Fairchild Republic A-10As and OA-10As (first A-10A received on 28 May 1991 and last OA-37B left on 23 August 1991).
15 Mar 1992: Unit designation changed to 172nd Fighter Squadron, 110th Fighter Group (172nd FS, 110th FG).
1 Jun 1992: As part of the Air Force restructuring program, gaining command changed to ACC.
1 Jul 1992: Completed conversion to A-10A/OA-10A.

Minnesota Air National Guard

As the first observation squadron in the National Guard to receive federal recognition (on 17 January 1921), the 109th Squadron occupies a special place in the history of military aviation in the United States. This unit is also one of the few Guard squadrons to have served on active duty on three occasions (during World War II, from February 1941 until November 1945; during the Korean War for 21 months; and during the Berlin Crisis for 11 months). Organized in

September 1948 as the 179th FS, the second Minnesota ANG unit also served on active duty in CONUS during the Korean War.

At the end of FY92, 2,509 officers and enlisted personnel manned 30 MN ANG units, including the 109th AS with C-130Es at Minneapolis-St Paul AFRS, and the 179th FS with F-16A/B ADFs at Duluth International Airport.

109th Airlift Squadron
133rd Airlift Wing

Lineage: *Organized at Kelly Field, TX, on 27 August 1917, as the 109th Aero Squadron, this Air Service unit moved to France in January 1918. It was redesignated the 639th Aero Squadron on 1 February 1918, served as a transportation unit with the AEF, and was demobilized at Mitchel Field, NY, on 23 June 1919. In 1936, its lineage and honors were consolidated with those of the 109th Squadron which had been activated as a Minnesota NG unit in January 1921.*
17 Jan 1921: 109th Squadron extended federal recognition at Holman Municipal Airport in St Paul as the aviation unit in the 34th Division, Minnesota NG. Began operations with a leased **Curtiss Oriole** and was equipped with **Curtiss Jennies** beginning in January 1922.
25 Jan 1923: Redesignated 109th OS.
1923-1940: Remaining based in St Paul, the 109th OS was equipped over the years with the mix of aircraft typical of prewar Guard units, including **Consolidated PT-1s; Dayton-Wright TW-3s; Douglas BT-1s, O-2s, O-38s** and **O-46s;** and **North American O-47s** and **BC-1s.** On 31 December 1940, it had one **BC-1A,** four **O-38B/Es** and eight **O-47A/Bs.**

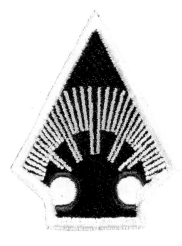

10 Feb 1941: Called to active duty, placed under the command of V Army Corps, and moved 17 days later to Camp Beauregard, LA.
World War II: Before being shipped to England in August 1942, the 109th OS moved twice in the US and briefly flew ASW patrols off the Georgia coast. Redesignated 109th TRS, equipped with **North American P-51/F-6s,** and assigned to the 67th TRG, Ninth Air Force, the unit flew reconnaissance missions in the ETO from December

The 109th FIS flew F-51Ds from Holman Field in St Paul until August 1956. It then became one of four Guard squadrons assigned T-28As as interim mission aircraft.

1943 until VE Day. Inactivated at Drew Field, FL, in November 1945, the squadron was redesignated the 109th FS and was allotted back to the Minnesota NG on 24 May 1946.
14 Sep 1946: 109th FS (SE) extended federal recognition at Holman Field, St Paul, MN, and soon equipped with **North American P-51Ds** (plus support

aircraft).
1 Mar 1951: Called to active duty as part of the Korean War call-up.
May 1951: Moved to Wold Chamberlain Field, Minneapolis, MN, and designated 109th FIS.
1 Dec 1952: Returned to state control at Holman Field, St Paul.
Aug 1956: Converted from F-51Ds to North American T-28As.
Jun 1957: Converted from T-28As to Lockheed F-94A/Bs.
Dec 1957: Converted from F-94A/Bs to Northrop F-89Hs.
Feb 1958: Moved to Minneapolis-St Paul IAP and converted form F-94A/Bs to Northrop F-89Hs.
Jan 1960: Began conversion from F-89Hs to **Boeing C-97As.**
22 Mar 1960: Redesignated 109th ATS (Heavy).
1 Jul 1960: Became MATS-gained upon implementation of gaining

On 2 January 1958, when the 432nd FIS was inactivated, Minnesota's 109th FIS was given the opportunity of taking over the facility and F-89Hs (including the last 10 Scorpions built by Northrop) of that active-duty squadron. Ever since, the 109th has remained based at the Minneapolis-St Paul IAP where one of its C-97Gs (to which the unit converted in 1960) was photographed in 1968.

command concept.

1 Oct 1961: Called to active duty as part of the Berlin Crisis call-up to conduct worldwide airlift missions from its base at Minneapolis-St Paul IAP.

31 Aug 1962: Returned to state control.

1 Jan 1966: Redesignated 109th MAS and became MAC-gained following MATS redesignation.

Winter 1970: Converted from C-97Gs to Lockheed C-130As.

20 Mar 1971: Redesignated 109th TAS and became TAC-gained.

1 Dec 1974: Became MAC-gained upon transfer of tactical airlift resources from TAC to MAC.

FY81: Converted from C-130As to C-130Es.

Aug 1990: Volunteers began flying missions in support of Operation Desert Shield.

15 Mar 1992: Unit designation changed to 109th Airlift Squadron, 133rd Airlift Wing (109th AS, 133rd AW).

1 Jun 1992: As part of the Air Force restructuring program, gaining command changed to AMC.

After flying C-130As for over 10 years, the 109th TAS coverted to less elderly C-130Es during FY81. In spite of much TLC on the part of the maintenance folks, these 'Herks' need to be replaced.

Peter B. Lewis

179th Fighter Squadron
148th Fighter Group

Right: Flying near Duluth, this F-89J was photographed in June 1966 as seven years of service with the Duluth unit were about to end.

Lineage: Constituted at Hamilton Field, CA, in May 1943, and activated in July of that year, the 393rd FS was assigned to the 367th FG, Ninth Air Force, with which it flew combat operations with Lockheed P-38Js in the ETO, beginning in May 1944, and with Republic P-47Ds, from February 1945. Inactivated at Seymour Johnson Field, NC, in November 1945, the squadron was reconstituted and redesignated the 179th FS before being allotted to the Minnesota NG on 24 May 1946.

18 Sep 1948: 179th FS (SE) extended federal recognition at Duluth Municipal Airport and, beginning in December of that year, equipped with North American F-51Ds (plus support aircraft).

1 Mar 1951: Called to active duty as part of the Korean War call-up but

The 'Deuce' made its debut with the 179th FIS in November 1966 but was replaced by the 'One-Oh-Wonder' four and a half years later. Flying F-102As, the Minnesotans took first place in their category at William Tell '70.

Maj. Gen. Wayne C. Gatlin

remained at Duluth MAP with F-51Ds.

1 Dec 1952: 179th FIS returned to state control.

Jul 1954: Converted from F-51Ds to Lockheed F-94A/Bs.

Apr 1957: Converted from F-94A/Bs to F-94Cs.

Jul 1959: Converted from F-94Cs to Northrop F-89Js.

1 Jul 1960: Became ADC-gained upon implementation of gaining command concept and reached group status with federal recognition of 148th FIG.

Nov 1966: Converted from F-89Js to

Below: Fall foliage in the northern US is a perfect background against which to photgraph jets. As shown by this portrait of McDonnell RF-4C, no one knows it better than Major General Gatlin, who spent 35 years with the Minnesota ANG.

MN ANG

Convair F/TF-102As.
Apr 1971: Converted from F/TF-102As to McDonnell F-101B/Fs.
Winter 1975: Converted from F-101B/Fs to McDonnell RF-4Cs.
10 Jan 1976: Redesignated 179th TRS and became TAC-gained.
FY83/84: Converted from RF-4Cs to F-4Ds.
15 Nov 1983: Redesignated 179th FIS.
Apr 1986-Apr 1987: Provided aircraft and personnel to Operation Creek Klaxon, the ANG's assumption of air defense commitment at Ramstein AB, Germany, while the 86th TFW, USAFE, was converting to F-16C/Ds.
Winter 1987: Sent a detachment to Loring AFB, ME, to take over alert commitment from the 101st FIS while the MA ANG unit was converting to F-15A/Bs.

Summer 1989: Sent detachments to Fresno ANGB and George AFB, CA, to take over alert commitment from the 194th FIS while the CA ANG unit was converting to F-16A/B ADFs.
Winter 1990: Completed conversion from F-4Ds (last flown out in April 1990) to General Dynamics F-16A/B ADFs.
15 Mar 1992: Unit designation changed to 179th Fighter Squadron, 148th Fighter Group (179th FS, 148th FG).
1 Jun 1992: As part of the Air Force restructuring program, gaining command changed to ACC.

ADF F-16s of the 179th Fighter Squadron carry the Little Dipper markings on the fin. The Duluth unit forms a link in the defensive chain round the United States.

Mississippi Air National Guard

As part of the pre-World War II expansion of the National Guard, Mississippi became the first state to be authorized to organize an aviation unit. Organized in September 1939, the 153rd Observation Squadron was placed on active duty 13 months later and ended the war as the 153rd Liaison Squadron in Germany. Allotted back to the Mississippi Guard in 1946, the 153rd initially served as a fighter unit but became a tactical reconnaissance squadron in December 1952 after serving on active duty in the United States during the Korean War. In this new role, it was joined seven months later by the 183rd TRS.

At the end of FY92, 2,908 officers and enlisted personnel manned 31 MS ANG units, including two flying squadrons (the 153rd ARS, with KC-135Rs at Key Field in Biloxi and the 183rd AS with C-141Bs at the Jackson Municipal Airport).

153rd Air Refueling Squadron
186th Air Refueling Group

Lineage: *Designated the 153rd Observation Squadron and allotted to the Mississippi NG on 18 August 1939.*
27 Sep 1939: 153rd OS activated in the Mississippi NG at Key Field, Meridian, and initially equipped with **Douglas O-38s**. Later added **Curtiss O-52s, North American O-47s** and **Stinson O-59s**.
15 Oct 1940: Called to active duty and placed under command of Fourth Corps Area. Soon after, moved to Wilmington, NC. On 31 December 1940, it had one **BC-1A**, five **O-38Es** and two **O-47As**.
World War II: Between November 1940 and August 1942 the squadron remained in the United States, first to undertake ASW patrols and then to train in preparation for overseas deployment. Still designated 153rd OS, the unit arrived at Membury, England, in September 1942. Redesignated 153rd Liaison Squadron on 31 May 1943 while

based at Keevil, England, it was assigned to the Ninth Air Force in December 1943 and was re-equipped with **Stinson L-5s** in April 1944. Between June 1944 and VE Day, the 153rd LS operated in support of ground forces in France, Belgium and Germany. Inactivated at Heidelberg, Germany, on 15 December 1945, the squadron was redesignated 153rd FS and was allotted to the Mississippi NG on 24 May 1946.
12 Sep 1946: 153rd FS (SE) extended federal recognition at Key Field, Meridian, and soon equipped with

Republic **P-47Ns** (plus support aircraft).
1 Mar 1951: Called to active duty.
Mar 1951: Moved to Turner AFB, GA, and assigned to the Second Air Force, SAC, as 153rd Fighter Escort Squadron.
11 Dec 1951: Moved to Godman AFB, KY, and assigned to the Ninth Air Force, TAC, as 153rd FBS.
27 Nov 1952: Returned to state control without aircraft.
1 Dec 1952: Redesignated 153rd TRS and re-equipped with North American **RF-51Ds**.
27 Dec 1953: Received first Lockheed

The RF-84F Thunderflash was one of the best subsonic reconnaissance jets and provided sterling service to the Guard, active-duty USAF units and allied air forces.

T-33A jet trainer.
Jun 1955: Converted from RF-51Ds to Lockheed RF-80As.
Oct 1956: Converted from RF-80As to Republic RF-84Fs.
Oct 1956-Mar 1958: Operations from Gulfport Permanent Training Site while Key Field's runway was being rebuilt for jet operations.
1 Jul 1960: Became TAC-gained upon

Taking part in Photo Derby '84 at NAS Fallon, Nevada, 66-0422 taxis at the start of a competition sortie on 9 October 1984. After leaving smoke trails in the sky for 13 years, the 173rd has now converted to KC-135Rs.

implementation of gaining command concept.
1 Oct 1961: Called to active duty during the Berlin Crisis but remained at home station.
20 Aug 1962: Returned to state control.

15 Oct 1962: Reached group status with federal recognition of the 186th TRG.
Nov 1970: Converted from RF-84Fs to McDonnell RF-101Cs.
Fall/Winter 1978: Converted from RF-101Cs (last RF-101 in USAF/ANG

inventory phased out on 13 Jan 1979) to McDonnell RF-4Cs.
FY91/FY92: Conversion from RF-4Cs to KC-135Rs (last RF-4Cs sent to AMARC on 14 Dec 1991, first two KC-135R maintenance trainers received in January 1992, and first KC-135R

mission flown on 8 Apr 1992).
1 Apr 1992: Unit redesignated 153rd Air Refueling Squadron, 186th Air Refueling Group, 153rd ARS, 186th ARG.
1 Jun 1992: As part of the Air Force restructuring program, gaining command changed to AMC.

183rd Airlift Squadron
172nd Airlift Group

1 Jul 1953: 183rd TRS (Night Photographic) extended federal recognition at Hawkins Field, Jackson. Squadron to be equipped with **Douglas RB-26B/Cs** (plus support aircraft).
Sep 1953: Began receiving its RB-26s.
Spring 1957: Pilots began training on **Republic RF-84Fs** in anticipation of proposed conversion to jets. Conversion not implemented due to lack of facilities suitable for jet operations.
15 Nov 1957: Redesignated 183rd Aeromedical Transport Squadron and became MAC-gained. Start of

conversion from RB-26s to **Fairchild C-119Fs** with receipt of first Flying Boxcar.
1 Jul 1960: Became MATS-gained upon implementation of gaining command concept.
1 Jul 1962: Redesignated 183rd Air Transport Squadron.
Jul 1962: Converted from C-119Fs to **Lockheed C-121Cs**.
19 Jan 1963: Permanent change of station from Hawkins Field to Jackson Municipal Airport (Allen C. Thompson Municipal Field).
11 Jan 1964: Reached group status

with federal recognition of the 172nd Air Transport Group.
1 Jan 1966: Redesignated 183rd MAS and became MAC-gained following MATS redesignation.
Feb 1967: Conversion from C-121Cs to Douglas C-124Cs initiated.
May 1972: Conversion from C-124Cs to Lockheed C-130Es initiated.
30 Jun 1972: Redesignated 183rd TAS/172nd TAG and became TAC-gained.
1 Dec 1974: Became MAC-gained upon transfer of tactical airlift resources from TAC to MAC.

Sunning its weary airframe at MASDC in May 1974, this ex-183rd MAS C-124C Globemaster II awaits the ultimate insult for aircraft with many years of good service.

FY81: Converted from C-130Es to C-130Hs.
1 Jul 1986: Redesignated 183rd MAS/172nd MAG with conversion from C-130Hs to **Lockheed C-141Bs**.
24 Aug 1990: Called to active duty as part of Operation Desert Shield call-up.
15 May 1991: Released from active duty after taking part in Desert Shield/Desert Storm.
15 Mar 1992: Unit designation changed to 183rd Airlift Squadron, 172nd Airlift Group (183rd AS, 172nd AG).
1 Jun 1992: As part of the Air Force restructuring program, gaining command changed to AMC.

Operating from the Allen C. Thomson Field in Jackson, the youngest flying squadron of the MS ANG, now reaching 40, became the first ANG unit to be assigned StarLifters and was redesignated from 183rd TAS to 183rd MAS on 1 July 1986 upon converting from C-130Hs to C-141Bs.

Missouri Air National Guard

Extended federal recognition in June 1923 and called to active duty in December 1940, Missouri's first flying unit served as the 110th TRS in New Guinea, the Philippines and Ie Shima from January 1944 until its inactivation in February 1946. Seven months later, the 110th was once again extended federal recognition in the Missouri Guard as a fighter squadron. In the immediate postwar period, the Missouri ANG was also to have organized a fighter squadron at Kansas City. The 180th, however, was activated at St Joseph as one of the National Guard's first bombardment squadrons.

During the Korean War, the 110th FBS served on FAD in the United States while the 180th BS went to France. During the Berlin Crisis, the 180th TRS was not activated, and it was the turn of the 110th TFS to go to France. Neither squadron was placed on FAD during the *Pueblo* Crisis.

At the end of FY92, 2,825 officers and enlisted personnel manned 34 MO ANG units, including the 110th FS with F-15A/Bs at the Lambert–St Louis International Airport and the 180th AS at the Rosecrans Memorial Airport in St Joseph with C-130Hs.

110th Fighter Squadron
131st Fighter Wing

Lineage: *Organized at Kelly Field, TX, on 14 August 1917 as the 110th Aero Squadron, Air Service, this maintenance and repair unit was redesignated 804th*

Aero Squadron on 1 February 1918, and remained at Kelly Field until demobilized on 18 November 1918. In 1936, its lineage and honors were consolidated with those of the 110th OS which had been activated as a Missouri NG unit in June 1923.
23 Jun 1923: *110th OS extended*

federal recognition at Anglum Airport, near Bridgeton, as the aviation unit in the 35th Division, Missouri NG, and initially equipped with **Curtiss JN-4Hs**.
Jul 1931: Moved to Lambert Field, St Louis.
1931-1940: Remaining based in St Louis, the 110th OS was equipped over

the years with the mix of aircraft typical of prewar Guard units, including **Consolidated PT-1s** and **O-17s; Curtiss JN-4Hs; JNSs** and **O-11s; Dayton-Wright TW-3s; Douglas BT-1s, O-2s** and **O-38s;** and **North American O-47s** and **BC-1s.**
23 Dec 1940: Called to active duty and

Douglas D. Olson

placed under the command of VII Army Corps. On 31 December 1940, it had one BC-1A, two O-38B/Ds and eight O-47A/Bs.

World War II: First relocated to Little Rock, AR, in January 1941, the mobilized Missouri NG unit changed station three more times, was redesignated on three occasions, flew ASW patrols off the California coast, and trained as a reconnaissance squadron before being shipped to Australia in October 1943. Redesignated 110th TRS in May 1944, assigned to the 71st TRG, Fifth Air Force, and successively equipped with Bell P-39s and North American P-51s, it flew combat operations in the Philippines and from Ie Shima between

Bearing the snorting Missouri mule insignia approved on 7 July 1949 for the 110th Fighter Squadron (SE), then equipped with F-51Ds, this F-100C transited at McClellan AFB on 28 September 1968.

Latest mounts of the 110th Fighter Squadron, McDonnell Douglas F-15 Eagles replaced F-4Es during the fall of 1991. The wing commander's F-15A-15-MC, 76-0030, had previously been assigned to the 405th TTW at Luke AFB, Arizona.

December 1944 and VJ Day. Inactivated at Ft William McKinley in the Philippines on 20 February 1946, the unit was redesignated 110th FS and was allotted back to the Missouri NG on 24 May 1946.

23 Sep 1946: 110th FS (SE) extended federal recognition at Lambert Field, St Louis, and soon equipped with North American P-51Ds (plus support aircraft).
1 Mar 1951: Called to active duty as part of the Korean War call-up and shortly thereafter moved to Bergstrom AFB, TX, for SAC duty.
Jul 1951: Transferred to TAC, moved to George AFB, CA, and redesignated 110th FBS.

1 Dec 1952: Returned to state control to be reorganized as the 110th BS (Light) and equipped with Douglas B-26B/Cs in early 1953.
Jan 1953: Partially converted from B-26B/Cs to Lockheed F-80Cs and redesignated 110th FIS.
Winter 1957: Converted from B-26B/Cs (last B-26C departed on 15 Dec 1957) and F-80Cs to Republic F-84Fs.
17 May 1959: Facilities at Lambert Field named Robertson ANGB.
1 Jan 1960: Redesignated 110th TFS.
1 Jul 1960: Became TAC-gained upon implementation of gaining command concept.
1 Oct 1961: Called to active duty as part of the Berlin Crisis call-up and moved to Toul-Rosières AB, France, later in that month for assignment to the 7131st TFW, USAFE.
20 Aug 1962: Returned to state control at Robertson ANGB, Lambert Field, St Louis, and re-equipped with North American F-100C/Fs during the

following month.
Dec 1971: Converted from F-100C/Fs to F-100D/Fs.
Early 1979: Converted from F-100D/Fs to McDonnell F-4Cs.
FY85: Converted from F-4Cs to F-4Ds.
FY91/FY92: Converted from F-4Es to McDonnell Douglas F-15A/Bs (first F-15A received in May 1991 and last F-4E left in Sep 1991).
15 Mar 1992: Unit designation changed to 110th Fighter Squadron, 131st Fighter Wing (110th FS, 131st FW).
1 Jun 1992: As part of the Air Force restructuring program, gaining command changed to ACC.

Carrying an AGM-65, this F-4E-41-MC is seen about to take off from Georgia AFB at the start of an Air Warrior sortie for the benefit of ground troops at the National Training Center.

Peter B. Lewis

Carl E. Porter

180th Airlift Squadron
139th Airlift Group

Lineage: *Constituted and activated at Barksdale Field, LA, in June 1942, the 438th BS (Medium) was assigned to the 319th BG, Twelfth Air Force, with which it flew combat operations with Martin B-26s and North American B-25s in the MTO between November 1942 and December 1944. Returned to CONUS and re-equipped with Douglas A-26B/Cs, the 438th BS and other squadrons of the 319th BG were reassigned to the Seventh Air Force in April 1945 and flew combat operations from Okinawa during the last month of World War II. Inactivated at Vancouver Barracks, WA, in December 1945, the squadron was redesignated 180th FS and was allotted to the Missouri NG on 24 May 1946.*
22 Aug 1946: 180th BS (Light)

extended federal recognition at Rosecrans MAP, St Joseph, MO, and soon equipped with Douglas A-26B/Cs (plus support aircraft).
1 Apr 1951: Called to active duty as part of the Korean War call-up.
Jul 1951: Moved to Bordeaux-Mérignac AB, France, as part of activated 126th BW.
May 1952: Moved to Laon AB, France.
1 Jan 1953: Returned to state control at Rosecrans MAP.
1 Jul 1955: Redesignated 180th BS (Tactical).
Spring 1957: Converted from B-26B/Cs to Lockheed F-80Cs.
15 Jun 1957: Redesignated 180th FIS.
Spring 1958: Converted from F-80Cs to Republic RF-84Fs.
10 Apr 1958: Redesignated 180th TRS.
1 Jul 1960: Became TAC-gained upon implementation of gaining command concept.
Mar 1962: First Boeing C-97F received

Peter B. Lewis

Above: The St Joseph unit is one of the few Guard squadrons to have flown -97s successively in the transport and tanker roles. 52-0288, a C-97G, was serving with the 180th MAS when photographed on 6 July 1988.

Left: With J47 auxiliary turbojets beneath the outer wing panels, this KC-97L of the 180th AREFS visited McClellan AFB in August 1974. Two years later, the Missouri unit converted from KC-97Ls to C-130As.

Peter B. Lewis

as squadron began its conversion from RF-84Fs to C-97F/Gs.

14 Apr 1962: Redesignated 180th ATS (Heavy) and became MATS-gained.

Summer 1969: Converted from C-97F/Gs to KC-97Ls.

6 Sep 1969: Redesignated 180th AREFS and became TAC-gained.

Summer/Fall 1976: Converted from KC-97Ls to Lockheed C-130As.

1 Oct 1976: Redesignated 180th TAS and became MAC-gained.

FY87: Converted from C-130As to C-130Hs.

Dec 1989: Participated in Operation Just Cause in Panama.

Aug 1990: Volunteers began flying missions in support of Operation Desert Shield.

27 Dec 1990: Called to active duty as part of Operation Desert Shield call-up.

30 May 1991: Released from active duty after taking part in Desert Shield/Desert Storm.

15 Mar 1992: Unit designation changed to 180th Airlift Squadron, 139th Airlift Group (180th AS, 139th AG).

1 Jun 1992: As part of the Air Force restructuring program, gaining command changed to AMC.

Currently equipped with C-130Hs and based at the Rosecrans Memorial Airport in St Joseph, the 139th Airlift Group not only has its 180th TAS flying regular airlift missions but also operates the Advanced Airlift Tactics Training Center for the benefit of ANG, AFRES and active-duty units.

Rick Morgan

Montana Air National Guard

The Montana ANG came into being in June 1947 when the 186th FS was federally recognized in Great Falls. With the exception of a period of 21 months, when it served on FAD in Georgia and California during the Korean War, the 186th has remained at that location. Throughout its existence, Montana's flying squadron has only flown fighters. It converted to F-16A/Bs during FY87. At the end of FY92, 1,093 officers and enlisted personnel manned 13 MT ANG units.

186th Fighter Squadron
120th Fighter Group

Lineage: *Constituted at the Richmond AAB, VA, in May 1943 and activated in July of that year, the 404th was assigned to the 371st FG, Ninth Air Force, with which it flew combat operations with Republic P-47Ds in the ETO from April 1944 until VE Day. Inactivated at Camp Shanks, NY, in November 1945, the unit was reconstituted and redesignated the 186th FS before being allotted to the Montana NG on 24 May 1946.*

27 Jun 1947: 186th FS (SE) extended federal recognition at Great Falls MAP, MT, and soon equipped with **North American P-51Ds** (plus support aircraft).

1 Apr 1951: Called to active duty as part of the Korean War call-up and soon thereafter moved to Moody AFB, GA, for SAC duty.

Nov 1951: Transferred to TAC, redesignated 186th FBS and moved to George AFB, CA.

1 Dec 1952: Returned to state control at Great Falls MAP.

Nov 1953: Converted from F-51Ds to North American F-86As and redesignated 186th FIS.

Photos of colorful Mustangs, Thunderjets, Starfires and Sabres (including this F-86A of the 186th FIS in October 1954) taking part in ANG Gunnery Meets at Gowen Field, Idaho, make one wish for a time machine.

Jun 1955: Converted from F-86As to Lockheed F-94As.

Apr 1956: Converted from F-94As to Northrop F-89Cs.

15 Apr 1956: Reached group status with federal recognition of the 120th FIG.

Apr 1958: Converted from F-89Cs to F-89Hs.

Mar 1960: Converted from F-89Hs to F-89Js.

1 Jul 1960: Became ADC-gained upon implementation of gaining command concept.

Jul 1966: Converted from F-89Js to Convair F/TF-102As.

Spring 1972: Converted from F/TF-102As to **Convair F-106A/Bs** (first Delta Darts received on 3 Apr 1972).

Mar 1973: F-106As upgraded to Block S standard with solid state avionics, expanded radar capabilities and clear canopies.

1 Apr 1980: Became TAC-gained following ADC inactivation.

Spring/Summer 1987: Converted from F-106A/Bs to **General Dynamics F-16A/Bs.**

FY91: F-16A/Bs brought up to ADF configuration.

15 Mar 1992: Unit designation changed to 186th Fighter Squadron, 120th Fighter Group (186th FS, 120th FG).

1 Jun 1992: As part of the Air Force restructuring program, gaining command changed to ACC.

As the 186th FIS began its conversion to the F-102A during the fall of 1965, it began sending its F-89Js to the Military Aircraft Storage and Disposition Center.

Pat Paulsen courtesy of David W. Menard

MT ANG

Above: In the immediate post-World War II period, the initial equipment of fighter squadrons included a variety of support aircraft such as this L-5E assigned to the 186th FS (SE).

Below: Photographed at the Sacramento Air Logistics Center during the ceremony marking the completion of the last F-106 overhaul, this F-106B was there to represent a major user of Sixes.

René J. Francillon

Peter B. Lewis

The C-130A operational support aircraft of the Montana ANG displayed its attractive tail markings when visiting Marana Air Park, Arizona, in November 1989. It has now been replaced by a Fairchild C-26B.

A General Dynamic F-16B-15-CF of the 186th FIS. The Montana unit had been expected to become the last Guard unit to fly F-106s, but conversion to Fighting Falcons was moved forward.

Nebraska Air National Guard

The 173rd FS, which on 26 July 1946 had become the second Guard flying squadron to be extended federal recognition, was also in the forefront of jet conversion as it first received F-80Cs during the spring of 1948. Again equipped with Mustangs during the Korean War when it served on FAD in the United States, the sole flying unit of the Nebraska ANG flew jet fighters from the fall of 1953 until its conversion to RF-84Fs in the spring of 1964.

At the end of FY92, 1,063 officers and enlisted personnel manned 13 NE ANG units, including the 173rd RS which flies RF-4Cs from Lincoln Municipal Airport.

173rd Reconnaissance Squadron
155th Reconnaissance Group

Lineage: *Constituted at Westover Field, MA, in May 1943 and activated two months later, the 401st FS trained with Republic P-47Ds. Assigned to the 370th FG, Ninth Air Force, it flew Lockheed P-38Js and North American P-51Ds in combat in the ETO from May 1944 until April 1945. It was inactivated at Camp Myles Standish, MA, in November 1945. Reconstituted and redesignated the 173rd FS, the unit was allotted to the Nebraska NG on 24 May 1946.*
26 Jul 1946: 173rd FS (SE) extended federal recognition at the Lincoln MAP and soon equipped with North American P-51Ds (plus support aircraft).
Spring 1948: Converted from F-51Ds

The 173rd has operated the RF-4C 'Rhino' for over 20 years, but is shortly to convert to tankers.

to Lockheed F-80Cs and redesignated 173rd FS (Jet).
1 Apr 1951: Called to active duty and soon re-equipped with F-51Ds.
Spring 1951: Moved to Bangor, ME, and assigned to SAC.
Nov 1951: Moved to Alexandria, LA, and transferred to TAC as 173rd FBS.
1 Jan 1953: Returned to state control to be reorganized as the 173rd FBS and equipped with F-51Ds.
Fall 1953: Redesignated 173rd FIS and converted back to F-80Cs.
1 Feb 1956: Moved to new facilities adjacent to Lincoln AFB.
Jan 1957: Converted from F-80Cs to North American F-86Ds.
Late 1959: Converted from F-86Ds to F-86Ls.
1 Jul 1960: Reached group status with federal recognition of the 155th FIG and became ADC-gained upon implementation of gaining command concept.
1 May 1964: Redesignated 173rd TRS/155th TRG as a TAC-gained unit and re-equipped with Republic RF-84Fs.
Feb 1972: Converted from RF-84Fs

(the last RF-84F in ANG service was flown to Davis-Monthan AFB for storage to MASDC) to McDonnell RF-4Cs.
15 Mar 1992: Unit designation changed to 173rd Reconnaissance Squadron, 155th Reconnaissance Group (173rd RS, 155th RG).
1 Jun 1992: As part of the Air Force restructuring program, gaining command changed to ACC.
FY94: Scheduled to convert from RF-4Cs to Boeing KC-135Rs and to become an AMC-gained air refueling unit.

Photographed in July 1971, seven months before Nebraska's 173rd Tactical Reconnaissance Squadron sent the last USAF RF-84Fs to MASDC, this Thunderflash had a bare metal airframe but carried a camouflaged ventral tank.

Nevada Air National Guard

The sole flying unit of the Nevada ANG was organized in April 1948 as a fighter squadron, flew F-51Ds on active duty in CONUS during the Korean War, and was equipped with jet interceptors from the fall of 1955 until the spring of 1961. Since that time, the 192nd has flown tactical reconnaissance aircraft, including RF-101Hs with which it served in Panama and Korea during its *Pueblo* Crisis activation, and RF-4Cs with which it flew 412 combat sorties during the Gulf War.

At the end of FY91, 1,110 officers and enlisted personnel manned 13 NV ANG units, including the 192nd TRS at Reno-Cannon International Airport (May ANGB). The 'High Rollers' (a nickname alluding to the fact that Reno, the hometown of the 192nd TRS, is a gambling town located on a high plateau in the Sierra Nevada), which have been equipped with RF-4Cs since July 1975, have achieved a high degree of readiness as evidenced by the fact that they won two of the last three biennial reconnaissance competitions.

192nd Reconnaissance Squadron
152nd Reconnaissance Group

Lineage: *Constituted and activated at Hamilton Field, CA, in October 1943, the 408th FS flew Bell P-39s, Curtiss P-40s and North American P-51s as an RTU in the ZI. Inactivated in November 1945. Reconstituted and redesignated the 192nd FS, the unit was allotted to the Nevada NG on 24 May 1946.*

12 Apr 1948: 192nd FS (SE) extended federal recognition at Reno AFB and soon equipped with North American P-51Ds (plus support aircraft).

1 Jan 1951: Reno AFB redesignated Stead AFB.

1 Mar 1951: Called to active duty and assigned to Tenth Air Force, CONAC.

9 Apr 1951: Moved to Bergstrom AFB, TX, redesignated 192nd FBS, and assigned to Eighth Air Force, SAC.

7 Aug 1951: Moved to George AFB, CA, and assigned to the Fifteenth Air Force, SAC.

16 Nov 1951: Remained at George AFB but transferred to TAC.

26 Aug-1 Sep 1952: Pilots from the 192nd ferried F-51Ds from George AFB to Keflavik, Iceland, via Tinker AFB, OK; Wright-Patterson AFB, OH; Otis AFB, MA; Presque Isle, ME; and Goose Bay, Labrador. The 24 aircraft which reached Iceland, some of their pilots, and some maintenance personnel flown in C-124s were then assigned to the newly-constituted 434th FIS. The 192nd FBS, however, remained officially based at George AFB until its inactivation.

1 Dec 1952: Returned to state control as 192nd FBS at Stead ANGB with F-51Ds.

1 Feb 1954: TDY relocated to Reno Municipal Airport.

1 Jun 1955: Redesignated 192nd FIS

Above: Initially equipped with RB-57B/Cs, the 192nd TRS was forced to switch to older RB-57As in May 1965 when the more recent models of the aircraft were needed in Vietnam.

Right: Between November 1971 and July 1975, the 192nd TRS gained the distinction of being the only squadron to fly RF-101Bs.

and began jet training with Lockheed T-33As.

Nov 1955: Converted from F-51Ds to North American F-86As.

Apr 1956: Permanent change of station to Reno Municipal Airport (May ANGB).

19 April 1958: Reached group status with federal recognition of the 152nd FIG.

Aug 1958: Converted from F-86As to F-86Ls.

1 Jul 1960: Became ADC-gained upon implementation of gaining command concept.

Feb 1961: Converted from F-86Ls to Martin RB-57B/Cs.

1 Mar 1961: Group redesignated 152nd TRG and became TAC-gained.

1 Apr 1961: Squadron redesignated 192nd TRS.

May 1965: Converted from RB-57B/Cs to RB-57As.

Oct 1965: Converted from RB-57As to McDonnell RF-101Hs.

26 Jan 1968: Called to active duty as part of the *Pueblo* Crisis call-up and soon moved to Richards-Gebaur AFB, MO. TDY deployments to Howard AFB, Panama, and deployment to Itazuke AB, Japan (18 Nov 1968 to 3 Feb 1969).

9 Jun 1969: Returned to state control.

Nov 1971: Converted from RF-101Hs to RF-101Bs.

Jul 1975: Converted from RF-101Bs to McDonnell RF-4Cs.

Nov 1986: Won RAM '86 competition.

Nov 1990: Won RAM '90 competition.

3 Dec 1990: Called to active duty as part of Operation Desert Shield call-up.

Jan-Mar 1991: Flew Desert Storm reconnaissance missions from Sheikh Isa AB, Bahrain.

20 Apr 1991: Released from active duty after taking part in Desert Shield/Desert Storm.

Summer 1991: Plans for the impending conversion from RF-4Cs to F-4Gs were cancelled (one F-4G was received and painted in 'High Rollers' markings but was later returned).

15 Mar 1992: Unit designation changed to 192nd Reconnaissance Squadron, 152nd Reconnaissance Group (192nd RS, 152nd RG).

1 Jun 1992: As part of the Air Force restructuring program, gaining command changed to ACC.

Below: Having replaced RF-101Bs during the summer of 1975, RF-4Cs have now been flown by the 'High Rollers' for more than 17 years. These RF-4Cs were photographed on a blustery winter day in March 1990.

Below: After the 192nd TRS returned from Bahrain, it was announced that it would become a 'Wild Weasel' unit. One F-4G was delivered in August 1991 and quickly received 'High Rollers' markings, but plans changed. The Nevadans will soldier on in RF-4Cs until at least FY94.

Above: ANG operational support turboprop aircraft are not attractive and most are 'plain Janes'. Hence, the 152nd RG merits plaudits for livening the world by applying its 'High Rollers' nickname to its C-12J.

New Hampshire Air National Guard

Organized in April 1947, the 133rd Squadron flew four types of single-engined fighters before becoming, in the summer of 1960, the first ANG unit to be equipped with four-engined aircraft. Since then, the 133rd has only flown 'heavies', converting from C-97s to

C-124s in 1967, to C-130s in 1971, and to jet tankers in 1975.

At the end of FY92, 1,061 officers and enlisted personnel manned 13 NH ANG units, including the 133rd ARS at Pease ANGS with KC-135Es.

133rd Air Refueling Squadron
157th Air Refueling Group

Lineage: *Constituted at Will Rogers Field, OK, in January 1942 and activated two months later, the 529th BS (Light) was redesignated 529th FBS immediately upon arriving in India in September 1943. Assigned to the 311th FG, Tenth Air Force, the squadron was redesignated the 529th FS in May 1944 and flew combat operations in the CBI from October 1943 to August 1945 with North American A-36s and P-51s. Inactivated at Ft Lawton, WA, in January 1946, the unit was reconstituted and redesignated the 133rd FS before being allotted to the New Hampshire NG on 24 May 1946.*
4 Apr 1947: 133rd FS (SE) extended federal recognition at Grenier Field, Manchester, NH, and soon equipped with Republic P-47Ds (plus support aircraft).
1 Feb 1951: Called to active duty as part of the Korean War call-up but remained at Grenier Field as the 133rd FIS.
1 Nov 1952: Returned to state control and converted from F-47Ds to North American F-51Hs.
Jun 1954: Converted from F-51Hs to Lockheed F-94A/Bs.
16 Apr 1956: Reached group status with federal recognition of 101st FIG.
Apr 1958: Converted from F-94A/Bs to North American F-86Ls.
Summer 1960: Converted from

F-86Ls to Boeing C-97As.
1 Sep 1960: Became MATS-gained, squadron redesignated 133rd ATS, and group renumbered and redesignated 157th ATG.
1 Oct 1961: Called to active duty as part of the Berlin Crisis call-up to conduct worldwide airlift missions from its base at Grenier Field.
31 Aug 1962: Returned to state control at Grenier Field.
Jan 1966: Moved to Pease AFB, redesignated 133rd MAS, and became MAC-gained following MATS redesignation.
Dec 1967: Converted from C-97As to Douglas C-124Cs.

Summer 1971: Converted from C-124Cs to Lockheed C-130As.
11 Sep 1971: Redesignated 133rd TAS and became TAC-gained.
1 Dec 1974: Became MAC-gained upon transfer of tactical airlift resources from TAC to MAC.
Summer 1975: Converted from C-130As to Boeing KC-135As.
1 Oct 1975: Redesignated 133rd AREFS and became SAC-gained.
FY84: Converted from KC-135As to KC-135Es.
Aug 1990: Volunteers began flying missions in support of Operation Desert Shield.
Sep 1990: Pease AFB inactivated,

Before concern over detectability in air combat became the norm, the USAF was not shy to apply conspicuous Dayglo markings, as carried by this F-86L of the 133rd FIS.

airfield transferred to local authorities, and Guard facilities designated Pease ANGS.
20 Dec 1990: Called to active duty as part of Operation Desert Shield call-up.
31 May 1991: Released from active duty after taking part in Desert Shield/Desert Storm.
15 Mar 1992: Unit abbreviation changed to 133rd ARS, 157th ARG.
1 Jun 1992: As part of the Air Force restructuring program, gaining command changed to AMC.

The 133rd AREFS converted to KC-135As during the summer of 1975 and obtained re-engined KC-135Es during FY84. This example in 1992 sports the new AMC mid-gray color scheme.

New Jersey Air National Guard

The 119th OS was organized in 1930 as the last of the initial group of 19 squadrons allotted to the National Guard. Called to active duty in September 1940, the 119th served stateside until its inactivation in May 1944. Postwar, the 119th FS and the 141st FS were allotted to the New Jersey Guard and were extended federal recognition in Newark and Trenton. Both were later relocated to the less noise-sensitive McGuire AFB when converting to jets. The 150th ATS was organized in February 1956 to take the place of the 119th FBS at Newark. The 119th moved to Atlantic City in 1958 and served on

FAD at that base during the Berlin Crisis. The 141st TFS served in France during that crisis and was joined at McGuire AFB by the 150th ATS in 1965.

At the end of FY92, 2,902 officers and enlisted personnel manned 37 NJ ANG units, including three flying squadrons (two at McGuire AFB, the 141st and 150th ARSs with F-4Es and the 150th AREFS with KC-135Es; and one at Atlantic City International Airport, the 119th FS with F-16A/B ADFs). In the fall of 1991, the 141st began its conversion from F-4Es to KC-135s.

119th Fighter Squadron
177th Fighter Group

Lineage: *Organized at Hampton, VA, on 5 June 1917, as the 5th Aviation School Squadron, this Air Service unit was redesignated 119th Aero Squadron on 2 September 1917, and Detachment No. 11, Air Service, Aircraft Production, on 31 July 1918. It remained at Hampton until demobilized on 29 May 1919. In 1936, its lineage and honors were consolidated with those of the 119th OS which had been activated as a New Jersey NG unit in January 1930.*

30 Jan 1930: 119th OS extended federal recognition at Newark Airport as the aviation unit in the 44th Division, New Jersey NG, and initially equipped with Consolidated PT-1s and O-17s, and Douglas BT-1s and O-2s.

1930-1940: Remaining based in Newark, the 119th OS retained the usual mix of aircraft, including Douglas O-38s and O-46s, and North American O-47s and BC-1s.

16 Sep 1940: Called to active duty and assigned to Second Corps Area. On 31 December 1940, it had one BC-1A, seven O-46As and three O-47A/Bs.

World War II: Remaining at Newark Airport until March 1942 and then moving six times before being inactivated at the Thomasville AAFld, GA, in May 1944. The unit was redesignated on four occasions, flew ASW patrols along the mid-Atlantic coast, and served as a P-39 RTU. Reconstituted and redesignated 119th FS, it was allotted back to the New Jersey NG on 24 May 1946.

29 Jan 1947: 119th FS (SE) extended federal recognition at the Newark Airport and soon equipped with Republic P-47Ds (plus support aircraft).

Feb 1952: Converted from F-47Ds to North American F-51Hs.

1 Sep 1952: Redesignated 119th FBS.

Jul 1954: Converted from F-51Hs to F-51Ds.

May 1955: Converted from F-51Ds to

Above: Based in Atlantic City, the 'New Jersey Devils' traded their Republic F-105Bs for Convair F-106As and F-106Bs until converting to F-16A/Bs in 1988, and flew their last three Delta Darts to the Aerospace Maintenance and Regeneration Center (AMARC) at Davis-Monthan AFB, Arizona, on 1 August 1988.

North American F-86Es.

1 Jul 1955: Redesignated 119th FIS.

Feb 1956: Moved to McGuire AFB.

Mar 1958: Converted from F-86Es to Republic F-84Fs.

Aug 1958: Moved to NAFEC Atlantic City.

Nov 1958: Redesignated 119th TFS.

1 Jul 1960: Became TAC-gained upon implementation of gaining command concept.

1 Oct 1961: Called to active duty as part of the Berlin Crisis call-up but remained at Atlantic City.

20 Aug 1962: Returned to state control.

15 Oct 1962: Reached group status

Above: The 119th Tactical Fighter Squadron was the only New Jersey ANG unit to fly Super Sabres.

Right: Photographed at Atlanta City on 26 June 1990, this F-16A-15M-CF of the 119th FIS had yet to be sent to be upgraded to ADF standard.

with federal recognition of 177th TFG.

Winter 1962: Converted from F-84Fs to North American F-86Hs.

Sep 1965: Began conversion from F-86Hs to North American F-100C/Fs.

26 Jan 1968: Called to active duty as part of the *Pueblo* Crisis call-up and moved to Myrtle Beach AFB, SC, to serve as an RTU.

18 Jun 1969: Returned to state control at Atlantic City.

Jun 1970: Began conversion from F-100C/Fs to Republic F-105Bs.

Winter 1972: Converted from F-105Bs to Convair F-106A/Bs.

27 Jan 1973: Redesignated 119th FIS and became ADC-gained.

1 Apr 1980: Became TAC-gained

following ADC inactivation.

Summer/Fall 1988: Converted from F-106A/Bs (last three Delta Darts sent to AMARC on 1 Aug) to General Dynamics F-16A/Bs (with which it went back on alert on 1 Nov).

FY91: F-16A/Bs brought up to ADF standard.

15 Mar 1992: Unit designation changed to 119th Fighter Squadron, 177th Fighter Group (119th FS, 177th FG).

1 Jun 1992: As part of the Air Force restructuring program, gaining command changed to ACC.

141st Air Refueling Squadron
108th Air Refueling Wing

Lineage: *Constituted and activated at Mitchel Field, NY, in September 1942, the 341st FS flew combat operations with Republic P-47Ds in the Southwest Pacific theater beginning in July 1943. Re-equipped with North American P-51Ds in January 1945, it was inactivated in Japan in May 1946. Reconstituted and redesignated the 141st FS, the unit was allotted to the New Jersey NG on 24 May 1946.*

26 May 1949: 141st FS (SE) extended federal recognition at Mercer County Airport, Trenton, and equipped with Republic F-47Ds (plus support aircraft).

1 Mar 1951: Ordered to active duty as part of the Korean War call-up and soon after transferred to Turner AFB, GA, where it was redesignated 141st FBS.

16 Nov 1951: Moved to Godman AFB, KY, while still on active duty.

1 Dec 1952: Returned to state control at Mercer County Airport, the 141st FBS was soon re-equipped with North American F-51Hs.

Feb 1954: Converted from F-51Hs to North American F-86As and permanent change of station to McGuire AFB.

Jul 1955: Redesignated 141st FIS.

Feb 1956: Converted from F-86As to F-86Es.

Mar 1958: Redesignated 141st FIS (Day) (SD).

Spring 1958: Converted from F-86Es to Republic F-84Fs.

Nov 1958: Redesignated 141st TFS (SD); the SD was later dropped from the designation.

1 Jul 1960: Became TAC-gained upon implementation of gaining command concept.

1 Oct 1961: Called to active duty as a result of the Berlin Crisis.

Nov 1961: Deployed to Chaumont AB,

Drag chute billowing in the J79's exhaust, an F-4E makes a 180° turn at the end of the runway.

Above: The 141st Tactical Fighter Squadron became the Guard's first squadron to fly Thunderchiefs when it converted from F-86Hs to F-105Bs in April 1964. 'Thunderhogs' were operated from McGuire AFB until the conversion to F-4Ds in the spring of 1981.

For the 'Tigers' of the 141st, the conversion in the fall of 1991 from F-4Es to KC-135Es, instead of the hoped-for F-16Cs, was a bitter pill to take.

France.

17 Aug 1962: Returned to state control without aircraft.

15 Oct 1962: Reached group status with federal recognition of the 108th TFG.

Oct 1962: 141st TFS re-equipped with North American F-86Hs.

Apr 1964: Converted from F-86Hs to Republic F-105Bs.

9 Dec 1974: 108th TFG inactivated and 141st TFS placed directly under the 108th TFW.

Spring 1981: Converted from F-105Bs to McDonnell F-4Ds.

Summer 1985: Converted from F-4Ds to F-4Es.

FY92/FY93: Converted from F-4Es to Boeing KC-135Es (first KC-135Es received on 27 Sep 1991 and last F-4E flown out on 7 Oct 1991).

19 Oct 1991: Redesignated 141st AREFS/108th AREFW.

15 Mar 1992: Unit abbreviation changed to 141st ARS, 108th ARW.

1 Jun 1992: As part of the Air Force restructuring program, gaining command changed to AMC.

1 Jan 93: Scheduled to complete conversion to KC-135Es.

150th Air Refueling Squadron
170th Air Refueling Group

Lineage: *Organized at Newark Airport to take over the facilities and much of the personnel of the 119th FBS which was being transferred to McGuire AFB.*

1 Feb 1956: 150th Air Transport Squadron (Medium) extended federal recognition at Newark Airport and equipped with **Curtiss C-46Ds**.

Feb 1957: Redesignated 150th Aeromedical Transport Squadron (Light).

Oct 1958: Converted from C-46Ds to Fairchild C-119G/MC-119Js.

1 Jul 1960: Became MATS-gained upon implementation of gaining command concept.

Oct 1962: Converted from MC-119Js to

On 23 June 1990, while most of its aircraft were deployed to England, the 150th AREFS kept two alert aircraft and this spare at McGuire AFB.

Beauty at rest: a Lockheed C-121G of the 150th MAS on the transient ramp at McClellan AFB, California, on 28 October 1967.

Lockheed C-121Cs.

18 Jan 1964: Reached group status with federal recognition of 170th Air Transport Group. Squadron redesignated 150th Air Transport Squadron (Heavy).

Jul 1965: Moved to McGuire AFB.

1 Jan 1966: Redesignated 150th MAS and became MAC-gained upon MATS redesignation.

Dec 1969: Redesignated 150th Aeromedical Airlift Squadron.

Spring 1973: Converted from C-121C/Gs to de Havilland Canada C-7A/Bs.

Jun 1973: Redesignated 150th TAS and became TAC-gained.

1 Dec 1974: Became MAC-gained upon transfer of tactical airlift resources from TAC to MAC.

Early 1977: Converted from C-7A/Bs to Boeing KC-135As.

1 Apr 1977: Redesignated 150th AREFS and became SAC-gained.

FY83: Converted from KC-135As to

KC-135Es.

Aug 1990: Volunteers began flying missions in support of Operation Desert Shield.

20 Dec 1990: Called to active duty as part of Operation Desert Shield call-up.

15 May 1991: Released from active duty after taking part in Desert Shield/Desert Storm.

15 Mar 1992: Unit abbreviation changed to 150th ARS, 170th ARG.

1 Jun 1992: As part of the Air Force restructuring program, gaining command changed to AMC.

New Mexico Air National Guard

Organized in July 1947 as the 188th FS, the flying unit of the New Mexico Guard has only used five types of mission aircraft in its 44-year history: the F-51D, F-80C, F-100A/C, A-7D/K and the F-16C/D. Nevertheless, two of its conversions made history, as in April 1958 the 188th FIS became the first Guard squadron to be assigned supersonic fighters (four years later one of its F-100As made

unfortunate headline news when a malfunction caused a Sidewinder missile to shoot down a B-52) and, as during the fall of 1973, the 188th TFS became the first Guard unit to receive A-7Ds.

At the end of FY92, 1,064 officers and enlisted personnel manned 13 NM ANG units, including the 188th FS which was converting to F-16C/Ds at Kirtland AFB.

N. Donald

188th Fighter Squadron 150th Fighter Group

Lineage: *Constituted at Key Field, MS, on 25 January 1943 and activated 10 days later as the 507th BS (Dive), this unit was redesignated 507th FS shortly after being shipped to England in the spring of 1944. Assigned to the 404th FG, Ninth Air Force, and equipped with Republic P-47Ds, it flew combat operations in the ETO between May 1944 and VE Day. Inactivated at Drew Field, FL, in November 1945, it was reconstituted and redesignated the 188th FS before being allotted to the New Mexico NG on 24 May 1946.*

7 Jul 1947: 188th FS (SE) extended federal recognition at Kirtland AAB, New Mexico, and soon equipped with **North American P-51Ds** (plus support aircraft).

1 Feb 1951: Called to active duty as part of the Korean War call-up but initially remained at Kirtland AFB.

20 Apr 1951: Moved to Long Beach MAP, CA, to serve as the 188th FIS with ADC.

1 Nov 1952: Returned to state control at Kirtland AFB.

Aug 1953: Began conversion from F/TF-51Ds to **Lockheed F-80Cs** (the first Shooting Stars were **F-80As** and **F-80Bs** which soon after were brought up to F-80C standard by LAS).

Sep 1955: North American F-86As borrowed from other ANG units were flown by pilots from the 188th FIS during the USAF Fighter Gunnery and Weapons Meet at Nellis AFB, NV. Although temporarily painted in NM ANG markings, these Sabres were not assigned to the 188th.

Apr 1958: Converted from F-80Cs to North American F-100As.

1 Jul 1960: Reached group status with federal recognition of 150th FIG and became TAC-gained upon implementation of gaining command concept.

Spring 1964: Converted from F-100As to F-100C/Fs.

1 Jul 1964: Redesignated 188th TFS.

26 Jan 1968: Called to active duty as part of the *Pueblo* Crisis call-up.

May 1968: Deployed to Tuy Hoa AB for combat operations in Vietnam.

5 Jun 1969: Returned to state control at Kirtland AFB.

Fall 1973: Converted from F-100C/Fs to LTV A-7Ds.

FY87: A-7Ds upgraded to LANA configuration.

15 Mar 1992: Unit designation changed to 188th Fighter Squadron, 150th Fighter Group (188th FS, 150th FG).

1 Jun 1992: As part of the Air Force restructuring program, gaining command changed to ACC.

New Mexico is another recent recruit to the long list of F-16C users. Its first F-16C arrived in May 1992.

FY92/FY93: Converting from A-7D/Ks to **General Dynamics Block 40 F-16C/Ds** (first F-16C received on 11 May 1992 and last A-7D left on 28 Sep 1992).

Douglas D. Olson

Above: The 188th FIS flew F-100As for six years beginning in April 1958. However, the New Mexico unit was redesignated the 188th TFS when converting to F-100Cs.

Right: 54-1639, the C-130A support aircraft of the 150th TFG, is seen on final approach to McClellan AFB in September 1987. It has now been replaced by a Fairchild C-26B.

Below: An A-7D-13-CV of the 188th TFS arrives at Kingsley Field.

Chris Jacquet

René J. Francillon

New York Air National Guard

Even though New York no longer is the most populous state in the union (having been surpassed in that respect by California in 1964), it has the largest Air National Guard, both in terms of personnel and number of units. At the end of FY92, 6,223 officers and enlisted personnel manned 71 NY ANG units, including five flying squadrons (the 102nd RQS at Suffolk County's Francis S. Gabreski Airport with HC-130Ps and HH-60Gs, the 136th FS with F-16A/B ADFs at Niagara Falls International Airport, the 137th AS with C-5As at Stewart IAP, the 138th FS at Syracuse's Hancock Field with F-16A/Bs, and the 139th AS at Stratton ANGS, Schenectady County Airport, with C/LC-130Hs).

Today's 102nd RQS can claim not only to be the oldest aviation unit in the National Guard (as it traces its ancestry to the Aviation Detachment, 1st Battalion, Signal Corps, which had been organized in the New York National Guard on 1 November 1915), but also to have served in a greater variety of roles (observation, bombardment, tactical reconnaissance, interception, aeromedical evacuation, transport, air refueling and air rescue) than any other ANG unit. Having served on FAD in the United States from October 1940 until April 1944, the 102nd was reorganized as a bombardment squadron after World War II when it was joined by a second bombardment squadron (the 114th) and four fighter squadrons (the 136th, 137th, 138th and 139th). As noted, five of these squadrons are still in existence but the 114th FIS was inactivated as a New York ANG unit in September 1958.

New York ANG

102nd Rescue Squadron
106th Rescue Group

Lineage: *The 102nd Aero Squadron was organized at Kelly Field, TX, on 23 August 1917. This Air Service unit moved to England in December 1917 and to France in January 1918 where it served as a transportation and aircraft repair and maintenance unit with the AEF. It was demobilized at Garden City, NY, on 1 May 1919. In 1936, its lineage and honors were consolidated with those of the 102nd Squadron which had been activated as a New York NG unit in November 1921. In February 1991, the lineage and honors of the 1st Aero Company, which had been part of the New York NG between 1 November 1915 and 23 May 1917, were consolidated with those of the 102nd ARS.*

17 Nov 1921: 102nd Squadron extended federal recognition at Hempstead as the aviation unit in the 27th Division, New York NG, and initially equipped with Curtiss JN-4H trainers.
4 Nov 1922: 102nd Squadron relocated to Miller Field, New Dorp, Staten Island.
25 Jan 1923: Redesignated 102nd OS.
1923-1940: Remaining based at Miller Field, the 102nd OS was equipped over the years with the mix of aircraft typical of prewar Guard units, including Consolidated PT-1s and O-17s; Curtiss O-11s; Dayton-Wright TW-3s; Douglas BT-1s, O-2s, O-25s, O-38s and O-46s; and North American O-47s and BC-1s.
15 Oct 1940: Called to active duty, assigned to the Second Corps Area, and moved 11 days later to Reilly Field, Ft McClellan, AL. On 31 December 1940, it had one BC-1A, six O-46As and two O-47A/Bs.
World War II: Remaining in CONUS until disbanded at Thermal AAFld, CA, on 15 April 1944, the federalized New York NG unit moved seven times, was redesignated on four occasions, flew ASW patrols along the California coast, and provided aerial support for ground forces in training. Reconstituted and designated 102nd BS, the squadron was allotted back to the New York ANG on 24 May 1946.
30 Nov 1947: 102nd BS (Light) extended federal recognition at Floyd Bennett Field (NAS Brooklyn), NY, and soon equipped with Douglas B-26B/Cs

(plus support aircraft).
1 Mar 1951: Called to active duty as part of the Korean War call-up.
May 1951: Converted from B-26B/Cs to Boeing B-29As, redesignated 114th BS (Medium), and moved to March AFB, CA.
1 Dec 1952: Returned to state control at Floyd Bennett Field to be organized once again as the 114th BS (Light) and equipped with B-26B/Cs.
Feb 1957: Converted from B-26B/Cs to Lockheed F-94Bs.
15 Jun 1957: Redesignated 102nd FIS.
Sep 1958: Converted from F-94Bs to Fairchild C/MC-119Js and redesignated 102nd Aeromedical Transport Squadron.

1 Jul 1960: Became MATS-gained upon implementation of gaining command concept.
Winter 1962: Converted from C/MC-119Js to Boeing C-97As.
1 Jan 1963: Redesignated 102nd Air Transport Squadron (Heavy).
1 Jan 1966: Redesignated 102nd MAS and became MAC-gained upon MATS redesignation.
Summer 1969: Converted from C-97As to KC-97Ls.
17 Sep 1969: Redesignated 102nd AREFS and became TAC-gained.
Jun 1970: Moved to Suffolk County Airport, Westhampton Beach.
Fall/Winter 1972: Converted from

Above: During the spring of 1975 the NY ANG squadron at the Suffolk County Airport switched from air defense to air rescue and was designated the 102nd AR&RS.

Right: During the late 1930s and early 1940s Douglas O-38s equipped 26 National Guard squadrons. This is an O-38 of the 102nd Observation Squadron, 27th Division, New York National Guard.

KC-97Ls to Convair F/TF-102As.
2 Dec 1972: Redesignated 102nd FIS and became ADC-gained.
Spring 1975: Converted from F/TF-102As to Lockheed HC-130H/Ps and Sikorsky HH-3Es.
14 Jun 1975: Redesignated 102nd ARRS and became MAC-gained.
1 Oct 1989: Redesignated 102nd ARS.
Fall 1990: Converted from HH-3Es to Sikorsky HH-60Gs but retained HC-130H/Ps.

Current equipment for New York's 102nd RQS include five Sikorsky HH-60G helicopters and four Lockheed HC-130P tankers.

114th Fighter
Interceptor Squadron

Lineage: *Constituted and activated at Barksdale Field, LA, in June 1942, the 439th BS (Medium) was assigned to the 319th BG, Twelfth Air Force, with which it flew combat operations with Martin B-26s and North American B-25s in the MTO between November 1942 and December 1944. Returned to CONUS and re-equipped with Douglas A-26B/Cs, the 439th BS and other squadrons of the 319th BG were reassigned to the Seventh Air Force in April 1945 and flew combat operations from Okinawa during the last month of World War II. Inactivated at Ft Lawton, WA, in January 1946, the squadron was redesignated 114th BS and was allotted to the New York NG on 24 May 1946.*

17 Jun 1947: 114th BS (Light) extended federal recognition at Floyd Bennett Field (NAS Brooklyn), NY, and soon equipped with Douglas A-26B/Cs (plus support aircraft).
1 Mar 1951: Called to active duty as

part of the Korean War call-up.
May 1951: Converted from B-26B/Cs to Boeing B-29As, redesignated 114th BS (Medium), and moved to March AFB, CA.
1 Dec 1952: Returned to state control at Floyd Bennett Field to be organized once again as the 114th BS (Light) and equipped with B-26B/Cs.
Spring 1957: Converted from B-26B/Cs to Lockheed F-94Bs.
Jun 1957: Redesignated 114th FIS.
14 Sep 1958: Inactivated at Floyd Bennett Field.

Extended federal recognition on 17 June 1947, the 114th Bombardment Squadron (Light) flew Douglas B-26Bs and B-26Cs until the spring of 1957. A little over a year after converting to Lockheed F-94Bs and being redesignated the 114th FIS, the unit was inactivated in the New York ANG.

136th Fighter Squadron
107th Fighter Group

Lineage: *Constituted at Hunter Field, GA, on 3 August 1943 and activated seven days later as the 482nd BS (Dive), this unit was redesignated 503rd FS shortly after being shipped to England in the spring of 1944. Assigned to the 339th FG, Eighth Air Force, and equipped with North American P-51Ds, it flew combat operations in the ETO between April 1944 and VE Day. Inactivated at Drew Field, FL, in November 1945, it was reconstituted and redesignated the 136th FS before being allotted to the New York NG on 24 May 1946.*

8 Dec 1948: 136th FS (SE) extended federal recognition at NAS Niagara Falls, NY, and soon equipped with Republic F-47Ds (plus support aircraft).
1 Mar 1951: Called to active duty as

The 136th FIS converted to F-16A/B ADFs during the summer of 1990 but is due to become an air refueling squadron during FY94.

part of the Korean War call-up and assigned to ADC, but remained at NAS Niagara Falls. Redesignated 136th FIS soon thereafter.
1 Dec 1952: Returned to state control and shortly after converted from F-47Ds to North American F-51Hs.
Feb 1954: Converted from F-51Hs to Lockheed F-94Bs.
Oct 1957: Converted from F-94Bs to North American F-86Hs.
10 Nov 1958: Redesignated 136th TFS.
Jun 1959: NAS Niagara Falls inactivated and airfield became Niagara Falls IAP.
1 Jul 1960: Became TAC-gained upon implementation of gaining command concept.
Aug 1960: Converted from F-86Hs to North American F-100C/Fs.
1 Oct 1961: Called to active duty as part of the Berlin Crisis call-up but remained based at Niagara Falls IAP.
25 Aug 1962: Returned to state control.
26 Jan 1968: Called to active duty as part of the *Pueblo* Crisis call-up.
Jun 1968: Deployed to Tuy Hoa AB for

combat operations in Vietnam.
11 Jun 1969: Returned to state control at Niagara Falls IAP.
Apr 1971: Began conversion from F-100C/Fs to McDonnell F-101B/Fs.
15 Jun 1971: Redesignated 136th FIS and became ADC-gained.
1 Apr 1980: Became TAC-gained following ADC inactivation.
Spring 1982: Converted from F-101B/Fs to McDonnell F-4Cs.
Fall 1986: Converted from F-4Cs to F-4Ds.
Spring/Fall 1990: Conversion from F-4Ds (last F-4D operational sorties flown on 31 August 1990) to General Dynamics F-16A/B ADFs.
15 Mar 1992: Unit designation changed to 136th Fighter Squadron, 107th Fighter Group (136th FS, 107th FG).

An F-101B-110-MC with an F-101B-105-MC in trail. The 136th Fighter Interceptor Squadron flew Voodoos for 11 years beginning in the spring of 1971.

1 Jun 1992: As part of the Air Force restructuring program, gaining command changed to ACC.
FY94: Scheduled to convert from F-16A/B ADFs to Boeing KC-135Rs and to become an AMC-gained air refueling unit.

McDonnell Douglas

Robert Pfannenschmidt

137th Airlift Squadron
105th Airlift Group

Lineage: *Constituted at Hunter Field, GA, on 3 August 1943 and activated seven days later as the 483rd BS (Dive), this unit was redesignated 504th FS shortly after being shipped to England in the spring of 1944. Assigned to the 339th FG, Eighth Air Force, and equipped with North American P-51Ds, it flew combat operations in the ETO between April 1944 and VE Day. Inactivated at Drew Field, FL, in November 1945, it was reconstituted and redesignated the 137th FS before being allotted to the New York NG on 24*

Boeing C-97s equipped 18 ANG squadrons during a 12-year period beginning in 1960. With New York's 137th Air Transport Squadron, C-97Gs replaced C-119Cs at the end of 1962 and were flown from the Westchester County Airport in White Plains until the squadron converted to U-3s.

May 1946.
24 Jun 1948: 137th FS (SE) extended federal recognition at Westchester County Airport, White Plains, NY, and soon equipped with Republic F-47Ds (plus support aircraft).
1 Sep 1952: Redesignated 137th FIS and converted from F-47Ds to North American F-51Hs.
Jun 1953: Converted from F-51Hs to Lockheed F-94A/Bs.
Feb 1958: Began conversion from F-94A/Bs to North American F-86Hs.
1 May 1958: Redesignated 137th TFS.
1 Jul 1960: Became TAC-gained upon implementation of gaining command concept.
Feb 1961: Redesignated 137th

Aeromedical Transport Squadron, converted from F-86Hs to Fairchild C-119Cs, and became MATS-gained.
Apr 1962: Boeing KC-97Gs obtained on loan from SAC to initiate crew training in preparation for conversion to Stratofreighters.
Dec 1962: Redesignated 137th Air Transport Squadron (Heavy) and converted from C-119Cs to Boeing C-97Gs.
1 Jan 1966: Redesignated 137th MAS and became MAC-gained following MATS redesignation.
Spring 1969: Converted from C-97Gs to Cessna U-3A/Bs.
28 May 1969: Redesignated 137th TASS and became TAC-gained.
Apr 1971: Converted from U-3A/Bs to Cessna O-2As.
Feb-Mar 1983: Moved to Stewart Reserve Training Center, Newburgh, NY.
1 May 1984: Redesignated 137th MAS

NY ANG

and became MAC-gained.
Jul 1985: Received first Lockheed C-5A.
FY86: Completed conversion from O-2As to Lockheed C-5As.
24 Aug 1990: Called to active duty as part of Operation Desert Shield call-up.
15 May 1991: Released from active duty after taking part in Desert Shield/Desert Storm.
15 Mar 1992: Unit designation changed to 137th Airlift Squadron, 105th Airlift Group (137th AS, 105th AG).
1 Jun 1992: As part of the Air Force restructuring program, gaining command changed to AMC.

During FY85 and FY86, after relocating to the Stewart Reserve Training Center, the 105th MAS underwent a remarkable conversion from O-2As to C-5As.

Geoffrey Le Baron courtesy of Marty Isham

138th Fighter Squadron
174th Fighter Wing

Lineage: *Constituted at Hunter Field, GA, on 3 August 1943 and activated seven days later as the 484th BS (Dive), this unit was redesignated 505th FS shortly after being shipped to England in the spring of 1944. Assigned to the 339th FG, Eighth Air Force, and equipped with North American P-51Ds, it flew combat operations in the ETO between April 1944 and VE Day. Inactivated at Drew Field, FL, in November 1945, it was reconstituted and redesignated the 138th FS before being allotted to the New York NG on 24 May 1946.*

28 Oct 1947: 138th FS (SE) extended federal recognition at Hancock Field, Syracuse, and soon equipped with Republic P-47Ds (plus support aircraft).
12 Jan 1950: Redesignated 138th FS (Jet) and converted from F-47Ds to Republic F-84Bs.
1 Nov 1950: Redesignated 138th FBS and converted from F-84Bs to North American F-51Hs.
1 Mar-30 Jun 1953: Maintained two

If you let me down you'll burn in a crash but if you are trustworthy and get me home safely you'll end up with a smelter ... After many years of good and loyal service with the 138th TFS, an F-86H awaits its undeserved fate at MASDC in 1965.

F-51Ds on alert from sunrise to sunset as part of an experiment to determine the feasibility of augmenting active ADC units with ANG squadrons.
29 Oct 1953: Redesignated 138th FIS.
Feb 1954: Converted from F-51Hs to Lockheed F-94A/Bs.
Dec 1957: Received first North American F-86H.
Summer 1958: Completed conversion from F-94A/Bs to F-86Hs.
1 Nov 1958: Redesignated 138th TFS.
1 Jul 1960: Became TAC-gained upon implementation of gaining command concept.
1 Oct 1961: Called to active duty as part of the Berlin Crisis call-up and moved to Phalsbourg AB, France, later in that month for assignment to USAFE.

21 Aug 1962: Returned to state control at Hancock Field.
15 Oct 1962: Reached group status with federal recognition of 174th TFG.
13 May 1968: Called to active duty as

Peter B. Lewis

part of the *Pueblo* Crisis call-up. Soon after, moved to Cannon AFB, NM, where it ran a forward air controller school and combat crew training school.
20 Dec 1968: Returned to state control at Hancock Field.
Fall 1970: Converted from F-86Hs to Cessna A-37Bs.
Summer 1979: Converted from A-37Bs to Fairchild-Republic A-10As.
31 Dec 1989: Completed conversion from A-10As to General Dynamics F-16A/Bs equipped to carry the GPU-5/A.

Below: Carrying live Mk 82 bombs, an A-10A of the 138th TFS taxis at Davis-Monthan AFB on 23 March 1983 on its way to the Barry M. Goldwater Range.

30-mm gun pod.
29 Dec 1990: Called to active duty as part of Operation Desert Shield call-up.
30 Jun 1991: Released from active duty after taking part in Desert Shield/ Desert Storm.
15 Mar 1992: Unit designation changed to 138th Fighter Squadron, 174th Fighter Wing (138th FS, 174th FW).
1 Jun 1992: As part of the Air Force restructuring program, gaining command changed to ACC.

Right: During Desert Storm combat operations, the 30-mm GPU-5/A gun pod was found to have limited value, as its use requires the F-16A to come within range of defenses.

Daniel Soulaine

Brian C. Rogers

139th Airlift Squadron
109th Airlift Group

Lineage: *Constituted and activated at Morris Field, NC, in July 1942, the 303rd FS was assigned to the 337th FG, Third Air Force, and served as a CONUS-based operational training unit. Successively equipped with Bell P-39s, Republic P-43s and P-47s, and Curtiss P-40s, it was disbanded at Sarasota, FL, on 1 May 1944. Reconstituted and redesignated the 139th FS, the unit was allotted to the New York NG on 24 May 1946.*
18 Nov 1948: 139th FS (SE) extended federal recognition at Schenectady Airport and soon equipped with Republic F-47Ds (plus support aircraft).
1951: Converted from F-47Ds to North American F-51Hs and redesignated 139th FIS.
1954: Converted from F-51Hs to Lockheed F-94Bs.
Spring 1957: Converted from F-94Bs to North American F-86Hs.
Nov 1957: Redesignated 139th TFS.
Jan 1960: Converted from F-86Hs to Boeing C-97As and redesignated 139th ATS.
1 Jul 1960: Became MATS-gained upon implementation of gaining command concept.
1 Oct 1961: Called to active duty as part of the Berlin Crisis call-up to conduct worldwide airlift missions from its Schenectady base.
31 Aug 1962: Returned to state control.
1 Jan 1966: Redesignated 139th MAS and became MAC-gained following

The 139th AS has four standard C-130Hs and, for use on Volant DEW missions, four LC-130Hs. For operations from snow-and-ice covered fields close to DEW Line radar stations in Greenland, the LC-130Hs have retractable skis.

The 139th FIS was one of the 17 Guard squadrons not called to active duty during the Korean War. Based at the Schenectady Airport, it converted from F-47Ds to F-51Hs in 1951.

MATS redesignation.
Early 1971: Converted from C-97As to Lockheed C-130As.
16 Mar 1971: Redesignated 139th TAS and became TAC-gained.
1 Dec 1974: Became MAC-gained upon transfer of tactical airlift resources

NY ANG

from TAC to MAC.
Summer 1975: Converted from C-130As to C-130Ds and C-130D-6s and assumed responsibility for the Volant DEW resupply mission to DEW-Line radar stations on the Greenland ice cap.
1 Jun 1985: Completed conversion from C-130D/D-6s (last C-130D transferred out on 4 Apr 1985) to C/LC-130Hs (operational ski trials

conducted on the Greenland ice cap in Mar 1985).
Aug 1990: Volunteers began flying Desert Shield support missions.
15 Mar 1992: Unit designation changed to 139th Airlift Squadron, 109th Airlift Group (139th AS, 109th AG).
1 Jun 1992: As part of the Air Force restructuring program, gaining command changed to AMC.

Jim Dunn

Above: Until recently, the 'Herks' *of the 139th TAS were finished in the usual dark camouflage, a rather inappropriate choice.*

Right: The Arctic camouflage, with *extensive use of red panels, is now applied to the C-130Hs (83-0488 illustrated) and LC-130Hs.*

North Carolina Air National Guard

For over 20 years, the 156th TAS has been flying C-130Bs from the Charlotte/Douglas International Airport. The only flying squadron in the North Carolina ANG was organized as the 156th FS in March 1948, flew Thunderjets in England during the Korean War, and became a transport unit in early 1961 when it was redesignated the 156th Aeromedical Transport Squadron.

At the end of FY92, 1,584 officers and enlisted personnel manned 19 NC ANG units, including the 156th AS.

156th Airlift Squadron 145th Airlift Group

Lineage: *Constituted and activated at Westover Field, MA, in December 1942, the 360th FG was assigned to the 356th FG, Eighth Air Force, with which it flew combat operations with Republic P-47Ds, from October 1943, and North American P-51Ds, from November 1944 until VE Day, in the ETO. Inactivated at Camp Kilmer, NJ, in November 1945, the unit was reconstituted and redesignated the 156th FS before being allotted to the North Carolina NG on 24 May 1946.*

15 Mar 1948: 156th FS (SE) extended federal recognition at Morris Field, Charlotte, NC, and soon equipped with Republic P-47Ds (plus support aircraft).
Dec 1949: Converted from F-47Ds to North American F-51Ds.
10 Oct 1950: Called to active duty as part of the Korean War call-up and moved 10 days later to Godman Field, KY, for assignment to TAC, redesignated to 156th FBS, and subsequently converted to Republic F-84Ds and then to F-84Es.
Nov 1951: Moved to RAF Manston, Kent, England.
10 Jul 1952: Returned to state control at Morris Field to be reorganized as the 156th FBS and equipped with F-51Ds.
Summer 1955: Converted from F-51Ds to North American F-86As.
1 Jul 1955: Redesignated 156th FIS.
1 Jul 1957: Reached group status with federal recognition of 145th FIG.
Oct 1957: Converted from F-86As to F-86Es.
Mar 1959: Converted from F-86Es to F-86Ls.
1 Jul 1960: Became ADC-gained upon implementation of gaining command concept.
1 Feb 1961: Redesignated 156th Aeromedical Transport Squadron and became MATS-gained.
May 1961: Completed conversion from F-86Ls to Fairchild C-119Cs.
Jun 1962: Converted from C-119Cs to Lockheed C-121C/Gs.
25 Jan 1964: Redesignated 156th ATS.
Winter 1965: Converted from C-121C/Gs to Douglas C-124Cs.
1 Jan 1966: Redesignated 156th MAS and became MAC-gained following MATS redesignation.
15 May 1971: Redesignated 156th TAS and became TAC-gained.
Spring/Summer 1971: Converted from C-124Cs to Lockheed C-130Bs.
1 Dec 1974: Became MAC-gained upon transfer of tactical airlift resources from TAC to MAC.
Jun 1986: Won Airlift Rodeo '86 competition.
Aug 1990: Volunteers began flying missions in support of Operation Desert Shield.
15 Mar 1992: Unit designation changed to 156th Airlift Squadron, 145th Airlift Group (156th AS, 145th AG).
1 Jun 1992: As part of the Air Force restructuring program, gaining command changed to AMC.
FY92: Contract awarded to Lockheed for 12 C-130HCs with which to replace the C-130Bs of the 156th AS.

With conversion to C-130Bs already *initiated, the 156th MAS sent its C-124Cs to MASDC where 53-0017 was photographed on 11 May 1971. Four days later the squadron was redesignated the 156th TAS.*

Peter B. Lewis

When flying MAFFS forest fire-fighting missions, the camouflaged *C-130Bs of North Carolina's 156th TAS, as well as those from Wyoming's 187th TAS and the C-130Es of California's 115th TAS, have markings and numbers applied in washable paint over their standard camouflage.*

North Dakota Air National Guard

There is no denying that the North Dakotans derive much pride from the 'Happy Hooligans' nickname earned by their Air Guardsmen during a particularly boisterous encampment, as their State Legislature has passed a resolution countermanding current ACC regulations and providing for this nickname to be boldly carried in full color on the fin and rudder of the aircraft of the 178th FIS (of course, ACC regulations would again apply if and when the unit were to be on FAD).

The 178th, which had been organized in January 1947 and served on active duty during the Korean War, has been a fighter interceptor Squadron since January 1953. At the end of FY92, when 1,217 officers and enlisted personnel manned 13 ND ANG units, the 178th FS was flying F-16A/B ADFs from Hector Field, Fargo, and from Klamath Falls.

178th Fighter Squadron 119th Fighter Group

Lineage: *Constituted at Hamilton Field, CA, in May 1943 and activated in July of that year, the 392nd FS was assigned to the 367th FG, Ninth Air Force, with which it flew combat operations with Lockheed P-38Js in the ETO, beginning in May 1944, and with Republic P-47Ds, from February 1945. Inactivated at Seymour Johnson Field, NC, in November 1945, the squadron was reconstituted and redesignated the 178th FS before being allotted to the North Dakota NG on 24 May 1946.*
16 Jan 1947: 178th FS (SE) extended federal recognition at Hector Field, Fargo MAP, ND, and soon equipped with North American P-51Ds (plus support aircraft).
1 Apr 1951: Called to active duty as part of the Korean War call-up and departed eight days later for Moody AFB, GA, for assignment to SAC.
1 Jun 1951: Redesignated 178th FBS.
Oct 1951: Moved to George AFB for assignment to TAC.
1 Dec 1952: Returned to state control at Hector Field.
1 Jan 1953: Redesignated 178th FIS.
Summer 1954: Converted from F-51Ds (last left on 14 Nov) to Lockheed F-94A/Bs (first received on 10 Jun).
Early 1956: Converted from F-94A/Bs

(last left on 17 Mar) to F-94Cs (first received on 19 Feb).
16 Apr 1956: Reached group status with federal recognition of 119th FIG.
Summer 1958: Converted from F-94Cs (last left on 21 Aug) to Northrop F-89Ds (first received on 28 Jun).
Fall 1959-Summer 1960: Converted from F-89Ds (last left on 7 Aug 1960) to F-89Js (first received on 1 Nov 1959).
1 Jul 1960: Became ADC-gained upon implementation of gaining command concept.
Summer-Fall 1966: Converted from

F-89Js (last left on 23 Nov) to Convair F/TF-102As (first received on 10 Jul).
Fall 1969: Converted from F/TF-102As (last left on 14 Dec) to McDonnell F-101B/Fs (first received on 17 Nov).
Spring 1977-Spring 1978: Converted from F-101B/Fs (last left on 16 Apr 1978) to McDonnell F-4Ds (first received on 15 Mar 1977).
1 Apr 1980: Became TAC-gained following ADC inactivation.
Apr 1986-Apr 1987: Provided aircraft and personnel to Operation Creek Klaxon, the ANG's assumption of air

defense commitment at Ramstein AB, Germany, while the 86th TFW, USAFE, was converting to F-16C/Ds.
FY90: Converted from F-4Ds (last left on 15 Jul 1990) to General Dynamics F-16A/B ADFs (with which alert status was resumed at Klamath Falls, OR, in Aug 1990).
15 Mar 1992: Unit designation changed to 178th Fighter Squadron, 119th Fighter Group (178th FS, 119th FG).
1 Jun 1992: As part of the Air Force restructuring program, gaining command changed to ACC.

Above: While ANG units were assigned C-131s as support aircraft, a healthy competition for the most spotless aircraft prevailed. North Dakota's VC-131D was a contender.

Right: F-4D 66-7498 was given special markings in 1989.

The Group Commander's F-16A ADF, complete with Teddy Roosevelt's 'Rough Riders' markings, poses during a visit to Colorado in August 1991.

Ohio Air National Guard

Even though it only ranks sixth in terms of state population, Ohio currently has five ANG flying squadrons (like New York, which has nearly 65 per cent more people), whereas the Air National Guard of four other more populous states either have four squadrons (California and Pennsylvania) or three squadrons (Illinois and Texas).

The first of the Ohio units, the 112th OS, was organized in June 1927 and served on active duty for five years beginning in November 1940 (lastly as the 112th Liaison Squadron in Europe). Postwar, the 112th BS was joined by three fighter squadrons, the 162nd, 164th and 166th; the 145th ATS was added in March 1956. During the Korean War activation, the 112th BS and 166th FS served in the United States; during the Berlin Crisis activation the 112th, 162nd and 164th

served stateside, while the 166th went to France; and during the *Pueblo* Crisis the 166th TFS was the only Ohio ANG unit to be called to active duty and went to Korea for one year; during Operation Just Cause the 112th TFS flew combat sorties in Panama; and during the Gulf War the 145th AREFS supported Desert Shield and Desert Storm operations.

At the end of FY92, 5,598 officers and enlisted personnel manned 66 OH ANG units, including five flying squadrons (the 112th FS flying F-16C/Ds from Toledo Express Airport, the 162nd FS flying A-7D/Ks but preparing to convert to F-16C/Ds at Springfield-Beckley Municipal Airport, the 166th FS undergoing conversion from A-7D/Ks to KC-135Rs at Rickenbacker ANGB, the 164th AS with C-130Hs at Mansfield-Lahm Airport, and the 145th ARS with KC-135Rs at Rickenbacker ANGB).

Ohio ANG

112th Fighter Squadron
180th Fighter Group

Lineage: *Organized at Kelly Field, TX, on 18 August 1917 as the 112th Aero Squadron, Air Service, this supply unit was redesignated 633rd Aero Squadron on 1 February 1918 and remained at Kelly Field until demobilized on 19 August 1919. In 1936, its lineage and honors were consolidated with those of the 112th OS which had been activated as an Ohio NG unit in June 1927.*
20 Jun 1927: 112th OS extended federal recognition at Hopkins Airport, Cleveland, as the aviation unit in the 37th Division, Ohio NG, and initially equipped with **Consolidated PT-1** trainers.
1927-1940: Remaining based in Cleveland, the 112th OS was equipped over the years with the mix of aircraft typical of prewar Guard units, including **Consolidated PT-1s and O-17s; Curtiss O-11s; Douglas BT-1s, O-2s and O-38s;** and **North American O-47s and BC-1s.**
25 Nov 1940: Called to active duty, assigned to the Fourth Corps Area, and moved seven days later to Pope Field, Ft Bragg, NC. On 31 December 1940, it had

one BC-1A, one O-38E and eight O-47A/Bs.
World War II: Remaining in CONUS until shipped to England in May 1944, the unit moved eight times, was redesignated twice, flew ASW patrols along the Atlantic coast, was inactive between October 1942 and April 1943, and was reorganized in April 1943 as the 112th Liaison Squadron in preparation for overseas deployment. Equipped with **Cessna UC-78s** and following troops on the European continent, it flew courier missions in the area to the rear of the front lines between June 1944 and VE Day. Inactivated at Drew Field, FL, in November 1945, the unit was redesignated 112th BS before being allotted back to the Ohio NG on 24 May 1946.
2 Dec 1946: 112th BS (Light) extended federal recognition at the Cleveland MAP and soon equipped with **Douglas A-26B/Cs** (plus support aircraft).
10 Oct 1950: Called to active duty as part of the Korean War call-up and moved to Lawson AFB, GA.
9 Jul 1952: Returned to state control

to be reorganized as the 112th FBS at Berea, OH, and equipped with **North American F-51Hs.**
Oct 1952: Relocated to Akron-Canton MAP in North Canton.
Jul 1955: Redesignated 112th FIS.
Apr 1956: Relocated to Toledo MAP and converted from F-51Hs to **North American T-28As** (with limited jet training using a few **Lockheed T-33As** and **Republic F-84Es**).
Jan 1959: Relocated to the Toledo Express Airport in Swanton and converted from T-28As to **Republic F-84Fs.**
1 Jul 1960: Became ADC-gained upon implementation of gaining command concept.
1 Oct 1961: Called to active duty as part of the Berlin Crisis call-up but remained at Toledo Express Airport.
20 Aug 1962: Returned to state control, redesignated 112th TFS, and became TAC-gained.
15 Oct 1962: Reached group status with federal recognition of 180th TFG.
Oct 1970: Converted from F-84Fs to North American F-100D/Fs.

The 112th TFS flew F-100Ds and F-100Fs between October 1970 and July 1979.

Summer 1979: Converted from F-100D/Fs to LTV A-7Ds.
Dec 1989: Flew 22 combat sorties during Operation Just Cause in Panama.
FY92/93: Converting from A-7D/Ks to General Dynamics Block 25 F-16C/Ds (first F-16D received on 29 Feb 1992 and last A-7D and last A-7K flown away on 18 May 1992).
15 Mar 1992: Unit designation changed to 112th Fighter Squadron, 180th Fighter Group (112th FS, 180th FG).
1 Jun 1992: As part of the Air Force restructuring program, gaining command changed to ACC.
31 Mar 1993: Scheduled to complete conversion to F-16C/Ds.

The Toledo 'Stingers' have joined the growing ranks of F-16 operators, with C Models. The 'OH' tailcode is shared with other Ohio squadrons.

With the emblem of the 112th TFS incorporating a cartoon representation of a yellow jacket, the nickname of the Ohio unit is 'Stingers'.

145th Air Refueling Squadron
160th Air Refueling Group

Lineage: *Organized at Akron-Canton MAP to take over the facilities and many of the personnel of the 112th FIS which was being transferred to Toledo MAP.*
17 Mar 1956: 145th ATS (Medium) extended federal recognition at Akron-Canton MAP and equipped with **Curtiss**

C-46Ds.
1 Feb 1958: Redesignated 145th Aeromedical Transport Squadron (Light) and converted from C-46Ds to **Fairchild C-119Js.**
1 Jul 1960: Became MATS-gained upon implementation of the gaining command concept.
8 Jul 1961: Reached group status with federal recognition of 160th AREFG, redesignated 145th AREFS, became TAC-gained, and relocated to Clinton County AFB.
Winter 1961: Converted from C-119Js

to **Boeing KC-97Fs** (first tanker received in Feb 1962).
1963: KC-97Fs replaced with KC-97Gs.
8-22 Aug 1964: Operation Ready Go: the 145th AREFS and the two other squadrons of the 126th AREFW (Illinois' 108th and Wisconsin's 126th) provided tankers to deploy 31 ANG fighters and reconnaissance aircraft from CONUS to Germany.
Spring/Summer 1965: Converted from KC-97Gs to KC-97Ls (first jet-augmented tanker received in Mar 1965).
Summer 1967/Spring 1975:

Participated four times a year in Operation Creek Party.
Sep 1971: Relocated to Lockbourne AFB.

Along with its KC-97Ls, the 145th AREFS had at least one C-97G. This transport-configured aircraft was photographed at St Joseph, Missouri, on 3 July 1971. Two months later, the Ohio squadron moved from Clinton County AFB to Lockbourne AFB. The later was renamed Rickenbacker AFB.

Right: Ohio and Wisconsin began the upgrading of ANG tanker assets with the introduction of the KC-135R. The 145th ARS will be joined by the 166th when it converts from A-7s.

Douglas D. Olson

May 1974: Lockbourne AFB renamed Rickenbacker AFB.
Apr 1975: Converted from KC-97Ls to Boeing KC-135As.
1 Jul 1976: Gaining command changed from TAC to SAC.
1 Apr 1980: Rickenbacker AFB transferred to Ohio ANG and redesignated Rickenbacker ANGB.
FY84: Converted from KC-135As to KC-135Es.
Aug 1990: Volunteers began flying missions in support of Operation Desert Shield.
20 Dec 1990: Called to active duty as part of Operation Desert Shield call-up.
15 May 1991: Released from active duty after taking part in Desert Shield/Desert Storm.
FY91/FY92: converted from KC-135Es to KC-135Rs (last KC-135E left on 4 Jun 1991 and first KC-135R received on 11

Right: 58-0017, a KC-135E of the 145th AREFS, was photographed at Forbes Field, Kansas, in September 1988.

Jerry Geer

Oct 1991).
15 Mar 1992: Unit abbreviation changed to 145th ARS, 160 ARG.
1 Jun 1992: As part of the Air Force restructuring program, gaining command changed to AMC.
Fall 1994: Will locate to Wright-Patterson AFB due to programmed closure of Rickenbacker ANGB.

162nd Fighter Squadron
178th Fighter Group

Lineage: *Constituted and activated at Hamilton Field, CA, in December 1942, the 362nd FS was assigned to the 357th FG, Eighth Air Force. Equipped with North American P-51Ds, it flew combat operations in the ETO from February 1944 until VE Day. Inactivated at Neubiberg, Germany, in August 1946, the unit was reconstituted and redesignated the 162nd FS before being allotted to the Ohio NG on 24 May 1946.*
2 Nov 1947: 162nd FS (SE) extended federal recognition at Cox-Dayton MAP in Vandalia and soon equipped with North American P-51Ds (plus support aircraft).
May 1950: Converted from F-51Ds to F-51Hs.
Oct 1952: Redesignated 162nd FBS.
1 Jul 1955: Redesignated 162nd FIS.
Sep 1955: Relocated to Springfield MAP and converted from F-51Hs to Republic F-84Es.
Mar 1958: Completed conversion from F-84Es to F-84Fs (first received in Nov 1957).
1 Jul 1960: Became ADC-gained upon implementation of gaining command concept.
1 Oct 1961: Called to active duty as part of the Berlin Crisis call-up but remained at Springfield MAP.
31 Aug 1962: Returned to state control.
15 Oct 1962: Reached group status with federal recognition of 178th TFG, redesignated 162nd TFS, and became TAC-gained.
Apr 1970: Converted from F-84Fs to North American F-100D/Fs.
Apr 1978: Converted from F-100D/Fs to LTV A-7Ds.
15 Mar 1992: Unit designation changed to 162nd Fighter Squadron, 178th Fighter Group (162nd FS, 178th FG).
1 Jun 1992: As part of the Air Force

In 1987, the A-7s of the three Ohio squadrons became the first ANG units to receive the gray and blue scheme illustrated by this A-7K.

restructuring program, gaining command changed to ACC.
FY93/FY94: Will become the last unit to convert from A-7D/Ks to General Dynamics Block 50 F-16C/Ds (A-7 operations will end in June 1993 and F-16 operations will commence in October 1993).

Peter B. Lewis

Above: Photographed on a sunless afternoon at McChord AFB, Washington, on 20 July 1968, this Republic F-84F-20-RE was one of the Thunderstreaks which equipped Ohio's 162nd Tactical Fighter Squadron between November 1957 and April 1970.

Douglas D. Olson

Ohio ANG

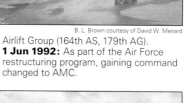

B. L. Brown courtesy of David W. Menard

164th Airlift Squadron
179th Airlift Group

Lineage: *Constituted and activated at Hamilton Field, CA, in December 1942, the 363rd FS was assigned to the 357th FG, Eighth Air Force. Equipped with North American P-51Ds, it flew combat operations in the ETO from February 1944 until VE Day. Inactivated at Neubiberg, Germany, in August 1946, the unit was reconstituted and redesignated the 164th FS before being allotted to the Ohio NG on 24 May 1946.*
20 Jun 1948: 164th FS (SE) extended federal recognition at Mansfield MAP and soon equipped with North American F-51Ds (plus support aircraft).
Jul 1949: Converted from F-51Ds to F-51Hs.
5 Nov 1952: Redesignated 164th FBS.
Sep 1953: Converted from F-51Hs to Lockheed F-80Cs.
Oct 1954: Converted from F-80Cs to Republic F-84Es.
Dec 1957: Converted from F-84Es to F-84Fs.
10 Nov 1958: Redesignated 164th TFS.
1 Jul 1960: Became TAC-gained upon implementation of gaining command concept.
1 Oct 1961: Called to active duty as part of the Berlin Crisis call-up but remained at Mansfield MAP.
20 Aug 1962: Returned to state control.
15 Oct 1962: Reached group status with federal recognition of 179th TFG.
9 Sep 1967: Mansfield MAP renamed Mansfield-Lahm Airport.
Feb 1972: Began conversion from F-84Fs to North American F-100D/Fs.
Winter 1975: Converted from F-100D/Fs to Lockheed C-130Bs.
5 Jan 1976: Redesignated 164th TAS and became MAC-gained.
Aug 1990: Volunteers began flying Desert Shield support missions.
Spring 1991: Converted from C-130Bs to C-130Hs (first C-130H received on 24 May and last C-130B flown out on 4 June).

Jan 1992: Completed conversion to C-130Hs.
15 Mar 1992: Unit designation changed to 164th Airlift Squadron, 179th Airlift Group (164th AS, 179th AG).
1 Jun 1992: As part of the Air Force restructuring program, gaining command changed to AMC.

Tom Brewer courtesy of David W. Menard

Above left: The 164th FBS flew F-84Es for three years in 1954-57.

Left: An F-100D bearing the yellow tail band of the 164th TFS on 12 May 1974, shortly before the squadron converted to A-7Ds.

Below: For the 164th the switch from the fighter mission to transport was made during the winter of 1975. Landing at McClellan AFB on 24 August 1981, 59-1525 was one of the last C-130Bs assigned to the 164th TAS.

Peter B. Lewis

166th Fighter Squadron
121st Fighter Wing

Lineage: *Constituted and activated at Hamilton Field, CA, in December 1942, the 364th FS was assigned to the 357th FG, Eighth Air Force. Equipped with North American P-51Ds, it flew combat operations in the ETO from February 1944 until VE Day. Inactivated at Neubiberg, Germany, in August 1946, the unit was reconstituted and redesignated the 166th FS before being allotted to the Ohio NG on 24 May 1946.*
21 Aug 1946: 166th FS (SE) activated at Port Columbus Airport and equipped with two North American T-6s and one Beech C-45 pending move to Lockbourne AFB.
26 Jan 1947: 166th FS (SE) extended federal recognition at Lockbourne AFB and equipped with North American P-51Ds (plus support aircraft).
Oct 1948: Converted from F-51Ds to F-51Hs.
Apr 1950: Converted from F-51Hs to Republic F-84Cs and redesignated 166th FS (Jet).
1 Feb 1951: Called to active duty as

part of the Korean War call-up and assigned ADC duty but initially remained based at Lockbourne AFB.
Jul 1952: Relocated to Youngstown MAP, OH.
1 Nov 1952: Returned to state control at Youngstown MAP to be reorganized as the 166th FBS and equipped with North American F-51Hs.
Mar 1954: Converted from F-51Hs to Lockheed F-80Cs.
Jan 1955: Converted from F-80Cs to Republic F-84Es.
1 Jul 1955: Redesignated 166th FIS.

Fall 1957: Converted from F-84Es to F-84Fs.
1 Nov 1958: Redesignated 166th TFS.
1 Jul 1960: Became TAC-gained upon implementation of gaining command concept.
1 Oct 1961: Called to active duty as part of the Berlin Crisis call-up.
Nov 1961: Moved to Etain AB, France, to serve with USAFE as part of the 7121st TFW.
16 Aug 1962: Returned to state control at Lockbourne AFB. F-84Fs left in France were replaced with North

American F-100C/Fs.
15 Oct 1962: Reached group status with federal recognition of 121st TFG.
26 Jan 1968: Called to active duty as part of the *Pueblo* Crisis call-up but remained at its home base for five months.
Jun 1968: Moved to Kunsan AB, Korea, and assigned to the 354th TFW.
19 Jun 1969: Returned to state control at Lockbourne AFB.
Nov 1971: Converted from F-100C/Fs to F-100D/Fs.
May 1974: Lockbourne AFB renamed

White-bordered blue fin bands, as carried by this F-100D, have long identified aircraft of the 166th.

Peter B. Lewis

154

Rickenbacker AFB.
10 Oct 1974: 121st TFG inactivated and 166th TFS placed directly under the 121st TFW.
Dec 1974: Converted from F-100D/Fs to LTV A-7Ds.
1 Apr 1980: Rickenbacker AFB transferred to Ohio ANG and redesignated Rickenbacker ANGB.
15 Mar 1992: Unit designation changed to 166th Fighter Squadron, 121st Fighter Wing (166th FS, 121st FW).
1 Jun 1992: As part of the Air Force restructuring program, gaining command changed to ACC.

This Republic F-84E-15-RE is preserved at Rickenbacker, wearing the blue trim and snake badge of the 166th FIS.

FY92/FY93: Converting from A-7D/Ks to Boeing KC-135Rs (last A-7D flown out on 23 Sep 1992 and first KC-135R scheduled for delivery in January 1993).
31 Dec. 1993: Planned date for redesignation to 166th ARS, 121st ARW, as an AMC-gained tanker unit.
Fall 1994: Will relocate to Wright-Patterson AFB due to programmed closure of Rickenbacker ANGB.

Douglas D. Olson

Charles T. Robbins

Carrying a dart target beneath its port wing, this A-7D of the 166th was at Davis-Monthan AFB in January 1987. In preparation for its conversion to KC-135Rs and its redesignation to 166th ARS, the squadron disposed of its last A-7D in September 1992.

Oklahoma Air National Guard

In 1946, the Oklahoma National Guard was allotted two fighter squadrons, its prewar 125th which had first been organized in November 1940 as the 125th FS and had been on active duty from January 1941 until December 1945 (lastly as the 125th Liaison Squadron in Europe), and the newly created 185th. Both squadrons served on active duty in the United States during the Korean War and the 125th was again activated during the Berlin Crisis.

At the end of FY92, 2,414 officers and enlisted personnel manned 29 OK ANG units, including the 125th FS at Tulsa International Airport with A-7D/Ks and the 185th AS at Will Rogers IAP, Oklahoma City, with C-130Hs.

125th Fighter Squadron
138th Fighter Group

Lineage: *Designated the 125th Observation Squadron and allotted to the Oklahoma NG on 30 July 1940.*
15 Nov 1940: 125th OS constituted in Tulsa.
31 Jan 1941: 125th OS extended federal recognition in Tulsa.
15 Sep 1941: Called to active duty, assigned to 68th OG, and moved five days later to Post Field, Ft Sill, OK. On 30 Nov 1941, it had two Douglas O-38Es, one North American O-47B and one North American BC-1A.
World War II: Remaining based in CONUS until May 1944, the mobilized Oklahoma NG unit moved seven times, was redesignated on three occasions, and was trained as a liaison squadron prior to being shipped to England. Designated 125th Liaison Squadron and equipped with Stinson L-5s, it flew combat operations in support of ground forces in northern Europe from August 1944 until VE Day. Inactivated at Frankfurt, Germany, in December 1945, the squadron was reconstituted and redesignated the 125th FS before being

allotted back to the Oklahoma NG on 24 May 1946.
15 Feb 1947: 125th FS (SE) extended federal recognition at Tulsa and soon equipped with North American P-51Ds (plus support aircraft).
Jun 1950: Converted from F-51Ds to Republic F-84Bs and redesignated 125th FS (Jet).
10 Oct 1950: Called to active duty as

part of the Korean War call-up.
Nov 1950: Moved to Alexandria AFB, LA, redesignated 125th FBS, and assigned to 137th FBG for service with TAC.
10 Jul 1952: Returned to state control in Tulsa to be re-equipped with North American F-51Ds.
FY54: Converted from F-51Ds to

Lockheed F-80Cs.
Summer 1957: Converted from F-80Cs to North American F-86Ls.
1 Aug 1957: Reached group status with federal recognition of 138th FIG and squadron redesignated 125th FIS.
Winter 1959-Spring 1960: Converted from F-86Ls to Boeing C-97Gs.

Peter B. Lewis

Framed against the row of SR-71 hangars at Beale AFB, this F-100D-45-NH, one of the last to equip the 125th TFS, was photographed at the California base on 5 May 1978. The Oklahoma unit was lucky to convert from C-124Cs to Huns during FY73 and flew F-100D/Fs until its conversion to A-7Ds.

Along with Iowa's 124th and New Mexico's 188th, Oklahoma's 125th TFS was one of three tactical fighter squadrons to be equipped with A-7Ds modified to carry the LANA pod.

FY73: Converted from C-124Cs to North American F-100D/Fs.
25 Jan 1973: Redesignated 125th TFS and became TAC-gained.
Jul 1978: Converted from F-100D/Fs to LTV A-7Ds.
FY87: A-7Ds upgraded to LANA configuration.
15 Mar 1992: Unit designation changed to 125th Fighter Squadron, 138th Fighter Group (125th FS, 138th FG).
1 Jun 1992: As part of the Air Force restructuring program, gaining command changed to ACC.
FY93: Scheduled to convert from A-7D/Ks to General Dynamics Block 50 F-16C/Ds.

15 Jan 1960: Redesignated 125th ATS.
1 Jul 1960: Became MATS-gained upon implementation of gaining command concept.

1 Oct 1961: Called to active duty as part of the Berlin Crisis call-up to conduct worldwide airlift missions from its base in Tulsa.

31 Aug 1962: Returned to state control.
Feb 1968: Converted from C-97Gs to Douglas C-124Cs.

Right: When it converted from Boeing C-97F/Gs to Douglas C-124Cs in April 1968, the 185th MAS retained its C-97E 'Talking Bird' airborne communications relay aircraft. This unique aircraft, serial 51-0224, was photographed at Will Rogers Field in Oklahoma City on 5 July 1968.

Below: During the summer of 1979, the 185th Tactical Airlift Squadron became the first ANG squadron to receive C-130Hs directly from the Lockheed plant in Georgia. 78-0313 is seen taxiing on one of the dirt strips at Fort Bragg, North Carolina, in June 1983.

185th Airlift Squadron 137th Airlift Wing

Lineage: *Constituted at Key Field, MS, on 25 January 1943 and activated 10 days later as the 506th BS (Dive), this unit was redesignated 506th FS shortly after being shipped to England in the spring of 1944. Assigned to the 404th FG, Ninth Air Force, and equipped with Republic P-47Ds, it flew combat operations in the ETO between May 1944 and VE Day. Inactivated at Drew Field, FL, in November 1945, it was reconstituted and redesignated the 185th FS before being allotted to the Oklahoma NG on 24 May 1946.*
13 Feb 1947: 185th FS (SE) extended federal recognition at Westheimer Field, Norman, OK, and soon equipped with North American P-51Ds (plus support aircraft).
Sep 1949: Relocated to Will Rogers Field, Oklahoma City MAP.
1 Feb 1951: Redesignated 185th TRS and converted from F-51Ds to RF-51Ds.
1 Apr 1951: Called to active duty as part of the Korean War call-up but initially remained at Will Rogers Field to complete conversion to tactical reconnaissance.
Jan 1952: Moved to Shaw AFB, SC, and converted from RF-51Ds to Lockheed RF-80As.
1 Jan 1953: Returned to state control to be reorganized as the 185th FBS and equipped with F-51Ds.
Spring 1953: Converted from F-51Ds to Lockheed F-80Cs.
May 1958: Redesignated 185th FIS and converted from F-80Cs to North American F-86Ls.
1 Jul 1960: Became ADC-gained upon implementation of gaining command concept.

FY61: Converted from F-86Ls to Boeing C-97F/Gs (plus one C-97E 'Talking Bird').
1 Apr 1961: Redesignated 185th ATS and became MATS-gained.
May 1965: C-97E 'Talking Bird' deployed to Ramey AFB, PR, to provide communications link with the Pentagon during the Dominican Republic Contingency.
1 Jan 1966: Redesignated 185th MAS and became MAC-gained following MATS redesignation.
Apr 1968: Converted from C-97F/Gs to Douglas C-124Cs but retained its C-97E 'Talking Bird'.
Fall-Winter 1974: Converted from C-97E/C-124Cs to Lockheed C-130As.
10 Dec 1974: Redesignated 185th TAS.
9 Feb 1975: 137th TAG inactivated and 185th placed directly under 137th TAW.

Summer 1979: Converted from C-130As to C-130Hs.
Aug 1990: Volunteers began flying missions in support of Operation Desert Shield.
15 Mar 1992: Unit designation changed to 185th Airlift Squadron, 137th Airlift Wing (185th AS, 137st AW).
1 Jun 1992: As part of the Air Force restructuring program, gaining command changed to AMC.

Oregon Air National Guard

Remaining briefly under state control following its organization in April 1941, the 123rd OS was called to active duty in World War II, and, after being organized as the 35th PRS, flew combat operations in the CBI theater of operations during the last 11 months of the war. The squadron was allotted back to Oregon in 1946 and has flown fighters ever since it received federal recognition as the 123rd FS in August 1946. During the Korean War it served on FAD at its home station. The other flying unit in the Oregon ANG, the 114th FS, was organized in February 1984 and since then has trained air defense crews for the Air National Guard.

At the end of FY92, 2,000 officers and enlisted personnel manned 20 OR ANG units, including the 114th FS at the Klamath Falls IAP with F-16A/B ADFs and the 123rd FS at Portland IAP with F-15A/Bs.

The Fairchild C-26 has gained a number of unflattering nicknames since winning the ANGOSTA competition. The most common are 'San Antonio sewer pipe' and 'San Antonio death tube'.

114th Fighter Squadron
142nd Fighter Group

Left: The 114th Tactical Fighter Training Squadron received federal recognition on 1 February 1984. Based at Kingsley Field, to which 63-7460 is seen returning in the afternoon of 6 July 1988, and equipped with F-4Cs, the 114th TFTS had been organized to serve as a replacement training unit for the benefit of Phantom-equipped ANG air defense units.

Below: The 114th FS continues its training tradition, producing pilots for the Guard's F-16 ADF force.

Lineage: *When in 1983 the Oregon ANG was authorized to organize a replacement training unit to train pilots and WSOs for the Guard's FISs, the new squadron was given the numerical designation of the 114th FIS which had been inactivated as a New York ANG unit on 14 September 1958.*
1 Feb 1984: 114th TFTS extended federal recognition at Kingsley Field, Klamath Falls, as TAC-gained RTU, and equipped with McDonnell F-4Cs.
Fall 1988: Converted from F-4Cs to General Dynamics F-16A/Bs.
1 Mar 1989: First F-16 upgraded to the ADF configuration delivered to Kingsley Field.
Fall 1989: Fully converted to F-16A/B ADFs.
15 Mar 1992: Unit designation

changed to 114th Fighter Squadron, 142nd Fighter Group (114th FS, 142nd FG).
1 Jun 1992: As part of the Air Force restructuring program, gaining command changed to ACC.

123rd Fighter Squadron
142nd Fighter Group

Lineage: *Designated the 125th Observation Squadron and allotted to the Oregon NG on 30 July 1940.*
18 Apr 1941: 123rd OS extended federal recognition at Swan Island Airport, Portland, and equipped with a mix of Douglas O-46s, North American O-47s and Stinson O-49s.
15 Sep 1941: Called to active duty and attached to the 70th OG. Ten days later the squadron moved to Gray Field, WA.
World War II: Between September 1941 and April 1944 the unit remained in the United States, changed location several times, was redesignated on four occasions, flew ASW patrols along the

Pacific northwest coast, and was eventually trained as a photographic reconnaissance unit. Equipped with Lockheed F-5 unarmed reconnaissance aircraft and redesignated 35th PRS, the squadron moved to India in the spring of 1944 for operations in the CBI theater. It flew combat operations in China with the Fourteenth Air Force and, briefly, with the Tenth Air Force between September 1944 and VJ Day. Shipped back to the United States in September 1945, the 35th PRS was inactivated in New Jersey on 7 November 1945.

The Portland-based 123rd had been designated an FIS ever since 1 March 1951 but, in the big designation shuffle of March 1992, became simply the 123rd FS.

Oregon ANG

Redesignated 123rd FS, it was allotted back to the Oregon NG on 24 May 1946.
30 Aug 1946: 123rd FS (SE) extended federal recognition at Portland MAP, and equipped with **North American P-51Ds**.
1 Mar 1951: Called to active duty as part of the Korean War call-up and redesignated 123rd FIS but remained based at Portland AFB. Most pilots transferred to other units and replaced by regular Air Force personnel.
Spring 1952: Converted from F-51Ds to **North American F-86Fs**.
1 Dec 1952: 123rd FIS returned to state control and once again equipped with F-51Ds.
Sep 1953: Converted from F-51Ds to F-86As at Portland IAP.
Oct 1955: Converted from F-86As to Lockheed F-94Bs.
Jun 1957: Converted from F-94Bs to Northrop F-89Ds.
Nov 1957: Converted from F-89Ds to F-89Hs.
1 Jul 1960: Became ADC-gained upon implementation of gaining command

Below: The 123rd FIS phased out the last ANG T-33As in October 1988 and the last ANG F-4Cs one year later.

concept.
Sep 1960: Converted from F-89Hs to F-89Js.
Jan 1966: Converted from F-89Js to Convair F/TF-102As.
Mar 1971: Converted from F/TF-102As to McDonnell F-101B/Fs.
1 Jul 1976: 142nd FIW transferred to the WA ANG and 142nd FIG extended federal recognition as parent unit for the 123rd FIS.
1 Apr 1980: Became TAC-gained following ADC inactivation.
FY82: Converted from F-101B/Fs to McDonnell F-4Cs.

Right: The 123rd FIS flew McDonnell Voodoos for 10 years beginning in March 1971. This F-101B-110-MC is about to touch down at Tyndall AFB after flying a William Tell sortie on 1 October 1978.

6 Oct 1988: Phased out last ANG T-33As.
24 May 1989: Received its first McDonnell Douglas F-15A/Bs.
24 Oct 1989: Phased out last ANG F-4Cs.
30 Jun 1990: Completed conversion from F-4Cs to F-15A/Bs.
15 Mar 1992: Unit designation changed to 123rd Fighter Squadron,

The 123rd successively flew three versions of the Scorpion: F-89Ds, F-89Hs, and F-89Js (including 53-2655).

142nd Fighter Group (123rd FS, 142nd FG).
1 Jun 1992: As part of the Air Force restructuring program, gaining command changed to ACC.

René J. Francillon

René J. Francillon

Pennsylvania Air National Guard

Over the years, Pennsylvania has had more ANG squadrons assigned (the 103rd, 117th, 140th, 146th, 147th, 148th and 193rd) than any other state. However, the PA ANG never had more than five flying squadrons at a time, as one of these units, the 117th FIS, was inactivated in January 1957 while another was renumbered/redesignated on three occasions (the 148th FBS being replaced by the 140th ATS in May 1956, and the 140th MAS being reorganized as the 193rd TEWS in September 1967).

The first of these units was organized in June 1924 as the 103rd OS and served on active duty between February 1941 and November

1945 (seeing combat in India and Burma as the 40th PRS). After World War II, the 103rd was reorganized as a bombardment squadron and was joined by the 117th BS, 146th FS, 147th FS and 148th FS.

At the end of FY92, 4,683 officers and enlisted personnel manned 56 PA ANG units, including four flying squadrons (the 103rd FS at NAS Willow Grove with OA-10As, the 146th and 147th ARSs at Greater Pittsburgh International Airport with A-7D/Ks, the 147th AREFS also at Greater Pittsburgh International Airport with KC-135Es, and the 193rd SOS at Harrisburg International Airport in Middletown with EC-130Es).

103rd Fighter Squadron
111th Fighter Group

Lineage: *Activated in Pennsylvania NG as 103rd Observation Squadron.*
27 Jun 1924: 103rd OS extended federal recognition at Philadelphia Airport as the aviation unit in the 28th Division, Pennsylvania NG, and initially equipped with **Curtiss JNS** trainers.
1924-1940: Remaining based in Philadelphia, the 103rd OS was equipped over the years with the mix of aircraft typical of prewar Guard units, including **Consolidated PT-1s** and **O-17s**; **Curtiss O-1s** and **O-11s**; **Douglas BT-1s**, **O-2s, O-38s** and **O-46s**; and **North American O-47s** and **BC-1s**. On 31 December 1940, it had one BC-1A, one O-38B, six O-46As and four O-47A/Bs.
17 Feb 1941: Called to active duty and placed under command of II Army Corps. Ten days later moved to Harrisburg MAP, PA.
World War II: Between December 1941 and May 1944 the unit remained in the United States, changed station several times, was redesignated on five occasions, flew ASW patrols along the New England coast, and was trained as a reconnaissance squadron before moving overseas. As the 40th PRS the unit arrived in India in July 1944 and, equipped with **Lockheed F-5s** and assigned to the 8th PRG, Tenth Air Force, flew combat operations in India and Burma between September 1944 and May 1945. Shipped back to the United States and inactivated at Camp Kilmer, NJ, on 2 November 1945, the squadron was redesignated 103rd BS and was allotted back to the Pennsylvania NG on 24 May 1946.
20 Dec 1948: 103rd BS (Light) extended federal recognition at Southwest Philadelphia Airport and equipped with **Douglas B-26B/Cs** (plus support aircraft).
1 Apr 1951: Called to active duty as part of the Korean War call-up and shortly thereafter moved to Fairchild

Right: Pennysylvania's 103rd TASS flew 'Blue Canoes', including this U-3B, as interim aircraft pending receipt of their O-2As.

Below: After flying OA-37Bs for eight years, the 103rd TASS converted to OA-10As.

AFB, WA, to be reorganized as the 103rd Strategic Reconnaissance Squadron (Medium) and equipped with **Boeing RB-29As**.
1 Jan 1953: Returned to state control to become the 103rd FBS and to be equipped with **North American F-51Ds**.
Oct 1954: Converted from F-51Ds to **Republic F-84Fs**.
1 Jul 1955: Redesignated 103rd FIS.
Jul 1956: Converted from F-84Fs to **Lockheed F-94A/Bs**.
Apr 1958: Converted from F-94A/Bs to F-94Cs.
Mar 1959: Converted from F-94Cs to

Northrop F-89H/Js.
1 Jul 1960: Became ADC-gained upon implementation of gaining command concept.
1 Apr 1962: Redesignated 103rd ATS (Heavy), re-equipped with **Boeing C-97s**, and became MATS-gained. Reached group status with federal recognition of the 111th ATG.
15 Mar 1963: Moved from Philadelphia IAP to NAS Willow Grove.
1 Jan 1966: Redesignated 111th MAS and became MAC-gained following MATS redesignation.
27 May 1969: Redesignated 103rd

TASS, equipped with **Cessna U-3A/Bs** pending availability of **Cessna O-2As**, and became TAC-gained.
1970: Converted from U-3A/Bs to O-2As.
FY82: Converted from O-2As to **Cessna OA-37Bs**.
31 Dec 1989: Completed conversion from OA-37Bs to **Fairchild OA-10As**.
15 Mar 1992: Unit designation changed to 103rd Fighter Squadron, 111th Fighter Group (103rd FS, 111th FG).
1 Jun 1992: As part of the Air Force restructuring program, gaining command changed to ACC.

117th Fighter
Interceptor Squadron

Lineage: *Constituted in June 1942 and activated at Barksdale Field, LA, on 16 June 1942, the 440th BS flew Martin B-26s and North American B-25s in the MTO as part of the 319th BG, Twelfth Air Force. Following its return to the United States in January 1945 and its conversion to Douglas A-26s, the 440th BS was transferred to the Seventh Air Force with which it operated from Okinawa between July and December 1945. Inactivated at Ft Lawton, WA, on 4 January 1946, it was redesignated 117th BS and allotted to the Pennsylvania ANG on 24 May 1946.*
20 Dec 1948: 117th BS (Light) extended federal recognition at Philadelphia MAP and equipped with **Douglas B-26B/Cs** (plus support aircraft).
1 Apr 1951: Called to active duty as part of the Korean War call-up and soon transferred to Langley AFB, VA, where it served as a B-26 training unit.
1 Jan 1953: Returned to state control to be reorganized at Philadelphia MAP as the 117th FBS and equipped with **Lockheed F-80Cs**.
1 Jul 1955: Redesignated 117th FIS.
Jan 1957: 117th FIS inactivated due to inability to maintain the required minimum personnel strength. Designation transferred to the Kansas ANG.

The 117th Squadron was a Pennsylvania ANG unit for just over eight years. As the 117th Bombardment Squadron (Light) it flew Douglas B-26Bs and B-26Cs for four years before converting to F-80Cs in January 1953.

Pennsylvania ANG

140th Military Airlift Squadron
168th Military Airlift Group

Lineage: *Organization of the 140th Air Transport Squadron (Medium) was announced in 1955. The new unit was to take over the facilities and most of the personnel of the 148th FBS, which was to be transferred to York County Airport in Admire.*

1 May 1956: 140th ATS (Medium) extended federal recognition at Spaatz Field, Reading, and equipped with Curtiss C-46Ds.

1 Feb 1957: Redesignated 140th Aeromedical Evacuation Squadron (Light).

Apr 1958: Converted from C-46Ds to Fairchild C-119Js (at least two were later modified to the MC-119J configuration).

1 Jul 1960: Became MATS-gained upon implementation of gaining command concept.

1 Feb 1961: 140th Aeromedical Evacuation Squadron relocated from Reading to Olmsted AFB in Middletown which had a longer runway and adequate glide slopes to enable the eventual conversion of the squadron to larger aircraft.

2 Nov 1962: First Lockheed C-121C assigned to the 140th which began its conversion from C-119Js.

16 Feb 1964: Reached group status with federal recognition of 168th ATG.

Nov 1964: The Air Force announced plans to inactivate Olmsted AFB thus threatening to leave the 140th ATS without a base from which to continue C-121 operations.

Aug 1965: Volunteers began participating in active Air Force aeromedical evacuation and cargo supply operations in support of the Southeast Asia War.

1 Jan 1966: Redesignated 140th MAS and became MAC-gained following MATS redesignation.

FY66: DoD announced plans to inactivate the 140th ATS and other ANG C-121 and C-97 airlift units during the following year but Congress overruled DoD and mandated that these squadrons be maintained or reorganized.

1 Jul 1967: The State of Pennsylvania took over the deed to the inactivated Olmsted AFB which became Olmsted State Airport.

17 Sep 1967: The 140th MAS and 168th MAG were reorganized as the 193rd TEWS, 193rd TEWG, and transferred from MAC-gained to TAC-gained status.

During the late 1950s and early 1960s, the 140th Aeromedical Evacuation Squadron flew MC-119Js first from Spaatz Field and then from Olmsted AFB.

146th Air Refueling Squadron
112th Air Refueling Group

Lineage: *Activated at Bushey Hall, England, on 1 October 1942, the 345th FS was equipped with Bell P-39s before moving to French Morocco to commence operations as part of the 350th FG. Remaining operational in the MTO until after VE Day and successively re-equipped with Lockheed P-38s and Republic P-47s, the squadron was*

During the late 1940s and early 1950s, P-47Ns (F-47Ns after June 1948) equipped 10 ANG squadrons in Connecticut, Delaware, Georgia (the 128th and 158th), Hawaii, Massachusetts, Mississippi, Pennsylvania (the 146th and 147th), and Puerto Rico.

inactivated in North Carolina on 7 November and, redesignated 146th FS, was allotted to the Pennsylvania NG on 24 May 1946.

18 Jun 1948: 146th FS (SE) extended federal recognition at Greater Pittsburgh Airport and equipped with Republic F-47Ns (plus support aircraft).

22 Apr 1949: 112th FG received federal recognition.

1 Nov 1950: Redesignated 146th FBS.

May 1951: Converted from F-47Ns to North American F-51Hs.

1 Oct 1952: Redesignated 146th FIS.

1 Dec 1952: Redesignated 146th FBS.

Jun 1954: Four North American F-86As assigned but proposed conversion from F-51Hs to F-86As cancelled soon afterward.

Oct 1954: Converted from F-51Hs to Republic F-84Fs.

1 Jul 1955: Redesignated 146th FIS.

Dec 1957: Converted from F-84Fs to North American F-86Ls.

1 Jul 1960: Became ADC-gained upon implementation of gaining command concept.

Nov 1960: Converted from F-86Ls to Convair F/TF-102As.

Apr 1975: Converted from F/TF-102As to LTV A-7Ds.

12 Apr 1975: Redesignated 146th TFS and became TAC-gained.

Summer 1991: Commenced conversion from A-7D/Ks to KC-135Es.

16 Oct 1991: Unit redesignated 146th

The 146th FIS converted from F-86Ls to F/TF-102As in November 1960 and flew 'Deuces' until converting to A-7Ds in April 1975. While flying F-102s, it compiled one of the best safety records in ADC.

A-7D-8-CV of the 146th TFS returns to its base at the Greater Pittsburgh IAP after a low-level training sortie.

AREFS/112th AREFG.
15 Mar 1992: Unit abbreviation changed to 146th ARS, 112th ARG.

1 Jun 1992: As part of the Air Force restructuring program, gaining command changed to AMC.

The 146th hoped to retain the fighter mission with F-16s, but in 1991 began conversion to KC-135Es.

147th Air Refueling Squadron
171st Air Refueling Wing

Lineage: *Activated at Bushey Hall, England, on 1 October 1942, the 346th FS was equipped with Bell P-39s before moving to French Morocco to commence operations as part of the 350th FG. Remaining operational in the MTO until after VE Day and successively re-equipped with Lockheed P-38s and Republic P-47s, the squadron was inactivated in North Carolina on 7 November and, redesignated 147th FS, was allotted to the Pennsylvania NG on 24 May 1946.*

22 April 1949: 147th FS (SE) extended federal recognition at Greater Pittsburgh Airport and equipped with **Republic F-47Ns** (plus support aircraft).

1 Oct 1952: Redesignated 147th FIS and converted from F-47Ns to **North American F-51Hs**.

Jul 1955: Converted from F-51Hs to Republic **F-84Fs**.

FY58: Converted from F-84Fs to **North American F-86Ls**.

1 Jul 1960: Became ADC-gained upon implementation of gaining command concept.

1 May 1961: Redesignated 147th Aeromedical Transport Squadron and equipped with **Fairchild C-119Js**.

18 Feb 1964: Redesignated 147th ATS and equipped with **Lockheed C-121Gs**.

1 Jan 1966: Redesignated 147th MAS and became MAC-gained following MATS redesignation.

19 Feb 1968: Redesignated 147th Aeromedical Airlift Squadron.

13 May 1968: Called to active duty as part of the *Pueblo* Crisis call-up to conduct worldwide aeromedical support operations from its Pittsburgh base.

13 Dec 1969: Returned to state control.

4 Oct 1972: Redesignated 147th AREFS and equipped with **Boeing KC-97Ls**. Gaining command changed from MAC to TAC.

1 Jul 1976: Gaining command changed from TAC to SAC.

Jul 1977: Conversion from KC-97Ls to **Boeing KC-135As** initiated.

FY83: Converted from KC-135As to KC-135Es.

Aug 1990: Volunteers began flying Desert Shield support missions.

20 Dec 1990: Called to active duty for Desert Shield.

15 May 1991: Released from active duty after taking part in Desert Shield/Desert Storm.

Above: After SAC decided that the Thunderstreak would not be suitable in the escort fighter role and relinquished its prior claim on F-84Fs, the 147th FBS became one of the first Guard units to convert to F-84Fs.

Left: A North American F-86L of the 147th FIS transits through Wright-Patterson AFB, Ohio. The Pittsburgh unit flew all-weather Sabres for nearly three years beginning in early 1958.

Below: A KC-135E of the 147th AREFS displays the new-style tanker markings as approved by AMC.

Pennsylvania ANG

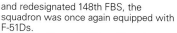

148th Fighter–Bomber Squadron

Lineage: *Activated at Bushey Hall, England, on 1 October 1942, the 347th FS was equipped with Bell P-39s before moving to French Morocco to commence operations as part of the 350th FG. Remaining operational in the MTO until after VE Day and successively* re-equipped with Lockheed P-38s and Republic P-47s, the squadron was inactivated in North Carolina on 7 November and, redesignated 148th FS, was allotted to the Pennsylvania NG on 24 May 1946.

27 Feb 1947: 148th FS (SE) extended federal recognition at Spaatz Field, Reading, and equipped with **Republic P-47Ds** (plus support aircraft).
Jul 1950: Redesignated 148th FIS.

Aug 1950: Converted from F-47Ds to **North American F-51Ds.**
1 Feb 1951: Placed on active duty as part of the Korean War call-up and moved to Dover AFB, DE, two weeks later.
1951-1952: While on active duty at Dover AFB, the 148th FIS successively converted to **North American F-86As** and **Lockheed F-94Bs.**
1 Nov 1952: Returned to state control

and redesignated 148th FBS, the squadron was once again equipped with F-51Ds.
1955: As Spaatz Field could not be extended for jet operations, plans were made to transfer the 148th FBS to York County Airport in Admire and to replace it at Spaatz Field with a transport squadron.
1 May 1956: 148th FBS placed on inactive status while awaiting transfer to York County Airport for re-equipment with jet fighters.
27 Jan 1957: Last F-51Ds of the 148th FBS retired.
31 Oct 1957: 148th FBS inactivated at Spaatz Field, Reading, after plans for its move to York County Airport foundered.

Pennsylvania's 148th flew only piston-engined fighters in its 10-year existence, apart from FAD during the Korean War.

193rd Special Operations Squadron
193rd Special Operations Group

Lineage: *Reorganization of the 140th Military Airlift Squadron and 168th Military Airlift Group into the 193rd Tactical Electronic Warfare Squadron, 193rd Tactical Electronic Warfare Group, was announced during the summer of 1967.*
17 Sep 1967: The 193rd TEWS and its parent 193rd TEWG were extended federal recognition at Olmsted State Airport (later renamed Harrisburg IAP) as TAC-gained units and took over the **C-121Cs** of the 140th MAS, 168th MAG.
Summer 1968: The first of five C-121Cs modified by Lockheed Air Service to the EC-121S configuration as airborne radio/television stations entered

Manned by volunteers, EC-130E 'Rivet Riders' played a discreet but important role during Desert Shield/Desert Storm.

service for the Coronet Solo mission.
26 Jul 1970-24 Dec 1970: In support of the Southeast Asia War, volunteers manned two EC-121S electronic warfare aircraft and deployed to Korat RTAFB, Thailand, for Operation Commando Buzz, while others flew C-121C support

The handful of 'Rivet Riders' have undergone a complete refit giving color broadcast capability.

missions to and from Thailand.
Apr 1971- Mar 1972: Transport-configured C-121Cs were based at

Torrejon AB, Spain, to take part in Operation Creek Airlift and provided scheduled passenger airlift for US forces in Europe.
1 Apr 1977: Group number and designation changed to 1st SOG.
5 Aug 1977: First **Lockheed C-130E** received as the unit began its conversion to Hercules.
9 Nov 1977: Last C-121C phased out but EC-121Ss retained pending conversion of the C-130Es to two classified configurations, the **EC-130E(RR) 'Rivet Rider'/'Comfy Levi'** airborne radio/television station for psychological warfare operations, and the **EC-130E(CL)** for Elint/ESM operations.
Dec 1977: Group number and designation changed back to 193rd TEWG.
16 Mar 1979: First Hercules modified to the EC-130E(RR) configuration redelivered to the 193rd TEWS.
14 May 1979: Last EC-121S flown to Davis-Monthan AFB for storage at MASDC.
6 Oct 1980: 193rd TEWS and 193rd TEWG redesignated 193rd Electronic Combat Squadron and 193rd ECG.
1 Mar 1983: The 193rd ECS and its parent 193rd ECG became MAC-gained units and the name of the classified

mission was changed from Coronet Solo to Volant Solo.

15 Nov 1983: 193rd ECS/193rd ECG redesignated 193rd SOS/193rd SOG.

Oct 1986: Volunteers flew EC-130Es in support of Operation Urgent Fury in Grenada.

Dec 1989: Volunteers flew EC-130Es in support of Operation Just Cause in Panama.

22 May 1990: The 193rd SOS and its parent 193rd SOG became AFSOC-gained units upon activation of this new major command.

Aug 1990-Spring 1991: Volunteers began flying EC-130Es in support of Operation Desert Shield.

Photography of 'Comfy Levi' EC-130Es with their aerials in place remains off limits; current 'Comfy Levi' photos show none of the distinctive features of this version.

Puerto Rico Air National Guard

Established in 1952, the Commonwealth of Puerto Rico is freely and voluntarily associated with the United States. Puerto Ricans elect their Governor, the members of their Legislative Assembly, and a non-voting Resident Commissioner to the US House of Representatives by direct vote. A plebiscite is to be held on 4 June 1993 to choose either statehood, independence or continued commonwealth status.

The flying unit of the Puerto Rico ANG (humorously referred to as the PRANG) was organized in November 1947 as the 198th FS. Remaining based in San Juan throughout its existence, first at the Isla Grande Airport and then at the International Airport, the 198th was never called to FAD. It did, however, lose aircraft to hostile action as pro-independence terrorists destroyed eight A-7Ds on 12 January 1981.

At the end of FY92, 1,415 officers and enlisted personnel manned 17 PR ANG units, including the 198th FS which was completing its conversion to F-16A/B ADFs at the Puerto Rico International Airport in San Juan.

198th Fighter Squadron 156th Fighter Group

Lineage: *Constituted and activated at Peterson Field, CO, in October 1944, the 463rd FS was assigned to the 507th FG, Twentieth Air Force, with which it flew combat operations with Republic P-47Ns in the western Pacific during the last two months of World War II. Inactivated at Yontan, Okinawa, in May 1946, the squadron was redesignated the 198th FS and was allotted to the Puerto Rico NG on 24 May 1946.*

23 Nov 1947: 198th FS (SE) extended federal recognition at the Isla Grande Airport, San Juan, and soon equipped with **Republic P-47Ns** (plus support aircraft).

15 Aug 1952: Redesignated 198th FBS.

16 Nov 1952: Redesignated 198th FIS.

Spring 1954: Facilities provided at the San Juan IAP to enable the 198th FIS to prepare for jet operations while the remainder of the unit stayed at the Isla Grande Airport.

Jul 1954: Converted from F-47Ns to

North American F-86Es.

May 1956: All 198th FIS activities consolidated at San Juan IAP.

10 Apr 1958: Reached group status with federal recognition of 156th FIG.

Aug 1958: Converted from F-86Es to F-86Ds.

1 Jul 1960: Became ADC-gained upon

implementation of gaining command concept.

Fall/Winter 1960: Converted from F-86Ds to F-86Hs.

1 Apr 1964: Redesignated 198th TFS and changed from ADC- to TAC-gained status, but retained sole responsibility for providing air defense for Puerto Rico.

Summer 1967: Converted from F-86Hs to Lockheed F-104C/Ds.

Summer 1975: Converted from F-104C/Ds to LTV A-7Ds.

12 Jan 1981: Eight A-7Ds destroyed in a terrorist attack at Muniz ANGS.

15 Mar 1992: Unit designation changed to 198th Fighter Squadron, 156th Fighter Group (198th FS, 156th FG).

1 Jun 1992: As part of the Air Force

Puerto Rico's 198th TFS was the only ANG unit to be equipped with the F-104C and F-104D versions of Lockheed's Mach 2 Starfighters.

restructuring program, gaining command changed to ACC.

FY92/FY93: Converting from A-7D/Ks to **General Dynamics Block 15 F-16A/B ADFs** (first F-16 received on 28 May 1992 and last A-7 flown out on 30 Jul 1992).

Jan 1993: Scheduled to complete conversion to F-16A/B ADFs.

The 198th changed mission when it replaced its 'SLUFs' with 'Vipers'. It now has the Air Defense Fighter version of the F-16.

71-0335, and A-7D-10-CV of the 198th Tactical Fighter Squadron, was photographed at Patrick AFB, Florida, on 22 April 1988.

Rhode Island Air National Guard

Smallest of the 50 states, Rhode Island was nevertheless one of the first to be allotted a Guard flying squadron. However, its inability to provide adequate facilities led to that unit, the 118th Observation Squadron, being instead organized in Connecticut in November 1923. Sixteen years later, Rhode Island was once again allotted a Guard flying unit and this time was successful in obtaining federal recognition for the 152nd Observation Squadron. Redesignated the 37th Photographic Reconnaissance Squadron while on active duty, this unit served in Italy during the last three months of World War II.

Returned to the State of Rhode Island after the war's end, the

152nd served as a fighter squadron for seven years beginning in September 1948. However, as facilities at the T. F. Green Airport could not be expanded to provide for safe jet operations, the 152nd FIS was transferred to the Arizona ANG and its place in the RI ANG was taken by the newly constituted 143rd Air Resupply Squadron. Since November 1955, the 143rd has flown a variety of piston- and turbo-prop-powered transport and utility aircraft.

At the end of FY92, 1,484 officers and enlisted personnel manned 16 RI ANG units, including the 143rd AS at the Quonset Point State Airport with C-130Es.

143rd Airlift Squadron
143rd Airlift Group

Lineage: *Organization of the 143rd Air Resupply Squadron was announced in 1955. The new unit was to take over the facilities and most of the personnel of the 152nd FIS at the T. F. Green Airport in Warwick.*
19 Nov 1955: 143rd Air Resupply Squadron extended federal recognition and equipped with **Curtiss C-46Ds** and Grumman SA-16As.
Summer 1958: C-46Ds phased out.
10 Oct 1958: Redesignated 143rd Troop Carrier Squadron (Medium).
1 Jul 1960: Became TAC-gained upon implementation of gaining command concept.
10 Jan 1962: Reached group status with federal recognition of 143rd TCG.
Early 1963: Converted from HU-16As to HU-16Bs.
1 Jul 1963: Redesignated 143rd Air Commando Squadron/Group.
Aug 1963: Helio U-10As added to HU-16Bs.
1965-1967: U-10As temporarily

replaced by de Havilland Canada U-6As.
Summer 1967: U-6As replaced by U-10Ds.
19 Aug 1968: Redesignated 143rd Special Operations Squadron/Group.
Fall 1971: Converted from HU-16Bs to Fairchild C-119Gs (later modified to C-119L standard) but U-10Ds retained.

This C-130E of the 130th Tactical Airlift Squadron was one of the competitors at Airlift Rodeo '90.

Summer 1975: Converted from C-119Ls and U-10Ds to **Lockheed C-130As.**
4 Oct 1975: Redesignated 143rd TAS and became MAC-gained.

15 Apr 1980: 143rd TAG relocated from T. F. Green Airport to Quonset State Airport in North Kingstown.
1 Jul 1980: 143rd TAS relocated to Quonset State Airport.
FY90: Converted from C-130As to C-130Es.
Aug 1990: Volunteers began flying missions in support of Operation Desert Shield.
23 Feb 1991: Called to active duty as part of Operation Desert Storm call-up.
10 Jun 1991: Released from active duty after taking part in Desert Shield/Desert Storm.
15 Mar 1992: Unit designation changed to 143rd Airlift Squadron, 143rd Airlift Group (143rd AS, 143rd AG).
1 Jun 1992: As part of the Air Force restructuring program, gaining command changed to AMC.

Beginning in 1963, Helio U-10s were assigned as mission aircraft to complement Grumman HU-16s and Fairchild C-119s serving with four air commando squadrons (redesignated special operations squadrons in August 1968) in California, Maryland, Rhode Island and West Virginia. Rhode Island's 143rd flew U-10As from 1963-1965, and is believed to have been the only ANG unit ever to fly floatplanes.

152nd Fighter Interceptor Squadron

Lineage: *Designated the 152nd Observation Squadron and allotted to the Rhode Island NG on 21 August 1939.*
13 Oct 1939: 152nd OS extended federal recognition at Hillsgrove and equipped with **Douglas O-38B/Es** and North American BC-1As and O-47As.
25 Nov 1940: Called to active duty and placed under command of First Corps Area but initially remained based at

Hillsgrove. On 31 December 1940, it had one **BC-1A**, eight **O-38B/Es** and three O-47As.
World War II: Between July 1941 and October 1943, the unit moved five times within CONUS, was redesignated on six occasions, flew ASW patrols along the New England coast, and trained in preparation for overseas deployment. As the 37th Photographic Reconnaissance Squadron, it was assigned to the 5th PRG, Fifteenth Air Force, in Italy, and flew **Lockheed F-5s** in combat from February 1945 until VE Day. Inactivated

at Camp Patrick Henry, VA, on 6 November 1945, it was redesignated 152nd FS and allotted back to the Rhode Island NG on 24 May 1946.
15 Sep 1948: 152nd FS (SE) extended federal recognition at Theodore Francis Green Airport in Warwick and equipped with **Republic F-47Ds** (plus support aircraft).
Summer 1952: Converted from F-47Ds to North American F-51D/Hs.
1 Sep 1952: Redesignated 152nd FIS.
1 Dec 1952: Redesignated 152nd FBS.
Early 1954: Partially converted to

Republic F-84Ds with these jets based at Bradley Field, CT, as the T. F. Green Airport was unsuitable for jet operations.
1 Jul 1955: Redesignated 152nd FIS.
19 Nov 1955: Unable to obtain jet facilities in its home state, the 152nd FIS was inactivated and its designation transferred to the Arizona ANG.

After a few months of split operations, with F-84Ds at Bradley Field, Connecticut, and F-51D/Hs in Rhode Island, the 152nd FIS was inactivated in November 1955.

RI ANG

South Carolina Air National Guard

The 157th FS received federal recognition in December 1946 but was reorganized as a tactical reconnaissance unit shortly after becoming one of the first Guard units called to active duty during the Korean War. After its return to state control in July 1952, the South Carolina ANG unit was once again equipped with fighters. Since then, the

157th has flown F-51Hs, F-80Cs, F-86Ls, F-104As (with which it deployed to Spain during its Berlin Crisis activation), F-102As, A-7Ds and F-16As. Having won the Gunsmoke '89 competition six years after becoming the first ANG unit to convert to Fighting Falcons, the 'Swamp Foxes' of the 157th TFS were well prepared for the tasks which awaited them upon their deployment to Saudi Arabia for Desert Storm combat operations.

At the end of FY92, 1,348 officers and enlisted personnel manned 14 SC ANG units, including the 157th FS at McEntire ANGB with F-16A/Bs.

157th Fighter Squadron
169th Fighter Group

Lineage: *Constituted in May 1943 and activated at Mitchel Field, NY, on 1 October 1942, the 350th FS was assigned to the 353rd FG, Eighth Air Force, with which it flew combat operations in the ETO with Republic P-47Ds (from August 1943) and North American P-51Ds (from October 1944 until VE Day). Inactivated at Camp Kilner, NJ, in October 1945. Reconstituted and redesignated the 157th FS, the unit was allotted to the South Carolina NG on 24 May 1946.*
9 Dec 1946: 157th FS (SE) extended federal recognition at Congaree AB, Columbia, SC, and soon equipped with North American P-51Ds (plus support aircraft).
10 Oct 1950: Called to active duty as part of the Korean War call-up and moved a few days later to Lawson AFB, GA, to be reorganized as the 157th TRS and equipped with RF-51Ds.
Jun 1951: Converted from RF-51Ds to Lockheed RF-80As.
Jan 1952: Moved to Fürstenfeldbrück AB, Germany.
10 Jul 1952: Returned to state control at Congaree AB to be reorganized as the 157th FIS and equipped with North American F-51Hs.
1 Dec 1952: Redesignated 157th FBS.
Jun 1953: F-51Hs supplemented with

With snow-covered Mt Baldy in the background, this 'Deuce' of the 157th FIS was photographed in March 1970 during a visit to California's 196th FIS at the Ontario International Airport.

North American F-86As.
Mar 1954: Converted from F-51Hs to Lockheed F-80Cs but retained a few F-86As.
Jan 1955: Last F-86As transferred out.
5 Sep 1957: Redesignated 157th FIS and reached group status with federal recognition of 169th FIG.
Early 1958: Converted from F-80Cs to North American F-86Ls (first received in Feb 1958).
Early 1960: Converted from F-86Ls to Lockheed F-104A/Bs (first received in Feb 1960).
1 Jul 1960: Became ADC-gained upon implementation of gaining command concept.
1 Nov 1961: Called to active duty as part of the Berlin Crisis call-up but remained at its home base for the first three weeks.
10 Nov 1961: Congaree AB renamed McEntire ANGB in honor of Brigadier General Barnie B. McEntire, the late commander of the SC ANG who had been killed on 25 May 1961 when he stayed in his crippled F-104A to avoid crashing in a populated area at Harrisburg, PA.
24 Nov 1961: Relocated to Moron AB, Spain.
15 Aug 1962: Returned to state control at McEntire ANGB.
Jun 1963: Converted from F-104A/Bs to Convair F/TF-102As.
Fall 1974/Spring 1975: Converted from F/TF-102As (last left on 5 Apr 1975) to LTV A-7Ds (first received in Oct 1974).
1 Apr 1975: Redesignated 157th TFS and became TAC-gained.
Jul 1983: Began conversion from A-7Ds to General Dynamics F-16A/Bs.
Oct 1989: Won Gunsmoke '89

USAF

The 157th FIS converted to F-104A/Bs in early 1960 but was forced to relinquish its Starfighters when it was released from FAD.

competition.
29 Dec 1990: Called to active duty as part of Operation Desert Shield call-up.
22 Jul 1991: Released from active duty after taking part in Desert Shield/Desert Storm.
15 Mar 1992: Unit designation changed to 157th Fighter Squadron, 169th Fighter Group (157th FS, 169th FG).
1 Jun 1992: As part of the Air Force restructuring program, gaining command changed to ACC.
FY94: Scheduled to convert from F-16A/Bs to F-16C/Ds.

Called to active duty on 29 December 1990, the 157th TFS deployed to the 'Camel Lot' at Al Kharj in Saudi Arabia, from where, as part of the 4th TFW(P), it flew 1,729 sorties without a combat or operational loss.

Randy Jolly

Peter B. Lewis

South Dakota Air National Guard

Since its organization in September 1946, the flying unit of the South Dakota ANG has remained based in its home state (including during its Korean War activation when it operated from Ellsworth AFB for 21 months). It served in the air-defense role until the spring of 1970 when the 175th became a Tactical Fighter Squadron upon converting from F-102As to F-100Ds. Since becoming a tactical fighter unit, the 175th has made several deployments overseas and during a 1989 deployment it flew combat missions in Panama in support of Operation Just Cause.

At the end of FY92, 1,004 officers and enlisted personnel manned 13 SD ANG units, including the 175th FS at Sioux Falls Municipal Airport with A-7D/Ks.

175th Fighter Squadron 114th Fighter Group

Lineage: *Constituted at Richmond AAB, VA, in April 1943 and activated one month later, the 387th FS was assigned to the 365th FG, Ninth Air Force. Equipped with Republic P-47Ds, it flew combat operations in the ETO from February 1944 until VE Day. Inactivated at Camp Myles, MA, in September 1945, the unit was reconstituted and redesignated the 175th FS before being allotted to the South Dakota NG on 24 May 1946.*

20 Sep 1946: 175th FS (SE) extended federal recognition at Sioux Falls MAP and soon equipped with North

On 17 July 1988, when it arrived at Gowen Field, Idaho, to take part in a five-day exercise, this A-7D of South Dakota's 175th TFS carried an unusual 'ordnance' beneath its starboard wing: a spare wheel!

American P-51Ds (plus support aircraft).
1 Mar 1951: Called to active duty as part of the Korean War call-up, redesignated 175th FIS, and assigned air-defense duty at Ellsworth AFB, SD.
1 Dec 1952: Returned to state control at Sioux Falls MAP.
Jun 1954: Converted from F-51Ds to Lockheed F-94A/Bs.
16 Apr 1956: Reached group status with federal recognition of 114th FIG.
May 1956: Converted from F-94A/Bs to F-94Cs.
Jan 1958: Converted from F-94Cs to Northrop F-89Ds.
Early 1960: Partially converted from F-89Ds to F-89Js.
1 Jul 1960: Became ADC-gained upon implementation of gaining command concept.
Fall 1960: Converted from F-89D/Js to Convair F/TF-102As (first received in Oct 1960).
Spring 1970: Converted from F/TF-102As (last left on 23 May 1970) to

North American F-100D/Fs.
23 May 1970: Redesignated 175th TFS and became TAC-gained.

FY77: Converted from F-100D/Fs to LTV A-7Ds.
Dec 1989: Flew 54 combat sorties during Operation Just Cause in Panama.
FY92: Converting from A-7D/Ks to General Dynamics Block 30 F-16C/Ds (first Fighting Falcon received on 14 Aug 1991 and last 'SLUF' flown out on 30 Jan 1992).
15 Mar 1992: Unit designation changed to 175th Fighter Squadron, 114th Fighter Group (175th FS, 114th FG).
1 Jun 1992: As part of the Air Force restructuring program, gaining command changed to ACC.
30 Sep 1992: Completed conversion to F-16C/Ds.

In keeping with the 'Lobos' nickname and wolf's head badge, the 175th FS has added fearsome tail markings to its F-16Cs.

Tennessee Air National Guard

Even though Tennessee only ranks 17th in terms of population, the 'Volunteer State' well deserves its historical nickname, as since 1957 it has had three ANG flying squadrons. Its first Guard flying unit was organized in 1921 as the 136th Squadron, was redesignated the 105th OS in January 1924, and served on active duty in the United States between September 1940 and August 1943. Post-World War II, the 105th and a second unit, the 155th, received federal recognition as

fighter squadrons. The third squadron, the 151st FIS, was organized in 1957. Tennessee Guardsmen served on active duty during the Korean War (the 105th and 155th both remaining stateside) and the Berlin Crisis (the 151st FIS flying F-104As in Germany), and the Gulf War.

At the end of FY92, 4,018 officers and enlisted personnel manned 45 TN ANG units, including the 105th AS at Nashville Metropolitan Airport with C-130Hs, the 151st ARS at McGhee-Tyson Airport in Knoxville with KC-135Es, and the 155th AS with C-141Bs, at Memphis International Airport.

105th Airlift Squadron 118th Airlift Wing

Lineage: *Organized at Kelly Field, TX, on 25 August 1917 as the 105th Aero Squadron, Air Service, this supply unit moved to France in December 1917 for service with the AEF. In 1936, its lineage and honors were consolidated with those of the 105th OS, a Tennessee NG unit which had been activated in December 1921 as the 136th Squadron.*

4 Dec 1921: 136th Squadron extended federal recognition at Blackwood Field, Nashville, as a Corps Aviation unit in the Tennessee NG and initially equipped with Curtiss JN-6Hs.
25 Jan 1923: Redesignated 136th OS.

16 Jan 1924: Redesignated 105th OS upon becoming part of the 30th Division.
1924-1940: Based successively at Blackwood Field in Nashville (from Dec 1921), in Memphis (from Nov 1930), at McConnell Field in Nashville (from Apr 1931), at Sky Harbor in Murfreesboro

(from 1932) and at Berry Field in Nashville (from Mar 1937), the 105th OS was equipped over the years with the mix of aircraft typical of prewar Guard units, including **Consolidated PT-1s** and **O-17s**; Dayton-Wright TW-3s; Douglas BT-1s, O-2s, O-25s, O-38s and O-46s;

and **North American O-47s and BC-1s.**
16 Sep 1940: Called to active duty, assigned to Fourth Corps Area, and moved eight days later to Columbia, SC. On 31 December 1940, it had one **BC-1A,** one **O-38B** and eight **O-47A/Bs.**
World War II: Remaining based in CONUS, the unit moved six times, was redesignated on two occasions, flew ASW patrols along the Carolinas coast, and served as a replacement training unit before being inactivated at Florence AAFld, SC, in August 1943. Reconstituted and redesignated the

Maintained by devoted and experienced 'wrench benders', old ANG aircraft – such as this 32-year-old C-130A of the 105th AS – remain remarkably reliable.

105th FS, the unit was allotted back to the Tennessee NG on 24 May 1946.
3 Feb 1947: 105th FS (SE) extended federal recognition at Berry Field,

Nashville MAP, and soon equipped with Republic P-47Ds (plus support aircraft).
1 Mar 1951: Called to active duty as part of the Korean War call-up but remained at Nashville for 15 months.
Apr 1951: Converted from F-47Ds to North American F-51Ds.
1 May 1951: Redesignated 105th FIS and F-51Ds supplemented during a nine-month period by four North American F-82Fs.
1 Jun 1952: Moved to McGhee Tyson Airport in Knoxville, TN.
1 Dec 1952: Returned to state control at Nashville MAP to be reorganized as the 105th TRS and equipped with North American RF-51Ds.

Sep 1954: Converted from RF-51Ds to Lockheed RF-80As.
1 Jul 1960: Became TAC-gained upon implementation of gaining command concept.
Spring 1961: Converted from RF-80As to Boeing C-97Gs.
1 Apr 1961: Redesignated 105th ATS (Heavy) and became MATS-gained.
1 Jan 1966: Redesignated 105th MAS and became MAC-gained following MATS redesignation.
Spring 1967: Converted from C-97Gs to Douglas C-124Cs.
Early 1971: Converted from C-124Cs to Lockheed C-130As.
26 Mar 1971: Redesignated 105th TAS

and became TAC-gained.
1 Dec 1974: Became MAC-gained upon transfer of TAC airlift resources to MAC.
9 Feb 1975: 118th TAG inactivated and 105th TAS placed directly under the 118th TAW.
FY90: Converted from C-130As to C-130Hs.
Aug 1990: Volunteers began flying Desert Shield support missions.
15 Mar 1992: Unit designation changed to 105th Airlift Squadron, 118th Airlift Wing (105th AS, 118th AW).
1 Jun 1992: As part of the Air Force restructuring program, gaining command changed to AMC.

151st Air Refueling Squadron
134th Air Refueling Group

Lineage: *New unit organized in the Tennessee ANG in 1957.*
15 Dec 1957: 151st FIS extended federal recognition at McGhee Tyson Airport in Knoxville and equipped with North American F-86Ds.
Jan 1960: Converted from F-86Ds to F-86Ls.
Jun 1960: Converted from F-86Ls to Lockheed F-104A/Bs.
1 Jul 1960: Became ADC-gained upon implementation of gaining command concept.
1 Nov 1961: Called to active duty as part of the Berlin Crisis call-up and F-104A/Bs airlifted to Ramstein AB, Germany, within a few days.

Above: Proudly emblazoned 'TENN AIR GUARD' and bearing the Air Defense Command shield on their tails, an F-104B and 12 F-104As are lined up at 'parade rest' shortly after the 151st FIS had converted from F-86Ls to Starfighters. During the 1961 Berlin Crisis activation, Tennessee's F-104s were airlifted to Ramstein AB, Germany.

19 Dec 1961: Assumed alert duty at Ramstein AB.
15 Aug 1962: Returned to state control at McGhee Tyson Airport.
Mar 1963: Converted from F-104A/Bs to Convair F/TF-102As.
Spring 1964: Converted from F/TF-102As (last left in Apr 1964) to Boeing KC-97Gs.
18 Apr 1964: Redesignated 151st AREFS and became TAC-gained.
Jun 1965: Converted from KC-97Gs to

KC-97Ls.
Jul 1976: Began participation in Operation Creek Party in Europe.
1 Jul 1976: Gaining command changed from TAC to SAC.
Summer/Fall 1976: Converted from KC-97Ls to Boeing KC-135As.

Above: During FY82, the KC-135As of the 151st AREFS were re-engined with JT3D turbofans. Like the other ANG KC-135E squadrons, the 151st played a vital role in the Gulf.

FY82: Converted from KC-135As to KC-135Es.
Aug 1990: Volunteers began flying Desert Shield support missions.
20 Dec 1990: Called to active duty for Desert Shield/Desert Storm.
1 Apr 1991: Released from active duty after taking part in Desert Shield/Desert Storm.
15 Mar 1992: Unit abbreviation changed to 151st ARS, 134th ARG.
1 Jun 1992: As part of the Air Force restructuring program, gaining command changed to AMC.
Beginning in July 1967, the 151st AREFS took part in Operation Creek Party and sent KC-97Ls and personnel on TDY to Europe. This KC-97L was photographed at Wright-Patterson AFB, Ohio, during a routine CONUS mission.

155th Airlift Squadron
164th Airlift Group

Lineage: *Constituted and activated at Westover Field, MA, in December 1942, the 359th FG was assigned to the 356th FG, Eighth Air Force, with which it flew combat operations with Republic P-47Ds*

(from October 1943) and North American P-51Ds (from November 1944 until VE Day) in the ETO. Inactivated at Camp Kilmer, NJ, in November 1945, the unit was reconstituted and redesignated the 155th FS before being allotted to the Tennessee NG on 24 May 1946.
23 Dec 1946: 155th FS (SE) extended federal recognition at Memphis MAP

and soon equipped with North American P-51Ds (plus support aircraft).
1 Apr 1951: Called to active duty as part of Korean War call-up but remained at Memphis MAP to be reorganized as the 155th TRS and converted from F-51Ds to RF-51Ds.
1 Jan 1953: Returned to state control to be reorganized as the 155th TRS

(Night Photographic) and converted from RF-51Ds to Douglas RB-26Cs.
Spring 1956: Converted from RB-26Cs to Republic RF-84Fs.
1 Apr 1956: Redesignated 155th TRS.
1 Jul 1960: Became TAC-gained upon implementation of gaining command concept.
Spring/Summer 1961: Converted

from RF-84Fs to **Boeing C-97As**.
1 Apr 1961: Redesignated 155th ATS (Heavy), reached group status with federal recognition of 164th ATG, and became MATS-gained.

The 155th MAS began its conversion from Boeing C-97As to Douglas C-124Cs in May 1967 and flew them for over seven years.

1 Jan 1966: Redesignated 155th MAS and became MAC-gained following MATS redesignation.
May 1967: Began conversion from C-97As to **Douglas C-124Cs**.

Fall/Winter 1974: Converted from C-124Cs to **Lockheed C-130As**.
10 Dec 1974: Redesignated 155th TAS.
Aug 1990: Volunteers began flying Desert Shield support missions.
FY91/FY92: Converted from C-130As to **Lockheed C-141Bs**.

C-141Bs are now the mission equipment, sporting the AMC mid-gray color scheme.

After flying C-130As since the end of 1974, the 155th Airlift Squadron completed its conversion to StarLifters during FY92.

16 Apr 1992: Unit redesignated 155th Airlift Squadron, 164th Airlift Group (155th AS, 164th AG).
1 Jun 1992: As part of the Air Force restructuring program, gaining command changed to AMC.

Texas Air National Guard

Federally recognized in June 1923 as the 111th OS, the first Texas Guard flying unit earned a distinguished war record both in World War II (when it flew combat operations in North Africa, Italy and France between November 1942 and VE Day) and during the Korean War (when its Thunderjets were flown from bases in Japan and Korea). Since 1955, the primary mission of the Houston-based squadron has been air defense, but the 111th FIS has also operated the ANG Jet Instrument School (between September 1957 and April 1976) and functioned as an operational training unit (between January 1970 and April 1976).

The 181st FS and 182nd FS were extended federal recognition in 1947. The former became a tanker unit in February 1965 and a tactical airlift unit in April 1978; it was first called to active duty in October 1990. The 182nd has always been in the fighter business; it served on active duty in Japan and Korea between June 1951 and July 1952, flew jet interceptors for 13 years beginning in August 1956, and was reorganized as the 182nd TFS in September 1969.

At the end of FY92, 3,882 officers and enlisted personnel manned 52 TX ANG units, including three flying squadrons (the 111th FS at Ellington Field in Houston with F-16A/Bs, the 181st AS at NAS Dallas with C-130Hs, and the 182nd FS at Kelly AFB with F-16As).

111th Fighter Squadron
147th Fighter Group

Lineage: *Organized at Kelly Field, TX, on 14 August 1917 as the 111th Aero Squadron, Air Service, this supply unit was redesignated 632nd Aero Squadron on 1 February 1918 but remained at Kelly Field until demobilized on 19 August 1919. In 1936, its lineage and honors were consolidated with those of the 111th OS which had been activated as a Texas NG unit in June 1923.*
29 Jun 1923: 111th OS extended federal recognition at Ellington Field, Houston, as the aviation unit in the 36th Division, Texas NG, and initially equipped with **Curtiss JN-4B** and **JN-4H** trainers.
Dec 1928: Relocated to Houston MAP.
1928-1940: Remaining based in Houston, the 111th OS was equipped over the years with the mix of aircraft

typical of prewar Guard units, including **Consolidated PT-1s, PT-3s** and **O-17s; Dayton-Wright TW-3s; Douglas O-2s, O-38s** and **O-43s;** and **North American O-47s** and **BC-1s.**
25 Nov 1940: Called to active duty and assigned to Eighth Corps Area but initially remained in Houston. On 31 December 1940, it had one **BC-1A,** six **O-43As** and five **O-47A/Bs.**
World War II: First moving to Brownwood, TX, in January 1941, the mobilized Texas NG unit moved three times and was redesignated on three occasions before being shipped to North Africa (via England) in the fall of 1942. In North Africa, it flew ASW, convoy and border patrols with **Douglas A-20As** before being reorganized as a reconnaissance unit. Successively equipped with A-36A, P-51 and F-6 versions of the North American Mustang, the 111th Reconnaissance

Squadron (Fighter)/Tactical Reconnaissance Squadron was assigned to the Twelfth Air Force and flew combat operations in the MTO and ETO from July 1943 until VE Day. Inactivated at Creil, France, in December 1945, it was reconstituted and redesignated the 111th FS before being allotted back to the Texas NG on 24 May 1946.
9 Feb 1947: 111th FS (SE) extended federal recognition at Ellington Field, Houston, and soon equipped with **North American P-51Ds** (plus support aircraft).
Apr 1949: Ellington Field became Ellington AFB.
10 Oct 1950: Called to active duty as part of the Korean War call-up and moved two weeks later to Langley AFB, VA, where it was redesignated 111th FBS and converted to **Republic F-84Es.**
May 1951: Personnel shipped to Japan to take over F-84Es of the 27th FES at Itazuke AB.

Jul 1951-Jul 1952: Combat operations with F-84Es from Itazuke AB and, beginning in Nov 1951, from Taegu AB (K-2) Korea.

Right: Yet to be brought up to ADF standard, this F-16A taxis out from the 114th TFTS ramp at Kingsley Field, Oregon, during the Sentry Eagle exercise in July 1990. The 111th FIS completed its conversion from F-4Ds to F-16As in 1989.

René J. Francillon

10 Jul 1952: Returned to state control at Houston MAP to be reorganized as 111th FIS and equipped with F-51Hs.
Jan 1953: Redesignated 111th FBS.
Jan 1955: Redesignated 111th FIS and converted from F-51Hs to Lockheed F-80Cs.
Oct 1956: Relocated to Ellington AFB.
Aug 1957: Converted from F-80Cs to North American F-86Ds.
9 Sep 1957: Became ANG Jet Instrument School, for which additional Lockheed T-33As were assigned, while retaining F-86Ds for air-defense duty.
17 May 1958: Reached group status with federal recognition of 147th FIG.
Jun 1959: Converted from F-86Ds to F-86Ls but retained T-33As for ANG Jet Instrument School.
1 Jul 1960: Became ADC-gained upon implementation of gaining command concept.
Aug 1960: Converted from F-86Ls to Convair F/TF-102As but retained T-33As for ANG Jet Instrument School.
Jul 1968: Ellington AFB inactivated and transferred to local authorities with Guard facilities becoming the Ellington ANGS.
1 Jan 1970: Group redesignated 147th Fighter Interceptor (Training) Group as the unit became the ANG F-102 CCTS while retaining T-33As to continue running the ANG Jet Instrument School.
May 1971: Added McDonnell F-101B/Fs.
1 Jan 1972: Unit also became the ANG F-101 CCTS while continuing as the F-102 CCTS and Jet Instrument School.

Right: With typical bravado, the Texans from Ellington Field claim to belong to the 'National Air Force of Texas'. In that spirit, the crew of this F-101F-91-MC flies the Texan flag while taxiing at Tyndall AFB during William Tell '76.

Jan 1975: F/TF-102As phased out.
30 Apr 1976: Duty as F-101 CCTS and ANG Jet Instrument School terminated but the 111th FIS continued to operate in the air-defense role.
1 Apr 1980: Became TAC-gained following ADC inactivation.
FY81: Converted from F-101B/Fs to McDonnell F-4Cs.
Jan 1987: Completed conversion from F-4Cs to F-4Ds.
1 Dec 1989: Began conversion from

Peter B. Lewis

F-4Ds to General Dynamics F-16A/Bs.
FY91: F-16A/Bs upgraded to ADF configuration.
15 Mar 1992: Unit designation

changed to 111th Fighter Squadron, 147th Fighter Group (111th FS, 147th FG).
1 Jun 1992: As part of the Air Force restructuring program, gaining command changed to ACC.

181st Airlift Squadron
136th Airlift Wing

Lineage: *Constituted in May 1943 and activated at Westover Field, MA, in June 1943, the 396th FS was equipped with Republic P-47Ds and assigned to 368th FG, Ninth Air Force. It flew combat operations in the ETO from Mar 1944 until VE Day. Inactivated at Straubing, Germany, in August 1946. Reconstituted and redesignated the 181st FS, the unit was allotted to the Texas NG on 21 Aug 1946.*
27 Feb 1947: 181st FS (SE) extended federal recognition at Hensley Field, NAS Dallas, and soon equipped with North American P-51Ds (plus support aircraft).
1950-1951: Partial conversion to Republic F-84Bs but jets were returned to active units and the 181st FIS converted to F-51Hs.
Jul 1952: Relocated to Love Field, Dallas.
Jan 1955: Converted from F-51Hs to Lockheed F-80Cs.
Aug 1957: Converted from F-80Cs to North American F-86Ds.
Jun 1959: Converted from F-86Ds to F-86Ls.
1 Jul 1960: Became ADC-gained upon implementation of gaining command concept.
Jul 1960: Relocated to NAS Dallas.
Jul 1964: Began conversion from F-86Ls to KC-97Gs.
Feb 1965: Redesignated 181st AREFS and became TAC-gained.
Mar 1965: Converted from KC-97Gs to KC-97Ls.
May 1967: Began participation in

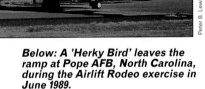

Operation Creek Party in Europe.
9 Dec 1974: 136th AREFG inactivated and 181st placed directly under the 136th AREFW.
1 Jul 1976: Gaining command changed from TAC to SAC.
Early 1978: Converted from KC-97Ls (last left in Jun 1978) to Lockheed C-130Bs (first received in Feb 1978).
1 Apr 1978: Redesignated 181st TAS and became MAC-gained.
FY87: Converted from C-130Bs to C-130Hs.
Dec 1989: Participated in Operation Just Cause in Panama.
Aug 1990: Volunteers began flying Desert Shield support missions.
5 Oct 1990: Called to active duty for Desert Shield/Desert Storm.
15 Apr 1991: Released from active duty after taking part in Desert Shield/Desert Storm.
15 Mar 1992: Unit designation changed to 181st Airlift Squadron, 136th

Above: After serving as an air defense unit, the Dallas squadron was redesignated the 181st AREFS in February 1965.

Below: A 'Herky Bird' leaves the ramp at Pope AFB, North Carolina, during the Airlift Rodeo exercise in June 1989.

René J. Francillon

Airlift Wing (181st AS, 136th AW).
1 Jun 1992: As part of the Air Force

restructuring program, gaining command changed to AMC.

Texas ANG

Peter B. Lewis

182nd Fighter Squadron
149th Fighter Group

Lineage: *Constituted in May 1943 and activated at Westover Field, MA, in June 1943, the 396th FS was equipped with Republic P-47Ds and assigned to 368th FG, Ninth Air Force. It flew combat operations in the ETO from Mar 1944 until VE Day. Inactivated at Straubing, Germany, in August 1946. Reconstituted and redesignated the 182nd FS, the unit was allotted to the Texas NG on 21 Aug 1946.*

6 Oct 1947: 182nd FS (SE) extended federal recognition at Brooks AFB, San Antonio, and soon equipped with **P-51Ds** (plus support aircraft).
10 Oct 1950: Called to active duty and moved to Langley AFB, VA, within two weeks.
Mar 1951: Converted from F-51Ds to Republic **F-84Es**.
May-Jun 1951: Moved to Itazuke AB, Japan.
Jun 1951-Jul 1952: Combat operations with F-84Es from Itazuke AB and, beginning in Nov 1951, from Taegu AB (K-2) Korea.

10 Jul 1952: Returned to state control to be reorganized as 182nd FBS and equipped with **F-51Hs** at Brooks AFB.
1 Aug 1956: Permanent change of station to Kelly AFB where the 182nd FBS converted from F-51Hs to Lockheed **F-80Cs**.
1 Jan 1957: Redesignated 182nd FIS.
Dec 1957: Converted from F-80Cs to North American **F-86Ds**, and, soon after, **F-86Ls**.
1 Jul 1960: Reached group status with federal recognition of the 149th FIG; was ADC-gained upon implementation of gaining command concept.

Having converted from Republic F-84F Thunderstreaks during the spring of 1971, the 182nd TFS flew North American F-100D and F-100F Super Sabres for eight years. The 'Huns' were exchanged for McDonnell F-4Cs.

Summer 1960: Converted from F-86Ls to Convair **F/TF-102As** (first received in Jul 1960).
Summer 1969: Converted from F/TF-102As (last left on 16 Sep 1969) to Republic **F-84Fs**.
14 Sep 1969: Redesignated 182nd TFS and became TAC-gained.
Spring 1971: Converted from F-84Fs to **North American F-100D/Fs**.
Spring 1979: Converted from F-100D/Fs to **McDonnell F-4Cs**.
1 Jul 1986: Completed conversion from F-4Cs to **General Dynamics F-16A/Bs**.
15 Mar 1992: Unit designation changed to 182nd Fighter Squadron, 149th Fighter Group (182nd FS, 149th FG).
1 Jun 1992: As part of the Air Force restructuring program, gaining command changed to ACC.

Brian C. Rogers

With training Sidewinders on the wingtips and BDU-33 practice bombs on the wing racks, a pair of F-16As prepares to train for the primary mission of the 182nd TFS.

Utah Air National Guard

After less than 15 years as a fighter squadron (including 21 months on active duty stateside during the Korean War), the 191st – Utah's only ANG flying squadron – converted to four-engined C-97s. It became

a tanker unit in the fall of 1972 when it exchanged its C-124Cs for KC-97Ls, and has flown Stratotankers since the spring of 1978 (its KC-135As being upgraded to KC-135E standard during FY82).

At the end of FY92, 1,657 officers and enlisted personnel manned 18 UT ANG units, including the 191st ARS at Salt Lake City International Airport with KC-135Es.

191st Air Refueling Squadron
151st Air Refueling Group

Lineage: *Constituted and activated at Hamilton Field, CA, in October 1943, the 407th FS flew Bell P-39s, Curtiss P-40s and North American P-51s as an RTU in the ZI. Inactivated in November 1945. Reconstituted and redesignated the 191st FS, the unit was allotted to the*

Utah NG on 24 May 1946.
18 Nov 1946: 191st FS (SE) extended federal recognition at Salt Lake City Airport and soon equipped with **North American P-51Ds** (plus support aircraft).
1 Apr 1951: Called to active duty as part of Korean War call-up and

redesignated 191st FBS, but initially remained in Salt Lake City.
Dec 1951: Moved to Clovis AFB, NM.
1 Jan 1953: Returned to state control

Peter B. Lewis

A KC-97L at the Salt Lake City IAP on 21 March 1974. Utah's 191st ATS/MAS had flown C-97C and C-97G transports for eight years beginning in the spring of 1961.

Brian C. Rogers

in Salt Lake City.
1 Jul 1955: Redesignated 191st FIS and converted from F-51Ds to North American F-86As.
24 Aug 1957: Reached group status with federal recognition of 151st FIG.
Aug 1958: Converted from F-86As to F-86Ls.
1 Jul 1960: Became ADC-gained upon implementation of gaining command concept.
Spring 1961: Converted from F-86Ls

to Boeing C-97C/Gs.
1 Apr 1961: Redesignated 191st ATS (Heavy) and became MATS-gained.
1 Jan 1966: Redesignated 191st MAS and became MAC-gained following MATS redesignation.
Feb 1969: Converted from C-97Gs to Douglas C-124Cs.
Fall 1972: Converted from C-124Cs to Boeing KC-97Ls.
20 Oct 1972: Redesignated 191st AREFS and became TAC-gained.

1 Jul 1976: Gaining command changed from TAC to SAC.
Apr 1978: Converted from KC-97Ls to Boeing KC-135As.
FY82: Converted from KC-135As to KC-135Es.
Aug 1990: Volunteers began flying missions in support of Operation Desert Shield.
20 Dec 1990: Called to active duty as part of Operation Desert Shield call-up.
15 May 1991: Released from active

During Desert Storm personnel and aircraft of the 191st AREFS were dispersed. This KC-135E was one of the aircraft assigned to the 1709th AREFW(P) in Jeddah.

duty after taking part in Desert Shield/Desert Storm.
15 Mar 1992: Unit abbreviation changed to 191st ARS, 151st ARG.
1 Jun 1992: As part of the Air Force restructuring program, gaining command changed to AMC.

Vermont Air National Guard

Since the organization of the 134th FS in August 1946, the flying unit of the Vermont ANG has remained based in Burlington but has had a diversified career. It served as a fighter interceptor squadron from July 1950 until June 1974 (and was placed on active duty in that capacity during the Korean War), and became a defense systems evaluation squadron in June 1974, a tactical fighter squadron in January

1982, and, again, a fighter interceptor squadron in July 1987. For a while, after its conversion to F-16s, the 134th FIS had intercepted more Soviet aircraft than any other ANG or USAF units based in CONUS, as its operations from Burlington IAP and, on detachment, from Bangor ANGB placed it in ideal positions to intercept Soviet aircraft transiting to and from Cuba.

At the end of FY92, 1,058 officers and enlisted personnel manned 13 VT ANG units, including the 134th FS at Burlington IAP with F-16A/B ADFs.

134th Fighter Squadron
158th Fighter Group

Lineage: *Constituted in January 1942 and activated at Will Rogers Field, OK, in March 1942, the 530th FS was initially equipped with Vultee A-31s but was soon re-equipped with North American A-36As. It was redesignated 384th BS (Dive) prior to moving to India during the summer of 1943 and became the 530th FBS before combat operations began while assigned to the 311th FBG, Tenth Air Force. Redesignated 530th FS on 30 May 1944, it flew North American P-51As and P-51Bs in China and India before being inactivated at Shanghai, China, on 16 February 1946. Reconstituted and redesignated the 134th FS, the unit was allotted to the Vermont NG on 24 May 1946.*
14 Aug 1946: 134th FS (SE) extended federal recognition at Burlington MAP and initially equipped only with support aircraft.
Apr 1947: First Republic P-47Ds assigned as mission aircraft.
Jul 1950: Converted from F-47Ds to F-51Ds and redesignated 134th FIS.
1 Feb 1951: Called to active duty but remained based at Burlington MAP (Ethan Allen AFB).
31 Oct 1952: Returned to state control.
Apr 1952: Converted from F-51Ds to Lockheed F-94A/Bs.
Apr 1958: Converted from F-94Bs to Northrop F-89Ds.
Jan 1960: Began participation in the ADC runway alert program.
1 Jul 1960: Reached group status with federal recognition of the 158th FIG and

With their state deriving its name from the French 'vert mont', the 'Green Mountain Boys' militiamen captured Fort Ticonderoga from the British in May 1775.

became ADC-gained upon implementation of gaining command

concept.
Summer 1965: Converted from F-89Ds to Convair F/TF-102As (first received on 12 Aug 1965).
9 Jun 1974: Redesignated 134th DSES/158th DSEG and converted from F/TF-102As to Martin EB-57B/Es.
1 Apr 1980: Became TAC-gained

following ADC inactivation.
1 Jan 1982: Redesignated 134th TFS/158th TFG after converting from EB-57B/Es to McDonnell F-4Ds.
Apr 1986: Began conversion from F-4Ds to General Dynamics F-16As.
1 Jul 1987: Redesignated 134th FIS/158th FIG.

Remaining ADC-gained after exchanging the intercept mission for that of defense systems evaluation, Vermont's 'Green Mountain Boys' flew EB-57s for seven and a half years.

Left: This pair of F-16As was photographed after the 134th TFS had converted from F-4Ds.

Below: Vermont's 134th FIS flew 'Deuces' between August 1965 and the spring of 1964.

1 Apr 1988: Det. 1 went on alert at Bangor IAP, ME.
FY90: F-16As brought up to F-16A ADF standard.
15 Mar 1992: Unit designation changed to 134th Fighter Squadron, 158th Fighter Group (134th FS, 158th FG).
1 Jun 1992: As part of the Air Force restructuring program, gaining command changed to ACC.

Virginia Air National Guard

At the end of FY92, 1,341 officers and enlisted personnel manned 14 VA ANG units, including the 149th FS which was flying F-16C/Ds from the Richmond International Airport. This flying unit, which had received federal recognition as the 149th FS in June 1947, served on active duty in Georgia and Kentucky during the Korean War, was a bombardment squadron between December 1952 and June 1957, and went through a confusing period between June 1957 and November 1958 when in quick succession it was redesignated from 149th BS to 149th FIS, to 149th TRS and finally to 149th TFS. Stability came back with that last redesignation and the Virginians then flew F-84Fs for nearly 13 years, before converting to F-105Ds in 1971, to A-7Ds in 1982, and to F-16C/Ds in 1991.

149th Fighter Squadron 192nd Fighter Group

Virginia replaced its trusty A-7Ds (below) after 10 years' service. Seen right is the current mission aircraft: the ubiquitous F-16, escorting an unmarked 'SLUF'.

Lineage: *Constituted in September 1942 and activated at Mitchel Field, NY, during the following month, the 328th FS was assigned to the 352nd FG, Eighth Air Force. It flew combat missions in the ETO with Republic P-47Ds (from September 1943) and North American P-51Ds (from April 1943 until VE Day). Inactivated at Camp Kilmer, NJ, in November 1945, the unit was reconstituted and redesignated the 149th FS before being allotted to the Virginia NG on 24 May 1946.*
21 Jun 1947: 149th FS (SE) extended federal recognition at Byrd Field, Sandston, VA, and soon equipped with Republic P-47Ds (plus support aircraft).
1 Mar 1951: Called to active duty as part of the Korean War call-up and moved within two weeks to Turner AFB, GA, for service with SAC.
Dec 1951: Transferred to TAC, redesignated 149th FBS, and moved to Godman AFB, KY.
1 Dec 1952: Returned to state control at Byrd Field to be reorganized as the 149th BS (Light) and equipped with Douglas B-26B/Cs.
15 Jun 1957: Redesignated 149th FIS and began conversion to North American F-86Es. Only three Sabres were received and the unit continued to fly B-26B/Cs.
10 Apr 1958: Redesignated 149th TRS

and began conversion to **Martin RB-57s,** but only one of these twin-jets was received.
14 Jun 1958: Redesignated 149th FIS and converted from B-26B/Cs to Republic F-84Fs.
10 Nov 1958: Redesignated 149th TFS.
1 Jul 1960: Became TAC-gained upon implementation of gaining command concept.
1 Oct 1961: Called to active duty as part of the Berlin Crisis call-up but

remained based at Byrd Field.
20 Aug 1962: Returned to state control.
15 Oct 1962: Reached group status with federal recognition of 192nd TFG.
19 Feb 1971: First Thunderchief received as unit began its conversion from F-84Fs to Republic F-105D/Fs.
FY82: Converted from F-105D/Fs to LTV A-7Ds.
FY91/92: Converted from A-7D/Ks to General Dynamics Block 30 F-16C/Ds

Preceding A-7Ds and A-7Ks in service with the 149th TFS, single-seat F-105Ds and two-seat F-105Fs served for 11 years.

(first F-16C received on 25 Jun 1991 and last A-7 left on 1 Oct 1991).
15 Mar 1992: Unit designation changed to 149th Fighter Squadron, 192nd Fighter Group (149th FS, 192nd FG).
1 Jun 1992: As part of the Air Force restructuring program, gaining command changed to ACC.
30 Jun 1992: Completed conversion to F-16C/Ds.

Peter B. Lewis

Virgin Islands Air National Guard

Purchased from Denmark in 1917, the US Virgin Islands are administered by the Department of the Interior. Virgin Islanders are US citizens and elect a Governor (who also is the Commander-in-Chief of the Virgin Islands Army National Guard and Air National Guard) and a non-voting member of the House of Representatives, but may not vote in Presidential elections.

The first unit of the Virgin Islands ANG, the 285th Combat Communications Flight, was activated at Christiansted, St Croix, on 7 May 1980. The ANG Headquarters was activated on 1 April 1983. At the end of FY92, the VI ANG had 34 officers and enlisted personnel to man three non-flying units.

Washington Air National Guard

Organized in 1924, the 116th OS served on active duty in the United States between September 1940 and November 1943. It was once again extended federal recognition in February 1947, converted to F-84s before being called to active duty during the Korean War (when it flew F-86s in England), and served in the air-defense role until July 1976. Since then, the 116th AREFS has flown Stratotankers, with its KC-135As being re-engined as KC-135Es in 1984.

Activation of a 'close air support detachment' was approved in February 1990. This detachment, which was initially manned by 15 full-time Washington Guardsmen, was organized at Gray Field, Ft Lewis, to provide maintenance and administrative support for up to 18 Air Force or ANG fighters on rotational detachments to provide close air support to Army units in training at Fort Lewis and the Yakima Firing Center. Early in 1993, this detachment was to have been expanded into a full fighter squadron equipped with 18 A-10As and six OA-10As but plans to activate this squadron were dropped during FY92.

At the end of FY92, 2,628 officers and enlisted personnel manned 30 WA ANG units, including the 116th ARS at Fairchild AFB with KC-135Es.

116th Air Refueling Squadron
141st Air Refueling Wing

Lineage: *Organized at Kelly Field, TX, on 29 August 1917, as the 116th Aero Squadron, this Air Service unit moved to France in January 1918. It was redesignated 637th Aero Squadron on 1 February 1918, served as a transportation and supply unit with the AEF, and was demobilized at Mitchel Field, NY, on 20 May 1919. In 1936, its lineage and honors were consolidated with those of the 116th OS which had been activated as a Washington NG unit in August 1924.*
6 Aug 1924: 116th OS extended federal recognition at Felts Field, Spokane, as the aviation unit in the 41st Division, Washington NG, and initially equipped with **Curtiss Jennies.**
1924-1940: Remaining based in Spokane, the 116th OS was equipped over the years with the mix of aircraft typical of prewar Guard units, including **Consolidated PT-1s** and **O-17s;** **Douglas BT-1s, O-2s** and **O-38s;** and **North American O-47s** and **BC-1s.**
16 Sep 1940: Called to active duty, assigned to Ninth Corps Area, and moved eight days later to Gray Field, Ft Lewis, WA. On 31 December 1940, it had one BC-1A, two O-38Es and eight O-47A/Bs.
World War II: Remaining based in CONUS until inactivated at Rogers Field, OK, in November 1943, the unit moved

Roger Cook courtesy of Dennis A. Pelthier

Above: While on FAD, the 116th FIS had flown Sabres in the UK.

Right: F-89Js were flown from 1960 until 1965 when they were retired.

four times, was redesignated on four occasions, flew ASW patrols along the Pacific northwest coast, and provided aerial support for ground forces in training. Reconstituted and redesignated the 116th FS, the unit was allotted back to the Washington NG on 24 May 1946.

Peter B. Lewis

Michael Pugh

With a Montana F-16A on the boom, a KC-135E makes a banking turn as it approaches the boundary of its assigned air refueling race track. The 116th AREFS came into being on 1 July 1976 when the Spokane unit traded F-101B/Fs for KC-135As.

10 Feb 1947: 116th FS (SE) extended federal recognition at Felts Field and soon equipped with North American P-51Ds (plus support aircraft).
Aug 1949: Relocated to Geiger Field, Spokane.
Jun 1950: Converted from F-51Ds to Republic F-84Bs and redesignated 116th FS (Jet).

1 Feb 1951: Called to active duty as part of the Korean War call-up and soon moved to Moses Lake AFB, WA, to be reorganized as the 116th FIS and converted from F-84Bs to North American F-86As.
Aug 1951: Moved to Shepherds Grove, Suffolk, England.
1 Nov 1952: Returned to state control at Geiger Field and re-equipped with North American F-51Hs.
Aug 1953: Converted from F-51Hs to North American F-86As.
Jun 1955: Converted from F-86As to Lockheed F-94A/Bs.
Oct 1957: Converted from F-94A/Bs to Northrop F-89Ds.
1 Jul 1960: Reached group status with federal recognition of 141st FIG and became ADC-gained upon implementation of gaining command concept.
Sep 1960: Converted from F-89Ds to F-89Js.
Summer 1965: Converted from F-89Js (last left in Aug 1965) to Convair F/TF-102As (first received on 30 Jun 1965).
Fall 1969: Converted from F/TF-102As (last left on 1 Dec 1969) to McDonnell F-101B/Fs.
30 Jun 1976: 141st FIG inactivated.
1 Jul 1976: Redesignated 116th AREFS, placed directly under the 141st AREFW, relocated to Fairchild AFB, and became SAC-gained.

Summer 1976: Converted from F-101B/Fs to Boeing KC-135As.
Spring 1984: Began conversion from KC-135As to KC-135Es.
Mar 1986: Last KC-135E received.
Aug 1990: Volunteers began flying missions in support of Operation Desert Shield.
20 Dec 1990: Called to active duty as part of Operation Desert Shield call-up.
15 Apr 1991: Released from active duty after taking part in Desert Shield/Desert Storm.
15 Mar 1992: Unit abbreviation changed to 116th ARS, 141st ARW.
1 Jun 1992: As part of the Air Force restructuring program, gaining command changed to AMC.

West Virginia Air National Guard

Organized in Charleston in March 1947, the first flying unit of the West Virginia ANG flew Thunderjets on active duty in England during the Korean War, was again equipped with Mustangs upon its return to state control, and moved to Martinsburg at the end of 1955 in preparation for its conversion to jets. Notwithstanding this move, the 167th TFS flew jets for less than four years, as it was reorganized as the 167th Aeromedical Transport Squadron in April 1961. Since

then, the 167th has remained a transport unit. That role has always been that of the 130th, the squadron which replaced the 167th in Charleston in October 1955.

At the end of FY92, 2,109 officers and enlisted personnel manned 27 WV ANG units, including the 130th AS flying C-130Hs from Yeager Airport in Charleston and the 167th AS flying C-130Es from Eastern West Virginia Regional Airport in Martinsburg.

130th Airlift Squadron
130th Airlift Group

Lineage: *When in 1955 the West Virginia ANG was authorized to organize a new squadron to replace its 167th FIS at Kanawha County Airport, the new unit was given the numerical designation of the 130th SRS (Medium), an ANG-manned unit which had been activated during the Korean War in August 1951 and had been assigned to the 111th SRW to serve alongside a Pennsylvania ANG squadron, the 103rd. The 130th SRS was inactivated on 1 January 1953 and the PA ANG unit was returned to state control.*
16 Oct 1955: 130th Air Resupply Squadron extended federal recognition at the Kanawha County Airport and equipped first with Curtiss C-46Ds and, within a year, with a mix of C-46Ds and Grumman SA-16As.
10 Oct 1958: Redesignated 130th TCS.

Moving into facilities left at the Kanawha County AP by the relocation of the 167th FIS, the 130th Air Resupply Squadron was initially equipped with Curtiss C-46s.

(Medium).
1 Jul 1960: Became TAC-gained upon implementation of gaining command concept.
Jan 1962: Converted from SA-16A/Bs to Fairchild C-119Cs (later C-119Gs and C-119Ls) and Helio U-10Bs.
1 Jul 1963: Redesignated 130th ACS.
Aug 1965: U-10Bs replaced with de Havilland Canada U-6As.
Jun 1967: U-6As replaced with U-10Ds.
8 Aug 1968: Redesignated 130th SOS.
Fall 1974-Fall 1975: Converted from U-10Ds (last left in Nov 1974) and C-119Ls (last left in Sep 1975) to Lockheed C-130Es (first received in Oct 1975).
4 Oct 1975: Redesignated 130th TAS and became MAC-gained.
FY86: Converted from C-130Es to C-130Hs.
Aug 1990: Volunteers began flying Desert Shield support missions.
5 Oct 1990: Called to active duty as part of the Desert Shield call-up.
26 May 1991: Released from active duty after taking part in Desert Shield/Desert Storm.

Doing it in the sand: participating in the Airlift Rodeo competition in June 1990, the West Virginians had no way of knowing that experience gained in the assault landing event would soon come in handy in Saudi Arabia.

USAF

15 Mar 1992: Unit designation changed to 130th Airlift Squadron, 130th Airlift Group (130th AS, 130th AG).

1 Jun 1992: As part of the Air Force restructuring program, gaining command changed to AMC.

Jim Dunn

Peter B. Lewis

Jim Dunn

167th Airlift Squadron
167th Airlift Group

Lineage: *Constituted and activated at Westover Field, MA, in January 1943, the 369th FS flew combat operations in the ETO with Republic P-47Ds (from December 1943) and North American P-51Ds (from November 1944 until VE Day) as part of the England-based 359th FG, Eighth Air Force. It was inactivated in November 1945. Reconstituted and redesignated 167th FS, the unit was allotted to the West Virginia NG on 24 May 1946.*

7 Mar 1947: 167th FS (SE) extended federal recognition at Kanawha County Airport, Charleston, and soon equipped with Republic P-47Ds (plus support aircraft).

Aug 1948: Converted from F-47Ds to North American F-51Ds.

Above: Graceful Super Constellations equipped the 167th Aeromedical Transport Squadron for nine years. This C-121G was photographed at Cheyenne, Wyoming, on 6 May 1967.

10 Oct 1950: Called to active duty as part of the Korean War call-up and moved 10 days later to Godman Field, KY, for assignment to TAC, redesignation to 167th FBS, and subsequent conversion to **Republic F-84Bs.**

Nov 1951: Moved to RAF Manston, England.

10 Jul 1952: Returned to state control at Kanawha County Airport to be reorganized as the 167th FIS and equipped with F-51Ds.

Dec 1955: Relocated to Martinsburg MAP, WV.

Oct 1956: Partially re-equipped with North American T-28As.

1 Mar 1957: Last ANG F-51Ds donated to Post 20 American Legion, in Charleston, WV.

Jul 1957: Converted from T-28As to F-86Hs.

10 Nov 1958: Redesignated 167th TFS.

1 Jul 1960: Became TAC-gained upon implementation of gaining command concept.

Spring 1961: Converted from F-86Hs to Fairchild C-119Cs.

1 Apr 1961: Redesignated 167th Aeromedical Transport Squadron (Light) and became MATS-gained.

Jul 1963: Received first Lockheed C-121Cs to start conversion from C-119Cs to C-121C/Gs.

18 Jan 1964: Redesignated 167th ATS (Heavy).

1 Jan 1966: Redesignated 167th MAS and became MAC-gained following MATS redesignation.

1 Aug 1968: Redesignated 167th Aeromedical Airlift Squadron.

Spring/Summer 1972: Converted from C-121C/Gs to **Lockheed C-130As.**

3 Jun 1972: Redesignated 167th TAS and became TAC-gained.

1 Dec 1974: Became MAC-gained upon transfer of TAC airlift resources to

Above: After trading its C-130Bs for C-130Es during the fall of 1989, the 167th TAS lost no time to qualify for Airlift Rodeo, where 62-1859 was photographed in June 1990.

MAC.

FY77: Converted from C-130As to C-130Bs.

Summer/Fall 1989: Converted from C-130Bs to C-130Es.

Aug 1990: Volunteers began flying Desert Shield support missions.

15 Mar 1992: Unit designation changed to 167th Airlift Squadron, 167th Airlift Group (167th AS, 167th AG).

1 Jun 1992: As part of the Air Force restructuring program, gaining command changed to AMC.

Wisconsin Air National Guard

Mustered in November 1940, the 126th OS served on active duty in the United States (from June 1941) and, as the 34th PRS, in the ETO (from March 1944). Post-World War II, it was allotted back to the Wisconsin Guard and received federal recognition as the 126th FS in June 1947. Until its conversion to tankers in March 1962, and including during a 21-month period when it served on active duty in its home state, the Milwaukee unit flew interceptors.

The second flying squadron of the Wisconsin ANG, the 176th, received federal recognition in Madison in October 1948 and was on

active duty at its home base between February 1951 and October 1952. After being returned to state control, the 176th served in the air-defense role for 22 years, became a tactical air support squadron in November 1974, and a tactical fighter squadron in November 1981.

At the end of FY92, 2,172 officers and enlisted personnel manned 26 WI ANG units, including the 126th ARS at General Billy Mitchell IAP in Milwaukee with KC-135Rs and the 176th FS at Truax Field in Madison with A-10As.

126th Air Refueling Squadron
128th Air Refueling Group

Lineage: *Designated the 126th Observation Squadron and allotted to the Wisconsin NG on 30 July 1940.*

12 Nov 1940: 126th OS activated at Milwaukee in the Wisconsin NG and equipped primarily with North American O-47A/Bs.

2 Jun 1941: Called to active duty and placed under command of II Army

Corps. Shortly thereafter moved to Ft Dix, NJ, with its O-47A/Bs supplemented by Douglas O-46As, Stinson O-59As and North American BC-1As.

World War II: Between January 1942 and March 1944 the unit remained in the United States, changed stations several times, was redesignated on four occasions, flew ASW patrols along the East Coast, and was trained as a

52-0828, a transport-configured C-97G, was used by the 126th AREFS as a 'bounce bird' trainer, freeing KC-97Ls for operations.

Peter B. Lewis

*This **KC-97L** was photographed on the ramp at the **General Mitchell Field** in Milwaukee, 17 months before the 126th **AREFS** received its first **KC-135As** to initiate its conversion to jet tankers.*

reconnaissance squadron before moving overseas. As the 34th PRS the unit moved to England in March 1944 and, equipped with **Lockheed F-5Es** (as well as a few **Douglas F-3s** and **North**

American F-10s), flew in combat with the 10th PRG, the Provisional Reconnaissance Group, and the 69th TRG from bases in England, France and Germany. Inactivated at Fürth, Germany, on 22 November 1945, the squadron was redesignated the 126th FS and was allotted to the Wisconsin NG on 24 May 1946.

25 Jun 1947: 126th FS (SE) extended federal recognition at General Mitchell Field, Milwaukee, and equipped with **North American P-51Ds** (plus support aircraft).

*A few months after returning from active duty during the Gulf War, the 126th **AREFS** became the first **ANG** unit to convert to 'big fan' **KC-135Rs**.*

29 Jun 1948: 128th FG extended federal recognition.
Sep 1949: Converted to Lockheed F-80As.
1 Feb 1951: Called to active duty as part of the Korean War call-up.
Mar 1951: Moved to Truax Field, Madison, WI.
31 Oct 1952: 126th FIS returned to state control to be re-equipped with F-51Ds at General Mitchell Field, Milwaukee.
Aug 1953: Converted from F-51Ds to North American F-86As.
Oct 1954: Converted from F-86As to Northrop F-89Cs (first F-89C received on 17 Oct).
Jan 1960: Converted from F-89Cs to F-89Js.
1 Jul 1960: Became ADC-gained upon

implementation of gaining command concept.
Aug 1961: Redesignated 126th AREFS, but not yet equipped with tankers, and became TAC-gained.
Mar 1962: Began training with Boeing KC-97Gs.
Nov 1962: Received first mission-ready KC-97Fs.
Dec 1963: Became first Guard squadron to be operationally ready as a tanker unit.
8-22 Aug 1964: Operation Ready Go: The 126th AREFS and the two other squadrons of the 126th AREFW (Illinois' 108th and Ohio's 145th) provided tankers to deploy 31 ANG fighters and reconnaissance aircraft from CONUS to Germany.
Mar/Aug 1965: Tankers brought up to jet-augmented KC-97L standard.
Jun 1967: First Creek Party assignment.
1 Jul 1976: Gaining command changed from TAC to SAC.
Dec 1976: Last Creek Party aircraft and crews returned from Germany.
2 Dec 1977: First Boeing KC-135A received.
FY83: Converted from KC-135As to KC-135Es.
Aug 90: Volunteers began flying Desert Shield support missions.
20 Dec 1990: Called to active duty as part of the Desert Shield call-up.
15 May 1991: Released from active duty after taking part in Desert Shield/Desert Storm.
Fall 1991: Converted from KC-135Es to KC-135Rs.
FY92: Converted from KC-135Es to KC-135Rs (first KC-135R received on 1 Oct 1991 and last KC-135E flown out on 12 Feb 1992).
15 Mar 1992: Unit abbreviation changed to 126th ARS, 128th ARG.
30 Apr 1992: Completed conversion to KC-135Rs.
1 Jun 1992: As part of the Air Force restructuring program, gaining command changed to AMC.

176th Fighter Squadron
128th Fighter Wing

Lineage: *Constituted and activated at Dale Mabry Field, FL, in July 1942, the 306th FS was assigned to the 338th FG, Third Air Force, and served as a CONUS-based replacement training unit. Successively equipped with Bell P-39s, Curtiss P-40s, North American P-51s and Republic P-47s, it was disbanded at Dale Mabry Field, FL, in May 1944. Reconstituted and redesignated the 176th FS, the unit was allotted to the Wisconsin NG on 24 May 1946.*
6 Oct 1948: 176th FS (SE) extended federal recognition at Truax Field, Madison, and equipped with **North American P-51Ds** (plus support aircraft).
1 Feb 1951: Called to active duty as part of the Korean War call-up.
Apr 1952: 176th FIS partially equipped with Northrop F-89As but retained its F-51Ds.
31 Oct 1952: 176th FIS returned to state control to be re-equipped with

*The 176th **FIS** converted from F-89Js to F-102As in the spring of 1966, 14 months before this 'Deuce' was photographed on the ramp at Truax Field, Madison.*

F-51Hs at Truax Field.
Oct 1954: Converted from F-51Hs to North American F-86As.
Oct 1955: Converted from F-86As to Northrop F-89B/Cs.
15 Apr 1956: Group status achieved with federal recognition of the 115th FIG.
Jul 1957: Converted from F-89B/Cs to F-89Ds.
1959: Converted from F-89Ds to F-89Hs.
Jan 1960: Converted from F-89Hs to F-89Js.
1 Jul 1960: Became ADC-gained upon implementation of gaining command concept.

Spring 1966: Converted from F-89Js to F/TF-102As (first received in May 1966).
9 Nov 1974: Redesignated 176th TASS and became TAC-gained; 115th TASG inactivated and 176th TASS placed under direct control of TAC-gained 128th TASW.
Fall 1974: Converted from F/TF-102As (last left on 9 Nov 1974) to Cessna O-2As.
Fall 1979: Converted from O-2As to Cessna OA-37Bs.
15 Nov 1981: Redesignated 176th TFS.
Fall 1981: Converted from OA-37Bs to Fairchild-Republic A-10As.

Carrying a TGM-65 Maverick training round, this A-10A of the 176th TFS was photographed on 1 October 1990. The 176th FS is scheduled to receive its first Block 30 F-16C in April 1993.

15 Mar 1992: Unit designation changed to 176th Fighter Squadron, 128th Fighter Wing (176th FS, 128th FW).

1 Jun 1992: As part of the Air Force restructuring program, gaining command changed to ACC.

FY93: Converting from A-10As to General Dynamics Block 30 F-16C/Ds (receipt of first Fighting Falcon programmed for 1 Apr 1993 and conversion scheduled to be completed on 30 Jun 1994).

Wyoming Air National Guard

Extended federal recognition as the 187th FS in August 1946, the only flying squadron in the Wyoming ANG flew fighters for nearly 15 years (including 21 months on active duty in the United States during the Korean War) prior to being reorganized as the 187th Aeromedical Transport Squadron. Since then, the 187th has been successively equipped with C-119Js, C-121Gs and C-130Bs.

At the end of FY92, 1,000 officers and enlisted personnel manned 14 WY ANG units, including the 187th AS at Cheyenne Municipal Airport with C-130Bs.

187th Airlift Squadron 153rd Airlift Group

Lineage: *Constituted at Westover Field, MA, in May 1943 and activated two months later, the 401st FS trained with Republic P-47Ds and, assigned to the 370th FG, Ninth Air Force, flew Lockheed P-38Js and North American P-51Ds in combat in the ETO for one year beginning in May 1944. It was inactivated at Camp Shanks, NY, in November 1945. Reconstituted and redesignated the 187th FS, the unit was allotted to the Wyoming NG on 24 May 1946.*

11 Aug 1946: 187th FS (SE) extended federal recognition at Cheyenne MAP and soon equipped with North American P-51Ds (plus support aircraft).

1 Apr 1951: Called to active duty and redesignated 187th FBS but remained at Cheyenne MAP for more than seven months.

Dec 1951: Moved to Clovis AFB, NM.

1 Jan 1953: Returned to state control at Cheyenne MAP.

Sep 1953: Converted from F-51Ds to Lockheed F-80Cs.

Summer 1957: Converted from F-80Cs to North American F-86Ls.

1 Jul 1957: Reached group status with federal recognition of 153rd FIG.

1 Jul 1960: Became ADC-gained upon implementation of gaining command concept.

Feb 1961: Began conversion from

This C-130B of the 187th TAS received appropriate markings for Wyoming's centennial.

Wyoming's 'Bucking Horse' insignia is proudly applied to this C-121G of the 187th MAS.

F-86Ls to **Fairchild C/MC-119Js.**

1 May 1961: Redesignated 187th Aeromedical Transport Squadron and became MATS-gained.

Apr 1963: Converted from C/MC-119Js to **Lockheed C-121Gs.**

8 Feb 1964: Redesignated 187th Air Transport Squadron (Heavy).

1 Jan 1966: Redesignated 187th MAS and became MAC-gained following MATS redesignation.

Spring 1972: Converted from C-121Gs to **Lockheed C-130Bs.**

13 Jul 1972: Redesignated 187th TAS and became TAC-gained.

1 Dec 1974: Became MAC-gained upon transfer of TAC airlift resources to MAC.

Dec 1989: Participated in Operation Just Cause in Panama.

Aug 1990: Volunteers began flying missions in support of Operation Desert Shield.

15 Mar 1992: Unit designation changed to 187th Airlift Squadron, 153rd Airlift Group (187th AS, 153rd AG).

1 Jun 1992: As part of the Air Force restructuring program, gaining command changed to AMC.

FY92: Contract awarded to Lockheed for eight C-130Hs with which to replace the C-130Bs of the 187th AS.

Mission Aircraft
of the Air National Guard

These mission aircraft (and support aircraft such as the Cessna U-3, Curtiss C-46, Douglas C-47 and Lockheed T-33, which served also as mission aircraft) are briefly described and their service with Guard units highlighted. Not included are aircraft which served, or are serving, only in a support role – such as Beech C-45s and C-12s; Convair T-29s and C-131s; Douglas C-54s; Fairchild C-26s; North American T-6s; Stinson L-5s; etc – nor which were operated by NG and ANG units during FAD periods – such as Aeronca O-58/L-3s; Bell P-39s; Boeing B-17s and B-29s; Consolidated B-24s; Curtiss A-18s and P-40s; Douglas A-20s, A-24s and B-18s; Lockheed F-4/F-5s and P-38s; North American B-25s and B-45s; Piper O-59/L-4s; Supermarine Spitfires; and Taylorcraft O-57s.

Peter B. Lewis

Boeing C-97 and KC-97 Stratofreighter

The development of a transport version of the B-29 Superfortress was undertaken by Boeing in 1942, and the first XC-97 flew on 15 November 1944. Eight additional transports derived from the B-29 followed prior to the final mass-produced version. Utilizing the taller fin and more powerful engines of the B-50 bombers, 879 transports and KC-97 tankers were built for the USAF until 1956.

With the ANG, C-97s equipped 18 transport and aeromedical evacuation squad-rons during a 12-year period commencing in 1960 when the type was delivered to the 133rd ATS, New Hampshire ANG, and ending in 1972 with its phase-out from the 197th MAS, Arizona ANG. In its KC-97 tanker version, the four-engined Boeing aircraft was operated by 10 air refueling squadrons starting with the 108th AREFS, Illinois ANG, in 1961 and ending with the 181st AREFS, TX ANG, in 1978. The Guard's most widely used model was the jet-augmented KC-97L.

Complete with underwing jets to augment take-off performance, this is a KC-97L of the 197th AREFS. The faithful KC-97 served with the Guard until 1978.

Squadron assignment
(C-97): 102nd NY (1963-1969), 103rd PA (1962-1969), 105th TN (1961-1967), 109th MN (1960-1971), 115th CA (1960-1970), 125th OK (1960-1968), 128th GA (1961-1965), 133rd NH (1960-1971), 137th NY (1961-1970), 139th NY (1960-1971), 142nd DE (1962-1971), 155th TN (1961-1967), 158th GA (1962-1967), 180th MO (1962-1969), 185th OK (1961-1963), 191st UT (1961-1969), 195th CA (1960-1970) and 197th AZ (1962-1972).

(KC-97): 102nd NY (1969-1972), 108th IL (1961-1976), 126th WI (1962-1977), 145th OH (1962-1975), 147th PA (1972-1976), 151st TN (1964-1976), 180th MO (1969-1976), 181st TX (1965-1978), 191st UT (1972-1978) and 197th AZ (1972-1977).

Specification
KC-97L
Type: tanker/transport powered by four piston engines and two auxiliary turbojets; max payload of 55,700 lb (25265 kg)
Powerplant: four 3,500-hp Pratt & Whitney R-4360-59 radial engines and two 5,970-lb (2708-kg) thrust General Electric J47-GE-25 turbojets
Performance: maximum speed 399 mph (642 km/h); climb rate 3,800 ft/min (19 m/sec); service ceiling 32,500 ft (9900 m); normal range 1,150 miles (1850 km)
Weights: empty 87,515 lb (39696 kg); gross 175,000 lb (79379 kg)
Dimensions: span 141 ft 3 in (43.05 m); length 110 ft 4 in (33.63 m); height 38 ft 3 in (11.66 m); wing area 1,720 sq ft (159.79 m²)
Armament: none

Boeing KC-135 Stratotanker

The transfer of Stratotankers to the ANG began during the summer of 1975 and their receipt marked the first association of the Guard with SAC. The design of a four-engined jet transport prototype capable of being developed into a commercial jetliner – the 707 series – and a military tanker/transport – the KC/C-135 series – was undertaken as a private venture by the Boeing Company in May 1952. The soundness of this venture was vindicated on 5 October 1954 when the USAF ordered an initial batch of 29 KC-135A tankers; subsequent contracts increased the total to 732 KC-135As and 88 other military versions. The first KC-135A flew on 31 August 1956, and delivery to the 93rd AREFS, SAC, began in June 1958. Seventeen years later, the type entered service with the 145th AREFS, Ohio ANG.

To improve performance and reduce noise when operating from some of the noise-sensitive ANG bases, all KC-135As in Guard service (as well as four KC-135Ds for the AK ANG) have been re-engined with 18,000-lb (8165-kg) thrust Pratt & Whitney TF33-P-102 turbofans. The first re-engined aircraft went to the 197th AREFS, Arizona ANG, in July 1982. KC-135Rs with 22,220-lb (10080-kg) thrust CFM F108-CF-100 turbofans were first assigned to ANG units in 1991.

Squadron assignment
(KC-135A): 108th IL (1976-1983), 116th WA (1976-1984), 117th KS (1978-1984), 126th WI (1977-1983), 132nd ME (1976-1985), 133rd NH (1975-1984), 145th OH (1975-1984), 147th PA (1976-1983), 150th NJ (1977-1983), 151st TN (1976-1982), 154th AR (1976-1984), 191st UT (1978-1982) and 197th AZ (1977-1982).

(KC-135E): 108th IL (from 1983), 116th WA (from 1984), 117th KS (from 1984), 126th WI (1983-1991), 132nd ME (from 1985), 133rd NH (from 1984), 141st NJ (from 1991), 145th OH (1984-1991), 147th PA (from 1983), 150th NJ (from 1983), 151st TN (from 1982), 154th AR (1984-1986), 168th AK (from 1986), 191st UT (from 1982) and 197th AZ (from 1982).

R. W. Harrison

Replacement of the KC-97 with the KC-135A Stratotanker began in 1975. Despite the hangar sign, this aircraft is from New Hampshire.

(KC-135R): 126th WI (from 1991), 145th OH (from 1991) and 153rd (from 1991).

Specification
KC-135A
Type: four-engined tanker
Powerplant: four 11,200-lb (5080-kg) thrust Pratt & Whitney J57-P-59W turbojets
Performance: maximum speed 585 mph (941 km/h); climb rate 2,000 ft/min (10 m/sec); service ceiling 50,000 ft (15240 m); normal range 1,150 miles (1850 km)
Weights: empty 98,446 lb (44654 kg); gross 297,000 lb (134717 kg)
Dimensions: span 130 ft 10 in (39.87 m); length 136 ft 3 in (41.53 m); height 38 ft 4 in (11.68 m); wing area 2,433 sq ft (226.03 m²)
Armament: none

All Guard KC-135s have been re-engined, most being KC-135Es featuring the TF33 turbofan.

James Benson

Cessna A-37 and OA-37 Dragonfly

After two T-37B jet trainers had been evaluated during 1962 by the Special Air Warfare Center, Cessna produced a specialized version with strengthened airframe, more powerful engines, and armament, including a Minigun in the nose and external stores on eight underwing pylons. Thirty-nine A-37As and 577 A-37Bs were built for the USAF and for the Mutual Aid Program.

In ANG service, A-37Bs equipped two squadrons during the 1970s, and OA-37Bs, with additional radios for air-to-ground communications, went to four squadrons beginning in 1979. The last OA-37Bs were phased out by the 176th FS in October 1992.

Squadron assignment

(A-37B): 104th MD (1970-1980) and 138th NY (1970-1979).

(OA-37B): 103rd PA (1982-1990), 169th IL (1979-1992), 172nd MI (1979-1992) and 176th WI (1979-1982).

Specification
A-37B

Type: two-seat light attack aircraft
Powerplant: two 2,850-lb (1293-kg) thrust General Electric J85-GE-17A turbojets
Performance: maximum speed 507 mph (816 km/h); climb rate 6,990 ft/min (35 m/sec); service ceiling 41,765 ft (12730 m); normal range 460 miles (740 km)
Weights: empty 6,211 lb (2817 kg); gross 14,000 lb (6350 kg)
Dimensions: span 35 ft 10½ in (10.93 m); length 29 ft 3 in (8.92 m); height 9 ft 2 in (2.79 m); wing area 184 sq ft (17.09 m²)
Armament: one 7.62-mm Minigun and 5,680 lb (2576 kg) of external stores

During the 1980s, the OA-37B was the main service version of the Dragonfly, employed on FAC duties. It has now been superseded by the OA-10A in this role.

Carl E. Porter

Cessna O-2 Super Skymaster

A militarized version of the Cessna 337 push-pull light aircraft, the O-2A was delivered to the USAF in 1967 to serve in the forward air control (FAC) role. For this mission the O-2A was flown as a two-seater and was equipped with four underwing hardpoints to carry gun/rocket pods or other stores. For light transport and liaison duty, the aircraft had provision for four removable passenger seats. A total of 501 O-2As, as well as 31 O-2Bs fitted for psychological warfare duty, were built by Cessna. The O-2A entered ANG service in 1970 with Pennsylvania's 103rd TASS and was phased out by New York's 137th TASS in 1985.

Squadron assignment
(O-2A): 103rd PA (1970-1982), 135th MD (1971-1977), 137th NY (1971-1985), 169th IL (1971-1980), 172nd MI (1971-1980), 176th WI (1974-1979) and 196th CA (1975-1982).

Specification
O-2A

Type: two-seat forward air control aircraft
Powerplant: two 210-hp Continental IO-360-C/D piston engines
Performance: maximum speed 199 mph (320 km/h); climb rate 1,100 ft/min (5.6 m/sec); service ceiling 18,000 ft (5490 m); normal range 1,060 miles (1705 km)
Weights: empty 2,848 lb (1291 kg); gross 5,400 lb (2450 kg)
Dimensions: span 38 ft 2 in (11.63 m); length 29 ft 9 in (9.07 m); height 9 ft 4 in (2.84 m); wing area 202.5 sq ft (18.81 m²)
Armament: provision for four 7.62-mm Minigun pods but armament normally restricted to target-marking rockets

Cessna's O-2 'Duck' was another FAC platform. This example served with the 196th TASS, CA ANG.

Peter B. Lewis

Cessna U-3

Pending delivery of their Cessna O-2As, three Tactical Air Support Squadrons were temporarily equipped with Cessna U-3As (with straight vertical surfaces) and/or U-3Bs (with swept fin and rudder). Nicknamed 'Blue Canoes', other U-3A/Bs served with ANG headquarters units.

Squadron assignment
(U-3A/B): 103rd PA (1969-1970), 137th NY (1969-1971) and 169th IL (1969-1970).

Specification
U-3A
Type: twin-engined, five-seat light transport
Powerplant: two 240-hp Continental O-470B piston engines
Performance: maximum speed 220 mph (354 km/h); climb rate 1,700 ft/min (8.6 m/sec); service ceiling 20,000 ft (6095 m); normal range 1,000 miles (1610 km)
Weights: empty 2,850 lb (1293 kg); gross 4,830 lb (2191 kg)
Dimensions: span 35 ft (10.67 m); length 27 ft (8.23 m); height 10 ft 6 in (3.2 m)
Armament: none

This U-3A was assigned to the Colorado ANG as an operational support aircraft.

Peter B. Lewis

Consolidated PT-1 and O-17

Developed by the Dayton-Wright Company from its civilian Chummy and military TA-3, 23 TW-3 primary trainers were built for the Air Service in 1922-23. A few were transferred to supplement Jennies in National Guard squadrons, the first going to California's 115th beginning in January 1925.

After acquiring design and production rights for the TW-3, Consolidated Aircraft developed several training and observation versions, including two which saw much service with the Guard and a third, the PT-3, of which at least one went to Texas' 111th Observation Squadron. The PT-1 trainer was essentially a refined TW-3 with tandem seating (instead of side-by-side accommodation), revised undercarriage and tail surfaces, and an uncowled 180-hp Wright E engine. The XO-17 prototype and the 29 O-17 light observation aircraft differed from the PT-1s primarily in being powered by the 220-hp Wright R-790-1 radial engine and in having a streamlined fuselage, revised tail surfaces, oleo shock absorbers, increased fuel capacity, and provision for a rear-mounted flexible gun.

Squadron assignment
(TW-3): 102nd (NY), 105th (TN), 106th (AL), 109th (MN), 110th (MO), 111th (TX), 115th (CA) and 118th (CT).

(PT-1): 101st (MA), 102nd (NY), 103rd (PA), 104th (MD), 105th (TN), 106th (AL), 108th (IL), 109th (MN), 110th (MO), 111th (TX), 112th (OH), 113th (IN), 115th (CA), 116th (WA), 118th (CT), 119th (NJ), 120th (CO) and 154th (AR).

(PT-3): 111th (TX).

(O-17): 101st (MA), 102nd (NY), 103rd (PA), 104th (MD), 105th (TN), 106th (AL), 108th (IL), 110th (MO), 111th (TX), 112th (OH), 113th (IN), 115th (CA), 116th (WA), 118th (CT), 119th (NJ) and 120th (CO).

Specification
O-17
Type: two-seat light observation aircraft
Powerplant: one 220-hp Wright R-790-1 radial engine
Performance: maximum speed 104 mph (167 km/h); climb rate 636 ft/min (3.2 m/sec); service ceiling 12,000 ft (3660 m); normal range 350 miles (565 km)
Weights: empty 1,881 lb (853 kg); gross 2,723 lb (1235 kg)
Dimensions: span 34 ft 6 in (10.52 m); length 27 ft 8 in (8.43 m); height 10 ft 3 in (3.12 m); wing area 295 sq ft (27.41 m²)
Armament: none normally fitted but provision for a flexible 0.30-in gun in the rear cockpit

Wearing the markings of the 107th Observation Squadron, Michigan NG, this PT-1 was typical of many which served with the Guard. Although basically a trainer, it was used for general spotting duties.

MI ANG

Convair F-102 and TF-102 Delta Dagger

With the ANG, as it had earlier with the USAF, the F-102 earned the distinction of being the service's first all-missile, delta-wing, supersonic interceptor. Developed, together with its Hughes MG-3 fire-control systems and Hughes Falcon air-to-air guided missiles, as part of the Air Defense Weapon System WS201A, the first YF-102 flew on 24 October 1953. Following a major redesign to correct performance deficiencies, 875 single-seat F-102A supersonic interceptors and 63 two-seat TF-102A subsonic combat trainers were built in San Diego between 1955 and 1958. Named Delta Dagger, the F-102A entered ADC service with the 327th FIS in June 1956.

F/TF-102As entered Guard service in early 1960 with the 182nd FIS, and this Texas ANG unit had fully converted to the type by July 1960. Twenty-two additional ANG interceptor squadrons were equipped with Delta Daggers and peak inventory was reached in the late 1960s. The 199th FIS, Hawaii ANG, became the last ANG unit to fly F-102As and retired its last Delta Daggers in October 1976.

Squadron assignment

102nd NY (1972-1975), 111th TX (1960-1975), 116th WA (1966-1969), 118th CT (1965-1971), 122nd LA (1960-1970), 123rd OR (1966-1971), 132nd ME (1969), 134th VT (1965-1974), 146th PA (1960-1975), 151st TN (1963-1964), 152nd AZ (1964-1969), 157th SC (1963-1975), 159th FL (1960-1974), 175th SD (1960-1970), 176th WI (1966-1974), 178th ND (1966-1969), 179th MN (1966-1972), 182nd TX (1960-1969), 186th MT (1966-1972), 190th ID (1964-1975), 194th CA (1964-1974), 196th CA (1965-1975) and 199th HI (1961-1976).

Specification
F-102A
Type: single-seat interceptor
Powerplant: one 16,000-lb (7257-kg) thrust Pratt & Whitney J57-P-23A turbojet

Right: The 'slippery' F-102 needed to employ its split-tail airbrakes to hold station with most photo-ships.

Performance: maximum speed 787 mph (1266 km/h); climb rate 21,050 ft/min (107 m/sec); service ceiling 52,800 ft (16095 m); normal range 670 miles (1080 km)
Weights: empty 19,350 lb (8777 kg); gross 31,276 lb (14187 kg)

Dimensions: span 38 ft 1½ in (11.60 m); length 68 ft 4⅔ in (20.83 m); height 21 ft 2 in (6.45 m); wing area 695 sq ft (64.57 m²)
Armament: six AIM-4C/D Falcon guided missiles, or two AIM-26B guided missiles and 24 unguided 2.75-in FFARs

Maj. Gen. Wayne C. Gatlin

Peter B. Lewis

Above: Completely destroying the fine lines of the mission aircraft, the bulged nose of the TF-102A housed two pilots in side-by-side seating, allowing the aircraft to be used for conversion and continuation training. In addition to its effect on the looks of the aircraft, the extra seat also damaged performance to the point where the trainer remained subsonic.

Right: A quartet of Delta Daggers from the 179th FIS, Minnesota ANG, puts up a fine formation. The 'Deuce' became the backbone of the ANG air defense effort, eventually retiring in 1976. Notable features of these aircraft are the red panels for high conspicuity should the aircraft be forced down over the snowy northern lands, and the 'O' prefix to the serial denoting an aircraft over 10 years old.

Maj. Gen. Wayne C. Gatlin

Convair F-106 Delta Dart

A derivative of the Delta Dagger with a more powerful engine, improved systems and substantially better performance, the Delta Dart was the last aircraft specially ordered by the USAF for the interception role. It entered ADC service in May 1959 with the 498th FIS and, before being phased out from ANG service more than 29 years later, had its systems progressively modernized. Convair built 277 F-106A single-seaters and 63 F-106B two-seaters.

Beginning in April 1972, when the first

F-106A/Bs were delivered to Montana's 186th FIS, and ending in August 1988, when New Jersey's 119th FIS sent its last to AMARC, Delta Darts equipped six Guard squadrons.

Squadron assignment

101st MA (1972-1987), 119th NJ (1973-1988), 159th FL (1974-1988), 171st MI (1972-1978), 186th MT (1972-1987) and 194th CA (1974-1984).

Specification
F-106A
Type: single-seat interceptor
Powerplant: one 17,200-lb (7802-kg) thrust Pratt & Whitney J75-P-17 turbojet
Performance: maximum speed 1,525 mph (2455 km/h); climb rate 50,200 ft/min (255 m/sec); service ceiling 57,000 ft (17375 m); normal range 1,150 miles (1850 km)
Weights: empty 23,646 lb (10725 kg); gross 38,250 lb (17350 kg)
Dimensions: span 38 ft 3½ in (11.67 m); length 70 ft 8¾ in (21.53 m); height 20 ft 3½ in (6.18 m); wing area 697.8 sq ft (64.83 m²)

Armament: one nuclear-tipped AIR-2A/B Genie unguided missile and/or four AIM-4F/G Falcon guided missiles; some aircraft modified to carry a 20-mm Vulcan cannon

Its lines a study in grace and elegance, the F-106 was also a highly potent interceptor and no mean brawler during close-in scraps. Relying initially on missile armament, some 'Sixes' were later given a cannon in place of the nuclear-tipped Genie, which was originally intended to destroy whole formations of bombers.

Curtiss C-46 Commando

One of the largest and heaviest twin-piston-engined transport aircraft ever built, the C-46 saw widespread service with the USAAF during World War II and with the USAF until the early 1960s. With the Guard, Commandos were first operated by the Territory of Hawaii National Guard, which used C-46Fs as part of the equipment of its 199th Utility Flight, beginning in 1947.

Eight years later, C-46Ds became the mission aircraft selected to equip new air resupply squadrons being formed in the Air National Guard to replace fighter squadrons at stations unsuitable for jet aircraft. Within four years, however, the C-46Ds were replaced by more modern equipment.

Squadron assignment

129th CA (1955-1958), 130th WV (1955-1958), 135th MD (1955-1958), 140th PA (1956-1958), 143rd RI (1955-1958), 145th OH (1956-1957) and 150th NJ (1956-1958).

Specification
C-46D
Type: twin-engined transport with max payload of 9,500 lb (4309 kg)
Powerplant: two 2,000-hp Pratt & Whitney R-2800-51 radial engines
Performance: maximum speed 241 mph (388 km/h); climb rate 10,000 ft (3050 m) in 13.4 min; service ceiling 23,150 ft (7055 m); normal range 1,525 miles (2455 km)
Weights: empty 30,765 lb (13955 kg); gross 51,900 lb (23541 kg)
Dimensions: span 108 ft (32.92 m); length 76 ft 4 in (23.27 m); height 21 ft 9 in (6.63 m); wing area 1,369 sq ft (127.18 m²)
Armament: none

The career of the C-46 in Guard service was relatively short. This C-46D served with the 129th Air Resupply Squadron, seen at Stockton in April 1958.

Curtiss Jenny

Deriving its popular name from its JN designation (the JN series combined the best features of two earlier Curtiss designs, the Models J and N), the Jenny was produced in large quantities between 1912 and 1919 as a trainer and light observation biplane. Still available in number in the early 1920s, the type was assigned to the first 16 observation squadrons.

The most important versions in Guard service were the JN-4Ds with 90-hp Curtiss OX-5 engines; the JN-4Hs and JN-6Hs with 150-hp Wright-Hispano As; and the JNS-1s which were JN-4s and JN-6s rebuilt in air depots after World War I with 150-hp Wright-Hispano 1 engines. As the small size of the forward cockpit of standard Jennies made it almost impossible for the pilot to bail out in an emergency, a number of Jennies were modified in Guard service. (The cowling between the two cockpits was cut away and new seats were installed to allow the pilot to slip back and out of the rear cockpit. This modification, first developed by California's 115th Observation Squadron, so impressed the Militia Bureau that it recommended its adoption by other Guard squadrons.) The first JN-4Ds were assigned to Maryland's 104th Squadron in July 1921 and the last JNS-1s were retired by Tennessee's 105th Observation Squadron in September 1927.

One of the 115th Observation Squadron's JN-4Hs displays the modified cockpits developed by this unit to ease emergency egress with a parachute.

Squadron assignment

101st (MA), 102nd (NY), 103rd (PA), 104th (MD), 107th (MI), 109th (MN), 110th (MO), 111th (TX), 115th (CA), 116th (WA), 118th (CT), 120th (CO), 135th/114th/106th (AL), 136th/105th (TN), 137th/113th (IN) and 154th (AR).

Specification
JN-6H
Type: two-seat trainer
Powerplant: one 150-hp Wright-Hispano A liquid-cooled engine
Performance: maximum speed 81 mph (130 km/h); service ceiling 6,000 ft (1830 m)
Weights: empty 1,886 lb (855 kg); gross 2,580 lb (1170 kg)
Dimensions: span 43 ft 7⅜ in (13.29 m); length 27 ft 4 in (8.33 m); height 9 ft 10⅝ in (3.01 m); wing area 352 sq ft (32.7 m²)
Armament: none normally fitted but provision in some aircraft for a forward-firing 0.30-in gun above the center wing and flexible guns in the rear cockpit

Curtiss O-11 and XO-12

Although its XO-1 lost the 1925 Air Service competition for Liberty-powered observation aircraft to the Douglas XO-2, Curtiss nevertheless was able to develop this biplane into a successful series of aircraft for the Air Service/Air Corps, the Navy, and civil and export customers. Sixty-six O-11s, powered by 435-hp Liberty engines instead of the 435-hp Curtiss D-12s of the Air Service/Air Corps O-1 series, were procured for the National Guard with FY27 and FY28 funds. One of these aircraft, 27-35, was re-engined with a 410-hp Pratt & Whitney R-1340-1 Wasp radial and, after being tested at McCook Field, was used by Massachusetts' 101st Observation Squadron and Connecticut's 118th Observation Squadron until scrapped in April 1933.

Squadron assignment
101st (MA), 102nd (NY), 103rd (PA), 104th (MD), 106th (AL), 110th (MO), 112th (OH), 113th (IN) and 118th (CT).

Specification
O-11
Type: two-seat observation biplane
Powerplant: one 435-hp Liberty V-1650-1 liquid-cooled engine
Performance: maximum speed 147 mph (236 km/h); climb rate 1,066 ft/min (5.4 m/sec); service ceiling 16,630 ft (5070 m); normal range 437 miles (705 km)
Weights: empty 3,012 lb (1366 kg); gross 4,532 lb (2056 kg)
Dimensions: span 38 ft (11.58 m); length 27 ft 3½ in (8.31 m); height 10 ft 3 in (3.12 m); wing area 351 sq ft (32.51 m²)
Armament: none normally fitted but provision for a forward-firing 0.30-in gun and a 0.30-in flexible gun in the rear cockpit plus 250 lb (113 kg) of bombs

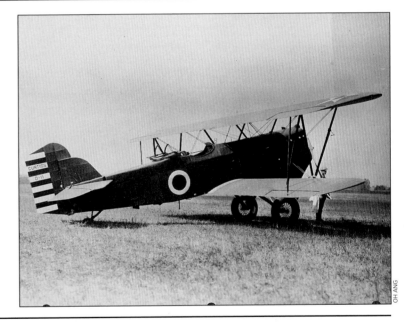

Curtiss O-11 of the 112th Observation Squadron, Ohio NG. The insignia represented the 'Buckeye State'.

Curtiss O-52 Owl

Ordered in FY40 and delivered beginning in the summer of 1941, the O-52s were intended to supplement late-model O-38 biplanes and more modern O-46 and O-47 monoplanes then equipping National Guard squadrons. Rather anachronistic with their high-mounted, strut-braced wings and manually-retracted undercarriage, they proved unsatisfactory and were quickly phased out.

Squadron assignment
105th (TN), 108th (IL), 111th (TX), 113th (IN), 119th (NJ), 152nd (RI) and 153rd (MS).

Specification
O-52
Type: two-seat observation monoplane
Powerplant: one 600-hp Pratt & Whitney R-1340-51 radial engine
Performance: maximum speed 208 mph (335 km/h); climb rate 10,000 ft (3050 m) in 8.2 min; service ceiling 21,000 ft (6400 m); normal range 700 miles (1130 km)
Weights: empty 4,231 lb (1919 kg); gross 5,364 lb (2433 kg)
Dimensions: span 40 ft 9 in (12.42 m); length 26 ft 4¾ in (8.04 m); height 10 ft (3.05 m); wing area 210 sq ft (19.51 m²)
Armament: one forward-firing 0.30-in gun and one 0.30-in flexible gun in the rear cockpit

This O-52 of the 111th Observation Squadron, Texas NG, is marked for the 1941 Louisiana Maneuvers.

de Havilland Canada C-7 Caribou

This STOL transport, designated DHC-4 by its Canadian manufacturer, was first ordered by the US Army in 1957 under the AC-1 designation. US orders totalled 164 aircraft, including five YAC-1s, 56 AC-1s (redesignated CV-2As in 1962), and 103 AC-1As (CV-2Bs after 1962). After being operated by the US Army for almost seven years, the CV-2A/Bs were transferred in 1967 to the USAF and were redesignated C-7As and C-7Bs. These aircraft saw much service during the Southeast Asia War.

After the war in Vietnam ended, the ANG obtained, in June 1973, a sufficient number of C-7A/Bs to equip New Jersey's 150th TAS/170th TAG. Less than four years later, these aircraft were transferred to the 135th TAS/135th TAG, Maryland ANG, which operated them until the end of 1980.

Squadron assignment
135th MD (1977-1980) and 150th NJ (1973-1977).

This C-7B was seen shortly after delivery to the New Jersey ANG. The 150th TAS flew the type until 1977, when the Caribous were passed on to the Maryland Guard for service until 1980.

Specification
C-7A
Type: twin-engined transport with max payload of 8,740 lb (3965 kg)

Powerplant: two 1,450-hp Pratt & Whitney R-2000-7M2 radial engines
Performance: maximum speed 216 mph (347 km/h); climb rate 1,355 ft/min (6.9 m/sec); service ceiling 24,800 ft (7560 m); normal range 850 miles (1370 km)

Weights: empty 18,260 lb (8283 kg); gross 31,300 lb (14197 kg)
Dimensions: span 95 ft 7½ in (29.15 m); length 72 ft 7 in (22.13 m); height 31 ft 9 in (9.68 m); wing area 912 sq ft (84.73 m²)
Armament: none

Frank MacSorley

de Havilland Canada U-6 Beaver

When, during the Southeast Asia War, the USAF needed all the Helio U-10s it could get, three ANG Air Commando Squadrons were temporarily forced to return their U-10s to the USAF. Beginning in September 1965, when the 135th ACS/135th ACG, Maryland ANG, traded its U-10Bs for U-6As, these three ANG squadrons flew Beavers as interim equipment.

Squadron assignment
129th CA (1966-1967), 135th MD (1965-1967) and 143rd RI (1965-1967).

During 1966/67, three ANG Air Commando Squadrons operated the U-6A Beaver as their mission equipment, while their U-10s were returned to active duty in the Southeast Asia war zone. They were used in a light transport role for support of Special Operations. This example was in the employ of the 143rd ACS, Rhode Island ANG.

Specification
U-6A
Type: single-engined utility transport

Powerplant: one 450-hp Pratt & Whitney R-985-AN-1 radial engine
Performance: maximum speed 163 mph (262 km/h); climb rate 1,020 ft/min (5.2 m/sec); service ceiling 18,000 ft (5485 m); normal range 455 miles (730 km)

Weights: empty 2,850 lb (1293 kg); gross 5,100 lb (2313 kg)
Dimensions: span 48 ft (14.63 m); length 30 ft 3 in (9.22 m); height 9 ft (2.74 m); wing area 250 sq ft (23.23 m²)
Armament: none

NGB/PA

Douglas A-26 (B-26 and RB-26) Invader

Designated A-26B, when fitted with a gun nose, and A-26C, when fitted with a transparent nose incorporating a bombardier station, the Douglas Invader was the most modern twin-engined, light bomber in USAAF service at the end of World War II. It was selected to equip 12 Bombardment Squadrons (Light) being formed in the National Guard, as well as to serve as a target-towing aircraft with the Guard's Fighter Squadrons.

The first Guard unit to receive A-26s as mission aircraft was the 180th BS (L), Missouri NG. Of the 12 A-26 (B-26 after June 1948) bombardment squadrons formed in the Guard during the late 1940s, six had been re-equipped with other types of aircraft by the end of the Korean War; however, two other squadrons received B-26s

at that time. In the reconnaissance role, four squadrons flew RB-26s.

As mission aircraft, the Invader was phased out of the Guard in 1958. The type, however, continued in limited use as a staff transport (VB-26B) and utility aircraft (TB-26B) for a number of years, with the last VB-26B being retired in 1972.

Squadron assignment
(A-26/B-26): 102nd NY (1947-1951 and 1952-1957), 103rd PA (1948-1951), 106th AL (1946-1951), 107th MI (1946-1950), 108th IL (1947-1952), 110th MO (1952-1957), 112th OH (1946-1952), 114th NY (1947-1951 and 1952-1957), 115th CA (1946-1951 and 1952), 117th PA (1948-1952), 122nd LA (1946-1957), 149th VA (1953-1958), 168th IL (1946-1957), and

180th MO (1946-1957).
(RB-26): 106th AL (1951-1957), 155th TN (1953-1956), 183rd MS (1953-1957) and 184th AR (1953-1956).

Specification
B-26B
Type: twin-engined light bomber
Powerplant: two 2,000-hp Pratt & Whitney R-2800-79 radial engines
Performance: maximum speed 322 mph (518 km/h); climb rate 1,070 ft/min (5.4 m/sec); service ceiling 24,500 ft (7470 m); normal range 1,680 miles (2705 km)
Weights: empty 22,362 lb (10143 kg); gross 41,800 lb (18960 kg)
Dimensions: span 70 ft (21.34 m); length 50 ft 8 in (15.44 m); height 18 ft

6 in (5.64 m); wing area 540 sq ft (50.17 m²)
Armament: 14 forward-firing 0.50-in guns, twin 0.50-in guns in dorsal and ventral turrets, and up to 6,000 lb (2722 kg) of bombs

Opposite page, top: Invaders from Alabama, Utah and Virginia line the apron of Las Vegas AFB during an exercise in March 1950. Although the B-26 served in numbers as a mission aircraft with bomber and reconnaissance units, these examples were serving at the time as support aircraft with F-51 and F-47 fighter outfits, chiefly to provide target-towing functions.

Douglas C-47 Skytrain

For almost 30 years, beginning in 1946, the venerable 'Gooney Bird' was operated as a support aircraft by most ANG flying squadrons, groups, and wings, as well as by state headquarters and the National Guard Bureau, thus helping the Guard to fulfill its mission. In addition, the 144th Air Transport Squadron (Light), Alaska ANG, operated six C-47As as its mission aircraft between July 1957 and April 1960.

Squadron assignment
144th AK (1957-1960).

Specification
C-47A
Type: twin-engined transport with max payload of 6,700 lb (3039 kg)
Powerplant: two 1,200-hp Pratt & Whitney R-1830-92 radial engines
Performance: maximum speed 230 mph (370 km/h); climb rate 10,000 ft (3050 m) in 9.6 min; service ceiling 24,000 ft (7315 m); normal range 1,600 miles (2575 km)
Weights: empty 17,865 lb (8103 kg); gross 31,000 lb (14061 kg)
Dimensions: span 95 ft 6 in (29.11 m); length 63 ft 9 in (19.43 m); height 17 ft (5.18 m); wing area 987 sq ft (91.7 m²)
Armament: none

Modified to VC-47D standards, this 'Gooney Bird' was typical of the many which served the Guard in a support function. The C-47's usage as a mission aircraft was restricted to six serving with the Alaska NG.

Douglas C-124 Globemaster II

Able to airlift large pieces of military equipment, C-124s continued to serve with the USAF and ANG for almost a quarter of a century after faster, but less capacious, turbine-powered transports had entered service. It was only with the availability, in MAC service, of the Lockheed C-5A, that the obsolete 'Old Shaky' could finally be retired.

In the ANG, the Globemaster II entered service in January 1966 with the 128th MAS/116th MAG, Georgia ANG. The other Georgia unit, the 158th MAS/165th MAG, became the last unit to phase out C-124Cs in September 1974.

Squadron assignment
105th TN (1967-1971), 125th OK (1968-1973), 128th GA (1966-1973), 133rd NH (1968-1971), 155th TN (1967-1974), 156th NC (1967-1971), 158th GA (1967-1974), 183rd MS (1967-1972), 185th OK (1968-1974) and 191st UT (1969-1972).

Specification
C-124C
Type: four-engined transport with max payload of 74,000 lb (33565 kg)
Powerplant: four 3,800-hp Pratt & Whitney R-4360-63A radial engines
Performance: maximum speed 304 mph (489 km/h); climb rate 760 ft/min (3.9 m/sec); service ceiling 21,800 ft (6645 m); normal range 4,030 miles (6485 km)
Weights: empty 101,165 lb (45888 kg); gross 194,500 lb (88224 kg)
Dimensions: span 174 ft 1½ in (53.07 m); length 130 ft 5 in (39.75 m); height 48 ft 3½ in (14.72 m); wing area 2,506 sq ft (232.82 m²)
Armament: none

Globemasters formed the backbone of the USAF's transport effort for many years. This C-124C served with the 128th MAS, GA ANG.

Douglas O-2, O-25 and BT-1

Winner of the 1925 Air Service competition for Liberty-powered Corps Observation airplane, the XO-2 was the progenitor of a long series of two-seat biplanes. The Militia Bureau first ordered 14 O-2Cs during FY26 to begin replacing Curtiss Jennies. That version, however, was found unsatisfactory and the O-2H version, which retained the 435-hp Liberty V-1650-1 engine but was fitted with staggered wings of unequal span (instead of the equal-span, non-staggered wings of the O-2C), was developed to improve stability. Fifty O-2Hs and 20 generally similar but unarmed O-2K trainers (soon redesignated BT-1s) were ordered by the Militia Bureau in Fiscal Years 1927, 1928 and 1930. They were supplemented in Guard service by O-2Hs, BT-1s and O-25s (which differed from O-2Hs primarily in being powered by 600-hp Curtiss V-1570-5 engines) transferred from the Air Corps.

O-2Cs entered service in 1927 and the last Liberty-powered aircraft, a BT-1, was retired in September 1935.

Squadron assignment

101st (MA), 102nd (NY), 103rd (PA), 104th (MD), 105th (TN), 106th (AL), 107th (MI), 108th (IL), 109th (MN), 110th (MO), 111th (TX), 112th (OH), 113th (IN), 115th (CA), 116th (WA), 118th (CT), 119th (NJ), 120th (CO) and 154th (AR).

A Douglas O-2H of the 119th Observation Squadron, New Jersey National Guard. The fuselage insignia was that of the 44th Division.

Specification
O-2H
Type: two-seat observation biplane
Powerplant: one 435-hp Liberty V-1650-1 liquid-cooled engine

Performance: maximum speed 134.5 mph (216 km/h); climb rate 1,075 ft/min (5.5 m/sec); service ceiling 16,900 ft (5150 m); normal range 512 miles (825 km)
Weights: empty 2,857 lb (1296 kg); gross 4,550 lb (2064 kg)

Dimensions: span 40 ft 10 in (12.45 m); length 30 ft (9.14 m); height 10 ft (3.05 m); wing area 362 sq ft (33.63 m²)
Armament: one forward-firing 0.30-in gun, one flexible 0.30-in rear-firing gun, and up to 400 lb (182 kg) of bombs

Douglas O-38 and BT-2

The first really satisfactory aircraft to be operated by the Guard was the Douglas O-38, which entered service in 1931 and was still in use 10 years later. Developed from the O-2H, but powered by a 525- to 625-hp radial engine, the aircraft of the O-38 series were reliable workhorses with respectable performance, including a top speed of 150 mph (241 km/h) for the O-38 model. The most important versions ordered for the National Guard were the O-38s and O-38Bs, both with open cockpits, and the O-38Es and O-38Fs, with canopy-covered cockpits.

The Militia/National Guard Bureau also operated as staff transports the sole O-38A and O-38D, the latter being the development aircraft for the O-38E/F versions. A small number of BT-2 trainers, which differed from O-38s in being powered by less powerful engines, was also operated by Guard squadrons.

Squadron assignment

101st (MA), 102nd (NY), 103rd (PA), 104th (MD), 105th (TN), 106th (AL), 107th (MI), 108th (IL), 109th (MN), 110th (MO), 111th (TX), 112th (OH), 113th (IN), 115th (CA), 116th (WA), 118th (CT), 119th (NJ), 120th (CO), 121st (DC), 122nd (LA), 124th (IA), 125th (OK), 127th (KS), 128th (GA), 152nd (RI) and 154th (AR).

The Douglas O-38 was an important aircraft to the Guard through the 1930s. This is an O-38E of the 116th Observation Squadron, WA NG, distinguished from earlier variants by having an enclosed cockpit, surely a welcome improvement for Washington's fliers in the grips of winter.

Specification
O-38
Type: two-seat observation biplane
Powerplant: one 525-hp Pratt & Whitney R-1690-3 radial engine

Performance: maximum speed 150 mph (241 km/h); climb rate 1,500 ft/min (7.6 m/sec); service ceiling 19,000 ft (5790 m); normal range 275 miles (440 km)
Weights: empty 3,070 lb (1393 kg); gross 4,456 lb (2021 kg)

Dimensions: span 40 ft (12.19 m); length 31 ft (9.45 m); height 10 ft 8 in (3.25 m); wing area 362 sq ft (33.63 m²)
Armament: one forward-firing 0.30-in gun, one flexible 0.30-in rear-firing gun, and up to 400 lb (182 kg) of bombs

Superseding but not completely replacing the O-38 was the Douglas O-46 parasol observation platform. This example carries the 'Flying Yankee' markings of the 118th Observation Squadron, CT ANG.

(O-43): 111th (TX).
(O-46): 101st (MA), 102nd (NY), 103rd (PA), 104th (MD), 105th (TN), 109th (MN), 115th (CA), 118th (CT), 119th (NJ), 121st (DC), 123rd (OR), 126th (WI), 127th (KS) and 128th (GA).

Specification
O-46A
Type: two-seat observation parasol monoplane
Powerplant: one 725-hp Pratt & Whitney R-1535-7 radial engine
Performance: maximum speed 200 mph (322 km/h); climb rate 1,765 ft/min (9 m/sec); service ceiling 24,150 ft (7360 m); normal range 435 miles (700 km)
Weights: empty 4,776 lb (2166 kg); gross 6,639 lb (3011 kg)
Dimensions: span 45 ft 9 in (13.94 m); length 34 ft 6¾ in (10.54 m); height 10 ft 8⅛ in (3.25 m); wing area 332 sq ft (30.84 m²)
Armament: one forward-firing 0.30-in gun and one flexible 0.30-in rear-firing gun

Douglas O-43 and O-46

Up to 1936, all the aircraft types operated by the National Guard had been biplanes. However, during that year the observation squadrons received the first Douglas O-46A parasol monoplanes ordered by the NGB during FY35. Powered by a 775-hp radial engine and fitted with a fully enclosed cockpit but retaining a fixed undercarriage, the O-46A had a top speed of 200 mph (322 km/h). Aircraft of this type were still in Guard service when the Observation Squadrons were activated one year prior to America's entry into World War II and saw limited wartime use on antisubmarine patrols.

Two earlier versions of the Douglas parasol monoplane, the O-31A and the O-43A, which were both powered by a liquid-cooled engine and fitted with a partially enclosed cockpit, were transferred to the National Guard by the Army Air Corps in the mid-1930s and were operated by Illinois' 108th and Texas' 111th Observation Squadrons.

Squadron assignment
(O-31): 108th (IL).

Fairchild C-119 and MC-119 Flying Boxcar

With its distinctive cargo/troop-carrying fuselage pod and twin-boom configuration, the C-119 was a more powerful and heavier version of the Fairchild C-82 which had first flown on 10 September 1944. Eight years after entering service with the USAF, Flying Boxcars were handed over to the newly organized Aeromedical Transport Squadrons of the ANG, beginning with Mississippi's 183rd. To suit them better for their use in the aeromedical evacuation role, a number of aircraft were modified to the MC-119J configuration with additional cabin soundproofing, accommodation for up to 35 litter patients, and a crew of six (pilot, co-pilot, flight mechanic, flight nurse and two medical technicians). In the medevac role, C-119s were replaced between 1961 and 1962 by quieter and more comfortable four-engined C-121s.

In its C-119C/G/L versions, the Flying Boxcar again saw Guard service as, beginning in July 1963 with California's 129th Air Commando Squadron, it equipped three air commando/special operations squadrons. The type was finally retired in September 1975.

Squadron assignment
102nd NY (1958-1962), 129th CA (1963-1975), 130th WV (1965-1975), 140th PA (1958-1962), 143rd RI (1971-1975), 145th OH (1957-1962), 147th PA (1961-1964), 150th NJ (1958-1961), 156th NC (1961-1962), 167th WV (1961-1963), 183rd MS (1957-1961) and 187th WY (1961-1963).

Specification
C-119J
Type: twin-engined transport with max payload of 20,000 lb (9070 kg)
Powerplant: two 3,500-hp Wright R-3350-89 radial engines
Performance: maximum speed 291 mph (468 km/h); climb rate 750 ft/min (3.8 m/sec); service ceiling 29,670 ft (9045 m); normal range 2,420 miles (3895 km)
Weights: empty 40,182 lb (18240 kg); gross 72,700 lb (33000 kg)
Dimensions: span 109 ft 3 in (33.29 m); length 86 ft 6 in (26.36 m); height 26 ft 6 in (8.08 m); wing area 1,447 sq ft (134.43 m²)
Armament: none

The C-119 Flying Boxcar had a long Guard career which finally ended in 1975. Most served as standard transports and aeromedical evacuation aircraft, but some were assigned to special operations duties with Air Commando Squadrons. This is one of the latter, flying with the 129th ACS.

Fairchild C-123 Provider

Fitted with skis and wingtip-mounted J44 auxiliary turbojets, the C-123J was ideally suited for Arctic operations. After equipping the 4083rd Strategic Wing, these aircraft were operated by the 144th Air Transport Squadron/Tactical Airlift Squadron, Alaska ANG, between 1960 and 1976.

Squadron assignment
144th AK (1960-1976).

Specification
C-123J
Type: ski-equipped transport with max payload of 8,345 lb (3785 kg)
Powerplant: two 2,500-hp Pratt & Whitney R-2800-99W radial engines and two 1,000-lb (454-kg) thrust Fairchild

J44-R-3 auxiliary turbojets
Performance: maximum speed 234 mph (377 km/h); climb rate 2,260 ft/min (11 m/sec); service ceiling 33,700 ft (10270 m); normal range 1,880 miles (3025 km)
Weights: empty 36,443 lb (16542 kg); gross 60,000 lb (27235 kg)
Dimensions: span 112 ft 6 in (34.29 m); length 79 ft 2½ in (24.14 m); height 35 ft (10.67 m); wing area 1,223 sq ft (113.62 m²)
Armament: none

An Alaskan rarity was the jet-equipped C-123J, which served only with the 144th ATS. The aircraft often operated with skis.

Peter B. Lewis

Fairchild-Republic A-10 Thunderbolt II

Beginning during the summer of 1979, tank-busting A-10As were delivered straight off the assembly line to replace A/OA-37Bs and F-100s equipping six ANG tactical fighter and tactical air support squadrons. Moreover, in 1989, OA-10As were delivered to Pennsylvania's 103rd TASS to replace OA-37Bs in the FAC role.

Squadron assignment
103rd PA (from 1989), 104th MD (from

1979), 118th CT (from 1979), 131st MA (from 1979), 138th NY (1979-1989), 172nd MI (from 1991) and 176th WI (1981-1982).

Specification
A-10A
Type: single-seat close air support aircraft
Powerplant: two 9,065-lb (4112-kg) thrust General Electric TF34-GE-100 turbofans

Performance: maximum speed 423 mph (681 km/h); climb rate 6,000 ft/min (30 m/sec); service ceiling 44,200 ft (13470 m); normal range 580 miles (935 km)
Weights: empty 20,796 lb (9433 kg); gross 50,000 lb (22680 kg)
Dimensions: span 57 ft 6 in (17.53 m); length 53 ft 4 in (16.26 m); height 14 ft 8 in (4.47 m); wing area 506 sq ft (47 m²)
Armament: one 30-mm gun and up to 16,000 lb (7250 kg) of external stores

A-10s were received new to equip Guard anti-armor squadrons, including the 176th TFS, Wisconsin ANG (below). The standard A-10 is in the process of being withdrawn from the attack mission, but some aircraft have been re-roled to act as forward air control aircraft under the designation OA-10A, although this does not entail any changes to the aircraft. Below left is an example from the 103rd TASS, Pennsylvania ANG, the first Guard unit to adopt the OA-10A.

René J. Francillon

Jim Dunn

General Dynamics F-16 Fighting Falcon

First assigned to South Carolina's 157th TFS during the summer of 1983 and equipping 34 squadrons in mid-1992, the F-16 is likely to remain the most numerous aircraft in Guard service well into the 21st century. In addition to being operated in the same tactical fighter configuration as aircraft assigned to active-duty squadrons, F-16s are operated by ANG squadrons in two unique configurations. New York's 138th TFS is, so far, the only squadron to be equipped with Fighting Falcons equipped with the 30-mm GPU-5/A gun pod for use in the tank-killing role, while 11 fighter interceptor squadrons were equipped with the F-16A/B ADF version specially developed for the ANG. F-16C/Ds were first assigned to ANG squadrons in 1991. Night-capable F-16C/Ds are entering Guard service in FY93.

Among the myriad of ANG F-16 units is the 121st FS, DC ANG, which employs the type on general battlefield duties.

Squadron assignment
(F-16A/B): 107th MI (from 1989), 111th TX (1989-1992), 114th OR (1988-1989), 119th NJ (1988-1991), 120th CO (from 1991), 121st DC (from 1989), 127th KS (1987-1991), 134th VT (1986-1991), 138th

NY (from 1988), 148th AZ (from 1985), 157th SC (from 1983), 159th FL (1987-1990), 160th AL (from 1987), 161st KS (1987-1991), 166th OH (from 1990), 170th IL (from 1988), 171st MI (1989-1991), 177th KS (1990-1991), 182nd TX (from

1985), 184th AR (from 1988) and 186th MT (1987-1991).

(F-16A/B ADF): 111th TX (from 1992), 114th OR (from 1989), 119th NJ (from 1991), 134th VT (from 1990), 136th NY (from 1990), 159th FL (from 1990), 169th IL (from 1992), 171st MI (from 1991), 178th ND (from 1989), 179th MN (from

Jim Dunn

René J. Francillon

1989), 186th MT (from 1991), 194th CA (from 1989) and 198th PR (from 1992).

(F-16C/D): 112th OH (from 1922), 113th IN (from 1991), 120th CO (from 1992), 127th KS (from 1990), 149th VA (from 1991), 161st KS (from 1990), 163rd IN (from 1991), 174th IA (from 1992), 175th SD (from 1992), 176th WI (from 1992), 177th KS (from 1990) and 188th NM (from 1992).

Specification
F-16A
Type: single-seat tactical fighter
Powerplant: one 23,840-lb (10814-kg) thrust Pratt & Whitney F100-P-200 turbofan
Performance: maximum speed 1,350 mph (2172 km/h); climb rate

Above: Defense of the US is now entrusted largely to the ANG's force of F-16A Block 15 ADFs, tailored to the interceptor mission.

Right: Second-generation F-16s now serve with the Guard in the form of F-16Cs and two-seat F-16Ds.

50,000 ft/min (254 m/sec); service ceiling 60,000 ft (18290 m); normal range 1,380 miles (2220 km)
Weights: empty 14,567 lb (6607 kg); gross 35,400 lb (16057 kg)
Dimensions: span 31 ft (9.45 m); length 49 ft 3 in (15.01 m); height 16 ft 8½ in (5.09 m); wing area 300 sq ft (27.87 m²)
Armament: one 20-mm cannon and up to 12,000 lb (5445 kg) of external stores

Robert B. Greby

Grumman SA-16 (HU-16) Albatross

The only amphibian to have served as mission aircraft in the ANG, the SA-16 (redesignated HU-16 in 1962) equipped four squadrons. The first two units received their Albatrosses in 1955 and kept them 16 years. In ANG service, the SA-16/HU-16s served as troop transports in support of Army Special Forces, whereas with the USAF they were used almost exclusively for air rescue duty.

Squadron assignment
129th CA (1956-1963), 130th WV (1956-1964), 135th MD (1955-1971) and 143rd RI (1955-1971).

Specification
HU-16B
Type: troop transport amphibian
Powerplant: two 1,425-hp Wright R-1820-76B radial engines

Performance: maximum speed 236 mph (379 km/h); climb rate 1,450 ft/min (7.4 m/sec); service ceiling 21,500 ft (6550 m); normal range 2,850 miles (4585 km)
Weights: empty 22,883 lb (10380 kg); gross 37,500 lb (17010 kg)
Dimensions: span 96 ft 8 in (29.46 m); length 62 ft 10 in (19.18 m); height 25 ft 10 in (7.87 m); wing area 1,035 sq ft (96.15 m²)
Armament: none

Normally thought of as an air rescue platform, the Albatross was used by the Guard for Special Forces support. This HU-16B served with the 143rd Special Operations Squadron, Rhode Island ANG.

RI ANG

189

Helio U-10 Super Courier

With its outstanding STOL performance, the U-10 was well suited to special operations and hence was a good complement to the C-119s and HU-16s which equipped air commando/special operations squadrons of the ANG. In Guard service, U-10As made their debut in 1963 and were later supplemented by extended-range U-10Bs and higher-weight U-10Ds (including float-equipped aircraft). Most, however, were transferred back to the USAF in 1965-1966 for duty in Vietnam. In 1967, U-10s were returned to the Guard and remained in service until 1975.

Squadron assignment
129th CA (1963-1966 and 1967-1975), 130th WV (1964-1974), 135th MD (1963-1965 and 1967-1971) and 143rd RI (1963-1965 and 1967-1975).

Specification
U-10A
Type: single-engined STOL light transport

Powerplant: one 195-hp Lycoming GO-480-G1D piston engine
Performance: maximum speed 176 mph (283 km/h); climb rate 1,350 ft/min (6.9 m/sec); service ceiling 20,500 ft (6250 m); normal range 670 miles (1080 km)
Weights: empty 2,037 lb (924 kg); gross 3,920 lb (1778 kg)
Dimensions: span 39 ft (11.89 m); length 30 ft 9 in (9.37 m); height 8 ft 10 in (2.69 m); wing area 231 sq ft (21.46 m²)
Armament: none

Often overlooked, the Helio U-10 Courier was instrumental in the development of airborne Special Forces techniques. The Guard operated four Special Operations Squadrons with the type, although these were temporarily reassigned to active-duty units. This U-10B served with the 129th SOS in California.

Courtesy of David W. Menard

Lockheed C-5 Galaxy

Heaviest aircraft in the Air Force inventory, the Galaxy entered ANG service in July 1985 after New York's 137th TASS was redesignated the 137th MAS and converted from the Cessna O-2A, the lightest aircraft in the Guard inventory.

Squadron assignment
137th NY (from 1985).

Specification
C-5A
Type: four-engined transport with max payload of 265,000 lb (120200 kg)
Powerplant: four 41,100-lb (18643-kg) thrust General Electric TF39-GE-1 turbofans
Performance: maximum speed

564 mph (907 km/h); climb rate 5,840 ft/min (30 m/sec); service ceiling 47,700 ft (14540 m); normal range 1,875 miles (3015 km) with max payload
Weights: empty 321,000 lb (145603 kg); gross 769,000 lb (348812 kg)
Dimensions: span 222 ft 8½ in (67.88 m); length 247 ft 9½ in (75.53 m); height 65 ft 1¼ in (19.84 m); wing area 6,200 sq ft (576 m²)
Armament: none

The 137th AS, NY ANG, is the Guard's only Galaxy unit, flying C-5As. Amazingly, the unit converted from the diminutive Cessna O-2.

Bill Curry

Lockheed C-121 and EC-121 Super Constellation

During the late 1940s and the 1950s, Lockheed Constellations and Super Constellations were among the best transport aircraft in both civilian and military service. The first aircraft in the series had been ordered by airlines prior to America's entry into World War II. They were completed, however, during the war as C-69 transports for the USAAF. In US military service, they were followed by C-121s (initially R7Vs with the USN) which served mainly in the transport role and as airborne early warning aircraft.

With the ANG, C-121s were first used in the aeromedical evacuation role, beginning in 1961 with the 183rd ATS, Mississippi ANG. Later, they also were used as personnel transports until being phased out in 1973.

In the electronic warfare role, the specialized EC-121S version was operated by the 193rd TEWS, Pennsylvania ANG, as an airborne TV and radio broadcasting station. The last of these 'Coronet Solo' aircraft was retired in May 1979.

Squadron assignment
(C-121): 140th PA (1962-1967), 147th PA (1963-1972), 150th NJ (1961-1973), 156th NC (1962-1967), 167th WV (1963-1972), 183rd MS (1961-1967), 187th WY (1963-1972) and 193rd PA (1967-1977).

(EC-121S): 193rd PA (1967-1979).

Specification
C-121C
Type: four-engined transport with max payload of 36,000 lb (16330 kg)
Powerplant: four 3,250-hp Wright R-3350-34 radial engines
Performance: maximum speed 376 mph (605 km/h); climb rate 1,150 ft/min (5.8 m/sec); service ceiling 22,300 ft

(6795 m); normal range 2,100 miles (3380 km)
Weights: empty 73,133 lb (33173 kg); gross 133,000 lb (60328 kg)
Dimensions: span 123 ft (37.49 m); length 116 ft 2 in (35.41 m); height 24 ft 9 in (7.54 m); wing area 1,654 sq ft (153.66 m²)
Armament: none

A classic of airline and USAF service alike, the Constellation was utilized by the Guard principally in the aeromedical evacuation and passenger transport roles, tasks to which the fast and long-legged aircraft was ideally suited. This is a C-121G of the 187th MAS, Wyoming ANG, seen at its Cheyenne base in 1971.

Peter B. Lewis

Lockheed C-130, EC-130 and HC-130 Hercules

First flown on 23 August 1954 and entering TAC service in December 1956, the 'Herky Bird' will remain the most important transport aircraft in the Air Force inventory well into the next century. Still in production, mostly for the ANG, the AFRES and export customers, the Hercules continues to serve military and civilian operators in a wide range of duties.

Since April 1970, when C-130As were first delivered to California's 115th TAS, C-130A/B/E/Hs have equipped 23 tactical airlift squadrons of the ANG (19 of which were still operating in FY92). Other Hercules versions in service with the ANG include ski-equipped aircraft (with New York's 139th TAS having operated C-130Ds between 1975 and 1985 and having been equipped since then with a mix of LC-130Hs and C-130Hs), tanker/rescue configured HC-130N/Ps (since 1975), and electronic warfare EC-130E 'Rivet Rider' and 'Comfy Levi' (since 1979 with Pennsylvania's 193rd).

Squadron assignment

(transport versions): 105th TN (from 1971), 109th MN (from 1971), 115th CA (from 1970), 130th WV (from 1975), 133rd NH (1971-1975), 135th MD (from 1980), 139th NY (from 1971), 142nd DE (from 1971), 143rd RI (from 1975), 144th AK (from 1976), 154th AR (from 1986), 155th TN (1974-1991), 156th NC (from 1971), 158th GA (from 1974), 164th OH (from 1976), 165th KY (from 1989), 167th WV (from 1972), 180th MO (from 1976), 181st TX (from 1978), 183rd MS (1972-1986), 185th OK (from 1974), 187th WY (from 1972), 193rd PA (1977-1979) and 195th CA (1970-1974).

Right: The three ANG rescue units all fly HC-130 sub-variants, these acting as long-range search platforms, command posts and tankers in the rescue mission.

Below: Backbone of the ANG airlift effort is the Hercules, here exemplified by a C-130E of the 115th AS, CA ANG. The aircraft also have a fire-fighting tasking.

(EC-130E): 193rd PA (from 1979).

(HC-130): 102nd NY (from 1975), 129th CA (from 1975), 210th AK (from 1990).

Specification
C-130H
Type: four-engined transport with max payload of 45,000 lb (20410 kg)
Powerplant: four 4,508-eshp Allison T56-A-15 turboprops

Performance: maximum speed 386 mph (621 km/h); climb rate 2,750 ft/min (14 m/sec); service ceiling 42,900 ft (13075 m); normal range 2,745 miles (4415 km)
Weights: empty 76,780 lb (34827 kg); gross 175,000 lb (79379 kg)
Dimensions: span 132 ft 7¼ in (40.42 m); length 97 ft 9⅝ in (29.81 m); height 38 ft (11.61 m); wing area 1,745.5 sq ft (162.16 m²)
Armament: none

Above: The shadowy 193rd SOG, PA ANG, operates two electronic versions of the Hercules. This is the EC-130E Rivet Rider, used for psy-war broadcasting.

Lockheed C-141 StarLifter

Built as C-141As and later upgraded to the stretched, air-refuelable C-141B configuration, StarLifters are the most numerous heavy transport aircraft in Air Force service. The C-141A version entered MAC service in August 1965, and the C-141Bs did so in January 1980, the latter first being assigned to Mississippi's 183rd MAS in 1986. A second Guard squadron, Tennessee's 155th, converted to C-141Bs during FY92.

Squadron assignment
155th TN (from 1991) and 183rd MS (from 1986).

Specification
C-141B
Type: four-engined transport with max payload of 89,150 lb (40438 kg)
Powerplant: four 21,000-lb (9525-kg) thrust Pratt & Whitney TF-33-P-7 turbofans
Performance: maximum speed 565 mph (909 km/h); climb rate 2,990 ft/min (15 m/sec); service ceiling 51,700 ft (15760 m); normal range 3,200 miles (5150 km) with max payload
Weights: empty 144,492 lb (65540 kg); gross 343,000 lb (155582 kg)
Dimensions: span 160 ft (48.77 m); length 168 ft 3½ in (51.29 m); height 39 ft 4 in (11.99 m); wing area 3,228.1 sq ft (299.9 m²)
Armament: none

Two Guard squadrons augment the active-duty C-141B StarLifter fleet on global transport missions. This example flies with the 183rd AS, and was seen on exercise in Honduras.

SMSgt Bob Mason/MS ANG

Lockheed F-80 and RF-80 Shooting Star

The first jet aircraft to be operated by ANG units, the F-80C was assigned to six squadrons prior to the Korean War. The distinction of being the first Guard unit to complete jet conversion went to California's 196th Fighter Squadron in June 1948. However, as jet aircraft were urgently needed by the USAF when war broke out in Korea, all six squadrons were divested of their Shooting Stars in 1950. In the post-Korean War period, F-80Cs, including F-80As and F-80Bs brought up to the same standards, again equipped 22 ANG squadrons. The last F-80s in the Guard were phased out in 1958.

While on active duty during the Korean War, the 157th (SC), 160th (AL) and 185th (OK) Tactical Reconnaissance Squadrons operated RF-80A reconnaissance aircraft; these units, however, converted back to Mustangs upon being returned to state control. Beginning in 1954, RF-80As were assigned to five Guard squadrons under state control and the type soldiered on with Tennessee's 105th TRS until 1961.

Squadron assignment
(F-80C): 110th MO (1957), 111th TX (1955-1957), 113th IN (1955-1956), 117th KS (1957-1958), 117th PA (1953-1956), 120th CO (1953-1957), 122nd LA (1957), 124th IA (1953-1956), 125th OK (1954-1957), 126th WI (1949-1951), 127th KS (1954-1958), 132nd ME (1948-1950), 144th AK (1954-1955), 157th SC (1955-1958), 158th GA (1948-1950), 159th FL (1948-1950 and 1955-1956), 163rd IN (1954-1956), 164th OH (1953-1954), 166th OH (1953-1954), 173rd NE (1948-1950 and 1953-1956), 174th IA (1953-1956), 182nd TX (1956-1957), 185th OK (1953-1958), 187th WY (1953-1958), 188th NM (1953-1958) and 196th CA (1948-1950).

(RF-80A): 105th TN (1954-1961), 153rd MS (1955-1957), 154th AR (1954-1957), 160th AL (1955-1956) and 184th AR (1956).

Specification
F-80C
Type: single-seat fighter
Powerplant: one 5,400-lb (2449-kg) Allison J33-A-35 turbojet
Performance: maximum speed 594 mph (956 km/h); climb rate 6,870 ft/min (35 m/sec); service ceiling 46,800 ft (14265 m); normal range 825 miles (1330 km)
Weights: empty 8,420 lb (3819 kg); gross 16,856 lb (7646 kg)
Dimensions: span 38 ft 9 in (11.81 m); length 34 ft 5 in (10.49 m); height 11 ft 3 in (3.43 m); wing area 237.6 sq ft (22.07 m²)
Armament: six 0.50-in guns and 2,000 lb of external stores

The F-80 was the ANG's first jet aircraft, serving briefly before the Korean War and then for some years after. This example is typical of the large numbers which served, shown in the colors of the 188th Fighter-Interceptor Squadron, New Mexico ANG.

Courtesy of Ben Knowles and David Menard

Lockheed F-94 Starfire

When, during the late 1940s, delays were experienced with the development of jet-powered, all-weather interceptors for the USAF, Lockheed stepped in with an interim design. Based on the airframe of the T-33A trainer, but fitted with a more powerful, afterburning engine, interception radar, and armament, the F-94A entered USAF service in May 1950. A total of 854 Starfires was built for the USAF.

First assigned, during the Korean War call-up, to three ANG squadrons (DC's 121st, Delaware's 142nd and Pennsylvania's 148th) serving on active duty with the Air Defense Command, the F-94A and B versions re-entered ANG service in June 1953 when Starfires replaced F-51Hs in the 137th FIS, New York ANG. With the F-94A/Bs later supplemented by F-94Cs, which had an all-rocket armament, Starfires equipped 21 interceptor squadrons of the Guard. The last F-94Cs were phased out in July 1959 by Minnesota's 179th FIS.

Squadron assignment
101st MA (1954-1958), 102nd NY (1957-1958), 103rd PA (1955-1959), 109th MN (1957), 114th NY (1957-1958), 116th WA (1955-1957), 118th CT (1956-1957), 123rd OR (1955-1957), 131st MA (1954-1958), 132nd ME (1954-1957), 133rd NH (1954-1958), 134th VT (1954-1958), 136th NY (1954-1957), 138th NY (1953-1957), 139th NY (1954-1957), 175th SD (1954-1958), 178th ND (1954-1958), 179th MN (1954-1959), 180th MO (1957-1958) and 190th ID (1955-1956).

Specification
F-94C

Type: two-seat all-weather interceptor

Powerplant: one 8,750-lb (3969-kg) thrust Pratt & Whitney J48-P-5 turbojet

Performance: maximum speed 640 mph (1030 km/h); climb rate 7,980 ft/min (41 m/sec); service ceiling 51,400 ft (15665 m); normal range 805 miles (1295 km)

Weights: empty 12,708 lb (5764 kg); gross 24,184 lb (10970 kg)

Dimensions: span 37 ft 4 in (11.38 m); length 44 ft 6 in (13.56 m); height 14 ft 11 in (4.55 m); wing area 232.8 sq ft (21.63 m²)

Armament: 48 2.75-in FFARs

The Lockheed F-94 was a stalwart of ANG interceptor units during the mid-1950s. One unit which flew the type was the 101st FIS of the Massachusetts Guard, which operated this F-94B. The later F-94C was also used, this featuring rocket armament in place of guns, revised nose contours and swept-back tailplanes.

Lockheed F-104 Starfighter

With several Allied air forces, notably in Western Europe and Japan, Starfighters were numerically the most important fighters beginning in the mid-1960s. With the USAF and the ANG, on the other hand, the F-104 saw only limited service even though it was the first Mach 2 American fighter.

Beginning in February 1960, when the 157th Fighter Interceptor Squadron, South Carolina ANG, received its first Starfighters, three Guard squadrons flew single-seat F-104As and two-seat F-104Bs, including during their deployment to Europe while on active duty for the Berlin Crisis. Their aircraft, however, were returned to the USAF in 1962-1963.

In the tactical role, F-104C/Ds were operated by Puerto Rico's 198th TFS for eight years beginning in the summer of 1967.

Squadron assignment

151st TN (1960-1963), 157th SC (1960-1963), 197th AZ (1960-1962) and 198th PR (1967-1975).

Specification
F-104A

Type: single-seat interceptor

Powerplant: one 15,800-lb (7167-kg) thrust General Electric J79-GE-3B turbojet

Performance: maximum speed 1,150 mph (1850 km/h); climb rate 54,000 ft/min (274 m/sec); service ceiling 58,000 ft (17680 m); normal range 850 miles (1370 km)

Weights: empty 12,760 lb (5788 kg); gross 27,853 lb (12634 kg)

Dimensions: span 21 ft 9 in (6.63 m); length 54 ft 8 in (16.66 m); height 13 ft 5 in (4.09 m); wing area 196.1 sq ft (18.22 m²)

Armament: one 20-mm cannon and two AIM-9B guided missiles

The 198th TFS was the only ANG operator of the F-104C/D, used for fighter-bomber duties.

The F-104 had two phases of ANG deployment, both of which were limited. For a short time from 1960 three states flew F-104A/Bs on interceptor duties, including South Carolina.

Lockheed T-33

When ANG fighter squadrons converted from propeller-driven aircraft to jets after the Korean War, they were assigned T-33A trainers to supplement their F-80s and F-84s. Thereafter, most fighter squadrons and several state support flights operated T-33As in support roles. Notably, fighter interceptor squadrons used T-33As to simulate enemy intruders until the late 1980s.

In addition to their assignment as support aircraft, T-33As were used by the 111th FIS, Texas ANG, between 1957 and 1976, to run the ANG Jet Instrument Training School.

Squadron assignment

111th TX (1957-1976).

Specification
T-33A

Type: two-seat jet trainer

Powerplant: one 5,400-lb (2450-kg) thrust Allison J33-A-35 turbojet

Performance: maximum speed 600 mph (965 km/h); climb rate 4,870 ft/min (25 m/sec); service ceiling 48,000 ft (14630 m); normal range 1,025 miles (1650 km)

Weights: empty 8365 lb (3794 kg); gross 15,061 lb (6832 kg)

Dimensions: span 38 ft 10½ in (11.85 m); length 37 ft 9 in (11.51 m); height 11 ft 8 in (3.55 m); wing area 234.8 sq ft (21.81 m²)

Armament: none

This 111th FIS T-33A was one of those used by the unit to provide jet instrument training. Other Guard T-birds served as hacks and adversaries.

LTV A-7 Corsair II

Designed as a carrier-based light attack aircraft, the Corsair II made its first flight on 27 September 1965 in the original A-7A version, and on 5 April 1968 in its land-based A-7D version for the USAF.

Beginning in October 1973, when New Mexico's 188th TFS acquired its first Corsair IIs, A-7Ds have been used to equip 16 Guard squadrons. Specially developed for the ANG, the two-seat A-7K combat trainer version was first delivered to Arizona's 152nd TFS in 1981.

During 1987/1988, a total of 78 A-7Ds and A-7Ks had their limited night/all-weather attack and navigation capability upgraded through the installation of the LANA (Low-Altitude Night Attack) system integrating the AN/AAR-49 FLIR, AN/APQ-126 radar, wide-angle HUD and automatic flight control system. LANA-equipped aircraft went to three squadrons, Iowa's 124th, New Mexico's 188th and Oklahoma's 125th. A-7s will be phased out in 1993 by the 162nd FS.

Squadron assignment

107th MI (1978-1990), 112th OH (1979-1992), 120th CO (1974-1991), 124th IA (from 1977), 125th OK (from 1978), 146th PA (1975-1991), 149th VA (1982-1991), 152nd AZ (1876-1991), 157th SC (1974-1983), 162nd OH (from 1977), 166th OH (1974-1992), 174th IA (1976-1992), 175th SD (1977-1992), 188th NM (1973-1992), 195th AZ (1984-1991), and 198th PR (1975-1992).

Specification

A-7D

Type: single-seat tactical fighter
Powerplant: one 14,250-lb (6464-kg) thrust Allison TF41-A-1 turbofan
Performance: maximum speed 698 mph (1123 km/h); climb rate 8,000 ft/min (41 m/sec); service ceiling 37,000 ft (11280 m); normal range 1,400 miles (2255 km)
Weights: empty 19,490 lb (8840 kg); gross 42,000 lb (19050 kg)
Dimensions: span 38 ft 8½ in (11.79 m); length 46 ft 1½ in (14.05 m); height 16 ft (4.88 m); wing area 375 sq ft (34.84 m²)
Armament: one 20-mm cannon and up to 15,000 lb (6805 kg) of external stores

Below: Until recently, the Corsair II was the standard attack aircraft of the ANG, but is now being fast replaced by the F-16.

Above: No less than three Ohio ANG squadrons were equipped with the 'SLUF', including the 162nd TFS.

Below: One of a small number of sub-types developed specifically for the Guard was the A-7K, a two-seat combat trainer version.

Martin B-57, EB-57 and RB-57

The prototype of the English Electric Canberra light bomber and reconnaissance aircraft made its first flight in England on 13 May 1949. Two years later, the British-designed twin-jet was placed in production under licence by the Glenn L. Martin Company and American-built RB-57As entered USAF service in April 1954. A total of 403 B/RB-57s was built for the USAF and the type served in the tactical bombing and reconnaissance, strategic reconnaissance, training and target-towing, night-interdiction, and electronic warfare training roles.

After serving with the 363rd TRW, TAC, RB-57As were handed over to the ANG in 1958 to equip four squadrons. Later supplemented by RB-57B/C/Es, these aircraft were used to equip a fifth tactical reconnaissance squadron in 1961. However, by early 1972, RB-57s were operated only by Kansas' 117th TRS. This squadron then converted to B-57Gs configured for night interdiction, and flew this version for two years. Beginning in 1974, the Martin twin-jet, in its EB-57 version, was operated by two defense systems evaluation squadrons, Kansas' 117th and Vermont's 134th. The last-mentioned unit retired the last Martin twinjets in the winter of 1981.

Squadron assignment

(B-57G): 117th KS (1972-1974).

(EB-57): 117th KS (1974-1978) and 134th VT (1974-1982).

(RB-57): 117th KS (1958-1972), 154th AR (1958-1965), 165th KY (1958-1965), 172nd MI (1958-1971) and 192nd NV (1961-1965).

Specification

RB-57B

Type: two-seat reconnaissance aircraft
Powerplant: two 7,220-lb (3275-kg) thrust Wright J65-W-5 turbojets
Performance: maximum speed 582 mph (936 km/h); climb rate 3,500 ft/min (18 m/sec); service ceiling 53,000 ft (16155 m); normal range 2,300 miles (3700 km)
Weights: empty 27,000 lb (12,247 kg); gross 55,000 lb (24948 kg)
Dimensions: span 63 ft 11½ in (18.40 m); length 65 ft 6 in (19.96 m); height 15 ft 7 in (4.75 m); wing area 960 sq ft (89.19 m²)
Armament: none

Although Kansas flew the B-57G Tropic Moon laser bomber and later joined Vermont in flying the EB-57 on DSE tasks, the US version of the Canberra was best-known in Guard service as the RB-57 reconnaissance platform. This aircraft is a B-57E of the 172nd TRS, a utility model which could undertake bombing, training or reconnaissance missions.

McDonnell F-4 Phantom II

First ordered by the Navy in 1954 as a carrier fighter, the F-4 became numerically the most important US military aircraft of the 1960s and early 1970s. Between 27 May 1958, when its XF4H-1 prototype made its first flight, and October 1979, when the last American-built F-4E was delivered to the RoKAF, a total of 5,068 Phantom IIs was built by McDonnell for the United States and allied nations. Fighter versions built for the USAF were the F-4C (first delivered to TAC in November 1963), F-4D and F-4E.

With the Guard, F-4Cs entered service with the 170th TFS, Illinois ANG, in January 1972 and were phased out by the 123rd FIS, Oregon ANG, in October 1989. F-4Ds, which first went to North Dakota's 178th FIS in March 1977, were retired by the 184th TFG, Kansas ANG, in March 1990. F-4Es initially equipped Missouri's 110th TFS and New Jersey's 141st TFS during the summer of 1985.

During 1991, the last F-4Es were phased out but a version new to the Guard, the F-4G 'Wild Weasel', entered service with the 190th TFS in Idaho.

Squadron assignment
110th MO (1979-1991), 113th IN (1979-1991), 114th OR (1984-1989), 121st DC (1981-1990), 122nd LA (1979-1985), 127th KS (1979-1990), 134th VT (1982-1987), 136th NY (1982-1990), 141st NJ (1981-1991), 160th AL (1983-1988), 163rd IN (1979-1991), 170th IL (1972-1989), 171st MI (1978-1990), 177th KS (1987-1990), 178th ND (1977-1990), 179th MN (1983-1990), 182nd TX (1979-1986), 184th AR (1979-1989), 190th ID (from 1991), 194th CA (1984-1989) and 199th HI (1976-1988).

Specification
F-4E
Type: two-seat tactical fighter
Powerplant: two 17,900-lb (8119-kg) thrust General Electric J79-GE-17 turbojets
Performance: maximum speed 1,485 mph (2389 km/h); climb rate 61,400 ft/min (312 m/sec); service ceiling 62,250 ft (18975 m); normal range 1,050 miles (1690 km)
Weights: empty 29,535 lb (13397 kg); gross 61,651 lb (27965 kg)
Dimensions: span 38 ft 4⅞ in (11.71 m); length 63 ft (19.20 m); height 16 ft 6 in (5.03 m); wing area 530 sq ft (49.24 m²)
Armament: one 20-mm cannon and up to 16,000 lb (7257 kg) of external stores

Robert S. Hopkins III

Below: The latest Phantom variant in Guard service is the F-4G 'Wild Weasel', employed on defense suppression tasks by the Idaho ANG at Boise.

Above: Like the F-16s which have replaced it, the F-4 served in both air defense and general battlefield roles. Representing the former is this 171st FIS F-4C.

Below: One of the last F-4E users was the 110th TFS of the Missouri ANG. This unit is based across the runway from the factory which built the Phantom.

René J. Francillon

Robert B. Greby

The 170th TFS of the Illinois ANG was the first Guard Phantom user, acquiring F-4Cs in 1972. These wore tactical three-tone camo to represent the battlefield role, as opposed to the air defense gray of the interceptor birds.

Bob Burgess

McDonnell RF-4 Phantom II

Whereas the USAF had first used Phantom IIs in the fighter role, the Guard initially received RF-4Cs, with Alabama's 106th TRS commencing its conversion in February 1971. Thereafter, RF-4Cs went to eight other ANG squadrons. At the end of FY90, RF-4Cs still equipped six squadrons and a training flight but, in 1991, two squadrons converted to other types.

Squadron assignment

106th AL (from 1971), 153rd MS (1979-1991), 160th AL (1971-1983), 165th KS (1976-1988), 173rd NE (from 1972), 179th MN (1976-1984), 190th ID (1975-1991), 192nd NV (from 1975) and 196th CA (from 1991).

Specification
RF-4C

Type: two-seat tactical reconnaissance aircraft
Powerplant: two 17,000-lb (7711-kg) thrust General Electric J79-GE-15 turbojets
Performance: maximum speed 1,459 mph (2348 km/h); climb rate 48,300 ft/min (245 m/sec); service ceiling 59,400 ft (18105 m); normal range 1,375 miles (2210 km)
Weights: empty 28,276 lb (12826 kg); gross 58,000 lb (26308 kg)
Dimensions: span 38 ft 4⅞ in (11.71 m); length 62 ft 10⅞ in (19.17 m); height 16 ft 6 in (5.03 m); wing area 530 sq ft (49.24 m²)
Armament: none

Above: ANG RF-4Cs, such as this Nevada aircraft, were commited to Desert Storm as the USAF's only tactical reconnaissance asset.

Below: RF-4C crews were happiest flying just above the trees, safe from enemy missiles. This early example flew with the 179th TRS.

McDonnell Douglas F-15 Eagle

First flown on 27 July 1972 and first delivered to the 555th TFTS, TAC, in November 1974, the Eagle remains the 'top of the line' fighter in the Air Force inventory. With the Guard, single-seat F-15As and two-seat F-15Bs were first assigned to the 122nd TFS, Louisiana ANG, during the summer of 1985, and now equip four tactical fighter squadrons and two fighter interceptor squadrons.

Squadron assignment

101st MA (from 1987), 110th MO (from 1991), 122nd LA (from 1985), 123rd OR (from 1989), 128th GA (from 1986) and 199th HI (from 1987).

Specification
F-15A

Type: single-seat tactical fighter
Powerplant: two 23,810-lb (10800-kg) thrust Pratt & Whitney F100-PW-100 turbofans
Performance: maximum speed 1,650 mph (2655 km/h); service ceiling 63,000 ft (19200 m)
Weights: empty 27,000 lb (12247 kg); gross 66,000 lb (29937 kg)
Dimensions: span 42 ft 9½ in (13.04 m); length 63 ft 9½ in (19.44 m); height 18 ft 7¼ in (5.67 m); wing area 608 sq ft (56.49 m²)
Armament: one 20-mm cannon and up to eight guided missiles (four AIM-7F/M, and four AIM-9L/M)

Above: Oregon's 123rd Fighter Squadron flies air defense from the Portland IAP and, on detachment, from McChord AFB in Washington.

Below: In alignment with active-duty units, ANG Eagles are changing to the 'Mod Eagle' low-visibility camouflage.

McDonnell F-101 Voodoo

Developed from the XF-88 experimental penetration fighter, the Voodoo was built for the USAF as a single-seater in the F-101A (escort), F-101C (tactical strike) and RF-101A/C (reconnaissance) versions, and as a two-seater in the F-101B (all-weather interception) and F-101F (operational training) versions. In its F-101A and RF-101A versions, the aircraft entered service with SAC and TAC in 1956. In its F-101B variant, it first went to ADC in 1959.

Beginning in November 1969 with units in Maine, North Dakota and Washington, seven ANG fighter interceptor squadrons flew two-seat Voodoos. Texas' 111th FIS retained F-101B/Fs until completing its conversion to F-4Cs in 1981.

Squadron assignment

111th TX (1971-1982), 116th WA (1969-1976), 123rd OR (1971-1981), 132nd ME (1969-1976), 136th NY (1971-1981), 178th ND (1969-1977) and 179th MN (1972-1975).

Partnering the F-106, the F-101B guarded US skies in ANG hands for 12 years, although Minnesota only had the type for four. Two of the mighty Genie nuclear air-to-air rockets could be carried in addition to radar- and IR-guided Falcons for the long-range interception role.

Specification
F-101B
Type: two-seat all-weather interceptor
Powerplant: two 16,900-lb (7666-kg) thrust Pratt & Whitney J57-P-55 turbojets

Performance: maximum speed 1,134 mph (1825 km/h); climb rate 49,200 ft/min (250 m/sec); service ceiling 54,800 ft (16705 m); normal range 1,520 miles (2445 km)
Weights: empty 28,970 lb (13141 kg); gross 52,400 lb (23768 kg)

Dimensions: span 39 ft 8 in (12.09 m); length 67 ft 5 in (20.55 m); height 18 ft (5.49 m); wing area 368 sq ft (34.19 m²)
Armament: six AIM-4F/G Falcon guided missiles, or two nuclear-tipped AIR-2A/B Genie unguided missiles and four AIM-4F/G Falcon guided missiles

Maj. Gen. Wayne C. Gatlin

McDonnell RF-101 Voodoo

With the ANG, the first Voodoos were the specially modified RF-101G/Hs which were obtained in 1965 by converting 61 F-101A/C airframes into tactical reconnaissance aircraft for assignment to Arkansas' 154th TRS, Kentucky's 165th TRS and Nevada's 192nd TRS. Later, seven ANG TRSs also flew RF-101As, RF-101Cs and RF-101Bs, this last being modified from 22 ex-Canadian CF-101B interceptors. The last RF-101s in the Air Force inventory were phased out by Mississippi's 153rd TRS in January 1979.

Squadron assignment

107th MI (1971-1972), 153rd MS (1970-1979), 154th AR (1965-1975), 165th KY (1965-1976), 171st MI (1971-1972), 184th AR (1970-1972) and 192nd NV (1965-1975).

Specification
RF-101C
Type: single-seat tactical reconnaissance aircraft
Powerplant: two 15,000-lb (6804-kg) thrust Pratt & Whitney J57-P-13 turbojets
Performance: maximum speed 1,012 mph (1629 km/h); climb rate 45,550 ft/min (231 m/sec); service ceiling 55,300 ft (16855 m); normal range 1,715 miles (2760 km)
Weights: empty 26,136 lb (11855 kg); gross 51,000 lb (23133 kg)
Dimensions: span 39 ft 8 in (12.09 m); length 69 ft 4 in (21.12 m); height 18 ft (5.49 m); wing area 368 sq ft (34.19 m²)
Armament: none

Thirty-one RF-101Hs (Nevada ANG illustrated) were produced from surplus F-101Cs for ANG use.

Peter B. Lewis

North American BC-1

Although not a mission aircraft, the North American BC-1A is included as it played an important part in the training of cadres provided to the USAAF by the National Guard in the early days of World War II. Its performance, notably its top speed of 207 mph (333 km/h), exceeded that of nearly all observation aircraft assigned at that time to Guard squadrons as mission aircraft. A generally similar AT-6A was delivered to the 121st Observation Squadron, DC ANG, before America's entry into World War II.

Postwar, various versions of the AT-6 (T-6 after June 1948) served as support aircraft with virtually all NG/ANG units until the early 1960s.

Squadron assignment

101st (MA), 102nd (NY), 103rd (PA), 104th (MD), 105th (TN), 106th (AL), 107th (MI), 108th (IL), 109th (MN), 110th (MO), 111th (TX), 112th (OH), 113th (IN), 115th (CA), 116th (WA), 118th (CT), 119th (NJ), 120th (CO), 122nd (LA), 124th (IA), 125th (OK), 126th (WI), 127th (KS), 128th (GA), 152nd (RI) and 154th (AR).

(AT-6A): 121st (DC).

Specification

Type: two-seat basic combat and instrument training aircraft
Powerplant: one 600-hp Pratt & Whitney R-1340-47 radial engine
Performance: maximum speed 207 mph (333 km/h); climb rate 10,000 ft (3050 m) in 7.9 min; service ceiling 23,300 ft (7100 m); normal range 1,100 miles (1770 km)
Weights: empty 4,090 lb (1855 kg); gross 5,200 lb (2359 kg)
Dimensions: span 42 ft 7 in (12.98 m); length 29 ft (8.84 m); height 12 ft 1 in (3.68 m); wing area 258 sq ft (23.97 m²)
Armament: provision for one forward-firing 0.30-in gun and one flexible rear-firing 0.30-in gun

Not strictly a mission aircraft, the BC-1 served in large numbers as a hack and, more importantly, as a trainer. This aircraft flew with the 115th Observation Squadron in California.

CA ANG

North American F-51 and RF-51 (P-51) Mustang

Assigned as mission aircraft to more Guard squadrons than any other type of aircraft, the P-51/F-51 Mustang, and its RF-51D photographic reconnaissance and TF-51D training versions, served in the ANG for 11 years. Deliveries started in 1946 when the first postwar fighter squadrons were formed, and Mustangs were in Guard service until March 1957, when the 167th FIS, West Virginia ANG, relinquished its last F-51Ds.

The design of the Mustang originated in January 1940 to meet the requirements of the British Purchasing Commission for an American-built fighter aircraft with performance equal or superior to that of the Curtiss Kittyhawk (P-40D). The first versions – including those built for the Royal Air Force, and the P-51/P-51A, A-36A and F-6B models for the USAAF (equipping, notably, some of the National Guard squadrons on FAD during World War II) – were powered by Allison V-1710 engines. However, it was the installation of Rolls-Royce Merlin engines, built under license by Packard, which turned built later versions of the Mustang into truly outstanding fighters excelling in the long-range, high-altitude, bomber-escort role. Until 1945, when production ended, a total of 15,868 Mustangs was built.

Large numbers of P-51Ds were available at the end of World War II to equip a majority of the fighter squadrons organized in the National Guard beginning in 1946. During the summer of 1950, how-

ever, the ANG lost some of its F-51Ds (the type symbol had been changed in June 1948 when the USAF dropped the P – pursuit designation for that of F – fighter) when the type became urgently needed to equip USAF squadrons in Korea. Later on, additional F-51Ds, as well as a smaller number of F-51Hs and RF-51Ds, were taken out of storage and were assigned to ANG squadrons to replace F-80s and F-84s being transferred to regular USAF units or to re-equip ANG squadrons after their return from active duty. Thus, no fewer than 75 Guard squadrons were equipped at one time or another with Mustangs; 44 of these squadrons had P-51Ds/F-51Ds as their first mission aircraft, 29 later converted from other types to F-51D/Hs, and seven were equipped with RF-51Ds.

Squadron assignment

(F-51D/H): 101st MA (1951-1954), 103rd PA (1953-1954), 104th MD (1951-1955), 107th MI (1952-1954), 108th IL (1952-1955), 109th MN (1946-1956), 110th MO (1946-1952), 111th TX (1947-1951 and 1952-1954), 112th OH (1952-1956), 113th IN (1947-1955), 115th CA (1953-1954), 116th WA (1947-1950 and 1952-1954), 118th CT (1952-1953), 119th NJ (1952-1955), 120th CO (1946-1953), 121st DC (1952-1954), 123rd OR (1946-1951 and 1952-1953), 124th IA (1946-1953), 125th OK (1947-1950 and 1952-1954), 126th WI

(1947-1949 and 1952-1953), 127th KS (1946-1950 and 1952-1954), 128th GA (1952), 131st MA (1951-1954), 132nd ME (1950-1954), 133rd NH (1952-1954), 134th VT (1950-1954), 136th NY (1952-1954), 137th NY (1952-1953), 138th NY (1950-1953), 139th NY (1951-1954), 141st NJ (1952-1955), 142nd DE (1952-1954), 146th PA (1951-1954), 147th PA (1951-1954), 148th PA (1950-1951 and 1952-1955), 152nd RI (1952-1955), 154th AR (1946-1950), 155th TN (1946-1951), 156th NC (1949-1951 and 1952-1953), 157th SC (1946-1950 and 1952-1954), 158th GA (1952-1953), 159th FL (1947-1948 and 1952-1955), 160th AL (1947-1950), 162nd OH (1948-1955), 163rd IN (1947-1954), 164th OH (1948-1953), 165th KY (1947-1951 and 1952-1956), 166th OH (1947-1950 and 1952-1954), 167th WV (1952-1957), 168th IL (1954-1955), 169th IL (1947-1956), 170th IL (1948-1953), 171st MI (1948-1950 and 1952-1955), 172nd MI (1947-1954), 173rd NE (1946-1948 and 1950-1953), 174th IA (1947-1950 and 1951-1953), 175th SD (1946-1954), 176th WI (1948-1952 and 1952-1953), 178th ND (1947-1954), 179th MN (1948-1954), 181st TX (1946-1950 and 1951-1954), 182nd TX (1947-1950 and 1952-1955), 185th OK (1947-1951 and 1953), 186th MT (1947-1953), 187th WY (1946-1953), 188th NM (1947-1953), 190th ID (1946-1953), 191st UT (1946-1955), 192nd NV (1948-1955), 194th CA (1949-1954), 195th CA (1946-1954), 196th CA (1946-1947 and 1952-

1954) and 197th AZ (1947-1950 and 1952-1953).
(RF-51D): 105th TN (1952-1954), 153rd MS (1952-1955), 154th AR (1952-1954), 155th TN (1951-1952), 160th AL (1952-1955) and 185th OK (1951).

Specification
F-51D
Type: single-seat fighter
Powerplant: one 1,490-hp Packard V-1650-7 liquid-cooled engine
Performance: maximum speed 437 mph (703 km/h); climb rate 10,000 ft (3050 m) in 3.3 min; service ceiling 41,900 ft (12770 m); normal range 950 miles (1530 km)
Weights: empty 7,125 lb (3230 kg); gross 11,600 lb (5260 kg)
Dimensions: span 37 ft 0½ in (11.29 m); length 32 ft 2¼ in (9.81 m); height 12 ft 2 in (3.71 m); wing area 272.3 sq ft (25.3 m²)
Armament: six 0.50-in guns and up to 2,000 lb (908 kg) of external stores

Inset: Distinguished by its taller fin and revised nose contours, the F-51H served in some numbers, this aircraft being assigned to the 104th FIS, Maryland ANG.

Below: Depicted at Boise during an ANG gunnery meet, this 165th F-BS F-51D sports the colorful markings associated with target-towing duties.

North American F-86A/E/F Sabre

First conceived in 1944 as a development of the straight-wing XFJ-1 Fury fighter of the US Navy, the F-86 (P-86 prior to June 1948) was the outstanding USAF fighter of the late 1940s and early 1950s. While its design was underway, North American and the USAAF agreed to modify it by incorporating swept wing and tail surfaces. With this characteristic feature, used for the first time on a US fighter, the prototype XP-86 was first flown on 1 October 1947. Including license production in Australia, Canada, Italy and Japan, and the FJ-2 through FJ-4 versions for the USN and USMC, a total of 9,386 aircraft was built. Main production versions for the USAF were the F-86A/E/F day fighters, the F-86H fighter-bomber and the F-86D/L interceptor fighters.

Seeing widespread (31 squadrons) but relatively short (less than seven years) service with the ANG, the air superiority versions of the Sabre (F-86A/E/F) had first gained fame over Korea where they thoroughly defeated the challenging MiG-15s. While serving on active duty in the US and Europe during their Korean War activation, three ANG squadrons (the 116th, 126th and 148th) were equipped with F-86As and the 123rd flew F-86Fs. With the ANG itself, F-86 day fighters were first assigned to the 186th FIS, Montana ANG, in November 1953 and were phased out in 1960 by California's 115th and 195th, and Colorado's 120th.

Squadron assignment

104th MD (1955-1957), 107th MI (1955-1956), 113th IN (1956-1958), 115th CA (1955-1960), 116th WA (1951-1952 and 1954-1955), 119th NJ (1955-1958), 120th CO (1958-1960), 121st DC (1954-1957), 123rd OR (1952 and 1953-1955), 126th WI (1951-1952 and 1953-1954), 141st NJ (1955-1958), 142nd DE (1954-1958), 144th AK (1955-1957), 152nd AZ (1956-1957), 156th NC (1954-1959), 163rd IN (1956-1958), 165th KY (1956-1958), 170th IL (1953-1955), 171st MI (1955-1956), 172nd MI (1954-1955), 176th WI (1953-1954), 186th MT (1953-1956), 190th ID (1953-1955), 191st UT (1955-1958), 192nd NV (1955-1958), 194th CA (1954-1958), 195th CA (1955-1960), 196th CA (1954-1958), 197th AZ (1953-1957), 198th PR (1954-1958) and 199th HI (1954-1958).

Specification
F-86A
Type: single-seat fighter
Powerplant: one 5,200-lb (2359-kg) thrust General Electric J47-GE-13 turbojet
Performance: maximum speed 679 mph (1093 km/h); climb rate 7,470 ft/min (38 m/sec); service ceiling 48,000 ft (14630 m); normal range 660 miles (1060 km)
Weights: empty 10,093 lb (4578 kg); gross 16,223 lb (7359 kg)
Dimensions: span 37 ft 1½ in (11.32 m); length 37 ft 6½ in (11.44 m); height 14 ft 8 in (4.47 m); wing area 287.9 sq ft (26.75 m²)
Armament: six 0.50-in guns and up to 2,000 lb (908 kg) of external stores

Many ANG units converted from the P-51 to another North American classic: the F-86 Sabre. Among these was the 197th FIS, which started its Sabre career with the F-86A (illustrated) before progressing to the F-86L.

Bernard J. Schulte courtesy of Picciani Aircraft Slides

North American F-86H Sabre

The less glamorous but longer lived F-86H version of the Sabre, which featured improved ground-attack capability, served with 14 ANG squadrons from 1957, when seven squadrons received F-86Hs, until 1970, when Maryland's 104th TFS and New York's 138th TFS were re-equipped with Cessna A-37Bs.

Squadron assignment

101st MA (1958-1964), 104th MD (1957-1970), 118th CT (1957-1959), 119th NJ (1962-1964), 121st DC (1957-1960), 131st MA (1958-1964), 136th NY (1957-1960), 137th NY (1958-1961), 138th NY (1957-1970), 139th NY (1957-1970), 141st NJ (1962-1964), 142nd DE (1958-1962), 167th WV (1957-1961) and 198th PR (1960-1967).

Specification
F-86H
Type: single-seat tactical fighter
Powerplant: one 8,920-lb (4046-kg) thrust General Electric J73-GE-3E turbojet

Performance: maximum speed 692 mph (1113 km/h); climb rate 12,900 ft/min (66 m/sec); service ceiling 50,800 ft (15485 m); normal range 1,040 miles (1675 km)
Weights: empty 13,836 lb (6276 kg); gross 24,296 lb (11020 kg)
Dimensions: span 39 ft 1½ in (11.93 m); length 38 ft 10 in (11.84 m); height 15 ft (4.57 m); wing area 313.4 sq ft (29.12 m²)
Armament: four 20-mm cannon and up to 4,000 lb (1816 kg) of external stores

The H-model Sabre featured strengthened wings for the carriage of air-to-ground stores, including tactical nuclear weapons, and LABS bombing equipment. Among the Guard units assigned the ground attack Sabre was the 167th TFS of the West Virginia ANG.

V. Reynolds courtesy of David W. Menard

North American F-86D/L Sabre

The all-weather interceptor versions of the Sabre – the original F-86D and the modified F-86L, with longer span and improved electronic systems – equipped 26 ANG fighter interceptor squadrons between August 1956, when F-86Ds were first assigned to Florida's 159th FIS, and May 1965, when California's 196th FIS last flew F-86Ls.

Squadron assignment

111th TX (1957-1960), 120th CO (1960-1961), 122nd LA (1957-1960), 124th IA (1958-1962), 125th OK (1957-1960), 127th KS (1958-1961), 128th GA (1960-1961), 133rd NH (1958-1960), 146th PA (1957-1960), 147th PA (1958-1961), 151st TN (1957-1960), 156th NC (1959-1960), 157th SC (1958-1960), 159th FL (1956-1960), 173rd (1957-1964), 181st TX (1957-1964), 182nd TX (1957-1960), 185th OK (1958- 1961), 187th WY (1958-1961), 190th ID (1959-1964), 191st UT (1958-1961), 192nd NV (1958-1961), 194th CA (1958-1964), 196th CA (1958-1965), 197th AZ (1957-1960), 198th PR (1958-1960) and 199th HI (1958-1961).

Specification
F-86L
Type: single-seat interceptor
Powerplant: one 7,650-lb (3470-kg) thrust General Electric J47-GE-33 turbojet

Performance: maximum speed 693 mph (1115 km/h); climb rate 12,200 ft/min (62 m/sec); service ceiling 48,250 ft (14705 m); normal range 550 miles (885 km)
Weights: empty 13,822 lb (6270 kg); gross 20,276 lb (9197 kg)
Dimensions: span 39 ft 9½ in (11.93 m); length 40 ft 3¼ in (12.27 m); height 15 ft (4.57 m); wing area 313.4 sq ft (29.12 m²)
Armament: 24 2.75-in FFARs

Fitting radar to the Sabre in the F-86D 'Dogship' and uprated F-86L versions provided the USAF with a limited all-weather interception capability. The Guard flew both types in sizable quantities, this F-86L flying with the 196th FIS.

North American F-100 Super Sabre

After serving in ANG squadrons for 21 years, the F-100 was finally phased out in 1979 (the last being those of Indiana's 113th TFS which were flown to MASDC in November 1979) by 10 of the 26 squadrons which had been equipped with this workhorse. This long career, during which ANG F-100 squadrons twice served on active duty and flew combat sorties in Vietnam, had begun in April 1958 when the 188th FIS, New Mexico ANG, had converted to F-100As.

The prototype of the F-100, the world's first operational fighter capable of level supersonic performance, had made its first flight on 25 May 1953. Produced in four main versions – the F-100A air super- iority fighter, the F-100C and F-100D tactical fighters, and the F-100F two-seat combat trainer – the Super Sabre became, during the late 1950s and early 1960s, the most important USAF tactical fighter. A total of 2,294 Super Sabres was built and all four principal versions served with ANG squadrons.

Squadron assignment

101st MA (1971-1972), 107th MI (1972-1978), 110th MO (1962-1979), 112th OH (1970-1979), 113th IN (1971-1979), 118th CT (1959-1966 and 1971-1979), 119th NJ (1964-1970), 120th CO (1961-1974), 121st DC (1960-1971), 122nd LA (1970-1979), 124th IA (1971-1976), 125th OK (1973-1978), 128th GA (1973-1979), 131st MA (1971-1979), 136th NY (1960-1971), 152nd AZ (1958-1964 and 1969-1978), 162nd OH (1970-1977), 163rd OH (1971-1979), 164th OH (1972-1975), 166th OH (1962-1974), 174th IA (1961-1977), 175th SD (1970-1977), 182nd TX (1971-1979), 184th AR (1972-1979) and 188th NM (1958-1973).

Specification
F-100D
Type: single-seat tactical fighter
Powerplant: one 16,950-lb (7688-kg) thrust Pratt & Whitney J57-P-21A turbojet

Performance: maximum speed 864 mph (1390 km/h); climb rate 16,000 ft/min (81 m/sec); service ceiling 56,100 ft (17100 m); normal range 1,500 miles (2415 km)
Weights: empty 21,000 lb (9525 kg); gross 34,832 lb (15800 kg)
Dimensions: span 38 ft 9⅓ in (11.81 m); length 49 ft 6 in (15.09 m); height 16 ft 2½ in (4.94 m); wing area 385.2 sq ft (35.79 m²)
Armament: four 20-mm cannon and up to 7,500 lb (3402 kg) of external stores

Strikingly painted, this F-100C flew with the 188th TFS, the first Guard unit to adopt the 'Hun' for operations in 1958. The last F-100 retired from ANG service 21 years later.

North American O-47

First ordered for National Guard squadrons during FY37, the O-47 was the first Guard airplane to combine such modern features as fully enclosed cockpits, cantilever monoplane configuration and retractable main undercarriage.

When, beginning in September 1940, Guard squadrons were activated for one year or the duration of World War II, the O-47A/Bs were the most advanced and numerous aircraft in their inventory. In 1941-1942, they saw widespread service in anti-submarine patrols along the US coast and were extensively flown in support of ground forces in training. Ten of these aircraft, manned by crews from as many National Guard squadrons, were shipped to Singapore in early 1942, but were diverted to Australia where they briefly flew on anti-submarine patrols.

Squadron assignment
101st (MA), 102nd (NY), 103rd (PA), 104th (MD), 105th (TN), 106th (AL), 107th (MI), 108th (IL), 109th (MN), 110th (MO), 111th (TX), 112th (OH), 113th (IN), 115th (CA), 116th (WA), 118th (CT), 119th (NJ), 120th (CO), 121st (DC), 122nd (LA), 123rd (OR), 124th (IA), 125th (OK), 126th (WI), 152nd (RI), 153rd (MS) and 154th (AR).

Specification
O-47A
Type: two-seat observation monoplane
Powerplant: one 975-hp Wright R-1820-9 radial engine
Performance: maximum speed 220.5 mph (355 km/h); climb rate 1,720 ft/min (8.7 m/sec); service ceiling 23,200 ft (7070 m); normal range 640 miles (1030 km)
Weights: empty 5,900 lb (2676 kg); gross 7,636 lb (3464 kg)
Dimensions: span 46 ft 4 in (14.12 m); length 33 ft 7 in (10.24 m); height 12 ft 2 in (3.71 m); wing area 350 sq ft (32.52 m²)
Armament: one forward-firing 0.30-in gun, one rear-firing flexible 0.30-in gun, and up to 650 lb (295 kg) of bombs

On entering World War II, the ANG was dominated by the O-47, and these performed well until late in 1942, flying coastal patrols and providing training. This example served with the 115th Observation Squadron of the California ANG.

William T. Larkins

North American T-28 Trojan

Piston-powered T-28A trainers served as mission aircraft with four ANG squadrons while these units awaited completion of runway lengthening at their bases to convert from F-51Ds to jet fighters. The Trojan was thus strictly an interim aircraft, as it lacked combat capability. It did, however, enable flight crews from these units to maintain their proficiency, improve their instrument flying technique, and familiarize themselves with tricycle undercarriage operations.

Winner of a design competition to provide the USAF with a replacement for the wartime North American T-6, the T-28 was first delivered to Air Training Command in 1950. Production totalled 1,987 aircraft and included 1,199 for the USAF (all but five of which were T-28As) and 788 for the USN.

Squadron assignment
109th MN (1956-1957), 112th OH (1955-1958), 167th WV (1956-1957) and 169th IL (1956-1958).

Specification
T-28A
Type: two-seat basic trainer
Powerplant: one 800-hp Wright R-1300-1A radial engine
Performance: maximum speed 283 mph (455 km/h); climb rate 1,870 ft/min (9.5 m/sec); service ceiling 24,000 ft (7315 m); normal range 1,000 miles (1610 km)
Weights: empty 5,111 lb (2318 kg); gross 6,365 lb (2887 kg)
Dimensions: span 40 ft 1 in (12.22 m); length 32 ft (9.75 m); height 12 ft 8 in (3.86 m); wing area 268 sq ft (24.90 m²)
Armament: none

MN ANG

A well-known type to many US Air Force officers, the T-28A Trojan was for many years the standard basic trainer, having replaced the ubiquitous T-6 Texan in the role. In Guard service it was used purely as a continuation trainer with four units to maintain proficiency and provide tricycle undercarriage conversion pending delivery of new jet fighters.

Northrop F-89 Scorpion

The design of this all-weather, two-seat interceptor was undertaken by Northrop in 1946 to provide the USAAF with a jet-powered successor to this company's P-61 Black Widow. Its prototype was first flown on 16 August 1948 and was followed by 1,190 production aircraft.

While on FAD during the Korean War, the 176th FIS, Wisconsin ANG, had first been assigned F-89As in April 1952. The 126th FIS, WI ANG, pioneered the use of Scorpions in the Air National Guard two and a half years later. Following the lead of this unit, 16 other ANG squadrons flew

Scorpions until 1969 when the 132nd FIS, Maine ANG, finally retired its last F-89s.

In ANG service, the Scorpions were used in five versions: the F-89B and C, with six nose-mounted 20-mm cannon; the F-89D, with armament consisting of FFARs in wingtip pods; the F-89H, armed with FFARs and Falcon guided missiles; and the F-89J, capable of launching two Genie unguided, nuclear-tipped rockets.

Squadron assignment
103rd PA (1959-1962), 107th MI (1956-1958), 109th MN (1957-1959), 116th WA (1957-1966), 123rd OR (1957-1966), 124th IA (1962-1969), 126th WI (1954-1962), 132nd ME (1957-1969), 134th VT (1958-1965), 171st MI (1956-1958), 172nd MI (1955-1958), 175th SD (1958-1960), 176th WI (1952 and 1954-1966), 178th ND (1958-1966), 179th MN (1959-1966), 186th MT (1956-1966) and 190th ID (1956-1959).

Specification
F-89D
Type: two-seat all-weather interceptor
Powerplant: two 7,200-lb (3266-kg) thrust Allison J35-A-41 turbojets
Performance: maximum speed 636 mph (1023 km/h); climb rate 8,360 ft/min (42 m/sec); service ceiling 49,200 ft (14995 m); normal range 850 miles (1370 km)
Weights: empty 25,194 lb (11428 kg); gross 42,241 lb (19160 kg)
Dimensions: span 59 ft 8 in (18.19 m); length 53 ft 10 in (16.41 m); height 17 ft 7 in (5.36 m); wing area 650 sq ft (60.39 m²)
Armament: 52 2.75-in FFARs

The Scorpion, unlovingly referred to as the 'Ramp Weight', had a long Guard career with interceptor squadrons. This F-89J served with the Montana ANG, and was preserved at the 186th FIS base at Great Falls. The J model was the last version, a rebuild of F-89Ds with Genie capability.

Peter B. Lewis

Republic F-47 (P-47) Thunderbolt

After providing excellent service as an escort fighter, the massive (by the standards of the time) Thunderbolt ended World War II as the outstanding American fighter-bomber. In the process, it earned an enviable reputation for its reliability and its ability to survive battle damage.

As 15,863 P-47s had been built between May 1941 and December 1945, Thunderbolts were available in large numbers to share responsibility with the Mustang in equipping fighter squadrons organized in the Guard after the war. Assigned to units on the East Coast, part

of the south, Puerto Rico, and Hawaii, late-model P-47Ds and P-47Ns were used as mission aircraft by 28 fighter squadrons. The first P-47 Guard squadron to be federally recognized was Connecticut's 118th, which received Thunderbolts in the second half of 1946, while Hawaii's 199th

gained, in 1954, the distinction of being the last US unit to fly the type.

Squadron assignment
101st MA (1946-1950), 104th MD (1946-1951), 105th TN (1947-1952), 118th CT (1947-1952), 119th NJ (1947-1952), 121st DC (1946-1949), 128th GA (1946-1952), 131st MA (1947-1951), 132nd ME (1947-1948), 133rd NH (1947-1952), 134th VT (1946-1950), 136th NY (1948-1952), 137th NY (1948-1952), 138th NY (1948-1950), 139th NY (1948-1951), 141st NJ (1949-1952, 142nd DE (1946-1950), 146th PA (1948-1951), 147th PA (1949-1951), 148th PA (1947-1950), 149th VA (1947-1953), 152nd RI (1948-1952), 153rd MS (1946-1952), 156th NC (1948-1949), 158th GA (1946-1948), 167th WV (1947-1951), 198th PR (1947-1954) and 199th HI (1947-1954).

Specification
F-47D
Type: single-seat fighter
Powerplant: one 2,300-hp Pratt & Whitney R-2800-59 radial engine
Performance: maximum speed 428 mph (689 km/h); climb rate 20,000 ft (6095 m) in 9 min; service ceiling 42,000 ft (12800 m); normal range 475 miles (765 km)
Weights: empty 10,000 lb (4536 kg); gross 19,400 lb (8800 kg)
Dimensions: span 40 ft 9 in (12.42 m); length 36 ft 1 in (11 m); height 14 ft 2 in (4.32 m); wing area 300 sq ft (27.87 m²)
Armament: eight 0.50-in guns, and up to 2,000 lb (908 kg) of bombs and/or rockets

Along with the Mustang, the Thunderbolt was the main ANG equipment immediately postwar. Here, F-47Ds of the 149th Fighter Squadron, Virginia ANG, line the ramp at Las Vegas AFB in 1950.

William T. Larkins

Republic F-84 Thunderjet

Having gained a strong reputation with the USAAF for its P-47 Thunderbolt, Republic was the recipient of one of the first contracts for jet fighters awarded by the War Department. The prototype which resulted from this contract, the XP-84, made its first flight on 28 February 1946, and was followed by 4,454 P/F-84s for the USAF and for NATO and other allied air forces.

At the time of the Korean War activation, early-model Thunderjets (F-84B/Cs), which had first been delivered to the 121st Fighter Squadron (Jet), DC ANG, had been assigned to no fewer than 14 Guard squadrons. Thus, the F-84 was outnumbering the other early jet, the Lockheed F-80, issued to the Air National Guard. Several of these squadrons converted to other types during the Korean War period, but nine other squadrons were assigned Thunderjets while they served on active duty. After the Korean War, Thunderjets were operated by 10 squadrons until the last three units completed, in 1958, their conversion to more modern equipment.

Squadron assignment

101st MA (1950-1951), 107th MI (1950-1952), 112th OH (1955-1958), 116th WA (1950-1951), 118th CT (1953-1956), 121st DC (1949-1951), 127th KS (1950-1952), 128th GA (1950-1952 and 1952-1955), 138th NY (1950), 142nd DE (1950-1951), 152nd RI (1955), 158th GA (1950-1952 and 1953-1957), 162nd OH (1955-1957), 164th OH (1954-1957), 166th OH (1950-1952 and 1955-1957), 171st MI (1950-1952), 174th IA (1950-1951 and 1956-1958) and 197th AZ (1950-1952).

Specification
F-84E
Type: single-seat fighter
Powerplant: one 4,900-lb (2223-kg) thrust Allison J35-A-17 turbojet
Performance: maximum speed 613 mph (986 km/h); climb rate 6,060 ft/min (31 m/sec); service ceiling 43,220 ft (13175 m); normal range 1,485 miles (2390 km)
Weights: empty 10,205 lb (4629 kg); gross 22,463 lb (10189 kg)
Dimensions: span 36 ft 5 in (11.10 m); length 38 ft 6 in (11.73 m); height 12 ft 7 in (3.84 m); wing area 260 sq ft (24.15 m²)
Armament: six 0.50-in guns and up to 4,000 lb (1816 kg) of external stores

Above: The 121st FS(Jet) was the first ANG squadron to fly the Thunderjet, acquiring the F-84C in late 1949 and flying them until 1951, when F-94Bs were delivered. F-84B/Cs were pure fighters.

Below: Compared to the F-84B/C, the F-84E had a longer fuselage, uprated engine, Sperry radar gunsight and provision for underwing bombs. These aircraft were employed by the 162nd FIS.

Republic F-84F Thunderstreak

Initially envisioned as a fairly straightforward development of the F-84, with swept wing and tail surfaces replacing the straight surfaces of the Thunderjet, the Thunderstreak evolved into a virtually new aircraft in spite of its designation in the F-84 series. Even though its prototype had first flown on 3 June 1950, the F-84F was not ready for service use until four years later. Even then, the type did not meet fully the expectation of the USAF and,

within eight months of receiving its first F-84Fs in January 1954, SAC began transferring virtually new aircraft to Pennsylvania's 146th FBS.

Fortunately, the long gestation of the Thunderstreak finally resulted in a reliable and fully combat-worthy tactical fighter. Thus, over an 18-year period, F-84Fs served with 24 ANG squadrons in the interceptor (limited use only), special delivery (nuclear) and tactical fighter roles.

Highlight of this long service was the deployment to Europe of four TFSs during the Berlin Crisis activation. The last Guard F-84Fs were phased out by Illinois' 170th TFS and Ohio's 164th TFS in the first quarter of 1972.

Squadron assignment
101st MA (1964-1971), 103rd PA (1955), 108th IL (1955-1961), 110th MO (1957-1962), 112th OH (1959-1970), 113th IN (1958-1962 and 1964-1971), 119th NJ (1958-1962), 124th IA (1969-1971), 128th GA (1955-1960), 131st MA (1964-1971), 141st NJ (1958-1962), 146th PA (1954-1957), 147th PA (1955-1958), 149th VA (1958-1971), 152nd AZ (1957-1958), 158th GA (1957-1962), 162nd OH (1957-1960), 163rd IN (1958-1962 and 1964-1971), 164th OH (1957-1972), 166th OH (1957-1962), 168th IL (1955-1958), 169th IL (1958-1969), 170th IL (1955-1972) and 182nd TX (1969-1971).

Specification
F-84F
Type: single-seat tactical fighter

Republic F-84F (continued)

Powerplant: one 7,220-lb (3275-kg)
thrust Wright J65-W-3 turbojet
Performance: maximum speed
695 mph (1118 km/h); climb rate 8,200 ft/
min (42 m/sec); service ceiling 46,000 ft
(14020 m); normal range 1,620 miles
(2605 km)
Weights: empty 13,645 lb (6189 kg);
gross 28,000 lb (12700 kg)
Dimensions: span 33 ft 7¼ in
(10.24 m); length 43 ft 4¾ in (13.22 m);
height 14 ft 4¾ in (4.39 m); wing area
325 sq ft (30.19 m²)
Armament: six 0.50-in guns and up to
6,000 lb (2722 kg) of external stores

*The tough and pugnacious
Thunderstreak was a Guard
stalwart throughout the late 1950s
and 1960s, performing a number of
missions including interception,
fighter-bomber and nuclear strike.
This F-84F-35-GK was on the
strength of the 110th TFS, Missouri
ANG.*

Courtesy of Cloud 9 Photography

Republic RF-84F Thunderflash

With wingroot intakes replacing the nose
intake of its fighter version, and photographic cameras in an elongated nose, the
RF-84F reconnaissance version of Republic's first swept-wing aircraft was operated by 11 ANG squadrons, beginning in
1956 with the 160th TRS, Alabama ANG,
and ending in 1972 with the 173rd TRS,
Nebraska ANG. In addition, the 113th and
163rd Tactical Fighter Squadrons, Indiana
ANG, flew RF-84Fs in 1962-64 when their
Thunderstreaks were retained temporarily by the USAF for assignment to active-
duty squadrons.

Squadron assignment

106th AL (1957-1971), 107th MI (1958-
1971), 113th IN (1962-1964), 153rd MS
(1957-1970), 154th AR (1957-1958), 155th
TN (1956-1961), 160th AL (1956-1971),
163rd IN (1962-1964), 171st MI (1958-
1971), 173rd NE (1964-1972), 174th IA
(1958-1961), 180th MO (1958-1962), and
184th AR (1957-1970).

Specification
RF-84F
Type: single-seat ractical
reconnaissance aircraft
Powerplant: one 7,800-lb (3538-kg)
thrust Wright J65-W-7 turbojet
Performance: maximum speed
679 mph (1093 km/h); climb rate
7,900 ft/min (40 m/sec); service ceiling
46,000 ft (14020 m); normal range
1,800 miles (2895 km)
Weights: empty 14,025 lb (6362 kg);
gross 27,000 lb (12247 kg)
Dimensions: span 33 ft 7¼ in
(10.24 m); length 47 ft 7¾ in (14.51 m);
height 15 ft (4.57 m); wing area 325 sq ft
(30.19 m²)
Armament: four 0.50-in guns

*The RF-84F Thunderflash was a
mainstay of ANG tactical
reconnaissance squadrons,
including the 172nd TRS.*

Peter B. Lewis

Republic F-105 Thunderchief

Affectionately nicknamed 'Thud' and, less
kindly, 'Lead Sled', the F-105 earned high
marks while serving with the USAF during
the Southeast Asia War. Originally conceived as a supersonic strike aircraft carrying a nuclear bomb in an internal bomb-
bay, the Thunderchief was developed into
an effective tactical fighter carrying
14,000 lb of external stores. The F-105 prototype first flew on 22 October 1955, and
its F-105B version entered USAF service
in 1958. Main production variants were
the single-seat F-105D and two-seat
F-105F. The F-105G was a later development of the F-105F fitted to serve in the
'Wild Weasel' defense-suppression role.

In Guard service, F-105Bs were operated by two New Jersey units (initial
assignment being to the 141st TFS in
1964), F-105D/Fs by three squadrons, and
F-105G/Fs by Georgia's 128th TFS (which
phased out the type in 1983).

*Continuing Republic's reputation
for producing tough, no-nonsense
fighter-bombers, the 'Thud' only
saw limited Guard service. This is
an F-105B, which flew with the 141st
TFS from McGuire AFB.*

Don Spering

Lindsay Peacock

Squadron assignment
119th NJ (1970-1973), 121st DC (1971-1981), 127th KS (1971-1979), 128th GA (1979-1983), 141st NJ (1964-1981) and 149th VA (1971-1982).

Specification
F-105D
Type: single-seat tactical fighter
Powerplant: one 24,500-lb (11113-kg) thrust Pratt & Whitney J75-P-19W turbojet
Performance: maximum speed

1,390 mph (2237 km/h); climb rate 34,500 ft/min (175 m/sec); service ceiling 52,000 ft (15850 m); normal range 1,840 miles (2960 km)
Weights: empty 27,500 lb (12474 kg); gross 52,546 lb (23834 kg)
Dimensions: span 34 ft 11¼ in (10.65 m); length 64 ft 3 in (19.58 m);

The last Thunderchiefs in service were the F-105G 'Wild Weasel' aircraft of the 128th TFS.

height 19 ft 8 in (5.99 m); wing area 385 sq ft (35.77 m²)
Armament: one 20-mm cannon and up to 14,000 lb (6350 kg) of external stores

Sikorsky CH-3 and HH-3 'Jolly Green Giant'

During the Southeast Asia War, the USAF had an urgent need for a long-range helicopter to rescue downed aircrew in the face of enemy opposition. To meet this specialized requirement, CH-3C twin-turbine helicopters were specially modified. Designated HH-3Es, these helicopters were heavily armored, fitted with an in-flight-refueling probe, external drop tanks and self-sealing internal tanks, and had provision for defensive armament.

After HH-3Es had been supplemented in USAF service with larger and heavier HH-53B/Cs, the type became available for ANG use and, beginning in 1975, was assigned to squadrons in California and New York along with supporting Lockheed HC-130P tankers. The two squadrons also operated a few CH-3Es lacking the air-refueling probe and other features peculiar to the rescue version.

Squadron assignment
102nd NY (1975-1990) and 129th CA (1975-1990).

Specification
HH-3E
Type: search and rescue helicopter
Powerplant: two 1,400-shp General Electric T58-GE-10 turboshafts
Performance: maximum speed 162 mph (261 km/h); climb rate 1,310 ft/

min (6.7 m/sec); service ceiling 12,000 ft (3660 m); normal range 625 miles (1005 km)
Weights: empty 13,255 lb (6012 kg); gross 18,000 lb (8165 kg)
Dimensions: rotor diameter 62 ft

(18.90 m); fuselage length 57 ft 3 in (17.45 m); height 18 ft 1 in (5.51 m)
Armament: two 0.30-in flexible guns

The ANG has in recent years maintained a rescue squadron on each coastline, and from 1975 these were equipped with the HH-3E. Here, an example from the 129th ARRS, CA ANG, refuels from one of the unit's HC-130 tankers.

René J. Francillon

Sikorsky HH-60 Pave Hawk

To replace the HH-3E in service with Air Rescue Squadrons, the Guard ordered in 1987 a specially developed version of the Army's UH-60A assault transport helicopter. Principal differences included the fitting of a refueling probe on the starboard side of the forward fuselage, auxiliary tanks in the rear of the cabin, radar in the nose, and a rescue winch. Initially designated MH-60G but redesignated HH-60G in the fall of 1991, the type was delivered to Alaska's 210th ARS in 1990.

Squadron assignment
102nd NY (from 1990), 129th CA (from 1990) and 210th AK (from 1990).

Specification
HH-60G
Type: search and rescue helicopter
Powerplant: two 1,543-shp General Electric T700-GE-700 turboshafts
Performance: maximum speed 192 mph (309 km/h); climb rate 450 ft/min (2.3 m/sec); service ceiling 19,000 ft (5790 m); normal range 375 miles (605 km)
Weights: empty 10,624 lb (4819 kg);

Replacing the HH-3E with the ANG rescue units is the HH-60G, similar to the active-duty MH-60G but with some Special Operations equipment deleted.

gross 20,250 lb (9185 kg)
Dimensions: rotor diameter 53 ft 8 in (16.36 m); fuselage length 50 ft 0¾ in (15.26 m); height 16 ft 10 in (5.13 m)
Armament: two 0.30-in Miniguns

Stinson O-49

To complement the relatively high-performance O-47 and O-52 observation aircraft procured for the observation squadrons during the late 1930s, the National Guard Bureau joined the Army Air Corps in ordering Stinson O-49s for use as artillery spotters and army cooperation aircraft. The first were delivered just when the Guard squadrons were being called to active duty.

Squadron assignment
101st (MA), 102nd (NY), 103rd (PA), 104th (MD), 105th (TN), 106th (AL), 107th (MI), 108th (IL), 109th (MN), 110th (MO), 111th (TX), 112th (OH), 113th (IN), 115th (CA), 116th (WA), 118th (CT), 119th (NJ), 120th (CO), 125th (OK), 153rd (MS) and 154th (AR).

Specification
O-49
Type: two-seat light observation monoplane
Powerplant: one 295-hp Lycoming R-680-9 radial engine

A Stinson O-49 of the 122nd Observation Squadron, LA ANG.

Performance: maximum speed 130 mph (209 km/h); climb rate 10,000 ft (3050 m) in 22.1 min; service ceiling 14,000 ft (4265 m); normal range

285 miles (460 km)
Weights: empty 2,595 lb (1177 kg); gross 3,325 lb (1508 kg)
Dimensions: span 50 ft 11 in

(15.52 m); length 33 ft 2 in (10.11 m); height 10 ft 2 in (3.10 m); wing area 329 sq ft (30.57 m²)
Armament: none

Thomas-Morse O-19

Development of a derivative of the Douglas O-2 observation biplanes, with corrugated sheet metal fuselage construction in place of the original fabric-covered fuselage, had been entrusted to the Thomas-Morse Company in 1925. Following the Liberty-powered XO-6 and XO-6B prototypes, Thomas-Morse was awarded several contracts for Wasp-powered O-19s between 1928 and 1931. A few of these aircraft were assigned to Colorado's 120th Observation Squadron during the late 1930s.

Squadron assignment
120th (CO).

Specification
O-19B
Type: two-seat observation biplane
Powerplant: one 450-hp Pratt & Whitney R-1340-7 radial engine
Performance: maximum speed 137 mph (220 km/h); climb rate 10,000 ft (3050 m) in 11.1 min; service ceiling 20,500 ft (6250 m); normal range

462 miles (745 km)
Weights: empty 2,722 lb (1235 kg); gross 3,800 lb (1724 kg)
Dimensions: span 39 ft 9 in (12.12 m); length 28 ft 4 in (8.64 m); height 10 ft 6 in (3.20 m); wing area 348 sq ft (32.33 m²)
Armament: one forward-firing 0.30-in gun and one rear-firing flexible 0.30-in gun

One of the primary roles of the Air National Guard has been the defense of the United States, with many Fighter Interceptor Squadrons (now just Fighter Squadrons) assigned to the task. Phantoms played their part in the 1980s with several squadrons, including the 123rd FIS from Portland, Oregon, which had the distinction of retiring the F-4C from service. This example is in full air defense configuration, with four Sparrows, four Sidewinders and a centerline cannon pod.

James Benson

Tables

INITIAL SQUADRON DESIGNATION	UNIT	STATE	ACTIVATION DATE
109th Squadron	34th Division	Minnesota NG	17 Jan 1921
	Redesignated 109th Obs Sqn on 25 Jan 1923		
104th Squadron	29th Division	Maryland NG	29 Jun 1921
	Redesignated 104th Obs Sqn on 25 Jan 1923		
137th Squadron	Corps Aviation	Indiana NG	1 Aug 1921
	Redesignated 113th Squadron and assigned to 38th Division on 3 Jan 1923, and 113th Obs Sqn on 25 Jan 1923		
102nd Squadron	27th Division	New York NG	17 Nov 1921
	Redesignated 102nd Obs Sqn on 25 Jan 1923		
101st Squadron	26th Division	Massachusetts NG	18 Nov 1921
	Redesignated 101st Obs Sqn on 25 Jan 1923		
136th Squadron	Corps Aviation	Tennessee NG	4 Dec 1921
	Redesignated 136th Obs Sqn on 25 Jan 1923, and then 105th Obs Sqn when assigned to the 30th Division on 16 Jan 1924		
135th Squadron	Corps Aviation	Alabama NG	21 Jan 1922
	Redesignated 135th Obs Sqn on 25 Jan 1923; 114th Obs Sqn when assigned to the 39th Division on 1 May 1923; and 106th Obs Sqn when assigned to the 31st Division on 16 Jan 1924		
110th Observation Squadron	35th Division	Missouri NG	23 Jun 1923
120th Observation Squadron	45th Division	Colorado NG	27 Jun 1923

INITIAL SQUADRON DESIGNATION	UNIT	STATE	ACTIVATION DATE
111th Observation Squadron	36th Division	Texas NG	29 Jun 1923
118th Observation Squadron	43rd Division	Connecticut NG	1 Nov 1923
115th Observation Squadron	40th Division	California NG	16 Jun 1924
103rd Observation Squadron	28th Division	Pennsylvania NG	27 Jun 1924
116th Observation Squadron	41st Division	Washington NG	6 Aug 1924
154th Observation Squadron	Corps Aviation	Arkansas NG	24 Oct 1925
107th Observation Squadron	32nd Division	Michigan NG	7 May 1926
112th Observation Squadron	37th Division	Ohio NG	20 Jun 1927
108th Observation Squadron	33rd Division	Illinois NG	1 Jul 1927
119th Observation Squadron	44th Division	New Jersey NG	30 Jan 1930
153rd Observation Squadron		Mississippi NG	27 Sep 1939
152nd Observation Squadron		Rhode Island NG	13 Oct 1939
126th Observation Squadron		Wisconsin NG	12 Nov 1940
125th Observation Squadron		Oklahoma NG	10 Feb 1941
124th Observation Squadron		Iowa NG	25 Feb 1941
122nd Observation Squadron		Louisiana NG	2 Mar 1941
121st Observation Squadron		DC NG	10 Apr 1941
123rd Observation Squadron		Oregon NG	18 Apr 1941
128th Observation Squadron		Georgia NG	1 May 1941
127th Observation Squadron		Kansas NG	4 Aug 1941

FISCAL YEAR	NUMBER OF FEDERALLY-RECOGNIZED SQUADRONS (30 June)	MANPOWER (30 June) OFFICERS	ENLISTED PERSONNEL	TOTAL	NUMBER OF AIRCRAFT ON STRENGTH	NUMBER OF FLIGHT HOURS PER YEAR
1921	2	20	90	110	0	0
1922	7	136	643	779	53	N.A.
1923	10	144	834	978	N.A.	N.A.
1924	13	240	1,269	1,509	N.A.	N.A.
1925	14	264	1,365	1,629	N.A.	N.A.
1926	16	239	1,307	1,546	N.A.	11,954
1927	17	330	1,636	1,966	147	15,706
1928	18	347	1,689	2,036	120	23,991
1929	18	328	1,664	1,992	136	25,375
1930	19	357	1,789	2,146	159	28,774
1931	19	362	1,853	2,215	180	39,341

FISCAL YEAR	NUMBER OF FEDERALLY-RECOGNIZED SQUADRONS (30 June)	MANPOWER (30 June) OFFICERS	ENLISTED PERSONNEL	TOTAL	NUMBER OF AIRCRAFT ON STRENGTH	NUMBER OF FLIGHT HOURS PER YEAR
1932	19	394	1,911	2,305	184	33,717
1933	19	393	1,904	2,297	N.A.	33,571
1934	19	387	1,891	2,278	113	33,059
1935	19	393	1,919	2,312	N.A.	40,214
1936	19	413	1,922	2,335	N.A.	45,852
1937	19	417	1,882	2,299	N.A.	N.A.
1938	19	430	1,910	2,340	N.A.	N.A.
1939	19	456	1,939	2,395	N.A.	N.A.
1940	21	469	2,426	2,895	N.A.	N.A.
1941	28	489	2,937	3,426	N.A.	N.A.

SOURCE: 1921 through 1932 – Annual Reports of the Chief of the Militia Bureau.
1933 through 1941 – Annual Reports of the Chief of the National Guard Bureau.

DATE	SQUADRON	INITIAL ASSIGNMENT DURING ACTIVE DUTY	SUBSEQUENT ASSIGNMENTS TO THEATERS OF OPERATIONS
16 Sep 1940	105th Obs Sqn, TN NG	Fourth Corps Area	ZI
16 Sep 1940	116th Obs Sqn, WA NG	Ninth Corps Area	ZI
16 Sep 1940	119th Obs Sqn, NJ NG	Second Corps Area	ZI
16 Sep 1940	154th Obs Sqn, AR NG	Eighth Corps Area	MTO, Fifteenth Air Force
15 Oct 1940	102nd Obs Sqn, NY NG	Second Corps Area	ZI
15 Oct 1940	107th Obs Sqn, MI NG	Fourth Corps Area	ETO, Eighth and Ninth Air Forces
15 Oct 1940	153rd Obs Sqn, MS NG	Fourth Corps Area	ETO, Ninth Air Force and IX Tactical Air Command
25 Nov 1940	101st Obs Sqn, MA NG	First Corps Area	ETO, Ninth Air Force and IX, XIX and XXIX Tactical Air Commands
25 Nov 1940	106th Obs Sqn, AL NG	Fourth Corps Area	PTO, Thirteenth Air Force
25 Nov 1940	111th Obs Sqn, TX NG	Eighth Corps Area	MTO, Twelfth and Fifteenth Air Forces
25 Nov 1940	112th Obs Sqn, OH NG	Fourth Corps Area	ETO, Ninth Air Force
25 Nov 1940	152nd Obs Sqn, RI NG	First Corps Area	MTO, Fifteenth Air Force
23 Dec 1940	110th Obs Sqn, MO NG	VII Army Corps	PTO, Fifth Air Force
6 Jan 1941	120th Obs Sqn, CO NG	Third Army	ZI
17 Jan 1941	113th Obs Sqn, IN NG	V Army Corps	ZI
3 Feb 1941	104th Obs Sqn, MD NG	II Army Corps	ZI
3 Feb 1941	108th Obs Sqn, IL NG	Second Army	Canal Zone
10 Feb 1941	109th Obs Sqn, MN NG	V Army Corps	ETO, Eighth and Ninth Air Forces
17 Feb 1941	103rd Obs Sqn, PA NG	II Army Corps	CBI, Tenth Air Force
24 Feb 1941	118th Obs Sqn, CT NG	IV Army Corps	CBI, Tenth and Fourteenth Air Forces
3 Mar 1941	115th Obs Sqn, CA NG	III Army Corps	CBI, Tenth Air Force
2 Jun 1941	126th Obs Sqn, WI NG	II Army Corps	ETO, Ninth Air Force and XII Tactical Air Command
1 Sep 1941	121st Obs Sqn, DC NG	65th Observation Group	MTO, Twelfth Air Force; and ETO, Ninth Air Force
15 Sep 1941	123rd Obs Sqn, OR NG	70th Observation Group	CBI, Tenth and Fourteenth Air Forces
15 Sep 1941	124th Obs Sqn, IA NG	II Air Support Command	ZI
15 Sep 1941	125th Obs Sqn, OK NG	68th Observation Group	ETO, Ninth Air Force and XXIX Tactical Air Command
15 Sep 1941	128th Obs Sqn, GA NG	II Air Support Command	MTO, Fifteenth Air Force
1 Oct 1941	122nd Obs Sqn, LA NG	68th Observation Group	MTO, Fifteenth Air Force
6 Oct 1941	127th Obs Sqn, KS NG	68th Observation Group	CBI, 2nd Air Commando Group; and PTO, Thirteenth and Seventh Air Forces

TABLE 4 ACTIVATED OBSERVATION SQUADRONS BASE & ASSIGNED AIRCRAFT 30 NOVEMBER 1941

	O-31B	O-38 B/D/E	O-43A	O-46A	O-47 A/B	O-49	O-52	O-57	O-58A/B	O-59	Other Types of Aircraft	TOTAL
101st Observation Squadron, Camp Edwards, MA	—	—	—	4	4	3	—	—	—	4	—	15
102nd Observation Squadron, Reilly Field, Ft McClellan, AL	—	—	—	6	2	3	—	1	—	—	1×C-45A	13
103rd Observation Squadron, Harrisburg, PA	—	—	—	6	3	3	—	1	—	—	—	13
104th Observation Squadron, Detrick Field, Frederick, MD	—	—	—	6	3	3	—	—	—	6	—	18
105th Observation Squadron, Columbia AAB, SC	—	1	—	—	1	5	10	—	—	—	—	17
106th Observation Squadron, Birmingham MAP, AL	—	—	—	—	9	3	—	—	—	—	—	12
107th Observation Squadron, Camp Beauregard, Alexandria, LA	—	—	—	—	5	1	—	—	—	—	1×C-45A	7
108th Observation Squadron, Chicago MAP, IL	1	—	—	—	7	3	3	—	—	—	—	14
109th Observation Squadron, Camp Beauregard, Alexandria, LA	—	—	—	—	7	2	—	—	6	—	—	15
110th Observation Squadron, Adams Field, Little Rock, AR	—	—	—	—	7	3	—	—	—	—	—	10
111th Observation Squadron, Brownwood MAP, TX	—	—	5	—	4	3	4	—	—	6	—	22
112th Observation Squadron, Pope Field, Ft Bragg, NC	—	—	—	—	8	3	—	1	—	—	—	12
113th Observation Squadron, Key Field, Meridian, MS	—	—	—	—	4	1	1	—	—	—	—	6
115th Observation Squadron, Paso Robles, CA	—	1	—	—	5	3	—	—	—	—	1×BC-1A	10
116th Observation Squadron, Gray Field, Ft Lewis, WA	—	—	—	—	8	3	—	—	—	—	—	11
118th Observation Squadron, Jacksonville MAP, FL	—	—	—	7	3	3	—	4	1	5	1×C-45A	24
119th Observation Squadron, Newark AP, NJ	—	—	—	—	3	3	10	—	—	—	—	16
120th Observation Squadron, Biggs Field, Ft Bliss, TX	—	—	—	—	7	3	—	—	—	—	—	10
121st Observation Squadron, Columbia AAB, SC	—	2	—	1	1	—	—	—	4	—	1×AT-6A	9
122nd Observation Squadron, New Orleans AAB, LA	—	3	—	1	1	—	—	—	—	—	1×BC-1A	6
123rd Observation Squadron, Gray Field, Ft Lewis, WA	—	—	—	1	—	—	—	—	—	—	1×BC-1A	2
124th Observation Squadron, Ft Leavenworth, KS	—	2	—	—	1	—	—	—	—	—	1×BC-1A	4
125th Observation Squadron, Post Field, Ft Sill, OK	—	2	—	—	1	—	—	—	—	—	1×BC-1A	4
126th Observation Squadron, Ft Dix, NJ	—	—	—	1	3	—	—	—	—	4	1×BC-1A	9
127th Observation Squadron, Ft Leavenworth, KS	—	1	—	1	—	—	—	—	—	—	1×BC-1A	3
128th Observation Squadron, Lawson Field, Ft Benning, GA	—	2	—	1	—	—	—	—	—	—	1×BC-1A	4
152nd Observation Squadron, Ft Devens, MA	—	—	—	—	2	3	9	—	6	—	1×BC-1A	21
153rd Observation Squadron, Key Field, Meridian, MS	—	—	—	—	3	3	4	—	1	—	—	11
154th Observation Squadron, Post Field, Ft Sill, OK	—	1	—	—	10	2	—	3	—	—	—	16
National Guard Bureau, Bolling Field, DC	—	—	—	—	1	—	—	1	—	—	1×A-17A 1×C-37 1×C-56	5
TOTAL	**1**	**15**	**5**	**35**	**113**	**59**	**41**	**11**	**18**	**25**	**16**	**339**

SOURCE: National Guard Aviation, 1940-41; Dr. Robert Krauskopf; AAHS Journal, Vol. 5, No. 1, Spring 1960

TABLE 5 PROPOSED ALLOTMENT OF NATIONAL GUARD AIR UNITS FISCAL YEAR 1946*

FIRST AIR FORCE
51st Wing, Boston, MA
101st Fighter Group, Augusta, ME
132nd Fighter Squadron, Bangor, ME
133rd Fighter Squadron, Manchester, NH
134th Fighter Squadron, Burlington, VT
102nd Fighter Group, Boston, MA
101st Fighter Squadron, Boston, MA
131st Fighter Squadron, Springfield, MA
103rd Fighter Group, Hartford, CT
118th Fighter Squadron, Windsor Locks, CT
152nd Fighter Squadron, Providence, RI
52nd Wing, New York, NY
106th Bombardment Group, New York, NY
102nd Bombardment Squadron, New York, NY
114th Bombardment Squadron, New York, NY
107th Fighter Group, Buffalo, NY
136th Fighter Squadron, Buffalo, NY
137th Fighter Squadron, Rochester, NY
138th Fighter Squadron, Syracuse, NY
139th Fighter Squadron, Albany, NY

108th Fighter Group, Newark, NJ
119th Fighter Squadron, Newark, NJ
141st Fighter Squadron, Trenton, NJ
142nd Fighter Squadron, Wilmington, DE

SECOND AIR FORCE
56th Wing, Chicago, IL
126th Bombardment Group (Composite), Chicago, IL
108th Bombardment Squadron, Chicago, IL
168th Bombardment Squadron, Chicago, IL
169th Fighter Squadron, Peoria, IL
170th Fighter Squadron, Springfield, IL
127th Fighter Group (Composite), Detroit, MI
107th Bombardment Squadron, Detroit, MI
171st Fighter Squadron, Detroit, MI
172nd Fighter Squadron, Battle Creek, MI
128th Fighter Group, Milwaukee, WI
126th Fighter Squadron, Milwaukee, WI
176th Fighter Squadron, Madison, WI
57th Wing, St Louis, MO
131st Fighter Group, St Louis, MO

110th Fighter Squadron, St Louis, MO
180th Fighter Squadron, Kansas City, MO
132nd Fighter Group, Des Moines, IA
124th Fighter Squadron, Des Moines, IA
174th Fighter Squadron, Sioux City, IA
175th Fighter Squadron, Sioux Falls, SD
133rd Fighter Group, St Paul, MN
109th Fighter Squadron, St Paul, MN
178th Fighter Squadron, Fargo, ND
179th Fighter Squadron, Duluth, MN
59th Wing, Denver, CO
140th Fighter Group, Denver, CO
120th Fighter Squadron, Denver, CO
127th Fighter Squadron, Wichita, KS
173rd Fighter Squadron, Omaha, NE
187th Fighter Squadron, Cheyenne, WY

FOURTH AIR FORCE
60th Wing, Seattle, WA
142nd Fighter Group, Portland, OR
116th Fighter Squadron, Spokane, WA

123rd Fighter Squadron, Portland, OR
186th Fighter Squadron, Butte, MT
190th Fighter Squadron, Boise, ID
61st Wing, San Francisco, CA
144th Fighter Group, San Francisco, CA
191st Fighter Squadron, Salt Lake City, UT
192nd Fighter Squadron, Reno, NV
194th Fighter Squadron, Oakland, CA
199th Fighter Squadron, Honolulu, TH
62nd Wing, Los Angeles, CA
146th Fighter Group (Composite), Los Angeles, CA
115th Bombardment Squadron, Los Angeles, CA
195th Fighter Squadron, Los Angeles, CA
196th Fighter Squadron, San Diego, CA
197th Fighter Squadron, Phoenix, AZ

TENTH AIR FORCE
58th Wing, Dallas, TX
136th Fighter Group, Dallas, TX
111th Fighter Squadron, Houston, TX
122nd Fighter Squadron, New Orleans, LA
181st Fighter Squadron, Dallas, TX
182nd Fighter Squadron, San Antonio, TX
137th Fighter Group, Tulsa, OK

125th Fighter Squadron, Tulsa, OK
154th Fighter Squadron, Little Rock, AR
185th Fighter Squadron, Oklahoma City, OK
188th Fighter Squadron, Albuquerque, NM

ELEVENTH AIR FORCE
53rd Wing, Philadelphia, PA
111th Bombardment Group, Philadelphia, PA
103rd Bombardment Squadron, Philadelphia, PA
117th Bombardment Squadron, Philadelphia, PA
112th Fighter Group, Pittsburgh, PA
146th Fighter Squadron, Pittsburgh, PA
147th Fighter Squadron, Reading, PA
148th Fighter Squadron, Scranton, PA
113th Fighter Group, Washington, DC
104th Fighter Squadron, Baltimore, MD
121st Fighter Squadron, Washington, DC
149th Fighter Squadron, Richmond, VA
55th Wing, Columbus, OH
121st Fighter Group (Composite), Columbus, OH
112th Bombardment Squadron, Cleveland, OH
162nd Fighter Squadron, Columbus, OH
164th Fighter Squadron, Cincinnati, OH
166th Fighter Squadron, Toledo, OH

122nd Fighter Group, Indianapolis, IN
113th Fighter Squadron, Indianapolis, IN
163rd Fighter Squadron, Ft Wayne, IN
123rd Fighter Group, Louisville, KY
165th Fighter Squadron, Louisville, KY
167th Fighter Squadron, Charleston, WV

FOURTEENTH AIR FORCE
54th Wing, Atlanta, GA
116th Fighter Group, Atlanta, GA
128th Fighter Squadron, Atlanta, GA
157th Fighter Squadron, Columbia, SC
158th Fighter Squadron, Savannah, GA
159th Fighter Squadron, Miami, FL
198th Fighter Squadron, Puerto Rico, PR
117th Fighter Group (Composite), Birmingham, AL
106th Fighter Squadron, Birmingham, AL
153rd Fighter Squadron, Meridian, MS
160th Fighter Squadron, Mobile, AL
118th Fighter Group, Nashville, TN
105th Fighter Squadron, Nashville, TN
155th Fighter Squadron, Memphis, TN
156th Fighter Squadron, Charlotte, NC

*When these units were eventually organized, several were federally recognized with a different designation or location (*e.g.,* the proposed 180th Fighter Squadron to be based in Kansas City, MO, received federal recognition on 22 August 1946 as the 180th Bombardment Squadron stationed at St Joseph, MO).

TABLE 6   POST-WORLD WAR II ANG FLYING SQUADRONS   CHRONOLOGICAL LISTING BY DATE OF FEDERAL RECOGNITION

INITIAL SQUADRON DESIGNATION	CURRENT SQUADRON DESIGNATION	STATE	DATE OF FEDERAL RECOGNITION	LINEAGE
120th FS (SE)	120th FS/140th FW	CO	30 June 1946	120th Obs Sqn, CO NG
173rd FS (SE)	173rd RS/155th RG	NE	26 July 1946	401st FS, 370th FG, 9th AF
118th FS (SE)	118th FS/103rd FG	CT	7 Aug 1946	118th Obs Sqn, CT NG
187th FS (SE)	187th AS/153rd AG	WY	11 Aug 1946	402nd FS, 370th FG, 9th AF
134th FS (SE)	134th FS/158th FG	VT	14 Aug 1946	530th FS, 311th FG, 14th AF
104th FS (SE)	104th FS/175th FG	MD	17 Aug 1946	104th Obs Sqn, MD NG
128th FS (SE)	128th FS/116th FW	GA	20 Aug 1946	128th Obs Sqn, GA NG
180th BS (L)	180th AS/139th AG	MO	22 Aug 1946	438th BS, 319th BG, 7th AF
101st FS (SE)	101st FS/102nd FW	MA	23 Aug 1946	101st Obs Sqn, MA NG
124th FS (SE)	124th FS/132nd FW	IA	23 Aug 1946	124th Obs Sqn, IA NG
154th FS (SE)	154th TS/189th AG	AR	24 Aug 1946	154th Obs Sqn, AR NG
123rd FS (SE)	123rd FS/142nd FG	OR	30 Aug 1946	123rd Obs Sqn, OR NG
142nd FS (SE)	142nd AS/166th AG	DE	6 Sep 1946	342nd FS, 348th FG, 5th AF
127th FS (SE)	127th FS/184th FG	KS	7 Sep 1946	127th Obs Sqn, KS NG
153rd FS (SE)	153rd ARS/186th ARG	MS	12 Sep 1946	153rd Obs Sqn, MS NG
109th FS (SE)	109th AS/133rd AW	MN	14 Sep 1946	109th Obs Sqn, MN NG
175th FS (SE)	175th FS/114th FG	SD	20 Sep 1946	387th FS, 365th FG, 9th AF
110th FS (SE)	110th FS/131st FW	MO	23 Sep 1946	110th Obs Sqn, MO NG
107th BS (L)	107th FS/127th FW	MI	29 Sep 1946	107th Obs Sqn, MI NG
195th FS (SE)	Inactivated in Sep 1974	CA	29 Sep 1946	410th FS, 373rd FG, 9th AF
121st FS (SE)	121st FS/113th FW	DC	2 Oct 1946	121st Obs Sqn, DC NG
115th BS (L)	115th AS/146th AW	CA	8 Oct 1946	115th Obs Sqn, CA NG
158th FS (SE)	158th AS/165th AG	GA	13 Oct 1946	351st FS, 353rd FG, 8th AF
190th FS (SE)	190th FS/124th FG	ID	13 Oct 1946	405th FS, 371st FG, 9th AF
199th FS (SE)	199th FS/154th CG	HI	4 Nov 1946	464th FS, 507th FG, 20th AF
196th FS (SE)	196th RS/163rd RG	CA	9 Nov 1946	411th FS, 373rd FG, 9th AF
191st FS (SE)	191st ARS/151st ARG	UT	18 Nov 1946	407th FS, 372nd FG, 3rd AF
106th BS (L)	106th RS/117th RW	AL	26 Nov 1946	106th Obs Sqn, AL NG
112th BS (L)	112th FS/180th FG	OH	2 Dec 1946	112th Obs Sqn, OH NG
174th FS (SE)	174th FS/185th FG	IA	2 Dec 1946	386th FS, 365th FG, 9th AF
122nd BS (L)	122nd FS/159th FG	LA	5 Dec 1946	122nd Obs Sqn, LA NG
157th FS (SE)	157th FS/169th FG	SC	9 Dec 1946	350th FS, 353rd FG, 8th AF
197th FS (SE)	197th ARS/161st ARG	AZ	12 Dec 1946	412th FS, 373rd FG, 9th AF
155th FS (SE)	155th AS/164th AG	TN	23 Dec 1946	359th FS, 356th FG, 8th AF
178th FS (SE)	178th FS/119th FG	ND	16 Jan 1947	392nd FS, 367th FG, 9th AF
108th BS (L)	108th ARS/126th ARW	IL	19 Jan 1947	108th Obs Sqn, IL NG
166th FS (SE)	166th FS/121st FW	OH	26 Jan 1947	364th TS, 357th FG, 8th AF
119th FS (SE)	119th FS/177th FG	NJ	29 Jan 1947	119th Obs Sqn, NJ NG
105th FS (SE)	105th AS/118th AW	TN	3 Feb 1947	105th Obs Sqn, TN NG
132nd FS (SE)	132nd ARS/101st ARW	ME	5 Feb 1947	528th FS, 311th FB, 10th AF
111th FS (SE)	111th FS/147th FG	TX	9 Feb 1947	111th Obs Sqn, TX NG
159th FS (SE)	159th FS/125th FG	FL	9 Feb 1947	352nd FS, 353rd FG, 8th AF
116th FS (SE)	116th ARS/141st ARW	WA	10 Feb 1947	116th Obs Sqn, WA NG
185th FS (SE)	185th AS/137th AW	OK	13 Feb 1947	506th FS, 404th FG, 9th AF
125th FS (SE)	125th FS/138th FG	OK	15 Feb 1947	125th Obs Sqn, OK NG
165th FS (SE)	165th AS/123rd AW	KY	16 Feb 1947	368th FS, 359th FG, 8th AF
131st FS (SE)	131st FS/104th FG	MA	24 Feb 1947	333rd FS, 318th FG, 7th AF
148th FS (SE)	Inactivated in May 1956	PA	27 Feb 1947	347th FS, 350th FG, 12th AF
181st FS (SE)	181st AS/136th AW	TX	27 Feb 1947	395th FS, 368th FG, 9th AF
167th FS (SE)	167th AS/167th AG	WV	7 Mar 1947	369th FS, 359th FG, 8th AF
133rd FS (SE)	133rd ARS/157th ARG	NH	4 Apr 1947	529th FS, 311th FG, 10th AF
113th FS (SE)	113th FS/181st FG	IN	14 Apr 1947	113th Obs Sqn, IN NG
114th BS (L)	Inactivated in Sep 1958	NY	17 June 1947	439th BS, 319th BG, 7th AF

INITIAL SQUADRON DESIGNATION	CURRENT SQUADRON DESIGNATION	STATE	DATE OF FEDERAL RECOGNITION	LINEAGE
149th FS (SE)	149th FS/192nd FG	VA	21 June 1947	328th FS, 352nd FG, 8th AF
169th FS (SE)	169th FS/182nd FG	IL	21 June 1947	304th FS, 337th FG, 3rd AF
126th FS (SE)	126th ARS/128th ARG	WI	25 June 1947	126th Obs Sqn, WI NG
186th FS (SE)	186th FS/120th FG	MT	27 June 1947	404th FS, 371st FG, 9th AF
188th FS (SE)	188th FS/150th FG	NM	7 July 1947	507th FS, 404th FG, 9th AF
172nd FS (SE)	172nd FS/110th FG	MI	16 Sep 1947	375th FS, 361st FG, 8th AF
160th FS (SE)	160th FS/187th FG	AL	1 Oct 1947	
182nd FS (SE)	182nd FS/149th FG	TX	6 Oct 1947	396th FS, 368th FG, 9th AF
163rd FS (SE)	163rd FS/122nd FW	IN	11 Oct 1947	365th FS, 358th FG, 9th AF
168th BS (L)	Inactivated in May 1958	IL	19 Oct 1947	437th BS, 319th BG, 7th AF
138th FS (SE)	138th FS/174th FW	NY	28 Oct 1947	505th FS, 339th FG, 8th AF
162nd FS (SE)	162nd FS/178th FG	OH	2 Nov 1947	362nd FS, 357th FG, 8th AF
198th FS (SE)	198th FS/156th FG	PR	23 Nov 1947	463rd FS, 507th FG, 20th AF
102nd BS (L)	102nd RQS/106th RQG	NY	30 Nov 1947	102nd Obs Sqn, NY NG
156th FS (SE)	156th AS/145th AG	NC	15 Mar 1948	360th FS, 356th FG, 8th AF
192nd FS (SE)	192nd RS/152nd RG	NV	12 Apr 1948	408th FS, 372nd FG, 3rd AF
171st FS (SE)	171st FS/191st FG	MI	25 Apr 1948	374th FS, 361st FG, 8th AF
146th FS (SE)	146th ARS/112th ARG	PA	18 June 1948	345th FS, 350th FG, 12th AF
164th FS (SE)	164th AS/179th AG	OH	20 June 1948	363rd FS, 357th FG, 8th AF
137th FS (SE)	137th AS/105th AG	NY	24 June 1948	504th FS, 339th FG, 8th AF
152nd FS (SE)	Inactivated in Nov 1955	RI	15 Sep 1948	152nd Obs Sqn, RI NG
179th FS (SE)	179th FS/148th FG	MN	18 Sep 1948	393rd FS, 367th FG, 9th AF
170th FS (SE)	170th FS/183rd FG	IL	30 Sep 1948	305th FS, 338th FG, 3rd AF
176th FS (SE)	176th FS/128th FW	WI	6 Oct 1948	306th FS, 338th FG, 3rd AF
139th FS (SE)	139th AS/109th AG	NY	18 Nov 1948	303rd FS, 337th FG, 3rd AF
136th FS (SE)	136th FS/107th FG	NY	8 Dec 1948	503rd FS, 339th FG, 8th AF
103rd BS (L)	103rd FS/111th FG	PA	20 Dec 1948	103rd Obs Sqn, PA NG
117th BS (L)	Inactivated in Jan 1957	PA	20 Dec 1948	440th BS, 319th BG, 7th AF
194th FS (SE)	194th FS/144th FW	CA	21 Mar 1949	409th FS, 372nd FG, 3rd AF
147th FS (SE)	147th ARS/171st ARW	PA	22 Apr 1949	346th FS, 350th FG, 12th AF
141st FS (SE)	141st ARS/108th ARW	NJ	26 May 1949	341st, 348th FG, 5th AF
144th FBS	144th AS/176th CG	AK	1 July 1953	
183rd RS	183rd AS/172nd AG	MS	1 July 1953	
184th RS	184th FS/188th FG	AR	15 Oct 1953	
129th ARS	129th RQS/129th RQG	CA	3 Apr 1955	
135th ARS	135th AS/135th AG	MD	10 Sep 1955	
130th TCS	130th AS/130th AG	WV	16 Oct 1955	
143rd ARS	143rd AS/143rd AG	RI	19 Nov 1955	
150th ATS	150th ARS/170th ARG	NJ	1 Feb 1956	
145th ATS	145th ARS/160th ARG	OH	17 Mar 1956	
140th ATS	Inactivated in Sep 1967	PA	1 May 1956	148th FBS, PA ANG
152nd FIS	152nd FS/162nd FG	AZ	18 May 1956	152nd FIS, RI ANG
117th FIS	117th ARS/190th ARG	KS	23 Feb 1957	117th FIS, PA ANG
151st FIS	151st ARS/134th ARG	TN	15 Dec 1957	
193rd TEWS	193rd SOS/193rd SOG	PA	17 Sep 1967	140th MAS, 168th MAG, PA ANG
114th TFTS	114th FS/142nd FG	OR	1 Feb 1984	114th FS, NY FG
177th TFTS	177th FS/184th FG	KS	1 Feb 1984	
195th TFTS	195th FS/162nd FG	AZ	1 Feb 1984	195th AS, 195th AG, CA ANG
148th TFTS	148th FS/162nd FG	AZ	15 Oct 1985	
168th AREFS	168th ARS/168th ARG	AK	1 Oct 1986	168th FS, IL ANG
161st TFTS	161st FS/184th FG	KS	1 July 1987	
210th ARS	210th RQS/176th CG	AK	4 Apr 1990	10th ARS, AAC
200th AS	200th AS	CO	15 Mar 1992	Det 1, HQ Colorado ANG
201st AS	201st AS	DC	15 Mar 1992	Det 1, DC ANG

TABLE 7 KOREAN WAR, 1950-1953 FLYING SQUADRONS CALLED TO ACTIVE DUTY

STATE	SQUADRON	AIRCRAFT	DURATION OF ACTIVE DUTY	MAIN STATIONS
Alabama	106th TRS	RB-26C	1 Apr 51 – 31 Dec 52	Birmingham MAP, AL Shaw AFB, SC
	160th TRS	F-51D/RF-80A	10 Oct 50 – 9 Jul 52	Birmingham MAP, AL Lawson AFB, GA Fürstenfeldbrück AB, Germany Neubiberg AB, Germany Toul-Rosières AB, France
Arizona	197th FS	F-84B/C/E	1 Feb 51 – 31 Oct 52	Luke AFB, AZ
Arkansas	154th FS	F-51D/F-84E	10 Oct 50 – 9 Jul 52	Langley AFB, VA Itazuke AB, Japan Taegu AB, Korea
California	115th BS	B-26B & C/B-45A	1 Apr 51 – 31 Dec 52	Langley AFB, VA
	195th FS	F-51D	1 Mar 51 – 30 Nov 52	Van Nuys MAP, CA
	196th FS	F-80C/F-84E	10 Oct 50 – 9 Jul 52	George AFB, CA Misawa AB, Japan
Colorado	120th FS	F-51D	1 Apr 51 – 31 Dec 52	Clovis AFB, NM
Connecticut	118th FS	F-47N	1 Feb 51 – 31 Oct 52	Suffolk County AP, NY
Delaware	142nd FS	F-84C/F-94B	1 Feb 51 – 31 Oct 52	New Castle County AP, DE
District of Columbia	121st FS	F-84C/F-94B	1 Feb 51 – 31 Oct 52	New Castle County AP, DE
Florida	159th FS	F-80C/F-84E	10 Oct 50 – 9 Jul 52	George AFB, CA Misawa AB, Japan
Georgia	128th FS	F-84C	10 Oct 50 – 9 Jul 52	Dobbins AFB, GA Alexandria AFB, LA

Tables

STATE	SQUADRON	AIRCRAFT	DURATION OF ACTIVE DUTY	MAIN STATIONS
Georgia (cont.)				
	158th FS	F-80C/F-84E	10 Oct 50 – 9 Jul 52	George AFB, CA
				Misawa AB, Japan
Idaho	190th FS	F-51D	1 Apr 51 – 31 Dec 52	Moody AFB, GA
				George AFB, CA
Illinois	108th BS	B-26B/C	1 Apr 51 – 31 Dec 52	Langley AFB, VA
				Bordeaux-Mérignac AB, France
				Laon AB, France
	168th BS	B-26B/C	1 Apr 51 – 31 Dec 52	Langley AFB, VA
				Bordeaux-Mérignac AB, France
				Laon AB, France
	170th FS	F-51D	1 Mar 51 – 30 Nov 52	Bergstrom AFB, TX
				George AFB, CA
Indiana	113th FS	F-51D	1 Feb 51 – 31 Oct 52	Sioux City, IA
				Ft Wayne, IN
				Scott AFB, IL
	163rd FS	F-51D	1 Feb 51 – 31 Oct 52	Ft Wayne, IN
Iowa	124th FS	F-51D	1 Apr 51 – 31 Dec 52	Dow AFB, ME
				Alexandria AFB, LA
	174th FS	F-84B/F-51D	1 Apr 51 – 31 Dec 52	Dow AFB, ME
				Alexandria AFB, LA
Kansas	127th FS	F-84C/G	10 Oct 50 – 9 Jul 52	Alexandria AFB, LA
				Chaumont AB, France
Kentucky	165th FS	F-51D/F-84E	10 Oct 50 – 9 Jul 52	Godman AFB, KY
				RAF Manston, England
Louisiana	122nd BS	B-26B/C	1 Apr 51 – 31 Dec 52	Langley AFB, VA
Maine	132nd FS	F-51D	1 Feb 51 – 31 Oct 52	Bangor, ME
Michigan	107th FS	F-84B/E	1 Feb 51 – 31 Oct 52	Luke AFB, AZ
	171st FS	F-84B/C/E	1 Feb 51 – 31 Oct 52	Luke AFB, AZ
	172nd FS	F-51D	1 Feb 51 – 31 Oct 52	Selfridge AFB, MI
Minnesota	109th FS	F-51D	1 Mar 51 – 30 Nov 52	Holman Field, MN
				Wold-Chamberlain Field, MN
	179th FS	F-51D	1 Mar 51 – 30 Nov 52	Duluth MAP, MN
Mississippi	153rd FS	F-47N	1 Mar 51 – 30 Nov 52	Turner AFB, GA
				Godman AFB, KY
Missouri	110th FS	F-51D	1 Mar 51 – 30 Nov 52	Bergstrom AFB, TX
				George AFB, CA
	180th BS	B-26B/C	1 Apr 51 – 31 Dec 52	Langley AFB, VA
				Bordeaux-Mérignac AB, France
				Laon AB, France
Montana	186th FS	F-51D	1 Apr 51 – 31 Dec 52	Moody AFB, GA
				George AFB, CA
Nebraska	173rd FS	F-51D	1 Apr 51 – 31 Dec 52	Dow AFB, ME
				Alexandria AFB, LA
Nevada	192nd FS	F-51D	1 Mar 51 – 30 Nov 52	Bergstrom AFB, TX
				George AFB, CA
New Hampshire	133rd FS	F-47D	1 Feb 51 – 31 Oct 52	Grenier Field, NH
New Jersey	141st FS	F-47D	1 Mar 51 – 30 Nov 52	Turner AFB, GA
				Godman AFB, KY
New Mexico	188th FS	F-51D	1 Feb 51 – 31 Oct 52	Long Beach MAP, CA
New York	102nd BS	B-29A	1 Mar 51 – 30 Nov 52	March AFB, CA
	114th BS	B-29A	1 Mar 51 – 30 Nov 52	March AFB, CA
	136th FS	F-47D	1 Mar 51 – 30 Nov 52	Niagara Falls, NY
North Carolina	156th FS	F-51D/F-84E	10 Oct 50 – 9 Jul 52	Godman AFB, KY
				RAF Manston, England
North Dakota	178th FS	F-51D	1 Apr 51 – 31 Dec 52	Moody AFB, GA
				George AFB, CA
Ohio	112th BS	F-51D/RB-26C	10 Oct 50 – 9 Jul 52	Lawson AFB, GA
	166th FS	F-84C	1 Feb 51 – 31 Oct 52	Lockbourne AFB, OH
				Youngstown MAP, OH
Oklahoma	125th FS	F-84B	10 Oct 50 – 9 Jul 52	Alexandria AFB, LA
	185th TRS	RF-51D/RF-80A	1 Apr 51 – 31 Dec 52	Shaw AFB, SC
Oregon	123rd FS	F-51D/F-86F	1 Mar 51 – 30 Nov 52	Portland MAP, OR
Pennsylvania	103rd BS	B-26/RB-29	1 Apr 51 – 31 Dec 52	Fairchild AFB, WA
	117th BS	B-26B/C	1 Apr 51 – 31 Dec 52	Langley AFB, VA
	148th FS	F-51D/F-86A/F-94A	1 Feb 51 – 31 Oct 52	Dover AFB, DE
South Carolina	157th TRS	RF-51D/RF-80A	10 Oct 50 – 9 Jul 52	Lawson AFB, GA
				Fürstenfeldbrück AB, Germany
South Dakota	175th FS	F-51D	1 Mar 51 – 30 Nov 52	Ellsworth AFB, SD
Tennessee	105th FS	F-47D	1 Mar 51 – 30 Nov 52	Nashville, TN
	155th TRS	RF-51D/RF-80A	1 Apr 51 – 31 Dec 52	Memphis, TN
				Shaw AFB, SC
Texas	111th FS	F-51D/F-84E	10 Oct 50 – 9 Jul 52	Langley AFB, VA
				Itazuke AB, Japan
				Taegu AB, Korea
	182nd FS	F-51D/F-84E	10 Oct 50 – 9 Jul 52	Langley AFB, VA
				Itazuke AB, Japan
				Taegu AB, Korea
Utah	191st FS	F-51D	1 Apr 51 – 31 Dec 52	Clovis AFB, NM
Vermont	134th FS	F-51D/H	1 Feb 51 – 31 Oct 52	Burlington, VT
Virginia	149th FS	F-47D	1 Mar 51 – 30 Nov 52	Turner AFB, GA
				Godman AFB, KY
Washington	116th FS	F-84B/F-86A	1 Feb 51 – 31 Oct 52	Moses Lake AFB, WA
				RAF Bentwaters, England
West Virginia	167th FS	F-47D/F-84B	10 Oct 50 – 9 Jul 52	Godman AFB, KY
				RAF Manston, England
Wisconsin	126th FS	F-80A/F-86A	1 Feb 51 – 31 Oct 52	Truax Field, WI
	176th FS	F-51D/F-89A/B	1 Feb 51 – 31 Oct 52	Truax Field, WI
Wyoming	187th FS	F-51D	1 Apr 51 – 31 Dec 52	Clovis AFB, NM

TABLE 8   AIR NATIONAL GUARD   GROWTH SINCE 1946

FISCAL YEAR (1)	NUMBER OF FEDERALLY-RECOGNIZED UNITS (2 & 3) ALL UNITS	(2 & 3) MISSION SQUADRONS	MANPOWER (UNDER STATE CONTROL ONLY) (2) OFFICERS	ENLISTED PERSONNEL	TOTAL	NUMBER OF AIRCRAFT ON STRENGTH (2)	NUMBER OF FLIGHT HOURS PER YEAR (1)
1946	4	1	N.A.	N.A.	108	1	N.A.
1947	257	57	2,742	7,599	10,341	1,965	N.A.
1948	393	73	4,242	25,088	29,330	N.A.	N.A.
1949	514	84	6,556	34,875	41,431	2,263	N.A.
1950	514	84	6,747	37,981	44,728	2,655	N.A.
1951	N.A.	17 (+67)	2,589	17,941	20,530	N.A.	N.A.
1952	N.A.	17 (+67)	1,527	13,361	14,888	N.A.	N.A.
1953	498	82	3,839	31,717	35,556	N.A.	N.A.
1954	554	87	5,741	44,104	49,845	1,812	N.A.
1955	572	87	6,698	54,608	61,306	2,060	358,275
1956	614	94	7,300	56,234	63,534	2,138	394,019
1957	588	94	8,033	59,917	67,950	2,027	458,999
1958	573	93	8,354	61,641	69,995	2,429	436,863
1959	567	92	8,473	62,521	70,994	2,421	464,256
1960	546	92	8,570	62,250	70,820	2,269	442,101
1961	584	92	8,718	62,177	70,895	2,039	434,455
1962	415 (+163)	61 (+31)	6,278	44,041	50,319	1,263	329,142
1963	670	92	9,650	64,675	74,325	1,658	387,423
1964	706	92	9,843	63,374	73,217	1,810	433,458
1965	728	92	10,268	66,142	76,410	1,772	455,180
1966	850	92	10,220	69,663	79,883	1,814	501,724
1967	856	92	10,566	73,192	83,758	1,811	540,060
1968	756 (+87)	78 (+14)	9,292	65,969	75,261	1,430	463,108
1969	858	92	10,281	73,133	83,414	1,703	415,953
1970	958	92	10,872	78,975	89,847	1,900	487,662
1971	985	92	11,210	74,479	85,689	1,938	455,645
1972	1,014	92	11,489	77,748	89,237	1,935	427,677
1973	1,041	92	11,564	78,807	90,371	1,859	N.A.
1974	1,046	92	11,669	82,215	93,884	1,800	405,427
1975	1,016	91	11,636	83,726	95,362	1,634	417,008
1976	1,018	91	11,341	79,865	91,206	1,615	511,877
1977	1,020	91	11,219	80,621	91,840	1,560	386,015
1978	1,033	91	11,157	80,517	91,674	1,540	382,115
1979	1,020	91	11,503	81,876	93,379	1,497	380,102
1980	1,054	91	11,897	84,386	96,283	1,550	393,252
1981	1,053	91	12,378	85,915	98,293	1,669	410,129
1982	1,054	91	12,517	88,140	100,657	1,630	411,167
1983	1,058	91	12,670	89,500	102,170	1,704	448,666
1984	1,073	94	12,628	92,066	104,694	1,684	424,563
1985	1,076	94	12,836	96,240	109,076	1,688	424,563
1986	1,079	95	13,153	99,102	112,255	1,782	415,645
1987	1,052	97	13,549	100,185	113,734	1,732	406,966
1988	1,180	97	13,715	100,957	114,672	1,730	438,090
1989	1,339	97	13,832	101,675	115,507	1,544	426,684
1990	1,372	98	14,149	103,521	117,670	1,535	429,897
1991	1,321	98	14,115	103,590	117,705	1,553	473,716 (4)
1992	1,378	100	14,282	104,641	118,923	1,547	442,821

SOURCE: Annual Reports of the Chief of the National Guard Bureau and data supplied by the Program Integration Branch, National Guard Bureau.

(1) For Fiscal Years 1946 through 1975, the period covered is from 1 July to 30 June (*e.g,* FY 1946 = 1 July 1945 to 30 June 1946); for Fiscal Year 1976, the period covered includes the Transitional Quarter and thus runs 15 months from 1 July 1975 to 30 September 1976; for the following Fiscal Years, the period covered is from 1 October to 30 September.

(2) Up to and including FY 1975 data are as of 30 June; thereafter, as of 30 September.

(3) The number of units and squadrons appearing in parentheses in these two columns indicate units and squadrons on federal active duty at the end of the Fiscal Year.

(4) Record number of hours flown during FY91 resulted from the ANG participation in Desert Shield and Desert Storm.

TABLE 9   BERLIN CRISIS, 1961-1962   FLYING SQUADRONS CALLED TO ACTIVE DUTY

STATE	SQUADRON	AIRCRAFT	DURATION OF ACTIVE DUTY	MAIN STATION	STATE	SQUADRON	AIRCRAFT	DURATION OF ACTIVE DUTY	MAIN STATION
Alabama	106th TRS	RF-84F	1 Oct 61 – 20 Aug 62	Chaumont AB, France	Mississippi	153rd TRS	RF-84F	1 Oct 61 – 20 Aug 62	*Key Field, Meridian, MS
	160th TRS	RF-84F	1 Oct 61 – 20 Aug 62	*Dannelly Field, AL	Missouri	110th TFS	F-84F	1 Oct 61 – 20 Aug 62	Toul-Rosières AB, France
Arizona	197th FIS	F-104A	1 Nov 61 – 15 Aug 62	Ramstein AB, Germany	New Hampshire	133rd ATS	C-97A	1 Oct 61 – 31 Aug 62	*Grenier Field, NH
Arkansas	184th TRS	RF-84F	1 Oct 61 – 15 Aug 62	*Ft Smith, AR	New Jersey	119th TFS	F-84F	1 Oct 61 – 17 Aug 62	Atlantic City NAFEC, NJ
California	115th ATS	C-97C	1 Oct 61 – 31 Aug 62	*Van Nuys, CA		141st TFS	F-84F	1 Oct 61 – 17 Aug 62	Chaumont AB, France
	195th ATS	C-97C	1 Oct 61 – 31 Aug 62	*Van Nuys, CA	New York	136th TFS	F-100C	1 Oct 61 – 24 Aug 62	*Niagara Falls MAP, NY
Colorado	120th TFS	F-100C	1 Oct 61 – 24 Aug 62	*Buckley ANGB, CO		138th TFS	F-86H	1 Oct 61 – 20 Aug 62	Phalsbourg AB, France
District of Columbia	121st TFS	F-100C	1 Oct 61 – 24 Aug 62	*Andrews AFB, MD		139th ATS	C-97A	1 Oct 61 – 31 Aug 62	*Schenectady City AP, NY
Illinois	169th TFS	F-84F	1 Oct 61 – 16 Aug 62	*Greater Peoria AP, IL	Ohio	112th TFS	F-84F	1 Oct 61 – 20 Aug 62	*Toledo Express AP, OH
	170th TFS	F-84F	1 Oct 61 – 24 Aug 62	*Capital AP, Springfield, IL		162nd TFS	F-84F	1 Oct 61 – 31 Aug 62	*Springfield MAP, OH
Indiana	113th TFS	F-84F	1 Oct 61 – 20 Aug 62	*Hulman Field, IN		164th TFS	F-84F	1 Oct 61 – 20 Aug 62	*Mansfield MAP, OH
	163rd TFS	F-84F	1 Oct 61 – 24 Aug 62	Chambley AB, France		166th TFS	F-84F	1 Oct 61 – 15 Aug 62	Etain AB, France
Massachusetts	101st TFS	F-86H	1 Oct 61 – 20 Aug 62	Phalsbourg AB, France	Oklahoma	125th ATS	C-97	1 Oct 61 – 31 Aug 62	*Tulsa MAP, OK
	131st TFS	F-86H	1 Oct 61 – 20 Aug 62	Phalsbourg AB, France	South Carolina	157th FIS	F-104A	1 Nov 61 – 15 Aug 62	Moron AB, Spain
Minnesota	109th ATS	C-97A	1 Oct 61 – 31 Aug 62	*Minneapolis-St Paul IAP, MN	Tennessee	151st FIS	F-104A	1 Nov 61 – 15 Aug 62	Ramstein AB, Germany
					Virginia	149th TFS	F-84F	1 Oct 61 – 20 Aug 62	*Byrd Field, Sandston, VA

NOTE: The * in front of the main station indicates that the squadron remained based at its home base.

TABLE 10 *PUEBLO* CRISIS, 1968-1969 FLYING SQUADRONS CALLED TO ACTIVE DUTY

STATE	SQUADRON	AIRCRAFT	DURATION OF ACTIVE DUTY	MAIN STATION
Arkansas	154th TRS	RF-101G/H	26 Jan 68 – 20 Dec 68	Richards-Gebaur AFB, MO Itazuke AB, Japan
Colorado	120th TFS	F-100C	26 Jan 68 – 30 Apr 69	Phan Rang AB, Vietnam
District of Columbia	121st TFS	F-100C	26 Jan 68 – 18 Jun 69	Myrtle Beach AFB, SC
Iowa	174th TFS	F-100C	26 Jan 68 – 28 May 69	Phu Cat AB, Vietnam
Kansas	127th TFS	F-100C	26 Jan 68 – 18 Jun 69	Kunsan AB, Korea
Kentucky	165th TRS	RF-101G/H	26 Jan 68 – 9 Jun 69	Richards-Gebaur AFB, MO Itazuke AB, Japan
Maryland	104th TFS	F-86H	13 May 68 – 20 Dec 68	Cannon AFB, NM
Nevada	192nd TRS	RF-101H	26 Jan 68 – 7 Jun 69	Richards-Gebaur AFB, MO Itazuke AB, Japan
New Jersey	119th TFS	F-100C	26 Jan 68 – 17 Jun 69	Myrtle Beach AFB, SC
New Mexico	188th TFS	F-100C	26 Jan 68 – 4 Jun 69	Tuy Hoa AB, Vietnam
New York	136th TFS	F-100C	26 Jan 68 – 11 Jun 69	Tuy Hoa AB, Vietnam
	138th TFS	F-86H	13 May 68 – 20 Dec 68	Cannon AFB, NM
Ohio	166th TFS	F-100C	26 Jan 68 – 18 Jun 69	Kunsan AB, Korea
Pennsylvania	147th AAS	C-121C	13 May 68 – 12 Dec 68	*Greater Pittsburgh AP, PA

NOTE: The * in front of the main station indicates that the 147th AAS remained based at its home base.

TABLE 11 AIR NATIONAL GUARD GAINING COMMANDS AND WING/GROUP/SQUADRON ALIGNMENT AS OF 30 SEPTEMBER 1991

AFSOC-gained unit
193rd SOG, 193rd SOS, PA ANG, Harrisburg IAP, Middletown EC-130E

MAC-gained units
118th Tactical Airlift Wing, TN ANG, Nashville Metropolitan AP
105th TAS C-130H
143rd TAG, 143rd TAS, RI ANG, Quonset Point State AP, North Kingstown C-130E
164th TAG, 155th TAS, TN ANG, Memphis IAP C-130A

123rd Tactical Airlift Wing, KY ANG, Standiford Field (ANG), Louisville
165th TAS C-130B
135th TAG, 135th TAS, MD ANG, Glenn L. Martin State AP, Baltimore C-130E
145th TAG, 156th TAS, NC ANG, Charlotte/Douglas IAP C-130B
179th TAG, 164th TAS, OH ANG, Mansfield-Lahm AP, Mansfield C-130H

133rd Tactical Airlift Wing, MN ANG, Minneapolis-St Paul AFRS, Minneapolis
109th TAS C-130E
167th TAG, 167th TAS, WV ANG, Eastern WVa Regional AP, Martinsburg C-130E
189th TAG, 154th TATS, AR ANG, Little Rock, AFB C-130E

136th Tactical Airlift Wing, TX ANG, NAS Dallas
181st TAS C-130H
139th TAG, 180th TAS, MO ANG, Rosecrans Memorial AP, St Joseph C-130H
166th TAG, 142nd TAS, DE ANG, New Castle County AP, Wilmington C-130H

137th Tactical Airlift Wing, OK ANG, Will Rogers World IAP, Oklahoma City
185th TAS C-130H
130th TAG, 130th TAS, WV ANG, Yeager AP, Charleston AP C-130H
165th TAG, 158th TAS, GA ANG, Savannah IAP C-130H

146th Tactical Airlift Wing, CA ANG, Channel Islands ANGS, Port Hueneme
115th TAS C-130E
153rd TAG, 187th TAS, WY ANG, Cheyenne MAP C-130B
176th COMPG, 144th TAS, AK ANG, Anchorage IAP C-130H

Unaligned Groups and Squadrons
105th MAG, 137th MAS, NY ANG, Stewart IAP, Newburgh C-5A
106th ARG, 102nd ARS, NY ANG, Francis S. Gabreski AP, Westhampton Beach .. HC-130H/P & HH-60G
109th TAG, 139th TAS, NY ANG, Stratton ANGS, Schenectady County AP, Scotia C-130H/LC-130H
129th ARG, 129th ARS, CA ANG, NAS Moffett Field .... HC-130H/P & HH-60G
172nd MAG, 183rd MAS, MS ANG, Allen C. Thompson Field, Jackson C-141B
176th COMPG, 210th ARS, AK ANG, Anchorage IAP .... HC-130H(N) & HH-60G

PACAF-gained units
Unaligned Group and Squadron
154th COMPG, 199th TFS, HI ANG, Hickam AFB F-15A/B

SAC-gained units
101st Air Refueling Wing, ME ANG, Bangor IAP
132nd AREFS KC-135E
134th AREFG, 151st AREFS, TN ANG, McGhee-Tyson AP, Knoxville KC-135E
157th AREFG, 133rd AREFS, NH ANG, Pease ANGS, Portsmouth KC-135E

126th Air Refueling Wing, IL ANG, O'Hare AFRS, Chicago
108th AREFS KC-135E
128th AREFG, 126th AREFS, WI ANG, General Mitchell IAP, Milwaukee KC-135E
151st AREFG, 191st AREFS, UT ANG, Salt Lake City IAP KC-135E

141st Air Refueling Wing, WA ANG, Fairchild AFB
116th AREFS KC-135E
161st AREFG, 197th AREFS, AZ ANG, Sky Harbor IAP, Phoenix KC-135E
168th AREFG, 168th AREFS, AK ANG, Eielson AFB KC-135D/E
190th AREFG, 117th AREFS, KS ANG, Forbes Field, Topeka KC-135E

171st Air Refueling Wing, PA ANG, Greater Pittsburgh IAP, Coraopolis
147th AREFS KC-135E
160th AREFG, 145th AREFS, OH ANG, Rickenbacker ANGB, Columbus KC-135E
170th AREFG, 150th AREFS, NJ ANG, McGuire AFB KC-135E

TAC-gained units
102nd Fighter Interceptor Wing, MA ANG, Otis ANGB, Falmouth
101st FIS F-15A/B
Det. 1, Loring AFB, ME
107th FIG, 136th FIS, NY ANG, Niagara Falls AFRS .... F-16 ADF
Det. 1, Charleston AFB, SC
125th FIG, 159th FIS, FL ANG, Jacksonville IAP .... F-16 ADF
Det. 1, Homestead AFB, FL
158th FIG, 134th FIS, VT ANG, Burlington IAP .... F-16A/B & ADF
Det. 1, Bangor IAP, ME
177th FIG, 119th FIS, NJ ANG, Atlantic City IAP .... F-16A/B & ADF
191st FIG, 171st FIS, MI ANG, Selfridge ANGB, Mount Clemens .... F-16A/B & ADF
Det. 1, Seymour Johnson AFB, NC

108th Tactical Fighter Wing, NJ ANG, McGuire AFB
141st TFS F-4E
175th TFG, 104th TFS, MD ANG, Glenn L. Martin State AP, Baltimore A-10A

113th Tactical Fighter Wing, DC ANG, Andrews AFB
121st TFS F-16A/B
159th TFG, 122nd TFS, LA ANG, NAS New Orleans F-15A/B
192nd TFG, 149th TFS, VA ANG, Richmond IAP A-7D/K

116th Tactical Fighter Wing, GA ANG, Dobbins AFB
128th TFS F-15A/B
169th TFG, 157th TFS, SC ANG, McEntire ANGB, Eastover F-16A/B
187th TFG, 160th TFS, AL ANG, Dannelly Field, Montgomery F-16A/B

117th Tactical Reconnaissance Wing, AL ANG, Sumpter Smith ANGS, Birmingham
106th TRS RF-4C
124th TRG, 190th TRS, ID ANG, Gowen Field, Boise Air Terminal RF-4C
189th TRTF, ID ANG, Gowen Field, Boise Air Terminal RF-4C
152nd TRG, 192nd TRS, NV ANG, Reno-Cannon IAP RF-4C
155th TRG, 173rd TRS, NE ANG, Lincoln MAP RF-4C
163rd TRG, 196th TRS, CA ANG, March AFB RF-4C
186th TRG, 153rd TRS, MS ANG, Key Field, Meridian RF-4C

121st Tactical Fighter Wing, OH ANG, Rickenbacker ANGB, Columbus
166th TFS A-7D/K
150th TFG, 188th TFS, NM ANG, Kirtland AFB A-7D/K
178th TFG, 162nd TFS, OH ANG, Springfield-Beckley MAP, Springfield A-7D/K
180th TFG, 112th TFS, OH ANG, Toledo Express AP, Toledo A-7D/K

122nd Tactical Fighter Wing, IN ANG, Ft Wayne MAP
163rd TFS F-4E
149th TFG, 182nd TFS, TX ANG, Kelly AFB F-16A/B
181st TFG, 113th TFS, IN ANG, Hulman Regional AP, Terre Haute F-4E
188th TFG, 184th TFS, AR ANG, Fort Smith MAP F-16A/B

127th Tactical Fighter Wing, MI ANG, Selfridge ANGB, Mount Clemens
107th TFS F-16A/B
110th TASG, 172nd TASS, MI ANG, WK Kellogg AP, Battle Creek OA-37B
112th TFG, 146th TFS, PA ANG, Greater Pittsburgh IAP, Coraopolis A-7D/K

128th Tactical Fighter Wing, WI ANG, Truax Field, Madison
176th TFS A-10A
111th TASG, 103rd TASS, PA ANG, NAS Willow Grove OA-10A
182nd TASG, 169th TASS, IL ANG, Greater Peoria MAP OA-37B

131st Tactical Fighter Wing, MO ANG, Robertson ANGS, Lambert Field, St Louis IAP
110th TFS F-4E
183rd TFG, 170th TFS, IL ANG, Capital MAP, Springfield F-16A/B

132nd Tactical Fighter Wing, IA ANG, Des Moines IAP
124th TFS A-7D/K
114th TFG, 175th TFS, SD ANG, Joe Foss Field, Sioux Falls MAP A-7D/K
185th TFG, 174th TFS, IA ANG, Sioux City MAP, Sergeant Bluff A-7D/K

140th Tactical Fighter Wing, CO ANG, Buckley ANGB, Aurora
120th TFS A-7D/K
138th TFG, 125th TFS, OK ANG, Tulsa IAP A-7D/K

144th Fighter Interceptor Wing, CA ANG, Fresno Air Terminal MAP
194th FIS .... F-16 ADF
Det. 1, George AFB, CA
119th FIG, 178th FIS, ND ANG, Hector Field, Fargo .... F-16 ADF
Det. 1, Klamath Falls IAP, OR
120th FIG, 186th FIS, MT ANG, Great Falls IAP .... F-16A/B & ADF
Det. 1, Davis-Monthan AFB, AZ
142nd FIG, 123rd FIS, OR ANG, Portland IAP F-15A/B
Det. 1, McChord AFB, WA
114th TFTS, OR ANG, Klamath Falls IAP .... F-16 ADF
147th FIG, 111th FIS, TX ANG, Ellington Field, Houston .... F-16A/B & ADF
Det. 1, Holloman AFB, NM
148th FIG, 179th FIS, MN ANG, Duluth IAP .... F-16 ADF
Det. 1, Tyndall AFB, FL

174th Tactical Fighter Wing, NY ANG, Hancock Field, Syracuse
138th TFS F-16A/B
103rd TFG, 118th TFS, CT ANG, Bradley ANGS, Windsor Locks A-10A
104th TFG, 131st TFS, MA ANG, Barnes MAP, Westfield A-10A

Unaligned Groups and Squadrons
156th TFG, 198th TFS, PR ANG, Puerto Rico IAP, San Juan A-7D/K
162nd TFG, 148th TFTS, AZ ANG, Tucson IAP F-16A/B
152nd TFS, AZ ANG, Tucson IAP F-16A/B
195th TFTS, AZ ANG, Tucson IAP F-16A/B
184th TFG, 127th TFS, KS ANG, McConnell AFB F-16C/D
161st TFTS, KS ANG, McConnell AFB F-16C/D
177th TFTS, KS ANG, McConnell AFB F-16C/D

TABLE 12   PRIMARY AIRCRAFT AUTHORIZATION BY FLYING SQUADRONS   AS OF 1 JUNE 1992

	CURRENT MISSION AIRCRAFT	ANNOUNCED CONVERSIONS		CURRENT MISSION AIRCRAFT	ANNOUNCED CONVERSIONS
ACC-gained aircraft			**AFSOC-gained aircraft**		
Fighters			193rd SOS, 193rd SOG, PA ANG	6 × EC-130E	
101st FS, 102nd FW, MA ANG	18 × F-15A/B				
103rd FS, 111th FG, PA ANG	18 × OA-10A		**AMC-gained aircraft**		
104th FS, 175th FG, MD ANG	18 × A-10A	add 6 × OA-10A	Airlift aircraft		
107th FS, 127th FW, MI ANG	24 × F-16A/B		105th AS, 118th AW, TN ANG	16 × C-130H	
110th FS, 131st FW, MO ANG	18 × F-15A/B		109th AS, 133rd AW, MN ANG	8 × C-130E	
111th FS, 147th FG, TX ANG	18 × F-16A/B ADF		115th AS, 146th AW, CA ANG	16 × C-130E	
112th FS, 180th FG, OH ANG	18 × F-16C/D		130th AS, 130th AG, WV ANG	8 × C-130H	
113th FS, 181st FG, IN ANG	18 × F-16C/D		135th AS, 135th AG, MD ANG	8 × C-130E	
114th FS, 142nd FG, OR ANG	18 × F-16A/B ADF		137th AS, 105th AG, NY ANG	11 × C-5A	
118th FS, 103rd FG, CT ANG	18 × A-10A	18 × F-16C/D	139th AS, 109th AG, NY ANG	4 × C-130H,	
119th FS, 177th FG, NJ ANG	18 × F-16A/B ADF			4 × LC-130H	
120th FS, 140th FW, CO ANG	24 × F-16C/D		142nd AS, 166th AG, DE ANG	8 × C-130H	
121st FS, 113th FW, DC ANG	24 × F-16A/B	18 × F-16A/B	143rd AS, 143rd AG, RI ANG	8 × C-130E	
122nd FS, 159th FG, LA ANG	24 × F-15A/B		154th TS, 189th AG, AR ANG	8 × C-130E	
123rd FS, 142nd FG, OR ANG	18 × F-15A/B		155th AS, 164th AG, TN ANG	4 × C-130A	
124th FS, 132nd FW, IA ANG	24 × A-7D/K	18 × F-16C/D		4 × C-141B	8 × C-141B
125th FS, 138th FG, OK ANG	18 × A-7D/K	18 × F-16C/D	156th AS, 145th AG, NC ANG	12 × C-130B	12 × C-130H
127th FS, 161st FS & 177th FS,	54 × F-16C/D	48 × F-16C/D	158th AS, 165th AG, GA ANG	8 × C-130H	
184th FG, KS ANG			164th AS, 179th AG, OH ANG	8 × C-130H	
128th FS, 116th FW, GA ANG	24 × F-15A/B		165th AS, 123rd AW, KY ANG	9 × C-130H	
131st FS, 104th FG, MA ANG	18 × A-10A	18 × F-16C/D	167th AS, 167th AG, WV ANG	12 × C-130E	
134th FS, 158th FG, VT ANG	18 × F-16A/B ADF		180th AS, 139th AG, MO ANG	8 × C-130H	
136th FS, 107th FG, NY ANG	18 × F-16A/B ADF	10 × KC-135R	181st AS, 136th AW, TX ANG	8 × C-130H	
138th FS, 174th FW, NY ANG	18 × F-16A/B	18 × F-16C/D	183rd AS, 172nd AG, MS ANG	8 × C-141B	
148th FS, 152nd FS, & 195th FS,	52 × F-16A/B		185th AS, 137th AW, OK ANG	8 × C-130H	
162nd FG, AZ ANG			187th AS, 153rd AG, WY ANG	8 × C-130B	8 × C-130H
149th FS, 192nd FW, VA ANG	24 × F-16C/D				
157th FS, 169th FG, SC ANG	24 × F-16A/B	24 × F-16C/D	Rescue aircraft		
159th FS, 125th FG, FL ANG	18 × F-16A/B ADF		102nd RQS, 106th RQG, NY ANG	4 × HC-130P,	
160th FS, 187th FG, AL ANG	18 × F-16A/B			5 × HH-60G	
162nd FS, 178th FG, OH ANG	18 × A-7D/K	18 × F-16C/D	129th RQS, 129th RQG, CA ANG	4 × HC-130H/P,	
163rd FS, 122nd FW, IN ANG	24 × F-16C/D			5 × HH-60G	
166th FS, 121st FW, OH ANG	24 × A-7D/K	10 × KC-135R			
169th FS, 182nd FG, IL ANG	18 × F-16A/B ADF		Tanker aircraft		
170th FS, 183rd FG, IL ANG	24 × F-16A/B		108th ARS, 126th ARW, IL ANG	10 × KC-135E	
171st FS, 191st FG, MI ANG	18 × F-16A/B ADF		116th ARS, 141st ARW, WA ANG	10 × KC-135E	
172nd FS, 110th FG, MI ANG	12 × A-10A,		117th ARS, 190th ARG, KS ANG	10 × KC-135E	
	6 × OA-10A		126th ARS, 128th ARG, WI ANG	10 × KC-135R	
174th FS, 185th FG, IA ANG	18 × F-16C/D		132nd ARS, 101st ARW, ME ANG	10 × KC-135E	
175th FS, 114th FG, SD ANG	18 × F-16C/D		133rd ARS, 157th ARG, NH ANG	10 × KC-135E	
176th FS, 128th FW, WI ANG	18 × A-10A	18 × F-16C/D	141st ARS, 108th ARW, NJ ANG	10 × KC-135E	
178th FS, 119th FG, ND ANG	18 × F-16A/B ADF		145th ARS, 160th ARG, OH ANG	10 × KC-135R	
179th FS, 148th FG, MN ANG	18 × F-16A/B ADF		146th ARS, 112th ARG, PA ANG	10 × KC-135E	
182nd FS, 149th FG, TX ANG	18 × F-16A/B		147th ARS, 171st ARW, PA ANG	10 × KC-135E	
184th FS, 188th FG, AR ANG	18 × F-16A/B		150th ARS, 170th ARG, NJ ANG	10 × KC-135E	
186th FS, 120th FG, MT ANG	18 × F-16A/B ADF		151st ARS, 134th ARG, TN ANG	10 × KC-135E	
188th FS, 150th FG, NM ANG	24 × A-7D/K	24 × F-16C/D	153rd ARS, 186th ARG, MS ANG	10 × KC-135R	
189th TF, 124th FG, ID ANG	6 × F-4G		191st ARS, 151st ARG, UT ANG	10 × KC-135E	
190th FS, 124th FG, ID ANG	18 × F-4G	24 × F-4G	197th ARS, 161st ARG, AZ ANG	10 × KC-135E	
194th FS, 144th FW, CA ANG	18 × F-16A/B ADF				
198th FS, 156th FG, PR ANG	18 × A-7D/K	18 × F-16A/B ADF	**PACAF-gained aircraft**		
			144th ARS, 176th CG, AK ANG	8 × C-130H	
Reconnaissance aircraft			168th ARS, 168th ARG, AK ANG	4 × KC-135D,	
106th RS, 117th RW, AL ANG	18 × RF-4C			4 × KC-135E	
173rd RS, 155th RG, NE ANG	18 × RF-4C		199th FS, 154th CG, HI ANG	24 × F-15A/B	
192nd RS, 152nd RG, NV ANG	18 × RF-4C		210th RQS, 176th 'CG, AK ANG	2 × HC-130H(N),	
196th TRS, 163rd RG, CA ANG	18 × RF-4C	10 × KC-135E		4 × HH-60G	
Support aircraft					
200th AS, 140th FW, CO ANG	4 × T-34A				
201st AS, 113th FW, DC ANG	4 × C-21A,				
	4 × C-22B				

TABLE 13   OPERATIONAL SUPPORT AIRCRAFT   AS OF 1 JUNE 1992

Alabama ....1 × C-130H (187th FG)	Illinois ....1 × C-26A (182nd FG)	Montana......................1 × C-26B (120th FG)	Puerto Rico.................1 × C-26B (156th FG)
Alaska.......................1 × C-26B (168th ARG)	Indiana......................1 × C-26A (122nd FW)	Nebraska ....1 × C-12F (155th RG)	Rhode Island.....................................NONE
Arizona ....1 × C-26B (162nd FG)	Iowa ....1 × C-12J (132nd FG)	Nevada ....1 × C-12J (152nd RG)	South Carolina ....1 × C-130H (169th FG)
Arkansas ....1 × C-12F (189th AG)	Kansas ....1 × C-12J (184th FG)	New Hampshire.................................NONE	South Dakota ....1 × C-12F (114th FG)
California .1 × C-26A & 1 × C-26B (144th FW)	Kentucky ....1 × C-12F (123rd AW)	New Jersey ....1 × C-26A (170th ARG)	Tennessee...NONE
Colorado....................1 × C-26B (140th FW)	Louisiana ....1 × C-130H (159th FG)	New Mexico ....1 × C-26B (150th FG)	Texas ....1 × UC-26C (OL-DI, 147th FG)
Connecticut ....1 × C-12F (103rd FG)	Maine ....NONE	New York ....1 × C-12J (109th AG)	Utah ....NONE
Delaware ....NONE	Maryland ....NONE	North Carolina ....NONE	Vermont......................1 × C-12F (158th FG)
DC/NGB ....NONE	Massachusetts ....1 × C-12J (102nd FW)	North Dakota ....1 × C-130B (119th FG)	Virginia ....1 × C-26A (192nd FW)
Florida........................1 × C-26A (125th FG)	Michigan ....1 × C-26B (127th FW)	Ohio ....1 × C-26A (121st FW)	Washington..................1 × C-12J (141st ARW)
Georgia.......................1 × C-26B (116th FW)	Minnesota ....1 × C-26B (148th FG)	Oklahoma ....NONE	West Virginia ....NONE
Hawaii........................1 × C-130H (154th CG)	Mississippi ....1 × C-26A (172nd AG)	Oregon ....1 × C-26A (142nd FG)	Wisconsin....................1 × C-26B (128th TW)
Idaho.........................1 × C-26A (124th RG)	Missouri.....................1 × C-12F (131st FW)	Pennsylvania..............1 × C-26A (111th FG)	Wyoming ....NONE

TOTAL BY TYPES   7 × C-12F   6 × C-12J   13 × C-26A   5 × C-130H   TOTAL 41 Operational support aircraft

Operational Support Aircraft

Thirty-nine states and Puerto Rico are assigned support aircraft to provide a utility transport capability, principally for the movement of Guard personnel. In addition, there are two airlift squadrons assigned to the Colorado ANG and the District of Columbia ANG. Apart from a few Hercules, most use off-the-shelf commercial aircraft types.

Right: The Beech C-12F is the military equivalent of the Super King Air B200C, powered by the PT6A-42 turboprop. It has a port-side cargo door and can carry eight passengers or cargo.

The USAF's Boeing T-43 fleet was originally procured solely for Air Training Command, but four aircraft now serve with the Colorado ANG on support missions and for supplying training to USAF Academy students.

A handful of C-130H Hercules remain in the OSA role with ANG units, although the older variants have recently been retired. This C-130B served with North Dakota, which now operates a C-26B.

The C-26A/B is the standard ANGOSTA, able to carry 19 passengers or 4,800 lb of cargo. The sole UC-26C is for drug interdiction, and is fitted with APG-66 radar, FLIR and extra communications.

The C-12J is based on the Beech 1900C, powered by the PT6A-65 turboprop. A stretched derivative of the Super King Air, the C-12J can accommodate up to 19 passengers in addition to the crew of two.

The C-21A (Learjet 35A) was chosen by the USAF to fulfil the VIP/staff/high-value light cargo transport mission. Six passengers is the normal load (seven is the maximum), or 800 lb of cargo.

Four ex-National/Pan Am Boeing 727-035s were purchased for use by the NGB, principally as staff transports. They are configured with 24 seats for VIPs in the first-class cabin and 66 standard seats in the rear.

TABLE 14   TAIL CODES ASSIGNED TO ANG UNITS

CODE	UNIT DESIGNATION WHEN CODE LAST APPLIED	CURRENT AIRCRAFT	PRIOR AIRCRAFT
AG	195th TAS, 195th TAG, CA ANG	No	C-130A
AL	160th FS, 187th FG, AL ANG	F-16A/B	F-4D
AZ	152nd TFTS and 195th TFTS, AZ ANG	No	A-7D/K
BC	172nd FS, 110th FG, MI ANG	A-10A/OA-10A	OA-37B
BH	106th RS, 117th RW, AL ANG	RF-4C	
BO	166th TFS, 354th TFW, OH ANG (on FAD)	No	F-100C/F
BP	127th TFS, 354th TFW, KS ANG (on FAD)	No	F-100C/F
CG	156th TAS, 145th TAG, NC ANG	No	C-130B
CO	120th FS, 140th FW, CO ANG	F-16C/D	A-7D/K
CS	138th TFS, 140th TFW, NY ANG (on FAD)	No	F-86H
CT	104th TFS, 140th TFW, MD ANG (on FAD)	No	F-86H
CT	118th FS, 103rd FG, CT ANG	A-10A	F-100D/F, F-86H
DC	121st FS, 113th FW, DC ANG	F-16A/B	
FL	159th FS, 125th FG, FL ANG	F-16A/B ADF	
FS	184th FS, 188th FG, AR ANG	F-16A/B	
FW	163rd FS, 122nd FW, IN ANG	F-16C/D	F-4C, F-4E
GA	128th FS, 116th FW, GA ANG	No	F-15A/B
HA	174th TFS, 37th TFW, IA ANG (on FAD)	No	F-100C/F
HA	174th FS, 185th FG, IA ANG	A-7D/K	
HF	113th TFS, 181st TFG, IN ANG	Changed to TH	F-4C, F-4E, F-100D
IA	124th FS, 132nd FW, IA ANG	No	A-7D/K
IL	169th FS, 182nd FG, IL ANG	F-16A/B ADF	OA-37B
JA	183rd TAS, 172nd TAG, MS ANG	No	C-130E
KE	153rd TRS, 186th TRW, MS ANG	No	RF-4C
KG	167th TAS, 167th TAG, WV ANG	No	C-130A
KY	165th TRS, 123rd TRW, KY ANG	No	RF-4C
MA	131st FS, 104th FG, MA ANG	A-10A	
MD	104th FS, 175th FG, MD ANG	A-10A	A-37B
MG	109th TAS, 133rd TAG, MN ANG	No	C-130A
MI	107th TFS, 127th TFW, MI ANG	F-16A/B	A-7D/K
MT	155th TAS, 164th TAG, TN ANG	No	C-130A
NG	105th AS, 118th AW, TN ANG	No	C-130A
NH	133rd FS, 157th TAG, NH ANG	No	C-130A
NJ	150th TAS, 170th TAG, NJ ANG	No	C-7A/B
NJ	141st ARS, 108th ARW, NJ ANG	KC-135E	F-4E
NM	188th FS, 150th FG, NM ANG	No	A-7D/K
NY	138th FS, 174th FW, NY ANG	F-16A/B	A-37B, A-10A
OH	112th FS, 180th FG, OH ANG	F-16A/B	A-7D/K
OH	162nd FS, 178th FG, OH ANG	F-16C/D	A-7D/K
OH	166th FS, 121st FW, OH ANG	A-7D/K	
OK	185th TAS, 137th TAW, OK ANG	No	C-130A
OK	125th FS, 138th FG, OK ANG	A-7D/K	
PA	103rd FS, 111th FG, PA ANG	OA-10A	OA-37B
PA	193rd TEWS, 193rd TEWG, PA ANG	No	C/EC-130E
PR	198th FS, 156th FG, PR ANG	F-16A/B ADF	A-7D/K
PT	146th TFS, 112th TFG, PA ANG	KC-135E	A-7D/K
RB	154th TFS, 123rd TRW, AR ANG (on FAD)	No	RF-101G/H
RG	165th TRS, 123rd TRW, KY ANG (on FAD)	No	RF-101G/H
RI	143rd TAS, 143rd TAG, RI ANG	changed to TN	C-130A
RJ	192nd TRS, 123rd TRW, NV ANG (on FAD)	No	RF-101G/H
SA	182nd FS, 149th FG, TX ANG	F-16A/B	
SC	157th TFS, 169th TFG, SC ANG	No	A-7D, F-16A/B
SD	175th FS, 114th FG, SD ANG	No	A-7D/K
SG	136th TFS, 31st TFW, NY ANG (on FAD)	No	F-100C/F
SG	139th TAS, 109th TAG, NY ANG	No	C-130A
SI	170th FS, 183rd FG, IL ANG	F-16A/B	
SK	188th TFS, 31st TFW, NM ANG (on FAD)	No	F-100C/F
SL	110th FS, 131st FW, MO ANG	F-15A/B	F-4E
SV	158th TAS, 165th TAG, GA ANG	No	C-130E
TH	113th FS, 181st FG, IN ANG	F-16C/D	(changed from HF code in 1991)
TL	125th FS, 138th FG, OK ANG	changed to OK	A-7D
TN	143rd TAS, 143rd TAG, RI ANG	No	C-130A (changed from RI)
VA	149th FS, 192nd FG, VA ANG	F-16C/D	A-7D/K
VG	115th TAS, 146th TAW, CA ANG	No	C-130A
VS	120th TFS, 35th TFW, CO ANG (on FAD)	No	F-100C/F
VT	134th TFS, 158th TFG, VT ANG	No	F-4D
WG	142nd TAS, 166th TAG, DE ANG	No	C-130A
WI	176th FS, 128th FW, WI ANG	A-10A	
WY	187th TAS, 153rd TAG, WY ANG	No	C-130B
XA	119th TFS, 113th TFW, NJ ANG (on FAD)	No	F-100C/F
XB	121st TFS, 113th TFW, DC ANG (on FAD)	No	F-100C/F
XD	HQ Flight, 113th TFW, DC ANG (on FAD)	No	F-100C/F

TABLE 15   GULF WAR, 1990-1991   DESERT SHIELD/DESERT STORM   FLYING SQUADRONS CALLED TO ACTIVE DUTY

STATE	SQUADRON	PROVISIONAL WING ASSIGNMENT	AIRCRAFT	DURATION OF ACTIVE DUTY	MAIN STATIONS
AZ	197th AREFS	1701st AREFW (P) 1712th AREFW (P) & 801st AREFW (P)	KC-135E	20 Dec 90-15 May 91	King Abdul Aziz IAP, Jeddah, Saudi Arabia; Abu Dhabi IAP, Abu Dhabi, UAE; Moron AB, Spain
DE	142nd TAS	1630th TAW (P)	C-130H	22 Jan 91-30 Jun 91	Al Dhafra AB, Abu Dhabi, UAE; then Al Kharj AB, Saudi Arabia
IL	108th AREFS	1712th AREFW (P) & 1709th AREFW (P)	KC-135E	20 Dec 90-31 May 91	Abu Dhabi IAP, Abu Dhabi, UAE; King Abdul Aziz IAP, Jeddah, Saudi Arabia
KS	117th AREFS	1701st AREFW (P)/ 1709th AREFW (P)	KC-135E	20 Dec 90-15 Apr 91	King Abdul Aziz IAP, Jeddah, Saudi Arabia
ME	132nd AREFS	1701st AREFW (P)/ 1701st SW (P) & 1713th AREFW (P)	KC-135E	20 Dec 90-30 May 91	King Abdul Aziz IAP, Jeddah, Saudi Arabia; Dubai IAP, Dubai, UAE
MO	180th TAS	1630th TAW (P)	C-130H	27 Dec 90-30 May 91	Al Dhafra AB, Abu Dhabi, UAE; then Al Kharj AB, Saudi Arabia
MS	183rd MAS	N/A	C-141B	24 Aug 90-15 May 91	*Jackson MAP, MS
NH	133rd AREFS	N/A	KC-135E	20 Dec 90-31 May 91	*Pease AFB, NH
NJ	150th AREFS	N/A	KC-135E	20 Dec 90-15 May 91	*McGuire AFB, NJ
NV	192nd TRS	35th TFW (P)	RF-4C	3 Dec 90-20 Apr 91	Sheikh Isa AB, Bahrain
NY	137th MAS	N/A	C-5A	24 Aug 90-15 May 91	*Stewart ANGB, NY
	138th TFS	4th TFW (P)	F-16A	29 Dec 90-30 Jun 91	Al Kharj AB, Saudi Arabia
OH	145th AREFS	1709th AREFW (P) 1712th AREFW (P) & 1713th AREFW (P)	KC-135E	20 Dec 90-15 May 91	King Abdul Aziz IAP, Jeddah, Saudi Arabia; Abu Dhabi IAP, Abu Dhabi, UAE; and Dubai IAP, Dubai, UAE
PA	147th AREFS	1713th AREFW (P)	KC-135E	20 Dec 90-15 May 91	Dubai IAP, Dubai, UAE
RI	143rd TAS	313th MAG	C-130E	23 Feb 91-10 Jun 91	RAF Mildenhall, UK, and Incirlik AB, Turkey
SC	157th TFS	4th TFW (P)	F-16A	29 Dec 90-22 Jul 91	Al Kharj AB, Saudi Arabia
TN	151st AREFS	1713th AREFW (P) & 1709th AREFW (P)	KC-135E	20 Dec 90-1 Apr 91	Dubai IAP, Dubai, UAE; King Abdul Aziz IAP, Jeddah, Saudi Arabia
TX	181st TAS	1630th TAW (P)	C-130H	5 Oct 90-15 Apr 91	Al Dhafra AB, Abu Dhabi, UAE; then Al Kharj AB, Saudi Arabia
UT	191st AREFS	N/A	KC-135E	20 Dec 90-15 May 91	*Salt Lake City IAP, UT
WA	116th AREFS	1701st ARFEW (P) & 1706th AREFW (P)	KC-135E	20 Dec 90-15 Apr 91	King Abdul Aziz IAP, Jeddah, Saudi Arabia; Cairo West AB, Egypt
WV	130th TAS	1630th TAW (P)	C-130H	5 Oct 90-26 May 91	Al Dhafra AB, Abu Dhabi, UAE; then Al Kharj AB, Saudi Arabia
WI	126th AREFS	1706th AREFW (P)	KC-135E	20 Dec 90-15 May 91	Cairo West AB, Egypt

NOTE: (1) The * in front of the main station indicates that these squadrons remained based at their home base. However, in most cases, crews, support personnel, and aircraft were forward deployed as required to provide logistic or tanking support for Operation Desert Shield and Operation Desert Storm.

(2) Not included in this table are flying units which served on a voluntary basis during Desert Shield/Desert Storm. Details concerning these units will be found in the main text.

Tables

ACC-gained units

Alabama ANG
106th RS, 117th RW, Birmingham IAP RF-4C
160th FS, 187th FG, Dannelly Field, Montgomery F-16A/B

Arizona ANG
148th FS, 162nd FG, Tucson IAP F-16A/B
152nd FS, 162nd FG, Tucson IAP F-16A/B
195th FS, 162nd FG, Tucson IAP F-16A/B

Arkansas ANG
184th FS, 188th FG, Fort Smith MAP F-16A/B

California ANG
196th RS, 163rd RG, March AFB RF-4C
(To complete conversion from RF-4Cs to KC-135Rs during the first quarter of FY94 and to become AMC-gained)
194th FS, 144th FW, Fresno Air Terminal MAP ....F-16A/B ADF
  Det. 1, March AFB, CA

Colorado ANG
120th FS, 140th FW, Buckley ANGB, Aurora F-16C/D
200th AS, 140th FW, Buckley ANGB, Aurora T-43A

Connecticut ANG
118th FS, 103rd FG, Bradley IAP, Windsor Locks A-10A
(To complete conversion from A-10As to F-16C/Ds during the third quarter of FY93)

District of Columbia ANG
121st FS, 113th FW, Andrews AFB, MD F-16A/B
201st AS, 113th FW, Andrews AFB, MD ....C-21A & C-22B

Florida ANG
159th FS, 125th FG, Jacksonville IAP ....F-16A/B ADF
  Det. 1, Homestead AFB, FL

Georgia ANG
128th FS, 116th FW, Dobbins AFRB, Marietta F-15A/B

Idaho ANG
189th TF, 124th FG, Gowen Field, Boise Air Terminal ....RF-4C & F-4G
(To complete conversion from RF-4Cs to F-4Gs during the third quarter of FY93)
190th FS, 124th FG, Gowen Field, Boise Air Terminal F-4G

Illinois ANG
169th FS, 182nd FG, Greater Peoria MAP ....F-16A/B ADF
170th FS, 183rd FG, Capital AP, Springfield F-16A/B

Indiana ANG
113th FS, 181st FG, Hulman Regional AP, Terre Haute F-16C/D
163rd FS, 122nd FW, Ft Wayne MAP F-16C/D

Iowa ANG
124th FS, 132nd FW, Des Moines IAP A-7D/K
(To complete conversion from A-7D/Ks to F-16C/Ds during the third quarter of FY93)
174th FS, 185th FG, Sioux City ANGB, Sergeant Bluff F-16C/D

Kansas ANG
127th FS, 184th FG, McConnell AFB F-16C/D
161st FS, 184th FG, McConnell AFB F-16C/D
177th FS, 184th FG, McConnell AFB F-16C/D

Louisiana ANG
122nd FS, 159th FG, NAS New Orleans F-15A/B

Maryland ANG
104th FS, 175th FG, Glenn L. Martin State AP, Baltimore A-10A
(Will add OA-10As during the first quarter of FY93)

Massachusetts ANG
101st FS, 102nd FW, Otis ANGB, Falmouth F-15A/B
  Det. 1, Loring AFB, ME
  (To move to Bangor IAP in July 1993)
131st FS, 104th FG, Barnes MAP, Westfield ....Converting
(To complete conversion from A-10s to F-16C/Ds during the first quarter of FY93)

Michigan ANG
107th FS, 127th FW, Selfridge ANGB, Mount Clemens F-16A/B
171st FS, 191st FW, Selfridge ANGB, Mount Clemens ......F-16A/B ADF
  Det. 1, Seymour Johnson AFB, NC
172nd FS, 110th FG, WK Kellogg AP, Battle Creek ....A-10A & OA-10A

Minnesota ANG
179th FS, 148th FG, Duluth IAP ....F-16A/B ADF
  Det. 1, Tyndall AFB, FL

Missouri ANG
110th FS, 131st FW, Lambert-St Louis IAP F-15A/B

Montana ANG
186th FS, 120th FG, Great Falls IAP ....F-16A/B ADF
  Det. 1, Davis-Monthan AFB, AZ

Nebraska ANG
173rd RS, 155th RG, Lincoln ANGS, Lincoln RF-4C
(To complete conversion from RF-4Cs to KC-135Rs during the second quarter of FY94 and to become AMC-gained)

Nevada ANG
192nd RS, 152nd RG, May ANGS, Reno-Cannon IAP RF-4C

New Jersey ANG
119th FS, 177th FG, Atlantic City IAP ....F-16A/B ADF

New Mexico ANG
188th FS, 150th FG, Kirtland AFB ....Converting
(To complete conversion from A-7D/Ks to F-16C/Ds during the first quarter of FY93)

New York ANG
136th FS, 107th FG, Niagara Falls AFRS ....F-16A/B ADF
  Det. 1, Charleston AFB, SC
  (To complete conversion from F-16As to KC-135Rs during the fourth quarter of FY94)
138th FS, 174th FW, Hancock Field, Syracuse F-16A/B

North Dakota ANG
178th FS, 119th FG, Hector Field, Fargo ....F-16A/B ADF
  Det. 1, Kingsley Field, OR

Ohio ANG
112th FS, 180th FG, Toledo Express AP, Toledo F-16C/D
162nd FS, 178th FG, Springfield-Beckley MAP, Springfield ....Converting
(To complete conversion from A-7D/Ks to F-16C/Ds during the second quarter of FY93)
166th FS, 121st FW, Rickenbacker ANGB, Columbus ....Converting
(To complete conversion from A-7D/Ks to KC-135Rs during the second quarter of FY93 and to become AMC-gained. Will relocate to Wright-Patterson AFB in FY94)

Oklahoma ANG
125th FS, 138th FG, Tulsa IAP A-7D/K
(To complete conversion from A-7D/Ks to F-16C/Ds during the fourth quarter of FY93)

Oregon ANG
114th FS, 142nd FG, Klamath Falls IAP ....F-16A/B ADF
123rd FS, 142nd FG, Portland IAP F-15A/B
  Det. 1, McChord AFB, WA

Pennsylvania ANG
103rd FS, 111th FG, Willow Grove ARFF OA-10A

Puerto Rico ANG
198th FS, 156th FG, Puerto Rico IAP, San Juan ....Converting
(To complete conversion from A-7Ds to F-16A/B ADFs during the first quarter of FY93)

South Carolina ANG
157th FS, 169th FG, McEntire ANGB, Eastover F-16A/B
(To complete conversion from F-16A/Bs to F-16C/Ds during the fourth quarter of FY94)

South Dakota ANG
175th FS, 114th FG, Joe Foss Field, Sioux Falls MAP F-16C/D

Texas ANG
111th FS, 147th FG, Ellington ANGS, Houston ....F-16A/B ADF
  Det. 1, Holloman AFB, NM
182nd FS, 149th FG, Kelly AFB F-16A/B

Vermont ANG
134th FS, 158th FG, Burlington IAP ....F-16A/B ADF
  Det. 1, Langley AFB, VA

Virginia ANG
149th FS, 192nd FG, Richmond IAP F-16C/D

Wisconsin ANG
176th FS, 128th FW, Truax Field, Madison ....Converting
(To complete conversion from A-10As to F-16C/Ds during the second quarter of FY93)

AFSOC-gained unit

Pennsylvania ANG
193rd SOS, 193rd SOG, Harrisburg IAP, Middletown EC-130E

AMC-gained units

Arizona ANG
197th ARS, 161st ARG, Sky Harbor IAP, Phoenix KC-135E

Arkansas ANG
154th TS, 189th AG, Little Rock AFB C-130E

California ANG
115th AS, 146th AW, Channel Islands ANGS, Port Hueneme C-130E
129th RQS, 129th RQG, NAS Moffett Field ....HC-130H/P & HH-60G

Delaware ANG
142nd AS, 166th AG, New Castle County AP, Wilmington C-130H

Georgia ANG
158th AS, 165th AG, Savannah IAP C-130H

Illinois ANG
108th ARS, 126th ARW, O'Hare ARFF, Chicago KC-135E

Kansas ANG
117th ARS, 190th ARG, Forbes Field, Topeka KC-135E

Kentucky ANG
165th AS, 123rd AW, Standiford Field, Louisville C-130H

Maine ANG
132nd ARS, 101st ARW, Bangor IAP KC-135E

Maryland ANG
135th AS, 135th AG, Glenn L. Martin State AP, Baltimore C-130E

Minnesota ANG
109th AS, 133rd AW, Minneapolis-St. Paul AFRS, Minneapolis C-130E

Mississippi ANG
153rd ARS, 186th ARG, Key Field, Meridian KC-135R
183rd AS, 172nd AG, Allen C. Thompson Field, Jackson C-141B

Missouri ANG
180th AS, 139th AG, Rosecrans Memorial AP, St. Joseph C-130H

New Hampshire ANG
133rd ARS, 157th ARG, Pease ANGS, Portsmouth KC-135E

New Jersey ANG
141st ARS, 108th ARW, McGuire AFB KC-135E
150th ARS, 170th ARG, McGuire AFB KC-135E

New York, ANG
137th AS, 105th AW, Stewart IAP, Newburgh C-5A
102nd RQS, 106th RQG, Francis S. Gabreski AP,
  Westhampton Beach ....HC-130H/P & HH-60G
139th AS, 109th AW, Stratton ANGS, Schenectady County AP, Scotia C-130H/LC-130H

North Carolina ANG
156th AS, 145th AG, Charlotte/Douglas IAP C-130B

Ohio ANG
145th ARS, 160th ARG, Rickenbacker ANGB, Columbus KC-135R
(To relocate to Wright-Patterson AFB in FY94)
164th AS, 179th AG, Mansfield-Lahm AP, Mansfield C-130H

Oklahoma ANG
185th AS, 137th AW, Will Rogers World IAP, Oklahoma City C-130H

Pennsylvania ANG
146th ARS, 112th ARG, Greater Pittsburgh IAP, Coraopolis KC-135E
147th ARS, 171st ARW, Greater Pittsburgh IAP, Coraopolis KC-135E

Rhode Island ANG
143rd AS, 143rd AG, Quonset Point State AP, North Kingstown C-130E

Tennessee ANG
105th AS, 118th AW, Nashville Metropolitan AP C-130H
151st ARS, 134th ARG, McGhee-Tyson AP, Knoxville KC-135E
155th AS, 164th AG, Memphis IAP C-141B

Texas ANG
181st AS, 136th AW, NAS Dallas C-130H

Utah ANG
191st ARS, 151st ARG, Salt Lake City IAP KC-135E

Washington ANG
116th ARS, 141st ARW, Fairchild AFB KC-135E

West Virginia ANG
130th AS, 130th AG, Yeager AP, Charleston AP C-130H
167th AS, 167th AG, Eastern WVa Regional AP, Martinsburg C-130E

Wisconsin ANG
126th ARS, 128th ARG, General Mitchell IAP, Milwaukee KC-135E

Wyoming ANG
187th AS, 153rd AG, Cheyenne MAP C-130B

PACAF-gained units

Alaska ANG
144th AS, 176th CG, Anchorage IAP C-130H
168th ARS, 168th ARG, Eielson AFB KC-135D/E
210th RQS, 176th CG, Anchorage IAP ....HC-130H(N) & HH-60G

Hawaii ANG
199th FS, 154th CG, Hickam AFB F-15A/B
New ARS, 154th CG, Hickam AFB KC-135R
(To be activated during the second quarter of FY93)

TABLE 17 CROSS REFERENCE FLYING SQUADRONS TO GROUPS/WINGS AND STATES

SQUADRON	GROUP/WING	STATE	SQUADRON	GROUP/WING	STATE
101st FS	102nd FW	Massachusetts	152nd FIS	—	Rhode Island
102nd RQS	106th RQG	New York	Inactivated on 19 Nov 55		
103rd FS	111th FG	Pennsylvania	152nd FS	162nd FG	Arizona
104th FS	175th FG	Maryland	153rd ARS	186th ARG	Mississippi
105th AS	118th AW	Tennessee	154th TS	189th AG	Arkansas
106th RS	117th RW	Alabama	155th AS	164th AG	Tennessee
107th FS	127th FW	Michigan	156th AS	145th AG	North Carolina
108th ARS	126th ARW	Illinois	157th FS	169th FG	South Carolina
109th AS	133rd AW	Minnesota	158th AS	165th AG	Georgia
110th FS	131st FW	Missouri	159th FS	125th FG	Florida
111th FS	147th FG	Texas	160th FS	187th FG	Alabama
112th FS	180th FG	Ohio	161st FS	184th FG	Kansas
113th FS	181st FG	Indiana	162nd FS	178th FG	Ohio
114th FIS	—	New York	163rd FS	122nd FW	Indiana
Inactivated on 14 Sep 58			164th AS	179th AG	Ohio
114th FS	142nd FG	Oregon	165th AS	123rd AW	Kentucky
115th AS	146th AW	California	166th FS	121st FW	Ohio
116th ARS	141st ARW	Washington	167th AS	167th AG	West Virginia
117th FIS	—	Pennsylvania	168th FS	—	Illinois
Inactivated in Jan 57			Inactivated on 31 May 58		
117th ARS	190th ARG	Kansas	168th ARS	168th ARG	Alaska
118th FS	103rd FG	Connecticut	169th FS	182nd FG	Illinois
119th FS	177th FG	New Jersey	170th FS	183rd FG	Illinois
120th FS	140th FW	Colorado	171st FS	191st FG	Michigan
121st FS	113th FW	District of Columbia	172nd FS	110th FG	Michigan
122nd FS	159th FG	Louisiana	173rd RS	155th RG	Nebraska
123rd FS	142nd FG	Oregon	174th FS	185th FG	Iowa
124th FS	132nd FW	Iowa	175th FS	114th FG	South Dakota
125th FS	138th FG	Oklahoma	176th FS	128th FW	Wisconsin
126th ARS	128th ARG	Wisconsin	177th FS	184th FG	Kansas
127th FS	184th FG	Kansas	178th FS	119th FG	North Dakota
128th FS	116th FW	Georgia	179th FS	148th FG	Minnesota
129th RQS	129th RQG	California	180th AS	139th AG	Missouri
130th AS	130th AG	West Virginia	181st AS	136th AW	Texas
131st FS	104th FG	Massachusetts	182nd FS	149th FG	Texas
132nd ARS	101st ARW	Maine	183rd AS	172nd AG	Mississippi
133rd ARS	157th ARG	New Hampshire	184th FS	188th FG	Arkansas
134th FS	158th FG	Vermont	185th AS	137th AW	Oklahoma
135th AS	135th AG	Maryland	186th FS	120th FG	Montana
136th FS	107th FG	New York	187th AS	153rd AG	Wyoming
137th AS	105th AG	New York	188th FS	150th FG	New Mexico
138th FS	174th FW	New York	189th TF	124th FG	
139th AS	109th AG	New York	190th FS	124th FG	Idaho
140th MAS	168th MAG	Pennsylvania	191st ARS	151st ARG	Utah
Reorganized as 193rd TEWS/193rd TEWG on 17 Sep 67			192nd RS	152nd RG	Nevada
141st ARS	108th ARW	New Jersey	193rd SOS	193rd SOG	
142nd AS	166th AG	Delaware	194th FS	144th FW	California
143rd AS	143rd AG	Rhode Island	195th TAS	195th TAG	California
144th AS	176th CG	Alaska	Inactivated on 30 Sep 74		
145th ARS	160th ARG	Ohio	195th FS	162nd FG	Arizona
146th FS	112th FG	Pennsylvania	196th RS	163rd RG	California
147th ARS	171st ARW	Pennsylvania	197th ARS	161st ARG	Arizona
148th F-BS	—	Pennsylvania	198th FS	156th FG	Puerto Rico
Reorganized as 140th ATS on 1 May 56			199th FS	154th CG	Hawaii
148th FS	162nd FG	Arizona	200th AS	140th FW	Colorado
149th FS	192nd FG	Virginia	201st AS	113th FW	District of Columbia
150th ARS	170th ARG	New Jersey	210th RQS	176th CG	Alaska
151st ARS	134th ARG	Tennessee			

TABLE 18 CROSS REFERENCE GROUPS/WINGS TO FLYING SQUADRONS AND STATES

WING	SQUADRON	STATE	GROUP	SQUADRON	STATE
101st ARW	132nd ARS	Maine	103rd FG	118th FS	Connecticut
102nd FW	101st FS	Massachusetts	104th FG	131st FS	Massachusetts
108th ARW	141st ARS	New Jersey	105th AG	137th AS	New York
113th FW	121st FS	District of Columbia	106th RQG	102nd RQS	New York
113th FW	201st AS	District of Columbia	107th FG	136th FW	New York
116th FW	128th FS	Georgia	109th AG	139th AS	New York
117th RW	106th RS	Alabama	110th FG	172nd FS	Michigan
118th AW	105th AS	Tennessee	111th FG	103rd FS	Pennsylvania
121st FW	166th FS	Ohio	112th ARG	146th ARG	Pennsylvania
122nd FW	163rd FS	Indiana	114th FG	175th FS	South Dakota
123rd AW	165th AS	Kentucky	119th FG	178th FW	North Dakota
126th ARW	108th ARS	Illinois	120th FG	186th FW	Montana
127th FW	107th FS	Michigan	124th FG	189th TF & 190th FS	Idaho
128th FW	176th FS	Wisconsin	125th FG	159th FS	Florida
131st FW	110th FS	Missouri	128th ARG	126th ARS	Wisconsin
132nd FW	124th FS	Iowa	129th RQG	129th RQS	California
133rd AW	109th AS	Minnesota	130th AG	130th AS	West Virginia
136th AW	181st AS	Texas	134th ARG	151st ARS	Tennessee
137th AW	185th AS	Oklahoma	135th AG	135th AS	Maryland
140th FW	120th FS	Colorado	138th FG	125th FS	Oklahoma
140th FW	200th AS	Colorado	139th AG	180th AS	Missouri
141st ARW	116th ARS	Washington	142nd FG	114th FS & 123rd FS	Oregon
144th FW	194th FS	California	143rd AG	143rd AS	Rhode Island
146th AW	115th AS	California	145th AG	156th AS	North Carolina
171st ARW	147th ARS	Pennsylvania	147th FG	111th FS	Texas
174th FW	138th FS	New York	148th FG	179th FS	Minnesota

Tables

(Air National Guard Groups)

GROUP	SQUADRON	STATE
149th FG	182nd FS	Texas
150th FG	188th FS	New Mexico
151st ARG	191st ARS	Utah
152nd RG	192nd RS	Nevada
153rd AG	187th AS	Wyoming
154th CG	199th FS	Hawaii
155th RG	173rd RS	Nebraska
156th FG	198th FS	Puerto Rico
157th ARG	133rd ARS	New Hampshire
158th FG	134th FS	Vermont
159th FG	122nd FS	Louisiana
160th ARG	145th ARS	Ohio
161st ARG	197th ARS	Arizona
162nd FG	148th FS, 152nd FS & 195th FS	Arizona
163rd RG	196th RS	California
164th AG	155th AS	Tennessee
165th AG	158th AS	Georgia
166th AG	142nd AS	Delaware
167th AG	167th AS	West Virginia
168th MAG	140th MAS	Pennsylvania
	Reorganized as 193rd TEWS/193rd TEWG on 17 Sep 67	
168th ARG	168th ARS	Alaska
169th FG	157th FS	South Carolina
170th ARG	150th ARS	New Jersey
172nd AG	183rd AS	Mississippi
175th FG	104th FS	Maryland
176th CG	144th AS & 210th RQS	Alaska
177th FG	119th FS	New Jersey
178th FG	162nd FS	Ohio
179th AG	164th AS	Ohio
180th FG	112th FS	Ohio
181st FG	113th FS	Indiana
182nd FG	169th FS	Illinois
183rd FG	170th FS	Illinois
184th FG	127th FS, 161st FS, & 177th FS	Kansas
185th FG	174th FS	Iowa
186th ARG	153rd ARS	Mississippi
187th FG	160th FS	Alabama
188th FG	184th FS	Arkansas
189th AG	154th TS	Arkansas
190th AG	117th ARS	Kansas
191st FG	171st FS	Michigan
192nd FG	149th FS	Virginia
193rd SOG	193rd SOS	Pennsylvania
195th TAG	195th TAS	California
Inactivated on 30 Sep 74		

TABLE 19   AIR NATIONAL GUARD BASES   (as of December 1992, 1993 conversions included)

Alabama
Birmingham AP	106th RS	RF-4C
Dannelly Field, Montgomery	160th FS	F-16A/B

Alaska
Base	Squadron	Aircraft
Anchorage IAP	144th AS / 210th RQS	C-130H / HH-60G/HC-130H(N)
Eielson AFB	168th ARS	KC-135D/E

Arizona
Davis-Monthan AFB	186th FS Det 1	F-16ADF
Sky Harbor IAP, Phoenix	197th ARS	KC-135E
Tucson IAP	148th FS, 152nd FS, 195th FS	F-16A/B

Arkansas
Base	Squadron	Aircraft
Little Rock AFB	154th TS	C-130E
Fort Smith MAP	184th FS	F-16A/B

California
Channel Islands ANGS, Port Hueneme	115th AS	C-130E
Fresno Air Terminal MAP	194th FS	F-16ADF
March AFB	194th FS Det 1 / 196th RS	F-16ADF / RF-4C
NAS Moffett Field	129th RQS	HH-60G/HC-130H/P

Colorado
Buckley ANGB, Aurora	120th FS / 200th AS	F-16C/D / T-43A

Connecticut
Base	Squadron	Aircraft
Bradley IAP, Windsor Locks	116th FS	F-16C/D

Delaware
New Castle County AP, Wilmington	142nd AS	C-130H

Florida
Homestead AFB	159th FS Det 1	F-16ADF
Jacksonville IAP	159th FS	F-16ADF
Tyndall AFB	179th FS Det 1	F-16ADF

Georgia
Base	Squadron	Aircraft
Dobbins AFRB, Marietta	128th FS	F-15A/B
Savannah IAP	158th AS	C-130H

Hawaii
Base	Squadron	Aircraft
Hickam AFB	199th FS / new ARS	F-15A/B / KC-135R

Idaho
Base	Squadron	Aircraft
Boise Air Terminal	189th TF / 190th FS	RF-4C, F-4G / F-4G

Illinois
Base	Squadron	Aircraft
Capital MAP, Springfield	170th FS	F-16A/B
Greater Peoria MAP	169th FS	F-16ADF
O'Hare AFRS, Chicago	108th ARS	KC-135E

Indiana
Ft Wayne MAP	163rd FS	F-16C/D
Hulman Regional AP, Terre Haute	113th FS	F-16C/D

Iowa
Des Moines IAP	124th FS	F-16C/D
Sioux City MAP, Sergeant Bluff	174th FS	F-16C/D

Kansas
Forbes Field, Topeka	117th ARS	KC-135E
McConnell AFB	127th FS, 161st FS, 177th FS	F-16C/D

Kentucky
Base	Squadron	Aircraft
Standiford Field, Louisville	165th AS	C-130H

Louisiana
Base	Squadron	Aircraft
NAS New Orleans	122nd FS	F-15A/B

Maine
Base	Squadron	Aircraft
Bangor IAP	132nd ARS	KC-135E
Loring AFB	101st FS Det 1	F-15A/B (to Bangor in 1993)

Maryland
Andrews AFB	121st FS / 201st AS	F-16A/B / C-21A/C-22B
Glenn L. Martin State AP	104th FS / 135th AS	A/OA-10A / C-130E

Massachusetts
Base	Squadron	Aircraft
Barnes MAP, Westfield	131st FS	F-16C/D
Otis ANGB, Falmouth	101st FS	F-15A/B

Michigan
Selfridge ANGB, Mount Clemens	107th FS / 171st FS	F-16A/B / F-16ADF
W.K. Kellogg AP, Battle Creek	172nd FS	A/OA-10A

Minnesota
Base	Squadron	Aircraft
Duluth IAP	179th FS	F-16ADF
Minneapolis-St Paul AFRS	109th AS	C-130E

Mississippi
Allen C. Thompson Field, Jackson	183rd AS	C-141B
Key Field, Meridian	153rd ARS	KC-135R

Missouri
Lambert Field-St Louis IAP	110th FS	F-15A/B
Rosecrans Memorial AP, St Joseph	180th AS	C-130H

Montana
Base	Squadron	Aircraft
Great Falls IAP	186th FS	F-16ADF

Nebraska
Base	Squadron	Aircraft
Lincoln MAP	173rd RS	RF-4C

Nevada
Base	Squadron	Aircraft
Reno-Cannon IAP	192nd RS	RF-4C

New Hampshire
Base	Squadron	Aircraft
Pease ANGS, Portsmouth	133rd ARS	KC-135E

New Jersey
Atlantic City IAP	119th FS	F-16ADF
McGuire AFB	141st ARS, 150th ARS	KC-135E

New Mexico
Holloman AFB	111th FS Det 1	F-16ADF
Kirtland AFB	188th FS	F-16C/D

New York
Francis S. Gabreski AP, Westhampton Beach	102nd RQS	HH-60G/HC-130P
Hancock Field, Syracuse	138th FS	F-16A/B
Niagara Falls AFRS	136th FS	F-16ADF
Schenectady County AP, Scotia	139th AS	C/LC-130H
Stewart IAP, Newburgh	137th AS	C-5A

North Carolina
Base	Squadron	Aircraft
Charlotte/Douglas IAP	156th AS	C-130B
Seymour Johnson AFB	171st FS Det 1	F-16ADF

North Dakota
Base	Squadron	Aircraft
Hector Field, Fargo	178th FS	F-16ADF

Ohio
Mansfield-Lahm AP, Mansfield	164th AS	C-130H
Rickenbacker ANGB, Columbus	145th ARS, 166th ARS	KC-135E
Springfield-Beckley MAP, Springfield	162nd FS	F-16C/D
Toledo Express AP, Toledo	112th FS	F-16C/D

Oklahoma
Tulsa IAP	125th FS	F-16C/D
Will Rogers World IAP, Oklahoma City	185th AS	C-130H

Oregon
Klamath Falls IAP	114th FS, 178th FS Det 1	F-16ADF
Portland IAP	123rd FS	F-15A/B

Pennsylvania
Greater Pittsburgh IAP, Coraopolis	146th ARS, 147th ARS	KC-135E
Harrisburg IAP, Middletown	193rd SOS	EC-130E (CL)/(RR)
NAS Willow Grove	103rd FS	OA-10A

Puerto Rico
Base	Squadron	Aircraft
Puerto Rico IAP, San Juan	198th FS	F-16ADF

Rhode Island
Base	Squadron	Aircraft
Quonset Point State Airport	143rd AS	C-130E

South Carolina
Base	Squadron	Aircraft
Charleston AFB	136th FS Det 1	F-16ADF
McEntire ANGB, Eastover	157th FS	F-16A/B

South Dakota
Base	Squadron	Aircraft
Joe Foss Field, Sioux Falls MAP	175th FS	F-16C/D

Tennessee
Base	Squadron	Aircraft
McGhee-Tyson AP, Knoxville	151st ARS	KC-135E
Memphis IAP	155th AS	C-141B
Nashville Metropolitan AP	105th AS	C-130H

Texas
NAS Dallas	181st AS	C-130H
Ellington Field, Houston	111th FS	F-16ADF
Kelly AFB	182nd FS	F-16A/B

Utah
Salt Lake City IAP	191st ARS	KC-135E

Vermont
Base	Squadron	Aircraft
Burlington IAP	134th FS	F-16ADF

Virginia
Langley AFB	134th FS Det 1	F-16ADF
Richmond IAP	149th FS	F-16C/D

Washington
Base	Squadron	Aircraft
Fairchild AFB	116th ARS	KC-135E
McChord AFB	123rd FS Det 1	F-15A/B

West Virginia
Eastern WVa Regional AP, Martinsburg	167th AS	C-130E
Yeager AP, Charleston	130th AS	C-130H

Wisconsin
General Mitchell IAP, Milwaukee	126th ARS	KC-135R
Truax Field, Madison	176th FS	F-16C/D

Wyoming
Base	Squadron	Aircraft
Cheyenne MAP	187th AS	C-130B

Bases of the Air National Guard

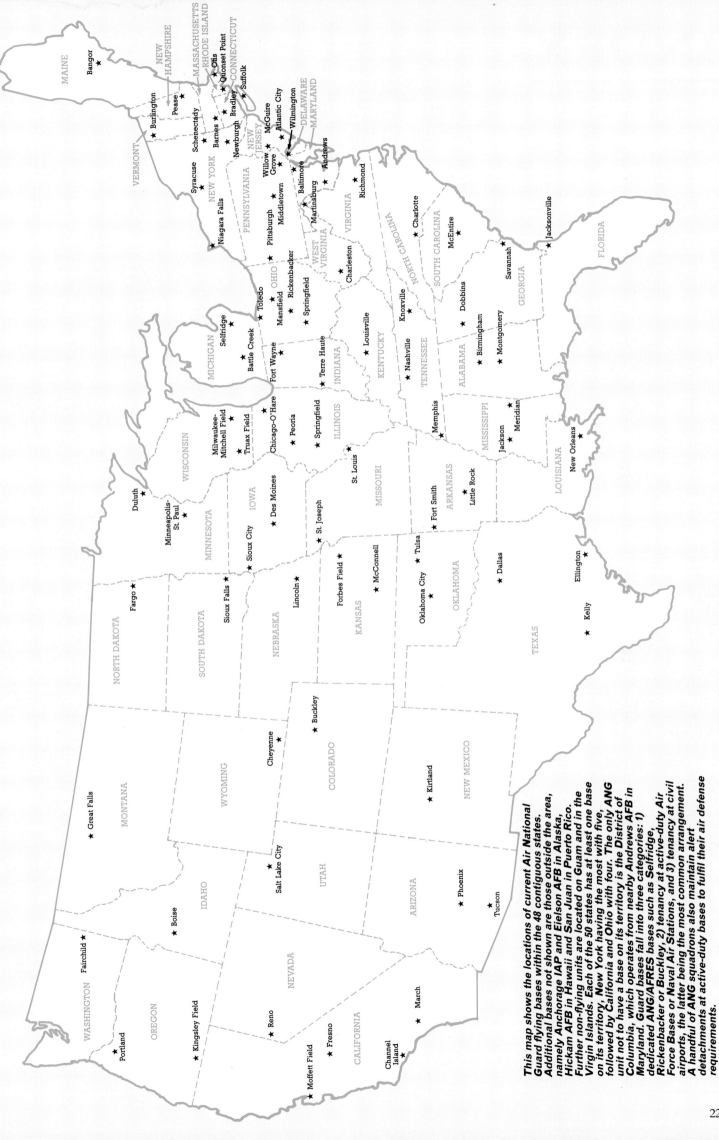

This map shows the locations of current Air National Guard flying bases within the 48 contiguous states. Additional bases not shown are those outside the area, namely Anchorage IAP and Eielson AFB in Alaska, Hickam AFB in Hawaii and San Juan in Puerto Rico. Further non-flying units are located on Guam and in the Virgin Islands. Each of the 50 states has at least one base on its territory, New York having the most with five, followed by California and Ohio with four. The only ANG unit not to have a base on its territory is the District of Columbia, which operates from nearby Andrews AFB in Maryland. Guard bases fall into three categories: 1) dedicated ANG/AFRES bases such as Selfridge, Rickenbacker or Buckley, 2) tenancy at active-duty Air Force Bases or Naval Air Stations, and 3) tenancy at civil airports, the latter being the most common arrangement. A handful of ANG squadrons also maintain alert detachments at active-duty bases to fulfil their air defense requirements.

221

INDEX